Law School Publications

of

WEST PUBLISHING COMPANY

St. Paul, Minnesota 55102

ACCOUNTING

Fiflis and Kripke's Accounting for Business Lawyers, 687 pages, 1971.

ADMINISTRATIVE LAW

Davis' Basic Text, about 700 pages, 1971.

Davis' Cases, Text and Problems, 2nd Ed., 609 pages, 1965.

ADMIRALTY

Healy and Currie's Cases and Materials on Admiralty, 872 pages, 1965.

AGENCY

Seavey and Hall's Cases, 431 pages, 1956.

Seavey's Studies, 451 pages, 1949.

Seavey's Text, 329 pages, 1964.

See Agency-Partnership.

AGENCY PARTNERSHIP

Seavey, Reuschlein & Hall's Cases, 599 pages, 1962.

Steffen's Cases, 3rd Ed., 733 pages, 1969.

BANKRUPTCY

MacLachlan's Text, 500 pages, 1956.

See Creditors' Rights.

BILLS AND NOTES

Aigler and Steinheimer's Cases, 670 pages, 1962.

Britton's Text, 2nd Ed., 794 pages, 1961.

See Commercial Transactions.

COMMERCIAL TRANSACTIONS

Speidel, Summers and White's Teaching Materials, 1144 pages, 1969.

COMMON LAW PLEADING

Koffler and Reppy on Common Law Pleading, 663 pages, 1969.

McBaine's Cases, Introduction to Civil Procedure, 399 pages, 1950.

Shipman's Text, 3rd Ed., 644 pages, 1923.

COMMUNITY PROPERTY

Burby's Cases, 4th Ed., 342 pages, 1955.

Huie's Texas Cases on Marital Property Rights, 681 pages, 1966.

Verrall and Sammis' Cases on California Community Property, 2nd Ed., 398 pages, 1971.

CONFLICT OF LAWS

Cramton and Currie's Cases—Comments—Questions, 915 pages, 1968.

Ehrenzweig's Text, 824 pages, 1962.

Ehrenzweig's Conflicts in a Nutshell, 2nd Ed., 392 pages, 1970.

Ehrenzweig and Louisell's Jurisdiction in a Nutshell, 2nd Ed., 315 pages, 1968.

Goodrich's Text, 4th Ed., 483 pages, 1964.

Scoles and Weintraub's Cases, 956 pages, 1967.

Selected Readings, 1151 pages, 1956.

Stumberg's Cases, 499 pages, 1956.

CONSTITUTIONAL LAW

Lockhart, Kamisar and Choper's Cases—Comments—Questions, 3rd Ed., 1,487 pages, 1970.

Lockhart, Kamisar and Choper's Cases and Materials on The American Constitution, 3rd Ed., 1970.

Lockhart, Kamisar and Choper's Annual Supplement.

Selected Essays, 971 pages, 1963.

See Constitutional Rights and Liberties.

CONSTITUTIONAL RIGHTS & LIBERTIES

Lockhart, Kamisar and Choper's Cases and Materials on Constitutional Rights and Liberties, 3rd Ed., 1970.

Lockhart, Kamisar and Choper's 1970 Supplement.

CONSUMER CREDIT

Kripke's Cases, 454 pages, 1970.

Young's Cases on Consumer Credit Pamphlet reprint from Dodyk, et al. Law and Poverty, 115 pages, 1969.

LAW SCHOOL PUBLICATIONS — Continued

CONTRACTS

Calamari & Perillo's Text, 621 pages, 1970.

Corbin's Cases, 3rd Ed., 1381 pages, 1947. 1953 Supplement, 36 pages.

Corbin's Text, Student Edition, 1224 pages, 1952.

Fuller and Braucher's Cases, 907 pages, 1964.

Simpson's Cases, 592 pages, 1956.

Simpson's Text, 2nd Ed., 510 pages, 1965.

COPYRIGHT

Nimmer's Cases on Copyright and Other Aspects of Law Pertaining to Literary, Musical and Artistic Works, about 877 pages, 1971.

CORPORATIONS

Henn's Text, 2nd Ed., 956 pages, 1970.

Stevens and Henn's Statutes, Cases and Materials on Corporations and Other Business Enterprises, 1448 pages, 1965.

Stevens and Henn's Practice Projects Supplement, 81 pages, 1965.

CREDIT TRANSACTIONS

Maxwell & Riesenfeld's California Cases on Security Transactions, 371 pages, 1957.

Maxwell & Riesenfeld's Supplement, 68 pages, 1963.

CREDITORS' RIGHTS

Riesenfeld's Cases on Creditors' Remedies and Debtors' Protection, 669 pages, 1967.

Riesenfeld's Statutory Supplement, 1969.

Riesenfeld's Case Supplement, 1970.

CRIMINAL LAW

Hall & Glueck's Cases, 2d Ed., 699 pages, 1958.

Miller's Text, 649 pages, 1934.

Stumberg's Texas Cases, 505 pages, 1954.

Stumberg and Maloney's Texas Cases Supplement, 117 pages, 1965.

CRIMINAL PROCEDURE

Hall, Kamisar, LaFave and Israel's Materials on Modern Criminal Procedure, 3rd Ed., 1456 pages, 1969.

Hall, Kamisar, LaFave and Israel's Materials on Basic Criminal Procedure, 3rd Ed., 617 pages, 1969.

Hall, Kamisar, LaFave and Israel's Annual Criminal Procedure Supplement.

Israel and LaFave's Constitutional Criminal Procedure in a Nutshell, 423 pages, 1971.

DAMAGES

Crane's Cases, 3rd Ed., 337 pages, 1955.

McCormick's Text, 811 pages, 1935.

DICTIONARIES

Black's, one volume.

Bouvier's, two volumes.

DOMESTIC RELATIONS

Clark's Cases, 870 pages, 1965.

Clark's Text, 754 pages, 1968.

Paulsen's Cases on Family Law and Poverty Pamphlet, reprint from Dodyk, et al. Law and Poverty, 266 pages, 1969.

See Juvenile Courts.

DRUGS AND DRUGGISTS

Arthur's Text, 4th Ed., 399 pp., 1955.

ENGINEERING LAW

Simpson & Dillavou's Text, 4th Ed., 506 pages, 1958.

Sweet's Legal Aspects of Architecture, Engineering and the Construction Process, 953 pages, 1970.

EQUITY

Cook's Cases, 4th Ed., 1192 pp., 1948.

McClintock's Text, 2nd Ed., 643 pages, 1948.

Van Hecke's Cases on Equitable Remedies, 651 pages, 1959.

See Remedies.

EVIDENCE

Cleary and Strong's Cases, 967 pages, 1969.

McCormick's Cases, 3rd Ed., 663 pages, 1956.

McCormick, Elliott & Sutton's Cases, 4th Ed., about 1100 pages, 1971.

McCormick's Text, 774 pages, 1954.

Rothstein's Evidence in a Nutshell, 406 pages, 1970.

Selected Writings, 1232 pages, 1957.

FEDERAL ANTI-TRUST LAWS

Oppenheim's Cases on Robinson-Patman Act, Pamphlet, 295 pages, 1967.

Oppenheim and Weston's Cases, 3rd Ed., 952 pages, 1968.

Oppenheim and Weston's Supplement, 1970.

FEDERAL ESTATE AND GIFT TAXATION

See Taxation.

FEDERAL INCOME TAXATION

See Taxation.

FEDERAL JURISDICTION AND PROCEDURE

Currie's Cases on Federal Courts, 823 pages, 1968.

Ehrenzweig and Louisell's Jurisdiction in a Nutshell, 2nd Ed., 315 pages, 1968.

Forrester, Currier and Moye's Cases, 2nd Ed., 933 pages, 1970.

Wright's Text, 2nd Ed., 745 pages, 1970.

FUTURE INTERESTS

Gulliver's Cases, 624 pages, 1959.

Powell's Cases, 3rd Ed., 1961.

Simes Text, 2nd Ed., 355 pages, 1966.

See Wills, Intestate Succession, Trusts, Gifts and Future Interests.

GRATUITOUS TRANSFERS

See Wills.

HOUSING AND URBAN DEVELOPMENT

Berger's Cases on Housing, Pamphlet reprint from Dodyk, et al. Law and Poverty, 277 pages, 1969.

Krasnowiecki's Cases, 697 pages, 1969.

Krasnowiecki's Statutory Supplement 1969.

See Land Use.

INSURANCE

Keeton's Cases on Basic Insurance Law, 655 pages, 1960.

Keeton's Basic Text, 712 pages, 1971.

Keeton's Case Supplement to Keeton's Basic Text, 398 pages, 1971.

Keeton & Keeton's Compensation Systems, Pamphlet Reprint from Keeton & Keeton's Cases on Torts, about 82 pages, 1971.

Vance's Text, 3rd Ed., 1290 pages, 1951.

INTERNATIONAL BUSINESS

Ebb's Cases, 885 pages, 1964.

Ebb's 1968 Supplement.

INTERNATIONAL LAW

Friedmann, Lissitzyn and Pugh's Cases, 1,205 pages, 1969.

INTRODUCTION TO LAW

Fryer and Orentlicher's Cases and Materials on Legal Method and Legal System, 1,043 pages, 1967.

Kimball's Historical Introduction to Legal System, 610 pages, 1966.

Kinyon's Introduction to Law Study and Law Examinations in a Nutshell, about 368 pages, 1971.

Smith's Cases on Development of Legal Institutions, 757 pages, 1965.

See Legal Method.

JURISPRUDENCE

Wu's Cases, 719 pages, 1958.

JUVENILE COURTS

Fox's The Law of Juvenile Courts in a Nutshell, 286 pages, 1971.

LABOR LAW

Sovern's Cases on Racial Discrimination in Employment, Pamphlet reprint from Dodyk et al. Law and Poverty, 188 pages, 1969.

LAND USE

Beuscher and Wright's Cases on Land Use, 788 pages, 1969.

Hagman's Text on Urban Planning and Land Development Control Law, about 542 pages, 1971.

LEGAL BIBLIOGRAPHY

Cohen's Legal Research in a Nutshell, 2nd Ed., about 220 pages, 1971.

How To Find The Law, with Special Chapters on Legal Writing, 6th Ed., 313 pages, 1965.

How To Find The Law Student Problem Book.

LEGAL ETHICS

Pirsig's Cases on Professional Responsibility, 2nd Ed., 447 pages, 1970.

Selected Readings Legal Profession, 565 pages, 1962.

LEGAL HISTORY

Kimball's Historical Introduction to Legal System, 610 pages, 1966.

Radin's Text, 612 pages, 1936.

Smith's Cases on Development of Legal Institutions, 757 pages, 1965.

LEGAL INTERVIEWING AND COUNSELING

Freeman's Cases, 253 pages, 1964.

LEGAL METHOD—LEGAL SYSTEM

Fryer and Orentlicher's Cases & Materials, 1043 pages, 1966.

See Introduction to Law.

LEGAL WRITING STYLE

Weihofen's Text, 323 pages, 1961.

See Legal Bibliography.

LEGISLATION

Nutting, Elliott and Dickerson's Cases 4th Ed., 631 pages, 1969.

LOCAL GOVERNMENT LAW

Michelman and Sandalow's Materials on Government in Urban Areas, 1216 pages, 1970.

Stason and Kauper's Cases, 3rd Ed., 692 pages, 1959.

See Land Use.

MASS COMMUNICATION LAW

Gillmor and Barron's Cases and Comment, 853 pages, 1969.

MORTGAGES

Osborne's Cases Secured Transactions, 559 pages, 1967.

Osborne's Text, 2nd Ed., 805 pages, 1970.

MUNICIPAL CORPORATIONS

Michelman and Sandalow's Materials on Government in Urban Areas, 1216 pages, 1970.

Stason and Kauper's Cases, 3rd Ed., 692 pages, 1959.

See Local Government Law.

See Land Use.

NATURAL RESOURCES

Trelease, Bloomenthal and Geraud's Cases and Materials on Natural Resources, 1131 pages, 1965.

OFFICE PRACTICE

A.B.A. Lawyer's Handbook, 557 pages, 1962.

See Legal Interviewing and Counseling.

OIL AND GAS

Hemingway's Text, 486 pages, 1971.
Huie, Walker and Woodward's Cases, 848 pages, 1960.
See Natural Resources.

PARTNERSHIP

Crane and Bromberg's Text, 695 pages, 1968.
See Agency-Partnership.

PERSONAL PROPERTY

Aigler, Smith and Tefft's Cases on Property, 2 Vols., 1339 pages, 1960.
Bigelow's Cases, 3rd Ed., 507 pages, 1942.
Fryer's Readings, 3rd Ed., 1184 pages, 1938.

PLEADING AND PROCEDURE

Brown, Karlen, Meisenholder, Stevens, and Vestal's Cases and Materials on Procedure Before Trial, 784 pages, 1968.

PLEADING AND PROCEDURE—Cont'd

Cleary's Cases on Pleading, 2d Ed., 434 pages, 1958.

Cound, Friedenthal and Miller's Cases on Civil Procedure, 1075 pages, 1968.

Cound, Friedenthal and Miller's Cases on Pleading, Discovery and Joinder, 643 pages, 1968.

Cound, Friedenthal and Miller's Civil Procedure Supplement, 1970.

Ehrenzweig and Louisell's Jurisdiction in a Nutshell, 2nd Ed., 315 pages, 1968.

Elliott & Karlen's Cases, 441 pages, 1961.

Hodges, Jones and Elliott's Cases on Texas Trial and Appellate Procedure, 623 pages, 1965.

Hodges, Jones, Elliott and Thode's Texas Judicial Process Prior to Trial, 935 pages, 1966.

Karlen's Cases on Trials and Appeals, 436 pages, 1961.

Karlen and Joiner's Cases and Materials on Trials and Appeals, 536 pages, 1971.

McBaine's Cases, Introduction to Civil Procedure, 399 pages, 1950.

POVERTY LAW

Dodyk, Sovern, Berger, Young and Paulsen's Cases on Law and Poverty, 1,234 pages, 1969.

Dodyk's Cases on Income Maintenance, Pamphlet reprint from Dodyk, et al. Law and Poverty, 379 pages, 1969.

REAL PROPERTY

Aigler, Smith & Tefft's Cases on Property, 2 Vols., 1339 pages, 1960.

Berger's Cases on Housing, Pamphlet reprint from Dodyk, et al. Law and Poverty, 277 pages, 1969.

Browder, Cunningham & Julin's Basic Property Law, 1209 pages, 1966.

Burby's Text, 3rd Ed., 490 Pages, 1965.

Jacobs' Cases Landlord and Tenant, 2nd Ed., 815 pages, 1941.

Moynihan's Introduction, 254 pages, 1962.

Phipps' Titles in a Nutshell—The Calculus of Interests, 277 pages, 1968.

Smith and Boyer's Survey of the Law of Property, 2nd Ed., 510 pages, 1971.
See Housing and Urban Development.

LAW SCHOOL PUBLICATIONS — Continued

REMEDIES

Cribbet's Cases on Judicial Remedies, 762 pages, 1954.

Wright's Cases, 498 pages, 1955.

York and Bauman's Cases, 1271 pages, 1967.

REVIEW MATERIALS

Ballantine's Problems.

Burby's Law Refreshers.

Nutshell Series.

Smith Reviews.

SALES

Nordstrom's Text, 600 pages, 1970.

Nordstrom and Lattin's Problems and Materials on Sales and Secured Transactions, 809 pages, 1968.

See Commercial Transactions.

SECURED TRANSACTIONS

See Commercial Transactions.

See Sales.

SURETYSHIP AND GUARANTY

Osborne's Cases, 221 pages, 1966.

Simpson's Cases, 538 pages, 1942.

TAXATION

Chommie's Text on Federal Income Taxation, 742 pages, 1968.

Chommie's Supplement, 1970.

Hellerstein's Cases on State and Local Taxation, 3rd Ed., 741 pages, 1969.

Kragen & McNulty's Cases on Federal Income Taxation, 1,182 pages, 1970.

Lowndes & Kramer's Text on Federal Estate and Gift Taxes, 2nd Ed., 951 pages, 1962.

Rice's Problems and Materials in Federal Estate & Gift Taxation, 504 pages, 1966.

Rice's Problems and Materials in Federal Income Taxation, 2nd Ed., about 502 pages, 1971.

TORTS

Green, Pedrick, Rahl, Thode, Hawkins and Smith's Cases, 1311 pages, 1968.

Green, Pedrick, Rahl, Thode, Hawkins and Smith's Cases on Injuries to Relations, 466 pages, 1968.

TORTS—Cont'd

Keeton and Keeton's Cases, about 1176 pages, 1971.

Prosser's Text, 4th Ed., 1208 pages, 1971.

Seavey, Keeton and Keeton's Cases, 2nd Ed., 1055 pages, 1964.

Seavey, Keeton and Keeton's Supplement, 1970.

TRADE REGULATION

See Federal Anti-Trust Laws.

See Unfair Trade Practices.

TRUSTS

Bogert's Text, 4th Ed., 528 pages, 1963.

Powell's Cases, Trusts and Wills, 639 pages, 1960.

Smith's Survey, 167 pages, 1949.

See Wills, Intestate Succession, Trusts, Gifts and Future Interests.

UNFAIR TRADE PRACTICES

Oppenheim's Cases, 783 pages, 1965.

Oppenheim and Weston's Supplement.

Oppenheim's Robinson-Patman Act Pamphlet, 295 pages, 1967.

WATER LAW

Trelease's Cases, 364 pages, 1967.

WILLS

Atkinson's Text, 2nd Ed., 975 pages, 1953.

Turrentine's Cases, 2nd Ed., 483 pages, 1962.

See Wills, Intestate Succession, Trusts, Gifts and Future Interests.

WILLS, INTESTATE SUCCESSION, TRUSTS, GIFTS AND FUTURE INTERESTS

Gulliver, Clark, Lusky and Murphy's Cases and Materials on Gratuitous Transfers: Wills, Intestate Succession, Trusts, Gifts and Future Interests, 1017 pages, 1967.

WORKMEN'S COMPENSATION

Malone and Plant's Cases, 622 pages, 1963.

HANDBOOK
OF THE LAW OF
REAL PROPERTY

By

WILLIAM E. BURBY

Professor of Law, California Western University

Professor Emeritus, University of Southern California

THIRD EDITION

HORNBOOK SERIES

ST. PAUL, MINN.
WEST PUBLISHING CO.
1965

This book is affectionately
dedicated to my daughter
Allene B.

*

PREFACE

The second edition of this book has not been revised. Rather, it has been completely rewritten. The lapse of ten years since publication of the second edition has made an expansion of the text necessary as a means by which to incorporate new material. The chapter on Homesteads has been omitted and there is expanded treatment of the subjects of Community Property and Future Interests. Long "reading footnotes" have been eliminated. It is believed that the detailed index will be of particular benefit to the readers.

WILLIAM E. BURBY

La Jolla, California,
July 6, 1965.

*

SUMMARY OF CONTENTS

SUMMARY OF CONTENTS

B. DERIVATIVE TITLE

PART 5. FUTURE INTERESTS

PART 6. RESTRAINTS PERTAINING TO ALIENATION

TABLE OF CONTENTS

PART 1. INTRODUCTION

CHAPTER 1. TENURE AND THE CLASSIFICATION OF ESTATES

CHAPTER 2. THE STATUTE OF USES

CHAPTER 3. REAL PROPERTY DEFINED

PART 2. RIGHTS IN LAND

A. RIGHTS INCIDENTAL TO POSSESSION

CHAPTER 4. WASTE

CHAPTER 5. INTERFERENCE WITH THE SUPPORT OF LAND AND STRUCTURES

CHAPTER 6. WATER RIGHTS

TABLE OF CONTENTS

B. RIGHTS IN THE LAND OF ANOTHER
CHAPTER 7. PROFITS AND EASEMENTS

CHAPTER 8. LICENSES

CHAPTER 9. COVENANTS IN DEEDS AND EQUITABLE LAND BURDENS

PART 3. POSSESSORY ESTATES

A. LESS THAN FREEHOLD ESTATES—LANDLORD AND TENANT

CHAPTER 10. INTRODUCTION

TABLE OF CONTENTS

CHAPTER 11. VARIOUS TYPES OF LEASEHOLD ESTATES

CHAPTER 12. CONDITIONS AND LIMITATIONS IN LEASES

CHAPTER 13. COVENANTS IN LEASES

CHAPTER 14. RENT

CHAPTER 15. SURRENDER OF LEASEHOLD ESTATES

TABLE OF CONTENTS

B. FREEHOLD ESTATES

CHAPTER 16. LIFE ESTATES

CHAPTER 17. ESTATES IN FEE

C. CONCURRENT OWNERSHIP

CHAPTER 18. COMMON LAW TYPES OF CONCURRENT OWNERSHIP

CHAPTER 19. COMMUNITY PROPERTY

TABLE OF CONTENTS

PART 4. TITLES

A. ORIGINAL TITLE

CHAPTER 20. ACQUISITION OF OWNERSHIP BY ADVERSE POSSESSION

B. DERIVATIVE TITLE

CHAPTER 21. MODE OF CONVEYANCE

CHAPTER 22. CONVEYANCE BY DEED AND BOUNDARY LINE AGREEMENTS

CHAPTER 23. COVENANTS IN DEEDS RESPECTING TITLE

CHAPTER 24. ESTOPPEL BY DEED

CHAPTER 25. THE RECORDING SYSTEM

TABLE OF CONTENTS

CHAPTER 26. TITLE REGISTRATION AND LIS PENDENS

PART 5. FUTURE INTERESTS

CHAPTER 27. VARIOUS TYPES OF FUTURE INTERESTS AND THEIR CHARACTERISTICS

CHAPTER 28. FUTURE INTERESTS IN CHATTELS

CHAPTER 29. THE CREATION OF FUTURE INTERESTS BY IMPLICATION

CHAPTER 30. CONTINGENCIES ATTACHED TO ESTATES (VESTING)

CHAPTER 31. ACCELERATION

TABLE OF CONTENTS

CHAPTER 32. GIFTS OVER IN CASE OF DEATH OR DEATH WITHOUT ISSUE

CHAPTER 33. CLASS GIFTS

CHAPTER 34. GIFTS TO "HEIRS," "ISSUE" AND "DESCENDANTS"

CHAPTER 35. POWERS OF APPOINTMENT

CHAPTER 36. RULE AGAINST PERPETUITIES

the personal allegiance of each landholder directly to the king.[1]

Feuds were granted by the king to his most important chieftains, tenants *in capite*. The chieftains, in turn, made grants of the land to other tenants, with the result that a landholder could have had the status of both a vassal and a lord. Such a dual status resulted in one's becoming a *mesne* or middle lord. Thus, a vast structure of tenure developed in which the king was lord paramount. The tenant actually in possession of the land was a tenant paravail. Land was not the subject of ownership; it was merely the subject of tenure.

The feudal system marks the beginning of our land law. Many modern rules of property law are understandable only in the light of this early setting. Whole volumes have been written about the feudal system and its political and social aspects. This discussion must, of necessity, be limited to a consideration of the more important phases of the feudal system and its relation to the development of the land law.

Forms of Tenure

A tenure which involved the rendition of services deemed appropriately to be rendered by a free man was a free tenure. Otherwise the tenure was unfree. Free tenures were those in chivalry, in socage and in frankalmoign.[2] Unfree tenure was that in villeinage, which later developed into copyhold tenure.

A tenure in chivalry that imposed an obligation to render military service was knight service. If the obligation was to render some personal honorary service to the king, such as carrying his sword, the tenure was grand serjeanty. If the service to the king did not involve military service but did involve some trivial thing associated with war, such as the yearly rendition of a bow or a sword, the tenure was that of petit serjeanty.

Socage tenure, a non-military tenure, imposed a duty to perform acts related to agriculture or to pay a fixed sum in lieu thereof (escuage). Frankalmoign tenure applied to land held by the church and contemplated the rendition of services of a religious nature, such as the saying of masses.

A tenure in villeinage—an unfree tenure—contemplated the rendition of menial services upon the lands of the overlord. Originally, the common law courts did not protect unfree tenure. The ancient actions, both proprietary and possessory, were available only to those holding land under free tenure. Eventually, however, the extent of the duties involved in a tenure in villeinage became fixed by custom, and the interest of the tenant was protected by the courts. The rights and obligations of tenants were made a matter of official record, and thereafter the tenure was known as copyhold tenure.[3]

In the course of time, the various kinds of services arising from tenure came to be regarded as owing from the land, and not from the one holding the land.[4] Thus it was that a designated area of land was bound to furnish a knight or other services. But while land might be burdened with an obligation to supply a certain number of knights or render other services, the tenant, by agreement with his overlord, might have been required to render a different type of service. Hence, it was important to distinguish the obligation of the land from the obligation of the tenant.

---

1. See Digby, History of the Law of Real Property (5th ed.) 36.

2. Holdsworth, History of English Law, 34–54.

3. Cheshire's Modern Real Property (9th ed.) 25.

4. I Poll. & Mait. History of English Law (2nd ed.) 237.

Incidents of Tenure

In the case of tenures in chivalry and socage, in addition to the rendition of services according to the type of tenure involved, there existed additional privileges in the lord and additional obligations on the tenant. Such additional privileges and obligations were incidents of tenure.

In the case of knight service, the personal relation between the overlord and his tenant was established by fealty and homage. Fealty consisted of an oath by the tenant to be faithful to his lord. Homage consisted of a solemn public ceremony by which the tenant acknowledged that he was the vassal of his lord, thus entitling the vassal to his lord's protection and warrant. Fealty, but not homage, was required in the case of socage tenure.[5]

Other incidents of tenure were aid, relief, wardship, marriage, and escheat. Aids were ransoms, or money payments, which the tenant was bound to make in order to secure the lord's release from prison, to help him knight his eldest son, and to provide a marriage portion for the lord's eldest daughter. Relief was a payment which a tenant's heir was required to make to the lord on succeeding to the inheritance. In the case of knight service, but not in the case of socage tenure, if the heir was under age, the lord had the right of wardship and the power to arrange for the marriage of the ward. Escheat was the termination of tenure if the tenant committed treason or a felony, or died without an heir.

Statutes and Decisions Affecting Tenure

One of the principal purposes of tenure was to fashion and perpetuate, through knight service, a dependable military society.[6] Knight service, however, in time, allowed for the privilege of scutage—the payment of money in lieu of such service. The result was that instead of developing a strong military society, the system of tenure gradually degraded into a system which had for its principal purpose the furtherance of the overlord's personal gain. Eventually, the pecuniary advantages to the overlord arising from the obligation of service declined to such an extent that their value became nominal.[7] The real advantages left to the overlord were in his right to the feudal incidents, especially wardship and marriage.[8] The influence of the landed gentry, who sought to safeguard those advantages, is discernible in the legislative acts and judicial decisions the force and effect of which are responsible for the rule in Shelley's case, the worthier title doctrine, and the Statute Quia Emptores, passed in 1290.[9] The judicial decisions expressed in the rule in Shelley's case [10] and the worthier title doctrine [11] are discussed under separate headings.

Prior to the enactment of the Statute Quia Emptores a tenant could alienate his land in one of two ways, either by substitution or by subinfeudation. In the case of alienation by substitution, the transferee was substituted in the stead of the tenant. The land remained subject to the rendition of feudal services, and the transferee became liable for the feudal incidents. However, the right of a tenant to so alienate without the consent of his overlord was not definitely established.[12] In the case of alienation by subinfeudation, the transferee was not a substitute for the tenant, but held under the tenant. Subinfeudation, therefore, was detrimental to the

---

5. 3 Holdsworth, History of English Law, 54.

6. 1 Poll. & Mait. History of English Law (2nd ed.) 252.

7. 2 Holdsworth, History of English Law, 348.

8. 2 Holdsworth, History of English Law, 348.

9. 18 Edw. I, cc. 1, 3 (1290).

10. See infra, § 138.

11. See infra, § 137.

12. 3 Holdsworth, History of English Law, 80.

interest of the overlord so far as feudal incidents were concerned. For example, the enfeoffment by A of a part of his land at a nominal yearly payment would result in lessening the value of the feudal incidents of A's overlord. The pecuniary benefits which the overlord could exact would be measured by the yearly payments reserved by A.

The purpose of the Statute Quia Emptores was to restore to the overlord the benefits flowing from the feudal incidents. Out of deference to the claims of tenants, the statute provided for the right of alienation by substitution, without the consent of the overlord; and further provided that where land was conveyed in fee simple absolute, the transferee would be deemed to hold directly from the overlord and not from his immediate transferor. The mesne, or middle, lords were thus eliminated. Put otherwise, the statute put an end to subinfeudation. The overlord could then look to the new owner for satisfaction of the feudal incidents,[13] and the vast structure of tenure which had developed under the feudal system was ended. The Statute of Tenures,[14] enacted in 1660, erased practically all of the feudal incidents. This statute not only converted tenure by knight service into socage tenure, but it abolished the more important feudal incidents of tenure, including wardship and marriage, aids, and fines for alienation.

Tenure in the United States

Colonial land grants from the Crown usually called for the payment of nominal rent and the land was held under socage tenure. After the revolution the state succeeded to the rights of the Crown as "lord paramount." However, the Statute Quia Emptores was considered to be a part of the local law. That

is to say, except in the landlord and tenant situations, the only tenure recognized was that between the state and the "owner" of the land.[15]

Statutes have been passed in many states disclaiming the fact that the state occupies the position of an overlord and declare that all land is allodial—held in absolute ownership, without recognizing any superior to whom any duty is owed because of tenure.

Even in states where tenure may be said to have survived, the only important incident of tenure is escheat in cases where the owner dies intestate and without heirs. As an incident of tenure escheat does not apply in the case of personal property because the feudal system concerned itself only with land. However, escheat statutes enacted in practically all of the states regulate matters of escheat both as to land and things other than land.

CLASSIFICATION OF ESTATES

2. An estate is an interest in land that is or may become possessory. According to the "scheme of estates" as developed in early English law, two or more persons may be the owners of separate and distinct estates in the same land and at the same time. However, only one possessory estate can exist at any given time. The other estates are called future interests.

Various types of estates. Freehold estates include estates in fee simple absolute, fee simple defeasible, fee simple conditional, fee tail and for life. Non-freehold estates are estates for years, from period to period, at will and at sufferance.

An estate in land is an interest that is or one that may become possessory, thus distinguishing it from an interest such as a profit or an easement. According to the "scheme

---

13. 2 Holdsworth, History of English Law, 348.

14. 12 Car. II, c. 24 (1660).

15. Van Rensselaer v. Hays, 1859, 19 N.Y. 68. That the Statute Quia Emptores may not be a part of the law in Pennsylvania and South Carolina, see Vance, The Quest for Tenure in the United States, 33 Yale Law Journal 248, 265 (1924).

of estates," as developed in early English law, two or more persons may be the owners of separate and distinct estates in the same land and at the same time. While there may be concurrent owners of a possessory estate, there can be but one possessory estate at any given time. The other estates are called future interests. For example, A, the "absolute owner" of land may convey it to B for life and direct that after the death of B the "absolute ownership" is to be in C. During the lifetime of B he may lease the land to D for a term of years. Assuming that the conveying instrument complies with the required formalities, the possessory estate is in B, subject to a term for years created in D. A future interest is created in C. Thus, "total ownership" of the land is separated into segments, each segment subject to enjoyment in possession during the time designated.

In the early development of the feudal system tenants holding under the important tenures (chivalry, socage and frankalmoign) were considered to be life tenants. In time it was recognized that a conveyance could be made to the tenant "and his heirs" and by such language assure that at the tenant's death the estate would pass to his heirs. These estates were called "freehold estates" because they were suitable estates for free men.

The tenant for life (freehold estate not of inheritance) and the tenant holding an inheritable estate (freehold estate of inheritance) were of vital importance in the administration of the feudal system. They were *seised* of the land and were responsible for the rendition of the feudal obligations. In this respect they differed from the villein who occupied manor land according to custom and who was under a duty to perform base and menial work in connection with the manor. Subsequently, the required services became fixed and the extent thereof was enrolled in the books of the manor. This was called copyhold tenure (a non-freehold estate). At the present time the important types of non-freehold estates are the estate for years, the estate from period to period, the estate at will and the estate at sufferance.[16]

Various Types of Estates

The word "fee" is used to describe an estate of inheritance, thus distinguishing it from a life estate.[17] An estate in fee is an estate which has a duration potentially infinite or is terminable upon an event which is not certain to occur within a fixed or computable period of time or within the duration of any specified life or lives.[18] That is the case, for example, in a conveyance A to B and his heirs so long as St. Paul's Cathedral stands.

An estate in fee simple absolute is the greatest estate known to the law. The word "simple" is used to indicate the fact that there are no restrictions with respect to the inheritable characteristics of the estate. The word "absolute" is used to indicate the fact that the estate is not defeasible upon the happening of any event. While the rules relating to the creation and characteristics of this and the other estates in fee are discussed under a separate heading,[19] the various estates in fee are defined in the following paragraphs.

First: A fee simple determinable (a qualified fee) is a fee simple defeasible, created by language indicating that the estate is to terminate automatically upon the happening of

16.   For discussion of the creation and characteristics of these estates, see infra, Chapter 2.

17.   2 Bl.Com. 106.

18.   1 Rest.Property, § 14.

19.   See infra, Chapter 17.

a stated event (a special limitation).[20] That is the case, for example, in a conveyance A to B and his heirs so long as the land is used for residential purposes.

Second: An estate in fee simple subject to a condition subsequent is a fee simple defeasible, created by language which confers upon the conveyor or his successors in interest a power to terminate the estate upon the happening of a named event. However, the estate continues in the grantee until this power is exercised.[21] Such an estate is created by a conveyance A to B and his heirs upon condition that the land is used for residential purposes. If the land is not used for residential purposes A may enter and terminate the estate.

Third: A fee simple subject to an executory limitation is a fee simple defeasible.[22] The estate terminates upon the happening of a named event and inures to the benefit of the owner of the executory interest, a person other than the conveyor or persons claiming under him. The creation of such an executory interest was made possible by the Statute of Uses, passed in 1536, and is discussed under a separate heading.

Fourth: An estate in fee simple conditional was recognized in England prior to the passage of the Statute De Donis in 1285.[23] In a conveyance A to B and the heirs of his body it was construed that B acquired a fee simple subject to a condition subsequent. The condition was birth of issue. Upon the happening of that event B's estate was, for practical purposes, an estate in fee simple.[24]

20. See 1 Rest.Property, § 23.

21. See 1 Rest.Property, § 24.

22. See 1 Rest.Property, § 16.

23. Stat. 13 Edw. I, c. 1 (1285).

24. See 1 Rest.Property, § 17.

Fifth: An estate in fee tail is an estate that involves restriction with respect to inheritance, and it owes its existence to the Statute De Donis, passed in 1285. It has been noted that prior to the passage of this statute, a conveyance A to B and the heirs of his body, created an estate in fee simple conditional. The condition was birth of issue capable of inheriting the property. But this was changed by the Statute De Donis. It was therein provided that a conveyance of this type created an estate that would pass by inheritance from generation to generation to the heirs of the body of the original grantee. If this line of inheritance should become extinct the estate reverted to the original grantor or those claiming under him.

Freehold Estates

Of inheritance

>Fee simple absolute
>Fee simple determinable
>Fee simple subject to a condition subsequent
>Fee simple subject to an executory limitation
>Fee simple conditional
>Fee tail

Not of inheritance

>Estate for one's own life
>Estate for the life of another (*pur autre vie*)
>Estate for one's own life and also for the life of another

Non-freehold Estates (Chattels Real)

>Estate for years
>Estate from period to period
>Estate at will
>Estate at sufferance

CHAPTER 2

THE STATUTE OF USES

THE SITUATION PRIOR TO THE STATUTE OF USES

3. Landowners resorted to the practice of vesting the legal title in another, upon the understanding that the land would be administered for the use and benefit of the transferor or for the use and benefit of his nominee. Equitable protection of the interests of such person early developed to a point where it could be said that he had "equitable ownership". Legal ownership might thus be separated from the equitable ownership—the "use".

The right to enjoy the benefits flowing from real or personal property is designated as the use. Usually, this right is an incident of legal ownership. Sometime in the thirteenth century the Franciscan friars, in order to comply with poverty vows, caused legal title to be held by others but retained the beneficial interest or use. Apparently, this was the beginning of a practice that involved the separation of legal title from beneficial ownership.

For a time this technique was also used to circumvent restrictions placed upon the making of gifts to religious corporations as pronounced in statutes of mortmain but this was expressly prohibited by a statute passed as early as in 1392. Private owners were quick to seize upon this device for personal benefit and used it for the following purposes, among others:

First: Some of the burdensome incidents of tenure could be avoided if the owner con-

veyed absolute ownership for designated uses. Assume the following disposition:

A ———————— B and his heirs

To the use of A for life

After the death of A to the use of A's children.

Upon the death of A the overlord would not be entitled to the feudal incidents of wardship, marriage or the money payment exacted upon the admittance of a new tenant (a fine). These obligations arose only upon the transmission of *a legal estate*. In the case under discussion A did not leave a legal estate at the time of his death. A *use* cannot properly be classified as a legal estate.

It is true, if B, the legal owner, should die the above mentioned feudal incidents would attach. However, this contingency could be avoided by conveying the legal estate to B and C *as joint tenants*. Upon the death of one joint tenant the ownership does not pass to his heirs. It *continues* in the surviving joint tenant. Successive joint tenancies could be created to prevent inheritance of the legal ownership.

Second: Prior to the passage of the Statute of Wills in 1540,[1] except by custom recognized in a few localities, a landowner did not have the privilege of disposing of his

---

1. 32 Hen. VIII c. 1 (1540).

freehold estates at the time of death. However, such estates could be conveyed to another to such uses as the one making the conveyance might designate by will.

Third: According to common law rules, a remainder was the only type of future interest that could be created in one other than the conveyor. As will be pointed out under a separate heading, highly technical restrictions surrounded the creation of a remainder.[2] However, there were no restrictions with respect to the creation of a use in a third party to take effect *in futuro*.

METHODS OF CREATING A USE

4. There are four methods by which a use can be created, namely, (1) by express provision under an effective common law conveyance, (2) by implication in favor of the conveyor if the conveyance is made without consideration and without an express use, (3) by bargain and sale, (4) by covenant to stand seised.

There were four methods by means of which a use can be created:

First: A use can be created by a common law conveyance accompanied by an express use. Thus, a conveyance can be made A to B and his heirs to the use of C and his heirs.

Second: If a conveyance is made without consideration and without an express statement as to the use there is a resulting use in favor of the conveyor. It is assumed that the conveyor did not intend to make a gift of the beneficial interest (use).[3] The prevailing American rule is that a conveyance made without consideration and without an express use is presumed to constitute a gift and no resulting use will arise.[4]

Third: The payment of consideration results in the creation of a use even in the absence of a conveyance. It is said that the use is raised by bargain and sale. The payment of consideration results in the creation of a use in the grantee even if the deed does not use words of bargain and sale.[5] Such payment negatives the claim of a resulting use.

Fourth: A use can be created by a covenant to stand seised. This involves the execution of an instrument under seal by the owner of property in which it is stated that he stands seised of the property to the use of a person related to him by blood or marriage. This is classified as "good consideration" as distinguished from "valuable consideration."[6] This method of creating a use was introduced after the passage of the Statute of Uses.[7] It is recognized in modern times and a seal is not required in those states that have abolished the distinction between sealed and unsealed instruments.[8]

ENFORCEMENT OF THE USE

5. A use is not a legal estate or interest in property but equity will enforce the use against any person who acquires the legal estate unless he qualifies as a *bona fide* purchaser for value and without notice.

Since a use is not a recognized legal estate or interest in property, a remedy at law is not available against a person to whom property was conveyed to uses even if he violates the confidence that had been reposed in him. However, as early as 1422 relief was made available in equity not only as against the person to whom the property was conveyed

---

2. See infra, § 138.

3. Armstrong v. Wolsey, [1755] 2 Wils. 19, 95 Eng. Rep. 662. *Cf.:* Shortridge v. Lamplugh, [1702] 2 Salk. 678, 90 Eng.Rep. 1244.

4. 2 Rest.Trusts, § 405.

5. Grey and Edward's Case, [1577] 4 Leon 110, 74 Eng.Rep. 763.

6. Roe d. Wilkinson v. Tranmer, [1757] 2 Wils. 75, 95 Eng.Rep. 694.

7. Sharington v. Strotten, [1565] 1 Plowd. 298, 75 Eng.Rep. 454.

8. Murray v. Kerney, 1911, 115 Md. 514, 81 A. 6.

but also as against his heirs.[9] Eventually, equitable relief was available against any person who acquired legal ownership of the property unless he qualified as a *bona fide* purchaser for value and without notice.

THE STATUTE OF USES

6. The Statute of Uses was passed for the purpose of abolishing dual ownership of land. That purpose, however, was not fully accomplished.

The Statute of Uses was passed in 1536 [10] and its purpose was to abolish the dual ownership of land. It was simply declared that henceforth the person having the use would be considered to be the legal owner. In the preamble of the statute it is stated that alleged abuses leading to its enactment included the creation of secret uses, informal testamentary dispositions of uses and loss of feudal benefits.

The statute was subjected to judicial interpretation with the result that its purpose was not accomplished.[11] Dual ownership of land continued to exist in the following situations.

First: The conclusion was reached that it was not the purpose of the statute to interfere in a case where a conveyance of legal title was made for *administrative purposes*. If it was necessary for one to whom a conveyance was made to retain the legal title in order to perform duties imposed upon him the statute did not operate to place the legal title in the person who had the use. Under such circumstances the use was classified as *active* (as distinguished from passive) and the statute did not apply.

In Anonymous (1545),[12] a feoffment was made to the use of the feoffor for life and "after his decease J. N. shall take the profits." The use was held to be passive and the statute operated to place the legal title in J. N. This followed from the fact that active duties respecting the land and the administration thereof were not placed in the hands of the feoffee. It is stated that a contrary result would have been reached if the feoffee had been directed to take the profits and deliver them to J. N.

The prevailing American view is that if the terms of a conveyance imposes an affirmative duty upon the grantee to convey or to protect the land, the use is active.[13]

Second: The Statute of Uses specifically provides that "where any person or persons stand or be seised, or at any time hereafter shall happen to be seised, * * * to the use, confidence or trust of any other person or persons, * * *" the person having the use shall be deemed the legal owner.

The above language justified the conclusion reached by the courts that the statute did not apply in the case of chattels because a person cannot, in legal contemplation, be seised of a chattel. Accordingly, the legal title to a chattel remains in the person to whom it is transferred regardless of expressions pertaining to the use.

While it is true that a person cannot be seised of a term for years (a chattel real), this does not mean that the statute may not operate with respect to a chattel real. For example, if land were conveyed to B and his heirs, to the use of C for ten years, the statute would operate to place the legal title to the ten year term in C. The language of the statute is complied with because *B is*

---

9. The Chancellor began to enforce the use probably as early as the reign of Henry V (1413–1422), but there is no record of relief prior to 1446. See Ames, Lectures on Legal History, 237.

10. 27 Hen. VIII, c. 10 (1536).

11. See Bordwell, The Repeal of the Statute of Uses, 39 Harv.Law Rev. 466, 470 (1926).

12. Anonymous [1545] Bro.Abr.Feoff. al Uses, pl. 52, March's Transl., 94.

13. 1 Rest.Trusts, § 69.

seised to the use of another—he being the owner of a freehold estate.[14]

Third: If a conveyance embodies two uses with respect to the same property and if they are not successive uses, only the first use will come within the scope of the Statute of Uses. The second use is considered to be repugnant and void.[15] For example, in a conveyance A to B and his heirs, to the use of B and his heirs, to the use of C and his heirs, the statute places the legal ownership in B and his heirs. The declared use to C and his heirs is repugnant and void.

The above stated rule was applied in Tyrrel's Case.[16] In consideration of the sum of four hundred pounds, Jane Tyrrel, a widow, conveyed described land to her son, G. Tyrrel and his heirs "to the use of the said Jane during her life * * * and immediately after her decease to the use of G. T. and the heirs of his body lawfully begotten; and in default of such issue, to the use of the heirs of the said Jane for ever." Payment of consideration raised a use in G. Tyrrel and the statute operated to place the legal title in him according to the terms of the deed. Any second use involved was repugnant and void. It is also suggested that the estate conveyed to G. Tyrrel according to the granting clause of the deed could not be limited or restricted by limitations contained in the habendum clause of the deed.

IMPORTANCE OF THE STATUTE OF USES IN MODERN LAW

7. If a use is not executed by the Statute of Uses the use may be enforced in equity as a trust.

    a. Trusts. The Statute of Uses did not arrest the development of equitable interests

in land that were eventually enforced as trusts.

    b. Conveyancing. The Statute of Uses furnished a new method by which to convey possessory estates in land.

    c. Future interests. The Statute of Uses made possible the creation of a new type of future interests called "executory interests."

In modern law the Statute of Uses is of importance in the areas of trusts, conveyancing and future interests. The various aspects are discussed in the following paragraphs.

Trusts

The Statute of Uses did not arrest the development of equitable interests in land, which interests later came to be recognized and administered as trusts. As has been stated, there were certain situations where the statute did not operate to place the legal title in the person having the use. But in Sambach v. Dalston,[17] it was held that the unexecuted use could be enforced in equity, thus giving effect to the intent of the conveyor. Like Tyrrel's case,[18] decided almost 100 years earlier, the Sambach case involved a use upon a use. But instead of holding that the second use was repugnant and void it was held to be enforceable in equity as a trust.

As a result of the rule that a second use was not within the scope of the Statute of Uses and yet could be enforced in equity as a trust, the operation of the statute could be prevented by the simple technique of declaring a second use in favor of an intended beneficial owner. Such a procedure was followed in Doe D. Lloyd v. Passingham.[19] The conveyance by deed was A to B and his heirs (lease and release) to the use of B and his heirs, to the use of C and his heirs. Even

---

14. Lutwich v. Mitton, [1620] Cro.Jac. 604, 79 Eng. Rep. 516.

15. See, Ames, Lectures on Legal History, p. 243.

16. 2 Dyer, 155a, 73 Eng.Rep. 336 (1557).

17. Tothill, 188, 21 Eng.Rep. 164 (1634).

18. 2 Dyer 155a, 73 Eng.Rep. 336 (1557).

19. 6 B. & C. 305, 108 Eng.Rep. 465 (1827).

though B acquired ownership according to common law rules (lease and release), the expressed use in favor of B and his heirs was operative as a first use and the second use in favor of C and his heirs was not executed by the Statute of Uses. Accordingly, C did not have a legal estate in the land. Any relief available to him would be in a court of equity to establish a trust because of the second use.

The prevailing rule is that the Statute of Uses is included as a part of the common law in the various American states.[20] If a use is not executed by the statute, as in the case of an active use,[21] a chattel interest[22] or a use on a use,[23] the unexecuted use is enforceable in equity as a trust. In some states the view is followed that the Statute of Uses does not form a part of the local common law.[24] However, even if this view is followed it is generally provided by statute that trusts may be created according to the intention of the parties.[25]

Conveyancing

The enactment of the Statute of Uses brought about a new method by means of which ownership in land could be conveyed. For example, payment of consideration by a proposed purchaser would raise a use in him (by bargain and sale). In the case of a passive use the statute would operate to convert the use into legal ownership. The same result would be accomplished if a use is raised by covenant to stand seised. If A conveys land to B and his heirs to the use of C and his heirs, the statute will operate to place the legal title in C and his heirs if the use is passive in nature.[26]

The method of conveying estates in land introduced by the Statute of Use furnishes the basis for the statutory methods of conveyancing established in a majority of the states.

Future Interests

The enactment of the Statute of Uses made possible the creation of a new type of future interest called an "executory interest." For example, in a conveyance it may be directed that a use is to arise in a designated person upon the happening of a stated event (springing use). So also, provision may be made for a use to shift from one person to another upon the happening of an event (shifting use) or the happening of the event may cause a use to result to the conveyor or his estate (resulting use). The statute may convert the use into a legal estate.

In the Maine case of Wyman v. Brown,[27] A conveyed an estate to B and his heirs but A was to have "quiet possession, and the entire income of the premises until her decease." The common law did not permit the conveyance of such an estate to commence *in futuro*. However, payment of consideration raised a use in B by bargain and sale and the Statute of Uses operated to convert this use into legal

---

20. 1 Bogert, Trusts and Trustees, § 208.

21. Kellogg v. Hale, 1883, 108 Ill. 164; 1 Rest.Trusts, § 69.

22. Ure v. Ure, 1900, 185 Ill. 216, 56 N.E. 1087; 1 Rest.Trusts, § 70.

23. Guest v. Farley, 1853, 19 Mo. 147; 1 Rest.Trusts, § 71.

24. See, for example, In re Estate of Fair, 1901, 132 Cal. 523, 60 P. 442, 64 P. 1000.

25. See, for example, West's Ann.Cal.Civ.Code, § 2220.

26. Witham v. Bronner, 1872, 63 Ill. 344. For detailed discussion of this method of conveying estates in land, see infra, § 116.

27. 50 Me. 139, 150 (1863).

ownership that would become possessory at the time fixed. Upon the happening of the event the use would "spring" from the conveyor A to B.[28]

Future interests of the type under discussion play an important part in the modern law of future interests, a topic discussed under a separate heading.[29]

28. See, Jackson ex dem. Wood v. Swart, 1822, 20 Johns. (N.Y.) 85.

29. See infra, § 141.

CHAPTER 3

REAL PROPERTY DEFINED

INTRODUCTORY STATEMENT

8. In the absence of severance, the physical extent of property in land includes surface rights, rights with respect to the area above the surface and the area beneath the surface. Ownership of the surface may include trees growing upon the land, chattels attached to the land and growing crops.

In the absence of a severance, the physical extent of property in land includes surface rights and rights with respect to the area above the surface and beneath the surface. Blackstone states it as follows: [1] "Land hath also, in its legal signification, an indefinite extent, upwards as well as downwards. *Cujus est solum ejus est usque ad coelum*, is the maxim of the law." [2] It includes minerals or fossils in their natural location. Because of the fugitive quality of oil and gas the prevailing rule is that it is not susceptible to ownership in place.

But a divided ownership may result if there is a severance. For example, ownership of the surface may be in one person and ownership of the area beneath the surface may be in another. So also, there may be a severance with respect to the surface and the area above the surface. Such a severance is accomplished if there is a separate interest in the space in a building, as in the case of a condominium. A California statute defines a condominium as an estate in real property consisting of an undivided interest in common "in a portion of a parcel of real property together with a separate interest in space in a residential, industrial or commercial building on such real property, such as an apartment, office or store. A condominium may include in addition a separate interest in other portions of such real property." [3]

The concept of ownership of the space above the surface has been questioned in litigation involving the right of the public to use such space for the purpose of air travel. The preferred view is that an invasion of the space does constitute a trespass but it is privileged when used for purpose of legitimate air travel. [4] The owner of the surface is entitled to recover to the extent of actual damage suffered by him. Some authorities have expressed the view that ownership extends only to the area above the surface that is in the "effective possession" of the owner of the surface. [5] In any event, land may be so located in reference to an airport or landing field that the "path of flight" is so close to the ground that its use substantially interferes with the enjoyment of the land. Such use by a governmental agency constitutes a

---

1. 2 Bl.Comm., 18.

2. See Herrin v. Sutherland, 1925, 74 Mont. 587, 241 P. 328, 42 A.L.R. 937 (causing a bullet to pass over the land of another constitutes a trespass).

3. West's Ann.Cal.Civ.Code, § 783. See also, §§ 1350–1359.

4. Burnham v. Beverly Airways, 1942, 311 Mass. 628, 42 N.E.2d 575; Rest.Torts, §§ 159, 194.

5. Hinman v. Pacific Air Transport, 9 Cir. 1936, 84 F.2d 755.

"taking of property," if only an easement, and entitles the landowner to compensation under constitutional provisions.[6] Such use by other agencies may constitute a trespass or a private nuisance.

The physical extent of property in land may also extend to chattels that have been attached to the land and to trees, crops etc., growing on the land. Ownership with respect to such items are discussed in the following sections.

TREES AND PERENNIAL BUSHES AND GRASSES (*Fructus Naturales*)

9. *Fructus naturales* **constitute a part of the land. Adjoining landowners are tenants in common of trees if the trunks of the trees are located in part upon the land of each owner.**

    a. Sale or mortgage of land. In the absence of written reservation, the ownership of *fructus naturales* **will pass with a conveyance of the land and will be included within the scope of a mortgage of the land.**

    b. Sale of *fructus naturales.* **A contract for the sale of** *fructus naturales* **is a contract for the sale of land within the Statute of Frauds unless severance is to be made by the vendor or immediate severance by the vendee is contemplated.**

    c. Crops produced by *fructus naturales.* **Growing crops of** *fructus naturales* **are classified as personal property.**

Trees and perennial bushes and grasses (*fructus naturales*) constitute a part of the land. Emphasis is placed upon the fact that such growths involve an aspect of permanency and usually require minimal care by man. These growths are to be distinguished from nursery stock. Such stock is considered to be personal property because the land is used only as a facility for preserving the merchandise and the element of permanency is lacking.[7]

Adjoining landowners are tenants in common of trees if the trunks of the trees are located in part upon the land of each owner.[8] There is authority for the view that the parties are tenants in common if the trunk of a tree is located entirely upon the land of one landowner and the roots extend into the land of the other.[9]

If the adjoining owners are tenants in common of boundary line trees, injunctive relief may be available to prevent one owner from destroying the trees. This relief was granted in Anderson v. Weiland (Cal.),[10] where eucalyptus trees formed a hedge that served the purpose of a windbreak.

Without reference to ownership as tenants in common, a landowner may be entitled to injunctive relief if the roots of trees encroach upon his land. As in the case of overhanging branches, this relief may be available upon proof of actual damages.[11]

Sale or Mortgage of Land

In the absence of written reservation, the ownership of *fructus naturales* will pass with a conveyance of the land and will be included within the scope of a mortgage of the land. There is authority for the view that this same rule applies with respect to "dead or down" timber that has not been removed from the land at the time of the conveyance

---

6. United States v. Causby, 1946, 328 U.S. 256, 106 Ct.Cl. 854, 66 S.Ct. 1062, 90 L.Ed. 1206.

7. Story v. Christin, 1939, 14 Cal.2d 592, 95 P.2d 925, 125 A.L.R. 1402; Swain Nelson & Sons Co. v. Department of Finance, 1937, 365 Ill. 401, 6 N.E.2d 632.

8. Robinson v. Clapp, 1895, 65 Conn. 365, 32 A. 939; Lennon v. Terrall, 1932, 260 Mich. 100, 244 N.W. 245.

9. Waterman v. Soper, [1789] 1 Ld.Raym. 737, 91 Eng.Rep. 1393.

10. 12 Cal.App.2d 730, 55 P.2d 1242 (1936).

11. Crance v. Hems, 1936, 17 Cal.App.2d 450, 62 P.2d 395.

or mortgage.[12] While this conclusion may be open to serious question it is supported by the argument that severance does not necessarily change the character of the growth, especially if the severance is wrongful or "accidental."

Sale of Fructus Naturales

The common law rule is that a contract for the sale of *fructus naturales* is a contract for the sale of an interest in land within the meaning of the real-property section (4th section) of the Statute of Frauds.[13] The recordation of such a contract operates to give constructive notice according to the provisions of a recording act relating to estates or interests in land.[14]

The interest acquired by the purchaser is a right to take the soil or a substance of the soil and, as such, the vendee acquires a profit.[15] If timber is reserved from the terms of the grant the vendor has such a profit. Frequently, provision is made for the removal of timber within a stated period of time. Such a provision would seem to limit the duration of the profit.[16] However, there is authority for the view that timber may be removed after that time and the only liabil-

ity will be limited to the damage caused to the land resulting from entry thereon.[17]

If the contract contemplates severance of timber by the seller, the contract is one by the seller to "bestow work and labor upon his own materials" and deliver it in its improved condition. Thus, the contract is not one that involves the conveyance of an interest in land. Rather, it involves the sale of chattels.[18]

Many early decisions follow the view that the transaction does not involve the conveyance of an interest in land if *immediate severance* of the timber is contemplated by the parties even if such severance is to be made by the buyer.[19] In some cases it is stated that such an agreement constitutes a constructive severance of the timber from the land.[20] In other cases it is held that the agreement confers a license upon the buyer to enter upon the land and that ownership of the timber passes to him only upon actual severance.[21] Under this view, only a breach of contract action can be maintained for wrongful revocation of the license. A sale of the land to a third party may result in such a revocation. It is also to be noted that circumstances may warrant the conclusion that the contract is one of employment rather than one for the sale of timber. That was the conclusion reached in the North Carolina case of Johnson v. Wallin.[22] A, the landowner, contracted with B, it being provided that B was to cut down certain trees, saw them into logs and cut them into timber. B was

---

12. Cockrill v. Downey, 1868, 4 Kan. 426; Brackett v. Goddard, 1866, 54 Me. 309.

13. Kirkeby v. Erickson, 1903, 99 Minn. 299, 96 N.W. 705 (wild grasses); Slocum v. Seymour, 1873, 36 N.J.L. 138 (standing timber to be removed within 1½ years); Green v. Armstrong, 1845, 1 Denio (N.Y.) 550 (standing timber to be removed within 20 years); Hirth v. Graham, 1893, 50 Ohio St. 57, 33 N.E. 90; Hundley v. Hulber, 1960, 201 Va. 847, 114 S.E.2d 738.

14. De Camp v. Wallace, 1904, 45 Misc. 436, 92 N.Y.S. 746 (sale is within provisions of recording statutes).

15. *Cf.:* Clap v. Draper, 1808, 4 Mass. 266 (purchaser acquires a "possessory estate" and may maintain trespass *quare clausum fregit* against the owner of the soil for cutting down the trees).

16. Saltonstall v. Little, 1879, 90 Pa. 422.

17. Irons v. Webb, 1879, 41 N.J.L. 203.

18. Killmore v. Howlett, 1872, 48 N.Y. 569.

19. *Accord:* Uniform Sales Act, § 76 (defining "goods").

20. Byassee v. Reese, 1863, 61 Ky. (4 Metc.) 372.

21. Drake v. Wells, 1865, 93 Mass. (11 Allen) 141.

22. 227 N.C. 669, 44 S.E.2d 83 (1947).

to retain part of the timber for his services. The court held that the contract was not one for the sale of standing timber.

Crops Produced by Fructus Naturales

Although *fructus naturales* may enhance the value of land over and above the value of the growing crop, profitable production depends upon cultivation, fertilization and care. This is reflected in the rule that a sale of a growing crop does not come within the scope of the real-property section (4th section) of the Statute of Frauds.[23] The crop may also be included in a chattel mortgage [24] although there is authority that the crop cannot be attached as a chattel.[25]

While *fructus naturales* constitutes a part of the land and cannot be classified as a part of the estate of a deceased life tenant,[26] a different rule is applied as to crops growing at the time of the death of a life tenant.[27] For example, hops growing from ancient roots but maturing shortly after the death of a life tenant belong to his estate.[28] A similar conclusion has been reached with respect to sugar cane.[29]

EMBLEMENTS *(Fructus Industriales)*

10. **Growing crops are usually classified as personal property.**

a. **Sale or mortgage of land.** Unless expressly excepted, growing crops will pass with a sale or mortgage of the land.

b. **Sale of growing crops.** A purported sale of growing crops is considered to be a contract to sell the crops when they come into existence.

c. **Intestate and testate succession.** If the owner of land dies intestate growing crops are considered to be personal property subject to administration. If the owner dies testate and make no specific provision otherwise the growing crops belong to the devisee of the land.

d. **Doctrine of emblements.** If a tenancy is one of uncertain duration, and is terminated without the fault of the tenant and not as the result of his act, the tenant is entitled to harvest crops planted during the period of the lease. If there are successive crops from one planting, the doctrine of emblements applies only to the first crop available after termination of the tenancy.

The doctrine of emblements applies in the case of a life estate but the right may be restricted by express provision in a deed or will that created the life estate.

Products of the earth which are *annual,* raised by yearly manurance and labor and essentially owe their existence to the cultivation by man, are called emblements or *fructus industriales.*

In general, such growing crops are classified as personal property. For example, they are subject to attachment according to procedures prescribed in the case of personal property.[30] However, if a court does not have jurisdiction to try title to land, it may

---

23. Vulicevich v. Skinner, 1888, 77 Cal. 239, 19 P. 424; Purner v. Piercy, 1874, 40 Md. 212; Frank v. Harrington, 1862, 36 Barb. (N.Y.) 415 (hops).

24. N Bar N Land & Livestock Co. v. Taylor, 1933, 94 Mont. 350, 22 P.2d 313 (alfalfa).

25. Sparrow v. Pond, 1892, 49 Minn. 412, 52 N.W. 36 (growing blackberries).

26. In re Chamberlain, 1893, 140 N.Y. 390, 35 N.E. 602.

27. For discussion of the doctrine of emblements as it relates to *fructus naturales,* see infra § 10.

28. Latham v. Atwood, [1635] Cro.Car. 515, 79 Eng. Rep. 1045.

29. Nawahi v. Hakalau Plantation Co., 1902, 14 Hawaii 460. See also, Florala Sawmill Co. v. Parrish, 1908, 155 Ala. 462, 46 So. 461 (turpentine "dip").

30. Polley v. Johnson, 1893, 52 Kan. 478, 35 P. 8; Dennett v. Hopkinson, 1873, 63 Me. 350; Penhallow v. Dwight, 1810, 7 Mass. 34; In re Anderson's Estate, 1908, 83 Neb. 8, 118 N.W. 1108. *Contra:* Ellithorpe v. Reidesil, 1887, 71 Iowa 315, 32 N.W. 238.

not have jurisdiction to try a case relating to growing crops.[31]

Sale or Mortgage of Land

Unless expressly excepted, growing crops will pass to the purchaser of the land [32] and are included within the scope of a mortgage of the land. Insofar as a purchaser of the land is concerned, the maturity or immaturity of the crop at the time of the sale is not a controlling factor.[33] There is an argument, however, that a crop ready for harvest should be considered the same as a harvested crop because it has ceased to depend upon nutriment from the soil.

The preferred view is that an oral reservation of a growing crop by the vendor or mortgagor of the land is not enforceable.[34] This conclusion cannot be based upon the Statute of Frauds because the transaction does not involve an interest in land insofar as the growing crops are concerned.[35] However, since a conveyance of land, by interpretation, includes crops growing on the land, an oral reservation of the crops cannot be shown because of the parol evidence rule.[36]

Usually, the mortgagor of land is entitled to remain in possession of the land until sale and conveyance under foreclosure proceedings and the expiration of the redemption period. The mortgagor is entitled to crops harvested during that period but he has no right to crops not so harvested.[37]

Sale of Growing Crops

According to common law rules, a contract of sale—as distinguished from a contract to sell—is void if it pertains to non-existing goods. However, a valid *contract of sale* may be made if the goods have potential existence. Thus, one in possession of land may make a present sale of crops to be grown on the land. At the present time the general rule is that a contract of sale which pertains to non-existing goods will be treated as a *contract to sell* the goods when they come into existence.[38] For this reason, the common law rule as to potential existence need not be applied. Of course, *a growing crop* has actual existence and may be the subject of a present sale.

A contract relating to the sale of emblements is not a contract for the sale of an interest in land within the meaning of the real-property (4th section) of the Statute of Frauds.[39]

---

31. See Bagley v. Columbus Southern Ry., 1896, 98 Ga. 626, 25 S.E. 638.

32. Newton County v. Boyd, 1919, 148 Ga. 761, 98 S.E. 347; Tripp v. Hasceig, 1870, 20 Mich. 254; Terhune v. Elberson, 1810, 3 N.J.L. 726, Reprint Ed. 297; Wilkins v. Vashbinder, 1838, 7 Watts (Pa.) 378. See, Herron v. Herron, 1890, 47 Ohio St. 544, 25 N.E. 420 (land acquired by wife from her husband in divorce proceedings).

33. Tripp v. Hasceig, 1870, 20 Mich. 254.

34. Davis v. Pancheri, 1951, 72 Idaho 28, 236 P.2d 716; Brown v. Thurston, 1868, 56 Me. 126; Austin v. Sawyer, 1828, 9 Cow. (N.Y.) 39. *Contra*: Kroh v. Dobson, 1949, 324 Mich. 384, 37 N.W.2d 144, 8 A.L.R.2d 561; Flynt v. Conrad, 1867, 61 N.C. 190. See, Dannefer v. Aurand, 1920, 106 Kan. 605, 189 P. 371; Garanflo v. Cooley, 1885, 33 Kan. 137, 5 P. 766.

35. Mitchell v. Weaver, D.Va.1953, 116 F.Supp. 707. See Wood v. Wood, 1947, 116 Colo. 593, 183 P.2d 889, 172 A.L.R. 812.

36. Austin v. Sawyer, 1828, 9 Cow. (N.Y.) 39; Flynt v. Conrad, 1867, 61 N.C. 190.

37. Beckman v. Sikes, 1886, 35 Kan. 120, 10 P. 592 (purchaser of the crop from the mortgagor); Farmers Bank of Hickory v. Bradley, 1926, 315 Mo. 811, 288 S.W. 774 (mortgagee of crop).

38. Uniform Sales Act, § 5(3).

39. Bull v. Griswold, 1858, 19 Ill. 631; Sainsbury v. Matthews, 1838, 4 M. & W. 343, 150 Eng.Rep. 1460.

Intestate and Testate Succession

If the owner of land dies intestate, growing crops are considered to be personal property and, as such, are subject to administration as in the case of other personal property.[40] Those who inherit the land are not entitled to the growing crops. However, if the owner of land dies testate, and makes no specific provision for the distribution of growing crops, they are considered to be a part of the land and belong to the devisee of the land.[41]

This preferential treatment of a devisee as opposed to an heir, is based upon the presumed intention of the testator. If his intention was to devise the land it is proper to presume that the intention was to include all benefits flowing from the land. However, the heir inherits the land, and emblements do not constitute a part of the land—there is no room for interpretation. As stated in Cooper v. Woolfitt (Eng.),[42] "A devisee takes more than the heir would have done; for he is not *'haeres factus,'* (a person who becomes the heir by gift or devise) but takes by conveyance. He is therefore entitled to everything which is appurtenant to the land, and as such to all crops growing on the land at the time of the testator's decease, unless it appears with certainty that the testator intended some one else to take them." The devisee is entitled even if the crop is ready for harvest at the time of the death of the testator.[43]

40. Marx v. Nelms, 1891, 95 Ala. 304, 10 So. 551; McGee v. Walker, 1895, 106 Mich. 521, 64 N.W. 482.

41. Dennett v. Hopkinson, 1873, 63 Me. 350; In re Andersen's Estate, 1908, 83 Neb. 8, 118 N.W. 1108; Smith v. Barham, 1833, 17 N.C. (2 Dev.) Eq. 420.

42. 2 H. & N. 122, 157 Eng.Rep. 51 (1857).

43. In re Estate of Andersen, 1908, 83 Neb. 8, 118 N.W. 1108.

Doctrine of Emblements

Under circumstances to be discussed, a tenant is entitled to crops planted during the continuance of his lease even if the crop is not ready for harvest at the termination of the tenancy. This does not result in an extension of the lease. The tenant has an irrevocable license to go upon the land to care for and harvest the crop.[44] The license is referable to the doctrine of emblements. It is applicable only as to crops planted during the continuance of the lease. It is not sufficient that the tenant merely prepared the land for planting.[45]

The doctrine of emblements is applicable only if a tenancy is one of uncertain duration and only if the tenancy is terminated through no fault on the part of the tenant.[46] Thus, it is applicable in the case of life estates, tenancies at will and from period to period.[47] The doctrine is applied as a means by which to encourage agricultural activities and out of fairness to tenants.

The doctrine of emblements is not applicable as to crops planted by a person in wrongful possession of the land. He is entitled to crops harvested during the period of his pos-

44. Edghill v. Mankey, 1907, 79 Neb. 347, 112 N.W. 570. See Commonwealth v. Galatta, 1917, 228 Mass. 308, 117 N.E. 343 (the tenant is the owner of the crop).

45. Price v. Pickett, 1852, 21 Ala. 741; Simpkins v. Rogers, 1854, 15 Ill. 397; Carman v. Mosier, 1898, 105 Iowa 367, 75 N.W. 323.

46. Brown v. Thurston, 1868, 56 Me. 126 (tenant at will); Davis v. Brocklebank, 1837, 9 N.H. 73 (tenant at will); Commonwealth v. Peterman, 1938, 130 Pa.Super. 497, 198 A. 687 (tenant from period to period); Kingsbury v. Collins, 1827, 4 Bing. 202, 130 Eng.Rep. 746 (tenant from period to period).

47. For explanation of these tenancies, see infra, §§ 49, 51, 84.

session [48] but is without further right.[49] Of course, he may be required to pay the reasonable rental value during the period of occupancy. Neither is the doctrine applicable in the case of a tenant for years (a fixed period).[50] As stated in Whitmarsh v. Cutting,[51] it is the tenant's folly to sow when he knows that his term will expire before he can reap. However, there is authority for the view that such a tenant is entitled to crops that are ready for harvest at the expiration of the lease if he acts promptly in completing the harvest.[52] By custom and usage in some states, the right of a tenant for years to "way-going" crops is recognized if special circumstances, such as an unusually late season, prevented harvest prior to the termination of the lease.[53]

A sublessee may be in a better position than the lessee insofar as the right to emblements is concerned. For example, if the headlease is terminated because of some default on the part of the lessee, the sublessee is entitled to harvest crops planted by him prior to such termination. His tenancy is one of uncertain duration because of the possibility of forfeiture and the forfeiture was brought about through no fault on the part of the sublessee.[54] This rule also applies in the case of a lessee of a life tenant where the life estate is brought to an end because of some act on the part of the life tenant.

The right of a lessee to emblements may constitute a breach of warranty against encumbrances contained in a deed conveying the land.[55] Additional rules are as follows:

First: The doctrine of emblements is applicable in situations where there are successive crops from one planting, such as in the case of *fructus naturales*, if the crop requires annual care and cultivation. This conclusion has been reached with respect to hops grown out of ancient roots [56] and as to sugar cane.[57] But the right of the tenant is limited to the first crop, however slight, that is available after the termination of the tenancy.[58] This constitutes a return for the labor incident to the care and cultivation of the trees, plants or vines.

Second: If a life estate is terminated by the death of a person who has an estate for his own lifetime, his personal representatives are entitled to harvest crops planted during the period of the life estate.[59] If A has an estate during the lifetime of B and B dies, A is entitled to harvest crops planted prior to the time of B's death.[60] If A has an estate during "widowhood" and the estate is terminated by remarriage benefits under the doctrine of emblements will be denied. This

---

48. Page v. Fowler, 1870, 39 Cal. 412; Robert Bros. v. Hurdle, 1849, 32 N.C. 490.

49. Stockwell v. Phelps, 1866, 34 N.Y. 363. But see Arnold v. Grigsby, 1923, 158 Ark. 232, 249 S.W. 584.

50. *Cf.:* Carmine v. Bowen, 1906, 104 Md. 198, 64 A. 932 (an estoppel situation).

51. 10 Johns. (N.Y.) 360 (1813).

52. See, for example, Opperman v. Littlejohn, 1911, 98 Miss. 636, 54 So. 77; Huggins v. Reynolds, 1908, 51 Tex.Civ.App. 504, 112 S.W. 116.

53. See, for example, Stultz v. Dickey, 1812, 5 Binn. (Pa.) 285. *Contra:* Miller v. Gray, 1941, 136 Tex. 196, 149 S.W.2d 582, 141 A.L.R. 1237.

54. Samson v. Rose, 1875, 65 N.Y. 411 (*dictum*). *Contra:* Agoure v. Plummer, 1917, 175 Cal. 543, 166 P. 311, noted in 6 Cal.Law Rev. 156 (1918).

55. Estep v. Bailey, 1919, 94 Or. 59, 185 P. 227.

56. Latham v. Atwood, [1638] Cro.Car. 515, 79 Eng. Rep. 1045.

57. Nawahi v. Hakalau Plantation Co., 1902, 14 Hawaii 460.

58. Graves v. Weld, [1833] 5 B. & Ad. 105, 110 Eng. Rep. 731. See Hendrixson v. Cardwell, 1876, 68 Tenn. (9 Baxt.) 389.

59. Edghill v. Mankey, 1907, 79 Neb. 347, 112 N.W. 570.

60. Sprick v. Beach, 1961, 188 Kan. 296, 362 P.2d 24.

follows from the fact that the estate was terminated by A's conduct.[61]

A life tenant may, of course, lease the land to another. However, unless the life tenant had a power authorizing the execution of a lease that would extend beyond his lifetime, the lease terminates upon the death of the life tenant. In that event, the tenant is entitled to harvest crops planted prior to the death of the life tenant.[62] However, the estate of the life tenant is not entitled to the benefits resulting therefrom. In other words, the life tenant is not a tenant in possession and is not entitled to benefits flowing from the doctrine of emblements. But if the life tenant enters into a sharecropping contract, his estate may claim benefits resulting from that contract.[63]

The right of a life tenant to benefits under the doctrine of emblements may be restricted by the express provisions in a deed or a will. For example, a deed may provide that after the death of a life tenant "all rents, profits and income" shall go to the grantee. Upon the death of the life tenant the grantee is entitled to growing crops because the profits therefrom accrue after the death of the life tenant.[64] Similar language may be embodied in a will.[65]

Third: The rights of one who purchases a growing crop from a tenant are measured by the rights of the tenant himself. If the tenancy is terminated prior to harvest the purchaser will be entitled to harvest the crop if and only if the tenant has such a right.[66]

Fourth: If land is encumbered after the execution of a lease the tenant's right to emblements will be protected except as to *bona fide* purchasers or mortgagees for value and without notice, actual or constructive.

If land is encumbered before the execution of a lease the prevailing rule is that the tenant is not entitled to benefits under the doctrine of emblements as against the creditor. He is only entitled to the crops harvested prior to sale under foreclosure proceedings and any period of redemption that may be allowed.[67] There is authority for the view that the tenant is entitled to harvest crops that mature within the stated period if the tenant acts promptly in completing the harvest.[68] There is also authority for the view that the tenant is entitled to crops harvested prior to the time when the purchaser *takes possession* of the land.[69]

Even if a judgment obtained against a landowner constitutes a lien on land owned by him, a tenant is entitled to emblements even if his lease was executed after the rendition of the judgment. This rule is based upon the fact that the purchaser at an execution sale acquires only the interest that the debtor has

---

61. Hawkins v. Skegg's Adm'r, 1848, 29 Tenn. (10 Humph.) 31.

62. Bradley v. Bailey, 1888, 56 Conn. 374, 15 A. 746 (when the crop was planted the lessee had reason to believe that the life tenant was near death).

63. In re Mischke's Estate, 1939, 136 Neb. 875, 287 N.W. 760, 125 A.L.R. 277; McCraw v. Simpson, 10 Cir. 1944, 141 F.2d 789; Restatement, Property, 1948 Supplement, § 121, *Comment bb.*

64. Williams v. Stander, 1960, 143 Colo. 469, 354 P.2d 492.

65. Lloyd v. First National Trust & Savings Bank, 1951, 101 Cal.App.2d 579, 225 P.2d 962. See Preston's Estate v. Preston, 1961, 59 Wash.2d 11, 365 P.2d 595 (trust income).

66. Debow v. Colfax, 1828, 10 N.J.L. 128.

67. Howell v. Schenck, 1853, 24 N.J.L. 89; Lane v. King, 1832, 8 Wend. (N.Y.) 584. *Contra:* Cassilly v. Rhodes, 1843, 12 Ohio 88 (on the theory that the tenant becomes a tenant at will).

68. Hecht v. Dettman, 1880, 56 Iowa 679, 7 N.W. 495, 10 N.W. 241; Myers v. Steele, 1916, 98 Kan. 577, 158 P. 660 (mortgagee of crop).

69. Schuchard v. St. Anthony & Dakota Elevator Co., 1928, 176 Minn. 37, 222 N.W. 292.

in the land and that interest is subject to the tenant's right to emblements.[70]

FIXTURES

11. A chattel may be placed on land under circumstances justifying the conclusion that it thereby became a part of the land. In that event it becomes a fixture.

a. Conversion of a chattel into a fixture. If the intention is to permanently improve the freehold a chattel may become a fixture even if it is not attached to the land by a mechanical device.

If a machine in an industrial plant is classified as a fixture that classification follows all of the essential parts of the machine.

Real property taxes are levied on the basis of land values augmented by fixtures.

Valuation of land taken in condemnation proceedings is computed on the basis of fixtures located on the land.

b. Severance of a fixture from the land. Classification as a fixture may continue even if a chattel is temporarily severed from the land or severed by accident, mistake or act of God.

The conditional seller of a chattel may lose his right to retake possession in case of default in payment if the chattel is converted into a fixture with his consent, express or implied, or if the chattel has become an integral part of the premises.

In general, the conditional seller's right to sever a chattel from the land is judged by reference to the rights of the possessor of the land.

The owner of a chattel has a right to sever it from the land of another if the chattel was attached without its owner's consent, express or implied.

c. Trade fixtures. In general, a tenant is entitled to remove fixtures if they were at-

tached by him for purposes of trade, ornament or domestic use.

The right of removal must be exercised during the period of the lease or during an extension thereof.

If the lease is one of uncertain duration removal may be made within a reasonable time after the termination of the lease.

A life tenant may remove trade fixtures during the continuance of the estate. A reasonable time for removal may be claimed by his executor or administrator.

Conversion of a Chattel Into a Fixture.

The traditional English rule is that a chattel is not converted into a fixture unless it is attached to the land by some mechanical device, such as by nails, bolts, screws or mortar.[71]

But this "attachment rule" is not absolute. For example, in the early English case of *Ex parte* Astbury,[72] the court states, "it is admitted that where there is a mortgage of a manufactory, and part of the machinery used in it is a fixture, that part passes." The issue in the case was whether or not duplicate rolls, fitted but not in place in rolling machines, would pass with a "mortgage of the manufactory." The conclusion is reached that the duplicate and fitted rolls, although not attached to the machine, would pass under such a mortgage. The situation involved a "constructive annexation."

The American rule is that the conversion of a chattel to that of a fixture depends upon the intention of the person making the annexation. A fixture results from an intention to "permanently improve the freehold." [73]

---

70. Dollar v. Roddenbery, 1895, 97 Ga. 148, 25 S.E. 410; Heavilon v. Farmers Bank of Frankfort, 1891, 81 Ind. 249.

71. King v. Otley, [1830] 1 B. & Ad. 161, 109 Eng.Rep. 747.

72. L.R. 4 Ch.App. 630 (1869).

73. Teaff v. Hewitt, 1853, 1 Ohio St. 511.

In the Connecticut case of Giuliano Construction Co. v. Simmons,[74] plaintiff purchased twenty building lots upon four of which were piles of topsoil. On lot number sixteen the pile was twenty feet high and forty feet long. Defendant purchased this lot without specific agreement as to the topsoil and claimed to be the owner thereof.

The court held that ownership of the topsoil remained in the plaintiff. When it was severed from its natural condition on the ground it became personal property and its ownership in the present case is governed by the law as it relates to fixtures. To constitute a fixture it must be shown that "a permanent accession to the freehold was intended to be made by the annexation of the article." The intention sought is not the subjective intention or undisclosed purpose of the annexor but is the intention manifested by his acts. In this case the size of the piles of topsoil, approximately the height of a two story building, was objective evidence that the topsoil had been piled on the lot for purposes other than permanent affixation.

A fixture may result if the chattel is attached to the land only by gravity, as in the case of heavy machinery or structures.[75] If a structure is placed on sills it may be assumed that the purpose was to prevent it from being considered as a fixture.[76]

The method by which a chattel is attached to land is one of the factors to be taken into consideration in resolving the intention-issue. Other factors to be considered include the purpose of the improvement as it relates to the use of the land, the nature of the annexor's interest in the land (owner in fee simple,

for life or tenant for years) and the extent of damage, if any, that would be caused by a severance of the chattel from the land.[77] Consideration is also given to the purpose for which a classification is made. A chattel may be classified as a fixture in litigation between the vendor and vendee of land or between the mortgagor and mortgagee of the land and be classified as personal property if the issue relates to taxation of the land or the amount of compensation in eminent domain proceedings.

If a chattel does not relate to the "normal use" of the land it may avoid classification as a fixture. For example, in the California case of M. P. Moller, Inc. v. Wilson,[78] a pipe organ was installed in a *private residence* and constructed to fit into a space specially provided. The conditional vendor of the organ claimed the organ because of default under the contract. His claim was resisted by a *bona fide* purchaser of the land under a deed of trust executed after the organ had been installed. Judgment was in favor of the conditional vendor upon the ground that the organ *did not become a fixture* when it was placed in the house. It was not essential to the ordinary and convenient use of the property as a residence.[79] In this respect the situation differs from one where an organ is installed in a place such as a church.

Chattels that are reasonably necessary to the use of land, or fixtures located thereon, may be classified as fixtures although not attached to the land by any mechanical means. This conclusion may be aided by proof of cus-

74. 147 Conn. 441, 162 A.2d 511 (1960).

75. Snedeker v. Warring, 1854, 12 N.Y. 170.

76. See, Scriven v. Bailey, 1940, 67 S.D. 169, 290 N.W. 486.

77. See, Kruse Metals Mfg. Co. v. Utility Trailer Mfg. Co., 1962, 206 Cal.App.2d 176, 23 Cal.Rptr. 514 (blower system installed by sublessee classified as personal property and, for that reason, did not subject the property to materialman's lien).

78. 8 Cal.2d 31, 63 P.2d 818 (1936).

79. *Contra*: Denvir v. Crowe, 1928, 321 Mo. 212, 9 S.W.2d 957.

tom and usage. Window screens, storm doors and windows, that have been fitted for the purpose, may be classified as fixtures although they are not in place.[80] This theory of "constructive annexation" may apply to such items as fencing material (wire and posts) placed on the land awaiting construction.

The prevailing view is that such items as gas stoves,[81] refrigerators, and electric light fixtures[82] may be classified as fixtures in spite of the fact that the "physical attachment" to the land may be slight. This is especially true in the case of an apartment building where the inclination is to apply a constructive-annexation rule.[83] While the cases are in conflict such unattached items as roll-a-way beds have been classified as fixtures.[84] This same classification has been applied in the case of wall-to-wall carpeting.[85]

The fact that a chattel is affixed to land does not necessarily mean that it thereby loses its characteristics as personal property. However, it may be affixed to land under circumstances justifying the conclusion that it does become a part of the land. In that event it is called a fixture.

The rights of a landowner with respect to a fixture are not absolute. A person other than the landowner may have a right to detach the chattel from the land and thereby restore it to its original condition as personal property. Such a right may be implied, as in the case of a lessee. This situation is discussed under the heading of trade fixtures. The right may be expressed such as in a case where the landowner purchases a chattel under a conditional sales agreement and thereafter affixes the chattel to the land thereby converting it into a fixture. If there is default under the conditional sales contract the conditional vendor may reclaim his property unless it is affixed to the land in such a manner as to become an integral part of the premises. In that event the identity of the chattel has been lost by integration.

Industrial machinery

If a machine in an industrial plant is classified as a fixture, essential parts of that machine follow the same classification even though the parts are not in place.[86]

In at least one state the theory of constructive annexation is extended to include unattached machinery that is essential to the operation of an industrial plant. Such a rule is declared in the Pennsylvania case of Titus v. Poland Coal Co.,[87] and is described as "the

80. Cunningham v. Seaboard Realty Co., 1904, 67 N.J.Eq. 210, 58 A. 812 (window screens made to order); E. M. Fish Co. v. Young, 1906, 127 Wis. 149, 106 N.W. 795.

81. Fratt v. Whittier, 1881, 58 Cal. 126 (gas fixtures installed in a hotel); Mortgage Bond Co. v. Stephens, 1937, 181 Okl. 419, 74 P.2d 361 (gas stoves, refrigerators and folding beds). *Contra*: Madfes v. Beverly Development Corp., 1929, 251 N.Y. 12, 166 N.E. 787 (gas ranges installed in an apartment house retained status as chattels).

82. Canning v. Owen, 1901, 22 R.I. 624, 48 A. 1033 (electric light fixtures installed in a hotel).

83. But see, Andrews v. First Realty Corp., 1935, 6 Cal.App.2d 407, 44 P.2d 628 (refrigerator equipment in apartment house classified as personal property).

84. Doll v. Guthrie, 1930, 233 Ky. 77, 24 S.W.2d 947. *Contra*: Gray v. Prudential Ins. Co., 1938, 182 Okl. 342, 77 P.2d 563.

85. Dean Vincent, Inc. v. Redisco, Inc., 1962, 232 Or. 170, 373 P.2d 995. But see, Dusenberry v. Taylor's, 1958, 7 Utah 2d 383, 325 P.2d 910.

86. In re Ginsburg, 3 Cir. 1958, 255 F.2d 358. See, Anderson v. Perpetual Bldg. & Loan Ass'n, 1937, 172 Md. 94, 190 A. 747, 109 A.L.R. 1419 (crane, drills and other minor units not physically affixed but considered to be integral parts of stone cutting and polishing machinery); Metropolitan Life Ins. Co. v. Kimball, 1939, 163 Or. 31, 94 P.2d 1101 (carts and trays essential parts of a prune dryer considered to be fixtures and necessary for the operation of a prune orchard).

87. 275 Pa. 431, 119 A. 540, 542 (1923).

assembled industrial plant doctrine." It is not applicable to nonproduction items in a plant, such as office equipment and trucks not used in connection with the manufacturing process.[88] This doctrine is applicable in the case of industrial mortgages (unless there is evidence that the parties did not intend to include this type of machinery)[89] and is used as a basis for valuation of land for the assessment of local real estate transactions. It is not applied in determining the value of land for the purpose of computing the amount of a tax assessed upon the sale of land (Realty Transfer Tax Act).[90]

A modified "industrial plant rule" is followed in New Jersey and is designated as "the institutional doctrine."[91] However, the doctrine is not applicable to the usual type of light-weight fixtures in a store.[92] In a number of states the "attachment-requirement" is reduced to a minimum. For example, a hookup to a power line may suffice for the purpose.[93]

Taxation

Real property taxes are levied on the basis of land values augmented by fixtures. The test to be applied in determining whether or not a chattel has been converted into a fixture is the same in an assessment case as it is in any other case. The intention of the one making the annexation, as determined by objective standards, is the controlling factor. If it is shown that such intention was to make a permanent improvement to the freehold then the valuation placed upon the land reflects the presence of the fixture.[94]

In behalf of the landowner it may be contended that this procedure is not equitable in a case where a person other than the landowner enjoys the beneficial rights of ownership. For example, the fixture may be subject to a right of severance in a tenant or a conditional vendor. Be that as it may, it is not for an assessor to pass upon the validity or invalidity of a claimed right of severance. The landowner is legally responsible for this condition of the land and if adjustments are necessary they should be made with persons who may have an interest such as the right of severance. The situation is not unlike that in the case where there are two or more estates in the same land. Usually, there is but one assessment and rules respecting the apportionment as to liability are not resolved by the assessor.

Of course, an issue may be raised as to the status of chattels placed upon land. For example, it may be contended that railroad tracks and other railroad equipment are not placed upon land with any intention to improve the freehold. Placement is for the simple purpose of conducting railroad operations. Further, the element of permanency is lacking because public convenience may require removal of the tracks etc., at any time.[95] The situation differs from one where a landowner places tracks, etc., on his land for the purpose

88. First Nat. Bank of Mt. Carmel v. Reichneder, 1952, 371 Pa. 463, 91 A.2d 277.

89. Delaware County Nat. Bank v. Montgomery, 3 Cir. 1935, 78 F.2d 616.

90. Commonwealth v. Haveg Industries, Inc., 1963, 411 Pa. 515, 192 A.2d 376.

91. Smyth Sales Corp. v. Norfolk B. & L. Ass'n, 1935, 116 N.J.L. 293, 184 A. 204, 111 A.L.R. 357.

92. Fahmie v. Nyman, 1961, 70 N.J.Super. 313, 175 A.2d 438 (purchaser of fixtures prevailed over a prior mortgagee of the land).

93. See, for example, Ottumwa Woolen Mill Co. v. Hawley, 1876, 44 Iowa 57.

94. Trabue Pittman Corp. v. Los Angeles County, 1946, 29 Cal.2d 385, 175 P.2d 512. But see, Zangerle v. Republic Steel Corp., 1945, 144 Ohio St. 529, 60 N.E.2d 170.

95. County of Placer v. Lake Tahoe Ry. Co., 1922, 58 Cal.App. 764, 209 P. 900.

of access to a mine.[96] Here, the installation does permanently improve the value of the mine and removal does not depend upon public convenience to the same extent as in the case of a public utility.

Condemnation

Valuation of land taken in condemnation proceedings is computed on the basis of fixtures located on the land. The intention test is applied in resolving the fixture-issue.[97] However, all of the furnishings of an apartment building are not to be classified as fixtures even if local custom and usage indicates that such furnishings would pass to a purchaser of the apartment building.[98]

Valuation to be placed upon the land and fixtures is not subject to variation by the fact that a third party, such as a tenant, may have a right to remove the fixtures. The reason for this rule is that in resolving a value issue the public authority is not entitled to rely upon the provisions of a privately negotiated contract between the landowner and a third party, such as a conditional vendor or a tenant. The tenant is entitled to share in an award to the extent of the value of fixtures subject to his right of removal.[99]

Many leases contain a waiver provision by the terms of which a tenant waives all claims against the lessor by reason of the taking of the leased land. In the absence of specific language to the contrary, such a clause does not amount to a waiver of the tenant's claim to compensation for the value of fixtures that are removable by him. Waiver is limited to a claim that might otherwise be asserted for the value of the unexpired term of his lease.[1]

Severance of a Fixture from the Land

In an early English decision, Wystow's Case,[2] a millstone, which was "parcel of a mill", was severed from the land for the temporary purpose of being repaired. While so severed its classification as a fixture was affirmed. At the time of severance it was not the intention of the owner to change the status from that of a fixture to that of personal property. That is also the case if severance is brought about by accident or act of God, as by a storm.[3]

According to one view, the promise of a landowner that if a chattel is affixed to land it can be removed at some subsequent date prevents the chattel from being converted into a fixture. According to another view such a promise merely authorizes the promisee to enter upon the land and perform an act that would otherwise be actionable. Under neither view is the promise within the scope of the real-property section of the Statute of Frauds. The promise is not one relating to an interest in land.

Early decisions declared the rule that if a chattel has been converted into a fixture, a sale of the fixture does involve the sale of an interest in land within the meaning of the Statute of Frauds.[4] It was so held in the Massachusetts case of Gibbs v. Estey,[5] where

---

96. Merritt & Bourne v. Judd & Byrne, 1859, 14 Cal. 59.

97. Los Angeles v. Klinker, 1933, 219 Cal. 198, 25 P.2d 826, 90 A.L.R. 148.

98. State by and through State Highway Commission v. Feves, 1961, 228 Or. 273, 365 P.2d 97.

99. Roffman v. Wilmington Housing Authority, Del. 1962, 179 A.2d 99; In re Whitlock Avenue in the City of New York, 1938, 278 N.Y. 276, 16 N.E.2d 281, reargument denied 278 N.Y. 714, 17 N.E.2d 135.

1. Roffman v. Wilmington Housing Authority, Del. 1962, 179 A.2d 99.

2. Y.B. 14 Hen. VIII, 25b (1523).

3. Rogers v. Gilinger, 1858, 30 Pa. 185. *Contra:* Buckout v. Swift, 1865, 27 Cal. 433.

4. Fuller v. Tabor, 1855, 39 Me. 519. But see, Adams v. Chamberlin, 1936, 54 Ga.App. 459, 188 S.E. 550.

5. 81 Mass. (15 Gray) 587 (1860).

the promise authorizing the removal of a house was not made until after the foundation of the house had been completed.[6] The Uniform Sales Act provides that a contract for the sale of a fixture is one pertaining to personal property if immediate removal is contemplated by the contracting parties.[7]

In the Minnesota case of Esbjornsson v. Buffalo Ins. Co.,[8] plaintiffs sold land the deed providing "except the buildings thereon which title the vendors reserve unto themselves with the right to remove" within a year. A building was not removed within the year. It was destroyed by fire and plaintiffs claimed under a fire insurance policy issued by defendant company.

It was contended that plaintiffs did not have an insurable interest. In denying this defense it is held that the buildings were *excluded* from the terms of the grant (excepted) and ownership remained in plaintiffs. Failure to remove the building within the year did not result in forfeiture of plaintiffs' ownership.

Loss of ownership by conditional seller of a chattel

In the event of default by the buyer under a conditional sales agreement, the seller's usual remedy is to repossess the chattel. If it has been converted into a fixture with the express or implied consent of the seller his right to retake possession may be lost be-

cause of intervening rights of third parties as discussed in the following paragraphs.

Regardless of other factors, the general rule is that repossession of the chattel will be denied if it has been affixed to land in such a manner as to become an integral part thereof. In that event it has lost its identity as a chattel.

Even if an identity situation is not involved, the preferred view is that a conditional seller is not entitled to regain possession of the chattel if it has been attached to the land of one other than the buyer and severance would cause *material* physical damage to the land or fixtures attached thereto. According to a minority rule physical damage to the land is not an appropriate test to be applied. For example, in the New Jersey case of Smyth Sales Corp. v. Norfolk Bldg. & Loan Ass'n,[9] the removal of oil burning equipment was denied upon the ground that it "became permanently essential to the completeness of the building" in which it has been installed. Thus, the court follows a "plant damage" rule rather than a "physical damage" rule. This "institutional doctrine", however, is not applicable to light-weight and common types of store fixtures.[10]

There is authority for the view that if a conditional seller is willing to pay the physical damage involved he is entitled to regain possession of the chattel even if the severance damage is considered to be material.[11] Application of this rule eliminates controversy as to whether or not a "material damage" is involved.

---

6. *Accord*: Baird v. Elliott, 1933, 63 N.D. 738, 249 N.W. 894, 91 A.L.R. 1274, noted in 18 Minn.Law Rev. 234 (contract for sale of building). *Contra*: Home Owners' Loan Corp. v. Gotwals, 1941, 67 S.D. 579, 297 N.W. 36 (oral exception of fixtures valid).

7. Uniform Sales Act, § 76 (defining the term "goods"). See, Cervadoro v. First Nat. Bank & Trust Co., 1944, 267 App.Div. 314, 45 N.Y.S.2d 738.

8. 252 Minn. 269, 89 N.W.2d 893 (1958).

9. 116 N.J.L. 293, 184 A. 204, 111 A.L.R. 357 (1936), noted in 22 Cornell Law Rev. 421 (1937).

10. Fahmie v. Nyman, 1961, 70 N.J.Super. 313, 175 A.2d 438 (conflicting claims asserted by a purchaser of the fixtures and a prior mortgagee of the land).

11. See, Uniform Commercial Code, § 9–313(2), comments 2, 3.

Vendor of land

One in possession of land under an executory contract of sale may purchase a chattel under a conditional sales contract and then default under both contracts. The general rule is that the conditional seller's right to sever the chattel is judged by reference to the rights of the possessor of the land. With exceptions already noted, the conditional seller is entitled to regain possession of the chattel.[12]

Bona fide purchaser or mortgagee of the land

A landowner may purchase a chattel under a conditional sales contract. If he converts it into a fixture, defaults under the contract and conveys the land to a *bona fide* purchaser or mortgagee, the conditional seller may lose his right to recover possession of the chattel. This conclusion is based upon the ground that the *bona fide* party has a right to rely upon the physical condition of the land as it appeared to be at the time of the sale or mortgage. Two additional points are as follows:

First: Statutes in some states make provision for the recordation of conditional sales contracts. According to one view, if a contract is properly recorded a subsequent purchaser or mortgagee of land to which a chattel has been affixed take with constructive notice of the seller's interest. But the preferred view is to the contrary. It is reasoned that while the recordation of a conditional sales contract operates to give constructive notice of the seller's interest to subsequent purchasers or mortgagees *of the chattel*, that is not the case with respect to purchasers or mortgagees of the land to which the chattel has been affixed. It is considered that the burden incident to a "search of the records"

would be intolerable in connection with a land-purchase or mortgage transaction because of the vast variety of chattels that constitute potential fixtures.[13] In some states this objection has been answered by a statutory requirement that the conditional sales contract be filed in records maintained for "real estate" transactions.[14]

Second: The general rule is that if land was mortgaged prior to the date upon which the chattel was affixed to the land, the seller under the conditional sales contract has a right to reclaim possession of the chattel as against the mortgagee.[15] Of course, this right of severance will be lost if the mortgaged land is sold to a *bona fide* purchaser after the chattel was affixed to the land.[16] Such a purchaser may acquire ownership subject to the prior mortgage.

It is obvious that in a pre-mortgage situation the mortgagee did not advance funds in reliance upon the fixture as security because the fixture was not there at the time of the mortgage. In some decisions it is also pointed out that the landowner cannot be presumed to have intended the chattel to become a fixture because of the existence of the mortgage. This is in accord with the rule that intention is determined by an objective standard. One of the matters that may be taken into consideration is the annexor's in-

12. See, Miller v. Waddingham, 1891, 91 Cal. 377, 27 P. 750.

13. See XX Century Heating etc., Co. v. Home Owners' Loan Corp., 1937, 56 Ohio App. 188, 10 N.E.2d 229, appeal dismissed 32 Ohio St. 476, 9 N.E.2d 2.

14. Massachusetts, Pennsylvania, Oregon and New York are listed in V Am.Law of Property, p. 52, fn. 23. See, Metropolitan Life Ins. Co. v. Kimball, 1939, 163 Or. 31, 94 P.2d 1101.

15. Intermountain Food Equipment Co., Inc. v. Waller, 1963, 86 Idaho 94, 383 P.2d 612; Blanchard v. Eureka Planing Mill Co., 1911, 58 Or. 37, 113 P. 55; V Am.Law of Property, § 19.12, p. 49.

16. See, Marine Midland Trust Co. v. Ahern, 1939, 16 N.Y.S.2d 656.

terest in the land. But in applying the general rule the right to remove a fixture should be denied if severance would impair the value of the security as it existed at the time when the mortgage was executed.[17]

The above reasoning is not applicable in a case where a landowner secures a "construction loan", it being understood that funds secured under the loan are to be used in the construction of a building and that the security is to be the "completed building." In a situation of this type the mortgagee will prevail as against the conditional seller of a chattel that is converted into a fixture after the execution of the mortgage.[18]

The minority rule is that a mortgagee will prevail as against the conditional seller of a chattel that is converted into a fixture either before or after the date of the mortgage. The only thing at issue is whether or not the chattel is properly classified as a fixture. That issue is not determined by reference to the time of annexation.[19]

Wrongful annexation and annexation by mistake

The owner of a chattel has a right to sever it from the land of another if it was affixed to the land without his consent express or implied.[20] This rule is followed unless the chattel has lost its identity by incorporation, such as in a case where a brick is embodied in a wall or a timber in a house.[21]

The common law rule is that the landowner reaps the benefit if fixtures are attached to his land even by one who acts under an innocent mistake as to ownership of the land.

In many states betterment statutes have been passed that afford some relief to the innocent actor in such a case. A usual provision is that improvements erected by mistake may be removed upon payment of damages that may thereby be caused to the physical condition of the land. But some statutes limit relief to an adverse possessor holding under color of title. So also, relief may be limited to amounts demanded by the landowner in a claim for the reasonable value of use and occupation.[22]

In some states equitable relief is made available under varying circumstances without the aid of a statute.[23] One theory is that if the landowner seeks equitable relief the court may impress a lien upon the land to the extent that the value of the land was enhanced because of improvements erected by an innocent party. It is concluded that one who seeks equity must do equity.

But equitable relief may be available if proceedings are instituted *against* the landowner. In the Michigan case of Ollig v. Eagles,[24] a builder brought a suit in equity to recover the value of a house that he erected upon defendant's land under the mistaken belief that the land belonged to plaintiff's wife. Having full knowledge of his own legal rights, the defendant stood by and acquiesced fully in plaintiff's acts without asserting a claim of ownership. It was held that defendant's silence served to estop him

---

17. Dauch v. Ginsburg, 1931, 214 Cal. 540, 6 P.2d 952.

18. Hammel Radiator Corp. v. Mortgage Guarantee Co., 1933, 129 Cal.App. 468, 18 P.2d 993.

19. See, for example, General Heat & Appliance Co. v. Goodwin, 1944, 316 Mass. 3, 54 N.E.2d 676; Holland Furnace Co. v. Trumbull Savings & Loan Co., 1939, 135 Ohio St. 48, 19 N.E.2d 273 (purchaser at foreclosure sale).

20. Eisenhauer v. Quinn, 1907, 36 Mont. 368, 93 P. 38.

21. See Shoemaker, Miller & Co. v. Simpson, 1876, 16 Kan. 43.

22. See, for example, West's Ann.Cal.Civ.Code, § 1013.5. For enumeration of statutes, see note, 41 Col.Law Rev. 1272, 1273 n. 5 (1941).

23. Pope v. Speiser, 1955, 7 Ill.2d 231, 130 N.E.2d 507. See, Rest.Restitution, § 161.

24. 347 Mich. 49, 78 N.W.2d 553 (1956).

from asserting his legal ownership as a defense.[25] It was also held that under the theory of implied contract, the court was justified in declaring a lien upon the land for the value of the improvement.

The prevailing rule is that the innocent improver is entitled to a lien to the extent that the improvement enhanced the value of the land even though estoppel is not involved.[26] Relief is denied, however, regardless of expenditures made, unless the improvement enhanced the value of the land.[27]

A court of equity may also authorize the removal of structures and other fixtures erected by the innocent plaintiff on the land of another upon condition that compensation is paid for any damage caused to the land.[28] An exchange of lots may be directed, if they are equal in value and advantage, and one owner innocently erected improvements on the wrong lot.[29]

Trade Fixtures

According to the common law rule, and with exceptions to be noted, a tenant is entitled to remove fixtures that he attached to leased land for purposes of trade. Removal was authorized if made at any time during the continuance of the lease. The rule was adopted as a means by which to encourage trade. In the early case of Elwes v. Maw

(Eng.),[30] it was held that the rule did not apply with respect to fixtures installed for agricultural purposes.[31] The prevailing American rule is that the trade fixture doctrine applies as to fixtures used for purposes of trade, agriculture, ornament or domestic use.[32]

It may be contended that a tenant who affixes a chattel to leased land does not usually entertain an intent to permanently improve the land and that the chattel should not be classified as a fixture. But this view has not been followed. If the chattel would be classified as a fixture if attached by the owner of the land it will be classified as a fixture if attached by the tenant.

By express agreement, a lessee may reserve the right to remove fixtures that he affixes to the leased land. In the face of such an agreement the right of the lessee and his successors in interest to remove a fixture is not made to depend upon the trade fixture doctrine. The agreement furnishes the basis for the right. The preferred view is that if a lease reserves a right in the tenant to remove fixtures he is not under a duty to exercise the right.[33] In other words, the creation of the right does not result in the creation of

---

25. *Accord:* Kish v. Beruth Holding Corp., 1961, 66 N.J.Super. 149, 168 A.2d 649.

26. See Meyers v. Canutt, 1951, 242 Iowa 692, 46 N.W.2d 72, 24 A.L.R.2d 1; Johnson v. Schwarz, Mo.1961, 349 S.W.2d 56.

27. Heim v. Shore, 1959, 59 N.J.Super. 78, 157 A.2d 146.

28. McCreary v. Lake Boulevard Sponge Exchange Co., 1938, 133 Fla. 740, 183 So. 7.

29. Voss v. Forgue, Fla.1956, 84 So.2d 563. See Paoli v. Casentini, 1961, 190 Cal.App.2d 52, 12 Cal. Rptr. 6 (reformation of conveying instruments); Meier v. Maguire, 1961, 172 Neb. 52, 108 N.W.2d 397 (reformation of conveying instruments).

30. 3 East 38, 102 Eng.Rep. 510 (1802).

31. *Contra:* Van Ness v. Pacard, 1829, 27 U.S. (2 Pet.) 137, 7 L.Ed. 374 (operation of a dairy).

32. Old Line Life Ins. Co. of America v. Hawn, 1937, 225 Wis. 627, 275 N.W. 542, noted in 22 Minn.Law Rev. 563 (1938).

33. Savage v. University State Bank, 1931, 263 Ill. App. 457; Arkansas Fuel Oil Co. v. Connellee, Tex.Civ.App.1931, 39 S.W.2d 99; Duvanel v. Sinclair Refining Co., 1951, 170 Kan. 483, 227 P.2d 88, 23 A.L.R.2d 649; Perry v. J. L. Mott Iron Works Co., 1911, 207 Mass. 501, 93 N.E. 798; Republic Investment Co. v. Naches Hotel Co., 1937, 190 Wash. 176, 67 P.2d 858; Cass v. Home Tobacco Warehouse Co., 1949, 311 Ky. 95, 223 S.W.2d 569; McKenzie v. Western Greenbrier Bank, 1962, 146 W.Va. 971, 124 S.E.2d 234.

a duty. An express agreement on the part of the lessee to remove fixtures attached to the land is necessary to accomplish such a purpose.

A tenant does not have a right to remove a chattel under the trade fixture doctrine if it is affixed to the land in such a manner as to justify the conclusion that it has become an integral part of the land.[34] Under such circumstance it has lost its identity by integration. However, there is authority that a tenant is entitled to remove buildings erected for the purpose of operating an oil and gasoline station.[35]

Estate for years (fixed term)

If a tenant is in possession under a lease for a fixed period of time, his right to remove trade fixtures will be lost unless exercised during the period of the lease or during any period during which the lease is *extended*.

The common law rule is that if a tenant enters into a new lease that results in a surrender of the old lease, or a renewal thereof, without making provision for the removal of fixtures that were attached during the term of the prior lease, his right to remove such fixtures is lost. This conclusion is based upon the ground that the terms of the new lease were presumably adjusted in accordance with the value of such fixtures to the lessor.[36] In some cases this is referred to as a "presumption of a gift." The common law

rule has been modified or abolished in a majority of the states. In other words, for the purpose under discussion a distinction is not made between an "extension" and a "renewal" of a lease.[37] In the New Jersey case of Greenspan-Greenberger Co. v. The Goerke Co.,[38] the court states that while the common law rule is followed in New Jersey, it is not applicable where store fixtures are involved.

Express provisions in a lease may authorize the removal of fixtures after the expiration of the lease. In the Michigan case of Davidson v. Crump Mfg. Co.,[39] the lease allowed removal of fixtures "at the end of this term." As construed by the court, this clause allowed the tenant a reasonable time after the expiration of the lease within which to remove fixtures. It is pointed out that the clause was not inserted in the lease to restrict the tenant's rights but, rather, to protect them. The clause was intended to mean something other than that the tenant had a right to remove fixtures during the continuance of the term because such a right would have existed in the absence of the clause. The obvious purpose of the clause was to extend and not to restrict the tenant's rights.[40]

Estates at will and from period to period (uncertain duration)

If an estate is one of uncertain duration, such as an estate at will or an estate from period to period, trade fixtures may be removed by the tenant within a reasonable time after the termination of his estate. This reason-

---

34. Alden v. Mayfield, 1912, 163 Cal. 793, 127 P. 44 (marble store front); Martin v. Pilaczynski, 1939, 63 Ohio App. 101, 25 N.E.2d 362, noted in 15 Notre Dame Lawyer 360 (1940) (building).

35. Murr v. Cohn, 1927, 87 Cal.App. 478, 262 P. 768 (including tank buried in the ground); Cameron v. Oakland County Gas & Oil Co., 1936, 277 Mich. 442, 269 N.W. 277, 107 A.L.R. 1142, noted in 35 Mich.Law Rev. 1178 (1937).

36. Watriss v. First Nat. Bank, 1878, 124 Mass. 571.

37. See, Woods v. Bank of Haywards, 1909, 10 Cal. App. 93, 106 P. 730; Radey v. McCurdy, 1904, 209 Pa. 306, 58 A. 558.

38. 111 N.J.Eq. 249, 162 A. 87 (1932).

39. 99 Mich. 501, 58 N.W. 475 (1894).

40. See also, Caperton v. Stege, 1891, 91 Ky. 351, 15 S.W. 870, 16 S.W. 84; Smith v. Park, 1883, 31 Minn. 70, 16 N.W. 490.

able-time rule is applicable if an estate for a fixed period is terminated upon the happening of some event, even forfeiture because of some default on the part of the tenant.[41]

Life estates

Since a life estate is an estate of uncertain duration, trade fixtures may be removed within a reasonable time after termination of the life estate.[42] If the estate is terminated because of the death of the life tenant his executor or administrator has a reasonable time within which to remove trade fixtures.

In the North Carolina case of Haywood v. Briggs,[43] a life tenant executed a lease by the terms of which the lessee was given the right to remove buildings that he might erect upon the land. After the death of the life tenant his lessee claimed a right to remove a large warehouse that had been erected upon the land and *this right was based upon the covenant in the lease*. In denying this right it is held that the lessee had no greater rights than those that could have been asserted by the life tenant.[44] The case is not decided upon the ground that the warehouse was or was not removable as a trade fixture. A fixture cannot properly be removed under that doctrine if it is attached in such a manner as to become an integral part of the premises.[45]

---

41. Getzendaner v. Erbstein, 1950, 341 Ill.App. 594, 94 N.E.2d 746. *Contra*: Pugh v. Arton, 1869, L.R. 8 Eq. 626.

42. Warrington v. Hignutt, 1943, 3 Terry 274, 31 A.2d 480; Lawton v. Lawton [1743] 3 Atk. 13, 26 Eng. Rep. 811.

43. 227 N.C. 108, 41 S.E.2d 289, 171 A.L.R. 480 (1946).

44. *Accord*: Chabon v. Lazarus, 1952, 18 N.J.Super. 443, 87 A.2d 435.

45. McCullough v. Irvine's Ex'rs, 1850, 13 Pa. 438 (brick house and barn, part stone and part frame); Cannon v. Hare, 1872, 1 Tenn.Ch. 22 (frame building on brick foundation); D'Eyncourt v. Gregory, 1866, L.R. 3 Eq. 382, 36 L.J.Ch. 107 (stone lions, stone seats and marble vases that were part of an architectural design). But see, Ray v. Young, 1913, 160 Iowa 613, 142 N.W. 393.

PART 2
RIGHTS IN LAND

A. RIGHTS INCIDENTAL TO POSSESSION
CHAPTER 4
WASTE

Sec.
12. Waste Defined.
13. Remedies for Waste.
14. Acts Constituting Waste.

WASTE DEFINED

12. The owner of a possessory estate in land is under a duty to use his possessory rights in a manner that is reasonable in nature. Unreasonable conduct that results in physical damage to the land is waste if it causes a substantial diminution in the value of estates owned by others in the same land.

a. Voluntary waste. Damage to the land that results from an affirmative act is voluntary waste. However, the tenant is not responsible for the acts of third parties not induced by him.

b. Permissive waste. Damage resulting from a possessor's failure to act in performance of a duty is permissive waste.

c. Equitable waste. Even if a possessor is immune from liability for legal waste he may be held accountable in equity if his conduct is considered to be unconscionable in nature. Responsibility is based upon equitable waste.

The owner of a possessory estate in land is not without restraint with respect to the use and enjoyment of land if a successive estate is involved, such as a remainder, reversion, possibility of reverter, power of termination or executory interest. He must refrain from *unreasonable conduct* resulting in physical damage to the land with resultant diminution in value. In many cases it is stated that waste consists of unprivileged conduct that causes "a permanent injury to the freehold." Unreasonable conduct in this respect is designated as waste.

A determination of the question as to whether or not an act constitutes waste involves a balancing of the right of the owner of the possessory estate against the right of the owner of the reversion, remainder, possibility of reverter or executory interest.

To constitute waste the act must involve an unreasonable exercise of the possessor's right of enjoyment and must result in a permanent and appreciable damage to the land. Trivial damage is not sufficient for the purpose.[1]

Statutes in some states provide that waste is not limited to conduct that causes a permanent damage to the land. In some instances the law of waste is made applicable to tenants in common and to joint tenants. For example, a California statute provides as follows: "If a guardian, tenant for life or years, joint tenant, or tenant in common of real property, commit waste thereon, any person aggrieved by the waste may bring an action against him therefor, in which action

---

1. Harrow School v. Alderton, 1800, 2 B. & P. 86, 126 Eng.Rep. 1170.

there may be judgment for treble damages." [2]

Voluntary Waste

Damage to the land which results from an affirmative act, if not privileged, constitutes voluntary waste. Usually, the possessor of land cannot be held responsible for the wrongful acts of others even though damage to the land is caused thereby. However, such damage may be traced to fault on the part of the possessor. For example, in the early Maryland case of White v. Wagner,[3] land was leased for residential purposes. The tenant used the land as a place for the publication of an unpopular political pamphlet and an enraged mob destroyed the house. The fact that the conduct of the tenant induced the destructive acts of third parties was held to be a sufficient basis upon which to establish liability for voluntary waste.

Permissive Waste

Damage to the land that results from the possessor's failure to act, when it was his duty to act, is permissive waste. For example, a possessor is usually under a duty to make the repairs that are necessary to protect the land, or structures thereon, from the elements, and failure to perform this duty constitutes permissive waste.

At one time a charge of permissive waste could be based upon damage caused by accident or by the wrongful act of a third party.[4] The present rule is that such liability can be established only by proof of fault on the part of the tenant.[5] Further, the claim of waste cannot successfully be based upon damage caused by act of God, public enemy or an act authorized by law.[6]

Equitable Waste

Insofar as legal rights are concerned, the owner of an estate in fee simple has complete freedom of action in connection with the management and control of the property. This is true even if his acts operate to impair the value of an executory interest. A provision in a conveying instrument declaring that the person acquiring a life estate or an estate for a period less than life is to take the estate "without impeachment of waste" creates an immunity insofar as legal waste would otherwise be involved.

But even if there is exemption of liability for legal waste it does not follow that the possessor of land has complete freedom of action in the use and enjoyment of the land. Conduct may be so outrageous in nature as to call for equitable relief in order to prevent threatened acts that would cause substantial damage to the land to the detriment of the owner of a future interest. Under such circumstances the conduct may be enjoined as equitable waste.

The claim of equitable waste may be based upon the ground that the threatened acts are motivated by wrongful intent and actuated by malice. But such claims must be substantiated by proof of the fact that the threatened acts do not conform to "standard conduct" of an owner.[7] Even the owner of an estate in fee simple may be held accountable for equitable waste at the instance of the owner of an executory interest.[8] But it takes a strong case, especially if the facts show

---

2. West's Ann.Code of Civ.Proc., § 732.

3. 4 Har. & J.(Md.) 373 (1818).

4. Co.Litt. 54a.

5. In re Stout's Estate, 1935, 151 Or. 411, 50 P.2d 768, 101 A.L.R. 672; Earle v. Arbogast, 1897, 180 Pa. 409, 36 A. 923 (not liable for damage caused by accidental explosion). See, Kirchwey, Liability for Waste, 8 Col.Law Rev. 624, 628 (1908).

6. U. S. v. Bostwick, 1876, 94 U.S. 53, 24 L.Ed. 65.

7. See, 1 Rest.Property, § 141, *Comment a* (pertaining to the right applicable to a life tenant).

8. 2 Rest.Property, § 193. See Turner v. Wright [1860] 2 DeG.F. & J. 234, 239, 45 Eng.Rep. 612. *Cf.*: Matthews v. Hudson, 1888, 81 Ga. 120, 7 S.E.

that there is little likelihood that the executory interest will ever become possessory.[9]

REMEDIES FOR WASTE

13. **The usual remedy for waste is an action at law to recover damages. In the absence of statute forfeiture of an estate cannot be declared because of waste. However, statutes in many states provide that under special circumstances double or triple damages may be recovered.**

Usually, an injunction may be secured to prevent acts of waste. This is the only remedy available for the protection of contingent interests. It is also the only remedy available if the tenant is immune from liability for legal waste.

At early common law the remedies for waste were the writ of prohibition and attachment and the writ of waste. At first, these writs were issuable only against tenants in dower, tenants by the curtesy, and guardians in chivalry, cases where the tenancy had been created by operation of law. It was considered that if a tenancy was created by act of the parties the matter could be regulated by an express provision in the instrument creating the estate.[10] But the statutes of Marlbridge [11] and Gloucester [12] made these remedies available against all tenants for life or for years. The Statute of Gloucester provided that the tenant's estate in the place wasted should be forfeited and allowed recovery of treble damages.

It is generally considered that these statutes applied to both voluntary and permissive waste.[13] Eventually, however, the penalties for waste as provided in the Statute of Gloucester were not applied in the case of permissive waste, or in cases where the damage was caused by a stranger and without the fault of the tenant.[14] The statutes did not change the rule that a tenant at will is not liable for permissive waste.[15] Voluntary waste terminates a tenancy at will and subjects the tenant to liability in an action for trespass.[16]

In the United States the law as it applies to waste is generally regulated by statute. The weight of authority is that the provisions embodied in the Statute of Gloucester do not constitute a part of the common law of the various states. The penalties therein declared for waste, especially the penalty of forfeiture, are not considered to be consistent with conditions existing in the various states.[17] While statutory provisions imposing a penalty for waste, such as double or triple damages, are not uncommon, there are only a few states where the statutes impose the penalty of forfeiture.[18]

286; Landers v. Landers, 1912, 151 Ky. 206, 151 S.W. 386.

9. See Hopper v. Barnes, 1896, 113 Cal. 636, 45 P. 874; Gannon v. Peterson, 1901, 193 Ill. 372, 62 N.E. 210, 55 L.R.A. 701; Dees v. Cheuvronts, 1909, 240 Ill. 486, 88 N.E. 1011; Brown v. Brown, 1921, 89 W.Va. 339, 109 S.E. 815.

10. Co.Litt. 54a. That the common law afforded some remedy for waste as against a tenant for life or for years where the estate was created by act of the parties, see Kirchwey, Liability for Waste, 8 Col.Law Rev. 425, 427 (1908).

11. 52 Hen. III, c. 23, § 2 (1267). The name Marlbridge was subsequently changed to Marlborough.

12. 6 Edw. I, c. 5 (1278).

13. 5 Law Quarterly Rev. 448 (1889).

14. Kirchwey, Liability for Waste, 8 Col.Law Rev. 624, 625 (1908).

15. Countess of Shrewsbury's Case, 1600, 5 Co.Rep. 13, 77 Eng.Rep. 68; Lothrop v. Thayer, 1885, 138 Mass. 466 (tenant at will not liable for destruction of building by fire which was caused by his negligent care of heating equipment. This was considered to be permissive waste).

16. Co.Litt. 57a.

17. See, for example, Smith v. Smith, 1951, 219 Ark. 304, 241 S.W.2d 113; Wise v. Potomac Nat. Bank, 1946, 393 Ill. 357, 65 N.E.2d 767; Schuman v. Schuman, 1921, 217 Mich. 184, 185 N.W. 717; Worthington Motors v. Crouse, 1964, —— Nev. ——, 390 P.2d 229.

18. In some states treble damages can be recovered only if the act was malicious or wanton in nature. See, for example, DeLano v. Tennemt, 1926, 138

A suit in equity to enjoin waste is an appropriate remedy even if an action at law can be maintained to recover damages. In some situations a suit in equity is the only remedy available. That is the case, for example, if there is a contingency attached to a future interest and the future interest may be damaged as a result of the threatened conduct.[19] Additional rules are as follows:

First: As has been noted, even the owner of an estate in fee simple may be enjoined from the commission of acts that would constitute equitable waste. Usually, the owner of an estate in fee simple has almost complete freedom of action with respect to the use and enjoyment of land. It is difficult to conceive of a case where a charge of equitable waste will be sustained if the conduct is consistent with that of "reasonable management". However, such a case is that of Pavkovich v. Southern Pacific Ry. Co.,[20] a California decision. Land was conveyed to defendant railroad in fee simple and was to be used for railroad purposes. The land was part of a rock quarry. The deed provided that the land was "to revert" to the grantors if not used for railroad purposes or if such use should at any time be abandoned. It was also provided that the railroad was to take gravel from the quarry only for railroad purposes. The owner of the possibility of reverter successfully enjoined defendant railroad from taking rock from the quarry for

other than railroad purposes. It is stated that the restriction as to rock was to protect the "contingent estate" and to prevent the land from being stripped of its most valuable asset.[21] From this decision it would seem that covenants and conditions in a conveying instrument are entitled to important consideration in resolving an issue as to whether or not questioned conduct should be classified as waste.

Second: Even if contingent interests are involved, in a suit to enjoin waste the court may order defendant to pay into court the amount of damage caused to the land. This money will be held in a court trust to await distribution to those who eventually qualify as distributees of the estate.[22]

Third: Even if the owner of a contingent interest may maintain a suit in equity to enjoin waste, the Statute of Limitations will not start to run in favor of the defendant until such time as interests are ascertained and the stage is set for an action at law to recover damages.[23]

Fourth: In many states it is provided by statute that demands against the estate of a deceased person must be filed against the estate within a stated time after the institution of probate proceedings. In some states it is held that such a claim must be filed if an accounting is sought against a deceased tenant arising out of acts of waste.[24]

Wash. 39, 244 P. 273, 45 A.L.R. 766. For an enumeration of statutes, see Rest.Property, 1948 Supplement, § 199, *Comments a, b and c.*

19. Ohio Oil Co. v. Daughetee, 1909, 240 Ill. 361, 88 N.E. 818; Latham v. Roanoke Ry. & Lumber Co., 1905, 139 N.C. 9, 51 S.E. 780; Roanoke Marble & Granite Co. v. Standard Gas & Oil Supply Co., 1930, 155 Va. 249, 154 S.E. 518.

20. 150 Cal. 39, 87 P. 1097 (1906).

21. But see, Davis v. Skipper, 1935, 125 Tex. 364, 83 S.W.2d 318.

22. Watson v. Wolff-Goldman Realty Co., 1910, 95 Ark. 18, 128 S.W. 581; 2 Rest.Property, § 189(1)(c).

23. Rhoda v. Alameda County, 1933, 134 Cal.App. 726, 26 P.2d 691.

24. See, for example, Steele v. Cross, Mo.1963, 366 S.W.2d 434.

ACTS CONSTITUTING WASTE

14. A change in the physical appearance of land does not constitute waste.

   a. Cutting timber. Unless authorized, a tenant for life or for a period less than life is guilty of waste if he cuts timber from the land. Usually, timber may be cut for purposes of making repairs. It may also be cut if this conforms with rules of good husbandry. It may be cut on a commercial basis if the conveyance was made for that purpose or if the land was used for that purpose at the time of the conveyance.

   b. Removal of earth or minerals from the land. In general, removal of earth or minerals by a tenant constitutes waste. Such acts are privileged, however, if the land was used for that purpose when the estate was created.

   c. Structural changes. Structural changes do not necessarily constitute waste. This is especially true if they result in an increase in the value of the land, security is posted for the costs involved and the one making the improvements is a life tenant or a tenant holding under a long term lease.

At one time land description depended upon the physical description of the land. Land was described as the "meadowland," "woodland" etc. Under such conditions it was held that an unauthorized change in the physical appearance of the land constituted waste.[25] This is not the case at the present time. Such changes do not constitute waste [26] if they are in accord with rules of good husbandry.[27]

Authorities support the view that default in performance of a duty to pay taxes may constitute waste. A charge of waste may also be sustained upon proof of the fact that a tenant defaulted in his duty to make repairs.[28] If a state of disrepair existed at the time of a testamentary disposition of a life estate the court may authorize a charge against the estate of the testator for the amount necessary to make the repairs.[29] Special situations involving waste are discussed in the following paragraphs.

Cutting Timber

With exceptions noted, unless a conveyance is made "without impeachment of waste" a tenant for life, or for a period less than life, is without authority to cut timber. Under some circumstances a tenant may not be authorized to cut timber yet the cutting of timber may not constitute waste. In that event the tenant is not entitled to retain the proceeds derived from a sale of the timber.[30] For example, in Bewick v. Whitfield (Eng.),[31] it was necessary to cut timber because of its decayed condition. The court held that the life tenant was not entitled to the proceeds derived from a sale of the timber. Of course a tenant is not entitled to benefits flowing from acts of waste in cutting timber.[32] Situations where the cutting of timber does not constitute waste are as follows:

First: A tenant is entitled to cut timber required for fuel, fencing or agricultural op-

---

25. Harrow School v. Alderton, [1800] 2 B. & P. 86, 126 Eng.Rep. 1170 (change of meadowland into a cultivated area).

26. J. H. Bellows Co. v. Covell, 1927, 28 Ohio App. 277, 162 N.E. 621, noted in 8 Bost.Univ.Law Rev. 312 (1928), 2 So.Cal.Law Rev. 399 (1929) (draining a lake to develop a golf course).

27. See Chapel v. Hull, 1886, 60 Mich. 167, 26 N.W. 874.

28. In re Stout, 1935, 151 Or. 411, 50 P.2d 768, 101 A.L.R. 672 (life tenant).

29. Savings Investment & Trust Co. v. Little, 1944, 135 N.J.Eq. 546, 39 A.2d 392; In re Collins' Will, 1946, 187 Misc. 188, 61 N.Y.S.2d 488. See Rest. Property, 1948 Supplement, § 127, *Comment a.*

30. Guest v. Guest, 1937, 234 Ala. 581, 176 So. 289. But see, Wilkinson v. Wilkinson, 1884, 59 Wis. 557, 18 N.W. 289.

31. 3 P.Wms. 267, 24 Eng.Rep. 1058 (1734).

32. 1 Rest. Property, § 119, *Comment c.*

erations. This privilege is the right to estovers. If a tenant is privileged to cut timber for the purpose of making repairs, he may cut timber and exchange it for lumber to be used for such purpose.[33] However, there is authority for the rule that it is waste for a life tenant to cut timber and exchange it for firewood.[34]

Second: A tenant of agricultural land may clear the land where this is reasonably necessary to prepare the land for cultivation and is not in violation of the rules of good husbandry.[35]

Third: Timber may be cut on a commercial basis if the conveyance was made for that purpose, if that is the only profitable use of the land or if the land was used for that purpose at the time of the conveyance.[36]

Removal of Earth or Minerals from the Land

With exceptions to be noted, if a conveyance is not made "without impeachment of waste," the removal of earth or minerals from the land constitutes waste.[37] Exceptions are as follows:

First: A tenant may enjoy all permanent uses to which the land was devoted at the time of the creation of the tenancy. This may include the right to remove earth or minerals.[38] For example, in the New Jersey case of Gaines v. Green Pond Iron Mining Co.,[39] mines had been opened, and operations started some sixty years prior to the creation of a life estate. But operations were continued only for a short period of time. The court held that the life tenant was entitled to operate the mines since it did not appear that the original operations were for a limited or restricted purpose. Neither did it appear that there had been an intention on the part of the former owner to abandon mining operations upon the land.[40]

A tenant is entitled to the rent which accrues under a mining lease where the lease was made prior to the creation of the estate even though mining operations were not started until after the estate was created.[41] In the Kentucky case of May v. Chinn,[42] a life tenant was denied the right to conduct mining operations. While the pit had been opened during the lifetime of the former owner in fee, such owner was not aware of that fact and there was merely a test tunnel or exploration.

Second: The removal of earth or minerals is privileged if that is reasonably necessary to accomplish the purpose of a lease. For example, if land is leased for agricultural purposes it is not waste for the tenant to remove stones from the land if that is reasonably necessary to prepare the land for cultivation.[43]

---

33. 1 Rest. Property, § 143, *Comment c.*

34. Padelford v. Padelford, 1828, 7 Pick. (Mass.) 152.

35. See Guest v. Guest, 1937, 234 Ala. 581, 176 So. 289, noted in 22 Minn.Law Rev. 574 (1938); Keeler v. Eastman, 1839, 11 Vt. 293.

36. 1 Rest. Property, § 144 (life tenant).

37. Marshall v. Mellon, 1897, 179 Pa. 371, 36 A. 201 (life tenant not entitled to take oil from the land); University v. Tucker, 1888, 31 W.Va. 621, 8 S.E. 410 (life tenant not entitled to take clay from the land for use in manufacturing bricks).

38. 1 Rest. Property, § 144 (life tenant).

39. 33 N.J.Eq. 603 (1881).

40. *Accord:* Lee & Bradshaw v. Rogers, 1921, 151 Ga. 838, 108 S.E. 371 (taking turpentine from trees).

41. Priddy v. Griffith, 1894, 150 Ill. 560, 37 N.E. 999; Youngman v. Shular, 1956, 155 Tex. 437, 288 S.W.2d 495 (oil lease); Graham v. Smith, 1938, 170 Va. 246, 196 S.E. 600; Koen v. Bartlett, 1895, 41 W.Va. 559, 23 S.E. 664 (oil lease).

42. 301 Ky. 732, 193 S.W.2d 149 (1946).

43. Lewis v. Godson, 1888, 15 Ont. 252.

Structural Changes

According to the early common law rule the unauthorized removal, alteration or replacement of a structure by a tenant for life, or by a tenant for a period less than life, constituted waste.[44] It was not material that the change did, in fact, increase the value of the land. Where such an increase did result the change was called "ameliorating waste." This rule was based in part upon the then existing law that a change in the physical appearance of land constituted waste.

The modern rule is that structural changes do not necessarily constitute waste.[45] This is in accord with an existing public policy in favor of community development. Various factors are taken into consideration. A structural change may be classified as waste if a short-term lease is involved whereas a different conclusion may be reached in the case of a long-term lease or a life estate.[46] It is proper to assume that the parties contemplated such changes in a long-term lease, or in case of a life estate.[47] This conclusion is especially true if there are changed conditions in the area and economic use cannot be made of the land in its then state.[48] In any event, if structural changes are to avoid the claim of waste it will be necessary for the tenant to prove that the property will be enhanced in value and he must protect the owners of future interests in the land from financial responsibility for the costs involved.[49]

44. Co.Litt. 53a.

45. See 1 Rest. Property, § 140, *Comment e.* A contrary rule declared in Brokaw v. Fairchild, 1931, 256 N.Y. 670, 177 N.E. 186, was subsequently changed by statute. See N.Y.Real Property Actions and Proceedings Law, § 803.

46. See Liability for Ameliorative Waste, 43 Harv. Law Rev. 1130, 1132 (1930).

47. See Northern Trust Co. v. Thompson, 1929, 336 Ill. 137, 168 N.E. 110; Doherty v. Allman, [1878] House of Lords, 3 App.Cas. 709. See also, Niehuss, Alteration or Replacement of Buildings by the Long-Term Lessee, 30 Mich.Law Rev. 386 (1932).

48. See Melms v. Pabst Brewing Co., 1899, 104 Wis. 7, 79 N.W. 738 (1899).

49. Rickaby v. McCrory Stores Corp., 6 Cir. 1929, 35 F.2d 14 (in this case the lease provided for the posting of such a bond).

CHAPTER 5

INTERFERENCE WITH THE SUPPORT OF LAND AND STRUCTURES

SUPPORT OF LAND

15. Lateral support is the support which land receives, or is entitled to receive, from surrounding land or the support that has been substituted for the natural condition. The common law rule is that an invasion of this right is actionable without proof of negligence.

a. Extent of area required for support. The area required for support cannot be extended by intervening excavations.

b. Fluid and semi-fluid substances. The support that land may receive from fluid substances, such as water or oil, is not protected by the law as it relates to lateral support. However, there is protection against withdrawal of semi-fluid substances.

c. Filled land. The right to lateral support is a right to support of land in substantially its natural condition. Filled-in land, if properly impacted, satisfies this requirement.

d. Independent contractors. Liability for withdrawal of lateral support cannot be avoided by employing an independent contractor to excavate the land.

e. Landlord and tenant. A landlord is not liable for damage caused by excavations on the land by his tenant.

f. Statute of Limitations. The Statute of Limitations does not start to run in favor of an excavator until such time as the land subsides.

Lateral support is the support which land receives, or is entitled to receive, from adjoining land or the support that has been substituted for the natural condition.

A right to lateral support from adjacent land is not a right in the adjacent land. In other words, it is not a right in the land of another. In this respect it differs from an easement. It is a right incident to the land that is entitled to support.

The common law rule is that an invasion of this right is actionable regardless of negligence.[1] However, liability will not arise if the withdrawal of lateral support is caused by an act of God. This refers to a situation where an act of God, such as a tidal wave, washes away the supporting land.[2] It does not apply to a situation where a man-made excavation causes a subsidence as the result of unprecedented rainfall.

Extent of Area Required for Support

The extent to which the surrounding area may be affected by the right of support that inheres in any one part of that area depends upon the structure of the soil. In the English case of Corporation of Birmingham v. Allen,[3] an area between plaintiff's land and the defendant's land had been excavated. Because of this excavation the subsequent excavation made on defendant's land caused the plaintiff's land to subside. In an action brought to recover damages judgment was

1. 4 Rest. Torts, § 817, *Comment b.*

2. Carrig v. Andrews, 1941, 127 Conn. 403, 17 A.2d 520, 132 A.L.R. 993, noted in 25 Minn.Law Rev. 633 (1941); 4 Univ. of Detroit Law Rev. 221 (1941).

3. L.R. 6 Ch.Div. 284 (1877).

rendered for the defendant, it being found that if the intervening land had been in its natural condition the defendant's act would not have caused the subsidence.[4] The area originally required for support cannot be enlarged by excavations on intervening land.

Fluid and Semi-fluid Substances

The support that land may derive from fluid substances, such as water or oil, is not protected by the law as it relates to lateral support.[5] A landowner does not have a legal right to claim such support because adjacent owners have a right to remove water or oil, or similar substances, that may be found beneath the surface of his own land even though the supply may be replenished by flow from the land of others. In addition, difficulties incident to regulation of the flow of such substances would be too great to justify the imposition of absolute liability. Certainly, the imposition of such liability would hamper land development to the detriment of the general community.

Many of the above arguments against the claim of a right to lateral support with respect to fluid substances are equally applicable where the right to such support is claimed with respect to semi-fluid substances, such as asphalt or quicksand. However, the general rule is that liability will arise if land subsides because of the withdrawal of semi-fluid substances.[6]

Filled Land

From a technical point of view it may be said that the common law duty of lateral support does not extend to filled land because the duty only exists with respect to land in its natural condition. However, from a practical point of view, if the fill is properly impacted the condition should be considered as "natural" for the purposes of lateral support. This is especially true after the lapse of time and exposure to the elements. This conforms to views expressed in the Pennsylvania case of Bradley v. Valicenti.[7] However, doubts are raised in a later case.[8]

Independent Contractors

Breach of duty as it relates to lateral support involves the invasion of a property right. There is also basis for the claim that one who excavates is engaged in work that is inherently dangerous. Both of these facts support the rule that a landowner cannot avoid responsibility for subsidence-damages by engaging the services of an independent contractor. Both the landowner and the independent contractor may be held liable for damages resulting from activities that deprived a plaintiff of lateral support.[9]

Landlord and Tenant

Ordinarily, a landlord is not responsible for the acts of a tenant as those acts relate to the use and enjoyment of the land. Accordingly, the landlord cannot be held liable for damages resulting from a subsidence of adjacent land because of an excavation made by a tenant that deprived adjacent land of lateral support.

In the New York case of Regal Shoe Co. v. Davies,[10] the defendants, as owners and lessors of land, delivered possession of the land to the tenant. The lease provided that the

---

4. *Accord:* 4 Rest. Torts, § 817, *Comment g, Illust.*7.

5. 4 Rest. Torts, § 818. See Popplewell v. Hodkinson, 1869, L.R. 4 Exch. 248.

6. Prete v. Cray, 1928, 49 R.I. 209, 141 A. 609, 59 A.L.R. 1241 (quicksand); Jordeson v. Gas Co., [1899] 2 Ch. 217 (quicksand); 4 Rest. Torts, § 818, *Comment b.*

7. 185 Pa.Super. 403, 138 A.2d 238 (1958).

8. Albert v. Wright, 1963, 410 Pa. 383, 189 A.2d 753.

9. Green v. Berge, 1894, 105 Cal. 52, 38 P. 539.

10. 150 Misc. 674, 268 N.Y.S. 731 (1933).

tenant should construct a building on the land and that the lessors would contribute a stated sum for that purpose. Plaintiff's land subsided as the result of an excavation made on the leased land. The court held that the lessors were not liable within the meaning of a statute placing liability upon persons "causing excavations to be made."

Statute of Limitations

If a landowner excavates on his own land he does not thereby violate any duty owing to adjoining landowners insofar as lateral support is concerned. The duty is one relating to support and not excavations. Accordingly, a breach of duty dates from the time of a subsidence. From this it follows that the Statute of Limitations will not start to run in favor of the one making an excavation until the date upon which the plaintiff's land subsides.[11] The one who excavates may be held liable even though he conveys the land to another.[12] His excavation resulted in a breach of duty dating from the time when the excavation caused a subsidence.

SUPPORT OF STRUCTURES

16. The common law right to lateral support does not include a right to support of structures that may be erected on the land.

If an excavation would have caused the land to subside even if a structure had not been erected thereon, then the excavator may be held liable for damage to the structure.

If an excavator is not under a duty to protect a structure he is not entitled to recover from its owner the expense incurred furnishing such protection. In so doing he acted as a volunteer.

In a number of states statutes have been enacted modifying the common law rules as they relate to lateral support in connection with damage caused to structures.

The common law right to lateral support is a right to the support of land in substantially its natural condition. It does not include a right to the support of both the land and structures that may be erected upon the land.[13] Of course, a defendant may be held liable for damage caused to structures if there is *proof of negligence* on his part.[14]

According to one view, even if the acts of defendant did deprive the plaintiff's land of lateral support, in the absence of negligence the defendant cannot be held liable for damages caused to structures as the result of a subsidence.[15] The liability is limited to land-damage because that is the measure of defendant's duty.

But the better reasoned cases are to the contrary. If it is shown that an excavation would have caused the land to subside even if no structures had been erected thereon, then liability will arise for damages caused to such structures by subsidence.[16] The subsidence—an invasion of a property right—was the proximate cause of the damage.

It seems clear that if the owner of a structure does not see fit to take necessary precautions to prevent its subsidence, the excavator is not entitled to proceed with the necessary work and recover the reasonable value thereof from the owner of the structure.[17]

---

13. 4 Rest. Torts, § 817(1), *Comment b.*

14. Hannicker v. Lepper, 1906, 20 S.D. 371, 107 N.W. 202; 4 Rest. Torts, § 819.

15. Gilmore v. Driscoll, 1877, 122 Mass. 199. See, Home Brewing Co. v. Thomas Colliery Co., 1922, 274 Pa. 56, 117 A. 542.

16. Prete v. Cray, 1928, 49 R.I. 209, 141 A. 609, 59 A.L.R. 1241; 4 Rest. Torts, § 817(2).

17. First Nat. Bank v. Villegra, 1891, 92 Cal. 96, 28 P. 97; Korogodsky v. Chimberoff, 1930, 256 Ill. App. 255; Braun v. Hamack, 1940, 206 Minn. 572, 289 N.W. 553, 129 A.L.R. 618, noted in 24 Minn.

11. Pollock v. Pittsburgh, B. & L. E. R. Co., 1923, 275 Pa. 467, 119 A. 547, 26 A.L.R. 1232; Backhouse v. Bonomi, [1862] 9 H.L.Cas. 503, 11 Eng.Rep. 825; 4 Rest. Torts, § 817, *Comment i.*

12. 4 Rest. Torts, § 817, *Comment j.*

In the first place, if the excavator is under a duty to support the structure such expenditures are on his own account. In the second place, if the excavator is not liable for the damage involved he must, of necessity, be acting as a volunteer. The decisions support the view that the owner of a structure cannot be held liable.

In a number of states statutes have been enacted or ordinances passed that modify, in some degree, the common law rules of liability in lateral-support situations. It is usually provided that one who contemplates excavation work must give reasonable notice to the owner of a structure in the danger zone as to the time and place of the contemplated activities. Failure to give such notice may justify the claim of negligence. Another usual provision is intended to relieve the owner of a structure from some of the responsibilities found to exist under common law rules. This is accomplished by the simple declaration that if the existing structure has a foundation of a standard depth (usually stated to be at the 12-foot level) then the excavator is under a duty to support the structure. In the performance of this duty the excavator is satisfying the statutory requirement and cannot use this as a basis upon which to recover expenses from the owner of the structure.[18]

SUBJACENT SUPPORT

17. Subjacent support is the support which land receives from the area beneath the surface or the support which has been substituted for the natural condition.

a. Structures. The right to subjacent support does not include a right to the sup-

port of structures that have been erected on the land.

b. Statute of Limitations. The Statute of Limitations does not start to run in favor of an excavator until the time of a subsidence.

Subjacent support is the support which land receives from the area beneath the surface or the support which has been substituted for the natural condition.

Problems with respect to subjacent support arise in cases of divided-ownership. For example, A may be the owner of a possessory estate of the surface and B may be the owner of a possessory estate of the area beneath the surface (or he may have a profit in the form of a right to dig coal or mine minerals). The owner of the surface may have a right to subjacent support or that right may be waived in favor of the owner of the area beneath the surface or the owner of a profit. In fact, the right to surface support may be in a third party. In the Pennsylvania case of Smith v. Glen Alden Coal Co.,[19] it is pointed out that there are *"three estates in land"*, namely, the coal, the surface, and the right of support to the surface, so that one person may own the coal, another the surface and a third the right to the surface support.

In the absence of express waiver, or one clearly implied, the grantee of coal or minerals takes the estate subject to the burden of surface support.[20]

Structures

As in the case of lateral support, a right to subjacent support does not include a right to the support of structures located on the land. It is a right to support of the land in substantially its natural condition.

Law Rev. 853 (1940), 88 Univ. of Pa.Law Rev. 1020 (1940), 50 Yale Law J. 1125 (1941); Warfel v. Vondersmith, 1954, 376 Pa. 1, 101 A.2d 736, noted in 27 Temple Law Qt. 512 (1954). *Contra:* Eads v. Gains, 1894, 58 Mo.App. 586.

18. See, James Stewart Co. v. Garden Plaza Building Corp., Inc., 1960, 88 Ariz. 286, 356 P.2d 31.

19. 347 Pa. 290, 32 A.2d 227 (1943).

20. See, Walker v. Forcey, 1959, 396 Pa. 80, 151 A.2d 601; Erwin v. Bethlehem Steel Corp., 1950, 134 W.Va. 900, 62 S.E.2d 337.

If a subsidence occurs, the person responsible may be held liable for damages caused to a structure if he acted negligently or if the land would have subsided had there been no structure thereon.[21] As a factual matter, liability for damage to structures may be established more readily in the case of the withdrawal of subjacent support than in the case of withdrawal of lateral support. In the case of subjacent support it is more difficult for a defendant to prove that structures erected on the land contributed to the subsidence since the weight of the structures is slight as compared with the weight of the supported land.[22]

Statute of Limitations

The general rule is that the owner of the surface who is entitled to subjacent support does not have a cause of action for an invasion of this right until a subsidence takes place. Accordingly, the Statute of Limitations does not start to run in favor of the defendant until that time.[23]

21. Ohio Collieries Co. v. Cocke, 1923, 107 Ohio 238, 140 N.E. 356, noted in 22 Mich.Law Rev. 75 (1923).

22. 4 Rest. Torts, § 820, *Comment d.*

23. 4 Rest. Torts, § 820, *Comment g.* *Contra:* Noonan v. Pardee, 1901, 200 Pa. 474, 50 A. 255, noted in 15 Harv.Law Rev. 574 (1902).

CHAPTER 6

WATER RIGHTS

NAVIGABLE BODIES OF WATER

18. A watercourse or lake is navigable if it is capable of use for purposes of commerce or if it can be made capable of such use by "reasonable improvements."

a. Ownership of the bed of navigable bodies of water. Where land borders upon the ocean or an arm thereof ownership of the littoral (riparian) owner extends to the mean high tide. Riparian rights may be separated from ownership of the land.

b. The shore. The area between the mean high tide and the mean low tide is called the shore. This area is held in trust by the state for the people of the state and cannot be conveyed or acquired by adverse possession.

c. Marginal sea. Insofar as the ocean is concerned, the area beyond the shore (the marginal sea) comes within the sovereignty of the United States.

d. Submerged land. If privately owned land is submerged by a navigable body of water a public right of navigation and fishing arises even though ownership of the land remains in private ownership subject to reclamation.

e. Inland bodies of water. The ownership of the bed of an inland body of water, if navigable, is in the state in which it is located.

f. Governmental regulations. The United States has power to legislate with respect to navigable bodies of water because it has power to regulate commerce. A riparian or littoral owner is not entitled to recover damages even if he suffers a loss due to legislation relating to navigation.

According to the English rule, a navigable body of water is one in which the tide ebbs and flows.[1] The Crown is the owner of the bed of all such waters.

The English test as to navigability is not suitable to conditions as they exist in the United States. Many watercourses and lakes are of particular value for purposes of navigation and yet they are not affected by any tide. According to the prevailing American rule, a watercourse or lake is navigable if it is capable of use for purposes of commerce, or if it can be made capable of such use by "reasonable improvements."[2]

In some cases it is stated that the term "navigable waters" has reference to commerce of a substantial and permanent character to be, or which may be, conducted thereon.[3] But this does not mean that the watercourse or lake must be susceptible of use by large vessels, or support a flow of

---

[1] Gould on Waters (3rd ed.) § 42.

[2] United States v. Appalachian Electric Power Co., 1940, 311 U.S. 377, 61 S.Ct. 291, 85 L.Ed. 243, noted in 21 Boston Univ.Law Rev. 344 (1941), 29 Cal. Law Rev. 761 (1941), 14 So.Cal.Law Rev. 322 (1941), 2 Wash. & Lee Law Rev. 272 (1941). *Cf.*: Haase v. Kingston Co-operative Creamery Ass'n, 1933, 212 Wis. 585, 250 N.W. 444 (public rights will not attach merely because a non-navigable body of water is made navigable in fact as a result of artificial conditions).

[3] Home Real Estate Loan & Ins. Co. v. Parmele, 1938, 214 N.C. 63, 197 S.E. 714, 717.

commercial traffic.[4] The claim of navigability has been sustained by proof that the stream was or had been used for floating logs ("floatable for timber"). But as one court has stated, a stream is not navigable if it is so difficult to get a row boat over it that "one had to push, cuss and holler at the same time to make it go." [5]

Ownership of the Bed of Navigable Bodies of Water

Where land borders upon the ocean or an arm thereof ownership of the littoral (riparian) owner extends to the mean or average high tide.[6] In some states it is held that ownership extends to the low water mark.[7] In any event, the owner of the upland is presumed to possess riparian rights, including the right to wharf out. Such rights are freely alienable and may be separated from the upland ownership.[8] Whether or not riparian rights are conveyed along with the grant of the uplands depends largely upon the intent of the grantor, with particular reference to the language in the deed. Other aspects of ownership are discussed in the following paragraphs.

The Shore

The area between the mean high tide and the mean low tide is the shore. The general rule is that the shore is held by the state in trust for the people of the state. It cannot be conveyed [9] and is not subject to acquisition by adverse possession.[10] In the California case of Muchenberger v. City of Santa Monica,[11] the defendant, a littoral owner, entered into an agreement with the City (acting under the authority of the State) by the terms of which the boundary line of defendant's land was fixed as a definite line. Prior thereto ownership extended to the mean high tide. The validity of the agreement was questioned upon the ground that it amounted to a conveyance of a portion of the shore, contrary to a provision in the State Constitution. The validity of the agreement was sustained upon the ground that it did not constitute a conveyance of land by the City. It merely operated to fix the boundary.

With exceptions to be noted, the littoral owner has a right to use the shore for purposes of access. To the extent that his activities do not interfere with the public right of navigation the littoral owner may erect structures, such as docks, to facilitate his use of the water. In many states such activities are regulated by statute. The littoral owner does not have a right to remove sand from the shore for the purpose of sale even if such use does not interfere with the public right of navigation.[12]

---

4. Green v. Eldridge, 1963, 230 Md. 441, 187 A.2d 674, 677.

5. Baker v. State, Fla.1056, 87 So.2d 497, 498.

6. United States v. State of Washington, 9 Cir. 1961, 294 F.2d 830 (the definition of mean high tide is the average elevation of all high tides as observed at a location through a complete tidal cycle of 18.6 years).

7. See, for example, Michaelson v. Silver Beach Improvement Ass'n, 1961, 342 Mass. 251, 173 N.E.2d 273, 275 (discussion of Mass. colonial ordinance of 1641–47); Conran v. Girvin, Mo.1960, 341 S.W.2d 75.

8. Mianus Realty Co. v. Greenway, 1963, 151 Conn. 128, 193 A.2d 713.

9. But see, Boone v. Kingsbury, 1928, 206 Cal. 148, 273 P. 797 (sustaining the validity of an oil-drilling agreement).

10. People v. Kerber, 1908, 152 Cal. 731, 93 P. 878.

11. 206 Cal. 635, 275 P. 803, 62 A.L.R. 219 (1929).

12. State v. Knowles-Lombard Co., 1936, 122 Conn. 263, 188 A. 275, 107 A.L.R. 1344. See Stewart v. Turney, 1922, 203 App.Div. 486, 197 N.Y.S. 81, noted in 36 Harv.Law Rev. 763 (1923) (the littoral owner does not have an exclusive right to the shore for the purpose of hunting).

Marginal Sea

In the case of the oceans the area beyond the shore (the marginal sea) comes within the sovereignty of the United States. In the absence of authorization by federal legislation the littoral state does not have a right to the oil and minerals that may be located beneath the surface.[13]

Submerged Land

If privately owned land is submerged by a navigable body of water, a public right of navigation and fishing arises even though ownership of this portion of the bed of the body of water remains in private ownership subject to reclamation.[14]

Inland Bodies of Water

The prevailing American rule is that the ownership of the bed of an inland body of water, if navigable, is in the state in which it is located.[15] In some states the riparian ownership extends to the high water mark. In other states ownership extends to the low water mark, described as the point to which the water recedes at its lowest ordinary stage.

Governmental Regulations

The general power of a state to legislate with respect to navigable bodies of water within the state is subject to the powers conferred upon the federal government by the United States Constitution. In the first place, federal jurisdiction may attach in admiralty and maritime litigation.[16] In the second place, the United States has power to regulate commerce with foreign nations and among the several states.[17] As a result of this authorization, the federal government has the power to legislate in matters relating to navigable bodies of water if interstate or foreign commerce is involved.

Usually, the owner of land that touches upon navigable water qualifies as a riparian owner. He is also designated as a littoral owner if the land touches upon tidal water, such as in the case of the ocean. The proprietary rights of a riparian or littoral owner are restricted because of the paramount public rights of navigation and fishing. If damage is suffered because of a proper exercise of these rights he is not entitled to recover compensation. Such an owner is also subject to possible damage as the result of legislation looking to the improvement of navigation.

In the California case of Miremar Co. v. City of Santa Barbara,[18] acting under state authority the city constructed a breakwater for the purpose of making a harbor for pleasure boats. Plaintiff, owner of a hotel on the beach some two miles away, claimed damages because the breakwater changed the ocean currents with the result that part of plaintiff's beach was washed away. Recovery was denied because the damages resulted from acts looking to the improvement of navigation. The recovery of damages will also be denied if improvements erected by a littoral owner on the shore (the area between mean high tide and the mean low tide) are destroyed. This is true even though the improvements did not interfere with the use of the water for purposes of navigation.[19]

---

13. U. S. v. State of California, 1947, 332 U.S. 19, 67 S.Ct. 1538, 91 L.Ed. 1877. See note, 36 Va.Law Rev. 806 (1950).

14. Bohn v. Albertson, 1951, 107 Cal.App.2d 738, 238 P.2d 128.

15. Pike Rapids Power Co. v. Minneapolis, St. P. & S. S. M. R. Co., 8 Cir. 1938, 99 F.2d 202. See United States v. State of California, 1965, —— U.S. ——, 85 S.Ct. 1401, —— L.Ed. ——.

16. U.S.Const. art. 3, § 2.

17. U.S.Const. art. 1, § 8, cl. 3.

18. 23 Cal.2d 170, 143 P.2d 1 (1943).

19. United States v. Chicago, M., St. P. & P. R. Co., 1941, 312 U.S. 592, 313 U.S. 543, 61 S.Ct. 772, 85

Compensation is required if land above the mean high tide (or the ordinary high water mark in non-tidal waters) is permanently flooded as the result of governmental activities even if for the purpose of improving navigation.[20] The federal government may also be held accountable for damages if activities are not related to navigation, such as in connection with a reclamation project.[21]

WATERCOURSES AND LAKES

19. **Riparian rights may arise with respect to water in a natural watercourse or lake or an artificial body of water if the water is not supplied by artificial means.**

　　a. **Riparian land. Riparian land is land so situated with respect to the body of water that, because of such location, the possessor is entitled to the benefits incident to the use of water. The land must touch upon the water and be under one ownership and within the watershed. If there is a severance of ownership the land that does not touch upon the water ceases to be riparian.**

　　b. **Accretion, reliction and avulsion. A riparian owner is entitled to land formed by accretion even if the deposit is brought about by artificial means provided he took no part in the creation of the condition. He is not entitled to land formed by avulsion.**

　　　　A boundary line is not changed by accretion or reliction if the land is described by a fixed boundary line as distinguished from a variable boundary line, as in a case where it is described by a watercourse or lake.

　　c. **Riparian use. A riparian owner is entitled to use all of the water if that is necessary for domestic purposes. But the**

reasonable use rule applies if water is used for irrigation purposes. Industrial use may qualify as a proper riparian use but the pollution of a watercourse or lake cannot be justified upon the ground that it is necessary in connection with an industrial activity.

　　d. **Prior appropriation doctrine. Under the prior appropriation doctrine, the water in a watercourse or lake belongs to the people of the state. Preferential rights do not attach by reason of the fact that land is riparian. An appropriator may acquire a prior right by following the procedure prescribed by statute.**

　　e. **Pueblo rights. The pueblo rights doctrine confers preferential rights upon a municipality in connection with the use of water for municipal purposes.**

Riparian rights may arise with respect to water in a natural or an artificial watercourse or lake. A watercourse is a body of water which flows in a known and well defined channel located on the surface of the earth or beneath the surface. It includes all springs, marshes and lakes which supply water to the watercourse.[22] It is not necessary that there be a constant flow of water.[23] However, water which flows through a ravine only during times of rain or melting snow does not constitute a watercourse.[24]

The prevailing rule is that the usual accretions which occur annually and regularly in their accustomed seasons (flood waters) constitute a part of the regular flow of a stream.[25] Assuming that a landowner does have a right to use any means available to him to prevent surface water from reaching

L.Ed. 1064, discussed in 14 So.Cal.Law Rev. 492, 494 (1941).

20. United States v. Cress, 1916, 243 U.S. 316, 37 S.Ct. 380, 61 L.Ed. 746 (*dictum*).

21. U. S. v. Gerlach Live Stock Co., 1950, 339 U.S. 725, 70 S.Ct. 955, 94 L.Ed. 1231, 20 A.L.R.2d 633.

22. 4 Rest.Torts, § 841(2).

23. Mogle v. Moore, 1940, 16 Cal.2d 1, 104 P.2d 785.

24. Eulrich v. Richter, 1875, 37 Wis. 226 (*dictum*).

25. Herminghaus v. Southern California Edison Co., 1926, 200 Cal. 81, 252 P. 607; Sparks Mfg. Co. v. Town of Newton, 1898, 57 N.J.Eq. 367, 41 A. 385. But see, Teass, Water and Watercourses, 18 Va. Law Rev. 223, 241 (1932).

his land,[26] he does not have a right to dam, obstruct or dike against ordinary flood water.[27] This right does exist in the case of extraordinary flood waters.

When the water in a watercourse reaches the end of its channel it may spread out over the surface of the earth. In that event it ceases to be a part of the watercourse and becomes surface water unless it returns to a well defined channel.[28] After such return it would again be a part of a watercourse.[29]

Water located in swamps and marshes is usually classified as surface water. Such water-areas are not lakes because the water is not confined to a reasonably well-defined bed.[30]

Except in cases where water is artificially supplied,[31] riparian rights may arise with respect to an artificial watercourse or lake.[32] For example, if an upper riparian owner diverts the flow of a stream, after the lapse of time, owners of land touching upon the watercourse in its new condition may have the rights of riparian owners. This conclusion is based upon the ground that where the artificially created condition is allowed to continue

for a long period of time, the condition will be considered to be a natural condition.[33] The period of time—by way of analogy—is that period which is prescribed for the acquisition of a prescriptive right.

According to some authorities, acquisition of a right to the use of water in an artificial-condition situation is based upon the ground that prescriptive rights have been acquired.[34] For example, if the owner of land abutting upon a stream erects a dam and thereby creates a millpond, the owners of land upon the newly formed body of water may acquire a prescriptive right to the use of the water.[35]

In the English case of Mason v. Shrewsbury & H. R. Co.,[36] a natural stream flowed over plaintiff's land. Defendant acquired an easement to divert water from this stream. After the lapse of a considerable time defendant discontinued diversion and returned the water to its original condition. Plaintiff claimed damages because of the fact that the bed of the stream, having been allowed to partly fill up, was not capable of caring for floodwaters. In denying recovery it is pointed out that in the absence of express stipulations regarding continuance, the owner of the dominant estate may, at any time, discontinue the user and not be held liable for damages resulting therefrom. A different result would be reached in a case such as this

---

26. See infra, § 21.

27. Pinkstaff v. Steffy, 1905, 216 Ill. 406, 75 N.E. 163; Sullens v. Chicago, R. I. & P. Ry. Co., 1888, 74 Iowa 659, 38 N.W. 545; Bahm v. Raikes, 1955, 160 Neb. 503, 70 N.W.2d 507. *Contra:* Taylor v. Fickas, 1878, 64 Ind. 167; Cass v. Dicks, 1896, 14 Wash. 75, 44 P. 113.

28. Everett v. Davis, 1941, 18 Cal.2d 389, 115 P.2d 821.

29. Macomber v. Godfrey, 1871, 108 Mass. 219.

30. See, 4 Rest.Torts, § 842, *Comment b.*

31. Wattson v. Eldridge, 1929, 207 Cal. 314, 278 P. 236; Wood v. Waud, [1849] 3 Exch. 748, 154 Eng. Rep. 1047.

32. Kray v. Muggli, 1901, 84 Minn. 90, 86 N.W. 882 (artificial pond). *Contra:* Goodrich v. McMillan, 1922, 217 Mich. 630, 187 N.W. 368, 26 A.L.R. 801, noted in 2 Wis.Law Rev. 181 (1923). See Whipple v. Nelson, 1943, 143 Neb. 286, 9 N.W.2d 288.

Burby Real Prop. 3rd Ed. HB—4

33. Natural Soda Products Co. v. City of Los Angeles, 1943, 23 Cal.2d 193, 143 P.2d 12, certiorari denied, 321 U.S. 793, 64 S.Ct. 790, 88 L.Ed. 1082, rehearing denied, 322 U.S. 768, 64 S.Ct. 942, 88 L.Ed. 1594; Shepardson v. Perkins, 1878, 58 N.H. 354 (based upon equitable estoppel). *Contra:* Drainage Dist. No. 2 v. City of Everett, 1933, 171 Wash. 471, 18 P.2d 53, 88 A.L.R. 123.

34. Murchie v. Gates, 1886, 78 Me. 300, 4 A. 698; Belknap v. Trimble, 1832, 3 Paige (N.Y.) 577 (change in bed of a watercourse).

35. Hammond v. Antwerp Light & Power Co., 1928, 132 Misc. 786, 230 N.Y.S. 621.

36. L.R. 6 Q.B. 578 (1871).

if plaintiff relied upon the fact that, because of long continued use and diversion of the water the "new condition" of the land should be considered as a natural condition.

Riparian Land

Riparian land is land so situated with respect to the ocean, a watercourse or a lake that, because of such location, the possessor is entitled to the benefits incident to the use of the water. These rights attach because possession of the riparian land carries with it a right of access to the water. If the bed of the body of water is in private ownership, a right of access is based upon ownership of that part of the area where access is claimed.[37] If the bed is in public ownership, as in the case of the ocean, ownership to the mean high tide confers riparian rights. Use of the area between the mean high tide and the mean low tide is based upon a public right.

Land is riparian only if it touches upon the body of water in question and is under one ownership. In addition, it must be within the watershed (the area which acts as a natural feeder for the body of water in question).[38] Rainfall within that area feeds the stream and, because of that fact, the land is entitled to preferential treatment. In at least one state, Oregon, this watershed-rule is not applied.[39]

In some states the lateral extent of riparian land is limited to land encompassed within the original government grant.[40] In the Nebraska case of McGinley v. Platte Valley Power & Irrigation District,[41] condemnation proceedings involved riparian land. The court refused to follow the usual rule as it relates to severance damages with the result that compensation was denied for loss of incidental benefits pertaining to the use of non-riparian land. The land was non-riparian because it was not included in the original government grant.

If there is a severance of ownership, that portion which does not touch upon the body of water ceases to be riparian. If subsequently the land which had ceased to be riparian again becomes a part of a riparian tract, held under a single title, there is a difference of opinion as to whether or not the riparian rights will re-attach.

Logically, whether or not land is riparian should be made to depend upon the situation of the land involved and not upon prior facts relating to unity of title.[42] But some authorities follow the view that once a portion of land is severed from that part of a tract which touches upon a body of water, the riparian characteristics of the severed portion is destroyed forever.[43] This rule is in furtherance of a policy followed in some states, especially in arid areas, to restrict the extent of riparian land. It has been held that

---

37. See, 4 Rest.Torts, § 843, *Comment b.*

38. Bathgate v. Irvine, 1899, 126 Cal. 135, 58 P. 442; Stratton v. Mt. Hermon Boys' School, 1913, 216 Mass. 83, 103 N.E. 87 (*dictum*), noted in 2 Cal.Law Rev. 340 (1914); Sayles v. City of Mitchell, 1932, 60 S.D. 592, 245 N.W. 390; Town of Gordonsville v. Zinn, 1921, 129 Va. 542, 106 S.E. 508, 14 A.L.R. 318.

39. Jones v. Conn, 1901, 39 Or. 30, 64 P. 855, 65 P. 1068.

40. Boehmer v. Big Rock Creek Irrigation Dist., 1897, 117 Cal. 19, 48 P. 908; Crawford Co. v. Hathaway, 1903, 67 Neb. 325, 93 N.W. 781; Watkins Land Co. v. Clements, 1905, 98 Tex. 578, 86 S.W. 733.

41. 132 Neb. 292, 271 N.W. 864 (1937).

42. Clark v. Allaman, 1905, 71 Kan. 206, 80 P. 571; Jones v. Conn, 1901, 39 Or. 30, 64 P. 855, 65 P. 1068.

43. Anaheim Union Water Co. v. Fuller, 1907, 150 Cal. 327, 88 P. 978; Watkins Land Co. v. Clements, 1905, 98 Tex. 578, 86 S.W. 733 (*dictum*); Yearsley v. Carter, 1928, 149 Wash. 285, 270 P. 804, noted in 27 Mich.Law Rev. 479 (1929).

the severance-rule is not applicable in a case where riparian land is partitioned as the result of judicial proceedings.[44]

Accretion, Reliction and Avulsion

If land is described by a variable boundary line, such as a body of water, the area is subject to change by accretion and reliction.[45] Accretion consists of the imperceptible deposit of silt, sand, gravel, etc. The land so deposited is called alluvion. Reliction is involved if the water gradually recedes. A temporary change in the water line, such as in the case of reliction caused by a seasonal drought, does not change the boundary line.[46] Neither is the boundary line changed by avulsion—a sudden change brought about by the action of the water.[47]

The right of a littoral or a riparian owner to land formed by accretion or reliction may be based upon public policy.[48] Such owner is the only one in a position to apply the area to a beneficial use because of the fact that the land is formed by a slow and imperceptible process. It is also a means by which the littoral or riparian owner can maintain a right of access to the water, a characteristic that is essential if the land is to remain riparian. It is also a fair rule because it is

compensation for the hazard of loss that may result from erosion.

The preferred view is that the accretion rule applies even if the deposit is brought about or accentuated by artificial means if the riparian or littoral owner took no part in the activities.[49]

In the Massachusetts case of Michaelson v. Silver Beach Improvement Ass'n, Inc.,[50] dredging operations under state authority resulted in the extension of a beach. A littoral owner was successful in establishing his claim of ownership to the newly formed land. The court expresses some doubt as to whether or not the dredging was justified as a means by which to improve navigation. But even assuming such justification, it did not follow that a man-made beach could be used as a means by which to impair the littoral owner's means of access to the water. The rules applicable in natural-accretion cases are applicable in a case of this type since the littoral owner took no part in the activities. It is to be noted that the change in this case was not brought about by accretion. The sand taken from the bottom of the water was deposited on the shore. The build-up was not by a slow and imperceptible process. A similar result was reached in the New York case of Tiffany v. Town of Oyster Bay,[51] where the build-up was accomplished by the littoral owner under the mistaken belief that he had received proper authorization from the public authorities.

Land described by a fixed boundary line is not subject to change by accretion or re-

---

44. Rancho Santa Margarita v. Vail, 1938, 11 Cal.2d 501, 81 P.2d 533, noted in 27 Cal.Law Rev. 92 (1938), 12 So.Cal.Law Rev. 222 (1939).

45. Strand Improvement Co. v. Long Beach, 1916, 173 Cal. 765, 161 P. 975 (littoral owner); Jefferis v. East Omaha Land Co., 1889, 134 U.S. 178, 10 S.Ct. 518, 33 L.Ed. 872.

46. Hillebrand v. Knapp, 1937, 65 S.D. 414, 274 N.W. 821, 112 A.L.R. 1104.

47. City of New York v. Realty Associates, 1931, 256 N.Y. 217, 176 N.E. 171, noted in 17 Iowa Law Rev. 263 (1932); Nolte v. Sturgeon, Okl.1962, 376 P.2d 616. But see, Hancock v. Moore, 1941, 135 Tex. 619, 146 S.W.2d 369.

48. See Gifford v. Yarborough, [1825] 5 Bing. 163, 130 Eng.Rep. 1023.

49. But see, Los Angeles Athletic Club v. City of Santa Monica, 1944, 63 Cal.App.2d 795, 147 P.2d 976.

50. 342 Mass. 251, 173 N.E.2d 273 (1961).

51. 234 N.Y. 15, 136 N.E. 224 (1922), noted in 71 Univ. of Pa.Law Rev. 157 (1923).

liction.[52] A contrary rule is followed in some states upon the ground that if land becomes riparian in fact it should be considered as riparian land regardless of a fixed-line description.[53] Under this view, if riparian land is lost in its entirety by erosion, the new riparian owner is entitled to land that is restored by accretion or reliction.

A riparian owner may be entitled to alluvion (land formed by accretion), because of the fact that he is the owner of riparian land to which it is formed or because he is the owner of the bed of the body of water where the formation took place, such as an island.[54] The general rule is that the state is the owner of the bed of an inland body of water if it is navigable. If it is non-navigable, the riparian owner may own to the thread of the stream or the center of a lake.[55]

The thread of a stream means the "geographical center of the stream at ordinary or medium state of the water, disregarding slight and exceptional irregularities in the banks. It is fixed without regard to the main channel of the stream; that is, the greater volume of water may flow and the greater depth of the water may lie on one side or other of the thread of the stream."[56] Boundary lines are extended at right angles with the "course of the river to the thread of the stream."[57] In the absence of special circumstances,[58] if a lake is involved ownership is determined by extending boundary lines to the geographical center of the lake.[59]

If the bed of the body of water is in public ownership, as in the case of the ocean and other bodies of water classified as navigable, the alluvion is apportioned on an equitable basis.[60] Importance is attached to the fact that the riparian characteristics of the land should be maintained and each riparian owner is entitled to his just share of the newly formed land for profitable use. Such an apportionment problem was involved in the Massachusetts case of Deerfield v. Arms.[61] The process of apportionment is stated to be as follows:

First: Measure "the whole extent of the ancient bank or line of the river, and compute how many rods, yards, or feet each riparian proprietor owned on the river line.

Second: "Supposing the former line, for instance, to amount to 200 rods, * * * divide the newly formed bank or river line into 200 equal parts, and appropriate to each proprietor as many portions of this new river line as he owned rods on the old. Then, to complete the division, lines are to be drawn from the points at which the proprietors respectively bounded on the old, to the points thus determined as the points of division on the newly formed shore. The new

---

52. Stratbucker v. Junge, 1951, 153 Neb. 885, 46 N.W. 2d 486; Ford v. Harris, Okl.1963, 383 P.2d 21; Allard v. Curran, 1918, 41 S.D. 73, 168 N.W. 761, noted in 17 Mich.Law Rev. 95 (1918). See Volcanic Oil & Gas Co. v. Chaplin, 1912, 27 Ont.Law Rep. 34 (not subject to loss by erosion).

53. Welles v. Bailey, 1887, 55 Conn. 292, 10 A. 565; Widdecombe v. Chiles, 1902, 173 Mo. 195, 73 S.W. 444; Wemmer v. Young, 1958, 167 Neb. 495, 93 N.W.2d 837.

54. See Perkins v. Adams, 1896, 132 Mo. 131, 33 S.W. 778. But see San Antonio River Authority v. Lewis, 1962, —— Tex. ——, 363 S.W.2d 444, 447.

55. 4 Rest.Torts, § 843, *Comment e.*

56. Bade, Title, Points and Lines in Lakes and Streams, 24 Minn.Law Rev. 305, 307 (1940).

57. Miller v. Hepburn, 8 Bush.(Ky.) 326 (1871).

58. See, Cutliff v. Densmore, 1958, 345 Mich. 586, 93 N.W.2d 307 (special circumstances because property was located on the bay of a lake); Rondesvedt v. Running, 1963, 19 Wis.2d 614, 121 N.W.2d 1.

59. See, Bade, Title, Points and Lines in Lakes and Streams, 24 Minn.Law Rev. 305, 306 (1940).

60. Grill v. Meydenbauer Bay Yacht Club, 1963, 61 Wash.2d 432, 378 P.2d 423.

61. 17 Pick.(Mass.) 41 (1835).

lines, thus formed, it is obvious, will be either parallel, or divergent, or convergent, according as the new shore line of the river equals or exceeds or falls short of the old." [62]

Riparian Use

The theory underlying riparian rights is that the water in a watercourse or lake may be used for the enjoyment and development of riparian land. The riparian owner cannot successfully assert ownership in the water itself. His right is usufructuary in nature—a right to use the water. [63]

The right of one riparian owner to use the water for riparian purposes is circumscribed by the fact that a similar right of use exists in other riparian owners. Considerable difficulty is encountered when it becomes necessary to adjust conflicting claims of riparian owners with respect to the use and enjoyment of water. It is generally stated that a riparian owner is entitled to make a "reasonable use" of the water. Among other things, reasonableness is judged upon the size of the watercourse, general usage and custom in the locality and the fact that other riparian owners have like rights of use. [64] A clash of interests may arise either because of the direct use of the water by one riparian owner or because of activities which cause pollution. These matters are discussed in the following paragraphs.

The outcome of litigation involving riparian rights will, in many cases, depend upon which of the two following rules is adopted by the court. According to the English rule, a riparian owner has a right to the flow of a watercourse in substantially its natural condition subject, [65] of course, to authorized use by upper riparian owners. [66] Any invasion of this right is actionable *without reference to actual damages* that may be involved. Under this view, if unauthorized use is allowed to continue for the statutory period the result may be the acquisition of a prescriptive right. [67] A technical wrong is involved if a riparian owner uses the water in a watercourse or lake for a purpose disassociated from the use of riparian land. [68]

While the English rule is followed in a majority of the American states, in a substantial number of states it is held that the rights of a riparian owner are not absolute. An invasion of his right does not occur until he suffers actual damages. This does not take place as long as there is sufficient water available to satisfy his riparian needs. The riparian right is limited to a reasonable beneficial use of water and any water in excess of this may be used by others. [69]

---

62. *Accord*: Hamilton v. Horan, 1936, 193 Ark. 85, 97 S.W.2d 637; Jennings v. Shipp, N.D.1962, 115 N.W.2d 12.

63. Federal Power Com'n v. Niagara Mohawk Power Corp., 1954, 347 U.S. 239, 74 S.Ct. 487, 98 L.Ed. 666.

64. Embry v. Owen, [1851] 6 Exch. 353, 155 Eng. Rep. 579. See Hoover v. Crane, 1960, 362 Mich. 36, 106 N.W.2d 563.

65. McCartney v. Londonderry, etc., Ry. Co., [1904] A.C. 301.

66. See Embrey v. Owen, [1851] 5 Exch. 353, 155 Eng.Rep. 579.

67. Appeal of Messinger, 1885, 109 Pa. 284, 4 A. 162. But see, Ulbricht v. Eufaula Water Co., 1889, 86 Ala. 587, 6 So. 78, where the court granted a modified injunction which vindicated the riparian owner's right but permitted the defendant's use of the water until such time as the riparian owner suffered actual damages.

68. Bank of Hopkinsville v. Western Kentucky Asylum for Insane, 1900, 108 Ky. 357, 56 S.W. 525; Garwood v. New York Central & H. R. R. Co., 1880, 83 N.Y. 400 (water used to supply needs of locomotives); Pennsylvania Rd. Co. v. Miller, 1886, 112 Pa. 34, 3 A. 780 (water used to supply needs of locomotives).

69. Stratton v. Mount Hermon Boys' School, 1913, 216 Mass. 83, 103 N.E. 87 noted in 12 Mich.Law Rev. 304 (1914); Minnesota Loan & Trust Co. v. St. Anthony Falls Water-Power Co., 1901, 82 Minn.

The doctrine as it relates to the reasonable beneficial use of water is a part of the statutory law in some states. In 1928 the California Constitution was amended to make application of this rule compulsory.[70] By force of this amendment a riparian owner cannot prevent such things as the construction of a dam to impound flood waters that would normally flow into the ocean. It may be that the riparian owner will lose the benefits of flood waters insofar as the deposit of silt on his land is concerned. He may also lose the benefits of flood waters for the purpose of cleansing his land of salt deposits in the lowlands that border upon the ocean. But the demand of flood water for such purposes properly cannot be classified as a reasonable beneficial use.[71]

Some of the important riparian uses are as follows:

First: A riparian owner is entitled to use all of the water that is necessary for domestic purposes even if this deprives a lower riparian owner of water required for the same purpose.[72] While a domestic use is involved if water is used for the care of livestock, that is not the case if livestock is raised for commercial purposes.[73] The domestic-use priority is not recognized in some localities where the industrial use of water is a predominant factor in community development.

There is authority for the view that a domestic use is involved in supplying water to an institution, such as a hospital,[74] or to supply the needs of the inhabitants of a community.[75] This conclusion as it relates to "city dwellers" is particularly objectionable because of the fact that they cannot qualify as riparian owners.

Second: Water in a watercourse or lake may properly be used to irrigate riparian land.[76] The reasonable use doctrine applies so the extent to which one riparian owner may be entitled to use water for this purpose depends upon the amount of water available, each owner being entitled to his proportionate share. The use of water for domestic purposes will be protected against claims of other riparian owners who assert the right to use the water for irrigation purposes.[77]

Third: The test of "reasonable conduct" is applied in resolving conflicting claims of riparian owners who conduct industrial activities. Usually, a riparian owner is not liable for damages that may result from the temporary interruption in the flow of water caused by the erection of a dam,[78] or the increase in

---

505, 85 N.W. 520; Meng v. Coffey, 1903, 67 Neb. 500, 93 N.W. 713; Gillis v. Chase, 1891, 67 N.H. 161, 31 A. 18; Texas Co. v. Burkett, 1927, 117 Tex. 16, 296 S.W. 273, 54 A.L.R. 1397.

70. Cal.Const. Art. XIV, § 3.

71. Peabody v. City of Vallejo, 1935, 2 Cal.2d 351, 40 P.2d 486. See, Gin S. Chow v. City of Santa Barbara, 1933, 217 Cal. 673, 22 P.2d 5, comment 22 Cal.Law Rev. 333 (1934), 8 Temp.Law Qt. 283 (1934). But see, Thompson v. New Haven Water Co., 1913, 86 Conn. 597, 86 A. 585.

72. Spence v. McDonough, 1889, 77 Iowa 460, 42 N.W. 371. For criticism of this view, see 10 Colo. Law Rev. 65 (1910).

73. Cowell v. Armstrong, 1930, 210 Cal. 218, 290 P. 1036 (*dictum*).

74. Filbert v. Dechert, 1903, 22 Pa.Super. 362 (900 persons).

75. City of Canton v. Shock, 1902, 66 Ohio St. 19, 63 N.E. 600. *Contra:* Stock v. City of Hillsdale, 1909, 155 Mich. 375, 119 N.W. 435; City of New Whatcom v. Fairhaven Land Co., 1901, 24 Wash. 493, 64 P. 735.

76. But see, Valmont Plantations v. State of Texas, 1962, 163 Tex. 381, 355 S.W.2d 502 (holding that Spanish and Mexican land grants did not confer, by implication, riparian irrigation rights). *Cf.*: San Antonio River Authority v. Lewis, 1963, —— Tex. ——, 363 S.W.2d 444.

77. Smith v. Corbit, 1897, 116 Cal. 587, 48 P. 725.

78. Dumont v. Kellogg, 1874, 29 Mich. 420.

the height of a dam.[79] A mill owner may properly close the gates of his dam during the night in order to secure a sufficient head of water to permit the operation of his mill.[80]

Ordinarily, the use of water is considered to be unreasonable if the quality of the water is impaired in a substantial degree. There is authority for the view that even heating the water in connection with industrial use is actionable if this prevents a lower riparian owner from using the water for the production of ice on a profitable basis.[81]

While the pollution of a watercourse or lake may be justified by custom or usage,[82] the pollution cannot be justified merely because it may be a necessary incident to industrial activity, such as the operation of a mine.[83] In Pennsylvania the rule is followed that although a riparian owner must submit to the pollution of a watercourse if mining operations are involved,[84] there is cause to complain if the pollution interferes with use of the water for public purposes.[85]

In the Maryland case of Helfrich v. Catonsville,[86] a riparian owner pastured cows in a field through which a stream flowed. This use caused a pollution of the water, making it unsuitable for drinking purposes, to the damage of a lower riparian owner that supplied drinking water from the watercourse to the inhabitants of a community. The court held that since the upper riparian owner was making a reasonable use of his pasture he incurred no liability. No point is made of the fact that the water company was using the water for non-riparian purposes. Of course, the activities of a riparian owner may be of such a nature as to constitute a public nuisance. As such, abatement may be ordered.[87]

Fourth: If a body of water is navigable in fact there is a public right to use the water for recreational purposes, such as fishing, swimming and boating. However, the weight of authority is that such a public right does not exist in the case of non-navigable waters. A contrary rule is followed in a few states where recreational use of inland lakes has taken on the aspects of a major industry.[88] While a public right may be acquired by dedication it cannot be acquired by prescription.

Riparian owners usually have a right to use a watercourse or lake for recreational purposes. However, there are two views as to the area of a body of water that may be used. According to the common law rule, the ownership of the bed of a non-navigable body of water carried with it the right to the exclusive use of the water within that area.[89] In

79. Pitts v. Lancaster Mills, 1847, 54 Mass.(13 Metc.) 156.

80. Bullard v. Saratoga Victory Mfg. Co., 1879, 77 N.Y. 525.

81. Sandusky Portland Cement Co. v. Dixon Pure Ice Co., 7 Cir. 1915, 221 F. 200.

82. Snow v. Parsons, 1856, 28 Vt. 459. See, Red River Roller Mills v. Wright, 1883, 30 Minn. 249, 15 N.W. 167. *Cf.*: Hayes v. Waldron, 1863, 44 N.H. 580.

83. Beach v. Sterling Iron & Zinc Co., 1895, 54 N.J. Eq. 65, 33 A. 286.

84. Pennsylvania Coal Co. v. Sanderson, 1886, 113 Pa. 126, 6 A. 453.

85. Pennsylvania Rd. Co. v. Sagamore Coal Co., 1924, 281 Pa. 233, 126 A. 386, 39 A.L.R. 882; comment, 34 Yale Law Jr., 670 (1925).

86. 74 Md. 269, 22 A. 72 (1891).

87. People v. Elk River Co., 1895, 107 Cal. 214, 40 P. 486 (stables etc., located on the land).

88. See, Rushton, Hoffmaster v. Taggart, 1943, 306 Mich. 432, 11 N.W.2d 193; Lamprey v. State, 1893, 52 Minn. 181, 53 N.W. 1139; Hillebrand v. Knapp, 1937, 65 S.D. 414, 274 N.W. 821, 112 A.L.R. 1104; 4 Rest. Torts, § 843, *Comment g.*

89. Baker v. Normanoch Ass'n, 1957, 25 N.J. 407, 136 A.2d 645 (owner of substantial portion of the bed may exclude owners of minimal portions of the bed); Smoulter v. Boyd, 1904, 209 Pa. 146, 58 A. 144. See Wickouski v. Swift, 1962, 203 Va. 467, 124 S.E.2d 892 (artificial body of water).

fact a fence barrier may be erected to assure such exclusive use. This is the rule followed in a majority of the states. According to the civil law rule, the reasonable use of a watercourse or lake by a riparian owner is not restricted by non-ownership of the bed. The use extends to the entire body of water. This rule is followed in a number of states where the recreational use of water is of prime importance to the economy.[90]

Prior Appropriation Doctrine

In some states the prior appropriation doctrine is applied with respect to the use of water.[91] The basic theory underlying this doctrine is that the water belongs to all of the people in the state. Preferential rights do not attach because of the fact that land is riparian to a watercourse.[92] However, a prior right to use the water may be acquired by one who first appropriates the water and, within a reasonable time, applies it to a beneficial use. In addition, the appropriator must conform to state statutes with respect to filing an application etc.

In a few states the prior appropriation doctrine is followed even though riparian rights are also recognized. For example, in California a prior appropriator cannot acquire rights that would deprive a riparian owner of his right to the reasonable beneficial use

of water in a watercourse or lake.[93] Only the surplus water is available for appropriation.[94]

Pueblo Rights

The Pueblo Rights Doctrine is followed in a few of the states that have a Spanish-Mexican origin. Application of this doctrine results in a priority in the use of water for municipal purposes.[95]

The doctrine dates from a time in 1789 when the King of Spain established the Town of Pictic in New Spain (Mexico). It was prescribed that the town was to have a preferential right to the use of water in any watercourse touching upon the boundaries of the town to the extent necessary for municipal purposes. The extent of the right expanded with the growth of the community. This arrangement was called the Plan of Pictic and was subsequently followed in the establishment of Indian villages (pueblos) in the area now comprising Arizona, California, New Mexico and Texas. The Pueblo Rights Doctrine is that municipalities located on the sites of these pueblos have succeeded to the rights of the pueblos as they relate to the use of water for municipal purposes. These rights are superior to claims of others as riparian owners or appropriators.

According to some authorities, application of this doctrine is mandatory in territory that came under the jurisdiction of the United States by force of the Treaty of Guada-

---

90. Duval v. Thomas, Fla.1959, 114 So.2d 791; Swartz v. Sherston, 1941, 299 Mich. 423, 300 N.W. 148, noted in 26 Minn.Law Rev. 569 (1942); Johnson v. Seifert, 1960, 257 Minn. 159, 100 N.W.2d 689; Snively v. Jaber, 1956, 48 Wash.2d 815, 296 P.2d 1015, 57 A.L.R.2d 560.

91. For an enumeration of the states following this view, see Wiel, "Priority" in Western Water Law, 18 Yale Law Jr. 189, fn. 3 (1909). See also, State ex rel. Emery v. Knapp, 1949, 167 Kan. 546, 207 P.2d 440, involving the 1945 Water Appropriation Act of Kansas.

92. Adams v. Portage Irr., Reservoir & Power Co., 1937, 95 Utah 1, 72 P.2d 648.

93. Palmer v. Railroad Comm., 1914, 167 Cal. 163, 138 P. 997. *Accord*: Crawford Co. v. Hathaway, 1903, 67 Neb. 325, 93 N.W. 781. The Nebraska cases are discussed in 15 Neb.Law Bulletin 271 (1937).

94. Cal.Const. Art. XIV, § 3, as amended 1928.

95. City of San Diego v. Cuyamaca Water Co., 1929, 209 Cal. 105, 287 P. 475; Cartwright v. Public Service Co., of New Mexico, 1958, 66 N.M. 64, 343 P.2d 654.

lupe Hidalgo between the United States and Mexico in 1848. Article VIII of the Treaty provides:

"In the said territories, property of every kind, now belonging to Mexico (*now*) established there, shall be inviolably respected."

PERCOLATING WATER

20. Percolating water is water beneath the surface of the earth that is not confined to a known and well defined channel or bed.

a. **Common law rule. The common law rule is one of absolute ownership of percolating water.**

b. **Reasonable use rule. Under the reasonable use rule all of the landowners have a correlative right with respect to percolating water located beneath the surface of their land.**

c. **Prior appropriation. Under the prior appropriation doctrine ownership of percolating water is in the state and is available to those who comply with state law as it relates to prior appropriation.**

d. **Interference with the flow of percolating water. In the absence of negligence a landowner cannot be held liable for activities that result in the obstruction of the flow of percolating water.**

e. **Causing the pollution of percolating water. A landowner who causes the pollution of percolating water can be held liable only upon proof of negligence or of the fact that it resulted from an unreasonable use of his land.**

Percolating water is water beneath the surface of the earth that is not confined to a known and well defined channel or bed. If it is so confined the water is classified as a watercourse or lake.[96]

Common Law Rule

The common law rule is one of absolute ownership. A landowner is not restricted in

96. Hale v. McLea, 1879, 53 Cal. 578.

the withdrawal of percolating water located beneath the surface of his land even if this causes the drainage of water from adjoining land to the damage of other landowners.[97]

According to some decisions, the above stated rule does not permit the taking of percolating water if it is not used for a beneficial purpose and the taking is by one who is actuated by malice.[98] A further restriction upon the use of the water is provided by statutes enacted in some states that prohibit the waste of percolating water.

Reasonable Use Rule

While the common law rule is applied in a majority of the early American decisions, an increasing number of states now apply the reasonable use rule. Under this rule the right of a landowner does not include unreasonable use of percolating water to the detriment of other landowners.

In applying the reasonable use rule there is a lack of uniformity as to what conduct does or does not constitute a reasonable use. Some decisions follow the rule that a landowner may use all of the percolating water that is available under his land if this is reasonably necessary for the beneficial enjoyment of his land. That this deprives other landowners of sufficient water for the beneficial use of their own land is not a controlling

97. Roath v. Driscoll, 1850, 20 Conn. 533; Chase v. Silverstone, 1873, 62 Me. 175; City of Corpus Christi v. City of Pleasanton, 1955, 154 Tex. 289, 276 S.W.2d 798; Fire District No. 1 v. Graniteville Spring Water Co., 1930, 103 Vt. 89, 152 A. 42; Chasemore v. Richards, [1859] 7 H.L.Cas. 349, 11 Eng.Rep. 140.

98. Chesley v. King, 1882, 74 Me. 164 (*dictum*); Greenleaf v. Francis, 1836, 18 Pick.(Mass.) 117 (*dictum*); Ryan v. Quinlan, 1912, 45 Mont. 521, 124 P. 512 (*dictum*). *Contra*: Chatfield v. Wilson, 1855, 28 Vt. 49; Huber v. Merkel, 1903, 117 Wis. 355, 94 N.W. 354.

factor.[99] Other authorities hold that such an absolute right does not exist. The rule applied is that all landowners have a right to the use of water that is located beneath the surface of the land. They are under an obligation to share in the use of the water on a correlative basis.[1] Thus, rights respecting use are similar to those of riparian owners.[2] In any event, the waste of percolating water may be enjoined.[3]

Under the reasonable use rule, percolating water may be sold or used for the benefit of land that does not overlie the area if this does not interfere with the requirements of other landowners who are entitled to use the water.[4] But the water cannot be sold or so used if such requirements are disturbed.[5] The sale or transportation of water is not an unreasonable use merely because this deprives other landowners of the opportunity to make a like use of the water.[6]

Prior Appropriation

Under the prior appropriation doctrine the ownership of percolating water is in the state and is available to those who comply with the state law as it relates to prior appropriators.[7] The first appropriator will be protected against a subsequent appropriator who impairs the available supply of water as conditions existed at the time of the first appropriation.[8]

Interference with the Flow of Percolating Water

An obstruction in the flow of percolating water may result from an activity that constitutes a normal and reasonable use of land, such as mining operations. This may cause damage to owners of adjoining land but, in the absence of negligence, is not an actionable wrong. This rule is followed in those states that follow the common law rule of absolute ownership of percolating water,[9] states that follow the rule of reasonable use [10]

99. Dunbar v. Sweeney, 1921, 230 N.Y. 609, 130 N.E. 913. See Meeker v. City of East Orange, 1909, 77 N.J.L. 623, 74 A. 379.

1. See Hudson v. Dailey, 1909, 156 Cal. 617, 105 P. 748.

2. 4 Rest.Torts, § 858.

3. Barclay v. Abraham, 1903, 121 Iowa 619, 96 N.W. 1080.

4. Cohen v. La Canada Land, etc., Co., 1907, 151 Cal. 680, 91 P. 584.

5. Katz v. Walkinshaw, 1903, 141 Cal. 116, 70 P. 663, 74 P. 766; Schenk v. City of Ann Arbor, 1917, 196 Mich. 75, 163 N.W. 109; Meeker v. City of East Orange, 1909, 77 N.J.L. 623, 74 A. 379, noted in 58 Pa.Law Rev. 303 (1910); Forbell v. New York, 1900, 164 N.Y. 522, 58 N.E. 644; City of Stillwater v. Cundiff, 1939, 184 Okl. 375, 87 P.2d 947; Township of Hatfield v. Lansdale Municipal Auth., 1961, 403 Pa. 113, 168 A.2d 333.

6. Merrick Water Co. v. City of Brooklyn, 1898, 32 App.Div. 454, 53 N.Y.S. 10, affirmed 160 N.Y. 657, 55 N.E. 1097. *Contra*: Rothrauff v. Sinking Spring Water Co., 1940, 339 P. 129, 14 A.2d 87, comment 26 Cornell Law Quarterly 154 (1940). *Cf.*: Hathorn v. Natural Carbonic Gas Co., 1919, 194

N.Y. 326, 87 N.E. 504 (where the abstraction of the water is by "unreasonable artificial means").

7. Bristor v. Cheatham, 1952, 73 Ariz. 228, 240 P.2d 185; Williams v. City of Wichita, 1962, 190 Kan. 317, 374 P.2d 578; State ex rel. v. Dority, 1950, 55 N.M. 12, 225 P.2d 1007; Wrathall v. Johnson, 1935, 86 Utah 50, 40 P.2d 755, 788.

8. Pima Farms Co. v. Proctor, 1926, 30 Ariz. 96, 245 P. 369; Noh v. Stoner, 1933, 53 Idaho 651, 26 P.2d 1112. See Volkmann v. Crosby, N.D.1963, 120 N.W.2d 18.

9. West Kentucky Coal Co. v. Dilback, 1927, 219 Ky. 783, 294 S.W. 478, noted in 16 Ky.Law Jr. 182; Logan Gas Co. v. Glasgo, 1930, 122 Ohio St. 126, 170 N.E. 874; Gallerani v. United States, D.Mass.1941, 41 F.Supp. 293; Acton v. Blondell, [1843] 12 Mees. & W. 324, 152 Eng.Rep. 1223.

10. Sloss-Sheffield Steel & Iron Co. v. Wilkes, 1936, 231 Ala. 511, 165 So. 764, 109 A.L.R. 385; Clinchfield Coal Corp. v. Compton, 1927, 148 Va. 437, 139 S.E. 308, 55 A.L.R. 1376; Evans v. City of Seattle, 1935, 182 Wash. 450, 47 P.2d 984. *Contra*: O'Leary v. Herbert, 1936, 5 Cal.2d 416, 55 P.2d 834.

and states that follow the doctrine of prior appropriation.[11] These various rules do not place restrictions upon the *use of land*. Restrictions, if any, relate to the *use of water*. However, there is authority for the view that a landowner may be held liable for an obstruction in the flow of percolating water if this is caused by an ultrahazardous activity, such as blasting operations.[12]

The improvement of land may necessitate the drainage of surface water. If the owner acts in a non-negligent manner he cannot be held liable even though the improvement results in the withdrawal of percolating water to the damage of an adjoining landowner.[13]

Causing the Pollution of Percolating Water

There are two views as to the liability of a landowner who causes the pollution of percolating water with resultant damage to another landowner who is entitled to make use of the water:

First: The prevailing rule is that a landowner who causes the pollution may be held liable only upon proof of fault on his part either because of the fact that he made an unreasonable use of his land or because he made a reasonable use of his land but acted in a negligent manner.[14]

In the Indiana case of City of Greencastle v. Hazelett,[15] the court refused to grant an injunction which would have prohibited the defendant from using his land as a burial ground even though it was alleged that such a use would destroy the utility of springs located on plaintiff's land.

Second: According to some authorities a landowner who causes the pollution of percolating water may be held liable for damages resulting therefrom even though he was free from negligence and even though he made only a reasonable use of his land.[16] The net result is liability without fault.

SURFACE WATER

21. Surface water is water that does not flow in a well defined channel and is not confined within a well defined basin.

A landowner is entitled to use surface water located on his land even if this deprives a lower landowner of benefits that would occur from the flow of the water.

a. Discharging surface water by artificial means. A landowner may be held liable for damage caused by the flow of surface water if the flow is changed or augmented by artificial means, such as by a ditch.

b. Obstructing the flow of surface water. According to the common law rule a landowner is privileged to prevent surface water from reaching his land. The civil law rule is that there is a natural servitude upon land to receive the natural flow of surface water. Under the reasonable conduct rule liability cannot be imposed upon a landowner who makes a reasonable use of his land.

If water on the surface of the ground does not flow in a well defined channel, as in the case of a watercourse, or is not confined within a well defined basin, as in the case of

11. See, N. M. Long & Co. v. Cannon-Papanikolas Const. Co., 1959, 9 Utah 2d 307, 343 P.2d 1100.

12. Richard v. Kaufman, D.Pa.1942, 47 F.Supp.2d 337.

13. N. M. Long & Co. v. Cannon-Papanikolas Const. Co., 1959, 9 Utah 2d 307, 343 P.2d 1100.

14. Long v. Louisville & N. R. Co., 1908, 128 Ky. 26, 107 S.W. 203; Rose v. Socony-Vacuum Corp., 1934, 54 R.I. 411, 173 A. 627. See, Schlichtkrull v. Mellon-Pollock Oil Co., 1930, 301 Pa. 553, 152 A. 829; Reinhart v. Lancaster Area Refuse Authority, 1963, 201 Pa.Super. 614, 193 A.2d 670.

15. 23 Ind. 186 (1864).

16. Gilmore v. Royal Salt Co., 1911, 84 Kan. 729, 115 P. 541; Berger v. Minneapolis Gaslight Co., 1895, 60 Minn. 296, 62 N.W. 336; Beatrice Gas Co. v. Thomas, 1894, 41 Neb. 662, 59 N.W. 925; Masten v. Texas Co., 1927, 194 N.C. 540, 140 S.E. 89.

a lake, it is classified as surface water.[17] Diffused surface water is water which ordinarily results from rainfall and melting snow and spreads over the surface of the earth. It ceases to be diffused surface water when it flows into a natural depression, draw, swale or other natural drainway.

A landowner may use surface water located on his land even though this deprives a lower landowner of the benefits that would otherwise accrue from the flow of this water.[18] Some authorities take the position that this rule applies only in situations where the water is used for a reasonable purpose. Also, it is not applicable if the appropriation is made merely for the purpose of causing damage to others.[19] Of course, if surface water has come to rest in a permanent bed, forming a pond or lake, the riparian rights of others may be involved.[20]

Discharging Surface Water by Artificial Means

A landowner may be liable for damages resulting from the flow of surface water if caused by changes made by him altering natural conditions. Of course, such changes may be justified by proof of a prescriptive right.[21] In the absence of prescription, a landowner does not have a right to change the directional flow of surface water as fixed by natural conditions. Except as noted, he does not have a right to construct drains or ditches with the result of a concentrated flow of surface water.[22] Liability may result if damage is caused by an accelerated flow.[23] An artificial drain substituted for a natural drain must have sufficient capacity to take care of the ordinary flow of surface water.[24]

Some variations or exceptions to the above stated rule are recognized. A landowner is entitled to erect improvements on his land or make use of it for agricultural purposes. In the absence of negligence he cannot be held liable for damages that may result from such activities insofar as surface-water drainage is concerned. It is frequently held that surface water may be drained by a ditch constructed according to the natural flow of surface water.[25] This is the statutory rule in some states.[26] It is also generally held that a riparian owner has a right to construct ditches and discharge surface water into the watercourse if that constitutes the natural drainage and does not result in a flow exceeding the capacity of the watercourse.[27] Un-

---

17. See Applegate v. Franklin, 1904, 109 Mo.App. 293, 84 S.W. 347 (a body of water was considered to be surface water although it varied in depth from three to six feet and covered an area of 2,500 acres).

18. Rogers v. Petsch, 1962, 174 Neb. 313, 117 N.W.2d 771 (spring water not flowing in a well-defined channel). See Kinyon and McClure, Interference With Surface Waters, 24 Minn.Law Rev. 891, 914 (1940).

19. 4 Rest.Torts, § 864, *Comment c.*

20. Schaefer v. Marthaler, 1886, 34 Minn. 487, 26 N.W. 726.

21. See Hargraves v. Wilson, Okl.1963, 382 P.2d 736.

22. Stone v. Ashurst, 1941, 285 Ky. 687, 149 S.W.2d 4; Kapayanis v. Fishbein, 1962, 344 Mass. 749, 181 N.E.2d 653 (gutters and roof drains attached to a structure); Yerex v. Eineder, 1891, 86 Mich. 24, 48 N.W. 875. See Rood, Surface Water in Cities, 6 Mich.Law Rev. 448, 464 (1908).

23. Inns v. San Juan Unified School District, 1963, 222 Cal.App.2d 174, 34 Cal.Rptr. 903; E. J. Hollingsworth Co. v. Jardel Co., 1962, 40 Del.Ch. 196, 178 A.2d 307 (paving a large parking lot).

24. See Harper v. Johannesen, 1962, 84 Idaho 278, 371 P.2d 842, 847 (not liable if damage is caused by unusual flood conditions). See Jorgensen v. City of Seattle, 1963, 62 Wash.2d 912, 385 P.2d 33.

25. See, for example, Stouder v. Dashner, 1951, 242 Iowa 1340, 49 N.W.2d 859.

26. See, for example, Johnson v. Metropolitan Life Ins. Co., 1946, 71 S.D. 155, 22 N.W.2d 737.

27. State of North Dakota v. State of Minnesota, 1923, 263 U.S. 365, 44 S.Ct. 138, 68 L.Ed. 342 (*dictum*), noted in 19 Ill.Law Rev. 344 (1925). See,

der some circumstances surface water may be classified as a "common enemy" which a landowner may discharge upon adjacent land if he adopts a method that does not cause "unreasonable damage."

Obstructing the Flow of Surface Water

Whether or not a landowner may, without liability, obstruct the flow of surface water and thus prevent it from reaching his land depends upon which of the following rules is adopted by the court.[28]

First: What is known as the common enemy rule, sometimes called the common law rule, originated in Massachusetts. According to this rule a landowner may use any available means to prevent surface water from reaching his land.[29] But this common enemy rule is applicable only in the case of diffused surface water, *i. e.*, water that is spread out over the surface of the earth. In the Nebraska case of Nichol v. Yocum,[30] Justice Carter states the rule as follows: "At common law the right to drain surface water into depressions, draws, swales, and drainways which existed in the state of nature was recognized. Lower lands are, at common law, under a natural servitude to receive the surface wa-

ter of higher lands flowing along natural depressions on the surface of the ground."

Second: Under the civil law rule all land is subject to a natural servitude to receive the *natural flow* of surface water. A landowner who obstructs such flow may be held liable for damages caused thereby.[31] However, a landowner does have a right to prevent *floodwaters* from reaching his land. That would be the case, for example, if the flow resulted from an extraordinary storm or extraordinary flood conditions of a watercourse.[32]

A flow of surface water does not cease to be a "natural flow" merely because the course or volume of the water was changed as the result of improvements erected upon land located in the area.[33] However, the one responsible for the augmented flow may be held liable for damages resulting from such acts.[34]

Third: An increasing number of decisions approve of the "reasonable conduct" rule. Insofar as drainage of surface water is concerned, a landowner cannot be held liable for damage caused in connection with the reasonable use of his land.[35] Application of this rule facilitates community development.

Manteufel v. Wetzel, 1907, 133 Wis. 619, 114 N.W. 91. *Cf.*: Bush v. City of Rochester, 1934, 191 Minn. 591, 255 N.W. 256.

28. For a classification of jurisdictions, see Kinyon and McClure, Interference With Surface Waters, 24 Minn.Law Rev. 891, 896, 902 (1940).

29. Levy v. Nash, 1908, 87 Ark. 41, 112 S.W. 173, 20 L.R.A.,N.S. 155 (urban property only); Dyer v. Starlhut, 1938, 147 Kan. 767, 78 P.2d 900 (urban property only); Bates v. Smith, 1868, 100 Mass. 181; Bowlsby v. Speer, 1865, 31 N.J.L. 351; Barkley v. Wilcox, 1881, 86 N.Y. 140; Bennett v. Cupina, 1930, 253 N.Y. 436, 171 N.E. 698, noted in 16 Corn. Law Qt. 109 (1930).

30. 173 Neb. 298, 113 N.W.2d 195, 200 (1962).

31. Gray v. McWilliams, 1893, 98 Cal. 157, 32 P. 976; Gormley v. Sanford, 1869, 52 Ill. 158; West v. Taylor, 1888, 16 Or. 165, 13 P. 665.

32. Wellman v. Kelley, 1953, 197 Or. 553, 252 P.2d 816. See Mogle v. Moore, 1940, 16 Cal.2d 1, 104 P.2d 785.

33. LeBrun v. Richards, 1930, 210 Cal. 308, 291 P. 825, 72 A.L.R. 336.

34. Andrew Jergens Co. v. Los Angeles, 1951, 103 Cal.App.2d 232, 229 P.2d 475.

35. Weinberg v. Northern Alaska Development Corp., Alaska, 1963, 384 P.2d 450; Whitman v. Forney, 1943, 181 Md. 652, 31 A. 630; Enderson v. Kelehan, 1948, 226 Minn. 163, 32 N.W.2d 286; Swett v. Cutts, 1870, 50 N.H. 439; Haskins v. Felder, Okl.1954, 270 P.2d 960. See Keys v. Romley, 1965, —— Cal.App.2d ——, 43 Cal.Rptr. 683.

B. RIGHTS IN THE LAND OF ANOTHER

CHAPTER 7

PROFITS AND EASEMENTS

PROFIT DEFINED

22. A profit is a nonpossessory interest in land and consists of a right to take the soil or a substance of the soil. If enjoyment of the right may be exercised only for the benefit of a dominant estate the right is a profit appurtenant. If the right is not so restricted it is a profit in gross.

a. **Distinguished from ownership of minerals in place.** The grant of an exclusive and unlimited right to minerals or other substances, such as coal, is a grant of the minerals in place. Because of the fungible nature of oil and gas the preferred view is that these substances are not subject to ownership in place.

b. **Distinguished from sale of personal property.** A contract for the sale of a certain percentage of oil that may be produced from a well is a contract for the sale of personal property. The right cannot be classified as a profit unless the purchaser acquires a right to take the oil as distinguished from a right to oil after it has been removed.

A profit, sometimes called a "profit a prendre," is a nonpossessory interest in land consisting of a right to take the soil or a substance of the soil, such as a right to take minerals, drill for oil or take wild game or fish.[1] If exercise of the right is restricted in the sense that it may be exercised only in connection with the use and enjoyment of described land (a dominant estate) the right is a profit appurtenant. If it is not so restricted it is a profit in gross.

Distinguished from Ownership of Minerals in Place

One person may have a possessory estate of the surface of land and another may have a possessory estate of the area beneath the

[1] Minnesota Valley Gun Club v. Northline Corp., 1940, 207 Minn. 126, 290 N.W. 222, noted in 24 Minn. Law Rev. 1000 (1940); Bingham v. Salene, 1887, 15 Or. 208, 14 P. 523; Frogley v. Earl of Lovelace, [1859], Johns.Ch. 333, 70 Eng.Rep. 450.

surface.[2] He may, for example, be the owner of minerals in place. If a grantee acquires ownership of minerals in place, as distinguished from a profit, he also acquires ownership of the space from which the minerals have been removed.[3]

There is a presumption that the grant of a right to take the soil or a substance of the soil, such as minerals, is not exclusive.[4] The grantor is not thereby excluded from the exercise of a similar right. In that event the grant results in the creation of a profit only. That is also the case if a grant confers a right to take minerals etc., only for a stated purpose.[5] However, the grant of an exclusive and unlimited right to dig coal or mine minerals is a grant of the coal or minerals in place.[6] That is also the nature of the interest even if the grant is for a limited time.[7] Upon the termination of the time fixed the grantor becomes revested with his former estate in whatever coal remains. The nature of the grant is not changed by the fact that the transfer is called a "lease". Since the conveyance of a freehold estate is involved, a covenant against assignment is null and void.[8]

While some authorities follow the view that the "ownership-in-place" rule applies in the case of oil and gas, the preferred view is that such substances are not susceptible to ownership in place.[9] Accordingly, a right to take oil or gas from the land constitutes a profit.

Distinguished from Sale of Personal Property

In the California case of Black v. Solano Co.,[10] A was engaged in drilling a well under an oil and gas lease. By a properly executed instrument he sold to B 5% of all oil to be produced from the well and B caused this instrument to be recorded. Thereafter, A entered into oil purchase contracts with C. B claimed that the recordation of the above mentioned instrument gave C constructive notice of B's interest. The local recording statute applied only to instruments conveying estates or interests in land. The court held that B did not acquire an interest in land and that the recordation of the instrument did not result in constructive notice.

B did not acquire a profit because the agreement did not confer upon him the right to drill for oil or take oil from the land. The agreement merely contemplated the sale of potential goods. Since the conveyance of an estate or interest in land is not involved such an agreement cannot be specifically enforced unless special circumstances are involved.[11]

---

2. In re Waltz, 1925, 197 Cal. 263, 240 P. 19.

3. Robinson v. Wheeling Steel & Iron Co., 1925, 99 W.Va. 435, 129 S.E. 311. See Simonton, Rights of Fee Simple Owner of Subjacent Mineral Stratum in the Containing Space, 32 W.Va. Law Quarterly 242 (1926). *Contra*: Clayborn v. Camilla Red Ash Coal Co., 1920, 128 Va. 383, 105 S.E. 117, 15 A.L.R. 946, criticized in 31 Yale Law Jr. 747 (1922).

4. Stanton v. T. L. Herbert & Sons, 1919, 141 Tenn. 440, 211 S.W. 353; Mountjoy's Case, [1583] Godb. 17, 78 Eng.Rep. 11.

5. Clement v. Youngman, 1861, 40 Pa. 341.

6. Caldwell v. Fulton, 1858, 31 Pa. 475. *Cf.*: Radke v. Union Pacific Rd. Co., 1959, 138 Colo. 189, 334 P.2d 1077 (exclusive right to *prospect for minerals* and remove the same if found held to create only a license).

7. In re Essex Coal Co., 1963, 411 Pa. 618, 192 A.2d 675.

8. In re Essex Coal Co., 1963, 411 Pa. 618, 192 A.2d 675.

9. See, for example, Callahan v. Martin, 1935, 3 Cal.2d 110, 43 P.2d 788, 101 A.L.R. 871; Rich v. Doneghey, 1918, 71 Okl. 204, 177 P. 86, 89, 3 A.L.R. 352.

10. 114 Cal.App. 170, 299 P. 843 (1931).

11. Richfield Oil Co. v. Hercules Gas Co., 1931, 112 Cal.App. 431, 297 P. 73. As to the nature of an

An agreement that confers a right to take oil from the land results in the creation of a profit. Such is the situation in the case of an oil and gas lease to continue for a stated period of time or for a stated time and as long thereafter as oil or gas, or either of them is produced.[12]

EASEMENT DEFINED

23. An affirmative easement is one that authorizes the doing of some act on the servient estate. A negative easement places a restriction on the activities that may be conducted on the servient estate.

    a. **Spurious easement.** A spurious easement is an easement that requires the doing of an affirmative act on the part of the owner of a servient estate.

    b. **Easement appurtenant and in gross.** An easement appurtenant is one created for use in connection with specific land (dominant estate). If use is not restricted to a dominant estate the easement is in gross.

An easement is a nonpossessory interest in land. It does not include the right to take the soil or the substance of the soil. In this respect it differs from a profit. It is an affirmative easement if it authorizes the doing of an act on the land of another (the servient estate).[13] This right may involve the use of a passageway, the maintenance of a ditch or drain or the right to interfere with the enjoyment of the land such as by causing noise or vibrations. It is a negative easement if it places a restriction upon the activities of the servient owner.[14] For example, in the case of an easement for light and air the owner of the servient estate does not have a right to erect a structure that would interfere with the enjoyment of this right. In the case of an easement for lateral support the owner of the servient estate is deprived of a right to excavate on his land in such a manner as to interfere with the enjoyment of the easement by the owner of the dominant estate.

There are many rights relating to the use of the land of another that cannot properly be classified as easements. For example, the various types of building restrictions are not recognized as easements. The enforcement of such interests remains flexible because governed by rules developed in equity and, for that reason, they are classified as equitable servitudes. It is also to be noted that a certain degree of *definiteness* is required if a privilege is to qualify as an interest in land, such as an easement.[15] It is doubtful that an easement can be created for "recreation and pleasure" with respect to a large area of land.[16] One cannot claim a possessory right under the guise of an easement. For example, one cannot claim an easement for the purpose of maintaining a garage on the land of another.[17]

The usual remedies available for wrongful interference with the use and enjoyment of a profit or an easement (incorporeal interests) are an action at law to recover damages or a

---

overriding oil royalty, see National Bank of Tulsa v. Warren, 1955, 177 Kan. 281, 279 P.2d 262; Davis v. Lewis, 1940, 187 Okl. 91, 100 P.2d 994; Danciger Oil & Refining Co. v. Burroughs, 10 Cir. 1935, 75 F.2d 855.

12. Dabney v. Edwards, 1935, 5 Cal.2d 1, 53 P.2d 962, 103 A.L.R. 822. See In re Broome's Estate, 1958, 166 Cal.App.2d 488, 333 P.2d 273. The reservation of a right to oil and gas creates a present interest and is not within the scope of the rule against perpetuities (Caffroy v. Fremlin, 1961, 198 Cal.App.2d 176, 17 Cal.Rptr. 668).

13. See 5 Rest. Property, § 451.

14. See 5 Rest. Property, § 452.

15. See 5 Rest. Property, § 450, *Comment m.*

16. See Drye v. Eagle Rock Ranch, Inc., 1963, —— Tex. ——, 364 S.W.2d 196. *Cf.*: In re Ellenborough Park [1956] Ch. 131.

17. Clements v. Sannuti, 1947, 356 Pa. 63, 51 A.2d 697. See Matteodo v. Ricci, 1936, 56 R.I. 208, 184 A. 573.

suit in equity for an injunction.[18] An action of ejectment will not lie because the purpose of such an action is to restore possession of land to the plaintiff. The owner of a profit or an easement is not entitled to such possession.[19]

Spurious Easement

The general rule is that an obligation imposing a duty to do an affirmative act is not classified as an easement. However, common law authority supports the view that the possessor of land may be under an obligation to maintain a boundary line fence and such an obligation is one that may be imposed upon subsequent owners of the land. Since the obligation does not conform to the usual standards for easements it is called a spurious (false) easement.[20] Statutes usually regulate obligations as they relate to fencing as between conterminous owners.

Easement Appurtenant and In Gross

An easement appurtenant is one created for use in connection with specific land designated as the dominant estate. If such a restriction as to use does not exist then the easement is in gross.

A construction that an easement was intended to be appurtenant is favored because if an easement is appurtenant uncertainties with respect to ownership are minimized. That ownership can be determined by ascertainment of the ownership of the dominant estate. It is not necessary that the instrument creating an easement expressly state that it is appurtenant nor need the dominant

estate be described.[21] It is not necessary that the two estates (dominant and servient) be contiguous or adjoining.[22] Whether or not the parties intended to create an easement appurtenant may be determined from a consideration of all the circumstances, including the purpose of the easement and its use as it relates to the use and enjoyment of land.[23] Two additional rules are as follows:

First: An easement may be appurtenant to a leasehold estate.[24] In Lebel v. Backman (Mass.),[25] such an easement existed for right of way purposes. An issue was raised as to the right of a sublessee to enforce the easement as against the original lessor. This issue was resolved in favor of the sublessee. The easement was appurtenant to the leasehold estate. The sublessee was not in a position to proceed against the original lessor on a contractual basis. There was neither privity of contract nor privity of estate as between the original lessor and the sublessee so enforcement would not be possible on the theory of covenants running with the land. However, an easement is an *in rem* interest

18. Waterbury Trust Co. v. G. L. D. Realty Co., 1938, 124 Conn. 191, 199 A. 106 (injunction denied after consideration of "comparative equities").

19. Waterbury Trust Co. v. G. L. D. Realty Co., 1936, 121 Conn. 50, 182 A. 466.

20. Bronson v. Coffin, 1871, 108 Mass. 175.

21. Hopper v. Barnes, 1896, 113 Cal. 636, 45 P. 874; Dennis v. Wilson, 1871, 107 Mass. 591; Sabins v. McAllister, 1950, 116 Vt. 302, 76 A.2d 106; 5 Rest. Property, § 453, *Comment a.*

22. Kaynor v. Fisch, 1951, 103 Cal.App.2d 832, 230 P.2d 418, 422; Graham v. Walker, 1905, 78 Conn. 130, 61 A. 98; Tide-Water Pipe Co. v. Bell, 1924, 280 Pa. 104, 124 A. 353, 40 A.L.R. 1516; Todrick v. Western Nat. Omnibus Co. [1934] 1 Ch. 561, noted in 48 Harv.Law Rev. 335 (1934). But see Steele v. Williams, 1944, 204 S.C. 124, 28 S.E.2d 644.

23. See Shingleton v. State, 1963, 260 N.C. 451, 133 S.E.2d 183; Bullock v. Phelps, 1905, 27 R.I. 164, 61 A. 589.

24. Anthony v. Chicopee Mfg. Corp., 1929, 168 Ga. 400, 147 S.E. 887 (ingress and egress); Doyle v. Lord, 1876, 64 N.Y. 432 (light and air). See Alabama Fuel & Iron Co. v. Courson, 1925, 212 Ala. 573, 103 So. 667, 43 A.L.R. 204.

25. 342 Mass. 759, 175 N.E.2d 362 (1961).

and enforcement is not made to depend upon contractual liability.[26]

Second: The conversion of an easement appurtenant into an easement in gross or an easement in gross into an easement appurtenant cannot be accomplished without the consent of the owner of the easement and the owner of the servient estate. An agreement for such a change relates to an interest in land and comes within the scope of the real-property section of the Statute of Frauds.

In Cadwalader v. Bailey,[27] an easement appurtenant was destroyed because of the fact that its use was dissociated from the use of the dominant estate.

ALIENABILITY AND APPORTIONABILITY OF PROFITS

24. If a profit is appurtenant it will follow ownership of the dominant estate. If it is admeasurable it will be apportioned by a sale of part of the dominant estate.

A profit in gross is assignable and transferable. Presumably, an exclusive profit in gross is apportionable. Presumably, however, a nonexclusive profit in gross is not apportionable.

If a profit is appurtenant and admeasurable, the right to use the profit may be asserted by the grantee or grantees of all or any part of the dominant estate and the right will pass without express words in the conveying instrument.[28]

In Hall v. Lawrence,[29] the owner of Blackacre had a right to take seaweed from Whiteacre to be used as fertilizer in connection with agricultural activities on Blackacre.

The court held that a person who acquired ownership in a part of Blackacre acquired a right to take the seaweed necessary to maintain the fertility of the land so acquired. The amount of seaweed necessary for this purpose could be ascertained so the profit was admeasurable. The amount of seaweed necessary for that purpose was not increased by a division of Blackacre into ownership by two or more persons.[30]

Some profits are not admeasurable and, for that reason, are not apportionable. In Tyrringham's case,[31] a right to pasture cattle (a profit) was appurtenant to described land (the dominant estate). The dominant estate and *a part of the servient estate* were subsequently acquired by one owner. The court held that the right of pasturage with respect to the other part of the servient estate was extinguished. The same result would be reached if a part of the servient estate was released from the burden.[32] This conclusion is based upon the ground that a release of part of the servient estate would place the full burden of pasturage on the remaining part of the servient estate. This result is inevitable if the profit is not admeasurable. The case differs from one where a right exists to pasture a stated number of animals.[33] Such a profit is admeasurable because the burden may be apportioned.

A profit in gross is exclusive if the owner has the sole right incident to its enjoyment. Not even the owner of the servient estate is entitled to use the land for the stated pur-

---

26. Relovich v. Stuart, 1931, 211 Cal. 422, 295 P. 819. *Cf.*: Coulter v. Sausalito Bay Water Co., 1932, 122 Cal.App. 480, 10 P.2d 780 (not an easement because there was no servient estate).

27. 17 R.I. 495, 23 A. 20, 14 L.R.A. 300 (1892).

28. Huntington v. Asher, 1884, 96 N.Y. 604.

29. 2 R.I. 218 (1852).

30. See Phillips v. Rhodes, 1843, 7 Metc. (Mass.) 322 (holding that the owner of the dominant estate had a right to sell the seaweed).

31. 4 Co.Rep. 36b, 76 Eng.Rep. 973 (1584).

32. Rotherham v. Green, [1597] Cro.Eliz. 593, 78 Eng. Rep. 836.

33. See Drury v. Kent, [1603] Cro.Jac. 14, 79 Eng. Rep. 13.

pose. Presumably, such a profit is apportionable. While a "divided ownership" may cause some inconvenience to the owner of the servient owner, it does not cause an increase in the burden insofar as a taking of the soil or a substance of the soil is concerned. In fact, if the owner of the profit is under a duty to pay royalties there is an advantage to the owner of the servient estate if the divided ownership results in increased activity.[34]

Presumably, a non-exclusive profit in gross is not apportionable.[35] A "divided ownership" would usually result in an increased burden on the servient estate. However, partial assignees may exercise the right in unison and divide the proceeds. Further, such a profit is alienable either by grant[36] or by descent.[37]

ALIENABILITY AND DIVISIBILITY OF EASEMENTS

25. Generally, ownership of an appurtenant easement follows ownership of the dominant estate. If the easement is divisible in nature one who acquires ownership of a part of the dominant estate will be entitled to rights of ownership in connection with the use of the easement.

The common law rule is that easements in gross are not alienable. Exception is made in the case of easements that require practically exclusive possession of the land to accomplish their purpose. In many states the rule is now followed that easements in gross are property interests and are alienable.

One who succeeds to the ownership of a dominant estate succeeds to ownership of an appurtenant easement.[38] Of course, this rule presupposes that the easement was in existence at the time of the conveyance, that the conveying instrument did not exclude the easement from the terms of the grant and that controlling exclusions did not attend the creation of the easement.

Normally, one who succeeds to a part of the dominant estate will succeed to his proportionate share of the easement-privileges.[39] However, this is not the case if the easement is not divisible. In the Iowa case of Loughman v. Couchman,[40] an easement was acquired by prescription and it involved the right to maintain a drain from a house then located on described land (the dominant estate) over the defendant's land (the servient estate). A part of the dominant estate was sold and another house was constructed thereon. Use of the drain was claimed in connection with the use of this new house. Such right was denied by the court upon the ground that this would result in an increase of the burden on the servient estate as it existed during the period of prescriptive use.

The common law rule is that easements in gross are not alienable.[41] Exception is

---

34. 5 Rest. Property, § 493 *Comment c.*

35. Stanton v. T. L. Herbert & Sons, 1919, 141 Tenn. 440, 211 S.W. 353; Grubb v. Bayard, 3 Cir. 1851, Fed.Cas.No.5,849; Mountjoy's Case, Godb., 17, 78 Eng.Rep. 11 (1583) *Cf.*: Hughes v. Devlin, 1863, 23 Cal. 501 (mining claim as distinguished from a mining right is apportionable).

36. Minnesota Valley Gun Club v. Northline Corp., 1940, 207 Minn. 126, 290 N.W. 222 (hunting privilege), noted in 24 Minn.Law Rev. 1000 (1940); Salene v. Isherwood, 1910, 55 Or. 263, 106 P. 18 (hunting privilege).

37. Bosworth v. Nelson, 1930, 170 Ga. 279, 152 S.E. 575. See 5 Rest. Property, § 491.

38. Huntington v. Asher, 1884, 96 N.Y. 604.

39. Cox v. Glenbrook Co., 1962, 78 Nev. 254, 371 P.2d 647 (easement for right of way purposes to 80 acre tract available to purchasers of lots when area was subdivided).

40. 242 Iowa 885, 47 N.W.2d 152 (1951).

41. Stockdale v. Yerden, 1922, 220 Mich. 444, 190 N.W. 225, noted in 32 Yale Law Jr. 813 (1923); Joachim v. Belfus, 1931, 108 N.J.Eq. 622, 156 A. 121 (easement to maintain poles for electric wires etc.); Boatman v. Lasley, 1873, 23 Ohio St. 614; Steele v. Williams, 1944, 204 S.C. 124, 28 S.E.2d 644.

made in the case of easements that require practically exclusive possession of the land and, for that reason, are akin to possessory estates. That is the case, for example, if the easement is for a railroad right of way,[42] pipe line purposes [43] or burial rights.[44]

In many states the rule is now followed that easements in gross are property interests and are alienable.[45] However, an easement in gross is not divisible. While it may be subject to concurrent ownership it is subject only to unity-enjoyment.[46] The Restatement of Property provides that easements in gross, like profits in gross, are alienable if they are of a commercial nature.[47] Otherwise, alienability is determined by reference to the manner or terms of their creation.[48]

CREATION OF PROFITS AND EASEMENTS BY EXPRESS GRANT

26. The creation or transfer of a profit or easement by express agreement can be accomplished only by a "deed of grant." This is true regardless of the duration of the interest.

According to common law rules, the only means by which a profit or an easement could be created or conveyed was by "deed of grant." [49] Being incorporeal interests (incorporeal hereditaments) a transfer could not be accomplished by a transfer of possession (livery of seisin), a means of conveyance that was available in the case of possessory estates.

The common law requirement of a "deed of grant" is followed at the present time regardless of the potential duration of the interest. In Duinneen v. Rich (Wis.),[50] an oral agreement did not result in the creation of an easement for a right of way even though an oral lease of the land for a like period would have been enforceable. This conclusion finds support in the Restatement of Property where it is explained as follows: [51] "It is arguable that the same policy which exempts short term leaseholds from any requirement as to writing would justify similar exemptions of short term easements.[52] In opposition to such an argument, it may be suggested that the visible taking of possession normally resulting from a lease affords a greater degree of security against unwarranted claims based upon parol evidence than would normally result from the informal creation of an easement. Also, in the case of an easement such as a mining right or an oil lease, it is conceivable that, even though the rights created thereby may be of short duration, their value may approximate that of the fee itself."

An intent to create a profit or an easement may be implied from language used in a deed. For example, in Hughes v. Lippincott (N. M.),[53] A conveyed described land to B and described it as being *adjacent to a passage-*

---

42. Garlick v. Pittsburgh & Western Ry. Co., 1902, 67 Ohio St. 223, 65 N.E. 896.

43. Standard Oil Co. v. Buchi, 1907, 72 N.J.Eq. 492, 66 A. 427, noted in 7 Col.Law Rev. 536 (1907).

44. Hook v. Joyce, 1893, 94 Ky. 450, 22 S.W. 651.

45. See, for example, Goodrich v. Burbank, 1866, 12 Allen (Mass.) 459; Poull v. Mockley, 1873, 33 Wis. 482.

46. See, Miller v. Lutheran Conference & Camp Ass'n, 1938, 331 Pa. 241, 200 A. 646, 130 A.L.R. 1245.

47. 5 Rest. Property, § 489.

48. 5 Rest. Property, § 491.

49. See Conard, The Requirement of a Sealed Instrument for Conveying Easements, 1940, 26 Iowa Law Rev. 41.

50. 22 Wis. 550 (1868).

51. 5 Rest. Property, § 467, *Comment g*, p. 2957.

52. See 5 Rest. Property, § 450, Special Note, providing as follows: "In this Restatement the term 'easement' is so used as to include within its meaning the special meaning commonly expressed by the term 'profit'."

53. 56 N.M. 473, 245 P.2d 390 (1952).

way. The passageway was located on a narrow strip of land retained by A. The court held that B acquired an easement in this land for passageway purposes.[54] Even if the passageway was not in existence at the time of the conveyance the grantor would be estopped to deny its existence.[55]

If land is conveyed by a deed that makes reference to a recorded plat the plat becomes a part of the deed under the doctrine of incorporation by reference. The result is that passageways indicated on the plat constitute easements appurtenant to the land conveyed.[56]

CREATION OF PROFITS AND EASEMENTS BY EXCEPTION AND RESERVATION

27. An incorporeal interest, such as a profit or an easement cannot be excepted from the terms of a deed. But such an exception is operative in the case of a *quasi*-profit or a *quasi*-easement.

A profit or an easement can be created by reservation. This is based upon the fiction that the one to whom a possessory estate is conveyed impliedly grants back to the grantor a profit or an easement according to the terms of the deed.

According to some authorities, an exception or reservation cannot be operative in favor of a person other than the grantor.

Usually, if a grantor "excepts" described land for a stated purpose, such as for railroad purposes, an easement as distinguished from a possessory estate arises out of the purported exception.

As discussed in the following paragraphs, there is a distinction between an "exception" and a "reservation" in connection with the creation of profits and easements. However,

it is not material whether a conveying instrument designates the transaction as an exception or a reservation. The terminology used is unimportant because the legal effect is determined by the nature of the conveyance.

Technical rules of construction relating to deeds may lead to the conclusion that words of exception do not result in the creation of any estate or interest in the grantor. For example, a warranty deed (a deed containing warranties respecting title) may contain a clause purporting to convey described land to the grantee (a granting clause). This clause may be followed by a provision "except the mineral or oil rights." It may be construed that this clause merely limits the liability of the grantor with respect to his warranties. In that event, mineral and oil rights, if any, will pass to the grantee.[57]

Additional problems are as follows:

First: An owner of land who conveys a possessory estate can except (exclude) a *corporeal interest* from the terms of his grant. For example, A (owner of land in fee simple) can convey the land to B in fee simple and except coal or minerals from the terms of the grant. In that event, A's ownership of the coal or minerals (in place) continues in its original quality. That is to say, A is the owner of the coal or minerals in fee simple even if the exception was not made to "A and his heirs." Assuming that these words (words of inheritance) are essential to the creation of an estate in fee simple, a new estate was not created in A. His ownership continued under the old title.[58]

According to one theory, a person may be the owner of oil and gas in place, just the same as he may be the owner of coal. Accordingly, oil and gas may be excepted from

---

54. But see, Lankin v. Terwilliger, 1892, 22 Or. 97, 29 P. 268.

55. Casella v. Sneirson, 1949, 325 Mass. 85, 89 N.E.2d 8.

56. Danielson v. Sykes, 1910, 157 Cal. 686, 109 P. 87.

57. Williams v. McCann, Okl.1963, 385 P.2d 788.

58. Whitaker v. Brown, 1863, 46 Pa. 197.

the terms of a grant.[59] However, a construction problem is involved as to the meaning of the word "minerals" in a deed whether the right to take oil and gas is based upon an exception or a reservation. Some decisions follow the view that a deed "excepting and reserving all coal, iron and minerals" includes oil and gas as well as solid materials.[60] According to another view, there is a rebuttable presumption that the word "minerals" does not include oil and gas.[61]

Second: The general rule is that an incorporeal interest, such as a profit or an easement, cannot be created by exception. If A conveys a possessory estate to B, A cannot except a profit or an easement from the estate conveyed and thereby make the land conveyed a servient estate. He may, of course, create a profit or an easement by reservation, a matter discussed in a following paragraph.

The rule that a profit or an easement cannot be created by an exception is a remnant of an ancient policy against the recognition of rights in property separate and distinct from the property itself. Maitland denies that this rule was based upon policy. He states that it grew out of "a mental incapacity, an inability to conceive that mere rights can be transferred." [62]

At the present time there is no sound reason why a profit or an easement cannot be created by exception.[63] This is consistent with the view that ownership of property consists of an aggregate of rights. In a conveyance the conveyor can except designated rights according to the understanding of the parties.

Third: According to some authorities a quasi-profit or easement has sufficient substance to come within the rule as it relates to exceptions. For example, in the Vermont case of Dee v. King,[64] A conveyed described land to B in fee simple. The deed provided, in part, that A was to have the "privilege of a pass (over the land conveyed) from the highway past the house to the railroad in my usual place of crossing." The words "in my usual place of crossing" evidenced the fact that, prior to the conveyance, A had used the land conveyed for passageway purposes. To this extent it enhanced the use and enjoyment of that portion of the land retained by him.

This prior use was not referable to an easement because A could not have an easement in the land separate and distinct from his possessory estate. However, the court describes the situation as involving a *quasi*-easement. The land conveyed by A was a *quasi*-servient estate and the land retained by him was a *quasi*-dominant estate. This fictional-existence of an easement was held to be a sufficient basis upon which to bring into play the law as it applies to excepting corporeal interests from the terms of a grant. After the conveyance A remained the owner of an easement with respect to the land conveyed and he was the owner of such interest in fee simple because that was the quality of

---

59. Elrod v. Heirs, Devisees, etc., 1952, 156 Neb. 269, 55 N.W.2d 673.

60. See, for example, Burdette v. Bruen, 1937, 118 W.Va. 624, 191 S.E. 360.

61. Highland v. Commonwealth of Pennsylvania, 1960, 400 Pa. 261, 161 A.2d 390 (The Dunham Rule, based on Dunham and Shortt v. Kirkpatrick, 1882, 101 Pa. 36).

62. Maitland, The Mystery of Seisin, 1886, 2 Law Quarterly Rev., 481, 489.

63. See, for example, Smith v. Furbish, 1894, 68 N.H. 123, 41 A. 398.

64. 77 Vt. 230, 59 A. 839 (1904).

his ownership of the possessory estate prior to the conveyance.[65]

Fourth: In the conveyance of a possessory estate the grantor can create a profit or an easement in the land conveyed by the "reservation" of such an interest in the grant. At early common law, only an interest arising out of the land, such as rent, could be created by reservation. But at the present time this is a means by which to create profits and easement.[66]

The creation of a profit or an easement by reservation is based upon the fiction that the one to whom the possessory estate is conveyed impliedly grants back to the grantor a profit or an easement according to the terms of the reservation clause in the deed.

As has been noted, the creation of a profit or an easement by reservation is based upon the fiction of a regrant from the one to whom the possessory estate is conveyed. Therefore, if words of inheritance are necessary to create a profit or an easement in fee simple, then the reservation must be in favor of the grantee of the profit or easement and his heirs. It is to be observed that the grantee of the profit or easement is, in fact, the grantor of the possessory estate. If such words of inheritance are not used the maximum duration of the interest is during the lifetime of the grantee (of the profit or easement).[67]

Statutes have been passed in many states providing that words of inheritance are not essential for the creation of estates or interests in fee simple. If such a statute is applicable it is of little importance whether a profit or an easement is created by exception or by reservation.

Fifth: There is substantial authority for the view that a reservation or exception cannot operate in favor of a "stranger to the deed." For example, if A conveys a possessory estate to B, a provision in the deed is inoperative that a third party, C, is to have an easement burdening the land conveyed.[68] However, to prevent a "windfall" to the grantee, the reservation or exception purporting to be in favor of a stranger operates in favor of the grantor and prevents the ownership of the reserved interest or excepted property from passing.[69]

Logically, a reservation or exception in favor of a person other than the grantor should be operative. Such third party is not a "stranger" to the deed because he is named as a grantee. The Restatement of Property, provides as follows: "By a single instrument of conveyance, there may be created as estate in land in one person and an easement (or profit) in another." [70]

Sixth: It may not be clear from the language used in a deed whether the grantor intended to except a possessory estate from the

65. *Accord:* Sabins v. McAllister, 1950, 116 Vt. 302, 76 A.2d 106. *Cf.:* Claflin v. Boston & Albany R. Co., 1892, 157 Mass. 489, 32 N.E. 659 (where proof was not made as to the existence of a quasi-easement).

66. See Doe d. Douglas v. Lock, [1835] 2 Ad. & E. 705, 111 Eng.Rep. 271.

67. Elwell v. Miner, 1961, 342 Mass. 450, 174 N.E.2d 43 (right of way).

68. Mott v. Nardo, 1946, 73 Cal.App.2d 159, 166 P.2d 37 (reservation); Herbert v. Pue, 1890, 72 Md. 307, 20 A. 182 (exception); Haverhill Savings Bank v. Griffin, 1903, 184 Mass. 419, 68 N.E. 839 (reservation); Hodgkins v. Bianchini, 1949, 323 Mass. 169, 80 N.E.2d 464 (exception); Choals v. Plummer, 1958, 353 Mich. 64, 90 N.W.2d 851 (reservation); Beardslee v. New Berlin Light & Power Co., 1912, 207 N.Y. 34, 100 N.E. 434; Erwin v. Bethlehem Steel Corp., 1950, 134 W.Va. 900, 62 S.E.2d 337 (reservation).

69. Allen v. Henson, 1919, 186 Ky. 201, 217 S.W. 120; Martin v. Cook, 1894, 102 Mich. 267, 60 N.W. 679; Wilson v. Gerard, 1952, 213 Miss. 177, 56 So.2d 471 (made in favor of a non-existent person); Stetson v. Nelson, N.D.1962, 118 N.W.2d 685; Joiner v. Sullivan, Tex.Civ.App.1953, 260 S.W.2d 439.

70. 5 Rest. Property, § 472.

terms of his grant or to reserve an easement. For example, in the California case of Coon v. Sonoma Magnesite Co.,[71] a deed of described land "excepted" a strip of land 40 feet wide for a road to be built. The court denied the claim of the grantor that he excepted a possessory estate in this area. The language resulted in the creation of an easement.[72] It is indicated that if the 40 foot strip had been specifically described a possessory estate would have been excepted. There is authority to the contrary, however, upon the ground that if a grantor intends to except a possessory estate he is not likely to go into detail in describing its intended use.[73]

The situation under discussion is similar to one where described land is conveyed for a stated purpose, such as "for a railroad," or for a "right of way." If a deed is otherwise sufficient to convey a possessory estate in fee simple, a grantee will acquire such an estate even if the deed also contains a clause that the land conveyed is to be used for railroad purposes or for a right of way.[74] This conclusion is in accord with the general rule that a statement in a deed as to the purpose of the conveyance does not purport to qualify the interest or estate conveyed.[75] If the language in a deed is ambiguous as to the quantum of the estate conveyed extrinsic evidence is admissible to ascertain the intention of the parties.[76]

Usually, in condemnation proceedings a limited interest or estate is acquired if that is sufficient for the purpose involved. Only an easement is acquired if land is condemned for a railroad right of way. However, statutes in some states authorize the acquisition of an estate in fee simple in right-of-way cases.[77]

CREATION OF PROFITS AND EASEMENTS BY IMPLICATION

28. **Profits and easements may be created by implication in connection with the conveyance of a possessory estate. Application of this rule requires the existence of a *quasi*-profit or a *quasi*-easement at the time of the contract of sale or at the time of the conveyance. In addition, it must be apparent, reasonably necessary for the enjoyment of the land retained or the land conveyed and continuous in nature.**

Circumstances surrounding the conveyance of a possessory estate may be sufficiently compelling to justify the conclusion that the parties intended the creation of a profit or an easement. The situation involves an exception to the Statute of Frauds.

The creation of a profit or an easement by implication presupposes the prior existence of a *quasi*-profit or *quasi*-easement and a severance of the *quasi*-dominant estate from the *quasi*-servient estate.[78] For example, in the Washington case of Bailey v. Hennessey,[79] the owner of a store building used a narrow strip of his land for access to the stores. While this use was not referable to an easement because a person cannot have an easement in his own land, it may be designated as a *quasi*-easement. The store building was a *quasi*-dominant estate and the pas-

---

71.   182 Cal. 597, 189 P. 271 (1920).

72.   See Pitcairn v. Harkness, 1909, 10 Cal.App. 295.

73.   Hinton v. Reynolds, 1943, 294 Ky. 525, 172 S.W. 2d 201.

74.   Biggs v. Wolfe, 1962, 40 Del.Ch. 212, 178 A.2d 482 ("for the purpose of a road").

75.   McCotter v. Barnes, 1958, 247 N.C. 480, 101 S.E.2d 330. But see, City of Glendora v. Faus, 1957, 148 Cal.App.2d 920, 307 P.2d 976 (where land was conveyed for railroad purposes *only*).

76.   Daugherty v. Helena & Northwestern Ry., 1952, 221 Ark. 101, 252 S.W.2d 546. *Cf.*: Swan v. O'Leary, 1950, 37 Wash.2d 533. 225 P.2d 199.

77.   See, for example, Lehigh Valley R. Co. v. Chapman, 1961, 35 N.J. 177, 171 A.2d 653.

78.   Rannels v. Marx, 1959, 357 Mich. 453, 98 N.W.2d 583 (common driveway); Stuart v. Lake Washington Realty Co., 1956, 141 W.Va. 627, 92 S.E.2d 981.

79.   112 Wash. 45, 191 P. 863 (1920).

sageway-land was a *quasi*-servient estate. The owner sold the store building to plaintiff and thereafter sold the passageway-land to the defendant. The court held that by selling the store building to plaintiff the grantor thereby conveyed to him, by implication, an easement over the passageway-land as a means of access to the store building. Thus, an easement was created by implied grant. There is authority for the view that prior use is not essential for the creation of a profit or an easement by implication. "Availability for use" will justify the conclusion that a profit or an easement was created by implication.[80] Of course, prior use is not necessary if land is purchased or leased by reference to plans that indicate the profit or easement in question. Under such circumstances the interest will be recognized on the basis of estoppel.[81]

It is sufficient if the *quasi*-profit or the *quasi*-easement existed at the time of the execution of the deed even though it did not exist at the time the owner entered into a contract to sell the land.[82] In fact, a profit or an easement may be created by implication if a *quasi*-profit or a *quasi*-easement existed at the time the owner entered into a contract to sell a part of his estate even though it did not exist at the time of the execution of the deed.[83] This result conforms to the general concepts of equitable conversion.

Rules relating to the creation of profits or easements by implication are applicable even though a conveyance is involuntary, such as in a mortgage foreclosure.[84] Problems involved in the creation of profits and easements by implication are discussed in the following paragraphs:

First: An interest is not created by implication unless the *quasi*-profit or the *quasi*-easement was apparent at the time of title-severance.[85] Some authorities take the position that to be "apparent" the *quasi*-profit or the *quasi*-easement must be readily visible. However, the weight of authority is to the contrary. It is sufficient if the situation is discoverable on a careful inspection of the alleged servient estate by one conversant with the claimed use of the land.[86] "Notorious visibility" is not essential. However, in the absence of actual knowledge of the facts, there must be some external evidence of a *quasi*-profit or *quasi*-easement as a foundation for the claim that a profit or an easement was created by implication.[87] In the Maryland case of Mitchell v. Houstle,[88] it is held that a *quasi*-easement consisting of a sewer line was not "apparent" within the meaning of the rule even though there were two cleanout pipes located on the servient estate that where about five inches in diameter and they extended out of the ground 8 or 10 inches.[89]

80. See, Mosier v. Mead, 1955, 45 Cal.2d 629, 290 P.2d 495, noted in 4 U.C.L.A.Law Rev. 300 (1956); White v. Berg, 1943, 19 Wash.2d 284, 142 P.2d 260.

81. Owsley v. Hamner, 1951, 36 Cal.2d 710, 227 P.2d 263, 24 A.L.R.2d 112. But see, Pyper v. Whitman, 1911, 32 R.I. 510, 80 A. 6.

82. Hubbard v. Grandquist, 1937, 191 Wash. 442, 71 P.2d 410, noted in 11 So.Cal.Law Rev. 379 (1938); 13 Wash.Law Rev. 58 (1938).

83. Toothe v. Bryce, 1892, 50 N.J.Eq. 589, 5 A. 182.

84. Lane v. Flautt, 1939, 176 Md. 620, 6 A.2d 228, noted in 4 Md.Law Rev. 88 (1939); German Sav. & Loan Society v. Gordon, 1909, 54 Or. 147, 102 P. 736.

85. Wiesel v. Smira, 1928, 49 R.I. 246, 142 A. 148, 58 A.L.R. 818.

86. See, Swarzwald v. Cooley, 1940, 39 Cal.App.2d 306, 103 P.2d 580; Van Sandt v. Royster, 1938, 148 Kan. 495, 83 P.2d 698; Dale v. Bedal, 1940, 205 Mass. 102, 25 N.E.2d 175.

87. Wolek v. Di Feo, 1960, 60 N.J.Super. 324, 159 A.2d 127 (sewer).

88. 217 Md. 259, 142 A.2d 556 (1958).

89. See Heatherdell Farms, Inc. v. Huntley Estates, 1954, 130 N.Y.S.2d 335.

Second: It must be shown that the *quasi*-profit or the *quasi*-easement was continuous in nature. Under the early view this required proof that the right was capable of enjoyment without any affirmative act on the servient estate. Accordingly, an easement for passageway purposes could not be acquired by implication.[90] At the present time the prevailing rule is that a *quasi*-profit or a *quasi*-easement is continuous if it is permanently adapted to the use of the *quasi*-dominant estate.[91]

Third: There must be proof that the *quasi*-profit or the *quasi*-easement was reasonably necessary for the enjoyment of the land sold or the land retained.[92] Proof of absolute necessity is not required.[93] The preferred view is that a profit or easement may be created by implied reservation as well as by implied grant.[94] It was so held in Pyer v. Carter (Eng.),[95] but later repudiated in Wheeldon

v. Burrows.[96] In some decisions it is stated that in an implied-reservation situation the plaintiff must establish a *firm case* as it relates to proof of reasonable necessity.

The minority rule is that, with exceptions noted, a profit or an easement cannot be created by implied reservation.[97] It is reasoned that a grantor should not be permitted to derogate (detract) from the terms of his own grant. Exception is made in a case of strict necessity, such as in a case where the land retained (the dominant estate) would be landlocked unless a right of way existed over the land conveyed.[98] Exception is also made if the situation involves reciprocal easements, such as in a case of a common driveway. It is also generally held that if the *quasi*-dominant estate and the *quasi*-servient estate are conveyed at the same time, either by deed or by will (simultaneous conveyances), profits and easements may arise by implication in favor of either or both of such grantees.[99]

Fourth: According to the English rule, an easement for light and air may be created by implication.[1] While this rule is followed in a few American states[2] it has, in general,

---

90. Milewski v. Wolski, 1946, 314 Mich. 445, 22 N.W. 2d 831, 164 A.L.R. 998; Caulfield v. Lobenstine, 1924, 123 Misc. 285, 205 N.Y.S. 150, noted in 25 Col.Law Rev. 234 (1925).

91. Adams v. Gordon, 1914, 265 Ill. 87, 106 N.E. 517; Eliason v. Grove, 1897, 85 Md. 215, 36 A. 844; German Savings & Loan Society v. Gordon, 1900, 54 Or. 147, 102 P. 736, 26 L.R.A.,N.S., 331; Brown v. Alabaster, 1887, 37 Ch.Div. 490.

92. Trunnell v. Ward, 1964, 86 Idaho 555, 389 P.2d 221.

93. Freightways Terminal Co. v. Industrial & Commercial Construction, Inc., Alaska, 1963, 381 P.2d 977, 984 (reasonably necessary); Liquid Carbonic Co. v. Wallace, 1908, 219 Pa. 457, 68 A. 1021 (highly convenient); Toothe v. Bryce, 1892, 50 N.J.Eq. 589, 25 A. 182 (convenient). But see Ketchel v. Ketchel, 1962, 367 Mich. 53, 116 N.W.2d 219.

94. Sieger v. Riu, 1937, 123 Conn. 343, 195 A. 735; Shandy v. Bell, 1934, 207 Ind. 215, 189 N.E. 627 (*dictum*); Van Sandt v. Royster, 1938, 148 Kan. 495, 83 P.2d 698, noted in 13 So.Cal.Law Rev. 525 (1940); 25 Va.Law Rev. 636 (1939); Tangner v. Brannin, Okl.1963, 381 P.2d 321; 5 Rest. Property, § 476, *Comment, c.*

95. 1 H. & N. 916, 156 Eng.Rep. 1472.

96. L.R. 12 Ch.D. 31 (1879).

97. Mitchell v. Seipel, 1879, 53 Md. 251; Adams v. Marshall, 1885, 138 Mass. 228; Brown v. Fuller, 1911, 165 Mich. 162, 130 N.W. 621; Blumberg v. Weiss, 1941, 129 N.J.Eq. 34, 17 A.2d 823; Mitchell v. Castellaw, 1952, 151 Tex. 56, 246 S.W.2d 163; Wheeldon v. Burrows, [1879] 12 Ch.D. 31.

98. Scheeler v. Dewerd, 1950, 256 Wis. 428, 41 N.W.2d 635. See, Mancuso v. Riddlemoser Co., 1911, 117 Md. 53, 82 A. 1051.

99. Mount Holyoke Realty Corp. v. Holyoke Realty Corp., 1933, 284 Mass. 100, 187 N.E. 227; Pearson v. Spencer, [1863] 3 B. & S. 761, 122 Eng.Rep. 285, noted in 8 Law Quarterly Rev. 111 (1892).

1. Palmer v. Fletcher, [1663] 1 Lev. 122, 83 Eng.Rep. 329.

2. Lane v. Flautt, 1939, 176 Md. 620, 6 A.2d 228, noted in 4 Md.Law Rev. 88 (1939); Fowler v. Wick, 1908, 74 N.J.Eq. 603, 70 A. 682; Nomar v. Ballard, 1950,

been repudiated. Its application would seriously hamper land development.[3]

Fifth: Extrinsic evidence is admissible to prove that the parties to a conveyance did not intend to create a profit or easement by implication.[4] An express provision in a deed creating a profit or an easement is some evidence of the fact that the parties did not intend to create other interests by implication.[5]

CREATION OF EASEMENTS OF NECESSITY

29. **Regardless of prior use, an easement may arise by implication if the existence of the easement is strictly necessary for the beneficial use of land. The creation of such an easement is based upon the presumed intent of the grantor and grantee. If the claim is made that the easement arose out of a prior conveyance there must be proof of the fact that at one time both the dominant and the servient estates were under one ownership.**

An easement of necessity continues only during the period of necessity and use during that time cannot furnish the basis for a claim of prescriptive right.

Regardless of prior use, an easement arises by implication if the existence of the easement is strictly necessary for the beneficial use of land sold or land retained.[6] That is the case, for example, if the only means of ingress and egress is over land sold or land retained. The preferred view is that proof

of *practical necessity* is a sufficient basis upon which to grant relief.[7] However, some authorities require proof of *actual necessity*. In the Maine case of Hildreth v. Googins,[8] the plaintiff's property was landlocked except to the extent that it was accessible by water. Declaration of an easement by implication was denied.[9]

The creation of an easement of necessity is based upon the presumed intention of the parties to a conveyance.[10] For that reason, one who claims the existence of such an easement must allege and prove that at one time both the dominant and the servient estates were under one ownership.[11] This common ownership need not be immediate.[12] It is sufficient if it existed at any point in the chain of title except that, according to some authorities, proof of a grant from the state or the United States is not sufficient to satisfy the requirement.[13]

An easement of necessity will continue only as long as the necessity continues.[14] In

7. See 19 Or.Law Rev. 362, 365 (1940).

8. 91 Me. 227, 39 A. 550 (1898).

9. Approved in Flood v. Earle, 1950, 145 Me. 24, 71 A.2d 55 (summer camp property that had always been reached by crossing the lake). See Elliott v. Ferguson, 1962, 104 N.H. 25, 177 A.2d 387.

10. Daywalt v. Walker, 1963, 217 Cal.App.2d 669, 31 Cal.Rptr. 899. But see Condry v. Laurie, 1945, 184 Md. 317, 41 A.2d 66, noted in 31 Cornell Law Qt. 516 (1946) (where deed expressly provided for a license).

11. Leonard v. Bailwitz, 1960, 148 Conn. 8, 166 A.2d 451. See Simonton, Ways by Necessity, 25 Col.Law Rev. 571, 575 (1925).

12. Crotty v. New River & Pocahontas Consol. Coal Co., 1913, 72 W.Va. 68, 78 S.E. 233.

13. Joyner v. Andrews, Fla.App.1962, 137 So.2d 870 (statutory rule).

14. Martinelli v. Luis, 1931, 213 Cal. 183, 1 P.2d 980; Collins v. Prentice, 1842, 15 Conn. 39 (*dictum*); Condry v. Laurie, 1945, 184 Md. 317, 41 A.2d 66, noted in 31 Corn.Law Qt. 516 (1946); Waubun

134 W.Va. 492, 60 S.E.2d 710 (implied reservation). In Owsley v. Hamner, 1951, 36 Cal.2d 710, 227 P.2d 263, 24 A.L.R.2d 112, the court indicates that this rule may be applicable in landlord and tenant cases.

3. Lynch v. Hill, Del.Ch.1939, 6 A.2d 614; Pica v. Cross County Construction Corp., 1940, 259 App. Div. 128, 18 N.Y.S.2d 470.

4. Rischall v. Bauchmann, 1946, 132 Conn. 637, 46 A.2d 898, 165 A.L.R. 559.

5. Joyce v. Devaney, 1948, 322 Mass. 544, 78 N.E.2d 641.

6. Hansen v. Smikahl, 1962, 173 Neb. 309, 113 N.W.2d 210.

view of the fact that the use of a right of way based on necessity is "of right" such use will not ripen into a prescriptive right.[15] According to the English rule, an easement of necessity may be used only for the purpose of the dominant estate as that estate existed at the time of the original conveyance.[16] Because of the fact that the necessity continues from day to day, the scope or extent of the easement should change with changes made in the use of the dominant estate.

Statutes have been passed in a number of states authorizing condemnation proceedings as a means by which to obtain a right of way.[17] However, the enactment of such a statute does not impair the common law right to obtain a right of way of necessity.[18] Resort may be had to condemnation in situations where such a common law right does not exist.

CREATION OF EASEMENTS BY ESTOPPEL

30. A vendor may be estopped to deny the right of his vendee to use the land for a stated purpose. Such use may restrict the rights of the vendor with respect to land retained by him. In that event, an easement is created by estoppel.

The vendor of land may be estopped to deny the right of his vendee to use the land for a purpose that was disclosed at the time of

the conveyance. This is true even though the intended use will restrict the rights of the vendor with respect to land retained by him. In such event the estoppel results in the creation of an easement, the retained land being the servient estate.

In the Michigan case of City of Battle Creek v. Goguac Resort Ass'n,[19] A was the owner of land that was riparian to a lake. He sold part of this land to the City of Battle Creek, knowing that the purpose of the City was to use the water from the lake for municipal purposes. Although A remained a riparian owner, he was estopped to use the lake for resort purposes with resultant contamination of the water. The easement acquired by the City was held to be enforceable as against subsequent purchasers of the servient estate. Theoretically, the rule under discussion is also applicable with respect to a profit.

Estoppel will not result in the creation of a profit or an easement unless it is shown that the land conveyed could not be used for the intended purpose without recognition of the fact that such an interest was created.[20]

CREATION OF A PROFIT OR AN EASEMENT BY PRESCRIPTION

31. A profit or easement may be acquired by prescription in a manner similar to that by which ownership of a possessory estate may be acquired by adverse possession.

a. When prescriptive period starts to run. The prescriptive period starts to run when the landowner has either a cause of action against the claimant or the physical means of preventing the use. In the case of a future interest this usually means that the statute does not start to run until the interest becomes possessory. However, a cause of action may arise prior to that

---

Beach Ass'n v. Wilson, 1936, 274 Mich. 598, 265 N.W. 474, 103 A.L.R. 983.

[15]. Bino v. City of Hurley, 1961, 14 Wis.2d 101, 109 N.W.2d 544.

[16]. Corp. of London v. Riggs, 1879, L.R. 13 Ch.Div. 798. For a criticism of this view see Simonton, Ways by Necessity, 25 Col.Law Rev. 571, 583 (1925).

[17]. See, for example, Leinweber v. Gallaugher, 1940, 2 Wash.2d 388, 98 P.2d 311. See also, Waggoner Estate v. Gleghorn, Tex.Civ.App.1963, 370 S.W.2d 786.

[18]. Reese v. Borghi, 1963, 216 Cal.App.2d 324, 30 Cal.Rptr. 868.

[19]. 181 Mich. 241, 148 N.W. 441 (1914).

[20]. Pwllbach Colliery Co., Ltd. v. Woodman, [1915] A.C. 634.

time if the damage to the land is permanent in nature.

b. Use must be adverse as distinguished from permissive. Acts performed in subordination to the rights of a landowner are permissive and not adverse.

c. Use must be open and notorious.

d. Use must be continuous and exclusive. In computing time the period of adverse use by one claimant may be tacked to the period of adverse use by a subsequent claimant provided there is privity of estate between them.

e. Riparian rights. An easement may be acquired by prescription to divert water from a watercourse or lake or to cause pollution.

f. Disabilities. If an owner is under a disability, such as minority or insanity, when a cause of action first accrues, the statute will not start to run until the disability is removed. However, the running of the statute is not interrupted by disabilities accruing after the cause of action first accrues.

A profit or an easement may be acquired by prescription in a manner similar to that by which ownership of a possessory estate may be acquired by adverse possession. However, in the absence of a statute to the contrary these prescriptive rights cannot be acquired against the United States, the state or agencies of the state.[21]

Historically, the doctrine of prescription was based upon the theory that the use of a profit or an easement for a time beyond memory was a worthy substitute for a grant. This period of time was independent of any time which the legislature might fix as the period of limitations. Because of the inconvenience of this rule, and to bring about a shorter time, a new device was invoked. It was held that use for a long period of time raised a presumption that a profit or an ease-

ment had been created by grant and that the grant was lost or destroyed.[22] The fiction of a "lost grant" has, in general, been discarded. The present theory is that the Statute of Limitations will bar the remedy of the owner with respect to whose land the right has been asserted.[23]

In a majority of the states, by analogy, the period for acquisition of a prescriptive right is fixed as the time required for the acquisition of title by adverse possession. A change in the statutory period fixed for adverse possession is also applicable in prescription cases.[24] In some states it is provided by statute that title cannot be acquired by adverse possession unless the claimant has complied with special rules relating to color of title, payment of taxes, etc. These special requirements are not usually applicable in prescription cases.[25]

In Maryland & Pennsylvania Railroad Co. v. Mercantile-Safe Deposit & T. Co. (Md.),[26] a strip of land had been used for a railroad right of way for a period of some seventy-five years when railroad operations ceased. The court denied the claim of the railroad that it had acquired a possessory estate in fee. The use resulted in the acquisition of an easement only and the easement was lost by abandonment. The nature of the use by the rail-

---

21. Verrill v. School City of Hobart, 1944, 222 Ind. 214, 52 N.E.2d 619.

22. See, 7 Holdsworth's History of English Law, 343–345.

23. For discussion of the distinction between the theories of a lost grant and prescription, see Big Cottonwood Tanner Ditch Co. v. Moyle, 1946, 109 Utah 213, 174 P.2d 148.

24. Klin Co., Inc. v. New York Rapid Transit Corp., 1936, 271 N.Y. 376, 3 N.E.2d 516, noted in 6 Bklyn. Law Rev. 251 (1936); 5 Fordham Law Rev. 509 (1936); 25 Geo.Law Jr., 193 (1936); 50 Harv.Law Rev. 527 (1937).

25. Hester v. Sawyers, 1937, 41 N.M. 497, 71 P.2d 646, 112 A.L.R. 536.

26. 224 Md. 34, 166 A.2d 247 (1960).

road company did not amount to possession of the land in question and that is essential to the acquisition of a possessory estate by adverse possession.

When the Prescriptive Period Starts to Run

In England and in a few states the statute starts to run if the owner of the "servient estate" is in a position to bring an action to protect his interest or if he has the physical means of preventing the use. For example, if A erects a building and draws additional lateral support from land owned by B (because of the structure), A may acquire a prescriptive right for lateral support. While B does not have a cause of action to prevent such use he does have, in theory, the physical means of preventing the use. He may excavate upon his own land and thereby deprive A of lateral support. A similar situation exists with respect to light and air. B cannot successfully maintain an action against A to prevent him from enjoying light and air from B's land. However, B does have, in theory, the physical means of preventing this use. He can erect a wall on his own land and thus interrupt the use of light and air.

The prevailing American rule is that an easement for light and air [27] or lateral support [28] cannot be acquired by prescription. The statute does not start to run until the servient owner has a cause of action or a practical means of preventing the use. As in the case of lateral support and light and air, a prescriptive right cannot be acquired for maintenance of trees on adjoining land even if the trees were used as a windbreak for the statutory period. [29]

In Sturges v. Bridgman (Eng.), [30] plaintiff, a physician, purchased land in 1865 and erected a consultation room in 1875. Defendant, a confectioner, owner of adjoining land, used machinery that caused vibrations which interfered with this use of plaintiff's land. Plaintiff sought to enjoin these acts upon the ground that they constituted a nuisance. Defendant's claim of prescriptive right was denied upon the ground that the vibrations did not interfere with plaintiff's use of the land until the consultation room was erected; and use after that time did not continue for the statutory period. It was considered that prior to the erection of the consultation room, the defendant's acts were neither preventable nor actionable.

This decision is questionable and is not in accord with the prevailing American rule. [31] Whether or not a defendant's conduct is actionable should not be made to depend upon the particular use to which a plaintiff devotes his land. Neither can the decision be justified under the *de minimus* rule because the invasion of plaintiff's right to the enjoyment of his land was substantial as evidenced by the fact that an injunction was granted. There was an actual invasion of a property right that continued for the statutory period. Of course, a prescriptive right cannot be acquired to commit a public nuisance. [32]

---

27. Kennedy v. Burnap, 1898, 120 Cal. 488, 52 P. 843; Lynch v. Hill, 1939, 24 Del.Ch. 86, 6 A.2d 614; Parker v. Foote, 1838, 19 Wend. (N.Y.) 309; Hubbard v. Town, 1860, 33 Vt. 295; Depner v. United States Nat. Bank, 1930, 202 Wis. 405, 232 N.W. 851.

28. Sullivan v. Zeiner, 1893, 98 Cal. 346, 33 P. 209; Tunstall v. Christian, 1885, 80 Va. 1.

29. See Rupp v. Hiveley, 1928, 94 Cal.App. 667, 271 P. 768.

30. 11 Ch. 852 (1879).

31. See, 13 Harv.Law Rev. 142 (1889). But see, Vowinckel v. N. Clark & Sons, 1932, 216 Cal. 156, 13 P.2d 733, holding that a prescriptive right was not acquired because the nuisance was continuous in nature and a new cause of action arose from day to day.

32. Bowen v. Wendt, 1894, 103 Cal. 236, 37 P. 149.

If land is in the possession of a tenant, the prescriptive period will not start to run against the owner of the reversion or remainder or executory interest until such time as he has a cause of action or the physical means of preventing the acts.[33] Usually, this does not arise until his estate becomes possessory. However, even prior to that time he does have a cause of action against the prescriptive claimant if the acts cause permanent damage to the land. Accordingly, in such a case the statutory period will run against the owner of the future interest. For example, in the California case of Heilbron v. Last Chance Water Ditch Co.,[34] the claim of a prescriptive right to take water from a watercourse was sustained although, during the time of prescriptive use, the land to which the water rights were attached was in the possession of a tenant. The court held that the taking of the water affected the fertility of the soil and amounted to an injury to the future interest.

Use Must be Adverse as Distinguished from Permissive

The claim of prescriptive right cannot successfully be based upon acts that are permissive as distinguished from adverse. Acts are permissive if they are performed in subordination to the rights of the landowner. If they are not performed in subordination to the rights of the landowner they are adverse. For example, if a landowner purports to grant a profit or an easement, exercise of the right by the grantee is not in subordination to the rights of the landowner even if the deed is void. Such use is adverse and may ripen into a prescriptive right.[35] The use

cannot properly be classified as permissive merely because the landowner consented to the acts involved.

The creation of a license by the landowner results in a permissive use. A licensee acts in subordination to the rights of the licensor. The use becomes adverse only after the revocation of the license or after notice to the landowner that the use thereafter would be exercised without reference to the license.[36] Use continued for the statutory period is presumed to be adverse if circumstances surrounding the origin of the use are not shown.[37]

The creation of a license requires mutual consent. Accordingly, a landowner cannot prevent the acquisition of a profit or an easement by merely posting a sign on his property stating that any use of the land by another is permissive and that the privilege may be revoked at any time.[38] However, the posting of such a sign may prevent the claim of a common law dedication. Local statutes may regulate matters pertaining to the posting of signs.

Circumstances may justify the implication that a use was permissive. That may be the case, for example, where uninclosed woodland is use for passageway purposes and this does not disturb the use and enjoyment of

---

33. 5 Rest.Property, § 458, *Comment g.*

34. 75 Cal. 117, 17 P. 65 (1888).

35. But see, Batts v. Greer, 1963, 71 N.M. 454, 379 P.2d 443.

36. Richardson v. Horn, 1940, 282 Ky. 5, 137 S.W.2d 394; Lustmann v. Lustmann, 1938, 204 Minn. 228, 283 N.W. 387; Faulkner v. Thorn, 1940, 122 W.Va. 323, 9 S.E.2d 140.

37. Sinnett v. Werelus, 1961, 83 Idaho 514, 365 P.2d 952; Petersen v. Corrubia, 1961, 21 Ill.2d 525, 173 N.E.2d 499; Predwitch v. Chrobak, 1958, 186 Pa. Super. 601, 142 A.2d 388. But see, Waterman Steamship Corp. v. McGill Inst., 1961, 274 Ala. 481, 149 So.2d 773; Cuillier v. Coffin, 1961, 57 Wash.2d 624, 358 P.2d 958.

38. Pratt v. Hodgson, 1949, 91 Cal.App.2d 401, 204 P.2d 934.

the land by the owner.[39] In Zinser v. Lucks
(Mo),[40] signs were maintained on uninclosed
woodland for the statutory period. A prescriptive right to maintain the signs was denied upon the ground that the landowner did
not know that such a claim was being asserted and the use was not of such a nature as to
justify the implication of notice. Usually, the
above stated rule as to uninclosed woodland
is not applicable in the case of urban land
even if uninclosed.[41]

Another type of "implied permissive use"
is involved in the Pennsylvania case of Shinn
v. Rosenberger.[42] A nonnavigable lake was
located in part on A's land and in part on B's
land. A conducted a summer resort and had
made use of the entire lake for boating, bathing and fishing for the statutory period and
claimed a prescriptive right. During this period both A and B made use of the entire lake
for these stated purposes. The court held
that the "mutual advantages" accruing to
the owners justified the conclusion that the
use was permissive. The same conclusion is
indicated in a situation where adjoining landowners make common use of a driveway that
is located in part upon their respective properties.[43]

---

39.   Trunnell v. Ward, 1964, 86 Idaho 555, 389 P.2d
221; Monroe v. Shrake, 1941, 376 Ill. 253, 33 N.E.2d
459; Lundberg v. Notre Dame, 1939, 231 Wis. 187,
282 N.W. 70, 285 N.W. 839, noted in Wis.Law Rev.
(1940) 87.

40.   361 Mo. 671, 235 S.W.2d 844.

41.   Shepard v. Gilbert, 1933, 212 Wis. 1, 249 N.W.
54, noted in 19 Cornell Law Qt. 337 (1934); 13 Or.
Law Rev. 78 (1933).

42.   347 Pa. 504, 32 A.2d 747 (1943).

43.   Banach v. Lawera, 1951, 330 Mich. 436, 47 N.W.2d
679, noted in 50 Mich.Law Rev. 776 (1952). But
see, De Forrest v. Bunnie, 1951, 201 Misc. 7, 107
N.Y.S.2d 396; Friend v. Holcombe, 1945, 196 Okl.
111, 162 P.2d 1008.

Use Must be Open and Notorious

In order to ripen into a prescriptive right
the use during the statutory period must be
open and notorious. This requirement is satisfied if the landowner has actual knowledge
of the use or if the circumstances are such
that he may be charged with knowledge.
This gives him an opportunity to protect his
interests. There is a minority rule that a
prescriptive right cannot be acquired upon
the basis of imputed knowledge. This is in
accord with the theory that the claim of a
prescriptive right is based upon acquiescence
in use, which raises a presumption of a "lost
grant." [44] Therefore, if a landowner was not
actually informed as to the use, it would not
be possible for him to acquiesce thereto.
Thus, the presumption of a lost grant is rebutted.

Use Must be Continuous and Exclusive

Acts upon which the claim of a prescriptive right is based must be continuous. This
requires that the acts relate to the same area.
For example, the claim of a prescriptive right
to a passageway will be denied if the use is
not confined to a definite area.[45] However,
slight deviations will not defeat the claim.[46]

A landowner's protests against use by the
prescriptive claimant will not interrupt the
running of the statute. A contrary conclusion has been reached in some cases upon the
ground that the doctrine of prescription is
based upon the presumption of a lost grant
and a protest is sufficient to overcome such a

---

44.   Village of Fairview v. Franklin Maple Creek
Pioneer Irr. Co., 1938, 59 Idaho 7, 79 P.2d 531.

45.   Slack v. Herrick, 1939, 226 Iowa 336, 283 N.W.
904.

46.   Murff v. Dreeben, Tex.Civ.App.1939, 127 S.W.2d
577.

presumption.[47] Statutes in some states provide that a written protest is sufficient to constitute an interruption. A physical prevention of use will, of course, interrupt the running of the statute. It is sufficient if the servient owner does some act that would be actionable if a profit or an easement did, in fact exist (a sueable act).[48] This is also the result of a judgment against the claimant sustaining the landowner's possessory rights.

The claim of prescriptive right depends upon proof of use by the person asserting the right. The claim cannot be sustained if it is founded upon the acts of others. This means that the use must be exclusive.[49] However, this does not mean that the claimant must prove that he was the only person who used the land for the purpose involved.[50] It is also to be noted that use by a tenant will inure to the benefit of the landlord if the lease purported to authorize such use by the tenant.[51]

In computing time, the period of adverse use by one claimant may be tacked to the period of adverse use by a subsequent claimant provided that there is privity of estate between such claimants. The requirement of privity of estate is satisfied if there is a relationship between the successive users,

such as that of grantor and grantee, ancestor and heirs, etc. It is not necessary that the profit or easement be included within the terms of the conveyance if the parties understood that the interest was intended to be included.[52]

Riparian Rights

A non-riparian owner, by agreement with a riparian owner, may acquire a right to use the water in a watercourse or lake. According to some authorities such an agreement creates a mere contract right as between the riparian owner and the other contracting party. Under this view, other riparian owners are not affected by the contract because it does not result in the creation of an easement.[53] The basis for this rule is that riparian rights cannot exist apart from riparian land. Other authorities take the position that such an agreement does result in the creation of an easement.[54] While the easement cannot operate to the prejudice of other riparian owners, the easement owner is entitled to rights commensurate with the rights of the riparian owner from whom the easement has been acquired.

47. Powell v. Bagg, 1857, 74 Mass. 441; Dartnell v. Bidwell, 1916, 115 Me. 227, 98 A. 743, 5 A.L.R. 1320.

48. Lehigh Valley Ry. Co. v. McFarlan, 1881, 43 N. J.L. 605.

49. Scott v. Weinheimer, 1962, 140 Mont. 554, 374 P.2d 91. See Schmidt v. Brown, 1907, 226 Ill. 590, 80 N.E. 1071. See Brannon v. Lewis and Clark County, 1964, 143 Mont. 200, 387 P.2d 706 (holding that the public can obtain a roadway by prescription).

50. Stix v. La Rue, 1962, 78 Nev. 9, 368 P.2d 167.

51. Totten v. Stuart, 1925, 143 Va. 201, 129 S.E. 217. *Cf.*: Deregibus v. Silberman Furniture Co., 1938, 124 Conn. 39, 197 A. 760; Abatiell v. Morse, 1948, 115 Vt. 254, 56 A.2d 464.

52. Trueblood v. Pierce, 1947, 116 Colo. 221, 179 P.2d 671, 171 A.L.R. 1270; Leonard v. Leonard, 1863, 7 Allen (Mass.) 277. *Contra*: Stewart v. Hunt, 1942, 303 Mich. 161, 5 N.W.2d 737.

53. Gould v. Eaton, 1897, 117 Cal. 539, 49 P. 577; City of Newcastle v. Harvey, 1913, 54 Ind.App. 243, 102 N.E. 878; York Haven Water & Power Co. v. York Haven Paper Co., 3 Cir. 1912, 201 F. 270, noted in 26 Harv.Law Rev. 661 (1913); Stockport Waterworks Co. v. Potter, [1864] 3 Hurl. & Co. 300, 159 Eng.Rep. 545 (non-riparian owner not entitled to recover damages caused by the pollution of a watercourse). *Cf.*: Gould v. Stafford, 1891, 91 Cal. 146, 27 P. 543 (riparian rights may be extinguished by grant).

54. Johnson v. Armour & Co., 1940, 69 N.D. 769, 291 N.W. 113, 127 A.L.R. 828; Hite v. Town of Luray, 1940, 175 Va. 218, 8 S.E.2d 369; Lawrie v. Silsby, 1904, 76 Vt. 240, 56 A. 1106.

But a prescriptive right may be acquired to divert water from a watercourse or lake[55] or to cause pollution.[56] The prescriptive period starts to run against riparian owners from the time such diversion or pollution constitutes an invasion of their legal rights.[57] Since a prescriptive right cannot be acquired to commit a public nuisance, to the extent that the pollution of water constitutes such a nuisance it may be enjoined regardless of the expiration of time.[58]

Even if a riparian owner is entitled to the use of water, he may choose to forego his right and allow the water to flow to a lower riparian owner. By using the water the lower owner cannot acquire a prescriptive right. This follows from the fact that the upper owner does not have a cause of action against the lower owner because the lower owner is not invading the legal rights of the upper owner. In explaining this rule it is sometimes stated that "prescription may not go upstream." But there is an exception to this rule. If the lower owner actually diverts water from the upper owner by going upon his land and constructing a ditch or installing a pipe, he may thereby gain a prescriptive right.[59] Of course, an upper owner may gain a prescriptive right as against a lower riparian owner.

In some states the rule is followed that the extent of an easement acquired by prescription is not only limited to the amount of water used during the statutory period but also to the amount of water actually applied to a beneficial use.[60]

Disabilities

Statutes fixing the time required for the acquisition of a possessory estate by adverse possession usually provide that certain disabilities of the landowner, such as minority or insanity, may extend that time. By way of analogy, the same rule is applicable in prescription cases.

In Tracy v. Atherton (Vt.),[61] the owner of land over which a right of way was claimed by prescription died before the full statutory period had expired. The land passed to his heir who was then under the disability of minority. It was contended that the period of such disability should not be included in computing the time required for the acquistion of a prescriptive right. Applying the same rule that is followed in adverse possession cases, the court held that since the disability did not exist when the cause of action first accrued it did not operate to interrupt the running of the statute.[62] The statutory period will not start to run if such a disability exists when the cause of action first accrues. But a subsequent disability either in the same owner or a subsequent owner will have no bearing upon the acquisition of a prescriptive right. In other words, there can be no tack-

---

55. Larsen v. Apollonia, 1936, 5 Cal.2d 440, 55 P.2d 196; Stock v. City of Hillsdale, 1909, 155 Mich. 375, 119 N.W. 435.

56. Masonic Temple Ass'n v. Harris, 1887, 79 Me. 250, 9 A. 737; Riggs v. City of Springfield, 1939, 344 Mo. 420, 126 S.W.2d 1144, 122 A.L.R. 1496.

57. See Meng v. Coffey, 1903, 67 Neb. 500, 93 N.W. 713, 720 (no invasion of a right if there is sufficient water to satisfy the needs of the riparian owners).

58. People v. Gold Run D. & M. Co., 1884, 66 Cal. 138, 4 P. 1152 (deposit of waste into a navigable water course); Bowen v. Wendt, 1894, 103 Cal. 236, 37 P. 149 (refuse from a slaughterhouse); Attorney General v. Grand Rapids, 1912, 175 Mich. 503, 141 N.W. 890 (city sewage).

59. Saxon v. DuBois, 1962, 209 Cal.App.2d 713, 26 Cal. Rptr. 196.

60. Pabst v. Finmand, 1922, 190 Cal. 124, 211 P. 11. See Akin v. Spencer, 1937, 21 Cal.App.2d 325, 69 P.2d 430, noted in 26 Cal.Law Rev. 718 (1938).

61. 36 Vt. 503 (1864).

62. *Accord*: Wallace v. Fletcher, 1855, 30 N.H. 434. *Contra*: Lamb v. Crosland, 1850, 4 Rich. (S.C.) 536.

ing of disabilities. If two or more disabilities exist at the time the cause of action accrues, such as minority and insanity, the statute will not start to run until the termination of the disability that continues for the longest time.[63]

If a profit or easement is acquired by prescription, the one who acquires the interest cannot be held liable for damages caused to the servient estate by the acts involved in connection with the acquistion of a prescriptive right.[64]

EXTENT OF PROFIT OR EASEMENT

32. The extent of a profit or easement is determined by the terms of the grant, if it was acquired by grant, or by the nature of the use if it was acquired by prescription.

The owner of a profit or easement has a right to do those things that are reasonably necessary for a proper enjoyment of the primary right.

Some easements require practically exclusive possession of the servient estate for their complete enjoyment. That is the case with respect to easements for a railroad right of way, pipe line purposes or burial rights.

> **a. Grant. A profit or easement can be used only for the purpose stated in a grant. A "change in use" cannot be justified upon the ground that it "would not increase the burden on the servient estate."**
>
> **b. Prescription. A change in the "extent of use" is not a change in the "nature of a use."**
>
> **c. Easements and profits appurtenant. Unless otherwise restricted, if an easement or profit is appurtenant it may be used for the general benefit of the dominant estate. However, use for the benefit of non-dominant property is not authorized and may be enjoined.**
>
> **d. Use of servient estate. The servient owner may use his land for any desired purpose as long as such use does not unrea-**

sonably interfere with the use of the easement or profit.

> **e. Scope of easement or profit enlarged by prescription. The extent of an easement or profit may be enlarged by prescription.**

The extent of a profit or easement is determined by the terms of the grant, if it was acquired by grant, or by the nature of the use if it was acquired by prescription. If acquired by implication the extent is determined by reference to the use as it existed at the time of the conveyance and such uses as the parties might reasonably have contemplated.[65]

The owner of a profit or an easement has a right to do those things considered to be reasonably necessary for the proper exercise of the primary right. For example, a profit that involves the taking of minerals includes a right to go upon the land and make tests for the presence of such substances [66] and prepare necessary passageways for successful operations. These rights are at times referred to as "secondary easements."

Some easements require practically exclusive possession of the land for their complete enjoyment. That is the case, for example, with respect to a railroad right of way [67] and easements for pipe lines and burial rights.[68] But mineral rights remain in the owner of the possessory estate.[69]

---

63. 5 Rest.Property, § 460, *Comment c.*

64. 5 Rest.Property, § 465.

65. Fristoe v. Drapeau, 1950, 35 Cal.2d 5, 215 P.2d 729; 5 Rest. Property, § 484, *Comment b.*

66. Beckwith v. Rossi, 1961, 157 Me. 532, 175 A.2d 732 (test for the presence of gravel).

67. See, Midland Valley R. Co. v. Sutter, 8 Cir., 1928, 28 F.2d 163, noted in 42 Harv.Law Rev. 963 (1929).

68. *Cf.*: Kesterson v. California-Oregon Power Co., 1924, 114 Or. 22, 228 P. 1092 (right of way for construction of high-tension power lines).

69. Magnolia Petroleum Co. v. Thompson, 10 Cir., 1939, 106 F.2d 217.

Grant

In Gray v. City of Cambridge (Mass.),[70] the grant was for an easement to place pipes for the conveyance of water "from Fresh Pond to the city reservoirs." An injunction was granted restraining the use of the pipes for the direct distribution of water to consumers. The grant did not include an easement for that purpose. It is of no concern that such a "change in use" would or would not increase the burden placed upon the servient estate. The grant of an easement to use a beach "for the purpose of boating, bathing, fishing and other recreation" does not include the right to use the land for the operation of a commercial business of renting boats.[71] An easement to install an "open ditch" does not carry a right to maintain a closed ditch.[72] If the easement is one to maintain a cement culvert along the ground the owner of the easement does not have a right to dig aprons under the ditch to permit the flow of surface water.[73]

While the grant of an easement for "foot-passage" properly may not be used for carriages or automobiles,[74] the grant of an easement for a "right to pass" is not limited to the type of vehicles customarily used at the time of the grant.[75] In Taylor v. Heffner (Pa.),[76] an easement was granted for a drive-way forty feet wide "as now used." The court held that this language merely described the location of the passageway and did not constitute a restriction on the manner in which it was to be used.[77]

Prescription

In Kerlin v. Southern Telephone & Telegraph Co. (Ga.),[78] a public utility maintained telephone poles and wires over described land and acquired an easement by prescription. The court held that the owners of the servient estate did not have a right to prevent the company from stringing two additional wires on poles, there being no change in the "outer limits" of the space utilized by the owner of the easement during the statutory period. The additional use of the servient estate was "in degree only" and not "in kind." A similar result was reached in Hopkins The Florist, Inc. v. Fleming (Vt.),[79] where a prescriptive right had been acquired to use a sewer pipe. During the statutory period the dominant estate had been occupied by but one family. Subsequent occupancy by two families did not impose an additional burden on the servient estate.

The purpose,[80] width [81] and location of an easement for a right of way is determined by the facts as they existed during the statutory period. While such a way may be acquired for the general purposes of the dominant estate, a cartway acquired by prescription does

---

70.   189 Mass. 405, 76 N.E. 195 (1905).

71.   Hewitt v. Perry, 1942, 310 Mass. 649, 39 N.E.2d 575.

72.   Allen v. San Jose Land & Water Co., 1891, 92 Cal. 138, 28 P. 215.

73.   North Fork Water Co. v. Edwards, 1898, 121 Cal. 662, 54 P. 69.

74.   Rowell v. Doggett, 1887, 143 Mass. 483, 10 N.E. 182.

75.   Copp v. Foster, 1963, 345 Mass. 777, 189 N.E.2d 521; Matteodo v. Capaldi, 1927, 48 R.I. 312, 138 A. 38, 53 A.L.R. 550.

76.   359 Pa. 157, 58 A.2d 450 (1948).

77.   *Contra:* Crew's Die Casting Corp. v. Davidow, 1963, 369 Mich. 541, 120 N.W.2d 238.

78.   191 Ga. 663, 13 S.E.2d 790 (1941).

79.   112 Vt. 389, 26 A.2d 96, 142 A.L.R. 463 (1942).

80.   Hawley v. McCabe, 1933, 117 Conn. 558, 169 A. 192, noted in 14 Boston Univ.Law Rev. 432 (1934) (hauling wood); Lawless v. Trumbull, 1962, 343 Mass. 561, 180 N.E.2d 80 (hauling wood). See Biggs v. Wolfe, 1962, 40 Del.Ch. 212, 178 A.2d 482.

81.   Northwest Cities Gas Co. v. Western Fuel Co., 1943, 17 Wash.2d 482, 135 P.2d 867.

not necessarily include a right to use the way for the purpose of driving cattle.[82]

Easements and Profits Appurtenant

In the absence of restrictions, if an easement or profit is appurtenant it may be used for the general benefit of the dominant estate.[83] It is assumed that the parties had in mind the normal development of the dominant estate. Accordingly, the "degree of use" may be augmented because of changes made in the use of the dominant estate.[84] A charge of "excessive use" may be sustained because of a change in the use of the dominant estate that cannot be characterized under the heading of "normal development." For example, if land is used for agricultural purposes, there is doubt whether an easement for right of way purposes can be used if the dominant estate is subsequently used as a "dumping ground," necessitating the use of heavy trucks etc.[85] Even assuming a proper use of the easement under such circumstances, a court of equity may direct procedures to be taken by those using the right of way in order to minimize the disturbances and inconveniences caused by noise, dust, etc., to the owner of the servient estate.[86]

Any attempt to use an appurtenant easement or profit for the benefit of non-dominant land may be enjoined. In D. M. Goodwillie Co. v. Commonwealth Electric Co.

(Ill.),[87] an easement for switch purposes was appurtenant to described land. A plant for generating electricity was constructed in part on the dominant estate and in part on non-dominant land. An essential part of the plant was thus located on the non-dominant land. The court held that the easement for switch purposes could not be used because such use, if permitted, would directly benefit the non-dominant land.[88]

An apparent attempt to benefit non-dominant land is beyond the scope of a profit or an easement. In the English case of Henning v. Burnet,[89] a passageway was appurtenant to land described as a "dwelling, coach-house, and stable." The easement did not authorize passage to a field that was not a part of the dominant estate. A passageway to Blackacre cannot properly be used to drive cattle to Blackacre and from there to other land.[90] But a *bona fide* use of a profit or easement is proper even if this results in some benefit to non-dominant land. For example, in the leading English case of Williams v. James,[91] hay, grown on non-dominant land, was stacked on the dominant estate and later was hauled over a passageway appurtenant thereto. The court held that this use was proper. The stacking of the hay on the dominant estate was a proper use of the land and

---

82. Ballard v. Dyson [1808] 1 Taunt. 279, 127 Eng. Rep. 841.

83. *Cf.:* Allan v. Gomme, [1840] 11 A. & E. 759, 113 Eng.Rep. 602 (description of dominant estate included a restriction as to use of right of way).

84. White v. Grand Hotel, Eastbourne, Ltd., [1913] 1 Ch. 113 (change from private dwelling to hotel).

85. See Wall v. Rudolph, 1961, 198 Cal.App.2d 684, 18 Cal.Rptr. 123.

86. Giles v. Luker, 1943, 215 Minn. 256, 9 N.W.2d 716. See Swensen v. Marino, 1940, 306 Mass. 582, 29 N.E.2d 15.

87. 241 Ill. 42, 89 N.E. 272 (1909).

88. *Accord:* McCullough v. Broad Exchange Co., 1905, 101 App.Div. 566, 92 N.Y.S. 533; Penn Bowling Recreation Center, Inc. v. Hot Shoppes, Inc., 1949, 86 App.D.C. 58, 179 F.2d 64, 16 A.L.R.2d 602 (easement suspended during continuance of the condition).

89. 8 Ex. 187, 155 Eng.Rep. 1313 (1852).

90. Howell v. King, [1674] 1 Mod. 190, 86 Eng.Rep. 821. See, Diocese of Trenton v. Toman, 1908, 74 N.J.Eq. 702, 70 A. 606; S. S. Kresge Co. of Michigan v. Winkelman Realty Co., 1952, 260 Wis. 372, 50 N.W.2d 920.

91. [1867] L.R. 2 C.P. 577, 16 L.T.R. 664.

was not done for the purpose of securing a benefit for the non-dominant land.

Use of Servient Estate

To the extent that privileges are conferred upon the owner of a profit or an easement, to that extent the privileges of use by the owner of the servient estate are diminished. As between the two, priority is given to the owner of the easement. The owner of the servient estate may use his land for any lawful purpose as long as such use does not unreasonably interfere with the enjoyment of the profit or easement. In City of Pasadena v. California-Michigan Land & Water Co. (Cal.),[92] a landowner granted to the city easements for the purpose of installing water pipes within an area five feet wide. Later, the landowner granted similar easements to another who installed pipes within the same five foot area. The court held that since the city's enjoyment of its easement was not disturbed it had no cause to complain. Specific situations are considered in the following paragraphs.

First: In some situations the existence of a profit or an easement result in some benefit to the owner of the servient estate. While the owner of the profit or easement is not under a duty to exercise his right of use,[93] he cannot make changes or alterations that would disturb the benefit enjoyed by the servient owner. It has been held, however, that the owner of an easement for an irrigation ditch has a right to improve the ditch to prevent seepage that resulted in a benefit to the servient owner. This does not result in a change in the nature of the use and it advances the interests of water conservation.[94]

Second: Ordinarily, the servient owner may construct fences along the sides of a right of way [95] and he may prevent such construction by the owner of the easement.[96] Also, the servient owner has a right to erect gates if this does not unreasonably interfere with the use of the right of way. It is immaterial whether the easement was acquired by grant [97] or by prescription.[98]

The servient owner has a right to erect a structure that projects over the right of way if this does not unreasonably interfere with the use for passageway purposes.[99] This obstruction-rule may not be applicable if an easement for light and air is involved.[1]

Scope of Easement or Profit Enlarged by Prescription

The scope of an easement or profit may be enlarged by prescription. In Gehman v. Erdman (Pa.),[2] the defendant had an easement

---

92. 17 Cal.2d 576, 110 P.2d 983, 133 A.L.R. 1186, noted in 29 Cal.Law Rev. 632 (1941).

93. Relovich v. Stuart, 1931, 211 Cal. 422, 295 P. 819.

94. Big Cottonwood Tanner Ditch Co. v. Moyle, 1946, 109 Utah 213, 174 P.2d 148, 172 A.L.R. 475.

95. Dolske v. Gormley, 1962, 58 Cal.2d 513, 25 Cal. Rptr. 270, 375 P.2d 174; Houghtaling v. Stoothoff, 1940, 259 App.Div. 854, 19 N.Y.S.2d 510; Dyba v. Borowitz, 1939, 136 Pa.Super. 532, 7 A.2d 500.

96. Doan v. Allgood, 1923, 310 Ill. 381, 141 N.E. 779.

97. Whitaker v. Yates, 1923, 200 Ky. 530, 255 S.W. 102, noted in 12 Ky.Law Jr. 172 (1924); Bakeman v. Talbot, 1865, 31 N.Y. 366; Gibbons v. Ebding, 1904, 70 Ohio St. 298, 71 N.E. 720. *Cf.:* Schaefer v. Burnstine, 1958, 13 Ill.2d 464, 150 N.E.2d 113.

98. Craig v. Kennedy, 1961, 202 Va. 654, 119 S.E.2d 320; Dyer v. Walker, 1898, 99 Wis. 404, 75 N.W. 79. *Contra:* Switzer v. Armantrout, 1939, 106 Ind. App. 468, 19 N.E.2d 858; Melton v. Donnell, 1938, 173 Tenn. 19, 114 S.W.2d 49.

99. Bitello v. Lipson, 1908, 80 Conn. 497, 69 A. 21; Atkins v. Bordman, 1840, 2 Metc. (Mass.) 457; Sutton v. Groll, 1886, 42 N.J.Eq. 213, 5 A. 901.

1. Attorney General v. Williams, 1885, 140 Mass. 329, 2 N.E. 80, 3 N.E. 214. In Mt. Holyoke Realty Corp. v. Holyoke Realty Co., 1935, 292 Mass. 332, 198 N.E. 242, 101 A.L.R. 1289, an easement was acquired for passageway in a building. It was held that the servient owner could be enjoined from covering up a skylight, because that would interfere with the use of the easement.

2. 105 Pa. 371 (1884).

which permitted him to maintain a dam at a stated level. He increased the height of the dam thus causing a larger area of the servient estate to be flooded. The increased height was maintained for the statutory period. The scope of the easement was enlarged by prescription.[3]

In a case of this type the use is referable to an existing easement. Therefore, in the absence of actual notice to the owner of the servient estate that an additional right is asserted, or in the absence of damages, from which notice may be implied, the claim that an easement has been enlarged by prescription will be denied. For example, in Lindokken v. Paulson (Wis.),[4] a right of way was acquired for the purpose of transporting milk to a factory. For the statutory period the owner of the easement used the road for all purposes necessary and convenient to the use of the dominant estate. The claim that the easement had been enlarged by prescription was denied. It did not appear that the owner of the servient estate had knowledge during the statutory period that the additional claim was being asserted and he suffered no damage as a result of the additional use.

IMPERFECT DESCRIPTION

33. If a deed creating a profit or an easement is ambiguous as to location, the ambiguity may be resolved by course of conduct. Otherwise, it will be resolved by the court, taking into consideration the intended purpose of the servitude and the necessities for its enjoyment.

A deed creating a profit or an easement may be ambiguous with respect to its location. In that event, the actual location used by the owner of the profit or easement, if with the consent of the owner of the servient

estate, resolves the ambiguity.[5] In Winslow v. City of Vallejo (Cal.),[6] the easement was for "any waterpipes or mains which may be laid by the city of Vallejo." A ten inch main was installed. Due to the growth of the community the capacity of this pipe became insufficient. The city threatened to install an additional fourteen inch pipe and an injunction was granted.[7] By the installation of the original pipe the scope and extent of the easement became fixed and certain. The rule of this case will be followed unless from the nature of the transaction and the purpose to be accomplished a contrary intent of the parties is apparent.[8] If the ambiguity cannot be resolved by reference to a course of conduct, in appropriate judicial proceedings the court, guided by the intended purpose of the profit or easement and the necessities for its enjoyment, will resolve the uncertainty.[9]

A grant is not "indefinite" within the meaning of the rule under discussion if the space to be occupied by the pipes is specified. In that event additional pipes may be placed within the specified area.[10] Also, the agreement may authorize replacement with a larger pipe where there is no limitation on

---

3. See Wheatley v. Chrisman, 1855, 25 Pa. 298.

4. 224 Wis. 470, 272 N.W. 453, 111 A.L.R. 910 (1937).

5. Caslani v. Aiken, 1936, 108 Vt. 106, 183 A. 489; Rhodes Cemetery Ass'n v. Miller, 1940, 122 W.Va. 139, 7 S.E.2d 659, noted in 47 W.Va.Law Qt. 61 (1940) (a reasonable width for a passageway was fixed by the court).

6. 148 Cal. 723, 84 P. 191 (1906).

7. *Accord:* Houston Pipe Line Co. v. Dwyer, 1964, — Tex. —, 374 S.W.2d 662; City of Lynchburg v. Smith, 1936, 166 Va. 364, 186 S.E. 51.

8. *Cf.:* Brookshire Oil Co. v. Casmalia, etc., Co., 1909, 156 Cal. 211, 103 P. 927.

9. Ingelson v. Olson, 1937, 199 Minn. 422, 272 N.W. 270, 110 A.L.R. 167; Graff v. Budgett, 1943, 69 S.D. 364, 10 N.W.2d 764.

10. Standard Oil Co. v. Buchi, 1907, 72 N.J.Eq. 492, 66 A. 427; Ozehoski v. Scranton Spring Brook Water Service Co., 1945, 157 Pa.Super. 437, 43 A.2d 601.

the size of the pipeline to be installed and there is authority to "construct, test, reconstruct, renew, operate, maintain, inspect, alter, repair and remove a pipeline." [11]

EASEMENTS FOR STREET AND HIGHWAY PURPOSES

34. The owner of land that abuts upon a public street or highway, whose ownership does not extend into the passageway, has easements for purposes of ingress, egress, light, air prospect and view. The use of these easements is restricted to the extent necessary for use of the areas for proper street and highway purposes.

The owner of land that abuts upon a public street or highway, whose ownership does not extend into the thoroughfare, has easements for ingress and egress, light and air, prospect and view.[12] However, enjoyment of these easements is subordinate to the public right to use the street or highway for proper highway purposes. As a safety measure, highway authorities may obstruct the view of signs if this is necessary to prevent the attention of motorists from being distracted from driving.[13] Ordinances may authorize the installation of parking meters.[14] However, there is some authority that an abutting owner cannot be deprived of the right to use the curb for loading and unloading purposes unless he is properly compensated.[15]

If the abutting owner's possessory estate extends into the thoroughfare he may, as owner of the servient estate, make use of the area for all purposes not inconsistent with the public use for proper highway purposes. He is entitled to trees cut from the thoroughfare in front of his land [16] and is entitled to compensation for additional servitudes that may be placed on the servient estate. Such would be the case if poles are erected and wires strung for the transmission of electricity.[17] In the Oklahoma case of Okmulgee Producers & Manufacturers Gas Co. v. Franks,[18] the public right was limited to the use of land for highway purposes. The court held that the construction of a pipeline along the way was not an additional burden for which the abutting owner would be entitled to compensation because this was a proper highway purpose in that it would relieve surface traffic.[19]

PARTY WALL EASEMENT

35. The creation of a party wall easement by express agreement requires compliance with the Statute of Frauds.

If a party wall is erected for the support of structures the strength of the wall properly cannot be impaired by openings made in the wall.

In the absence of an agreement to the contrary, the owner of an easement created by express agreement has authority to increase the height of the wall. However, he may be held

11.　Weaver v. Natural Gas Pipeline Co., 1963, 27 Ill. 2d 48, 188 N.E.2d 18, 19.

12.　Williams v. Los Angeles Ry. Co., 1907, 150 Cal. 592, 89 P. 330; Kane v. Metropolitan Elevated Ry. Co., 1891, 125 N.Y. 164, 26 N.E. 278.

13.　Perlmutter v. Greene, 1932, 259 N.Y. 327, 182 N.E. 5, 81 A.L.R. 1543.

14.　Gilsey Buildings, Inc. v. Great Neck Plaza, 1939, 170 Misc. 945, 11 N.Y.S.2d 694; Kimmel v. Spokane, 1941, 7 Wash.2d 372, 109 P.2d 1069, noted in 29 Cal.Law Rev. 651 (1941). But see, City of Birmingham v. Hood-McPherson Realty Co., 1937, 233 Ala. 352, 172 So. 114, 108 A.L.R. 1140, noted in 22 Minn. Law Rev. 111 (1937); M. H. Rhodes, Inc. v. City of Raleigh, 1940, 217 N.C. 627, 9 S.E.2d 389, comment, 19 No.Car.Law Rev. 70 (1940).

15.　See, Eisenmann v. Tester, 1934, 47 Ohio App. 275, 191 N.E. 839, noted in 48 Harv.Law Rev. 339 (1934).

16.　Brooks v. Bess, 1937, 135 Me. 290, 195 A. 361.

17.　Cathey v. Arkansas Power & Light Co., 1936, 193 Ark. 92, 97 S.W.2d 624.

18.　177 Okl. 456, 60 P.2d 771 (1936).

19.　*Contra:* Hofius v. Carnegie-Illinois Steel Corp., 1946, 146 Ohio St. 574, 67 N.E.2d 429.

liable for any damage that may be caused thereby.

A party wall is a wall so located as to support structures that may be erected upon the land of adjoining owners. There is authority for the rule that "support of structures" is not a necessary ingredient of a party wall. Under this view a structure may be classified as a party wall even though used only as a curtain wall to obtain protection from the elements or to prevent the spread of fire.[20] A party wall involves cross-easements if it is located in part upon the land of adjoining owners.

The creation of a party-wall easement by express agreement requires compliance with the provisions of the Statute of Frauds. However, if a party wall is erected in reliance upon an oral agreement there is sufficient part performance to take the case out of the operation of the Statute of Frauds. Such an agreement may even be implied if a landowner remains silent knowing that such a structure is being erected in part on his land by an adjoining owner.[21] Not only may the silent-owner be estopped to deny the existence of the easement but he may be required to pay his proportionate share of the costs of erecting the wall if he subsequently makes use of the wall—such a promise to pay may be implied.[22]

If a party wall is erected for the support of structures the strength of the wall cannot be impaired by windows or other openings in the wall.[23] If the easement is acquired by grant, and in the absence of a provision to the contrary, either party has a right to increase the height of the wall (as distinguished from extending its length) if this can be accomplished without causing damage to the wall or the adjoining structures.[24] However, the potential height may be limited, such as in a case where the party wall agreement provides that each owner may erect a building to a stated height.[25]

If a party-wall easement is acquired by prescription the owner of the easement does not have a right to increase the height of the party wall. This follows from the fact that the scope and extent of such an easement is determined by reference to the use as continued for the statutory period.

One landowner may tear down a party wall if he replaces it with a wall furnishing equivalent support. In so doing, he may be held liable for any damage caused to the adjoining structure.[26]

While an owner is entitled to post signs on that part of the wall located on his land,[27] he does not have a right to use a party wall for that purpose if the area of the wall involved is on the land of an adjoining owner.[28] This follows from the fact that the easement

20. Gimbel Bros., Inc. v. Markette Corp., 3 Cir. 1962, 307 F.2d 91.

21. Brandhagen v. Burt, N.D.1962, 117 N.W.2d 696.

22. Day v. Caton, 1876, 119 Mass. 513.

23. Graves v. Smith, 1888, 87 Ala. 450, 6 So. 308; Kuh v. O'Reilly, 1914, 261 Ill. 437, 104 N.E. 5; Normille v. Gill, 1893, 159 Mass. 427, 34 N.E. 543.

24. Sorensen v. J. H. Lawrence Co., 1951, 194 Md. 546, 71 A.2d 292, 24 A.L.R.2d 1047; Everett v. Edwards, 1898, 149 Mass. 588, 22 N.E. 52; Brooks v. Curtis, 1872, 50 N.Y. 639.

25. Frowenfeld v. Casey, 1903, 139 Cal. 421, 73 P. 152.

26. Putzel v. Drovers' & Mechanics' Nat. Bk., 1894, 78 Md. 349, 28 A. 276, 22 L.R.A. 632; Mary Jane Stevens Co. v. First Nat. Bldg. Co., 1936, 89 Utah 456, 57 P.2d 1099, comment, 35 Mich.Law Rev. 976 (1937), (holding that the builder will be liable to the adjoining owner for damage caused to his land only if there is a showing of negligence).

27. Lappan v. Glunz, 1925, 140 Mich. 609, 104 N.W. 26. See, Wilensky v. Robinson, 1948, 203 Ga. 423, 47 S.E.2d 270, 2 A.L.R.2d 1129.

28. Wait v. Newman, 1938, 284 Mich. 1, 278 N.W. 742. See, Varriale v. Brooklyn Edison Co., 1929, 252 N.Y. 222, 169 N.E. 284.

is one for support of a structure and not one for advertising.

DUTY TO REPAIR

36. The owner of a profit or easement is under a duty to keep the servient estate in repair insofar as the profit or easement area is concerned.

The owner of a profit or easement is under a duty to keep the servient estate in repair insofar as the profit or easement area is concerned.[29] This rule is followed even if a condition of disrepair developed through the activity of the servient owner if his use of the land was reasonable.[30] There is a privilege to enter upon the land for the purpose of making necessary repairs or improvements. Liability will not arise if these activities are conducted in a reasonable manner.[31]

EXTINGUISHMENT OF EASEMENTS AND PROFITS

37. An easement or profit is extinguished when ownership of the servitude and the servient estate are united in the same person other than in a representative capacity.

a. By estoppel. An easement or a profit may be extinguished or modified by estoppel. That is the case, for example, if there is an apparent abandonment of the interest and the servient owner erects improvements in reliance thereon.

b. Fulfillment of purpose. An easement or profit terminates upon the fulfillment of the purpose for which it was created.

c. By abandonment. Failure to use an easement or profit will not result in its extinguishment. However, that may result upon proof of an intention to abandon the interest if this is accompanied by physical acts affecting either the dominant or the servient estate.

d. By prescription. An easement or profit may be extinguished by prescription.

e. Destruction of servient estate. A destruction of the servient estate will result in extinguishment of an easement or profit.

f. Tax sale of servient estate. A tax sale of the servient estate will not result in the extinguishment of an easement or profit.

An easement or a profit is extinguished when the ownership thereof and the ownership of the servient estate are united in the same person. The non-possessory interest merges into the possessory estate.[32] If the non-possessory interest is of longer duration than that of the possessory estate the merger applies only during the continuance of the possessory estate.[33] It is also to be noted that the merger rule does not apply where one or the other of the interests is acquired in a representative capacity,[34] or as a mortgagee.[35] Other methods of extinguishment are discussed in the following paragraphs.

By Estoppel

Apparent abandonment of an easement or profit may result in its extinguishment if the servient owner, in reliance thereon, erects improvements on his land. This result will follow if the expenditures are substantial in

29. Maddock v. Chase, 1947, 94 N.H. 241, 51 A.2d 145 (easement in a structure).

30. Durfee v. Garvey, 1889, 78 Cal. 546, 21 P. 302 (cattle, pastured upon the servient estate, caused some obstruction to a drain).

31. Guillet v. Livernois, 1937, 297 Mass. 337, 8 N.E.2d 921, 112 A.L.R. 1300 (to surface and grade a passageway); Mt. Holyoke Realty Corp. v. Holyoke Realty Corp., 1935, 292 Mass. 332, 198 N.E. 242, 101 A.L.R. 1289 (to install lighting fixtures in a hallway); Edgett v. Douglass, 1891, 144 Pa. 95, 22 A. 868 (to repair a dyke).

32. Dimoff v. Laboroff, 1941, 296 Mich. 325, 296 N.W. 275; Read v. Jones, 1928, 152 Va. 226, 146 S.E. 263, noted in 15 Va.Law Rev. 716 (1929).

33. Dority v. Dunning, 1886, 78 Me. 381, 6 A. 6.

34. Pearce v. McClenaghan, 1851, 5 Rich. (S.C.) 178; Thomas v. Thomas, [1835] 2 C.M. & R. 34, 150 Eng. Rep. 15.

35. Ritger v. Parker, 1851, 8 Cush. (Mass.) 145.

ements are interests in land
of the Statute of Frauds.
exceptions noted, the re-
such interests to the owner
estate must be in writing.
extinguishment of these in-
nment are as follows:

e intention to abandon a
ement will not result in its
¹ In a few states the rule
a profit or an easement was
escription non-use for the
will result in its extinguish-
sis of abandonment.[42] This
conflict with the provisions
Frauds and draws an illogi-
tween profits and easements
he manner of acquisition. It
however, that application of
es some protection to inno-
of the servient estate. Re-
are not applicable if a profit
acquired by prescription.
haser of the servient estate
l of notice that might other-
the physical condition of the
or easement has been aban-
period of time.[43]

scher, 1930, 112 Conn. 5, 151 A. 351,
h.Law Rev. 376 (1931); Haigh v.
239 Ill. 227, 87 N.E. 962, comment,
83 (1910); Dubinsky v. Cama, 1927,
261 Mass. 47, 158 N.E. 321; Crew's Die Casting
Corp. v. Davidow, 1963, 369 Mich. 541, 120 N.W.2d
238; Sabins v. McAllister, 1950, 116 Vt. 302, 76 A.2d
106; Ward v. Ward, [1852] 7 Ex. 838, 155 Eng.Rep.
1189; Cook v. Mayor & Corp. of Bath, [1868] L.R.
6 Eq. 177. *Cf.*: Mathwes Slate Co. of N. Y. Inc.,
v. Advance Industrial Supply Co., 1918, 185 App.
Div. 74, 172 N.Y.S. 830, noted in 32 Harv.Law Rev.
735 (1919).

42. See, Rhodes v. Whitehead, 1863, 27 Tex. 304;
West's Ann.Cal.Civ.Code, § 811(4).

43. See City of Harrodsburg v. Cunningham, 1944, 299
Ky. 193, 184 S.W.2d 357.

Browne v. Trustees of
1872, 37 Md. 108; Moore v. Rawson, 3 B. & C. 332,
107 Eng.Rep. 756 (1824). But see, Blenis v. Utica
Knitting Co., 1911, 73 Misc. 61, 130 N.Y.S. 740,
noted in 11 Col.Law Rev. 777 (1911); Rogers v.
Stewart, 1833, 5 Vt. 215.

37. 84 Me. 33, 24 A. 432 (1891).

38. See Dillman v. Hoffman, 1875, 38 Wis. 559.

39. 125 Misc. 584, 211 N.Y.S. 217 (1925), noted in 35
Yale Law J. 234 (1925).

40. See also, Griffin v. Dwyer, 1937, 181 Okl. 71, 72
P.2d 349; Hopkins The Florist, Inc. v. Fleming,
1942, 112 Vt. 389, 26 A.2d 96.

The homestead of Frank De La
Rosa as the Home Tract in
(Name)
Nueces County, Texas

1511 N. McCampbell

Home 449-1219
office 449-1415

Second: The prevailing rule is that a profit or an easement may be extinguished by abandonment if the intention to abandon the interest is accompanied by acts furnishing some outward manifestation of the intention and thereby satisfying the policy of the Statute of Frauds.

Of course there must be proof of an intention to abandon the interest. Non-use for a long period of time is strong evidence of such an intention. Even payment for the privilege in the form of rental may be sufficient to prove this intention.[44] However, an oral understanding that the location of an easement is to be changed, or acquiescence in such a change, is not evidence of abandonment. Such an agreement is enforceable if acted upon by the parties.[45]

Assuming proof of an intention to abandon a profit or an easement, this purpose may be accomplished if accompanied by acts reflected in the physical condition of either the dominant or the servient estates. For example, in Jones v. Van Bochove (Mich.),[46] a cement company acquired an easement as a means by which to transport marl to its plant. Intending to abandon the easement the company removed the rails and ties located on the dominant estate and demolished the factory building. The court held that these acts brought about an extinguishment of the easement.[47] Even failure to act may be sufficient for the purpose if this is reflected in the physical condition of the land. That is the case, for example, if improvements essential for the enjoyment of the easement are allowed to fall into a state of disrepair and remain in that condition for a long period of time.[48] There is authority for the view that the act involved need not relate to the physical condition of the land. For example, in McKinney v. Pennsylvania R. Co. (Pa.),[49] it is held that a passageway-easement had been extinguished because the owner of the easement participated in public proceedings that resulted in the establishment of a public way over the area in question.[50]

Rights of the public in land dedicated for use as a public cemetery may be lost by non-use.[51] However, a contrary rule is followed in the case of a private burial ground. In such a case only the removal of the remains will be sufficient to constitute an abandonment of the easement.[52]

By Prescription

A profit or easement may be modified or extinguished by prescription. To the extent that the owner of the servient estate prevents the use of a profit or easement for the statutory period, to that extent the profit or easement is modified or extinguished.[53]

---

44. See note, 38 Harv.Law Rev. 523 (1925).

45. Bagley v. Petermeier, 1943, 233 Iowa 505, 10 N.W. 2d 1. See Rivas & Rivas, Inc. v. River Road Swimming Club, 1962, 40 Del.Ch. 249, 180 A.2d 282.

46. 103 Mich. 98, 61 N.W. 342 (1894).

47. *Accord:* Norton v. Duluth Transfer Ry. Co., 1915, 129 Minn. 126, 151 N.W. 907, noted in 13 Mich.Law Rev. 701 (1915); Arena v. Prisco, 1948, 81 N.Y.S.2d 627. *Cf.:* Cook v. Mayor & Corp. of Bath, L.R., 6 Eq. 177 (1868).

48. Kraft v. Miller, 1946, 314 Mich. 390, 22 N.W.2d 857.

49. 222 Pa. 48, 70 A. 946 (1908).

50. See, Skelton v. Schenetzky, 1924, 82 Ind.App. 432, 144 N.E. 144, noted in 23 Mich.Law Rev. 72 (1924).

51. Clinton Chamber of Commerce v. Jacobs, 1948, 212 Ark. 776, 207 S.W.2d 616; A. F. Hutchinson Land Co. v. Whitehead Bros. Co., 1926, 218 App.Div. 682, 219 N.Y.S. 413.

52. Frost v. Columbia Clay Co., 1924, 130 S.C. 72, 124 S.E. 767, noted in 38 Harv.Law Rev. 688 (1925), 23 Mich.Law Rev. 423 (1925). But see, Johnson v. Kentucky-Virginia Stone Co., 1941, 286 Ky. 1, 149 S.W.2d 496.

53. Glatts v. Henson, 1948, 31 Cal.2d 368, 188 P.2d 745; Goodwin v. Bragaw, 1913, 87 Conn. 31, 86 A. 668 (modified); Illinois Central R. Co. v. Houghton, 1888, 126 Ill. 233, 18 N.E. 301; Jennison v. Walker,

Destruction of Servient Estate

Destruction of a servient estate usually results in the extinguishment of a profit or easement. Thus, an easement in a structure, such as a party wall, is destroyed if the structure is destroyed or rendered useless for the intended purpose without the fault of the servient owner. For example, it may be declared unsafe by public authority and ordered demolished.[54]

In Sherred v. Cisco (N.Y.),[55] a party wall was destroyed by fire and plaintiff, one of the co-owners, built a new wall on the foundation of the one destroyed. Thereafter the defendant, the other co-owner, made use of the wall. Plaintiff claimed a right to recover one-half the cost of the new wall. Recovery was denied upon the ground that the easements were extinguished by the destruction of the original wall and that defendant acquired title by accession to the portion of the new wall erected on his land.[56]

According to the general rule, a party wall easement is not extinguished by damage caused to the wall even if the utility of the wall is impaired as to some but not as to all of the co-owners.[57] A contrary conclusion is indicated in some decisions in cases where the easement was acquired by grant. It is reasoned that the purpose of the grant is mutual in nature. The duration of the respective easements should be measured by the duration of the mutual purpose. Failure of purpose as to one party results in an ex-

tinguishment of the easement. Under this view it may be contended that if, as the result of changed conditions, a party wall is not suitable to support a structure which can produce an adequate return on existing land values the easements are extinguished.[58]

The rules applicable in party wall situations are, in general, applicable in the case of easements in other types of structures. For example, in Shirley v. Crabb (Ind.),[59] a building subject to an easement for passageway purposes was destroyed by fire. The court held that the easement could not be claimed with respect to a new building constructed on the same site.[60] An economic advantage to the servient owner is not justification for his voluntary destruction of a building with resultant extinguishment of easements.[61]

Tax Sale of Servient Estate

Sale of the servient estate pursuant to default in the payment of taxes will not result in extinguishment of a profit or easement. The assessment against the servient estate does not contemplate a levy against the easement or profit.[62] This is true even if the local statute expressly provides that a tax deed passes the absolute title "free from all incumbrances."[63]

1858, 11 Gray (Mass.) 423; Loumar Development Co. v. Redel, Mo.1963, 369 S.W.2d 252.

54. See In re State Fire Marshal, 1963, 175 Neb. 66, 120 N.W. 549.

55. 4 Sandf. (N.Y.) 480 (1851).

56. *Accord:* Antomarchi's Ex'r v. Russell, 1879, 63 Ala. 356; Orman v. Day, 1853, 5 Fla. 385; Bowhay v. Richards, 1908, 81 Neb. 764, 116 N.W. 677.

57. Commercial Nat. Bk. of Ogden v. Eccles, 1913, 43 Utah 91, 134 P. 614.

58. See, S. S. Kresge Co. v. Garrick Realty Co., 1932, 209 Wis. 305, 245 N.W. 118, 85 A.L.R. 283.

59. 138 Ind. 200, 73 N.E. 130 (1894).

60. *Accord:* Muzio v. Erickson, 1919, 41 Cal.App. 413, 182 P. 974; Rudderham v. Emery Bros., 1924, 46 R.I. 171, 125 A. 291, 34 A.L.R. 602, noted in 23 Mich. Law Rev. 73 (1924); 34 Yale Law J., 211 (1924). But see, Douglas v. Coonley, 1898, 156 N.Y. 521, 51 N.E. 283.

61. Rothschild v. Wolf, 1942, 20 Cal.2d 17, 123 P.2d 483.

62. Ross v. Franko, 1942, 139 Ohio St. 395, 40 N.E.2d 664.

63. Smith v. Smith, 1913, 21 Cal.App. 378, 131 P. 890; Alamogordo Imp. Co. v. Prendergast, 1939, 43 N.M. 245, 91 P.2d 428, 122 A.L.R. 1277 (equitable servitude). But see, Young v. Thendara, Inc., 1950, 328 Mich. 42, 43 N.W.2d 58.

CHAPTER 8

LICENSES

LICENSE DEFINED

38. A license authorizes the use of land that is in the possession of one other than the licensee. It is created by mutual consent and is thus to be distinguished from a privilege conferred by law or one that is incident to an estate in land.

A license personal is one wherein the use of the land is incidental to the main purpose of the license. A license real is involved if the main purpose of the license involves the use of the land itself.

In general, the difference between a license and a profit or an easement is that a license may be revoked at the will of the licensor.

A license authorizes the use of land that is in the possession of one other than the licensee. It is based upon mutual consent. In this respect it differs from a privilege to go upon land that is conferred by law, such as in a case where a person may go upon land to abate a public nuisance or to serve legal process.[1] It also differs from a privilege to go upon land that is incident to an estate in the land, such as the privilege of a former tenant at will to go upon the land after the termination of his estate to harvest crops planted by him during the period of the lease (doctrine of emblements).[2] A license differs from an easement only because it is terminable at the will of either party, a matter discussed in the following paragraphs.

While a license may confer a privilege in connection with the use of land, the use of land may be clearly incidental to the main purpose of the license.[3] That is the case, for example, if a person has a privilege to go upon land for the purpose of entertainment, such as to witness a sporting event or to attend a theatre. At times such a license is called a license personal to distinguish it from a license real wherein the main purpose of the license involves the use of the land itself.[4]

A license personal may be irrevocable for reasons of public policy. For example, while the general rule is that a license to visit a place of amusement may be revoked,[5] even if this may result in contractual liability, statutes have been passed in some states declaring such a privilege to be irrevocable except for cause.[6] It is generally recognized that a license personal is irrevocable if it is coupled with an interest. In Wood v. Manley (Eng.),[7] the defendant purchased hay that was stacked on land leased to the plaintiff. The court held

---

1. See, 5 Rest.Property, § 512, *Comment h.*

2. See supra, § 10.

3. See Thomas v. Sorrell, [1673] Vaugh. 330, 124 Eng.Rep. 1089, 1109.

4. See Conard, An Analysis of Licenses in Land, 42 Col.Law Rev. 809 (1942).

5. See Marrone v. Washington Jockey Club, 1913, 227 U.S. 633, 33 S.Ct. 401, 57 L.Ed. 679; Wood v. Leadbitter, [1845] 13 M. & W. 838, 153 Eng.Rep. 351; Revocability of Licenses—The Rule of Wood v. Leadbitter, 13 Mich.Law Rev. 401 (1915); Conard, The Privilege of Forcibly Ejecting an Amusement Patron, 90 Univ. of Pa.Law Rev. 809 (1942).

6. See, for example, the application of a California statute in Western Turf Ass'n v. Greenberg, 1907, 204 U.S. 359, 27 S.Ct. 384, 51 L.Ed. 520.

7. 11 Ad. & E. 34, 113 Eng.Rep. 325 (1839).

that defendant could not be held liable as a trespasser even though he went upon the land and removed the hay without plaintiff's consent. The Restatement of Property defines a license coupled with an interest as one which is incidental to the ownership of an interest in a chattel personal located on the land with respect to which the license exists.[8] If a contract for the sale of standing timber does not pass ownership of the timber until it is severed from the land, a license to go upon the land may be revoked prior to that time.[9]

ORAL LICENSE ACTED UPON

39. The creation of an easement or profit must ordinarily comply with the formalities prescribed by the Statute of Frauds.

a. **Oral license acted upon: extinguishment of an easement or profit. If an oral license is acted upon it may result in the extinguishment of an easement or profit.**

b. **Oral license acted upon: creation of an easement or profit. If a licensee expends funds in erecting improvements, acting in reliance on an oral license, the license may be converted into an easement or profit.**

A license that contemplates a direct use of land is a license real and, to this extent, is not distinguishable from an easement or a profit. If the understanding is that such a license may be revoked at will it may be created by an oral agreement. The creation of such a minimal interest in land is not within the scope of the real-property section of the Statute of Frauds. If a more extended duration is contemplated a profit or easement is involved and there must be compliance with the common law requirement of a "deed of grant." Otherwise, except as noted, the li-

cense may be revoked at any time. In some cases it is stated that if the parties failed to comply with the prescribed formalities the intent was probably to create only a license.[10]

Oral License Acted Upon: Extinguishment of an Easement or Profit

An easement or a profit may be extinguished by an oral license acted upon. In Winter v. Brockwell (Eng.),[11] A was the owner of an easement for light and air and B was the owner of the servient estate. A orally authorized B to erect a skylight that would, if erected, interfere with A's easement. The court held that A could not revoke the license after B had acted in reliance thereon and expended funds in erecting the improvement.[12] There was sufficient outward manifestations of the intention of the parties to satisfy the policy of the Statute of Frauds. In addition, the decision resulted in the extinguishment of an easement. Application of this rule tends to "clear land titles."

Oral License Acted Upon: Creation of an Easement or Profit

If a licensor and licensee intend to create only a license, revocation by the licensor may come at any time regardless of expenditures made by the licensee in reliance on the agreement.[13]

A license implied by law may also be revoked at any time regardless of expenditures made by the licensee. In West River Power Co. v. Bussino (Vt.),[14] plaintiff erected poles

---

8. 5 Rest.Property, § 513.

9. Emerson v. Shores, 1901, 95 Me. 237, 49 A. 1051; Drake v. Wells, 1865, 11 Allen (Mass.) 141; Burkhart v. Cartwright, 1960, 221 Or. 26, 350 P.2d 185.

10. See Emerson v. Shores, 1901, 95 Me. 237, 49 A. 1051; Smyth v. Brooklyn Union Elevated R. Co., 1907, 121 App.Div. 282, 105 N.Y.S. 610.

11. 8 East. 308, 103 Eng.Rep. 359 (1807).

12. *Accord:* Vogler v. Geiss, 1879, 51 Md. 407.

13. St. Louis Nat'l Stockyards v. Wiggins Ferry Co., 1884, 112 Ill. 384.

14. 111 Vt. 137, 11 A.2d 263 (1940).

and strung wires on defendants' land. No express license had been given but one of the defendants knew that the improvements were being erected and made no objection. The court held that the license implied by law, resulting from failure on the part of defendants to object, could be revoked.

The preferred view is that an oral license acted upon may be converted into an easement or profit if evidence does not show that the parties intended to create a license only.[15] This conversion may result because of the fact that the licensee expended substantial amounts in erecting improvements in reliance on the license. Acts incident to the erection of improvements constitute a sufficient outward manifestation of intent to satisfy the policy of the Statute of Frauds. Thus, specific performance of the agreement is justified. If the oral agreement was silent as to consideration then the case may call for an application of the doctrine of promissory estoppel. The avoidance of hardship is an important factor leading to this conclusion.

The duration of the profit or easement should conform with the terms of the oral agreement. If no time was agreed upon, the duration should be measured by the life of the improvement erected.[16] Although there is authority to the contrary, the owner of the easement should have the right to make necessary repairs even though he may not have a right to make replacements.[17] If revocation of the oral license is denied solely because of the hardship involved, the duration of the profit or easement should be limited to a term which would afford the licensee compensation for his expenditures.[18]

Because of the Statute of Frauds, many authorities follow the view that an oral license may be revoked at any time regardless of improvements erected by the licensee. This conclusion avoids the creation of a profit or easement by parol.[19] However, in Brehm v. Richards (Md.),[20] as a condition of revocation the licensor was required to compensate the licensee to the extent that the improvements increased the value of the land. This unjust-enrichment rule is not applicable to one who may purchase the land from the licensor.[21]

---

15. Flickinger v. Shaw, 1890, 87 Cal. 126, 25 P. 268 (consideration); Stoner v. Zucker, 1906, 148 Cal. 516, 83 P. 808 (no consideration); Brantley v. Perry, 1904, 120 Ga. 760, 48 S.E. 332; Stoering v. Swanson, 1918, 139 Minn. 115, 165 N.W. 875; Fitzsimmons v. Gilmore, 1938, 134 Neb. 200, 278 N.W. 262; Powers v. Coos Bay Lumber Co., 1954, 200 Or. 329, 263 P.2d 913; Rerick v. Kern, 1826, 14 Serg. & R.(Pa.) 267. See Conrad, Easements, Licenses and the Statute of Frauds, 15 Temple Univ. Law Qt. 222, 233 (1941).

16. Grimshaw v. Belcher, 1891, 88 Cal. 217, 26 P.2d 84; Carleton v. Redington, 1850, 21 N.H. 291; Phillips v. Cutler, 1915, 89 Vt. 233, 95 A. 487.

17. See, Grimshaw v. Belcher, 1891, 88 Cal. 217, 26 P. 84; Carleton v. Redington, 1850, 21 N.H. 291.

18. See, 5 Rest. Property, § 519, *Comment to Subsection (4) (g)*.

19. Baird v. Westberg, 1931, 341 Ill. 616, 173 N.E. 820, criticized in 26 Ill.Law Rev. 436 (1931); Cook v. Stearns, 1814, 11 Mass. 533; Crosdale v. Lanigan, 1892, 129 N.Y. 604, 29 N.E. 824; Henry v. Dalton, 1959, 89 R.I. 150, 151 A.2d 362; Fentiman v. Smith, [1803] 4 East. 107, 102 Eng.Rep. 770; Hewlins v. Shippan, [1826] 5 Barn. & C. 221, 108 Eng.Rep. 82.

20. 152 Md. 126, 136 A. 618, 56 A.L.R. 1103 (1927).

21. Mayor etc., of Baltimore v. Brack, 1939, 175 Md. 615, 3 A.2d 471, 120 A.L.R. 543, noted in 25 Va.Law Rev. 735 (1939).

CHAPTER 9

COVENANTS IN DEEDS AND EQUITABLE LAND BURDENS

COVENANTS IN DEEDS

40. At common law, covenants in deeds other than those pertaining to title are not enforceable as contractual obligations by and against remote parties in the absence of privity of estate. However, enforcement may be available in equity.

The common law rule is that privity of estate does not arise merely because there is a grantor-grantee relationship. The prevailing American rule is that privity of estate may arise because of that relationship. As such, covenants in deed that touch and concern the land may be enforceable by and against remote parties.

   a. Covenants affecting profits or easements. Privity of estate exists between the owner of an easement or profit and the owner of the land that is burdened with the servitude.

   b. Covenants between the owner of a possessory estate and the owner of an equitable interest in the same land. Privity of estate exists between the owner of a possessory estate and the owner of an equitable interest in the same land.

The general rule is that a person cannot be held liable for breach of contract unless it is shown that he was a party to the contract. In other words, contractual obligations are personal in nature and privity of contract is essential for the establishment of such liability. Variations or exceptions to this rule are to be found in the law as it relates to the assignment of contract rights and contracts made for the benefit of third parties.

This concept of privity of contract cannot be ignored merely because of the fact that a plaintiff seeks to establish contractual liability based on a covenant contained in a lease or in a deed. However, there is a recognized substitute for privity of contract. It is called privity of estate.

It is well established that certain types of covenants contained in a *lease* may be enforced by and against those who may succeed to the estates of the original contracting parties. The existence of tenure satisfies the requirement of privity of estate. It is also generally recognized that if the contracting parties have mutual and coexisting interests in the same land their successors in interest may be bound by covenants that relate to the "common interest." For example, a covenant on the part of the owner or a profit or an easement and the owner of the servient estate may be enforced by and against their successors in interest.[1]

There is a difference of opinion as to the rights and liabilities of remote parties with respect to covenants contained in a deed that conveys an estate in fee simple. Since the passage of the statute *Quia Emptores*[2] tenure does not exist as between the grantor and the grantee and certainly does not exist as between the grantor or his successors and one who may succeed to the estate of the

---

1. See cases cited in note 18, **infra.**

2. 18 Edw. I, cc. 1, 3 (1290).

grantee. And after the conveyance it cannot correctly be said that there are "mutual and coexisting interests" in the land conveyed.

Except in the case of covenants relating to title, a matter discussed under a separate heading,[3] the common law rule is that covenants in deeds are not enforceable, as such, by or against remote parties. The reason given for this conclusion is that there is neither privity of contract nor privity of estate in such a situation. But the lack of privity of estate is an excuse for the conclusion reached rather than a reason. A *fictitious* "privity of estate" could be found because of the grantor-grantee relationship.[4] It might even be held that privity of estate is not necessary for enforcement of such covenants.[5] But, as a matter of policy, it was considered desirable to deny legal relief for breach of such covenants and leave enforcement, if any, in the area of equitable relief, such as in the case of equitable servitudes and covenants enforceable in equity upon the ground of unjust enrichment.

The common law rule is followed in the California case of Los Angeles Terminal Land Co. v. Muir.[6] A covenant included in a deed conveying land in fee simple provided that no saloon should ever be maintained on the land conveyed and that the land should not be used for business purposes, other than for a hotel or lodging house. The court held that the covenant could not be enforced by the grantor against the defendant who acquired the estate from the original grantee with notice of the covenant.[7] The covenant did not create an *in rem*

interest, such as a profit or an easement. The grantee did not acquire a qualified fee. Privity of estate could not be shown and the restrictions were not created with the formalities required for enforcement as equitable servitudes.

The prevailing American rule probably is that privity of estate can be established out of a grantor-grantee relationship.[8] For example, in Georgia Railroad Co. v. Reeves (Ga.),[9] A conveyed part of his land to B and it was to be used as a railroad right of way. The deed contained a covenant that a depot and station would be erected on the land for the benefit of A and his assigns. Ownership of the land conveyed passed from B to C. The court held that C could be held liable for breach of the covenant.[10] It is usually considered that such a covenant is not binding upon remote parties (does not "run with the land") unless it affects the use and enjoyment of the land (it must "touch and concern" the land).[11] Early New York decisions held that only "restrictive covenants" could be enforced against remote parties.[12] However, the present New York rule is that affirmative covenants may be enforceable by and against remote parties.[13]

[3.] See infra, § 126.

[4.] 5 Rest.Property, § 534(a).

[5.] See 2, American Law of Property, § 9.11, p. 369.

[6.] 136 Cal. 36, 68 P. 308 (1902).

[7.] *Accord:* McIntosh v. Vail, 1943, 126 W.Va. 395, 28 S.E.2d 607, 151 A.L.R. 804.

[8.] 5 Rest.Property, § 534(a). See Chesapeake & Ohio Ry. Co. v. Willis, 1958, 200 Va. 299, 105 S.E.2d 833 (covenant to maintain fences considered to be a covenant running with the land, rather than an easement, and ceased to run with the land when a cause of action for breach was outlawed by the Statute of Limitations).

[9.] 64 Ga. 492 (1880).

[10.] See note, 23 Harv.Law Rev. 298 (1910).

[11.] Epting v. Lexington Water Power Co., 1935, 177 S.C. 308, 181 S.E. 66, 102 A.L.R. 773, noted in 13 N.Y.Univ.Law Quarterly Rev. 313 (1936).

[12.] Miller v. Clary, 1913, 210 N.Y. 127, 103 N.E. 1114, L.R.A.1918E, 222.

[13.] See Nicholson v. 300 Broadway Realty Corp., 1959, 7 N.Y.2d 240, 164 N.E.2d 832 (covenant to furnish heat).

Because of the existence of "privity of contract," the liability of a promisor may continue even after he has parted with his interest in the land with respect to which the promise was made.[14] This is especially true if the promise relates to the payment of money as distinguished from a specific use of the land.[15] However, if a covenant operates to create a profit or an easement, the original covenantor cannot be held liable for subsequent breach of covenant by one who acquires the servient estate.[16]

Covenants Affecting Profits or Easements

Even according to the common law rule, privity of estate exists between the owner of a profit or an easement and the owner of the land which is burdened with the servitude. This conclusion is based upon the fact that there are co-existing interests in the servient estate. A covenant entered into between such parties that pertains to the profit or easement may be enforced by or against their successors in interest.

It is immaterial whether the covenant imposes an affirmative obligation upon the covenantor or whether it is merely restrictive in nature. In Morse v. Aldrich (Mass.),[17] an easement in a body of water was created for the purpose of maintaining fish ponds. The servient owner covenanted to drain the water from the pond at specified periods each year. A subsequent purchaser of the servient estate was bound by the covenant.[18]

If an agreement relates to a party wall, a covenant by one party to pay a proportionate share of the value or cost of the wall may be enforced against his successors in interest. The benefit side of the covenant (a right to receive payment) may be enforced by one who succeeds to the interest of the covenantee if the parties intended that result.[19] This intent may be manifested by the fact that the covenants are made in behalf of the "heirs, administrators, executors and assigns."[20] The original covenantee may, of course, expressly reserve the right to enforce payment.[21] In New York a distinction is made between a case where immediate construction of the wall is contemplated and one where construction is to be at some future time. In the former situation the benefit side of the covenant is presumed to be personal to the covenantee. In the latter situation the purchaser of the land from the covenantee is presumably entitled to payment.[22]

In Lincoln v. Burrage (Mass.),[23] executors conveyed one of two adjoining lots upon which a party wall had been constructed. The grantee covenanted for himself, his heirs and assigns, to pay to the executors, or their successors, the value of a party wall which was located on the land conveyed if the covenan-

---

14. 5 Rest.Property, § 538.

15. See, for example, City of Glendale v. Barclay, 1963, 94 Ariz. 358, 385 P.2d 230.

16. Goldberg v. Nicola, 1935, 319 Pa. 183, 178 A. 809, 98 A.L.R. 774.

17. 36 Mass.(19 Pick.) 449 (1837).

18. See Carlson v. Libby, 1950, 137 Conn. 362, 77 A.2d 332; Everett Factories & Terminal Corp. v. Oldetyme Dist. Corp., 1938, 300 Mass. 499, 15 N.E.2d 829, 118 A.L.R. 965 (to pay part of expenses in

connection with the maintenance of a spur track); Shaber v. St. Paul Water Co., 1883, 30 Minn. 179, 14 N.W. 874 (apparently an easement in gross). *Cf.*: Wiggins Ferry Co. v. Ohio & Mississippi Railway Co., 1879, 94 Ill. 83.

19. McCormick v. Stonehart, Tex.Civ.App.1917, 195 S.W. 883.

20. Southworth v. Perring, 1905, 71 Kan. 755, 81 P. 481, 82 P. 785. *Contra:* Gibson v. Holden, 1885, 115 Ill. 199, 3 N.E. 282. See Aigler, Agreements to Pay for Party Walls, 10 Mich.Law Rev. 187, 200 (1912).

21. Conduitt v. Ross, 1885, 102 Ind. 166, 26 N.E. 198.

22. Crawford v. Krollpfeiffer, 1909, 195 N.Y. 185, 88 N.E. 29.

23. 177 Mass. 378, 59 N.E. 67 (1901).

tee should make use of the wall. Thereafter, the defendant acquired ownership of the land and made use of the wall. Action was brought by the covenantees to recover payment. Recovery was denied. At the time of the sale to the original covenantor the executors (covenantees) did not have any interest in the adjoining lot, having previously sold that lot to a third party. Accordingly, neither privity of contract nor privity of estate could be established as between the plaintiffs and defendant. Plaintiffs retained no interest in the land that would support the claim of privity.

Covenants between the Owner of a Possessory Estate and the Owner of an Equitable Interest in the same Land

Privity of estate exists as between the owner of a possessory estate and the owner of an equitable interest in the land. Therefore, a covenant entered into between such owners pertaining to the equitable interest may be enforced by or against successors to the interest of the covenantor or the covenantee. In Sacramento Suburban Fruit Lands Co. v. Whaley (Cal.),[24] a mortgagee covenanted to release from the lien of the mortgage any ten acres of the encumbered land upon the payment of a stated amount. It is held that the one who acquired the interest of the mortgagor was entitled to the benefit of the covenant as against a transferee of the mortgagee.

EQUITABLE SERVITUDES

41. Building restrictions and restrictions relating to land use may be enforceable in equity by and between landowners in the restricted area. In that event the restrictions are called equitable servitudes.

a. Dominant estate. Equitable servitudes can be created only for the use and enjoyment of land (a dominant estate).

24. 50 Cal.App. 125, 194 P. 1054 (1920).

b. Restrictive covenant. Only restrictive covenants are enforceable as equitable servitudes.

c. Creation of equitable servitudes. A writing is necessary for the creation of equitable servitudes but they may be implied from the establishment of a general building plan or scheme.

d. Reserved right to release restrictions. A general power to release restrictions, reserved by the grantor, is inconsistent with the creation of equitable servitudes.

e. Power of termination. Equitable servitudes may be created even if the grantor reserves the power to terminate an estate for breach of the restrictions (power of termination).

f. Construction of deed. It is not necessary that restrictions embodied in a deed that conveys a possessory estate be set forth in the granting clause.

g. Denial of equitable relief. Equitable relief will be denied if the defendant qualifies as a *bona fide* purchaser for value and without notice.

Restrictions may not be enforceable because of estoppel, waiver or abandonment of rights by the plaintiff or because of the relative hardships involved or because of changed conditions.

Restrictions pertaining to land-use may be susceptible of effective enforcement in equity in two types of situations. *First:* When the equitable enforcement is supplementary to the legal remedies at law for breach of contract or the invasion of a property right. *Second:* When the restriction is cognizable only in equity. The former is merely a plan of the general law for equitable relief. The latter is peculiarly a problem of property law.

Historically, the common law courts adopted a strict and rigid attitude against restrictions relating to land-use in the case of estates in fee simple. Only certain types of restrictions were recognized as, for instance, restrictions occasioned by easements and profits [25] and those that might inhere in a fee simple determinable or in a fee simple subject to a condition subsequent.[26]

The needs of a developing society required that judicial recognition be extended to restrictions of other types. For example, land for residential purposes could more readily be sold if the new owner could be assured that the land would retain its characteristic as "residential property." Public policy favored this type of community development. The purpose could best be accomplished by recognizing restrictions that could be enforced by and against the landowners in the restricted area, *i.e.* enforced among themselves (*inter sese*).

Building restrictions and restrictions as to the use of land could have been enforced if the common law courts had seen fit to recognize such interests as easements, but such recognition was denied. Of course, an easement for light and air is recognized and there is no reason why restrictions relating to setback lines should not be enforceable as easements.[27] Restrictions relating to land-use may be enforced if embodied as limitations or conditions in the conveyance of an estate in fee simple determinable or an estate in fee simple subject to a condition subsequent. But this technique would not place enforcement in the hands of the various landowners.

In the early leading English case of Tulk v. Moxhay,[28] A sold part of his land to B in fee simple and B covenanted for himself, his heirs and assigns, that designated restrictions would be observed with respect to the land sold. Thereafter, B conveyed the land to C in fee simple and he took with notice of the restrictions. The court held that the restrictions could be enforced against C, this relief being granted on the basis of unjust enrichment. It was assumed that the price which C paid for the land was fixed upon the hypothesis that the restrictions were enforceable. If not so enforceable, C would receive a benefit which he had not contemplated and A, the original grantor, would lose the benefits that the restrictions would afford the land retained by him.[29] Thus, the enforcement of the restrictions was placed on an *in personam* basis. Subsequent decisions, however, indicate that such restrictions result in the creation of an equitable interest in the land (an *in rem* interest). It was held, for example, that restrictions could be enforced against one who acquired title to land by adverse possession.[30]

American decisions are in conflict as to the nature of the restrictions under discussion, usually referred to as equitable servitudes. A number of decisions follow the view that only *in personam* rights are involved. It is held, for example, that a landowner is not entitled to compensation if other land is taken in eminent domain proceedings for a use that is in violation of restrictions.[31] However, the preferred view is that equitable servi-

---

25. For discussion of easements and profits, see supra, Chapter 7.

26. For discussion of the various types of estates in fee, see supra, § 2.

27. Hogan v. Barry, 1886, 143 Mass. 538, 10 N.E. 253; Muzzarelli v. Hulshizer, 1894, 163 Pa. 643, 30 A. 291. *Contra:* Cotton v. Cresse, 1912, 80 N.J. Eq. 540, 85 A. 600. See Stone, The Equitable Rights and Liabilities of Strangers to a Contract, 18 Col.Law Rev. 291, 293, n. 3 (1918).

28. 2 Ph. 774, 41 Eng.Rep. 1143 (1848).

29. See, Clark, Equitable Servitudes, 16 Mich.Law Rev. 90, 91 (1917).

30. In re Nisbet and Pott's Contract, [1906] 1 Ch. 386.

31. Friesen v. City of Glendale, 1930, 209 Cal. 524, 288 P. 1080 (*dictum*); Sackett v. School District, 1931, 118 Cal.App. 254, 5 P.2d 23; Anderson v. Lynch, 1939, 188 Ga. 154, 3 S.E.2d 85, 122 A.L.R. 1456. *Cf.:* Moses v. Hazen, 1934, 63 App.D.C. 104, 69 F.2d 842, 98 A.L.R. 386. See Comment, 14 Wash. Law Rev. 137 (1939).

tudes involve *in rem* interests in the nature of equitable easements. The interest is considered to be enforceable against one who acquires the restricted area under an original title, such as a tax deed.[32] If the restricted area is acquired in eminent domain proceedings for a use that is in violation of restrictions, those entitled to benefits under the restrictions are entitled to compensation.[33] A suit to enjoin violations may be maintained at any time within the statutory period applicable in the case of prescriptive rights. The right is not barred by the ordinary Statute of Limitations relating to actions for breach of contract or damage to land.[34]

Dominant Estate

An equitable servitude implies that a correlative benefit to land must flow from the imposition of the servitude. Hence, the existence of a dominant estate (land that will benefit through the enforcement of a restriction) is essential.[35]

In London County Council v. Allen (Eng.),[36] A applied to the Council for permission to construct a road. The permission was granted in reliance upon A's covenant that neither he nor his heirs or assigns would erect buildings on A's land that was adjacent to the contemplated road. The Council owned no land in that locality. Thereafter, A conveyed the land to B who purchased with notice of the covenant. Because a dominant estate was not involved the court held that the restriction could not be enforced as an equitable servitude.[37] It has been suggested that the land which the Council owned in the abutting street could have been considered to be the dominant estate.[38] Land which may be acquired under a specifically enforceable contract may qualify as a dominant estate.[39]

Restrictive Covenant

Courts have always been loath to enforce a covenant which would tend unduly to burden titles or impose upon the courts the burden of supervision. Therefore, only restrictive covenants, as distinguished from those requiring affirmative acts by the covenantee, are considered as creating equitable servitudes.[40]

---

32. Schlafly v. Baumann, 1937, 341 Mo. 755, 108 S. W.2d 363, noted in 3 Mo.Law Rev. 326 (1938); Northwestern Improvement Co. v. Lowry, 1937, 104 Mont. 289, 66 P.2d 792, 110 A.L.R. 605, noted in 12 Wash.Law Rev. 300 (1937); Crawford v. Senosky, 1929, 128 Or. 229, 274 P. 306; Hayes v. Gibbs, 1946, 110 Utah 54, 169 P.2d 781, 168 A.L.R. 513. *Contra:* Nedderman v. City of Des Moines, 1936, 221 Iowa 1352, 268 N.W. 36.

33. Town of Stamford v. Vuono, 1928, 108 Conn. 359, 143 A. 245; Allen v. City of Detroit, 1911, 167 Mich. 464, 133 N.W. 317; Peters v. Buckner, 1921, 288 Mo. 618, 232 S.W. 1024, 17 A.L.R. 543; Hayes v. Waverly & Passaic R. Co., 1893, 51 N.J.Eq. 345, 27 A. 648; Flynn v. New York, Westchester & Boston Railway Co., 1916, 218 N.Y. 140, 112 N.E. 913, noted in 30 Harv.Law Rev. 89 (1916).

34. McLaughlin v. Neiger, Mo.App.1956, 286 S.W.2d 380; Jinkins v. City of Jal, 1963, 73 N.M. 173, 386 P.2d 599.

35. But see Metropolitan Investment Co. v. Sine, 1962, 14 Utah 2d 36, 376 P.2d 940 (purpose of restriction was the protection of a business). The

restriction may be imposed for the protection of land owned by a third party (Vogeler v. Alwyn Imp. Corp., 1928, 247 N.Y. 131, 159 N.E. 886).

36. 3 K.B. 642 [1914], noted in 13 Mich.Law Rev. 150 (1914).

37. *Accord:* Foreman v. Sadler's Ex'rs, 1911, 114 Md. 574, 80 A. 298; Orenberg v. Johnston, 1929, 269 Mass. 312, 168 N.E. 794, noted in 39 Yale Law Jr. 911 (1930); Wilmurt v. McGrane, 1897, 16 App. Div. 412, 45 N.Y.S. 32. *Contra:* Van Sant v. Rose, 1913, 260 Ill. 401, 103 N.E. 194. See Simpson, Fifty Years of American Equity, 50 Harv.Law Rev. 171, 215 (1936).

38. See note 28 Harv.Law Rev. 201 (1914).

39. Bessinnett v. White, 1926, 58 Ont.Law Rep. 125, noted in 39 Harv.Law Rev. 775 (1926).

40. See 3 Tiffany, Real Property (3rd ed.) § 756.

Creation of Equitable Servitudes

Usually, equitable servitudes are created as the result of covenants relating to the use of land that are embodied in a deed that conveys a possessory estate. However, the conveyance of a possessory estate in land is not essential to the creation of equitable servitudes any more than it is essential to the creation of profits or easements. Landowners in a specific area may join together in the execution of a document placing restrictions upon their land that are enforceable *inter sese* (among themselves).[41]

In jurisdictions following the view that an equitable servitude is an interest in land, its creation must be in writing because of the real-property section of the Statute of Frauds.[42] In jurisdictions following the view that equitable servitudes involve mere contract rights, a written instrument is necessary because the Statute of Frauds usually provides that a contract not to be performed within a year must be in writing.[43] In some cases oral promises respecting the use of land have been enforced, apparently upon the ground of estoppel.[44]

Usually, equitable servitudes are created in connection with the conveyance of a possessory estate. This requires proof of the fact that the grantor and the grantee intend-

ed the creation of such interests. In Doerr v. Cobbs (Mo.),[45] A, the owner of two lots that were separated by an alley, conveyed lot #1 to B and his heirs. The deed contained a restriction against building within forty feet of the street. Some time later A conveyed lot #2 to C and his heirs, and this deed contained a restriction identical in form to the one contained in B's deed. The court held that a subsequent purchaser of lot #1 could not enforce the restriction as against a subsequent purchaser of lot #2. When A conveyed lot #1 he did not insert any provision in the deed that would evidence the fact that he intended the restriction to attach to the land retained by him (lot #2). An express covenant restricting the use of land conveyed does not raise, by implication, a corresponding covenant restricting the use of land retained by the common grantor.[46] According to some decisions, however, such an implication may arise.[47]

The most satisfactory way to create equitable servitudes is by apt language in a deed or recorded plat[48] that sets forth the restrictions and expresses the intent of the parties. There should be a statement that the restrictions are binding with respect to the land conveyed as well as to the land retained by the grantor and the land so retained should be

41. Wayt v. Patee, 1928, 205 Cal. 46, 269 P. 660; Jones v. Eilenstine, Kan.App.1963, 369 S.W.2d 278; O'Neal v. Vose, 1944, 193 Okl. 451, 145 P.2d 411. See 5 Rest. Property, § 539, *Comment i.*

42. Waterhouse v. Capital Inv. Co., 1960, 44 Hawaii 235, 353 P.2d 1007; Sprague v. Kimball, 1913, 213 Mass. 380, 100 N.E. 622; Miller v. Babb, Tex.Civ. App.1924, 263 S.W. 253, noted in 3 Tex.Law Rev. 101 (1924).

43. Long v. Cramer Meat & Packing Co., 1909, 155 Cal. 402, 101 P. 297.

44. Tallmadge v. East River Bank, 1862, 26 N.Y. 105. See Reeves v. Morris, 1942, 155 Kan. 231, 124 P.2d 488.

45. 146 Mo.App. 342, 123 S.W. 547 (1909).

46. McKenrick v. Savings Bank of Baltimore, 1938, 174 Md. 118, 197 A. 580; Mission Covenant Church v. Nelson, 1958, 253 Minn. 230, 91 N.W.2d 440; McNichol v. Townsend, 1907, 73 N.J.Eq. 276, 67 A. 938.

47. Weil v. Hill, 1915, 193 Ala. 407, 69 So. 438; Ball v. Millikin, 1910, 31 R.I. 36, 76 A. 789; Boyden v. Roberts, 1907, 131 Wis. 659, 111 N.W. 701.

48. See Wischmeyer v. Finch, 1952, 231 Ind. 282, 107 N.E.2d 661. But declaration of tract restrictions, even though of record, is not effective to impose equitable servitudes until at least one lot has been conveyed (Girard v. Miller, 1963, 214 Cal.App.2d 266, 29 Cal.Rptr. 359).

specifically described.[49] In a few states the creation of equitable servitudes depends upon compliance with these formalities.[50] This assures certainty both with respect to the intent of the parties and the extent of the land that is to be subject to restrictions.[51]

The prevailing rule is that expressions of intent to create equitable servitudes need not be embodied in a deed or recorded plat. The intention may be implied from the fact that the landowner established a "general building plan or scheme" of development.[52] This may be shown by the fact that similar restrictions were imposed upon land similarly located.[53] Restrictions in a subdivided area need not be uniform in order to establish a

general building plan or scheme. Some areas may be restricted for residential use and others for parks, places of amusement or business.

Reserved Right to Release Restrictions

The preferred view is that a reservation by a common grantor of a *general power* to release restrictions is inconsistent with the creation of equitable servitudes.[54] If such a power exists the restrictions are not mutually enforceable by and between the owners of land in the restricted area. However, such interests may exist if the grantor reserved a *limited power*, such as a power to release one lot from the restrictions.[55] This is true to the extent that an exercise of the limited power would not disturb the existence of "the general plan or scheme" of development.

Power of Termination

The reservation of a power of termination is compatible with the creation of equitable servitudes.[56] However, the release of such a power to the owners of land in the restricted area will not prejudice other landowners in their enforcement of the restrictions. Of course, a conveyance of land subject to "conditions, restrictions and reservations," is not

49. But see Buckley v. Mooney, 1954, 339 Mich. 398, 63 N.W.2d 655 (must be made binding upon *present as well as future owners* of the land retained).

50. See Palermo v. Allen, 1962, 91 Ariz. 57, 369 P.2d 906; Werner v. Graham, 1919, 181 Cal. 174, 183 P. 945.

51. *Cf.:* McCurdy v. Standard Realty Corp., 1943, 295 Ky. 587, 175 S.W.2d 28 (where dispute related to extent of the restricted area).

52. Virgin v. Garrett, 1936, 233 Ala. 34, 169 So. 711; Bachman v. Colpaert Realty Corp., 1935, 101 Ind. App. 306, 194 N.E. 783; Allen v. City of Detroit, 1911, 167 Mich. 464, 133 N.W. 317; De Gray v. Monmouth Beach Club House Co., 1892, 50 N.J. Eq. 329, 24 A. 388, followed in La Fetra v. Beveridge, 1938, 124 N.J.Eq. 24, 199 A. 70; Anderson v. Marshall-Malaise Lumber Co., 1935, 66 N.D. 216, 263 N.W. 721; Frey v. Poynor, Okl.1962, 369 P.2d 168; Bethea v. Lockhart, Tex.Civ.App.1939, 127 S.W.2d 1029; Cheatham v. Taylor, 1927, 148 Va. 26, 138 S.E. 545, discussed in 17 Va.Law Rev. 607 (1931); Stein v. Endres Home Builders, Inc., 1938, 228 Wis. 620, 280 N.W. 316; Nottingham Patent Brick & Tile Co. v. Butler [1885] 15 Q.B. 261. See Strachan, Restrictive Covenants Affecting Land, 46 Law Quarterly Rev. 159 (1930). *Cf.:* Snow v. Van Dam, 1935, 291 Mass. 477, 197 N.E. 224; Solar v. Ruehlman, 1929, 33 Ohio App. 224, 168 N.E. 861.

53. See King v. James, 1950, 88 Ohio App. 213, 97 N.E. 2d 235. But the restrictions need not be identical (Hooker v. Alexander, 1942, 129 Conn. 433, 29 A.2d 308; Hartt v. Rueter, 1916, 223 Mass. 207, 111 N.E. 1045.

54. Palermo v. Allen, 1962, 91 Ariz. 57, 369 P.2d 906; Rankin v. Brown, 1948, 142 N.J.Eq. 180, 59 A.2d 645; Suttle v. Bailey, 1961, 68 N.M. 283, 361 P.2d 325; Rose v. Jasima Realty Corp., 1926, 218 App.Div. 646, 219 N.Y.S. 222; Humphrey v. Beall, 1939, 215 N.C. 15, 200 S.E. 918; Price v. Anderson, 1948, 358 Pa. 209, 56 A.2d 215, 2 A.L.R.2d 593. *Contra:* Burkhardt v. Lofton, 1944, 63 Cal.App.2d 230, 146 P.2d 720; Stein v. Endres Home Builders, Inc., 1938, 228 Wis. 620, 280 N.W. 316. *Cf.:* Hall v. Gulledge, 1962, 274 Ala. 105, 145 So.2d 794 (one of the factors to be considered); Patrone v. Falcone, 1963, 345 Mass. 634, 189 N.E.2d 228.

55. Mangini v. Oak Park Trust and Savings Bank, 1963, 43 Ill.App.2d 318, 193 N.E.2d 479.

56. Robertson v. Nichols, 1949, 92 Cal.App.2d 201, 206 P.2d 898.

a sufficient expression of intention to create equitable servitudes.[57]

Construction of a Deed

It is not necessary that restrictions embodied in a deed be set forth in the granting clause.[58] In some states it is held that the estate conveyed in the granting clause cannot be qualified by provisions in other parts of the deed.[59] But equitable servitudes do not qualify the estate conveyed. They merely relate to the use of the land.

Denial of Equitable Relief

A donee of land takes subject to equitable servitudes even though he acquires ownership without notice.[60] But equitable servitudes cannot be enforced against a *bona fide* purchaser for value and without notice. The purchaser may be charged with constructive notice if the instrument creating equitable servitudes is recorded as authorized by law and is in his chain of title.[61] Notice may also be charged to him if the physical condition of the land evidences the existence of restrictions.[62] Other situations that involve enforcement problems are as follows:

First: The granting of equitable relief depends upon proof of the fact that defendant's conduct constitutes a violation of the restriction. In Boston-Edison Protective Ass'n v. Paulist Fathers (Mich.),[63] land was to be used only for a "single dwelling house" and "dwelling house purposes only." Claimed violation of the restriction consisted of occupancy by five priests and two servants. In denying this claim it is pointed out that a place may be used as a dwelling even though the occupants are not related by blood or marriage.[64] But the construction of a house for use by a college fraternity violates a restriction limiting use of the property to "one single private dwelling house."[65] So also, use of property as a rooming house violates a restriction that limits use to a "one-family" dwelling.[66]

A restriction that property is to be used only as a "single dwelling house" is to be distinguished from a restriction of use to "one family." The word "family" is usually restricted to persons who are related by blood or marriage.[67] However, in construing restrictive covenants, occupancy of property by an incidental dweller, such as a roomer or boarder, may not be considered to be a violation of such a restriction.[68]

---

57. King v. Snyder, 1961, 189 Cal.App.2d 482, 11 Cal.Rptr. 328.

58. Cleveland Realty Co. v. Hobbs, 1964, 261 N.C. 414, 135 S.E.2d 30.

59. See for example, Carllee v. Ellsberry, 1907, 82 Ark. 209, 101 S.W. 407, 12 L.R.A.,N.S., 956. The prevailing rule is that a deed is construed as a whole and that one part is not given priority over another part of the instrument (McCullock v. Holmes, 1892, 111 Mo. 445, 19 S.W. 1096. However, if there is an irreconcilable conflict, provisions in the "premises" will prevail over provisions in a subsequent part of the deed, such as the "habendum" (Bennett v. Langham), 1964, — Tenn. —, 383 S.W.2d 16).

60. See Bridgewater v. Ocean City R. Co., 1901, 62 N.J.Eq. 276, 49 A. 801, affirmed, 63 N.J.Eq. 798, 52 A. 1130.

61. See infra, § 131.

62. Hegna v. Peters, 1925, 199 Iowa 259, 201 N.W. 803.

63. 306 Mich. 253, 10 N.W.2d 847, 148 A.L.R. 364 (1943).

64. See Wallace v. St. Clair, 1962, — W.Va. —, 127 S.E.2d 742 (the word "dwelling" and the words "single dwelling" refer not only to type of building but also to permissible use).

65. Seeley v. Phi Sigma Delta House Corp., 1928, 245 Mich. 252, 222 N.W. 180.

66. Hooker v. Alexander, 1942, 129 Conn. 433, 29 A.2d 308. *Cf.:* Nerrerter v. Little, 1932, 258 Mich. 462, 243 N.W. 25.

67. Simons v. Work of God Corporation, 1962, 36 Ill.App.2d 199, 183 N.E.2d 729.

68. See Southampton Civic Club v. Couch, 1959, 159 Tex. 464, 322 S.W.2d 516.

There are conflicting views as to the scope of a restriction prohibiting the erection on the land of anything except a "dwelling house." According to one view this limits construction to a single-family dwelling.[69] In other decisions such a restriction is not considered to be violated by the erection of a building to house two or more families.[70] This conclusion is reached upon the ground that a rule of strict construction should be followed as a means by which to curtail the creation of "land burdens" that tend to place restraints upon alienation.

In Bove v. Giebel (Ohio),[71] land in a subdivision was restricted "for residential purposes only." The owner of land in this restricted area claimed a right to construct a road across his land in order to establish a means of ingress and egress to land that he owned outside the restricted area. The court held that this proposed use would not violate the restriction if residential-use restrictions were placed on the land to which access was claimed.

Second: Equitable relief may be denied upon the ground that the complaining party participated in restriction-violations. The defense of waiver may be available if complaint had not been made of known violations.[72] However, this is not true if the violations were in other blocks or on other streets of the restricted area where the use was not directly injurious to him.[73] Evidence may also establish the fact that an intent to impose restrictions was abandoned, such as where restrictions were not imposed in connection with the sale of a substantial part of the area involved.[74]

Even if the intent to impose restrictions is not abandoned, violations of restrictions may be so extensive as to justify the conclusion that the entire scheme of development as conceived and established has been abandoned. This issue of abandonment must be resolved by reference to the number and seriousness of the violations and the extent to which they have infected the entire restricted area.[75]

Third: Injunctive relief against violations of equitable servitudes may be denied "if the harm done by granting the injunction will be disproportionate to the benefit secured thereby."[76] This process of "balancing the equities" is followed in equitable servitude cases the same as in a case where injunctive relief is sought against the continuance of a private nuisance. Public interest may weigh heavily against injunctive relief if the economic interest of a community is involved. That would be the case if an injunction would hamper the operation of a key industry. An award of damages may be made as a substitute for injunctive relief.

Fourth: Usually, equitable servitudes are created as a means by which to preserve the residential character of a particular area.

---

69. Schadt v. Brill, 1913, 173 Mich. 647, 139 N.W. 878, noted in 11 Mich.Law Rev. 521 (1913).

70. Bear v. Bernstein, 1948, 251 Ala. 230, 36 So.2d 483, 14 A.L.R.2d 1372; Bruno v. Hanna, 1960, 63 N.J.Super. 282, 164 A.2d 647; Charlotte Consol. Const. Co. v. Cobb, 1928, 195 N.C. 690, 143 S.E. 522.

71. 169 Ohio St. 325, 159 N.E.2d 425 (1959).

72. Wischmeyer v. Finch, 1952, 231 Ind. 282, 107 N.E.2d 661; Burns v. Beckenhauer, 1962, 368 Mich. 516, 118 N.W.2d 263; De Martini v. Hayhurst, 1936, 154 Or. 663, 62 P.2d 1 (unreasonable delay in enforcement).

73. Brideau v. Grissom, 1963, 369 Mich. 661, 120 N.W.2d 829; Barham v. Reames, Tex.Civ.App.1963, 366 S.W.2d 257.

74. Logan v. Sprinkle, 1961, 256 N.C. 41, 123 S.E.2d 209.

75. See Guyton v. Yancey, 1961, 240 La. 794, 125 So.2d 365.

76. See 5 Rest.Property, § 563.

They may be imposed as a means by which to regulate business operations and may even prohibit residential use. But a change in the nature of a locality insofar as use is concerned may be so "drastic" or "fundamental" as to nullify the purpose. In that event enforcement may be denied because this would be inequitable and unjust.[77] If unenforceable because of changed conditions, equitable servitudes, as interests in land, cease to exist. Enforcement will also be denied even if equitable servitudes are considered to be enforceable as contract rights. The contractual obligations are enforceable only if benefits accrue according to the intent of the original contracting parties.

A "drastic" or "fundamental" change may be brought about by conditions that develop from within or from without the restricted area.[78] According to one view, the restrictions may be destroyed by erosion.[79] This means that the restrictions may be enforceable in part of a restricted area and not in another part. Gradually, the entire area may be infected. According to another view, changed conditions will not be a sufficient justification for the denial of equitable relief unless it is shown that the change affects substantially all of the land in the restricted area.[80] Under either view it would seem that

while some restrictions may not be enforceable because of changed conditions it does not follow that other restrictions may not be enforced. For example, if a restriction relates to residential use only, a prohibition against operating a rooming house may be lifted because of changed conditions. It does not follow, however, that use of the land for other commercial purposes will be sanctioned.[81]

Enforcement of equitable servitudes will not be denied merely because of the fact that land may be more valuable if unrestricted as to use.[82] So also, restrictions cannot be destroyed by the enactment of a zoning ordinance authorizing a use other than that specified in the restrictions.[83] This may be true even if a zoning ordinance specifically prohibits the only use authorized according to the terms of the restrictions.[84] The fact that a zoning ordinance authorizes the use of land for business purposes may be some evidence of the fact that there has been a "drastic" or "fundamental" change in the area insofar as land-use is concerned.

The owner of land in a restricted area may quiet title against restrictions if they are not enforceable because of changed conditions.[85] Some decisions proceed upon the theory that this relief is available only by the payment of damages by the one seeking such

---

77. Key v. McCabe, 1960, 54 Cal.2d 736, 8 Cal.Rptr. 425, 356 P.2d 169; Anness v. Freeman, Ky.App. 1956, 294 S.W.2d 77; Jackson v. Stevenson, 1892, 156 Mass. 496. *Cf.:* Jones v. Eilenstine, Kan.App. 1963, 369 S.W.2d 278.

78. Downs v. Kroeger, 1927, 200 Cal. 743, 254 P. 1101, noted in 16 Cal.Law Rev. 58 (1927); Trustees of Columbia College v. Thacher, 1882, 87 N.Y. 311; Dunlap v. Beaty, 1961, 239 S.C. 196, 122 S.E.2d 9.

79. Atlas Terminals, Inc. v. Sokol, 1962, 203 Cal.App. 2d 68, 21 Cal.Rptr. 293. *Cf.:* Taylor Ave. Improvement Ass'n v. Detroit Trust Co., 1938, 283 Mich. 304, 278 N.W. 75.

80. Continental Oil Co. v. Fennemore, 1931, 38 Ariz. 277, 299 P. 132.

81. Morgan v. Matheson, 1961, 362 Mich. 535, 107 N.W.2d 825.

82. Ockenga v. Alken, 1942, 314 Ill.App. 389, 41 N.E. 2d 548.

83. Murphey v. Gray, 1958, 84 Ariz. 299, 327 P.2d 751; Whiting v. Seavey, 1963, 159 Me. 61, 188 A.2d 276.

84. See Bernard v. Schneider, 1962, 264 Minn. 104, 117 N.W.2d 755.

85. Marra v. Aetna Const. Co., 1940, 15 Cal.2d 375, 101 P.2d 490; Dunlap v. Beaty, 1961, 239 S.C. 196, 122 S.E.2d 9. See Simpson, Fifty Years of American Equity, 50 Harv.Law Rev. 171, 217 (1936).

relief. This conclusion is open to question because the restrictions are nullified by changed conditions.[86]

COVENANTS IN EQUITY

42. Even if a covenant may not be enforceable at law by and against remote parties, it may be enforceable in equity as a means by which to prevent unjust enrichment.

Regardless of privity of estate, a covenantee may be afforded equitable relief if there is a breach of the covenant with resultant unjust enrichment.[87] Injunctive relief may be available to prevent breach of a covenant respecting the use of personal property.[88] An equitable lien may be imposed upon land to assure payments according to the terms of a contract made by a prior owner. For example, in Fresno Canal etc., Co. v. Rowell (Cal.),[89] a landowner covenanted for himself and his assigns to take water at a stipulated rate and for a stated period. It was held that the covenant to pay for water created a lien enforceable against subsequent purchasers of the land with notice.[90] A lien may also arise out of a contract involving the sale of crops.[91] A lien may be imposed because of promises made by prior owners of the land to pay a proportionate share of the costs incident to maintenance of streets, lights and other improvements in the area.[92]

Equity may prevent the breach of an economic covenant. For example, in Dick v. Sears-Roebuck & Co. (Conn.),[93] A conducted a retail furniture store. He conveyed neighboring land to B who covenanted for himself and his assigns not to use the land acquired for the purpose of conducting a furniture store. The land was subsequently acquired by C who had notice of the covenant. The court held that he was bound by the covenant.[94] This covenant was not enforceable as an equitable servitude because it was not intended for the benefit of any land (there was no dominant estate).[95] It was not enforceable as an equitable lien because it did not involve the payment of money. A similar restriction may be enforced against a lessee who acquired his estate with notice.[96] According to some authorities, economic-benefit covenants are enforceable in equity even though

---

86. See McClure v. Leaycraft, 1905, 183 N.Y. 36, 75 N.E. 961; Hysinger v. Mullinax, 1958, 204 Tenn. 181, 319 S.W.2d 79.

87. See Russell v. Palos Verdes Properties, 1963, 218 Cal.App.2d 754, 32 Cal.Rptr. 488.

88. See, for example, Nadell & Co. v. Grasso, 1959, 175 Cal.App.2d 420, 346 P.2d 505.

89. 80 Cal. 114, 22 P. 53 (1889).

90. *Accord:* Orchard Homes Ditch Co. v. Snavely, 1945, 117 Mont. 484, 159 P.2d 521. See Maher v. Cleveland Union Stockyards Co., 1936, 55 Ohio App. 412, 9 N.E.2d 995, noted in 4 Ohio St.Univ. Law Jr., 93 (1937); 47 Yale Law Jr. 821 (1938) (promise to pass assessments that might be levied against the grantor's adjoining land because of the opening of a street).

91. See Arndt, Co-operative Marketing Associations, 9 Cal.Law Rev. 44, 49 (1920).

92. See Neponsit Property Owners' Ass'n, Inc. v. Emigrant Industrial Savings Bank, 1938, 278 N.Y. 248, 15 N.E.2d 793, reargument denied 278 N.Y. 704, 16 N.E.2d 852, 118 A.L.R. 982, noted in 38 Col.Law Rev. 1299 (1938), 16 N.Y.Univ.Law Quarterly Rev. 164 (1938); Collins v. Lyon, 1943, 181 Va. 230, 24 S.E.2d 572 (10% of purchase price of subdivision lots to be used to maintain improvements constituted a charitable trust); Queen City Park Ass'n v. Gale, 1938, 110 Vt. 110, 3 A.2d 529.

93. 115 Conn. 122, 160 A. 432 (1932).

94. *Accord:* Langenback v. Mays, 1950, 206 Ga. 859, 60 S.E.2d 240; Oliver v. Hewitt, 1950, 191 Va. 163, 60 S.E.2d 1, 23 A.L.R. 516. *Contra:* Shade v. O'Keefe, Inc., 1927, 260 Mass. 180, 156 N.E. 867.

95. But see, Raney v. Tompkins, 1950, 197 Md. 98, 78 A.2d 183, noted in 35 Marg.Law Rev. 205 (1951).

96. Pappadatos v. Market Street Bldg. Corp., 1933, 130 Cal.App. 62, 19 P.2d 517.

they relate to personal property.[97] Whether such a covenant relates to land or personal property, equitable relief may be denied upon grounds of public policy. This involves a consideration of the monopolistic tendencies involved.[98]

97. Pratte v. Balatsos, 1955, 99 N.H. 430, 113 A.2d 492; Waring v. WDAS Broadcasting Station, 1937, 327 Pa. 433, 194 A. 631 (criticized in 22 Minn.Law Rev. 559 (1938); P. Lorrillard Co. v. Weingarden, D.C.1922, 280 F.2d 238, noted in 36 Harv.Law Rev. 107 (1922). *Contra:* National Skee-Ball Co. v. Seyfried, 1932, 110 N.J.Eq. 18, 158 A. 736, noted in 16 Minn.Law Rev. 865 (1932). *Cf.:* Sandullo v. La Brunna, 1932, 111 N.J.Eq., 4, 160 A. 834.

98. Burdell v. Grandi, 1907, 152 Cal. 376, 92 P. 1022; Dean v. Montell, 1951, 361 Mo. 1204, 239 S.W.2d 337. *Cf.:* Messett v. Cowell, 1938, 194 Wash. 646, 79 P.2d 337, noted in 37 Mich.Law Rev. 651 (1939).

PART 3

POSSESSORY ESTATES

A. LESS THAN FREEHOLD ESTATES—LANDLORD AND TENANT

CHAPTER 10

INTRODUCTION

THE NATURE OF A LEASE

43.   While a lease usually involves contractual aspects, it results in the creation of an estate in the lessee. The general rule is that the rights and liabilities of the lessor and lessee are determined on the basis of property law rather than by reference to the rules of contract law.

According to the common law of England, a lessee does not acquire an estate until he takes possession of the land. Until that time he has a "mere interest in the term (an *interesse termini*)." The prevailing American rule is that the acquisition of an estate is not made to depend upon the acquisition of possession.

a. Anticipatory breach of contract. The doctrine of anticipatory breach of contract is not applicable in the case of a lease.

b. Intestate succession and testamentary capacity. In the absence of a statute to the contrary, upon the death of a lessee his leasehold estates are distributed as in the case of chattels.

c. Inheritance and estate taxes. Only the state in which the land is situated has jurisdiction to assess inheritance or estate taxes on the interest of a lessee.

In the early development of the law a lessee had no remedy against a stranger to the title who wrongfully evicted him from the land. The lessee's only remedy was against the lessor for breach of warranty if such a warranty had, in fact, been made. Eventually, such a warranty was implied. Even a wrongful eviction by the lessor could be redressed only by an action of covenant with a resultant award of damages or, if the term had not expired, the leasing contract might be specifically enforced.

Such restricted remedies available to the lessee that would not give him specific recovery of possession is the basis for the conclusion that during this period a lessee's interest was purely contractual in nature. This is in accord with the civil law rule according to which a lease is a contract for the continuing exchange of performances.[1] Subsequently, ejectment actions were made available to a lessee who was wrongfully evicted. By 1499 it was determined that he had a right to recover possession of the

[1]   Rials v. Davis, 1947, 212 La. 161, 31 So.2d 726.

111

land itself.[2] After this remedy was made available he had an interest in the land as well as contractual rights (an *in rem* interest called a chattel real). In spite of this dual nature of a lease, the general rule is that the rights and liabilities of a lessor and lessee are determined on the basis of property law rather than on the basis of contract law.[3] Variations and exceptions to this rule are discussed in the following paragraphs.

Various reasons are given for the "late development" of the common law remedy that affords specific recovery of land by a lessee with the resultant change in the nature of his interest from that of a mere contract right to that of an estate in the land. In 2 Blackstone's Commentaries, p. 141, it is stated that these "estates were originally granted to mere farmers or husbandmen, who every year rendered some equivalent in money, provisions, or other rent, to the lessors or landlords; but, in order to encourage them to manure and cultivate the ground, they had a permanent interest granted them, not determinable at the will of the lord. And yet their possession was esteemed of so little consequence, that they were rather considered as the bailiffs or servants of the lord, who were to receive and account for the profits at a settled price, than as having any property of their own." It is also to be noted that during the twelfth and thirteenth centuries leases for years were used primarily as securities for loans made by lessees and it was not contemplated that the lessees would desire possession of the land. Accordingly, during this period there was no urgency with respect to a specific action by

lessees looking to recovery of possession of the land.[4] That urgency did arise with a change in social and economic conditions under which the primary purpose of a lease was to confer a possessory right to land.

According to the English common law, the creation of an estate in the lessee depends upon his entry upon the land and acquisition of actual possession. Prior to such entry he has a mere interest in the term (an *interesse termini*).[5] Until such entry the lessee is not in a position to maintain an action of trespass even though he can maintain ejectment if he is entitled to possession. Ejectment is based upon a fictitious admission of entry upon the land by the defendant. Under some circumstances a lessee could acquire an estate in the land prior to his entry[6] by force of the Statute of Uses,[7] a matter discussed under a separate heading.[8]

While American authorities are to be found that support the old rule as it relates to "entry by the lessee,"[9] there is no modern justification for the doctrine that the acquisition of an estate by the lessee depends upon his entry upon the land.

Anticipatory Breach of Contract

In view of the fact that a lease involves the conveyance of an estate in land, the doctrine of anticipatory breach of contract is not applicable. If a lessee abandons the leased land the lessor is entitled to recover rent only

---

2. Digby, History of the Law of Real Property (5th ed.) p. 241. For discussion of the early history, see note 20 Geo.Law Rev. 521 (1932).

3. See 1 Tiffany, Landlord and Tenant, § 16, p. 160; 5 Williston on Contracts (rev. ed.) § 1329.

4. See Gulliver, Cases and Materials on the Law of Future Interests, p. 33.

5. Lewis v. Baker, [1905] 1 Ch.Div. 46, 74 L.Jr.Ch. 39.

6. Lutwich v. Mitton, [1620] Cro.Jac. 604, 79 Eng. Rep. 516; Compleat Attorney, ed. 1656, 315.

7. 27 Hen. VIII, c. 10 (1536).

8. See supra, Chapter 2.

9. See, for example, Caldwell v. Center, 1866, 30 Cal. 539; Simon v. Kirkpatrick, 1927, 141 S.C. 251, 139 S.E. 614, 54 A.L.R. 1348.

as it accrues. A covenant in the lease may provide that under such circumstances the lessor may treat the lease as terminated and recover the difference between the rent called for in the lease and the reasonable rental value of the balance of the term. Some authorities follow the view that an *inter vivos* lease is a bilateral contract with dependent promises. If the lessee abandons the leased land the lessor may recover for breach of the lease on the basis of anticipatory breach of contract.[10]

Under provisions of the Bankruptcy Act,[11] the debts of a bankrupt may be proved and allowed against the estate if they are "claims for anticipatory breach of contract, executory in whole or in part, including unexpired leases of real or personal property: Provided, however, that the claim of a landlord for damages for injury resulting from the rejection of an unexpired lease of real estate or for damages or indemnity under a covenant contained in such lease shall in no event be allowed in an amount exceeding the rent reserved by the lease, without acceleration, for the year next succeeding the date of the surrender of the premises to the landlord or the date of reentry of the landlord, whichever first occurs, whether before or after bankruptcy, plus an amount equal to the unpaid rent accrued, without acceleration, up to such date: * * *."

Intestate Succession and Testamentary Capacity

In the absence of a statute to the contrary, upon the death of a lessee his leasehold estates are distributed as in the case of chattels.[12]

Testamentary capacity to dispose of a leasehold estate is governed by the law applicable in the case of chattels. While a person under the age of twenty-one may not have capacity to make a testamentary disposition of "lands, tenements or incorporeal hereditaments," he may have capacity to make a testamentary disposition of personal property, including a chattel real.[13]

Inheritance and Estate Taxes

Only the state in which the land is located has jurisdiction to assess inheritance or estate taxes on the interest of a lessee. The matter is not governed by the law of the domicile of the lessee at the time of his death.[14]

STATUTE OF FRAUDS

44. A lease involves the conveyance of an estate in land within the meaning of the real-property section of the Statute of Frauds. A writing may also be required under the statute pertaining to contracts if the lease is not to be performed within a year "from the making thereof."

Requirements of the Statute of Frauds are satisfied if a writing identifies the lessor and the lessee, describes the leased land, states the duration of the lease and the amount of rent, if any.

The Statute of Frauds is applicable whether an agreement purports to be a lease or to be a contract to make a lease. A properly executed contract may be specifically enforceable in equity. Even if the contract is not executed in the manner required by the statute, it may be specifically enforceable under the part performance doctrine.

---

10. Novak v. Fontaine Furniture Co., 1929, 84 N.H. 93, 146 A. 525; Hawkinson v. Johnston, 8 Cir., 1941, 122 F.2d 724, 137 A.L.R. 420, noted in 40 Mich. Law Rev. 1263 (1942).

11. 11 U.S.C.A. § 103(a) (9).

Burby Real Prop. 3rd Ed. HB—8

12. Rood on Wills (2nd Ed.), § 828. See Jones v. Magruder, D.C.Md.1941, 42 F.Supp. 193 (ground rent lease.)

13. Holzman v. Wagner, 1911, 114 Md. 322, 79 A. 205.

14. In re Barclay's Estate, 1939, 1 Wash.2d 82, 95 P.2d 393.

A memorandum will be viewed as a mere "preliminary step" in the negotiation of a lease if it fails to provide for all of the necessary terms of the lease.

"Due execution of a lease" requires the signature of the lessor. A local statute may also require acknowledgement and recordation. The preferred view is that the signature of the lessee is not required. His acceptance of the lease binds him to the terms and conditions thereof.

A lease involves the conveyance of an estate in land within the meaning of the real-property section of the Statute of Frauds. However, statutes usually exempt short-term leases, such as leases that do not exceed the period of one year.[15] But an otherwise valid oral lease is brought within the purview of the statute if it contains an option for extension or renewal and the total period might exceed the time permitted for an oral lease. This follows from the fact that a lease is a present demise for the full term to which it may be extended or renewed.[16] Important authorities also support the view that a lease is a contract within the meaning of a statute providing that a contract not to be performed within one year "from the making thereof" must be in writing.[17]

Requirements of the Statute of Frauds are satisfied if a writing identifies the lessor and the lessee, describes the leased land, states the duration of the lease and the amount of rent, if any, to be paid. A memorandum will be viewed as a mere "preliminary step" in negotiations for a lease if it fails to provide for all of the necessary terms of the lease. For example, this construction is indicated if improvements are contemplated and the writing fails to fix the liability for the costs involved.[18]

Due execution of a lease requires the signature by the lessor or by his duly authorized agent and delivery of the lease to the lessee. A local statute may prescribe additional formalities, such as acknowledgement and recordation.[19] Although the cases are in conflict, the preferred view is that "due execution" does not require the signature of the lessee. He is bound by the terms of a lease because of his acceptance.[20]

Provisions of the Statute of Frauds are applicable whether the written instrument purports to be a lease or a memorandum or contract to execute a lease. Of course, a memorandum or contract to execute a lease does not result in the creation of an estate. For example, execution does not give the proposed lessee a right to maintain ejectment.[21] However, the memorandum or con-

---

15. See Caplis v. Monroe, 1924, 228 Mich. 586, 200 N.W. 123.

16. Wright v. Allred, 1946, 226 N.C. 113, 37 S.E.2d 107; Weatherford v. Lee, Tex.Civ.App.1963, 364 S.W.2d 730.

17. Wickson v. Monarch Cycle Mfg. Co., 1900, 128 Cal. 156, 60 P. 764, 79 Am.St.Rep. 36; Nelson v. Street, 1938, 148 Kan. 587, 83 P.2d 793, 119 A.L.R. 1222; Sutton v. Staton, 1938, 275 Ky. 658, 122 S.W.2d 509; Unglish v. Marvin, 1891, 128 N.Y. 380, 28 N.E. 634; *Contra:* Northrup v. Nicklas, 1946, 115 Colo. 207, 171 P.2d 417; Baie v. Nordstrom, 1947, 238 Iowa 866, 29 N.W.2d 211; Sullivan v. Bryant, 1913, 40 Okl. 80, 136 P. 412; Hayes v. Arrington, 1902, 108 Tenn. 494, 68 S.W. 44; Clark Development Co. v. Sonnenberg, 1920, 86 W.Va. 375, 103 S.E. 199.

18. Hansen v. Catsman, 1963, 371 Mich. 79, 123 N.W. 2d 265 (uncertainties respecting contemplated improvements); Upsal Street Realty Co. v. Rubin, 1937, 326 Pa. 327, 192 A. 481.

19. See, for example, Hyatt v. Romero, 1948, 190 Md. 500, 58 A.2d 899 (required if lease is for a longer period than seven years).

20. Chandler v. Hart, 1911, 161 Cal. 405, 119 P. 516; Midland R. Co. v. Fisher, 1890, 125 Ind. 19, 24 N. E. 756; Finley v. Simpson, 1850, 22 N.J.L. 311; Atlantic Dock Co. v. Leavitt, 1873, 54 N.Y. 35; Central Bldg. Co. v. Keystone Shares Corp., 1936, 185 Wash. 645, 56 P.2d 697 (lessee failed to acknowledge lease). *Contra:* Hinsdale v. Humphrey, 1843, 15 Conn. 431; Davis v. Gerson, Mo.App.1949, 219 S.W.2d 748.

21. Jackson ex dem. Bulkley v. Delacroix, 1829, 2 Wend.(N.Y.) 433.

tract may be specifically enforceable in equity with the result that the lessee acquires the estate according to the terms of the writing.[22] For this purpose, the memorandum or contract must be signed by the party sought to be charged. It must set forth the terms of the proposed lease with sufficient certainty to satisfy the provisions of the Statute of Frauds. This means that the parties must be identified, the land described and the duration of the proposed lease specified. But even if the writing does satisfy the requirements of the Statute of Frauds, it may not be specifically enforceable. It must also be clear that the parties reached final agreement on the terms and conditions of the proposed lease. Any "unfinished business" is fatal to a claim for specific performance.[23]

Even if a lease or contract to lease is not executed with the formalities prescribed by the Statute of Frauds, under some circumstances it may be specifically enforceable under the part performance doctrine. This relief may be available if the lessee takes possession of the leased land and, in reliance upon the leasing agreement, pays rent and changes his position to such an extent that substantial hardship would follow if the agreement is not enforced. According to some authorities, proof of hardship alone may justify specific performance.

There is a difference of opinion as to whether or not the continued possession of a lessee under a prior lease may be used as a basis for the granting of specific performance of a new lease that does not comply with the provisions of the Statute of Frauds. According to one view specific per-

formance is denied upon the ground that the lessee's possession of the land is not referable to the new agreement.[24] According to another view this relief may be granted if there is proof of substantial hardship that would follow the denial of equitable relief.[25]

Usually, specific performance is sought by the lessee. But this relief may be available to a lessor if the lessee takes possession of the land under the leasing agreement and the lessor is in a position to prove elements of hardship if the agreement is not enforced.[26] Additional points are as follows:

First: The part performance doctrine is applied only in equity. For that reason, a plaintiff cannot rely upon this doctrine if he brings an action at law to recover damages or rent. However, a contrary rule is followed in the Florida case of Lipkin v. Bonita Garden Apts., Inc.[27] In an action to recover rent for an apartment the defendant lessee relied upon the fact that the lease had not been executed with the formalities prescribed by the Statute of Frauds. Judgment for plaintiff was sustained upon the ground that there had been sufficient part performance to take the case out of the operation of the statute and that, under the circumstances, defendant was "estopped" to set up the invalidity of the lease.

---

22. See Levin v. Saroff, 1921, 54 Cal.App. 285, 201 P. 961.

23. See H. M. Weill Co. v. Creveling, 1917, 181 App. Div. 282, 168 N.Y.S. 385, affirmed 223 N.Y. 672, 119 N.E. 1048 (1918).

24. Lapedus v. Weinberg, 1940, 292 Mich. 439, 290 N.W. 859; Cauthron v. Goodwin, Okl.1955, 287 P. 2d 893.

25. Halsey v. Robinson, 1942, 19 Cal.2d 476, 122 P. 2d 11; S. Lemel, Inc. v. 27th Ave. Farmers Market, Inc., Fla.App.1961, 126 So.2d 167; Walter C. Pressing Co. v. Hogan, 1954, 99 Ohio App. 319, 133 N.E. 2d 419.

26. Seaman v. Aschermann, 1881, 51 Wis. 678, 8 N. W. 818; Hoffman v. F. H. Duehay, Inc., C.A.D.C. 1933, 65 F.2d 839. *Cf.:* Hacienda Gift Shop, Inc. v. Las Vegas Hacienda, Inc., 1960, 76 Nev. 86, 349 P.2d 613; Rawlinson v. Ames, [1925] 1 Ch. 96.

27. 122 So.2d 623 (Fla.App.1960).

Second: A decree of specific performance extends to all of the provable terms of a lease, including an option to renew.[28]

Third: In Minsky's Follies of Florida, Inc. v. Sennes (Fed.),[29] a leasing agreement involving a nightclub and restaurant was not in writing as required by the Statute of Frauds. At the request of the named lessor the named lessee incurred expenses in obtaining a liquor license, hiring a watchman and in counsel fees in connection with the preparation of a lease. The court held that these expenditures were recoverable in an action of implied assumpsit. It was not of controlling importance that the expenditures were collateral to an unenforceable lease. It was sufficient that the expenditures were made at defendant's request and for his benefit.[30]

LEASEHOLD ESTATE DISTINGUISHED FROM OTHER INTERESTS

45. A lease creates a possessory estate in land. It is this characteristic that distinguishes a lease from such interests as a license, a profit or an easement.

   a. Cropping contract. Unlike a lease, a cropping contract does not create an estate or interest in land.

   b. Incorporeal interests in land. The grant of an incorporeal interest in land, such as a right to drill for oil, is usually referred to as a lease. It is not a lease in a technical sense because it does not create a possessory estate.

By definition, a lease creates a possessory estate in land. It is this characteristic that distinguishes a leasehold estate from other types of interests.[31] For example, a guest in a hotel cannot usually be classified as a lessee because he does not have a right to possession of the land. Instead, he is considered to be a business guest.[32] However, the relationship may be that of lessor and lessee if it is understood that the occupant has a right of control with respect to the area in question. This may be implied if the occupancy is not on a temporary basis. This is especially true if the occupant assumes responsibilities respecting care and maintenance of the room or rooms. It may also be indicated by the fact that he supplied some or all of the furnishings.[33]

It is well recognized that an employment contract may include the right of the employee to occupy living quarters in a structure owned by the employer. If the employee is given the right to exclusive possession of the area then the relationship is that of lessor and lessee as well as that of employer and employee. For example, in Simons v. Lebrun (N. Car.),[34] a person employed to manage two rooming houses was considered to be a lessee with respect to rooms occupied under the employment contract.[35] However,

---

28. Crossman v. Fontainebleau Hotel Corp., 5 Cir. 1959, 273 F.2d 720.

29. 206 F.2d 1 (5 Cir. 1953).

30. See Nelson v. Street, 1938, 148 Kan. 587, 83 P. 2d 793, 119 A.L.R. 1222.

31. But see Bryant v. Marstelle, 1946, 76 Cal.App. 2d 740, 173 P.2d 846 (holding that an agreement does not constitute a lease unless it provides for the payment of rent).

32. Dewar v. Minneapolis Lodge etc., 1923, 155 Minn. 98, 192 N.W. 358, 32 A.L.R. 1012. See Johnson v. Kolibas, 1962, 75 N.J.Super. 56, 182 A.2d 157 (roomer).

33. See Brin v. Sidenstucker, 1943, 232 Iowa 1258, 8 N.W.2d 423, 145 A.L.R. 359; State v. Bowman, 1938, 202 Minn. 44, 279 N.W. 214; Mason v. Hotel Grand Union, 1943, 41 N.Y.S.2d 309. *Cf.:* Sawyer v. Congress Square Hotel Co., 1961, 157 Me. 111, 170 A.2d 645.

34. 219 N.C. 42, 12 S.E.2d 644 (1941).

35. *Accord:* Najewitz v. City of Seattle, 1944, 21 Wash.2d 656, 152 P.2d 722, noted in 20 Wash.Law Rev. 169 (1945) (watchman and caretaker of a gravel pit).

if occupancy is "incident to the employment" the employee is considered to be a licensee rather than a lessee.[36] Under such circumstances, possession of the property remains in the employer.

A person may also retain possession of land even though he may confer a license upon another to conduct a business on the land or to place a vending machine on the land.[37] For example, the operator or a hotel or night club may grant a license to another authorizing the operation of a checkroom or the use of space for the sale of merchandise.[38] Such an arrangement (a concession) differs from a lease because of the fact that the space to be used for the purpose is subject to change at any time at the will of the one who confers the privilege.[39]

Cropping Contract

A landowner may engage the services of a person to plant, cultivate and harvest a crop paying him, as compensation, a share of the crop. Such a cropping contract does not create a possessory right in the land and, for that reason, does not create a leasehold estate. The person so engaged may be a servant,[40] an independent contractor[41] or even a joint venture may be involved. However, the agreement may result in the creation of a leasehold estate the rent being payable in crops. In that event, ownership of the crop remains in the lessee until division is made.[42] However, some authorities follow the view that the parties are tenants in common of the crops.[43]

The terms of the agreement determines whether it constitutes a cropping contract or a lease.[44] If the landowner confers possessory rights upon the other contracting party the relationship is that of lessor and lessee. Such an intention may be indicated by the fact that the agreement is designated as a lease and requires the payment of "rent." In Sherwin v. Bogosian (Cal.),[45] a lessor claimed that his lessee had breached a covenant in the lease that prohibited subleasing. The lessee contended that his agreement with the third party (the alleged sublessee) was nothing but a cropping contract. The court held that the arrangement constituted a sublease. It conferred possessory rights with respect to the land.[46]

Incorporeal Interests in Land

The grant of incorporeal interests in land, such as a right to drill for oil or mine minerals, is usually referred to as a lease. But such a lease does not result in the creation of a landlord and tenant relationship because the lessee does not acquire a possessory estate in the land.[47] These rights

---

36. Jump v. Pilgrim Properties, Inc., 1947, 118 Ind. App. 164, 75 N.E.2d 165; Davis v. Long, 1920, 45 N.D. 581, 178 N.W. 936, 14 A.L.R. 796 (farmhand); Turner v. Mertz, 1925, 55 App.D.C. 177, 3 F.2d 348, 39 A.L.R. 1140.

37. Timmons v. Cropper, Del.Ch.1961, 172 A.2d 757.

38. R. H. White Co. v. Jerome H. Remick & Co., 1908, 198 Mass. 41, 84 N.E. 113; Senrow Concessions, Inc. v. Shelton Properties, Inc., 1961, 10 N.Y.2d 320, 178 N.E.2d 726; Frank Warr & Co., Ltd. v. London County Council, [1904] 1 K.B. 713, 73 L.J.K.B. 362. See Walsh, Licenses and Tenancies for Years, 19 N.Y.Univ.Law Quarterly Rev. 333, 338 (1942).

39. But see Beckett v. City of Paris Dry Goods Co., 1939, 14 Cal.2d 633, 96 P.2d 122.

40. Huff v. Watkins, 1880, 15 S.C. 82.

41. Duncan v. Anderson, 1876, 56 Ga. 398.

42. Warner v. Abbey, 1873, 112 Mass. 355.

43. Smith v. Thibault, 1961, 122 Vt. 256, 168 A.2d 729.

44. See Smith v. McNew, Mo.App.1964, 381 S.W.2d 369.

45. 112 Cal.App. 359, 296 P. 641 (1931).

46. See, Birmingham v. Rogers, 1885, 46 Ark. 254.

47. *Cf.:* Jordan v. Indianapolis Water Co., 1902, 159 Ind. 337, 64 N.E. 680, noted in 16 Harv.L.Rev. 225 (1902).

to take the soil or a substance of the soil are defined as profits. It is also generally considered that the grant of a privilege to pasture livestock results in the creation of a profit. However, there is authority for the view that a "grazing permit," if exclusive in nature, results in the creation of a possessory estate in the land. It has been so held with respect to the lease of federal land for grazing purposes pursuant to provisions of the federal Taylor Grazing Act.[48]

If the exclusive right to possession is granted, even though the use of the land is restricted, a possessory estate is conveyed with the resultant relationship of landlord and tenant.[49] Usually, the grant of a right to maintain a sign on the land of another results in the creation of a license or an easement.[50] However, a possessory estate may be acquired even though use of the land is restricted to this one purpose.[51] The imposition of restrictions and controls respecting the use of land may cause what would otherwise qualify as a possessory estate to fade into an incorporeal interest, such as a license.[52]

LIABILITY FOR DAMAGE CAUSED TO THE LAND

46. While a lessee may be held liable for waste, he is not liable to the lessor for damage caused to the land by accident, extraordinary force of nature or by the wrongful act of others without his participation.

48. Sproul v. Gilbert, 1961, 226 Or. 392, 359 P.2d 543 (construing 43 U.S.C.A. § 315m).

49. Rendall v. Pioneer Hotel, Inc., 1950, 71 Ariz. 10, 222 P.2d 986.

50. Thomas Cusack Co. v. Myers, 1920, 189 Iowa 190, 178 N.W. 401, 10 A.L.R. 1104 (easement).

51. See Wunsch v. Donnelly, 1939, 302 Mass. 286, 19 N.E.2d 70.

52. See Thiokol Chemical Corp. v. Morris County Bd. of Taxation, 1964, 41 N.J. 405, 197 A.2d 176.

If a third party does cause damage to the land the lessee is entitled to recover damages only to the extent that he has suffered a loss.

While a lessee is entitled to the "issues and profits" from the land, unless privileged,[53] he is not entitled to use the land in a manner that will diminish the value of interests owned by others in the same land. An improper use of the land in this respect constitutes waste, a matter discussed under a separate heading.[54]

In the absence of a covenant in the lease that imposes liability, a lessee is not responsible for damages caused to the land by the wrongful act of a third party, by accident or by an extraordinary force of nature.[55] If a third party does cause damage to the leased land, the lessee is entitled to recover damages to the extent that he has suffered a loss.[56] The lessee's liability may arise because of his covenant to repair.[57] The minority rule is that the lessee is entitled to recover to the full extent of the damage caused to the land.[58] In that event he is under a duty to account to the owners of other estates in the land.

53. See, for example, Heywood v. Fulmer, 1902, 158 Ind. 658, 32 N.E. 574, 18 L.R.A. 491 (lessee expressly authorized to remove sand and gravel from the land).

54. See supra, Chapter 4.

55. Winfree v. Jones, 1905, 104 Va. 39, 51 S.E. 153; United States v. Bostwick, 1876, 94 U.S. 53, 24 L.Ed. 65. See Kirchwey, Liability for Waste, 8 Col. Law Rev. 624, 628 (1908).

56. Elliott v. Missouri Pac. Ry. Co., 1898, 8 Kan.App. 191, 55 P. 490; Weston v. Gravlin, 1877, 49 Vt. 507; California Dry-Dock Co. v. Armstrong, 9 Cir., 1883, 17 F. 216.

57. Stapp v. Madera Canal & Irrigation Co., 1917, 34 Cal.App. 41, 166 P. 823.

58. Ulrich v. McCabe, 1856, 1 Hilt. (N.Y.) 251.

TORT LIABILITY

47. In general, a lessor is not liable for injuries resulting from a defective condition of the leased land.

  a. **Areas under the control of the lessor.** A lessor may be held liable for injuries resulting from a defective condition if the situation involves an area over which the lessor retained control.

  b. **Known defective conditions.** The liability of a lessor may arise with respect to defective conditions if he knew of the condition at the time of the lease and failed to disclose the facts to the lessee.

  c. **Public use rule.** If land is leased for a purpose that involves admission of the public in connection with an activity conducted by the lessee the lessor is under a duty to see that the premises are in a safe condition at the time of the lease.

  d. **Covenant to repair.** According to one view, a lessor may be held liable in damages for personal injuries resulting from default in the performance of a covenant to make repairs.

  e. **Voluntary repairs.** If a lessor volunteers to make repairs the work must be done with reasonable care. Default in this respect may result in liability for personal injuries resulting therefrom.

  f. **Statutory liability.** In many states statutes have been passed imposing a duty upon lessors to maintain leased premises in a state of repair. Breach of this duty may result in liability for personal injuries.

In general, a lessor is not liable for injuries resulting from a defective condition of the leased land.[59] The lessee assumes responsibilities incident to the physical condition of the land and the activities conducted thereon. This follows from the fact that the lessee has a right to possession and control of the land. Some authorities take the position that in the lease of a furnished house for a short period of time there is an implied warranty that the house and its appointments are suitable for occupancy. A breach of this warranty may result in liability for breach of contract. However, a tort action cannot be maintained against the lessor on the basis of alleged negligence.[60]

However, there are situations where duties respecting maintenance are imposed upon the lessor. Default in the performance of such a duty may result in tort liability on the basis of negligence. These situations are discussed in the following paragraphs. Where such a duty does exist there are conflicting views as to the validity of a contractual provision that would relieve the lessor from liability for default in the performance of this duty. According to the prevailing rule such an exculpatory clause may relieve the lessor from liability for ordinary negligence.[61] The concept of freedom of contract sanctions such validity except in situations where the public interest is considered to be a predominant factor. However, in some states the invalidity of such an exculpatory clause is declared by statute.[62]

If the default relates to repairs of the leased land, the release-by-contract is bind-

---

59. As for liability of a lessor with respect to the physical condition of a public sidewalk adjacent to the leased land, see Lee v. Ashizawa, 1964, 60 Cal.2d 862, 37 Cal.Rptr. 71, 389 P.2d 535.

60. Zatloff v. Winkleman, 1960, 90 R.I. 403, 158 A.2d 874. *Cf.:* Ackarey v. Carbonaro, 1946, 320 Mass. 537, 70 N.E.2d 418.

61. Eastern Avenue Corp. v. Hughes, 1962, 228 Md. 477, 180 A.2d 486; Bryans v. Gallagher, 1962, 407 Pa. 142, 178 A.2d 766. See Werner v. Knoll, 1948, 89 Cal.App.2d 474, 201 P.2d 45; Mitterlehner v. Mercantile National Bank, Tex.Civ.App.1964, 378 S.W.2d 137. *Contra:* Papaklos v. Shaka, 1941, 91 N.H. 265, 18 A.2d 377.

62. See, for example, Ill.Rev.Stat. ch. 80, § 15a (1959); Billie Knitwear, Inc. v. New York Life Ins. Co., 1940, 174 Misc. 978, 22 N.Y.S.2d 324, affirmed 262 A.D. 714, 27 N.Y.S.2d 328, appeal granted 262 A.D. 743, 28 N.Y.S.2d 726, affirmed 288 N.Y. 682, 43 N.E.2d 80.

ing upon the lessee, the members of his family [63] and persons on the land with the consent of the lessee, express or implied. The rights of such third parties are based upon the rights of the lessee. A different rule applies if the default relates to the lessor's failure to maintain areas over which he retains control, such as common walks, halls and stairways. While the lessee may contract for himself he cannot limit the rights of third parties by such a contract. Their rights are not derived "through the lessee." [64]

Areas Under the Control of the Lessor

A lessor who has several tenants in the same building is under a duty to keep the areas used in common by the lessees in a reasonably safe condition.[65] The minority rule is that his duty is to keep the areas used in common in the same condition that they were in at the time the leases were executed.[66]

The above stated duty is based upon the fact that the lessor retains control over the areas in question, such as hallways, stairs and walks. But the lessor is not an insurer. His liability depends upon proof of fault on his part. For example, if a lessee slips and falls because of the presence of some foreign substance on the floor, stairs or walk, the lessor can be compelled to respond in damages only if he can be charged with responsibility for creating the condition, knew of the condition and failed to take corrective measures or can be charged with constructive notice.[67]

The constructive-notice rule applies in a case where the condition existed a sufficient length of time prior to the accident to permit the lessor, in the exercise of reasonable care, to find and correct it. The liability may arise because of a dangerous condition resulting from the natural accumulation of snow or ice.[68]

The duty on the part of the lessor extends to the lessee, members of the lessee's family and all persons on the land at the invitation of the lessee, express or implied.[69]

Known Defective Conditions

A lessor is under a duty to disclose to his lessee the existence of any known latent defect existing at the time of the lease.[70] A breach of this duty results if there is a concealed hazard—a hazard not disclosed by the physical condition of the land. For example, a lessee may be charged with notice of the fact that a door may lead to a basement but he may not be charged with knowledge of the fact that there is a concealed hazard consisting of a "precipitous basement stairway" without a platform at the top of the steps and without a railing.[71]

---

63. Deen v. Holderfield, 1963, 275 Ala. 360, 155 So.2d 314 (wife of tenant).

64. See, for example, Valentin v. D. G. Swanson & Co., 1960, 25 Ill.App.2d 285, 167 N.E.2d 14 (tenant's wife injured on a common stairway).

65. Reiman v. Moore, 1940, 42 Cal.App.2d 130, 108 P.2d 452; United Shoe Machine Corp. v. Paine, 1 Cir., 1928, 26 F.2d 594, 58 A.L.R. 1398.

66. Andrews v. Williamson, 1906, 193 Mass. 92.

67. McGuire v. Valley National Bank of Phoenix, 1963, 94 Ariz. 50, 381 P.2d 588; Berardo v. Am-

brozy, 1942, 128 N.J.L. 295, 25 A.2d 538. See Brown v. Frontier Theatres, Inc., 1963, —— Tex. ——, 369 S.W.2d 299 (property damage caused by defective wiring in space occupied by the lessor).

68. Reardon v. Shimelman, 1925, 102 Conn. 383, 128 A. 705, 707, 39 A.L.R. 287; Young v. Saroukos, (Del., 1963) 189 A.2d 437. *Contra:* Bell v. Siegel, 1922, 242 Mass. 380, 136 N.E. 109, 25 A.L.R. 1261.

69. Coupe v. Platt, 1899, 172 Mass. 458, 52 N.E. 526; Karp v. Barton, 1912, 164 Mo.App. 389, 144 S.W. 1111; Stern v. Miller, 1908, 60 Misc. 103, 111 N.Y.S. 659.

70. Powell v. Stivers, 1951, 108 Cal.App.2d 72, 238 P.2d 34; Cowen v. Sunderland, 1887, 145 Mass. 363, 14 N.E. 117; Miller v. Vance Lumber Co., 1932, 167 Wash. 348, 9 P.2d 351.

71. Merrill v. Buck, 1962, 58 Cal.2d 552, 25 Cal.Rptr. 456, 375 P.2d 304.

Public Use Rule

Generally, a lessor may escape responsibility for defective conditions respecting the leased land if he informs his lessee of the facts. But this is not true if land is leased for a purpose that involves the admission of the public in connection with an activity conducted by the lessee. In such a case the lessor may be held liable for personal injuries suffered by a member of the public.[72] This is true if the injuries resulted from a defective condition, artificial in nature, existing when the lessee took possession of the land. For this purpose the evidence must show that the lessor knew or should have known of the condition and realized or should have realized the hazards involved and had no reason to expect that the lessee would correct the condition before use by the public. Additional rules are as follows:

First: A "dangerous condition *of the premises*" does not exist if the danger arises because of some article that properly cannot be classified as a fixture, such as a portable gas heater not furnished under the terms of the leasing agreement.[73]

Generally, a lessor cannot be held liable for injuries resulting from *activities* conducted by the lessee. However, a lessor may be held liable if the leased land is not suitable for the purpose of such activity. For example, if land is leased for the purpose of conducting "hot rod" races, the lessor may be held liable if the barriers and guards are not sufficient for the protection of spectators.[74] This liability is not based upon alleged negligence of the lessee in the operation of racing. Rather, it is based upon the lessor's own breach of duty as it relates to the condition of the premises.

Second: The liability of the lessor does not extend to conditions that develop after the lessee takes possession of the land.[75]

Covenant to Repair

The authorities are fairly evenly divided as to whether or not a lessor may be held liable for personal injuries suffered as a result of his breach of contract to repair. The traditional rule is against such recovery. It is reasoned that in a breach of contract action recovery is limited to damages that were reasonably within the contemplation of the parties and damages of the type under consideration does not qualify.[76] However, an increasing number of decisions point out that the disrepair enhances the risk of personal injury to persons upon the land. This is a matter that was within the contempla-

---

72. Hayes v. Richfield Oil Corp., 1952, 38 Cal.2d 375, 240 P.2d 580 (gasoline service station); Gilligan v. Blakesley, 1933, 93 Colo. 370, 26 P.2d 808 (doctor's office); Turner v. Kent, 1932, 134 Kan. 574, 7 P.2d 513 (grocery store); 2 Rest. Torts, § 359. *Contra:* Trondle v. Ward, 1942, 129 N.J.L. 179, 28 A.2d 509 (hotel); Sacks v. Sunset Hill Realty Corp., 1937, 250 App.Div. 778, 294 N.Y.S. 127, affirmed 276 N.Y. 668, 13 N.E.2d 54 (26-room dwelling house); Hayden v. Second Nat. Bank of Allentown, 1938, 331 Pa. 29, 199 A. 218 (public garage).

73. Goodman v. Harris, 1953, 40 Cal.2d 254, 253 P.2d 447. See also, Manning v. Leavitt Co., 1939, 90 N.H. 167, 5 A.2d 667, 122 A.L.R. 249 (permanent wave machine in a beauty parlor).

74. Gibson v. Shelby County Fair Ass'n, 1950, 241 Iowa 1349, 44 N.W.2d 362. See also, Larson v. Calder's Park Co., 1919, 54 Utah 325, 180 P. 599, 4 A.L.R. 731 (shooting gallery).

75. Anderson v. Valley Feed Yards, Inc., 1963, 175 Neb. 719, 123 N.W.2d 839.

76. See Spinks v. Asp, 1921, 192 Ky. 550, 234 S.W. 14; Jacobson v. Leventhal, 1930, 128 Me. 424, 148 A. 281, 68 A.L.R. 1192; Jordan v. Miller, 1919, 179 N.C. 73, 101 S.E. 550.

tion of the parties.[77] Additional rules are as follows:

First: Since tort liability is involved, the duty of a lessor extends not only to the lessee and members of his family but as well to persons on the premises with his consent, express or implied.[78] There is a minority rule that privity of contract must exist as between the plaintiff and the lessor.[79]

Second: An issue as to consideration for such a promise may arise if the promise is not embodied in the leasing agreement. However, a promise made in the face of a threat by the lessee to move creates a sufficient consideration to support the promise.[80]

Voluntary Repairs

Even in the absence of a repair-covenant, a lessor who volunteers to make repairs must act with reasonable care. Default in this respect may result in liability if the negligence is the proximate cause of personal injuries either to the lessee or to a person on the premises with the consent of the lessee, express or implied.[81]

According to one view, liability will arise only if the acts of the lessor made the premises more dangerous or created a deceptive appearance.[82] The preferred view is that the injured party need prove only that what was wrong continued to be wrong although the exercise of prudence would have made it right.[83]

Statutory Liability

In many states statutes have been passed imposing a duty upon lessors to maintain leased premises in a state of repair. This is especially true with respect to multiple dwellings.[84] A California statute provides that the lessor of a building intended for the occupation of human beings must, in the absence of an agreement to the contrary, put it into a condition fit for such occupation, and repair all subsequent dilapidations thereof, which render it untenantable (with exceptions).[85] But the statute does not create tort liability. If there is default in the performance of the statutory duty, and after reasonable notice to the lessor, the lessee may either vacate the premises or make the repairs and charge the lessor to the extent of one month's rent.[86]

77. Scholey v. Steele, 1943, 59 Cal.App.2d 402, 138 P.2d 733; Scibek v. O'Connell, 1945, 131 Conn. 557, 41 A.2d 251; Williams v. Davis, 1961, 188 Kan. 385, 362 P.2d 641; Zuroski v. Strickland, 1964, 176 Neb. 633, 126 N.W.2d 888. See 2 Rest. Torts, § 357 (if disrepair creates an unreasonable risk).

78. Sontag v. O'Hare, 1898, 73 Ill.App. 432; Barron v. Liedloff, 1905, 95 Minn. 474, 104 N.W. 289; Merchants' Cotton Press & Storage Co. v. Miller, 1916, 135 Tenn. 187, 186 S.W. 87; Ross v. Haner, Tex. Civ.App., 1922, 244 S.W. 231 (plaintiff was tenant's minor child).

79. Tuttle v. George H. Gilbert Mfg. Co., 1887, 145 Mass. 169, 13 N.E. 465; Kohnle v. Paxton, 1916, 268 Mo. 463, 188 S.W. 155; Dustin v. Curtis, 1907, 74 N.H. 266, 67 A. 220; Schick v. Fleischauer, 1898, 26 App.Div. 210, 49 N.Y.S. 962; Soulia v. Noyes, 1940, 111 Vt. 323, 16 A.2d 173. See Ripple v. Mahoning Nat. Bank, Ohio App.1943, 56 N.E.2d 942.

80. Farley v. Yerman, 1963, 231 Md. 444, 190 A.2d 773.

81. Continental Oil Co. v. Ryan, Okl.1964, 392 P.2d 492.

82. See 2 Rest. Torts, § 362.

83. Olsen v. Mading, 1935, 45 Ariz. 423, 45 P.2d 23; Janofsky v. Garland, 1941, 42 Cal.App.2d 655, 109 P.2d 750; Bartlett v. Taylor, 1943, 351 Mo. 1060, 174 S.W.2d 844.

84. For interpretation of such a statute, see Daniels v. Brunton, 1950, 9 N.J.Super. 294, 76 A.2d 73.

85. West's Ann.Cal.Civ.Code, § 1941.

86. West's Ann.Cal.Civ.Code, § 1942.

CHAPTER 11

VARIOUS TYPES OF LEASEHOLD ESTATES

ESTATE FOR YEARS

48. An estate for years is an estate the maximum duration of which is measured by one or more years or by a fraction of a year.

    a. **Date of commencement.** Date for the commencement of the lease must be designated with reasonable certainty.

    b. **Definite termination date.** An estate may be classified as one for years even though it may terminate prior to the time fixed upon the happening of a named event.

    c. **Notice to terminate.** Notice is not required for the termination of an estate for years.

An estate for years is an estate the maximum duration of which is measured by one or more years, or by a fraction of a year.[1] Thus, an estate for one week, one month etc., qualifies as an "estate for years." The estate may be terminable upon the happening of a stated event or it may be subject to a condition subsequent.[2] In many states the maximum duration of an estate for years is fixed by statute.[3]

Date of Commencement

The date fixed for the commencement of the lease must be designated with reasonable certainty. There are two reasons for this rule. In the first place, it cannot be said that a lease is for a fixed period of time if there is uncertainty as to the starting date. In the second place, the common law rule is that an estate does not vest in the lessee until he takes possession of the land. Until that time he has a mere *interesse termini,* defined as an interest in the term. However, this reason ceased to be applicable in those situations where the Statute of Uses operated to confer legal ownership of a leasehold estate in the lessee prior to actual entry upon the land, a matter discussed under a separate heading.[4] Uncertainty respecting the starting date of a lease is removed if the event happens that embodied the contingency.[5] It is also to be noted that a definite date may be fixed for the beginning of a lease even though it is provided that there is to be an abatement of the rent until the happening of a named event, such as the completion of improvements.[6]

Definite Termination Date

The duration of an estate for years must be capable of measurement in terms of years

---

1. Co.Litt. 45b.

2. 1 Rest. Property, § 19, *Comment c.*

3. See, for example, West's Ann.Cal.Civ.Code, §§ 717, 718, and statutes construed in Western Union Tel. Co. v. Louisville & N. R. Co., 1918, 202 Ala. 542, 81 So. 44; Stewart v. Gorter, 1889, 70 Md. 242, 16 A. 644; Clark v. Barnes, 1879, 76 N.Y. 301; Piper v. Taylor, 1922, 48 N.D. 967, 188 N.W. 171. See also, The Long Term Ground Lease: A Survey, 48 Yale Law Jr. 1400 (1939).

4. See supra, Chapter 2.

5. See Wunsch v. Donnelly, 1939, 302 Mass. 286, 19 N.E.2d 70.

6. Dunbar v. R. E. Williams Co., Inc., Ky.App.1962, 358 S.W.2d 536.

or fractions thereof. An estate may be classified as an estate for years even though it may terminate prior to the time fixed upon the happening of a named event. For example, the estate may be one for 10 years, terminable prior to that time by the happening of a named event. But such a lease differs from the one involved in National Bellas-Hess, Inc. v. Kalis (Fed.).[7] The lease was for a term "commencing October 1, 1943, and ending sixty (60) days after the signing of the treaty of peace upon the close of the war with Germany and/or with Japan, whichever treaty of peace is the latest * * *." The court held that the lessee occupied the land as a tenant at will only.[8] The lease failed to create an estate for years because of the uncertainty respecting its potential duration. This conclusion is not affected by the fact that the event was one certain to happen and the uncertainty related only to the time when the event would happen. It is not the certainty of the happening of the event which is to end the term but the certainty of the date on which the termination of the lease will take place that is the determining factor. It is held in some cases, however, that such a lease creates an estate for years.[9]

The prevailing rule is that a lease for a definite period of time constitutes an estate for years even though it may be terminated before the time fixed at the option of either the lessor or the lessee.[10] According to some

decisions, however, such a provision for termination results in the creation of an estate at will.[11] This conclusion is apparently based upon the questionable ground that mutuality requires that if a lease is terminable at the will of one party it is also terminable at the will of the other party. While this mutuality of obligation rule is of importance in the area of contract law there is no basis for its application in connection with the classification of estates. In many cases the argument relating to mutuality is not applicable because termination is made to depend upon the happening of some event, such as a sale of the land by the lessor or the erection of improvements by him.[12]

Notice to Terminate

Notice is not required for the termination of an estate for years because the expiration date is fixed and certain. However, notice may be an important factor if the lease provides for automatic renewal. For example, a lease may provide for renewal at the expiration date unless, prior to that date, the landlord or the tenant gives notice that the lease is not to be renewed.[13] A New York statute provides that such an automatic renewal clause is not binding on the tenant unless the landlord gives the tenant notice of its existence in the lease at least 15 and not more than 30 days prior to the time within which the tenant is required to give such notice of termination. A provision in the

---

7. 191 F.2d 739 (8 Cir., 1951), certiorari denied 342 U.S. 933, 72 S.Ct. 377, 96 L.Ed. 695.

8. *Accord*: Stanmeyer v. Davis, 1944, 321 Ill.App. 227, 53 N.E.2d 22.

9. Beeson v. La Vasque, 1920, 144 Ark. 522, 223 S.W. 355; Rupp Hotel Operating Co. v. Donn, Fla.1947, 29 So.2d 441; Wilcox v. Bostick, 1899, 57 S.C. 151, 35 S.W. 496; Hammond v. Barton, 1896, 93 Wis. 183, 67 N.W. 412; Smith's Transfer & Storage Co., Inc. v. Hawkins, D.C.Mun.App.1946, 50 A.2d 267.

10. Southeastern Land Co. v. Clem, 1931, 239 Ky. 417, 39 S.W.2d 674 (*dictum*); Peoples Park & Amuse-

ment Ass'n, Inc. v. Anrooney, 1939, 200 Wash. 51, 93 P.2d 362.

11. United States v. Pacific Market Co., D.C.Wyo. 1930, 51 F.2d 348. For discussion of estates at will, see §§ 108, 109, post.

12. See David Roth's Sons, Inc. v. Wright & Taylor, Inc., Ky.App.1961, 343 S.W.2d 389.

13. Epes v. Palmieri, 1943, 181 Va. 332, 25 S.E.2d 279.

lease purporting to waive this requirement is contrary to public policy.[14]

In Warnecke v. Rabenau's Estate (Mo.),[15] the landlord filed a claim against the estate of his deceased tenant that involved rent allegedly due for a suite of offices in an office building. The decedent was a certified public accountant and died prior to the expiration of his two year lease. The estate claimed that his death operated as a termination of the lease. The court sustains this claim. It is pointed out that generally, in the absence of an express provision in the lease, the death of a tenant does not result in the termination of a lease. However, in this case provisions in the lease justified the conclusion that it was "personal in nature." It was expressly provided that the premises "were to be used and occupied as office for certified accountants, but for no other purpose." There was a covenant against assignment without the written consent of the landlord and it could not otherwise be assigned "voluntarily or by operation of law." There was also a covenant against subleasing. It is pointed out that the only purpose of the lease was to make it possible for the tenant to carry on a profession not open to the public at large. It is concluded that the landlord must have contemplated that the tenant remain alive during the period of the lease.[16]

ESTATE AT WILL

49. An estate at will is an estate which is terminable at the will of the lessor and also at the will of the lessee and has no other fixed period of duration.

a. **Creation of an estate at will.** An estate at will may be created by express agreement. It may also be created by operation of law, such as in a case where a tenant takes possession of the land under a lease that is not in writing as required by the Statute of Frauds. If a lease is terminable at the will of the lessor it is, by implication, also terminable at the will of the lessee.

b. **Termination of an estate at will.** An estate at will is terminated by operation of law upon the death of the lessor or the death of the lessee, or upon a conveyance or assignment of their interests. A local statute may require notice of termination under varying circumstances.

An estate at will is an estate which is terminable at the will of the lessor, and also at the will of the lessee, and which has no other designated period of duration.[17] An estate at will may exist even though reasonable notice of termination may be required.[18]

A lease may provide that the estate is to continue "until further agreement of the parties." This understanding does not sanction termination by unilateral action. The termination requires agreement by both the lessor and the lessee. Accordingly, if there is compliance with the formalities prescribed by the Statute of Frauds a determinable life estate is created.[19]

Creation of an Estate at Will

An estate at will may be created by express agreement, such as in a lease expressly providing that the estate is "at will." It may also be created by operation of law. That is the case, for example, if a lessee takes pos-

---

14. Boyd H. Wood Co. v. Horgan, 1943, 291 N.Y. 422, 52 N.E.2d 932.

15. Warnecke v. Rabenau's Estate, Mo.App.1963, 367 S.W.2d 15.

16. *Cf.*: Israel v. Beale, Admr., 1930, 270 Mass. 61, 169 N.E. 777, 68 A.L.R. 588.

17. 1 Rest. Property, § 21.

18. Say v. Stoddard, 1875, 27 Ohio St. 478.

19. Disley v. Disley, 1910, 30 R.I. 366, 75 A. 481. *Contra*: Lepsch v. Lepsch, 1949, 275 App.Div. 412, 90 N.Y.S.2d 157, noted in 19 Fordham Law Rev. 104 (1950) (estate at will).

session of land under an oral lease that is unenforceable because of the Statute of Frauds.[20] The same conclusion is indicated if a person is in possession of land during the time that the parties are negotiating for a lease [21] or in possession under a contract for the sale of the land that cannot be enforced because of the Statute of Frauds.[22]

The following declaration by Lord Coke has greatly influenced the modern law as it relates to estates at will: "It is regularly true, that every lease at will must in law be at the will of both parties, and therefore when the lease is made, to have and to hold at the will of the lessor, the law implyeth it to be at the will of the lessee also; for it cannot be only at the will of the lessor, but it must be at the will of the lessee also. And so it is when the lease is made to have and to hold at the will of the lessee, this must be also at the will of the lessor; and so are all the books that seem prima facie to differ, clearly reconciled." [23] No reasons are given for the conclusions so indicated. Assuming compliance with the formalities prescribed by the Statute of Frauds, a conveyance of the type mentioned by Lord Coke should result in the creation of a determinable life estate. Differences of opinion on the matter,

as reflected in modern decisions, are set forth in the following propositions:

First: The weight of authority is that if an estate is terminable at the will of the lessor it is, by implication, terminable at the will of the lessee. This is in accord with the first proposition declared by Lord Coke.

It is usually stated that this rule is based upon the concept of mutuality of obligation. It is reasoned that if the lease is not binding on the lessor it is not binding on the lessee. But the validity of this argument is open to question. In the first place, the rule as to mutuality of obligation is applicable to contractual obligations and has no place in a situation that involves the conveyance of an estate. In the second place, lack of mutuality means lack of consideration. Usually, a price is paid by the lessor for the retained privilege of termination. This is reflected in the price he receives for the conveyance. It is also to be noted that an estate at will does not result if some condition is attached to the privilege of revocation retained by the lessor.[24]

Second: A number of decisions support the rule declared by Lord Coke that if a lease is terminable at the will of the lessee it is, by implication, also terminable at the will of the lessor and results in the creation of an estate at will.[25] However, the weight of authority is that such a conveyance is not terminable at the will of the lessor and results in the creation of a determinable life

---

20. Sikes v. Carter, 1923, 30 Ga.App. 539, 118 S.E. 430 (by statute); Fisher v. Heller, 1928, 174 Minn. 233, 219 N.W. 79; Davis v. Lovick, 1946, 226 N.C. 252, 37 S.E.2d 680. *Cf.*: Cochran v. Ward, 1892, 5 Ind.App. 89, 29 N.E. 795, 31 N.E. 581.

21. Lyon v. Cunningham, 1884, 136 Mass. 532; Huntington v. Parkhurst, 1891, 87 Mich. 38, 49 N.W. 597. *Contra*: Pacific Coast Joint Stock Land Bank v. Jones, 1939, 14 Cal.2d 8, 92 P.2d 390, 123 A.L.R. 695 (considered to be a licensee and not entitled to the benefit of the doctrine of emblements).

22. Harris v. Frink, 1872, 49 N.Y. 24. *Contra*: Arnold v. Fraser, 1911, 43 Mont. 540, 117 P. 1064.

23. Co.Litt., 55a.

24. Gunsenhiser v. Binder, 1910, 206 Mass. 434, 92 N.E. 705.

25. Morgan v. Morgan, 1949, 309 Ky. 581, 218 S.W.2d 410; Foley v. Gamester, 1930, 271 Mass. 55, 170 N.E. 799; Nimmer v. Chewning, 1930, 155 S.C. 528, 152 S.E. 702; Holcombe v. Lorino, 1935, 124 Tex. 446, 79 S.W.2d 307, noted in 14 Tex.Law Rev. 109 (1935). See Freedline v. Cielensky, 1961, 115 Ohio App. 138, 184 N.E.2d 433 (oral lease).

estate.[26] Ruling out the application of contract law as it relates to mutuality of obligation, there are no legal barriers to the creation of such an estate in compliance with the intention of the parties.

Third: A lease for a fixed period, such as for ten years, is not reduced to an estate at will even if provision is made for termination at the will of the lessor [27] or at the will of the lessee.[28]

Termination of an Estate at Will

At common law an estate at will may be terminated at the will of either the lessor or the lessee. In the case of agricultural land, upon termination by the lessor the lessee is allowed a reasonable time within which to harvest and remove crops growing upon the land at the time of termination.[29] The tenancy does not continue until the crops have been removed.[30] The privilege is regarded as a license and not an estate.[31]

The estate at will grew out of what was considered to be a personal relationship. From this it followed that the estate terminated by operation of law upon the death of either the lessor or the lessee or in case of an assignment of the reversion [32] or the leasehold estate. While this personal relationship is not terminated by a sublease,[33] some decisions indicate that a sublease results in the termination of an estate at will at the election of the lessor.[34]

In many states statutes provide that notice must be given to terminate an estate at will. Some statutes require either the lessor or the lessee to give such notice.[35] Other statutes require notice only on the part of the lessor.[36] However, the general rule is that notice is not required if the estate is terminated by operation of law.[37]

There is authority for the view that a provision in the lease may abrogate the necessity of notice as specified in a statute.[38] There is, of course, a public-policy argument against such a rule.

ESTATE AT SUFFERANCE

50. If a lessee wrongfully holds over after the expiration of his lease he becomes a tenant at sufferance unless he asserts a claim of ownership that makes him an adverse possessor.

Notice is not required to terminate an estate at sufferance. However, it is usually pro-

---

26. Gunnison v. Evans, 1933, 136 Kan. 791, 18 P.2d 191; Sweetser v. McKenney, 1875, 65 Me. 225; Thompson v. Baxter, 1909, 107 Minn. 122, 119 N.W. 797; Lindlay v. Raydure, D.Ky.1917, 239 F. 928.

27. Southeastern Land Co. v. Clem, 1931, 239 Ky. 417, 39 S.W.2d 674 (*dictum*). *Contra:* United States v. Pacific Market Co., D.C.Wyo.1930, 51 F.2d 348.

28. Cleveland Wrecking Co. v. Aetna Oil Co., 1941, 287 Ky. 542, 154 S.W.2d 31, 137 A.L.R. 352 (lease for one year and then from year to year, with option in lessee to terminate on sixty days' notice); Peoples Park & Amusement Ass'n, Inc. v. Anrooney, 1939, 200 Wash. 51, 93 P.2d 362.

29. See supra § 10.

30. See Humphries v. Humphries, 1843, 25 N.C. 362.

31. 1 Rest.Torts, § 179.

32. Souza v. Becker, 1938, 302 Mass. 28, 18 N.E.2d 350, 120 A.L.R. 1002. *Cf.:* Ferrigno v. O'Connell, 1944, 315 Mass. 536, 53 N.E.2d 384.

33. Public Service Co. v. Voudomas, 1930, 84 N.H. 387, 151 A. 81, 70 A.L.R. 480, noted in 15 Minn.Law Rev. 120 (1930).

34. See, Anderson v. Ries, 1946, 222 Minn. 408, 24 N.W.2d 717, 167 A.L.R. 1033.

35. See, for example, Ga.Code, § 61–105 (one month notice by lessee and two months notice by lessor). See, Sikes v. Carter, 1923, 30 Ga.App. 539, 118 S.E. 430.

36. See, for example, West's Ann.Cal.Civ.Code, § 789. For an analysis of such statutes, see 26 Iowa Law Rev. 76 (1940).

37. Seavey v. Cloudman, 1897, 90 Me. 536, 38 A. 540; Howard v. Merriam, 1851, 59 Mass. 563.

38. Kirk v. Eastern Coal Corp., 1941, 285 Ky. 422, 148 S.W.2d 289.

vided by statute that a lessor is not entitled to regain possession of his land by self-help. He may maintain ejectment or remedies available under a local Unlawful Entry and Detainer statute.

If a lessee wrongfully holds over after the expiration of his lease he thereby becomes a tenant at sufferance unless he asserts a claim of ownership that makes him an adverse possessor. He cannot be held liable as a trespasser because he entered upon the land rightfully and his interest is possessory in nature. Statutes in some states provide that if a lessee of agricultural land holds over and remains in possession for a stated period, such as sixty days, without notice by the lessor to deliver up possession, it is implied that the lessee is holding possession with the permission of the lessor. He is then entitled to hold possession under the terms of the prior lease for another full year.[39]

Notice is not required to terminate an estate at sufferance. In some states it is provided by statute that a lessor cannot terminate an estate at sufferance without notice.[40] However, such statutes require notice only if the lessee has remained in possession after the expiration of his lease with the consent of the lessor, express or implied.[41] Under such circumstances a new tenancy has supplanted the tenancy at sufferance.

If a lessor is entitled to possession of the leased land he cannot be held liable in an action of trespass if he takes possession of the land by force.[42] However, a remedy may be available to the lessee under a local unlawful entry and detainer statute. According to some decisions, statutes of this type do not deprive the lessor of a right to regain possession without resort to legal action if this can be done without the use of force.[43] The preferred view is that the use of force cannot be justified even if it is authorized by a provision in the lease.[44]

ESTATE FROM PERIOD TO PERIOD (PERIODIC TENANCY)

51. An estate from period to period (periodic tenancy) is an estate which continues from year to year, or for successive fractions of a year, until terminated by proper notice. It is also designated as a tenancy from year to year. A series of separate estates is not involved. The original tenancy continues until terminated by proper notice.

a. Creation of a periodic tenancy. A periodic tenancy may be created by express agreement or by implication. While an estate at will created by express agreement will not evolve into a periodic tenancy, that result may follow if the tenancy at will is created by implication.

If a lessee takes possession under a lease that is not executed with the formalities prescribed by the Statute of Frauds he becomes a tenant at will. Upon the payment of rent on a periodic basis he may become a periodic tenant.

If a lease does not fix the period of duration the lessee becomes a tenant at will. However, if rent is fixed on a periodic basis he may become a periodic tenant.

Under some circumstances a lessor has an option to treat a tenant at sufferance as a periodic tenant.

b. Notice of termination. Notice is required to terminate a periodic tenancy. The common law rule is that the notice

---

39. See, for example, Ky.Rev.Stats. 383.160. For application of such a statute, see Nye v. Dotta, 1952, 112 Cal.App.2d 129, 245 P.2d 529.

40. See, for example, Felt v. Methodist Educational Advance, 1930, 251 Mich. 512, 232 N.W. 178.

41. Smith v. Littlefield, 1873, 51 N.Y. 539.

42. Gower v. Waters, 1926, 125 Me. 223, 132 A. 550, 45 A.L.R. 309; Low v. Elwell, 1876, 121 Mass. 309; Shorter v. Shelton, 1945, 183 Va. 819, 33 S.E.2d 643.

43. See, for example, Snitman v. Goodman, D.C.Mun. App.1955, 118 A.2d 394.

44. Howe v. Frith, 1908, 43 Colo. 75, 95 P. 603.

must be as long as the period itself but not exceeding six months. The time of notice must be synchronized with the beginning of a new period. Usually, the matter is regulated by statute.

c. **Controlling covenants in a periodic tenancy.** If a lease evolves into a periodic tenancy the covenants in the foundation lease are carried over into the new relationship if they are consistent with the form of the tenancy and the parties did not evidence an intention to the contrary. The prevailing rule is that an option to purchase contained in the foundation lease is not carried over into a periodic tenancy.

An estate from period to period (periodic tenancy) is an estate which continues from year to year, or for successive fractions of a year, until terminated by proper notice.[45] Thus, the estate may be one from year to year, from month to month, from week to week or even from day to day. At times the estate is designated as one "from year to year" without reference to the length of the period involved. This form of tenancy was recognized as a means by which to alleviate the hardship incident to a tenancy at will where either the lessor or the lessee may terminate the estate without notice.[46]

If a periodic tenancy is created by express agreement it is not one that involves a series of separate tenancies. The original tenancy continues until terminated by proper notice. That is the case, for example, if L leases to T from month to month or from year to year etc. That is also the case if a lease is silent as to duration (a general letting) and rent is made payable on a periodic basis, such as by the year. Under such circumstances, if a lessor brings an action to recover rent he must include in his claim all rent that has

accrued at the time of his action. This conclusion is based upon the rule that a litigant cannot split his cause of action. Further, a statute regulating leases may violate constitutional rules if it purports to apply to a periodic tenancy created prior to its passage.[47]

There is authority for the view that if a periodic tenancy is created by implication, each period is considered to be a separate and distinct tenancy.[48] However, once a periodic tenancy is created it should be governed by the same rules whether created by express agreement or by implication. In the case of Shack v. Weissbard (N.J.),[49] a periodic tenancy was created by implication when a tenant held over after the expiration of his lease. At that time a statute provided that three months notice was necessary to terminate the tenancy. The court held that the notice-requirement could not be changed by a statute enacted after the estate was created.

Creation of a Periodic Tenancy

A periodic tenancy may be created by express agreement or by implication. In a lease "for one year and then from year to year" the lessee acquires a lease for one year certain and then from year to year. The minimum duration of such a lease is two years.

The general rule is that a periodic tenancy may be created by implication although statutes in some states provide otherwise.[50] Sit-

---

45. 1 Rest. Property, § 20.

46. Right ex dem. Flower v. Darby, K.B.1786, 1 Term Rep. 159, 99 Eng.Rep. 1029. See, Foster, Nebraska Landlord and Tenant, 4 Neb.Law Bulletin 317 (1926).

47. Spiritwood Grain Co. v. Northern Pacific Ry. Co., 8 Cir.1950, 179 F.2d 338.

48. See Alexander v. Harris, 1808, 4 Cranch (U.S.) 299, 302, 2 L.Ed. 627. See Mellows v. Low, [1923] 1 K.B. 522.

49. 130 N.J.L. 472, 33 A.2d 571 (1943).

50. For application of such statutes, see Brown v. Markham, 1950, 56 Fla. 202, 48 So. 39; Welch v. Rice, 1945, 61 Wyo. 511, 159 P.2d 502. A Washington statute requires an express written contract (11 Rem. Rev.Stats., § 10618).

uations involving the creation of this tenancy by implication are discussed in the following paragraphs.

Estate at will

An estate at will created by express agreement will not evolve into a periodic tenancy. For example, if a lease expressly provides that the lessee will give up possession of the land upon demand the estate remains an estate at will regardless of the payment of rent on a periodic basis.[51]

Under some circumstances, an estate at will created by implication may develop into a periodic tenancy. Two such situations are as follows:

First: The general rule is that a person who takes possession of land under a lease that is not executed with the formalities prescribed by the Statute of Frauds is a tenant at will.[52] However, upon the payment of rent this tenancy evolves into a tenancy from period to period. The length of the period is determined by reference to the time fixed for the payment of rent. If the rent is fixed on a yearly basis the tenancy is one from calendar year to calendar year even though it is payable on an installment basis such as by the month.[53] Of course, the fact that an oral lease is specifically enforceable may prevent its evolution into a periodic tenancy if request is made for specific performance.[54]

Statutes in some states provide that all interests or estates in land, created by parol, shall have the force and effect of estates at will *only*. According to one view, a statute of this type prevents the tenancy at will from evolving into a periodic tenancy by possession and payment of rent.[55] According to another view, a periodic tenancy may result.[56] It is reasoned that the statute does not purport to control the type of tenancy that may result from the tenancy at will by force of events that take place *after* the tenant takes possession.

Second: A "general letting" is involved if a lease does not fix the period of its duration. One taking possession under such a lease becomes a tenant at will. However, if the rent is fixed on a periodic basis, such as by the year, the tenant becomes a periodic tenant.[57] The tenancy is from calendar year to calendar year if the rent is computed on a yearly basis even if it is payable in installments.[58] Some authorities determine the period by reference to the period fixed for the *payment* of rent. The implication of a periodic tenancy is not possible in a situation where the agreed rental is not payable on a periodic basis.[59]

Statutes in some states provide that a lease without a fixed period of duration is a lease for one month only if the rent is payable on a monthly basis. Holding over after the ex-

---

51. Humphries v. Humphries, 1843, 25 N.C. 362.

52. But see Cochran v. Ward, 1892, 5 Ind.App. 89, 29 N.E. 795, 31 N.E. 581 (that he is a periodic tenant); Secor v. Pestana, 1865, 37 Ill. 525 (becomes a tenant for years).

53. Griswold v. Town of Branford, 1908, 80 Conn. 453, 68 A. 987 (monthly); Arbenz v. Exley, Watkins & Co., 1903, 52 W.Va. 476, 44 S.E. 149 (quarterly).

54. Sorrells v. Goldberg, 1904, 34 Tex.Civ.App. 265, 78 S.W. 711. For a discussion of this view, see 19 Tex. Law Rev. 338 (1941).

55. Davis v. Thompson, 1836, 13 Me. 209; Ellis v. Paige, 1822, 1 Pick. (Mass.) 43.

56. Barlow v. Wainwright, 1894, 22 Vt. 88.

57. But see, Norman v. Morehouse, Tex.Civ.App.1922, 243 S.W. 1104, noted in 23 Col.Law Rev. 79 (1923) (held to be tenant at will).

58. *Cf.:* McNulty v. Windham, 1937, 182 S.C. 462, 189 S.E. 754 (rent paid weekly and held to be a tenant from year to year).

59. Leonard v. Spicer Mfg. Co., 1927, 103 N.J.L. 391, 139 A. 15, 55 A.L.R. 284.

piration of the month is not evidence of a further lease.[60]

Holdover tenant

If a lessee wrongfully holds over after the expiration of his lease the lessor may consider him to be a tenant at sufferance and institute proceedings to recover possession of the land. Instead, the lessor may outline the terms of a new leasing agreement that may be deemed accepted if the lessee continues in possession of the land.[61] There is a third possibility. With exceptions to be noted, the lessor may elect to consider the tenant as a periodic tenant.

Historically, the implication of a periodic tenancy is based upon the presumed intention of the parties. In line with this view there is early English authority that a periodic tenancy will not result if the holdover tenant evidences the fact that such was not in accord with his intention.[62] But the prevailing American rule is that the election is with the lessor regardless of the intention of the lessee.[63] Circumstances do not warrant the conclusion that the law relating to "implied contracts" furnishes the basis for the obligation imposed upon the lessee. Rather, the duty is one imposed by law because of the wrongful act of the lessee in holding over after the expiration of his term.[64]

The lessee may avoid the "penalty" imposed by law by proof of the fact that he held over after the expiration of his term for a very short period of time as justified by local custom or usage.[65] His conduct may also be excused if there is proof of the fact that he held over because of the illness of a family member and that moving would impair that person's life or health.[66] There must be proof that moving would worsen conditions.[67] Additional points are as follows:

First: A periodic tenancy will not arise if the lessee held over with the consent of the lessor, such as in a case where the delay in giving up possession resulted from the fact that the parties were negotiating for a new lease.[68] In any event, a provision in the lease may negative the implication of a new lease under the circumstances.[69]

Second: A lessor's option to treat a lessee as a tenant at sufferance may be lost if there is an unreasonable delay on his part in asserting his right to possession. This is a statutory rule in some states if agricultural leases are involved.[70]

---

60. See, for example, Corthouts v. Connecticut Fire Safety Services Corp., 1963, 2 Conn.Cir. 34, 193 A.2d 909 (construing Gen.Stats. § 47–22).

61. Donnelly Advertising Corp. v. Flaccomio, 1958, 216 Md. 113, 140 A.2d 165.

62. Jones v. Shears, [1836] 4 Ad. & E. 832, 111 Eng. Rep. 997. See Dougal v. McCarty, [1893] Q.B. 736.

63. A. H. Fetting Mfg. Jewelry Co. v. Waltz, 1930, 160 Md. 50, 152 A. 434, 71 A.L.R. 1443; Schuyler v. Smith, 1873, 51 N.Y. 309; Finif v. Gearing, 1932, 106 Pa.Super. 419, 162 A. 325, noted in 7 Temp.Law Qt. 519. *Contra:* Benton v. Williams, 1909, 202 Mass. 188, 88 N.E. 843.

64. See Herter v. Mullen, 1899, 159 N.Y. 28, 53 N.E. 700.

65. *Cf.:* Unger v. Kern, 1939, 123 N.J.L. 348, 8 A.2d 824 (custom justified retention of possession until noon of the day following termination of the lease).

66. Herter v. Mullen, 1899, 159 N.Y. 28, 53 N.E. 700.

67. In re Garland's Estate, 1940, 173 Misc. 832, 19 N.Y.S.2d 411.

68. Lawson v. West Virginia Newspaper Publishing Co., 1944, 126 W.Va. 470, 29 S.E.2d 3.

69. Kokalis v. Whitehurst, 1952, 334 Mich. 477, 54 N.W.2d 628; Montgomery v. Willis, 1895, 45 Neb. 434, 63 N.W. 794.

70. See, for example, Nye v. Dotta, 1952, 112 Cal.App. 2d 129, 245 P.2d 529, construing West's Ann.Cal.Code Civ.Proc. § 1161(2)—60 days; Ky.—KRS 383.160 (90 days).

Third: If the original term was for one year or more, the periodic tenancy will be from calendar year to calendar year.[71] If the original term was for a period of less than one year, a like period will apply in the new tenancy.[72] According to some authorities, the length of the period is determined by reference to the "installment-periods" fixed for the payment of rent in the prior lease rather than by reference to the term of the lease itself. In other words, if the prior lease was for a period of one year with rent payable monthly, the periodic tenancy will be one from month to month.[73]

Fourth: In a few states a periodic tenancy does not arise if a lessee holds over after the expiration of his lease. It is considered that the prior lease is renewed at the election of the lessor for a period not exceeding one year. This tenancy continues only for the time fixed. Notice of termination is not necessary.[74]

Notice of Termination

A periodic tenancy continues until proper notice of termination is given by the lessor or by the lessee.[75] However, some authorities recognize an exception to this rule if a periodic tenancy evolves from the possession of a lessee under a lease not executed with the formalities prescribed by the Statute of Frauds.[76] While notice may be necessary to terminate the tenancy prior to the time agreed upon, it terminates automatically at the end of that period. It is reasoned that the Statute of Frauds is not concerned with such an "executed oral agreement."

A New York statute provides that as to land located in New York City, the lessee has the privilege of terminating the tenancy at the end of any period without the necessity of giving notice.[77]

While matters pertaining to notice are usually regulated by statute, some of the important aspects are as follows:

First: The common law rule is that the length of notice given must equal the length of the period measuring the duration of the

71. Clinton Wire Cloth Co. v. Garner, 1881, 99 Ill. 151 (5 year lease at a monthly rental); Kearns v. Clark, 1945, 159 Kan. 353, 154 P.2d 479, construing G.S.1935, § 67–502; Viator v. Moses, 1939, 186 Miss. 419, 191 So. 412; Maier v. Champion, 1922, 97 N.J.L. 493, 117 A. 603 (three year lease at a monthly rental); In re Garland's Estate, 1940, 173 Misc. 832, 19 N.Y.S.2d 411; Deitz v. County Court, 1940, 122 W.Va. 296, 8 S.E.2d 884; Ramnik Corp. v. Wallace, 1938, 61 R.I. 282, 200 A. 765 (statutory rule).

72. Heun v. Hanson, 1947, 331 Ill.App. 82, 72 N.E.2d 703, noted in 26 Chicago-Kent Law Rev. 174 (1948). See Foster, Nebraska Landlord and Tenant, 4 Neb. Law Bulletin 217, 339 (1926).

73. Hellebush v. Tischbein Apothecaries, Inc., 1936, 54 Ohio App. 162, 6 N.E.2d 584, noted in 11 Cinn. Law Rev. 427 (1937); Elkins National Bank v. Nefflen, 1936, 118 W.Va. 29, 188 S.E. 750, 108 A.L.R. 1460, noted in 6 Ford.Law Rev. 319 (1937), 23 Va. Law Rev. 716 (1937), 43 W.Va.Law Qt. 339 (1937).

74. Rice v. Atkinson, Deacon, Elliott Co., 1921, 215 Mich. 371, 183 N.W. 762, 19 A.L.R. 1399, noted in 20 Mich.Law Rev. 340 (1922); Bateman v. Maddox, 1894, 86 Tex. 546, 26 S.W. 51 *(dictum)*, discussed in

Bobbitt, Tenancy from Year to Year and Related Estates, 8 Tex.Law Rev. 325, 331 (1930).

75. That "personal service" may be made by mail, see Univ. of So. Calif. v. Weiss, 1962, 208 Cal.App. 2d 759, 25 Cal.Rptr. 475.

76. Adjmi v. Ginter Restaurant Co., 1935, 291 Mass. 224, 196 N.E. 842; Teft v. Hinchman, 1889, 76 Mich. 672, 43 N.W. 680; Vanderhoff v. Lawrence, Mo.App.1947, 201 S.W.2d 509, affirmed 206 S.W.2d 569 (1947); Doe d. Tilt v. Stratton, [1828] 4 Bing. 446, 130 Eng.Rep. 839. *Contra:* Tracy v. Donovan, 1918, 37 Cal.App. 350, 174 P. 113; Darling Shops Del. Corp. v. Baltimore Center Corp., 1949, 191 Md. 289, 60 A.2d 669, 6 A.L.R.2d 667.

77. T. I. B. Corp. v. Repetto, 1940, 174 Misc. 501, 20 N.Y.S.2d 744, affirmed, 261 App.Div. 813, 25 N.Y.S. 2d 782 (1941) with lease to appeal denied, 261 App. Div. 943, 27 N.Y.S.2d 185 (1941).

lease, with a maximum notice of six months.[78] Thus, one month's notice is required to terminate a tenancy from month to month. Six months' notice is required to terminate a tenancy from calendar year to calendar year. Statutes in some states provide for a maximum period of less than six months, such as one month or thirty days.[79]

Except to the extent that public policy is involved, notice requirements may be regulated by provisions in the lease. There is authority for the view that a leasing agreement may provide for termination of the lease at any time without notice.[80] However, such a provision would result in the creation of a tenancy at will rather than a periodic tenancy.

Second: Notice must be given the required length of time prior to the anniversary of the lease.[81] For example, if a tenancy is from one calendar year to another and starts on January 1st, notice of termination must be served at least six months prior to January 1st of any given year.[82]

In a number of states the above stated rule has been changed by statute. For example, a Michigan statute provides that in all cases of tenancies from year to year, notice to quit, given at any time, shall be sufficient to terminate the tenancy at the expiration of one year from the time of the service of such notice.[83] A California statute provides that a tenancy from *month to month* may be terminated by thirty (30) days notice given

at any time.[84] Similar provision is not made in the case of other tenancies, such as a tenancy from year to year.

A notice is not necessarily defective merely because it is given a longer time before the expiration date of the period than is required by law.[85]

Third: In Besdine v. Leitner (N. Y.),[86] a lessor's notice to his month to month tenant was that the tenant should remove from the land or pay an increased rental. The lessee remained in possession but refused to pay the increased rent. The court held that the notice did not result in termination of the tenancy because the demand for rent was inconsistent with the demand for possession.[87] In view of the fact that the lessee does not have a right to occupy the land except on terms fixed by the lessor, if the terms are not acceptable to the lessee he can vacate. Accordingly, the preferred view is that the terms of the lease can be changed by notice.[88]

Fourth: If a lessor terminates a periodic tenancy by proper notice, and the lessee holds over, the lessor may elect to treat him as a tenant at sufferance or as a periodic tenant.[89] This means that the lessor may consider his notice of termination as a nullity. However, there is authority for the view that the notice of termination stands and a new

---

78. Maniatty v. Carroll Co., 1945, 114 Vt. 168, 41 A.2d 144, 156 A.L.R. 1306.

79. See, for example, West's Ann.Cal.Civ.Code, § 1946.

80. Bailey v. Lund, 1938, 134 Neb. 319, 278 N.W. 506.

81. Heun v. Hanson, 1947, 331 Ill.App. 82, 72 N.E.2d 703, noted in 26 Chicago-Kent Law Rev. 174 (1948).

82. Right ex dem. Flower v. Darby, [1786] 1 Term Rep. 159, 99 Eng.Rep. 1029.

83. Mich.Comp.Laws 1948, § 554.134.

84. West's Ann.Cal.Civ.Code, § 1946.

85. Wright v. Zachgo, 1937, 222 Iowa 1368, 271 N.W. 512; Medical Professional Bldg. Corp. v. Ferrell, Tex.Civ.App.1939, 131 S.W.2d 683.

86. 166 Misc. 658, 2 N.Y.S.2d 271 (1938).

87. See, Welk v. Bidwell, 1950, 136 Conn. 603, 73 A.2d 295. *Cf.*: Williams v. Seder, 1940, 306 Mass. 134, 27 N.E.2d 708 (notice served on a tenant at will).

88. Abraham v. Gheens, 1924, 205 Ky. 289, 265 S.W. 778, 40 A.L.R. 186; Bhar Realty Corp. v. Becker, 1958, 49 N.J.Super. 585, 140 A.2d 756. See, West's Ann.Cal.Civ.Code, § 827.

89. Douglass v. Whitaker, 1884, 32 Kan. 381, 4 P. 874; Moshier v. Reding, 1835, 12 Me. 478; Providence County Sav. Bank v. Hall, 1888, 16 R.I. 154, 13 A. 122.

agreement will be required for the creation of a periodic tenancy.[90]

Controlling Covenants in a Periodic Tenancy

A periodic tenancy may evolve from a tenancy at will, a lease that is unenforceable because of the Statute of Frauds or an expired lease if the lessee holds over. In general, promises and covenants in these "foundation leases" will form a part of the periodic tenancy if they are consistent with the new relationship. These include covenants to repair,[91] to pay rent,[92] not to assign or sublease [93] and covenants relating to the planting of crops,[94] removal of fixtures [95] and the termination of the tenancy upon the happening of some event.[96]

If a lease is unenforceable because of the Statute of Frauds, provision as to the duration of the lease will not form a part of the periodic tenancy. There is authority for the view that the date fixed for the termination of the lease will be operative and the periodic tenancy will terminate at that time regardless of notice.[97] This conclusion is not sound for two reasons. In the first place, the Statute of Frauds prohibits application of this aspect of the oral lease. In the second place, a fixed period of duration is inconsistent with the existence of a periodic tenancy that has the important characteristic of termination by notice.[98]

In the Illinois case of Wanous v. Balaco,[99] a tenant took possession under a lease that provided in part: "Lessors agree to give Lessee the right to purchase the premises * * * during any part of the term * *." The lease expired and the tenant continued to occupy the land as a periodic tenant. He claimed that the option to purchase carried over into the new tenancy. This claim was denied upon the ground that the duration of the option was, by implication, limited to the duration of the foundation lease and was not applicable to the new tenancy and the new condition of things. The same conclusion may be supported upon the ground that such an option is not a part of the lease itself. It is a collateral and independent covenant and does not become one of the terms of the periodic tenancy.[100]

---

90. Neumeister v. Palmer, 1880, 8 Mo.App. 491; Emmons v. Scudder, 1874, 115 Mass. 367; Ibbs v. Richardson, [1839] 9 A. & E. 849, 112 Eng.Rep. 1436.

91. Martin v. Smith, 1874, L.R. 9 Exch. 50.

92. Ferri v. Liberatoscioli, 1940, 338 Pa. 454, 13 A.2d 45.

93. Hall v. Henry J. Robb, Inc., D.C.Mun.App.1943, 32 A.2d 707 (subleasing).

94. Millage v. Spahn, 1946, 115 Colo. 444, 175 P.2d 982.

95. Knox v. Wolfe, 1946, 73 Cal.App.2d 494, 167 P.2d 3.

96. Gostin v. Needle, 1946, 185 Md. 634, 45 A.2d 772, 163 A.L.R. 1013.

97. Secor v. Pestana, 1865, 37 Ill. 525; Doe d. Tilt v. Stratton, [1828], 4 Bing. 446, 130 Eng.Rep. 839.

98. See, Tracy v. Donovan, 1918, 37 Cal.App. 350, 174 P. 113.

99. 412 Ill. 545, 107 N.E.2d 791 (1952).

100. *Accord:* Spaulding v. Yovino-Young, 1947, 30 Cal. 2d 138, 180 P.2d 691; Libin v. Peters, 1947, 118 Ind. App. 27, 75 N.E.2d 162; Glocksine v. Malleck, 1963, 372 Mich. 115, 125 N.W.2d 298; Wright v. Barclay, 1949, 151 Neb. 94, 36 N.W.2d 645; Andreula v. Slovak Gymnastic Union, 1947, 140 N.J.Eq. 171, 53 A.2d 191. *Contra:* Ardito v. Howell, 1947, 29 Del.Ch. 467, 51 A.2d 859; Gressitt v. Anderson, 1947, 187 Md. 586, 51 A.2d 159; Rubin v. Gochrach, 1947, 186 Va. 786, 44 S.E.2d 1; Last v. Puehler, 1963, 19 Wis. 2d 291, 120 N.W.2d 120 (first refusal).

CHAPTER 12

CONDITIONS AND LIMITATIONS IN LEASES

IN GENERAL

52. A lease is subject to a condition subsequent if the lessor reserves the power to terminate the lease upon the happening of a named event. A determinable lease is one wherein it is provided that the lease is to terminate automatically upon the happening of a named event.

A lease may provide for automatic termination upon the happening of a named event or it may contain a provision authorizing the lessor to terminate the lease at that time. Usually, in line with a strict construction against forfeiture, there must be clear language in a lease if premature termination is contemplated.[1] In the Massachusetts case of Wheeler v. Dascomb,[2] a covenant provided that the lessee would "deliver up said premises" upon receiving three months notice and upon payment of a stipulated sum by the lessor. Since there was no express provision relating to the termination of the lease for breach of this covenant the lessor's sole remedy was for breach of contract. There is no discussion of the question as to whether or not this type of a covenant may be specifically enforced. The covenant differs from one where the lessor reserves the *right to terminate the lease* upon the happening of a named event (a power of termination).[3]

In many states it is provided by statute that a lessor may follow statutory procedure and thereby terminate a lease for breach of a covenant to pay rent. A California statute provides for such termination for breach of any covenant in the lease.[4] In case of the premature termination of a lease the lessee is discharged from liability except as to covenants in default at the time of termination.[5] This rule has been applied in a case where the lease expressly provided that the termination was "without prejudice to any remedies for arrears of rent or breach of covenant." This clause did not authorize the recovery of future rentals.[6]

Leases are subject to the implied condition that the lessee will not deny the title of his lessor. In the event of such denial the lessor may terminate the lease.[7]

---

1. Beck v. Giordano, 1960, 144 Colo. 372, 356 P.2d 264; Brown's Adm'rs v. Bragg, 1864, 22 Ind. 122.

2. 3 Cush. (Mass.) 285 (1849).

3. Gunsenhiser v. Binder, 1910, 206 Mass. 434, 92 N.E. 705.

4. West's Ann.Cal.Code Civ.Proc., § 1161, subd. 3, applied in McCarty v. Raso, 1951, 102 Cal.App.2d 909, 228 P.2d 577.

5. Blond v. Hoffman, 1938, 343 Mo. 247, 121 S.W.2d 137.

6. Rohrt v. Kelley Mfg. Co., 1961, 162 Tex. 534, 349 S.W.2d 95.

7. Jones v. Stiffler, 1939, 137 Pa.Super. 133, 8 A.2d 455 *(dictum)*.

CONSTRUCTION

53. Even if a lease specifically provides that it is to terminate upon some default on the part of the lessee, the termination is at the option of the lessor. This rule of construction is followed in compliance with the presumed intention of the parties and as a means by which to prevent a lessee from gaining an advantage by reason of his own default.

If it is provided that the lessor may terminate a lease if he should sell the property, a sale made for the mere purpose of avoiding the lease will not warrant termination. Further, an option to purchase does not constitute a "sale" within the meaning of such a condition or limitation.

In construing the provisions of a lease the courts disregard technical language and attempt to give effect to the intention of the parties as gathered from a consideration of the entire lease.[8] In the Minnesota case of Lowenthal v. Newlon,[9] a lease provided that in case of default in the payment of rent or in the performance of any other covenant "then and from thenceforth this lease shall become ended and determined" and all rights of the lessee forfeited. There was also provision for right of re-entry. The court denied the lessee's claim that default on his part brought an end to the lease without reference to the intention of the lessor. If, as here, the provision for automatic termination is based upon a contemplated breach of the lease by the lessee it is obvious that the provision was inserted for the benefit of the lessor only. Therefore, if the lessee defaults the lease is not terminated unless the lessor elects that result.[10] Otherwise, a lessee might

benefit from his own default. In a few decisions it is held that if a lease provides for termination upon the happening of a named event the lease terminates at that time regardless of default on the part of the lessee.[11]

If it is provided that a lessor can terminate the lease if he should sell the property, a sale made for the mere purpose of avoiding the lease will not warrant termination.[12] The condition contemplates good faith on the part of the lessor.[13]

While the execution of an option to purchase does not constitute a "sale" within the meaning of such a condition,[14] an oral contract of sale may warrant termination of the lease. This is true if there is sufficient part performance to take the contract out of the operation of the Statute of Frauds.[15]

Assuming a *bona fide* sale of the land, the lessee must surrender possession to the purchaser even though the lessor was under a duty to pay the lessee the value of improvements erected upon the land and defaulted in the performance of this duty.[16] Of course, a provision in the lease may make payment a condition of surrender. If possible, the lease

---

8. Markey v. Smith, 1938, 301 Mass. 64, 16 N.E.2d 20, 118 A.L.R. 274, noted in 25 Va.Law Rev. 102 (1938).

9. 138 Minn. 248, 164 N.W. 905 (1917).

10. Bank of America v. Moore, 1937, 18 Cal.App.2d 522, 64 P.2d 460; Vincent v. Kaser Construction Co., 1963, 253 Iowa 1141, 125 N.W.2d 608 ("failure to make any such payments shall terminate this lease");

Cohen v. Afro-American Realty Co., 1908, 58 Misc. 199, 108 N.Y.S. 998 (lease was to terminate if any legal process was filed against the lessee); Clark v. Jones, 1845, 1 Denio (N.Y.) 516 (failure to pay rent). But see, Murray Realty Co. v. Regal Shoe Co., 1934, 265 N.Y. 332, 193 N.E. 164.

11. See, for example, Weill v. Centralia Service & Oil Co., 1943, 320 Ill.App. 397, 51 N.E.2d 345.

12. Muzzy v. Allen, 1856, 25 N.J.L. 471.

13. Yontz v. McDowell, 1923, 197 Ky. 770, 247 S.W. 948.

14. Diamond Cattle Co. v. Clark, 1937, 52 Wyo. 265, 74 P.2d 857, 116 A.L.R. 912.

15. Luse v. Elliott, 1927, 204 Iowa 378, 213 N.W. 410.

16. Miami Co-Operative Mining Co. v. Cherokee Coal Co., 1924, 96 W.Va. 11, 122 S.E. 286, 35 A.L.R. 514.

will be construed in such a manner as to require such payment as a condition.[17]

CONDITIONS NOT SUSCEPTIBLE OF SUCCESSIVE BREACHES

54. Some conditions are not susceptible of successive breaches and for that reason are "entire in nature." For example, if a lease contains a condition against assignment without the consent of the lessor the condition is abrogated if an assignment is made with consent. This follows from the fact that an assignment terminates the estate of the lessee.

Modern authorities support the view that if such a condition is expressly made binding upon the lessee *and his assigns*, the provision operates to create successive conditions. As such, the condition may be imposed upon assignees.

Some conditions are not susceptible of successive breaches and for that reason are said to be "entire in nature." [18] For example, if a lease contains a condition against assignment without the consent of the lessor, the condition is abrogated if an assignment is made with consent. This follows from the fact that a lessee can make but one assignment because after an assignment his interest is terminated.

In Dumpor's case,[19] a lease contained a provision (construed to be a condition) that the lessee "or his assigns" should not "alien the premises" without the license of the lessors. The lessee, Bolde, after securing consent, assigned the lease to Tubbe, who devised the lease to his son. The son died testate and the administrator of his estate assigned the lease to defendant. The lessor claimed a right to enter for breach of the condition. This claim was denied upon the ground that a condition is entire and indivisible and, hav-

ing once been waived, cannot be enforced again.[20] Of course, the consent of the lessor may be qualified. That is, it may be given on condition that subsequent assignments are not to be made without the consent of the lessor.[21]

Because of the fact that in Dumpor's case the condition against assignment was expressly made binding upon the lessee "or his assigns" argument may be made that the provision created "successive conditions" binding upon successive assignees. However, the court held otherwise.[22] The decision was probably influenced by the fact that conditions were not looked upon with favor because they involve the forfeiture of estates. This is indicated by the fact that in some decisions a distinction is drawn between conditions and covenants.[23]

The rule in Dumpor's case has been repudiated in a number of states.[24] That is to say, if the condition is expressly made binding upon the lessee "and his assigns" the language is held to be sufficiently expressive to create successive conditions. However, if assignees are not named they are not bound by the original condition. This is designated as the "singleness-of-covenant" rule.[25]

20. *Accord*: Aste v. Putnam's Hotel Co., 1923, 247 Mass. 147, 141 N.E. 666, 31 A.L.R. 149.

21. Kew v. Trainor, 1894, 150 Ill. 150, 37 N.E. 223; Springer v. Chicago Real Estate Loan & Trust Co., 1903, 202 Ill. 17, 66 N.E. 850.

22. The rule in Dumpor's case was abolished by an English statute enacted in 1859 (22 & 23 Vict., c. 35).

23. Williams v. Dakin, 1839, 22 Wend.(N.Y.) 201. *Contra*: Reid v. John F. Wiessner Brewing Co., 1898, 88 Md. 234, 40 A. 877, noted in 12 Harv.Law Rev. 272 (1898).

24. See, for example, Investors' Guaranty Corp. v. Thompson, 1924, 31 Wyo. 264, 225 P. 590, 32 A.L.R. 1071, noted in 19 Ill.Law Rev. 463 (1925).

25. Kendis v. Cohn, 1928, 90 Cal.App. 41, 265 P. 844; Barber v. Hyder, 1948, 52 N.M. 421, 200 P.2d 717.

17. Diepenbrock v. Luiz, 1913, 159 Cal. 716, 115 P. 743.

18. See McGlynn v. Moore, 1864, 25 Cal. 384, 395.

19. 4 Coke, 119b, 76 Eng.Rep. 1110 (1603).

CONDITIONS SUSCEPTIBLE OF SUCCESSIVE BREACHES

55. If a condition is susceptible of successive breaches the lessor may waive his right to declare a forfeiture for one breach but insist upon subsequent compliance with the terms of the lease. Under some circumstances it may be necessary for him to give notice to the lessee of his intention to enforce the condition (reinstate the condition).

Many conditions are susceptible of successive breaches. In other words, they are not "entire in nature." This is true with respect to conditions relating to the timely payment of rent, conditions prohibiting subleasing [26] etc. A lessor may waive his right to declare a forfeiture for breach of such a condition [27] (such as by the acceptance of rent accruing after a known breach) but insist upon subsequent compliance with the terms of the lease.[28] For this purpose, however, it may be necessary for him to give notice to the lessee of his intention to enforce the condition involved and thereby "reinstate the condition" as set forth in the lease.[29]

In Doe dem Ambler v. Woodbridge (Eng.),[30] there was a condition that rooms could be used only for "bed or sitting rooms" by the lessee and members of his family. The lessee allowed a lodger to occupy part of the area and the lessor accepted rent with knowledge of the breach of condition. The court held that this constituted a waiver of the condition only as to breaches that occurred prior to the acceptance of rent. The condition was continuous in nature and a new breach occurred each and every day that the lodger remained.[31]

EQUITABLE RELIEF AGAINST FORFEITURE

56. Equitable relief against forfeiture may be available under a variety of circumstances in situations involving an innocent default.

A court of equity may grant relief against forfeiture under a variety of circumstances, such as in a case where the lessee was the victim of fraud, accident or mistake.[32] The relief is usually available if there has been substantial compliance with the conditions set forth in the lease.[33] In general, equitable relief is not indicated in the case of a wilful default.[34] It is usually granted in the case of an innocent default.[35] This is especially true if the default involved the payment of money and timely tender was made.[36] In some states it is provided by statute that equitable relief against forfeiture may be granted on

---

26. Miller v. Newton-Humphreville Co., N.J.Ch.1920, 116 A. 325. But see, Wertheimer v. Hosmer, 1890, 83 Mich. 56, 47 N.W. 47.

27. Lucas Hunt Village Co. v. Klein, Mo.App.1948, 212 S.W.2d 480; Woolard v. Schaffer Stores Co., Inc., 1936, 272 N.Y. 304, 5 N.E.2d 829, 109 A.L.R. 1262, noted in 15 N.Y.Univ.Law Qt.Rev. 286 (1938). See, Potter v. Henry Field Seed Co., 1948, 239 Iowa 920, 32 N.W.2d 385.

28. London v. Tebo, 1923, 246 Mass. 360, 141 N.E. 234, 29 A.L.R. 1037; Zotalis v. Cannellos, 1917, 138 Minn. 179, 164 N.W. 807.

29. See Famous Permanent Wave Shops, Inc. v. Smith, 1939, 302 Ill.App. 178, 23 N.E.2d 767, noted in 28 Georgetown Law Jr. 1137 (1940).

30. 9 B. & C. 376, 109 Eng.Rep. 140 (K.B.1829).

31. See Zotalis v. Cannellos, 1917, 138 Minn. 179, 164 N.W. 807.

32. City Garage & Sales Co. v. Ballenger, 1926, 214 Ala. 516, 108 So. 257; Galvin v. Southern Hotel Corp., 4 Cir. 1946, 154 F.2d 970. See Comment, Relief from Forfeitures for Non-payment of Rent, 28 Georgetown Law Jr., 1137 (1940).

33. City Garage & Sales Co. v. Ballenger, 1926, 214 Ala. 516, 108 So. 257.

34. Bonfils v. Ledoux, 8 Cir. 1920, 266 F. 507, 16 A.L.R. 430; Darvirris v. Boston Safe Deposit & Trust Co., 1920, 235 Mass. 76, 126 N.E. 382, 16 A.L.R. 429.

35. Lundin v. Schoeffel, 1897, 167 Mass. 465, 45 N.E. 933.

36. Moore v. Richfield Oil Corp., 1962, 233 Or. 39, 377 P.2d 32; Galvin v. Southern Hotel Corp., 4 Cir. 1946, 154 F.2d 970.

the basis of hardship if application is made within a specified time.[37] In general, the rules relating to equitable relief against forfeiture are also applicable in the case of a determinable lease.[38]

ENFORCEMENT OF CONDITION OR LIMITATION

57. Even if a lessor is entitled to the possession of land because of the termination of a lease, he is not entitled to regain possession by

self-help. **He must follow the statutory procedure that is made available for this purpose.**

Even if a lessor is entitled to the possession of land because of the termination of a lease, he is not entitled to regain possession by self-help. He must resort to appropriate judicial proceedings usually prescribed in unlawful entry and detainer statutes.[39] In some states it is also necessary to serve notice of termination on the lessee a stated period of time prior to bringing action.[40]

---

37. See, for example, West's Ann.Cal.Code Civ.Proc. § 1179.

38. See, Niles, Conditional Limitations in Leases in New York, 11 N.Y.Univ.Law Qt.Rev., 15, 30 (1933).

39. See, for example, Jordan v. Talbot, 1961, 55 Cal.2d 597, 12 Cal.Rptr. 488, 361 P.2d 20.

40. See, for example, Igauye v. Howard, 1952, 114 Cal.App.2d 122, 249 P.2d 558, applying West's Ann. Cal.Civ.Code, § 791 (three days' notice required).

CHAPTER 13

COVENANTS IN LEASES

THEORIES UNDERLYING LIABILITY OF PARTIES

58. Privity of contract exists as between a lessor and lessee. The execution of a lease also creates a tenurial relationship designated as privity of estate. Privity of estate exists only while the lessor and lessee, or their assignees, are the owners of the identical estates created by the lease.

An assignment is involved if the lessee conveys the identical estate he acquired under the lease. If a lesser estate is conveyed the transaction constitutes a sublease. There are conflicting views as to whether or not a conveyance constitutes an assignment if a power of termination (right of re-entry) is reserved.

a. Privity of contract. Privity of contract is not destroyed by an assignment. If the assignee expressly assumes the obligations according to the terms of the lease there is privity of contract between the lessor and the assignee. Otherwise, the liability of an assignee depends upon privity of estate.

b. Lessee estopped to deny title of his lessor. With various exceptions, in an action brought by the lessor for breach of covenant the lessee is estopped to deny the title of the lessor. This estoppel applies as against assignees and sublessees and may be asserted by the assignee of the lessor or by the heirs of the lessor.

Contractual obligations are personal. Except in cases involving third party beneficiary contracts and in assignment situations, privity of contract is essential for contractual liability. But privity of contract is not essential when it comes to the enforcement of covenants in a lease.

There is, of course, privity of contract between a lessor and a lessee. But the execution of a lease also creates a tenurial relationship arising out of the fact that the lessor and the lessee have co-existing, mutually exclusive, interests in the same land that are created by the lease. This tenure is described as *privity of estate* and may be used as a substitute for privity of contract in litigation involving liability for breach of covenants in a lease. Restrictions on the type of covenants that may be enforced on the basis of privity of estate are discussed under a separate heading.

Privity of estate exists only while the lessor or the lessee or any third party was the owner of the *identical estate* created by the lease. For example, if the lessor assigns the reversion there is privity of estate as between the assignee and the lessee. If the les-

140

see transfers the *identical estate* he acquired under the lease privity of estate exists as between this party and the owner of the reversion. A conveyance of the identical estate constitutes an assignment. A conveyance of anything less than that constitutes a sublease.[1] A conveyance of the identical estate in a part of the land results in an assignment *pro tanto*.[2] A tenurial relationship does not exist as between the lessor and a sublessee.

The reservation of rent by a conveyor will not prevent the transfer from being classified as an assignment.[3] It is not material whether the rent is more or less than the rent specified in the lease. This follows from the fact that a right to rent may exist separate and distinct from a reversion. According to the common law rule, an assignment results even if the conveyor retains a right of entry (power of termination) for breach of a named condition. This conforms to the historical view that a right of entry is not an interest in land. It is something in the nature of a "mere possibility" and is simply a means by which to enforce the terms of a lease.[4] While

this common law rule is followed in many states the preferred view is that a right of entry is an estate in land. The retention of this estate results in a sublease.[5]

At common law covenants were enforceable by and against an assignee of the leasehold estate but they were not enforceable by or against an assignee of the reversion. During the reign of Henry VIII legislation was enacted which provided that the assignee of the reversion was in the same position as the assignee of the leasehold estate.[6] Thus, privity of estate made enforcement of covenants possible by and against remote parties taking by assignment. This rule is followed in all of the American states.[7]

Privity of Contract

The privity of contract existing between the lessor and lessee is not destroyed by an assignment. Their liability remains unchanged whether a breach of covenant occurs before or after an assignment. If the assignee of a lease *expressly assumes* the obligations according to the terms of the lease the lessor thereby becomes a third party beneficiary under the contract of assignment. The liability of the assignee is then based upon privity of contract and extends to a breach

---

1. McKinley Realty & Const. Co. v. Rosenblum, 1933, 149 Misc. 730, 268 N.Y.S. 67. But see Jaber v. Miller, 1951, 219 Ark. 59, 239 S.W.2d 760 (whether or not a conveyance results in an assignment or a sublease depends upon the *intention* of the parties).

2. Bancroft v. Vizard, 1919, 202 Ala. 618, 81 So. 560; Cook v. Jones, 1894, 96 Ky. 283, 28 S.W. 960; Craig v. Summers, 1891, 47 Minn. 189, 49 N.W. 742; New Amsterdam Cas. Co. v. National Union Fire Ins. Co., 1935, 266 N.Y. 254, 194 N.E. 745, 99 A.L.R. 216. *Contra*: Fulton v. Stuart, 1825, 2 Ohio 215; Shannon v. Grindstaff, 1895, 11 Wash. 536, 40 P. 123. *Cf.*: McNeil v. Kendall, 1880, 128 Mass. 245.

3. Johnson v. Moxley, 1927, 216 Ala. 466, 113 So. 656.

4. Backus v. Duffy, 1930, 103 Cal.App. 775, 284 P. 954; Sexton v. Chicago Storage Co., 1889, 129 Ill. 318, 21 N.E. 920; Craig v. Summers, 1891, 47 Minn. 189, 49 N.W. 742; Wilson v. Cornbrooks, 1928, 104 N.J.L. 418, 140 A. 292; Gillette Bros., Inc. v. Aristocrat Restaurant, Inc., 1924, 239 N.Y. 87, 145 N.E. 748, noted in 34 Yale Law Jr. 913 (1925); Sheridan

v. Doherty, Inc., 1919, 106 Wash. 561, 181 P. 16, noted in 20 Col.Law Rev. 95 (1920). *Cf.*: Smiley v. Van Winkle, 1856, 6 Cal. 605. See Groth v. Continental Oil Co., 1962, 84 Idaho 409, 373 P.2d 548.

5. Essex Lunch, Inc. v. Boston Lunch Co., 1918, 229 Mass. 557, 118 N.E. 899 (lessee, as owner of a reversion, entitled to enjoin acts of waste); Saling v. Flesch, 1929, 85 Mont. 106, 277 P. 612; Davis v. Vidal, 1912, 105 Tex. 444, 151 S.W. 290; Voloudakis v. Commissioner of Internal Revenue, 9 Cir. 1960, 274 F.2d 209 (sublease so lessee not entitled to treat payments received as capital gains rather than ordinary income).

6. 32 Hen. VIII, c. 34 (1540).

7. See Abbot, Covenants in a Lease which Run with the Land, 31 Yale Law Jr. 127, 128 (1921).

of covenant that occurs even after a re-assignment.[8]

In the absence of an assumption agreement the liability of an assignee depends upon privity of estate. For that reason he cannot be held liable for the breach of a covenant that occurred prior to the assignment.[9] For the same reason, he cannot be held liable for the breach of a covenant that occurred after a surrender [10] or re-assignment [11] of the lease. There is some authority that mere abandonment of the land by an assignee relieves him from liability for breach of a covenant that occurs after the abandonment.[12] Theoretically, this conclusion is not sound because the estate survives an abandonment. However, the conclusion is a practical one in view of the fact that the assignee may rid himself of the estate at any time by making an assignment to a person without financial responsibility.

Privity of estate as between the lessor and the assignee of the leasehold estate may exist even if the assignee does not take actual possession of the land. It has been so held in a case where the assignee recognized the validity of the assignment by paying rent.[13]

Lessee Estopped to Deny Title of His Lessor

With exceptions to be noted, in an action brought by the lessor for breach of a covenant in the lease, the lessee is estopped to deny the title of his lessor. This estoppel applies as against assignees and sublessees and may be asserted by an assignee of the lessor or by the heirs of the lessor. The estoppel results from the conduct of the lessee in taking possession of the land by and with the consent of the lessor (estoppel *in pais*).

First: A claim of estoppel will not be sustained as to matters arising after the surrender of a lease because, in that event, possession of the land is not referable to the consent of the lessor. A lessee may deny the title of the lessor if the lessee did not take original possession under the lease but, while otherwise in lawful possession, he was fraudulently induced to take a lease.[14]

Second: Estoppel is not applicable as to changes in ownership of the land that took place after the execution of the lease. For example, the lessee may show that the estate of the lessor expired during the continuance of the lease either because the lessor had a limited estate or because the lessor conveyed the estate to another. In that event the duty of the lessee is owing to one other than the lessor.[15] The lessee may show that he acquired the estate from the lessor after the execution of the lease.[16]

8. Bank of America v. Moore, 1937, 18 Cal.App.2d 522, 64 P.2d 460 (the assignment provided that the assignee ". . . is to accept, assume and agree to perform all of the terms, conditions and limitations contained in said lease.")

9. Washington Natural Gas Co. v. Johnson, 1889, 123 Pa. 576, 16 A. 799.

10. Lincoln Fireproof Warehouse Co. v. Greusel, 1929, 199 Wis. 428, 224 N.W. 98, 227 N.W. 6, 70 A.L.R. 1096, noted in 15 Iowa Law Rev. 213 (1930); 28 Mich.Law Rev. 773 (1930).

11. A. D. Juilliard & Co. v. American Woolen Co., 1943, 69 R.I. 215, 32 A.2d 800, 148 A.L.R. 187. *Contra*: Waggoner v. Edwards, Tex.Civ.App.1935, 83 S.W.2d 386; Marathon Oil Co. v. Edwards, Tex.Civ.App.1936, 96 S.W.2d 551, error dismissed.

12. Treff v. Gulko, 1932, 214 Cal. 591, 7 P.2d 697. *Contra*: Baston v. Davis, 1959, 229 Ark. 666, 318 S.W.2d 837.

13. Tate v. Neary, 1900, 52 App.Div. 78, 65 N.Y.S. 40.

14. Knowles v. Robinson, 1963, 60 Cal.2d 620, 36 Cal. Rptr. 33, 387 P.2d 833.

15. Beach v. Boettcher, 1944, 323 Ill.App. 79, 55 N.E.2d 104. But see Quon v. Sanguinetti, 1943, 60 Ariz. 301, 135 P.2d 880.

16. Corrigan v. City of Chicago, 1893, 144 Ill. 537, 33 N.E. 746. But see, Colette v. Tidwell, 1944, 112

Third: A lessee may set up his own title if, by the form of his action, the lessor put his own title in issue, such as in a quiet title action.[17]

THE RULE IN SPENCER'S CASE

59. **According to the two propositions declared in Spencer's case, an assignee of either the reversion or of the leasehold estate cannot be held liable for breach of covenant, (1) if the covenant pertained to a thing not** *in esse,* **unless the covenant was in terms made binding upon assignees, or (2) if the covenant is of a type that "does not touch and concern the land."**

The modern law relating to liability on covenants in leases has been influenced by two propositions declared in Spencer's case,[18] an early English decision.

First: If the covenant pertains to a thing that is not in existence (*in esse*), a remote party will not be bound by the covenant unless it includes him in its terms. For example, if a covenant requires the lessee to build a wall, an assignee of the lessee will not be bound unless the original covenant was made binding upon the lessee *and his assigns.*[19] The burden incident to a covenant of this type is particularly heavy so the intention to bind remote parties should be clearly expressed. Of course, this formal method of expressing intention is not necessary if the covenant pertains to a thing *in esse,* such as in a case where the covenant is to repair a building or a wall that may be erected upon the land.[20]

A requirement relating to the use of technical language is not generally looked upon with favor. A number of authorities express the view that the intention of the parties for the purpose under discussion can be determined by reference to surrounding circumstances as well as by reference to technical words.[21]

Second: Remote parties are not concerned with a covenant in a lease unless it is closely associated with estate involved, *i. e.,* the leasehold estate or the reversion. This requirement is usually expressed by the statement that the covenant must "touch and concern the land."

There seems to be no universally accepted test as to when a covenant does touch or concern the land. Professor Bigelow has presented a workable test. If the covenant tends to increase or diminish the rights, privileges, or powers of the tenant in connection with his enjoyment of the leased land, then the covenant is one that touches and concerns the leasehold estate and may be enforced by and against any subsequent assignee of the estate.[22] The same test is applicable in determining whether or not a covenant touches and concerns the reversion.

A covenant may touch and concern both the leasehold estate and the reversion. For example, an option to purchase contained in a lease increases the value of the leasehold estate and restricts the powers and privileges of the owner of the reversion. Thus, the benefit side of the covenant runs with an assignment of the leasehold estate and the

Colo. 117, 146 P.2d 891; Brydges v. Millionair Club, Inc., 1942, 15 Wash.2d 714, 132 P.2d 188.

17. Collier v. Johnson, 1926, 79 Cal.App. 322, 249 P. 217.

18. 5 Co.Rep. 16A, 77 Eng.Rep. 72 (K.B. 1583).

19. See, West's Ann.Cal.Civ.Code, § 1464.

20. Minshull v. Oakes, [1858] 2 H. & N. 793, 157 Eng. Rep. 327.

21. Purvis v. Shuman, 1916, 273 Ill. 286, 112 N.E. 679, noted in 1 Ill.Law Bulletin 60 (1917); 15 Mich. Law Rev. 79 (1916); Sexauer v. Wilson, 1907, 136 Iowa 357, 113 N.W. 941; Masury v. Southworth, 1859, 9 Ohio St. 340.

22. Bigelow, The Content of Covenants in Leases, 12 Mich.Law Rev. 639 (1914). See First Nat. Bank v. Hazelwood Co., 1917, 85 Or. 403, 166 P. 955.

burden side of the covenant runs with an assignment of the reversion.[23] But it is not necessary that both the benefit and the burden side of a covenant run with the land.[24] A further discussion of these matters will be found in sections pertaining to specific covenants.

ASSIGNING AND SUBLEASING

60. While conditions and covenants against assigning or subleasing are sanctioned they involve a restraint upon alienation and are strictly construed.

    a. **Covenant distinguished from condition or limitation. The breach of a condition or limitation that prohibits assigning or subleasing may result in the termination of a lease. Termination cannot be declared for breach of a covenant.**

    b. **Strict construction. A prohibition against assigning or subleasing is strictly construed. A restriction against assignment is not breached by a sublease and *vice versa*. A general prohibition against assignment will not prevent an assignment by operation of law.**

    c. **Corporations. A prohibition against assigning or subleasing is not violated by a transfer in management of a corporate lessee resulting from the sale of corporate stock.**

    d. **Partnership. A prohibition against assignment is breached if there is a withdrawal of a partner of a lessee partnership if he was a member of the partnership at the time of the lease.**

In the absence of restrictions in the lease a lessee may assign or sublease without the consent of the lessor.[25] However, this is not true if a lease involves elements of personal trust and confidence.[26] Further, statutory restrictions have been enacted in some states.[27]

Some question may be raised as to why prohibitions against assigning or subleasing should be tolerated. They involve restraints upon alienation and the lessor is protected from a financial point of view because privity of contract exists between the lessor and his lessee. This means that a lessee cannot escape liability for breach of the covenants in a lease by making an assignment or a sublease.

But a lessor may properly be motivated by considerations wholly apart from security with respect to the payment of rent or the performance of other covenants in the lease. The future value of his property depends in large measure upon many things incident to the mode of occupancy. A lessor has a right to determine the person or persons who are to occupy his land. This reflects the common law concept of "personal relationship" existing between the lessor and the lessee. The execution of a lease evidences approval as to the lessee. This is the reason for the rule that a reassignment to the original lessee

23. Hollander v. Central Metal & Supply Co., 1908, 109 Md. 131, 71 A. 442; Texas Co. v. Butler, 1953, 198 Or. 368, 256 P.2d 259 (burden side); Hagar v. Buck & Griffin, 1872, 44 Vt. 285 (benefit side). *Contra*: Woodall v. Clifton, [1905] 2 Ch. 257.

24. Thruston v. Minke, 1870, 32 Md. 487 (benefit side did not run with assignment of the reversion); American Strawboard Co. v. Haldeman Paper Co., 6 Cir. 1897, 27 C.C.A. 634, 83 F. 619. But see Congleton v. Pattison, [1808] 10 East 130, 103 Eng. Rep. 725; Vyvyan v. Arthur, [1823] 1 B. & C. 410, 107 Eng.Rep. 152.

25. Braunstein, Inc. v. McCrory Stores Corp., 1922, 93 N.J.Eq. 419, 116 A. 707, 23 A.L.R. 133.

26. Crump v. Tolbert, 1946, 210 Ark. 920, 198 S.W.2d 518; Nassau Hotel Co. v. Barnett & Barse Corp., 1914, 162 App.Div. 381, 147 N.Y.S. 283, affirmed 212 N.Y. 568, 106 N.E. 1036 (1914).

27. See, for example, Keefer v. Spohrer, 1949, 168 Kan. 331, 212 P.2d 230 and Jones & Oglebay v. Kansas City Board of Trade, 1903, 99 Mo.App. 433, 78 S.W. 843 (assignment without consent prohibited if lease does not exceed the period of two years); Grossmann v. Barney, Tex.Civ.App.1962, 359 S.W.2d 475, refused n. r. e. (Art. 5237, Vernon's Ann.Tex. Civ.Stats., prohibits assignments and subleases without the lessor's consent).

does not constitute a breach of a covenant not to assign without the consent of the lessor.[28] Undoubtedly there are limitations on this "freedom of choice." For example, there may be constitutional or statutory restrictions on a choice that is based upon the race or color of the proposed tenant.[29]

If an assignment or sublease is prohibited without the consent of the lessor he may withhold his consent arbitrarily.[30] Reason must be shown, however, if the lease provides that consent shall not be arbitrarily or unreasonably withheld, or words of similar import.[31]

Covenant Distinguished from Condition or Limitation

In the absence of statute,[32] the breach of a covenant not to assign or sublease does not give the lessor a right to terminate the lease. A tenant in possession under an unauthorized assignment is entitled to share in the award if the leased land is taken in eminent domain proceedings.[33]

Usually, the lease specifically provides that the lessor may terminate the lease in case of an unauthorized assignment or sublease, or that the lease will terminate automatically upon the happening of the event.[34] In the face of such provisions the assignee should not be allowed to share in an award in the absence of a waiver of the unauthorized assignment.

Strict Construction

Since restrictions upon the right of a lessee to assign or sublease constitute a restraint upon alienation they are not favored and are subject to strict construction. A prohibition against assignment is not breached by a sublease[35] and a prohibition against a sublease is not breached by an assignment.[36] However, in Marcelle, Inc. v. Sol. & S. Marcus Co. (Mass.),[37] it is held that because of the close business relationship existing between the lessor and the lessee in connection with the use of the leased land, a prohibition against assignment includes a prohibition against subleasing.

A general prohibition against assignment will not prevent an assignment by operation of law resulting from the death or bankruptcy of the lessee.[38] Such an assignment is pro-

---

28. Donaldson v. Strong, 1910, 195 Mass. 429, 81 N.E. 267; Coulos v. Desimone, 1949, 34 Wash.2d 87, 208 P.2d 105.

29. See Abstract Investment Co. v. Hutchinson, 1962, 204 Cal.App.2d 242, 22 Cal.Rptr. 309.

30. Jacobs v. Klawans, 1961, 225 Md. 147, 169 A.2d 677; Dress Shirt Sales, Inc. v. Hotel Martinique Associates, 1963, 12 N.Y.2d 339, 239 N.Y.S.2d 660, 190 N.E.2d 10. See Grossmann v. Barney, Tex. Civ.App.1962, 359 S.W.2d 475, refused n. r. e.

31. See Sarner v. Kantor, 1924, 123 Misc. 469, 205 N.Y.S. 760.

32. See West's Ann.Cal.Code Civ.Proc., § 1161, subd. 3.

33. In re Mackie's Petition, 1961, 365 Mich. 322, 112 N.W.2d 573 (covenant and not a condition). See also, In re Mackie's Petition, 1963, 372 Mich. 104, 125 N.W.2d 482.

34. See Nelson v. Seidel, Tex.Civ.App.1959, 328 S.W. 2d 805, refused n. r. e. (termination is at the election of the lessor).

35. Burns v. Dufresne, 1912, 67 Wash. 158, 121 P. 46. See, Fairbanks v. Power Oil Co., 1945, 81 Ohio App. 116, 77 N.E.2d 499 (these covenants not breached by a tenant who creates a non-possessory estate, such as a license).

36. Rogers v. Hall, 1947, 227 N.C. 363, 42 S.E.2d 347; Willenbrock v. Latulippe, 1923, 125 Wash. 168, 215 P. 330; Goldman v. Daniel Feder & Co., 1919, 84 W.Va. 600, 100 S.E. 400, 7 A.L.R. 246, noted in 20 Col.Law Rev. 223 (1920), 68 Univ. of Pa.Law Rev. 189 (1920), 29 Yale Law Jr. 568 (1920). But see Dillingham v. Williams, Tex.Civ.App.1942, 165 S.W. 2d 524, error refused.

37. 274 Mass. 469, 175 N.E. 83, 74 A.L.R. 1012 (1931).

38. Farnum v. Hefner, 1889, 79 Cal. 575, 21 P. 955; Buddon Realty Co. v. Wallace, 1945, 238 Mo.App. 900, 189 S.W.2d 1002; Gazlay v. Williams, 1908, 210 U.S. 41, 28 S.Ct. 687, 52 L.Ed. 950. See Stratford Co. v. Continental Mortgage Co., 1925, 74 Cal.App.

hibited if the lease provides against assignment "by act of the parties or by operation of law [39]." If a lease creates an estate in two or more lessees, a covenant that the *lessees* will not assign is not breached by an assignment made by only one of the lessees.[40]

A prohibition against assignment relates only to a technical assignment and is not breached by a mortgage or deed of trust on the leasehold estate given by the lessee. This is especially true in connection with a mortgage if it operates to create a lien only and does not transfer ownership.[41]

Corporations

It is proper to assume that one who leases land to a corporation places little if any reliance upon the personal characteristics of the lessee. It is a well known fact that matters relating to management and control of a corporation are subject to continual change. Accordingly, a prohibition against assigning or subleasing is not breached by a transfer in management resulting from a sale of corporate stock.[42] In a strict sense, corporate ownership is not lost if the corporate lessee is involved in a merger or a consolidation. This is especially true in the case of a merger where the identity of the corporate lessee is

not completely lost.[43] A lease may specifically provide for termination by the lessor if a "change in the control" of the corporation results during the period of the lease by a transfer of shares by those having control at the time of the lease. The validity of such a provision has been sustained.[44]

Partnership

If a lease is made to a partnership the lessor has a right to rely upon the personal characteristics of all of the partners responsible for performance at the time of the lease. Financial responsibility is assured because of privity of contract. A prohibition against assignment is violated if a corporation is organized to take over the partnership assets.[45] That is also the case if a change in the partnership organization results in the withdrawal of a partner who was a member of the firm at the time of the lease.[46] However, this is not a prohibition against the admission of new partners.[47]

There is authority for the view that a covenant or condition against assignment is not breached even if some *but not all* of the original partners withdraw. It is considered that

551, 241 P. 429; Medinah Temple Co. v. Currey, 1896, 162 Ill. 441, 44 N.E. 839; Paddell v. Janes, 1914, 84 Misc. 212, 145 N.Y.S. 868.

39. But see Burns v. McGraw, 1946, 75 Cal.App. 481, 171 P.2d 148.

40. Spangler v. Spangler, 1905, 11 Cal.App. 321, 104 P. 995; Hunt v. Shell Oil Co., 10 Cir. 1941, 116 F.2d 598 (*dictum*).

41. Chapman v. Great Western Gypsum Co., 1932, 216 Cal. 420, 14 P.2d 758, 85 A.L.R. 917; West Shore R. Co. v. Wenner, 1904, 70 N.J.L. 233, 57 A. 408, affirmed 71 N.J.L. 682, 60 A. 1134 (1905). But see, Crouse v. Mitchell, 1902, 130 Mich. 347, 90 N.W. 32.

42. Burrows Motor Co., Inc. v. Davis, D.C.Mun.App. 1950, 76 A.2d 163.

43. Dodier Realty & Inv. Co. v. St. Louis Nat. Baseball Club, 1951, 361 Mo. 981, 238 S.W.2d 321, 24 A.L.R.2d 683; Segal v. Greater Valley Terminal Corp., 1964, 83 N.J.Super. 120, 199 A.2d 48. *Cf.*: Lord Baltimore Filling Stations, Inc. v. Hoffman, D.C.Mun.App.1955, 117 A.2d 397 (breach of covenant against assignment resulted when parent corporation succeeded to rights under the lease upon dissolution of the corporate lessee, a wholly owned subsidiary).

44. Associated Cotton Shops, Inc. v. Evergreen Park Shopping Plaza, 1960, 27 Ill.App.2d 467, 170 N.E.2d 35 (space in a shopping center leased to a corporation).

45. Emery v. Hill, 1893, 67 N.H. 330, 39 A. 266.

46. Saxeney v. Panis, 1921, 239 Mass. 207, 131 N.E. 331 (*dictum*).

47. Miller v. Pond, 1921, 214 Mich. 186, 183 N.W. 24, 17 A.L.R. 179.

the "personal element" is satisfied if even one of the original partners remains.[48] It is assumed that at the time of the lease the lessor was satisfied with the personal characteristics of all the partners, individually. Having made his choice he has no cause to complain if that relationship continues to exist in whole or in part.

DELIVERY OF POSSESSION TO LESSEE

61. A lessor is not subject to an implied covenant to deliver possession of leased land to the lessee.

A lessor impliedly covenants that the lessee will have a legal right to possession of the leased land at the beginning of the term. Therefore, a lessor must respond in damages to his lessee if the tenant is prevented from taking possession according to the terms of his lease either by act of the lessor or by the owner of a title paramount.[49] Some decisions follow the view that the lessor's default constitutes a breach of an implied covenant of quiet enjoyment.[50]

According to the English rule, a lessor impliedly covenants that he will deliver possession of the leased land to the lessee at the commencement of the lease.[51] Thus, the obligation of the lessor is not satisfied merely because the lessee has a legal right to possession. The lessor is under an obligation to see that a former tenant vacates the premises in time to make the premises available for the new tenant. While this English rule is fol-

lowed in many American states,[52] the prevailing rule is that a lessor's duty does not include the obligation of delivering possession of the leased land to the tenant.[53] Statutory remedies are usually available by means of which the new tenant can gain possession of the land. In addition, the wrongdoer may subject himself to damages for unwarranted interference with the contractual relationship existing between the lessor and the lessee.[54]

QUIET ENJOYMENT

62. The relationship of landlord and tenant raises an implied covenant for quiet enjoyment. This affords protection to a lessee in his enjoyment of the leased land as against wrongful acts of the lessor or by one who has a title paramount. Interference with possession by a stranger (one not claiming under the lessor or under a title paramount) does not constitute a breach of this covenant.

The relationship of lessor and lessee imposes a contractual duty upon the lessor to refrain from interfering with the lessee's reasonable enjoyment of the leased land.[55]

---

48. Hoops v. Tate, 1951, 104 Cal.App.2d 486, 231 P.2d 560; Borgen v. Wiglesworth, 1962, 190 Kan. 367, 375 P.2d 601.

49. Boltz v. Crawford & North Ave.'s Theatre Co., 1938, 294 Ill.App. 258, 13 N.E.2d 844.

50. See Riley v. Hale, 1893, 158 Mass. 240, 33 N.E. 491; Garrison v. Hutton, 1907, 118 App.Div. 455, 103 N.Y.S. 265.

51. Coe v. Clay, [1829] 5 Bing. 440, 130 Eng.Rep. 1131.

52. King v. Reynolds, 1880, 67 Ala. 229; Cheshire v. Thurston, 1950, 70 Ariz. 299, 219 P.2d 1043; Stewart v. Murphy, 1915, 95 Kan. 421, 148 P. 609; Adrian v. Rabinowitz, 1936, 116 N.J.L. 586, 186 A. 29; Barfield v. Damon, 1952, 56 N.M. 515, 245 P.2d 1032; Sloan v. Hart, 1909, 150 N.C. 269, 63 S.E. 1037; Dieffenbach v. McIntyre, 1953, 208 Okl. 163, 254 P.2d 346. *Cf.*: Brown v. Wall, 1914, 186 Mo. App. 150, 171 S.W. 586.

53. See Teitelbaum v. Direct Realty Co., 1939, 172 Misc. 48, 13 N.Y.S.2d 886; Hannan v. Dusch, 1930, 154 Va. 356, 153 S.E. 824, 70 A.L.R. 141; 3 Mo. Law Rev. 299 (1938).

54. Reichman v. Drake, 1951, 89 Ohio App. 222, 100 N.E.2d 533.

55. Stewart v. Murphy, 1915, 95 Kan. 421, 148 P. 609 (*dictum*); Winchester v. O'Brien, 1929, 266 Mass. 33, 164 N.E. 807, 64 A.L.R. 895; Hannan v. Harper, 1926, 189 Wis. 588, 208 N.W. 255, 45 A.L.R. 1119. *Contra*: Lovering v. Lovering, 1843, 13 N.H. 513 (*dictum*); Mershon v. Williams, 1899, 63 N.J.L. 398, 44 A. 211, noted in 13 Harv.Law Rev. 307 (1899). See Implied Covenants for Quiet Enjoyment, 3 Col.Law Rev. 43 (1903).

This implied warranty for quiet enjoyment is recognized even if a statute provides that covenants are not to be implied "in a conveyance of real property" [56] or "real estate." [57] A lease is not a conveyance of real property or real estate within the meaning of such statutes. They are limited in their operation to the conveyance of freehold estates.

A breach of covenant for quiet enjoyment, whether the covenant is expressed or implied, occurs if the lessee's enjoyment of the leased land is disturbed in a substantial manner either by the lessor [58] or by the owner of a title paramount.[59] A disturbance caused by a stranger does not constitute a breach of this covenant.[60]

An express covenant for quiet enjoyment may be general or it may be restricted. If the covenant is general, any substantial disturbance with enjoyment of possession may be actionable. The covenant may specifically provide that a wrongful action by the lessor to recover possession of the land constitutes an eviction.[61] In any event, the provisions of an express covenant are controlling.[62]

Breach of a covenant for quiet enjoyment may justify equitable relief by way of an injunction.[63] It may result in a constructive eviction if the lessee gives up possession of the leased land. In that event the lessee cannot be held liable for rent that accrues subsequent to the relinquishment of possession. These remedies are in addition to the tenant's right to recover damages for breach of the covenant.[64] But if the tenant remains in possession difficulties may be encountered in ascertaining the actual damage suffered.[65]

FITNESS

63. **In general, the lessor does not impliedly warrant that the leased land is suitable for a specific purpose. So also, warranties are not implied by the lessee with respect to his fitness to occupy the property.**

a. **Building under construction. If a building under construction is leased for a particular purpose there is an implied covenant by the lessor that it will be suitable for such purpose, unless, of course, the defect is obvious at the time of the lease.**

b. **Furnished dwelling. According to some decisions, if a short term lease is involved the lessor of a furnished dwelling impliedly warrants that it is reasonably fit for occupancy.**

c. **Public nuisance. A lessor is under a duty to abate a public nuisance if he has knowledge of its existence prior to the time fixed for the beginning of the lease.**

---

56. Jeffers v. Easton, Eldridge & Co., 1896, 113 Cal. 345, 45 P. 680; Fifth Ave. Bldg. Co. v. Kernochan, 1917, 221 N.Y. 370, 117 N.E. 579 (*dictum*), noted in 18 Col.Law Rev. 89 (1918).

57. Northern Brewery Co. v. Princess Hotel, 1915, 78 Or. 453, 153 P. 37. *Contra:* Minnis v. Newbro-Gallogly Co., 1913, 174 Mich. 635, 140 N.W. 980.

58. Levitzky v. Canning, 1867, 33 Cal. 299; Winchester v. O'Brien, 1929, 266 Mass. 33, 164 N.E. 807, 64 A.L.R. 895; Hubble v. Cole, 1891, 88 Va. 236, 13 S.E. 441. *Cf.:* Levy v. Cohen, 1941, 27 N.Y.S.2d 385.

59. Ganz v. Clark, 1929, 252 N.Y. 92, 169 N.E. 100. See In re O'Donnell, 1925, 240 N.Y. 99, 147 N.E. 541 (attornment to a claim of title paramount proper basis for breach of covenant for quiet enjoyment).

60. Hockersmith v. Sullivan, 1912, 71 Wash. 244, 128 P. 222. See Branger v. Manciet, 1860, 30 Cal. 625 (where covenant expressly covered acts of strangers to the title).

61. Paddell v. Janes, 1915, 90 Misc. 146, 152 N.Y.S. 948.

62. Burr v. Stenton, 1871, 43 N.Y. 462; Line v. Stephenson, [1838] 4 Bing.(N.C.) 678, 132 Eng.Rep. 950.

63. Winchester v. O'Brien, 1929, 266 Mass. 33, 164 N.E. 807, 64 A.L.R. 895.

64. Kane v. Mink, 1884, 64 Iowa 84, 19 N.W. 852; Winchester v. O'Brien, 1929, 266 Mass. 33, 164 N.E. 807, 64 A.L.R. 895; Hubble v. Cole, 1891, 88 Va. 236, 13 S.E. 441.

65. See Matzger v. Arcade Bldg. & Realty Co., 1918, 102 Wash. 423, 173 P. 47.

d. Illegality. If land is leased for a particular purpose the lessee may avoid the lease if the use is illegal because of structural defects.

With exceptions to be noted, covenants relating to the "fitness" of the leased land for a specific purpose are not implied in a lease. A lease constitutes a sale of an estate in land and the doctrine of *caveat emptor* applies (let the buyer beware).[66] Of course, a lessee may avoid a lease if he was induced to enter into the transaction as the result of fraudulent representations made by the lessor. But mere failure on the part of the lessor to disclose a condition that would impair the utility of the land for a particular use does not constitute fraud. This is true even though the intended use is made known to the lessor.[67] To show fraud the lessee must prove that the lessor was under a duty to speak. This duty exists only in special situations, such as in a case where the lessee had a right to rely upon the unexpressed judgment of the lessor.

In Humphreys v. Miller,[68] a lessee engaged rooms for occupancy by a person suffering from leprosy. The lessor claimed damages for breach of an alleged implied warranty by the lessee of the tenant's fitness to inhabit the land. The claimed existence of such a warranty was denied.

Building Under Construction

If a building under construction is leased for a particular purpose there is an implied covenant by the lessor that it will be suitable for such purpose.[69] This rule applies in a situation where, at the time of the lease, the construction has not progressed far enough for the tenant to ascertain, by inspection, the suitability for the intended use.[70]

Furnished Dwelling

In Smith v. Marrable (Eng.),[71] it is held that there is an implied warranty of fitness by the lessor in the case of a short term lease of a furnished dwelling. This exception proceeds upon the theory that the furnishings (personal property) constitute the principal part of the lease and the chief subject of the warranty. However, the warranty does extend to structural defects.[72] The rule has found considerable support in the American decisions.[73] It is to be noted that the warranty does not apply as to conditions that develop after the effective date of the lease.[74] Application of the exception has also been denied in the case of a partially furnished dwelling.[75]

66. Dutton v. Gerrish, 1851, 63 Mass.(9 Cush.) 89; Daly v. Wise, 1892, 132 N.Y. 306, 30 N.E. 837; Ph. Chaleyer, Inc. v. Simon, D.N.J., 1950, 91 F.Supp. 5. See Naumberg v. Young, 1882, 44 N.J.L. 331 (evidence of oral warranty not admissible).

67. Anderson Drive-In Theatre, Inc. v. Kirkpatrick, 1953, 123 Ind.App. 388, 110 N.E.2d 506.

68. 2 K.B. 122, 116 Times L.R. 668 [1917], noted in 17 Col.Law Rev. 251 (1917); 16 Mich.Law Rev. 50 (1917).

69. J. D. Young Corp. v. McClintic, Tex.Civ.App.1930, 26 S.W.2d 460, noted in 44 Harv.Law Rev. 132 (1930).

70. See Oliver v. Hartzell, 1926, 170 Ark. 512, 280 S.W. 979.

71. 11 M. & W. 5, 152 Eng.Rep. 693 (1843).

72. Ackarey v. Carbonaro, 1946, 320 Mass. 537, 70 N.E.2d 418.

73. Young v. Povich, 1922, 121 Me. 141, 116 A. 26, 29 A.L.R. 48, noted in 22 Col.Law Rev. 595 (1922); Hacker v. Nitschke, 1942, 310 Mass. 754, 39 N.E.2d 644, 139 A.L.R. 257; Delamater v. Foreman, 1931, 184 Minn. 428, 239 N.W. 148, noted in 17 Iowa Law Rev. 543 (1932) (*dictum* that rule applies to unfurnished apartment in a multiple dwelling); Morgenthau v. Ehrich, 1912, 77 Misc. 139, 136 N.Y.S. 140.

Contra: Fisher v. Lighthall, 1885, 15 D.C.(4 Mackey) 82; Murray v. Albertson, 1888, 50 N.J.L. 167, 13 A. 394.

74. Davenport v. Squibb, 1947, 320 Mass. 629, 70 N.E.2d 793.

75. Bolieau v. Traiser, 1925, 253 Mass. 346, 148 N.E. 809.

Public Nuisance

A lessor is under a duty to abate a public nuisance if he has knowledge of its existence prior to the time fixed for the beginning of the term. He may be compelled to respond in damages if the lessee is compelled by public authority to give up possession of the land.[76]

Illegality

If land is leased with the understanding that it is to be used for a particular purpose, the lessee may avoid liability under the lease if use for the particular purpose is illegal because of structural defects.[77]

REPAIRS

64. In the absence of statute, and in the absence of a controlling covenant, a lessor is not under a duty to maintain leased land in a state of repair.

a. Lessee. Unless a lessee covenants to make repairs his duty with respect to maintenance is defined by the law as it relates to waste.

> **If a lessee installs fixtures as authorized by the lease he cannot be held liable for failure to remove fixtures at the termination of the lease.**

> **A covenant by the lessee to keep the premises in repair does not impose a duty to rebuild. There is authority for the view that such a duty is imposed by a covenant to "maintain and keep" the premises in repair.**

b. Remote parties. Unless a specific time is fixed for performance, both the benefit and the burden side of a covenant to repair may be enforced by and against remote parties. If a specific time for performance is fixed, assignees of estates after that time are not involved.

In the absence of statute, and in the absence of a controlling covenant, a lessor is not under a duty to make repairs with respect to the leased land.[78] There is some authority that a lessor may be bound by an implied covenant to repair because of a limited duty to repair placed upon the lessee. For example, if a covenant requires a lessee to make all repairs "excluding the roof," there is an implied covenant on the part of the lessor to keep the roof in repair. This is especially true if the lessor "recognized the obligation" by making repairs.[79]

Even if a lessor does covenant to repair this does not impose a duty upon him to rebuild in the event that structures are destroyed. In this respect the covenant differs from one to "repair or restore." [80] The minority rule is that a general and unqualified covenant by the lessor to repair imposes a duty to rebuild. However, even under this view, a limited covenant to repair, such as a covenant to keep the roof in repair, does not impose a duty to rebuild.[81] A lessee cannot successfully defend an action for rent upon the ground that the lessor defaulted in performing a covenant to repair. Historically, covenants by the lessor and covenants by the lessee are independent unless evidence is clear that the parties intended otherwise.[82] However, breach of a

---

76. Steefel v. Rothschild, 1904, 179 N.Y. 273, 72 N.E. 112.

77. Economy v. S. B. & L. Bldg. Corp., 1930, 138 Misc. 296, 245 N.Y.S. 352.

78. Friedman v. LeNoir, 1952, 73 Ariz. 333, 241 P.2d 779.

79. Jersey Silk & Lace Stores v. Best Silk Shops, 1929, 134 Misc. 315, 235 N.Y.S. 277. *Contra:* Plate Glass Underwriters' Mutual Ins. Co. v. Ridgewood R. Co., 1925, 219 Mo.App. 186, 269 S.W. 659. See Fischer v. Collier, Fla.App.1962, 143 So.2d 710.

80. Leonardi v. Furman, 1957, 83 Ariz. 61, 316 P.2d 487; Mattal v. American Trust Co., 1962, 208 Cal. App.2d 645, 25 Cal.Rptr. 517; Manufacturers Trust Co. v. Bach, 1961, 32 Misc.2d 858, 223 N.Y.S.2d 86.

81. Miller v. Miller, 1953, 217 Miss. 650, 54 So.2d 739, 38 A.L.R.2d 674.

82. Frazier v. Riley, 1926, 215 Ala. 517, 111 So. 10; Hosang v. Minor, 1962, 205 Cal.App.2d 269, 22 Cal.

repair-covenant by the lessor may be suffi-ciently serious in nature to furnish the basis for a constructive eviction.[83]

Statutes in an increasing number of states impose a duty to repair upon the lessor of multiple dwellings.[84] The usual statute requires the lessor to obtain a certificate from designated public officials to the effect that the buildings conform to public regulations. Some statutes provide that a lessor cannot recover rent from his tenants unless such a certificate is secured.[85]

Under the New York Multiple Dwelling Law,[86] a lessor of apartments is liable for damages resulting from failure to keep the dwelling in repair. Under a California statute the lessor of a building intended for occupancy by human beings is under a duty to maintain the leased land in a reasonably fit condition for human habitation.[87] While this statute does not impose either a contractual duty or declare a rule of tort liability,[88] if repairs are not made after reasonable notice the lessee may either vacate the land and thereby avoid further liability under the lease or expend not to exceed one month's rent in making repairs.[89]

Lessee

Unless a lessee covenants to make repairs his duty with respect to maintenance is defined by the law as it relates to waste, a matter discussed under a separate heading.[90] He is under a duty, non-contractual in nature, to return the leased land without substantial change in its physical condition during the period of the lease. Failure to exercise reasonable care to protect the premises from the elements constitutes permissive waste. It has also been noted that if a lessee fails to make repairs he may incur tort liability for injuries suffered by third parties.[91]

Under some circumstances a lessor is under a duty to keep certain areas of leased land in a state of repair, such as stairs, halls, walks, parking lots, etc., that are reserved for the common use of tenants.[92] A lease may provide that the lessee "will save the lessor harmless" from "any and all" liability arising out of a default in the performance of this duty. The purpose of the covenant is to cast upon the lessee the duty of making repairs. However, an injured party is not entitled to an action against the lessee for breach of this contract. The lessor and lessee did not intend to execute a contract for the benefit of a third party. The purpose of the contract was to protect the lessor "in certain circumstances by holding him free from liability."[93] An indemnity type of contract is involved.

If a lessee installs fixtures as authorized by the lease he cannot be held liable for failure to remove the fixtures at the end of the term unless he has bound himself to do so by a

Rptr. 794; Masser v. London Operating Co., 1932, 106 Fla. 474, 145 So. 72; Brady v. Brady, 1922, 140 Md. 403, 117 A. 882; Stone v. Sullivan, 1938, 300 Mass. 450, 15 N.E.2d 476. See Medico-Dental Co. v. Horton and Converse, 1942, 21 Cal.2d 411, 132 P.2d 457.

83. Oppenheimer v. Szulerecki, 1921, 297 Ill. 81, 130 N.E. 325, 28 A.L.R. 1439. See infra § 76.

84. See, for example, Barsky v. Litwin, 1939, 289 Mich. 672, 287 N.W. 339.

85. See, for example, Second Nat'l Bank of New Haven v. Loftus, 1936, 121 Conn. 454, 185 A. 423, noted in 35 Mich.Law Rev. 1183 (1937).

86. McKinney's N.Y. Multiple Dwelling Law, § 78.1.

87. West's Ann.Cal.Civ.Code, § 1941.

88. Green v. Redding, 1891, 92 Cal. 548, 28 P. 599.

89. West's Ann.Cal.Civ.Code, § 1942.

90. See supra, Chapter 4.

91. See supra, § 47.

92. See supra, § 47.

93. Silverman v. Food Fair Stores, Inc., 1962, 407 Pa. 507, 180 A.2d 894, 895.

specific covenant.[94] Rules respecting specific covenants are as follows:

First: A covenant by the lessee to keep the premises in repair, reasonable wear and tear excepted, applies even if repairs are made necessary through no fault on his part.[95] However, this covenant does not impose upon the lessee a duty to rebuild or replace structures.[96] Neither does it impose a duty to make structural changes as demanded by public authority except in cases where the changes are made necessary by the special use to which the land is subjected by the lessee.[97]

This covenant imposes a continuing duty upon the lessee. If he fails to make the repairs within a reasonable time he may be held liable in damages in an action brought by the lessor before the expiration date of the lease. Under ordinary circumstances the measure of damages is based upon the cost of repairs.[98] Improvements made by a tenant may not be set off against damages caused by breach of the covenant.[99]

Second: A covenant by the lessee to "maintain and keep" the premises in repair is broader in scope than a covenant to repair. It imposes an obligation to make necessary replacements.[1] A lessor may recover for breach of this covenant prior to the expiration of the lease.[2]

Third: A covenant to surrender the premises after the expiration of the lease in as good condition as they were in at the time of the lease, ordinary wear and tear excepted, is more restricted in scope than a general covenant to repair. The lessee is not under a duty to repair if the disrepair resulted from the act of a third party and without the fault of the lessee.[3] It is also to be noted that the lessor cannot successfully maintain an action for breach of this covenant until the expiration of the lease.[4]

94. Savage v. University State Bank, 1931, 263 Ill. App. 457; Duvanel v. Sinclair Refining Co., 1951, 170 Kan. 483, 227 P.2d 88, 23 A.L.R.2d 649; Cass v. Home Tobacco Warehouse Co., 1949, 311 Ky. 95, 223 S.W.2d 569; Perry v. J. L. Mott Iron Works Co., 1911, 207 Mass. 501, 93 N.E. 798; Lamonica v. Bosenberg, 1964, 73 N.M. 452, 389 P.2d 216; Arkansas Fuel Oil Co. v. Connellee, Tex.Civ.App. 1931, 39 S.W.2d 99; Republic Invest. Co. v. Naches Hotel Co., 1937, 190 Wash. 176, 67 P.2d 858; McKenzie v. Western Greenbrier Bank, 1962, 146 W. Va. 971, 124 S.E.2d 234.

95. Dolack v. Pioche, 1868, 35 Cal. 416; Leominster Fuel Co. v. Scanlon, 1922, 243 Mass. 126, 137 N.E. 271, 24 A.L.R. 1459.

96. Realty & Rebuilding Co. v. Rea, 1920, 184 Cal. 565, 194 P. 1024; Wattles v. South Omaha Ice & Coal Co., 1897, 50 Neb. 251, 69 N.W. 785, 36 L.R.A. 424. *Contra:* Publishers Bldg. Co. v. Miller, 1946, 25 Wash.2d 972, 172 P.2d 489 *(dictum)* (there was also a covenant to quit and surrender the premises in good condition, reasonable wear and tear and damage by fire excepted). *Cf.:* Anderson v. Ferguson, 1943, 17 Wash.2d 262, 135 P.2d 302.

97. 140 West Thirty Fourth St. Corp. v. Davis, 1936, 158 Misc. 470, 285 N.Y.S. 957. See Wolfe v. White, 1948, 114 Utah 39, 197 P.2d 125.

98. Corbett v. Derman Shoe Co., 1959, 338 Mass. 405, 155 N.E.2d 423; Cruzan v. Franklin Stores Corp., 1963, 72 N.M. 48, 380 P.2d 190. *Cf.:* United States v. Flood Building, D.Cal.1957, 157 F.Supp. 438; Realty Associates, Inc. v. United States, 1956, 134 Ct.Cl. 167, 138 F.Supp. 875.

99. Willoughby v. Atkinson Furnishing Co., 1899, 93 Me. 185, 44 A. 612; Cruzan v. Franklin Stores Corp., 1963, 72 N.M. 48, 380 P.2d 190 (where improvements were required by the terms of the lease); Atlantic Coastline Rd. Co. v. United States, 1954, 129 Ct.Cl. 137.

1. Arnold-Evans Co. v. Hardung, 1925, 132 Wash. 426, 232 P. 290, 45 A.L.R. 9.

2. Avelez Hotel Corp. v. Milner Hotels, Inc., 1956, 227 Miss. 808, 87 So.2d 63; Wanamaker v. Butler Mfg. Co., 1910, 136 App.Div. 265, 120 N.Y.S. 1000; City Hotel Co. v. Aumont Hotel Co., Tex.Civ.App. 1947, 107 S.W.2d 1094.

3. Kirby v. Davis, 1923, 210 Ala. 192, 97 So. 655, noted in 8 Minn.Law Rev. 261 (1924).

4. Massachusetts Home Missionary Society v. Sirlanni, 1925, 252 Mass. 352, 147 N.E. 823.

Remote Parties

Both the benefit and the burden of a covenant to repair may be enforced by and against assignees of the leasehold estate and assignees of the reversion. The repair-covenant touches and concerns the land because it is necessarily related to the use and enjoyment of the leasehold estate and is reflected in the value of the reversion.[5]

In Gerzebek v. Lord (N. J.),[6] the lessor covenanted to paint and clean the house and to make stated repairs during the continuance of the lease. Some two years after the execution of the lease the lessor conveyed the reversion to defendant and the lessee sought to recover damages from the assignee for breach of the covenant. In denying recovery it is pointed out that the covenant to paint and clean the house was a covenant to prepare the house for occupancy. As such, it was breached, if at all, *prior to the grant of the reversion* to the defendant. Accordingly, he could not be held liable therefor. No time was fixed for the performance of the covenant to make the stated repairs. A duty to make these repairs did not arise until notice was given by the tenant. Plaintiff failed to prove that the defendant had been given such notice.

A general covenant to repair is continuous in nature. Accordingly, an assignee of the leasehold estate cannot avoid liability for breach of such a covenant by proof of the fact that the premises were in a state of disrepair at the time of the assignment.[7]

---

5. *Cf.:* Willcox v. Kehoe, 1905, 124 Ga. 484, 52 S.E. 896 (a covenant to make reimbursement for repairs made by the lessee).

6. 33 N.J.L. 240 (1869).

7. Mascals Case, [1857] 1 Leo. 62, 74 Eng.Rep. 58. But see, Foss v. Stanton, 1904, 76 Vt. 365, 57 A. 942 (assignee of reversion denied recovery for breach of covenant to repair because premises in a state of disrepair at the time of the assignment).

INSURANCE

65. **Unless the duty is imposed by covenant, neither the lessor nor the lessee is under a duty to insure against damage or loss by fire or other hazard. A lessor need not use insurance money received by him in rebuilding.**

A covenant by the lessee to insure is enforceable against an assignee of the leasehold estate. The benefit of such a covenant may be enforced by an assignee of the reversion.

In the absence of a covenant to the contrary a lessee is not under an obligation to carry insurance on the leased land.[8] If he secures such insurance in the name of the lessor he acts as a mere volunteer and is not entitled to reimbursement to the extent of premiums paid.

If the lease imposes a duty on the lessee to obtain insurance and there is a breach of this covenant the lessee may be held accountable for actual damage caused to the leased land that is not compensated for by insurance. His liability is not limited to the amount of premiums involved.[9] However, if the lessor is aware of the fact that the lessee has failed to insure, the lessor is under an obligation to secure the insurance in order to mitigate damages. He may, of course, hold the tenant liable to the extent of the premiums involved.

If the insured buildings are destroyed, and the lessor is compensated by insurance, in the absence of a covenant to the contrary the lessor is not under a duty to use the insurance money to repair or rebuild. A covenant by the lessor to repair does not impose an obligation to rebuild.[10]

If a covenant provides that the insurance proceeds are to be used to repair or rebuild the covenant may be enforced by and against

---

8. Hart v. Hart, 1903, 117 Wis. 639, 94 N.W. 890.

9. Franck v. Stout, 1909, 139 Wis. 223, 120 N.W. 867.

10. Saylor v. Brooks, 1923, 114 Kan. 493, 220 P. 193.

remote parties.[11] It is a covenant that involves the preservation of the estate and, for that reason, touches and concerns the land within the meaning of the rule declared in Spencer's case.[12]

If insurance money is not to be used in restoration it may be contended that the covenant to obtain insurance is a personal covenant and not binding on remote parties. However, the duty to insure is a duty that can be evaluated in terms of money and, in effect, is reflected in the amount of rent agreed to be paid. As such, it is a covenant to pay rent and is enforceable by and against remote parties.[13] A similar type of covenant is involved in the North Dakota case of Northern Pacific Ry. Co. v. McClure.[14] A railroad company leased land to defendant at a nominal rental. The defendant lessee covenanted to save the lessor harmless in case of the destruction of chattels located on the land if caused by fire resulting from railroad operations. Plaintiff, assignee of the reversion, was entitled to the benefit of the covenant.[15]

RESTRICTIONS RESPECTING THE USE OF LAND

66. **If a lease does not place a restriction on the use of leased land it may be used for any lawful purpose. A provision authorizing a** specific use is considered to be permissive and not restrictive.

   a. **Compulsory use. A lease may specifically provide that the land is to be used only for a designated purpose. In general, such a clause does not impose a duty on the lessee to use the land for that purpose.**

   b. **Economic advantage. A lease may contain a clause restricting the business activities of either the lessor or the lessee. Under varying circumstances, such an "economic-benefit" covenant may be enforced by and against the successors in interest of the original covenanting parties.**

If a lease does not place a restriction on the use of leased land it may be used for any lawful purpose. Generally, a provision authorizing a specific use is considered to be permissive and not restrictive. In Borgen v. Wiglesworth (Kan.),[16] a lease provided that the lessees "shall construct a car washing building at their own expense upon said land." The court held the lease did not restrict the use of the building to that of "car washing." This conclusion is fortified by the fact that the lease specifically prohibited use of the land for the purpose of operating any kind of "cafe or restaurant business." The expression of one thing is the exclusion of another (*expressio unius est exclusio alterius*).

Some authorities take the position that if a particular use is stated in the lease the lessee does not have a right to use the land for any other purpose.[17] This construction gives some meaning to the language in the lease. A permissive-clause is not necessary to confer the right upon the tenant.

---

11. Masury v. Southworth, 1859, 9 Ohio St. 340; Northern Trust Co. v. Snyder, 76 F. 34, 7 Cir., 1896; Vernon v. Smith, 1821, 5 Barn. & Ald. 1, 106 Eng. Rep. 1094; *Contra:* Griffin v. W. L. Pfeffer Lumber Co., 1918, 285 Ill. 19, 120 N.E. 583.

12. See supra, § 59.

13. St. Regis Restaurant v. Powers, 1927, 219 App. Div. 321, 219 N.Y.S. 684, noted in 36 Yale Law Jr. 1187 (1927); Voight v. Southern Ohio Sav. Bank & Trust Co., 1939, 63 Ohio App. 56, 25 N.E.2d 304.

14. 9 N.D. 73, 81 N.W. 52, 47 L.R.A. 149 (1899).

15. *Contra:* Atwood v. Chicago, M. & St. P. Ry. Co., 1924, 313 Ill. 59, 144 N.E. 351, noted in 19 Ill.Law Rev. 581 (1924). *Cf.:* Shank v. Gerrard Wire Tying Machines Co., Inc., 1928, 250 Ill.App. 346.

16. 189 Kan. 261, 369 P.2d 360 (1962).

17. Davis v. Des Moines & Ft. D. R. Co., 1912, 155 Iowa 51, 135 N.W. 356; Grinnell Bros. v. Asiuliewicz, 1927, 241 Misc. 186, 216 N.W. 388; Collins v. Truman, 1929, 223 Mo.App. 186, 14 S.W.2d 526; Weinkrantz v. Southwestern Life Ins. Co., Tex.Civ. App.1924, 264 S.W. 550.

Compulsory Use

A lessor may specifically provide in his lease that the leased land is to be used *only* for a designated purpose, a provision that is not uncommon in commercial leases. The lease may also provide that the land *is to be used* for that purpose. But, except as noted, a compulsory-covenant is not implied.[18]

In many cases it is urged that such a covenant should be implied in commercial leases if the rental is computed on a percentage basis. However, this claim is usually denied if the lessee is required to pay an unconditional minimum rental that is *substantial in nature* in light of all the surrounding circumstances.[19] There is authority for the view that if the lease includes the *good will of a business* there is an implied covenant that the tenant will exercise reasonable diligence in promoting the interests of both the lessor and the lessee. Certainly there is an implied covenant that the lessee will not open a competing business in the immediate vicinity and thereby divert customers to the prejudice of the lessor.[20]

In Dover Shopping Center, Inc. v. Cushman's Sons, Inc. (N. J.),[21] defendant, a well known bakery company, leased a store in a shopping center for the purpose of conducting a retail business. Defendant covenanted to keep the store open daily for the customary business hours (except holidays and Sundays). There was a substantial minimum rental plus a shifting percentage of gross sales in excess of the minimum. Defendant found it less expensive to pay the minimal rental than to operate the store. This suit was brought to compel defendant to operate the business according to the terms of the lease. A mandatory order was granted. The contract did not require the rendition of personal services by the defendant. Court supervision would be required only as to fundamental matters such as keeping the store open. No direction is made as to the method of operating the business or as to quality of the product to be sold.[22] While some claim may be made that the remedy at law by way of damages is adequate in a case of this type that is open to question. In the first place, there are difficulties in determining damages because of the percentage method of computing the rent. But more important, it is impossible to estimate the damage that would come from the withdrawal of one of the members of a "semi-cooperative enterprise like a shopping center." This damage cannot be accurately ascertained.

Economic Advantage

The purpose of a covenant may be to suppress competition. The advantage sought may be in favor of the lessor or it may be in

---

18. Rogers v. Jones, 1959, 38 Del.Ch. 288, 150 A.2d 327; Dickey v. Philadelphia Minit-Man Corp., 1954, 377 Pa. 549, 105 A.2d 580; Floste Corp. v. Marlemes, Fla.1951, 53 So.2d 538; Congressional Amusement Corp. v. Weltman, D.C.Mun.App., 1947, 55 A.2d 95. *Contra:* Asling v. McCallister-Fitzgerald Lumber Co., 1926, 120 Kan. 455, 244 P. 16.

19. Jenkins v. Rose's 5, 10 and 25¢ Stores, Inc., 1938, 213 N.C. 606, 197 S.E. 174; Kretch v. Stark, Ohio 1962, 193 N.E.2d 307; Monte Corp. v. Stephens, Okl.1958, 324 P.2d 538; Weil v. Ann Lewis Shops, Inc., Tex.Civ.App.1955, 281 S.W.2d 651. See Lippman v. Sears Roebuck & Co., 1955, 44 Cal.2d 136, 280 P.2d 775 (minimum rental not considered to be "substantial" within the meaning of the rule); Stemmler v. Moon Jewelry Co., Inc., Fla.App.1962, 139 So.2d 150.

20. Seggebruch v. Stoser, 1941, 309 Ill.App. 385, 33 N.E.2d 159. *Cf.:* Masciotra v. Harlow, 1951, 105 Cal.App.2d 376, 233 P.2d 586 (good will not involved insofar as the lessor was concerned). But see Stern v. Dunlap Co., 10 Cir. 1955, 228 F.2d 939.

21. 63 N.J.Super. 384, 164 A.2d 785 (1960).

22. *Cf.:* Security Builders, Inc. v. Southwest Drug Co., Inc., 1962, 244 Miss. 877, 147 So.2d 635; Price v. Herman, 1948, 81 N.Y.S.2d 361, affirmed 275 App.Div. 675, 87 N.Y.S.2d 221 (1949) (involved operation of a bakery and not merely an outlet store).

favor of the lessee. Enforcement of these covenants involves important matters of public policy. These and other problems are as follows:

First: A restrictive covenant for the benefit of the lessor may prohibit use of the leased land for a business that would be in competition with a business conducted by the lessor. The covenant may provide that the leased land is to be used only for a stated purpose, such as for the sale of gasoline, oil and related products, and the only products to be sold are those supplied by the lessor.

The validity of these restraints is generally recognized. The restrictive covenant is ancillary to a legitimate business transaction (the lease), is reasonable and necessarily related to the main purpose of the lease.[23] Restrictions of this type furnish an exception to the rule that restraints upon trade are contrary to public policy and void. A similar exception is recognized in situations where the restrictive covenant is for the economic interest of the lessee.[24]

In view of the fact that the restrictive covenant restricts the use of the leased land it does touch and concern the leasehold estate and the burden side of the covenant "runs with the land" and may be enforced as against an assignee of the leasehold estate.[25] But the benefit side of the covenant does not "touch and concern" the reversion. It is of benefit to the lessor because of the fact that he is the *owner of a business* and not because of the fact that he is the owner of the reversion. One who acquires the reversion from the lessor is not in a position to enforce the covenant. In addition, he would not be damaged by a breach. However, if the assignee of the reversion also purchases the business there may be an implied assignment of rights under the covenant.

Second: If land is leased for the purpose of conducting a particular type of business the lease may validly provide that the lessor will not engage in a competing business in connection with the use of other described land (such as in a shopping center) during the period of the lease.[26] The lease may restrict the kind of merchandise to be sold by the lessee and provide that the lessor will not lease other land for the sale of similar merchandise.[27] However, a rule of strict construction is applicable because the covenant is one in restraint of trade. Accordingly, in the absence of express provision, the restraint is not applicable as to the lessor [28] or one to whom he may subsequently convey the land.[29] In fact, according to common law rules such a covenant is not enforceable at law as against a subsequent purchaser of land from the lessor.[30] However, it may be enforceable

---

23. See United States v. Addyston Pipe & Steel Co., 6 Cir. 1898, 85 F. 271, 282.

24. *Cf.:* Irving Investment Corp. v. Gordon, 1949, 3 N.J.Super. 385, 66 A.2d 54, affirmed 3 N.J. 217, 69 A.2d 725; Stewart v. Stearns & Culver Lumber Co., 1908, 56 Fla. 570, 48 So. 19; Donohue v. Peterson, 1939, 161 Or. 65, 87 P.2d 770, 122 A.L.R. 1025; Schnitzer v. Southwest Shoe Corp., 1963, — Tex. —, 364 S.W.2d 373.

25. See American Strawboard Co. v. Haldeman Paper Co., 6 Cir. 1897, 83 F. 619.

26. Uptown Food Store, Inc. v. Ginsberg, 1963, 255 Iowa 462, 123 N.W.2d 59.

27. Parker v. Levin, 1934, 285 Mass. 125, 188 N.E. 502, 90 A.L.R. 1446. See Vanover v. Justice, 1918, 180 Ky. 632, 203 S.W. 321; Freedman v. Seidler, 1963, 233 Md. 39, 194 A.2d 778.

28. Stockton Dry Goods Co. v. Girsh, 1951, 36 Cal. 2d 677, 227 P.2d 1, 22 A.L.R.2d 1460; Sylvester v. Hotel Pasco, 1929, 153 Wash. 175, 279 P. 566, noted in 29 Col.Law Rev. 1161 (1929).

29. Postal Tel.-Cable Co. v. Western Union Tel. Co., 1895, 155 Ill. 335, 40 N.E. 587.

30. See Leonard v. Lavigne, 1964, 245 La. 1004, 162 So.2d 341.

as a covenant running with the land in equity.[31]

While a covenant relating to competition will not be implied, the restriction may arise because of technical language used in the lease. For example, in Belvedere Hotel Co. v. Williams (Md.),[32] the lease involved a barber shop and manicuring "concession" in a hotel and was for the period of two years. The court held that the word "concession" evidenced an intention to "convey more than a mere part of the building." It carried, by construction, a covenant on the part of the lessor not to lease other space in the hotel for similar purposes.

An exclusive merchandising right in a shopping center is not limited to the stores constructed at the time of the lease. The first-built units are not insulated from those constructed at a later date. This rule is certainly applicable to two adjoining portions of the same tract owned and managed by the same owner.[33] There is authority for the view that it applies with respect to stores constructed on adjacent land even if the land was not owned by the lessor at the time of the first lease.[34]

An exclusive-merchandising covenant is violated by the lessor's submission to the forbidden use by another tenant.[35] Usually, equitable relief is available to the injured tenant. Proceedings may be instituted against the lessor and the lessee who violates the covenant is a proper party defendant.

Such lessee may be enjoined from violating the restriction if he acquired his estate with notice, actual or constructive.[36] The difficulties incident to injunctive relief may warrant cancellation of the lease.[37]

TAXES

67. A lessee is not under a duty to pay taxes. A covenant to pay "taxes" does not impose an obligation to pay special assessments. Usually, a covenant to pay taxes or special assessments may be enforced by and against remote parties.

Except as noted, in the absence of a covenant to the contrary a lessee is not under an obligation to pay taxes on the leased land. This is true even in the case of a long term lease.[38] Taxes are not usually levied against a limited estate in land such as a leasehold estate. However, there is authority for the view that a tenant occupying land without an obligation to pay rent is under a duty to pay taxes.[39] Also, in the case of a perpetual lease the tax-obligation is with the tenant because such a lease is tantamount to a fee.[40] A statute which provides that taxes are to be levied against a lessee as an "owner" in fee does not

31. See supra, § 42.

32. 137 Md. 665, 113 A. 335, 14 A.L.R. 622 (1921).

33. Slice v. Carozza Properties, Inc., 1958, 215 Md. 357, 137 A.2d 687.

34. Carter v. Adler, 1955, 138 Cal.App.2d 63, 291 P.2d 111, 115. See Parker v. Lewis Grocer Co., 1963, 246 Miss. 873, 153 So.2d 261.

35. Snavely v. Berman, 1923, 143 Md. 75, 121 A. 842.

36. Pappadatos v. Market Street Bldg. Corp., 1933, 130 Cal.App. 62, 19 P.2d 517; Farm Food Stores, Inc. v. Gianeschi, 1944, 320 Ill.App. 582, 51 N.E.2d 792; Vaughan v. General Outdoor Advertising Co., Inc., Ky.App.1962, 352 S.W.2d 562. But see Harris v. Siegel, Tex.Civ.App.1934, 68 S.W.2d 330, noted in 13 Tex.Law Rev. 133 (1934) (remedy at law considered to be adequate).

37. Rental Development Corp. of America v. Lavery, 9 Cir. 1962, 304 F.2d 839.

38. Deutsch v. Frey, 1930, 36 Ohio App. 226, 173 N.E. 40 (five year lease).

39. Kelley v. Ball, 1892, 14 Ky.Law Rep. 132, 19 S.W. 581; Willard v. Blount, 1850, 33 N.C. 624.

40. Hughes v. Young, 1832, 5 Gill. & J. (Md.) 67 (renewable 99 year lease); Piper v. Meredith, 1827, 83 N.H. 107, 139 A. 294, 55 A.L.R. 148 (perpetual lease).

change the obligation as it exists between the lessor and the lessee.[41]

While a lessee may covenant to pay taxes, he is not thereby under an obligation to pay special assessments unless his covenant specifically includes such obligations.[42] Taxes are levies made to obtain necessary funds for usual governmental operations. Special assessments are levies that, in legal contemplation, make funds available for the payment of improvements that increase the value of the land in question, such as in the case of curbing, grading or paving a street. A covenant to pay all taxes "ordinary as well as extraordinary of every kind that may be levied upon or assessed against said premises" is not broad enough to impose an obligation on the tenant to pay taxes for special assessments.[43] Liability will arise if the covenant is to pay "assessments." [44]

A covenant to pay taxes is a covenant to protect the land against a public sale for taxes. Therefore, the covenant is one that touches and concerns both the reversion and the leasehold estate within the meaning of the rule in Spencer's Case. As such, the covenant is enforceable by and against remote parties.[45] Of course this is not true if the covenant requires payment of taxes on other than the leased land.[46] Even in that situation there is an argument that the covenant is, in effect, a rent covenant that is enforceable by and against remote parties.

Neither the benefit nor the burden of a tax-covenant are applicable to remote parties if there was default at the time of assignment.[47] When the obligation becomes due and payable it is an existing cause of action and the only interested parties are the then existing debtor and creditor. The obligation accrues when taxes become due and payable and not at the time of the assessment.[48]

RENEWAL OR EXTENSION

68. **Technically, the renewal of a lease, as distinguished from an extension, requires the execution of a new lease. The judicial trend is to disregard this distinction.**
   a. **Perpetual lease. In the absence of specific language to the contrary, a covenant to renew or extend a lease is limited to one renewal or one extension.**
   b. **First refusal. A covenant that the lessee has a "first refusal" for an additional term merely gives the lessee a right to renew if the lessor desires to lease the land upon the expiration of the first lease.**
   c. **Certainty as to duration and rent. If the option is silent as to such matters as the duration of the new period or the rent to be paid, reference is made to the basic lease.**
   d. **Notice. Unless otherwise provided by statute, it is not necessary for the lessee to make personal service of his notice of intention to renew or extend a lease.**

Theoretically, a covenant for the renewal of a lease, if exercised, requires the execution of a new leasing agreement.[49] A covenant to ex-

---

41. Boston Molasses Co. v. Commonwealth, 1907, 193 Mass. 387, 79 N.E. 827.

42. DeClercq v. Barber Asphalt Paving Co., 1897, 167 Ill. 215, 47 N.E. 367.

43. Blake v. Metropolitan Chain Stores, 1929, 247 Mich. 73, 225 N.W. 587, 63 A.L.R. 1386. But see Efros v. Russo, 1962, 71 N.J.Super. 602, 177 A.2d 565.

44. Milligan v. E. R. Darlington Lumber Co., 1908, 145 Ill.App. 518; Theo. Hamm Brewing Co. v. Northwestern Trust Co., 1917, 135 Minn. 314, 160 N.W. 792; Swetland Bldg. Co. v. Children's Home, 1928, 127 Or. 188, 270 P. 927.

45. Mason v. Smith, 1881, 131 Mass. 510 (assignee of leasehold estate liable).

46. Gower v. Postmaster-General, Ch.Div.1887, 57 L. T.Rep.,N.S., 527.

47. Wills v. Summers, 1890, 45 Minn. 90, 47 N.W. 463.

48. Security System Co. v. S. S. Pierce Co., 1926, 258 Mass. 4, 154 N.E. 190; Trask v. Graham, 1891, 47 Minn. 571, 50 N.W. 917.

49. Leavitt v. Maykel, 1909, 203 Mass. 506, 89 N.E. 1056.

tend a lease contemplates that the original lease will be continued in force for the additional period without the formality of a new lease.[50]

The distinction between a "renewal" and an "extension" is technical in nature. The judicial trend is to disregard the distinction and dispense with the requirement of a "new lease" in renewal cases.[51] Even if the technical rule is followed, in construing the provisions of a lease it may be found that the parties used the word "renew" as being synonymous with the word "extend." [52]

There are situations where the distinction between "renew" and "extend" may still be a matter of importance. For example, if the option is for an "extension" of the lease and the lessee holds over after the expiration of the basic lease it may be concluded that by so doing he has exercised the option. In that event he cannot be classified as a tenant at sufferance or as a periodic tenant. While this conclusion may be reached even if the lease provides for a "renewal," it is particularly indicated if provision is made for an "extension" of the existing lease without the necessity of notice.[53] Even if notice is required the

formality is for the benefit of the lessor and may be waived by him.[54]

By executing a sublease for a period extending beyond the term of the basic lease the lessee may become obligated to his sublessee to exercise an option to renew or extend the lease so that the sublessee may be protected for the full period of the sublease. This duty has been imposed upon the lessee even though a sublease contained an express provision to the effect that the sublease would automatically terminate upon the termination, cancellation or expiration of the basic lease.[55]

Perpetual Lease

Usually, covenants and conditions contained in the basic (first or primary) lease are carried over into a renewed or extended lease. But this is not true with respect to renewal or extension covenants. In the absence of specific language to the contrary, a covenant to renew or extend a lease is limited to *one renewal* or *one extension*. Otherwise there would be no end to the matter with the result —a perpetual lease. A perpetual lease is created by language in a lease for a fixed period, such as ten years, that is to be "automatically renewed for a further period of 10 years, and likewise at the expiration of any renewal period, unless the lessee gives notice to the lessors 90 days prior to the expiration date that he does not intend to exercise the renewal privilege." [56]

Even if a perpetual lease is not prohibited by the Rule against Perpetuities, or some

50. Straus v. Shaheen, Inc., 1942, 310 Mass. 646, 39 N.E.2d 573. See Murray v. Odman, 1939, 1 Wash.2d 481, 96 P.2d 489.

51. Orr v. Doubleday, Page & Co., 1918, 223 N.Y. 334, 119 N.E. 552, 1 A.L.R. 338; Haddad v. Tyler Production Credit Ass'n, Tex.Civ.App.1948, 212 S.W.2d 1006.

52. Ackerman v. Loforese, 1930, 111 Conn. 700, 151 A. 159, noted in 26 Ill.Law Rev. 445 (1931); Klein v. Auto Parcel Delivery Co., 1921, 192 Ky. 583, 234 S.W. 213; Seefeldt v. Keske, 1961, 14 Wis.2d 438, 111 N.W.2d 574.

53. Klein v. Auto Parcel Delivery Co., 1921, 192 Ky. 583, 234 S.W. 213, noted in 35 Harv.Law Rev. 621 (1922) (word "renew" used as meaning "extend"); Straus v. Shaheen, Inc., 1942, 310 Mass. 646, 39 N.E.2d 573.

54. Gordon v. Tennant, Adm'x, 1940, 108 Ind.App. 326, 26 N.E.2d 559 (retention of possession by sublessee); Wherry v. Lacey, 1964, 236 Or. 307, 388 P.2d 279. See Tay-Holbrook, Inc. v. Tutt, 1933, 218 Cal. 600, 24 P.2d 463.

55. Texas Co. v. Adelman, 1939, 186 Okl. 663, 99 P.2d 874, 127 A.L.R. 945.

56. In re Mackie's Petition, 1963, 372 Mich. 104, 125 N.W.2d 482, 483.

other positive rule of law, matters discussed under a separate heading,[57] it is not looked upon with favor. If the purpose is to create successive rights with respect to renewals or extensions this purpose must be expressed in specific language.[58] It is not found from the fact that the right is expressed in the plural, such as "renewals" or "extensions." [59] Of course, a lease may provide for a specific number of renewals or extensions.

First Refusal

A covenant that the lessee has a "refusal" for an additional term constitutes an option and the lessee may demand a renewal.[60] However, if the provision is that the lessee has a "first refusal" it merely gives the lessee a right to a renewal if the lessor desires to lease the land upon the expiration of the basic lease.[61] This rule of construction gives some meaning to the word "first."

A provision that written notice is to be given in the event that either the lessor or the lessee desires to renew the lease does not, standing alone, constitute an option to renew.[62]

Certainty as to Duration and Rent

If the option is silent as to such matters as the duration of the new period or the rent to be paid, reference is made to the basic lease.[63] If that lease was for a period of one year then the renewal or extension is for a like period and the same rental prevails.

A provision for renewal or extension for a rental "to be agreed upon" invalidates the option because of the uncertainty involved.[64] However, there is authority for the view that such an option may be sustained and it calls for the payment of "reasonable rental" as determined by the court.[65]

Notice

Unless otherwise provided by statute it is not necessary for the lessee to make personal service of his notice of intention to exercise an option to renew or extend a lease.[66] But mailing such notice is not sufficient unless it is actually received by the lessor within the time fixed.[67] However, a clause in the lease

---

57. See infra, § 87.

58. Albany Savings Bank v. R. E. Gigliotti Motor Sales of Utica, 1937, 162 Misc. 468, 295 N.Y.S. 779; Lawson v. West. Va. Newspaper Pub. Co., 1944, 126 W.Va. 470, 29 S.E.2d 3.

59. Gray v. Stadler, 1938, 228 Wis. 596, 280 N.W. 675. See Syms v. New York, 1887, 105 N.Y. 153, 11 N.E. 369.

60. Callahan Co. v. Michael, 1910, 45 Ind.App. 215, 90 N.E. 642; Tracy v. Albany Exchange Co., 1852, 7 N.Y. 472; McAdoo v. Callum, 1882, 86 N.C. 419.

61. Ablett v. Clauson, 1954, 43 Cal.2d 280, 272 P.2d 753; Landowners Co. v. Pendry, 1940, 151 Kan. 674, 100 P.2d 632, 127 A.L.R. 890; Cloverdale Co. v. Littlefield, 1921, 240 Mass. 129, 133 N.E. 565; Laevin v. St. Vincent De Paul Society, 1949, 323 Mich. 607, 36 N.W.2d 163, 6 A.L.R.2d 815; Hill v. Prior, 1919, 79 N.H. 188, 106 A. 641. *Contra:* Callahan Co. v. Michael, 1910, 45 Ind.App. 215, 90 N.E. 642 (first refusal); Stetler v. North Branch Transit Co., 1917, 258 Pa. 299, 101 A. 980. In Fergen v. Lyons, 1916, 162 Wis. 131, 155 N.W. 935, noted in 14 Mich.Law Rev. 514 (1916), such a provision is held to be ambiguous and explainable by surrounding circumstances.

62. Gardella v. Greenburg, 1922, 242 Mass. 405, 136 N.E. 106, 26 A.L.R. 1411.

63. Mutual Paper Co. v. Hoague-Sprague Corp., 1937, 297 Mass. 294, 8 N.E.2d 802.

64. Ablett v. Clauson, 1954, 43 Cal.2d 280, 272 P.2d 753; Beal v. Dill, 1953, 173 Kan. 879, 252 P.2d 931; Batavia National Bank v. S. & H., Inc., 1958, 3 Wis.2d 565, 89 N.W.2d 309.

65. Moss v. Olson, 1947, 148 Ohio St. 625, 76 N.E.2d 875; Young v. Nelson, 1922, 121 Wash. 285, 209 P. 515, 30 A.L.R. 568.

66. James v. Hutchinson, Mo.App.1948, 211 S.W.2d 507.

67. Bluthenthal v. Atkinson, 1910, 93 Ark. 252, 124 S.W. 510; Alger v. Community Amusement Corp., 1943, 320 Ill.App. 184, 50 N.E.2d 594; McCrory Stores Corp. v. Goldberg, 1923, 95 N.J.Eq. 152, 122 A. 113; J. M. Wilcox & Co. v. Scott-Burr Stores Corp., D.Tex.1951, 97 F.Supp. 792, affirmed 194 F.2d 989 (1952).

may require mailing only. The notice must be definite, unconditional and unqualified.[68]

In case of the lessor's death, and in the absence of statute, notice must be given to the heirs. The administrator does not have authority to act in behalf of the heirs.[69]

OPTION TO PURCHASE

69. The obligations assumed by a lessee furnish the required consideration to support an option to purchase. If it does not violate the rule against perpetuities, is sufficiently definite as to terms and executed with the formalities required by the Statute of Frauds, it may be specifically enforced.
   a. First privilege to purchase. An unqualified right to demand a conveyance is not created by a "first privilege" to purchase. It is qualified by the owner's right to withdraw the property from the market.
   b. Exercise of option. Unless provided otherwise, an option to purchase may be exercised during the period of an extension or renewal.
      Usually an option provision requires that the lessee give the lessor written notice of his intention to exercise the option.

The obligations assumed by a lessee usually furnish the required consideration to support an option to purchase as set forth in the lease.[70] If the option does not violate the Rule against Perpetuities,[71] is sufficiently definite as to terms and executed with the formalities prescribed by the Statute of Frauds, it may be specifically enforced.[72] It is lacking in definiteness if it merely provides that the purchase price is to be paid "as

mutually agreed by both parties." [73] The option may be assigned separate and distinct from the leasehold estate.[74] It may be enforced by and against remote parties.[75] Authorities support the view that an unexecuted option cannot be used as a means by which to increase the award to which a lessee may be entitled in eminent domain proceedings. For this purpose an option does not create an estate or interest in land.[76]

Unless the lessor has properly terminated a lease for breach of condition,[77] default in the performance of covenants and conditions by the lessee will not necessarily prevent him from exercising his option to purchase.[78] It seems clear that an exercise of the option to purchase cures any default that relates to the value of the reversion, such as a default in connection with a covenant to repair. Generally, a lessee with an option to purchase can avoid the consequences of waste by exercising his option.[79] Under such circumstances the relationship of the parties changes from that of lessor and lessee to that of vendor and vendee and the default does not result in

---

68. Pope v. Goethe, 1935, 175 S.C. 394, 179 S.E. 319, 99 A.L.R. 1005.

69. O'Connor v. Chiascione, 1943, 130 Conn. 304, 33 A.2d 336, 148 A.L.R. 169.

70. Tebeau v. Ridge, 1914, 261 Mo. 547, 170 S.W. 871.

71. See infra, § 187.

72. See 5 Williston on Contracts (rev. ed.) § 1419.

73. Roberts v. Adams, 1958, 164 Cal.App.2d 312, 330 P.2d 900.

74. Mott v. Cline, 1927, 200 Cal. 434, 253 P. 718, (*dictum*). The lower court decision is discussed in 15 Cal.Law Rev. 56 (1926).

75. Hollander v. Central Metal & Supply Co., 1908, 109 Md. 131, 71 A. 442; Rogers v. Graves, 1937, 254 App.Div. 467, 5 N.Y.S.2d 967; Humble Oil & Refining Co. v. Lennon, (R.I., 1962), 182 A.2d 306.

76. Keogh v. Peck, 1925, 316 Ill. 318, 147 N.E. 266, 269, 38 A.L.R. 1151; Phillips Petroleum Co. v. City of Omaha, 1960, 171 Neb. 457, 106 N.W.2d 727.

77. London v. Tebo, 1923, 246 Mass. 360, 141 N.E. 234, 29 A.L.R. 1037.

78. Crowell v. Braly, 1959, 169 Cal.App.2d 352, 337 P. 2d 211; Gassert v. Anderson, 1937, 201 Minn. 515, 276 N.W. 808.

79. Keogh v. Peck, 1928, 316 Ill. 318, 147 N.E. 266, 38 A.L.R. 1151; Powell v. Dayton Ry. Co., 1888, 16 Or. 33, 16 P. 863.

damage to the vendor.[80] This same rule should apply even if the default does not affect the value of the reversion, such as in a default in the payment of rent, if the lessee tenders the amount due. However, in some cases specific performance of the covenant has been denied upon the ground that a petitioner in default is not entitled to equitable relief.[81]

First Privilege to Purchase

In R. I. Realty Co., Inc. v. Terrell (N. Y.),[82] a lease gave the lessee the "first privilege to buy said property." The court held that a sale was at the election of the lessor. If he did elect to sell then the lessee could take advantage of his "first privilege" to purchase. This conclusion gives meaning to the language "*first* privilege." However, other language in the lease may justify the conclusion that the option given to the lessee was intended to be absolute.[83]

In some decisions it is indicated that a "first option", "right of first refusal" or "first chance to buy" are too uncertain and incomplete to warrant enforcement.[84] However,

the general rule is to the contrary. Unless the context of the agreement indicates otherwise, such provisions confer a right to purchase at the same price and upon the same terms as contained in any *bona fide* offer from a third party that is acceptable to the lessor.[85] But such an interpretation is not indicated if there is a further provision in the lease that the price is "to be negoitated and to be agreeable between the parties at the time of sale." This makes the option unenforceable because of uncertainty.[86]

Exercise of Option

Unless provided otherwise, an option to purchase may be exercised during the period of an extension [87] or renewal [88] of a lease because the option is an integral part of the lease. While an option to renew a lease may not be included in the renewal period, other covenants and conditions are extended into the new period. The minority rule is that an option to purchase is a "separate and independent" covenant in the lease and unrelated to the lease itself. It is considered

80. Chapman Drug Co. v. Chapman, 1960, 207 Tenn. 502, 341 S.W.2d 392.

81. Helbig v. Bonsness, 1938, 227 Wis. 52, 277 N.W. 634, 115 A.L.R. 373, noted in Wis.Law Rev.1939, p. 87.

82. 254 N.Y. 121, 172 N.E. 262 (1930), noted in 15 Minn.Law Rev. 119 (1930).

83. See Associated Truck Lines v. Bae, 1956, 346 Mich. 106, 77 N.W.2d 384 (date given after which the option could be exercised); Schroeder v. Gemeinder, 1875, 10 Nev. 355; Tantum v. Keller, 95 N.J.Eq. 466, 123 A. 299 affirmed 96 N.J.Eq. 672, 126 A. 925 (1924) (fixed price and lessee had the first privilege to purchase "at any time" during the lease).

84. See Folsom v. Harr, 1905, 218 Ill. 369, 75 N.E. 987; Wolf v. Lodge, 1913, 159 Iowa 162, 140 N.W. 429; Fogg v. Price, 1888, 145 Mass. 513, 14 N.E. 741; McClung Drug Co. v. City Realty & Investment Co., 1919, 91 N.J.Eq. 216, 108 A. 767.

85. Nelson v. Reisner, 1958, 51 Cal.2d 161, 331 P.2d 17; Jurgensen v. Morris, 1920, 194 App.Div. 92, 185 N.Y.S. 386; Tamura v. De Tuliis, 1955, 203 Or. 619, 281 P.2d 469.

86. King v. Dalton Motors, Inc., 1961, 260 Minn. 124, 109 N.W.2d 51.

87. Schaeffer v. Bilger, 1946, 186 Md. 1, 45 A.2d 775, 163 A.L.R. 706; Moore v. Maes, 1949, 214 S.C. 274, 52 S.E.2d 204; Moiger v. Johnson, 1950, 86 U.S. App.D.C. 219, 180 F.2d 777; Sherwood v. Tucker, [1924] 2 Ch. 42, noted in 23 Mich.Law Rev. 75 (1924).

88. Hindu Incense Mfg. Co. v. MacKenzie, 1949, 403 Ill. 390, 86 N.E.2d 214; Meadow Heights Country Club v. Hinckley, 1925, 229 Mich. 291, 201 N.W. 190; Trustees of Congregation of Sons of Abraham v. Gerbert, 1895, 57 N.J.L. 395, 31 A. 383; Masset v. Ruh, 1923, 235 N.Y. 462, 139 N.E. 574. But see, Gulf Oil Corp. v. Buram Realty Co., Inc., 1962, 11 N.Y.2d 233, 182 N.E.2d 608 (limited to period of basic lease where option was to be exercised "at any time during the term of this lease").

that while an option to purchase survives if a lease is "extended" that is not the case if a lease is "renewed." [89] The preferred view is that the technical distinction between an "extension" and a "renewal" should not be applied in resolving the issue under discussion.[90] It is true that, technically speaking, the extension of a lease does not require the execution of a new leasing agreement. The period of the old lease is merely extended. A renewal requires the execution of a new leasing agreement.

Usually an option provision requires that the lessee give the lessor written notice of his intention to exercise the option. The notice must be given within the time specified otherwise it is considered that the option is withdrawn. In this respect time is of the essence even in the absence of a specific provision to that effect.[91] Unless a lease provides otherwise, notice to exercise an option is effective only upon its receipt by the party to be notified.[92] If the lessee is given an option to purchase "during the term of this lease" it is contemplated that notice must be given and payment so made that the purchase and sale contract will have been completed within the lease term.[93] Formalities, such as the requirement of written notice, may be waived by the lessor.[94]

[89]. Pettit v. Tourison, 1925, 283 Pa. 529, 129 A. 587, 39 A.L.R. 1106; Batchelor v. Murphy, [1924] 2 Ch. Div. 252.

[90]. Sisco v. Rotenberg, Fla.1958, 104 So.2d 365.

[91]. Rosenaur v. Pacelli, 1959, 174 Cal.App.2d 673, 345 P.2d 102.

[92]. Starr v. Holck, 1947, 318 Mich. 452, 28 N.W.2d 289, 172 A.L.R. 413; Hoban v. Hudson, 1915, 129 Minn. 335, 152 N.W. 723; McCrory Stores Corp. v. Goldberg, 1923, 95 N.J.Eq. 152, 122 A. 113.

[93]. Cities Service Oil Co. v. National Shawmut Bank, 1961, 342 Mass. 108, 172 N.E.2d 104.

[94]. Bio-Ramo Drug Co., Inc. v. Abrams, 1962, 229 Md. 494, 184 A.2d 831.

CHAPTER 14

RENT

RENT, IN GENERAL

70. **Rent is the consideration agreed to be paid for an estate in land. The payment of rent is not involved if money is paid to a lessor as a bonus for execution of a lease or paid to a lessee as consideration for an assignment or a sublease.**

a. **Payments made to third party. In general, a covenant by the lessee to make fixed payments to a third party does not constitute rent.**

b. **Deposits. A deposit of money with the lessor by the lessee may be as security for the faithful performance of the terms of the lease. However, the deposit may be made as an advance payment of rent.**

c. **Theories underlying liability. If the liability of a lessee is based upon an express promise to pay rent, he remains liable for payments that may accrue after an assignment. If his liability is based upon an implied promise his liability for unaccrued rent ceases if the lease is assigned with the consent of the lessor, express or implied.**

Liability of an assignee of the leasehold estate is usually based upon privity of estate. However, an assumption agreement may fix liability on the basis of privity of contract.

Blackstone defines rent as " * * * a certain profit issuing yearly out of lands and tenements corporeal." [1] It may be payable in money, services or in profits derived from the use of land.

Ground rent is rent reserved by the owner of unimproved land where improvements are to be erected by the owner of the possessory estate. According to the common law rule land may be conveyed in fee simple with the reservation of a yearly rent to the grantor and his heirs.[2] In the absence of statute there are no restrictions upon the creation of irredeemable ground rent. In the Pennsylvania case of In re Crean's Estate,[3] land was conveyed in fee simple, the grantor reserving yearly ground rent of $8,000. The ground rent was extinguishable "at any time after 15 years" at the option of the purchaser by payment of $200,000. This was a valid ground rent under a statute that prohibited the crea-

---

1. 2 Bl.Com. 41. See T. Cyprian Williams, The Incidence of Rent, 11 Harv.Law Rev. 1, 3 (1897). Consideration to be paid for a license is not rent (Hancock v. Austin, Court of Common Pleas 1863, 14 C.B.,N.S., 634). But the law of constructive eviction has been applied in such a case (Thomas Cusack Co. v. Pratt, 1925, 78 Colo. 28, 239 P. 22. 44 A.L.R. 55, noted in 24 Mich.Law Rev. 511 (1926)).

2. Van Rensselaer v. Ball, 1859, 19 N.Y. 100.

3. 321 Pa. 216, 183 A. 915 (1936).

tion of irredeemable ground rents with a provision that the time of extinguishment may not be postponed longer than 21 years, or life or lives in being at the time of its creation.

In modern times rent is usually associated with non-freehold estates. The consideration agreed to be paid for the estate (rent) is generally payable in money or in crops to be raised on the land. The preferred view is that if rent is payable in crops the lessor and the lessee are tenants in common of the crops.[4] Frequently, the amount of rent may include a fixed percentage of the income derived from a business conducted on the land.[5]

In some instances rent consists of a legal detriment assumed by the lessee. For example, in the North Dakota case of Northern Pacific Ry Co. v. McClure,[6] the lessee of land from a railroad company covenanted to hold the company harmless for any damage caused to chattels located on the leased land if the damage resulted from railroad operations. This was construed to be a rent covenant. The parties intended this result and the consideration could be measured in terms of money (cost of insurance).[7]

As has been stated, rent is the consideration promised for the conveyance of an estate in land. If a leasing agreement is applicable to both land and chattels, and provides for unsegregated payments of consideration, the entire amount is classified as rent.[8] In Welch

v. Ashby (Mo.),[9] a lump sum was fixed as rent for land and live stock. The lessor instituted a summary action to recover possession of the land. According to a local rule of procedure the action was proper only if the lessor had made a demand for the *rent due*. While it is recognized that rent is payable only for the use of land, it is held that the lessee was estopped to claim that a segregated payment of the sum should be made as between the land and the live stock and that, therefore, only part of the amount was payable as rent.

The obligation to pay rent must have its origin in an agreement. If land is occupied without the owner's consent, express or implied, the occupant may be held liable in damages for the *mesne profits* from the land but not for rent.[10] However, there is some authority that the landowner may waive the tort and sue the occupant on an implied promise to pay the reasonable rental value of the land.[11]

Since the obligation to pay rent has its origin in an agreement, one might expect that liability would be governed by the rules of contract law. In fact, such a view is followed in many of the decisions.[12] However, the law as it relates to rent took shape before there was much development in the field of contracts and the law, as thus developed, is of controlling importance in modern litigation.

Accrued rent, that is, rent that is **due and** payable, is a chose in action and properly

---

4. Farmers Mutual Mfg. & Ginning Co. v. Thompson, 1942, 60 Ariz. 37, 131 P.2d 413; Leis v. Beckmark, 1937, 133 Neb. 467, 275 N.W. 679.

5. Jackson v. Pepper Gasoline Co., 1939, 280 Ky. 226, 133 S.W.2d 91, 126 A.L.R. 1370. See comment, The Percentage Lease—Its Functions & Drafting Problems, 61 Harv.Law Rev. 317 (1948).

6. 9 N.D. 73, 81 N.W. 52 (1899).

7. *Accord:* Kennedy Bros. v. Iowa State Insurance Co., 1902, 119 Iowa 29, 91 N.W. 831; Northern Pacific Ry. Co. v. McClure, 1899, 9 N.D. 73, 81 N.W. 52. *Contra:* Atwood v. Chicago, Milwaukee & St.

Paul Ry. Co., 1924, 313 Ill. 59, 144 N.E. 351, noted in 19 Ill.Law Rev. 581 (1925), 23 Mich.Law Rev. 76 (1924). *Cf.:* M. E. Blatt Co. v. United States, 1938, 305 U.S. 267, 59 S.Ct. 186, 83 L.Ed. 167.

8. Mickle v. Miles, 1856, 31 Pa. 20; Farewell v. Dickenson, [1827] 6 B. & C. 251, 108 Eng.Rep. 446.

9. 88 Mo.App. 400 (1901).

10. See 2 Tiffany, Landlord and Tenant, p. 1859.

11. See, for example, Ransch v. Arp, 1919, 39 Cal. App. 580, 179 P. 694.

12. See infra, § 80.

classified as personal property. Unaccrued rent is classified as an interest in land. Therefore, a statute which levies a tax on intangible personal property is not applicable to unaccrued rent.[13]

Payments Made to a Third Party

Authorities support the position that a covenant by the lessee to make fixed payments *to a third party* does not classify as a rent covenant. For example, in Evans v. Lincoln Co. (Pa.),[14] the lessee covenanted to pay for gas used on the land and all water taxes that might be assessed. These payments were to be made to the creditors. The court held that since payments were not to be made to the lessor the amounts involved did not constitute rent.[15] In view of the fact that these payments operated to reduce the liability of the lessor they should be classified as rent.[16] The fact that payments were to be made to a third party is immaterial.

Deposits

The payment of rent is not involved if money is paid to the lessor as a bonus for the execution of a lease. That is also the case if money is paid to a lessee as consideration for the assignment of a lease or as a bonus for the execution of a sublease.[17] In all such situations the amounts so paid are not recoverable and the payor is not entitled to credit for payments so made in satisfaction of a rent-covenant.[18] Other types of deposits are as follows:

First: Money or securities may be deposited with the lessor by the lessee as security for the faithful performance of the terms of the lease. This may result in a debtor-creditor relationship or the lessor may be classified as a trustee.[19]

There may be agreement that the funds so deposited are to be forfeited to the lessor in the event of default by the lessee in the performance of the terms of the lease. In that event, rules pertaining to "liquidated damages" are applicable. To be valid the amount of deposit must bear some reasonable relationship to the potential damage that may be suffered by the lessor in case of default and it must be shown that the actual damages involved could not be ascertained with reasonable certainty.[20] If the actual damages flowing from a breach can be ascertained with reasonable certainty in light of facts as they exist at the time of the execution of the lease, then anything in excess of that amount would fall within the classification of a *penalty* and this would nullify the claim of the lessor.[21]

While both the benefit and the burden side of a covenant to pay rent is enforceable against remote parties that is not the case with respect to security-deposits. A covenant by a lessor to return a security deposit is

---

13. State v. Royal Mineral Ass'n, 1916, 132 Minn. 232, 156 N.W. 128.

14. 204 Pa. 448, 54 A. 321 (1903).

15. *Accord:* Korn v. Johnson, Tex.Civ.App.1938, 117 S.W.2d 844, noted in 17 Tex.Law Rev. 221 (1939) (covenant to carry insurance on the leased land). *Cf.:* Lamoine Mott Estate v. Neiman, 8 Cir. 1935, 77 F.2d 744, 99 A.L.R. 1097 (lessor's lien for rent did not include amount of taxes which the lessee had covenanted to pay).

16. Irving Trust Co. v. Burke, 4 Cir. 1933, 65 F.2d 730, 88 A.L.R. 877.

17. Wood v. Hipwell, 1930, 107 Cal.App. 680, 290 P. 1040.

18. See Comment, 27 Cal.Law Rev. 83 (1938).

19. Mallory Associates, Inc. v. Barving Realty Co., Inc., 1949, 300 N.Y. 297, 90 N.E.2d 468, 15 A.L.R.2d 1193 (trustee by force of statute), reargument denied 300 N.Y. 680, 91 N.E.2d 331. See Green v. Frahm, 1917, 176 Cal. 259, 168 P. 114.

20. Stuco Corp. v. Gates, Fla.App.1962, 145 So.2d 527; Southern Motor Supply Co. v. Shelburne Motor Co., 1935, 172 Okl. 495, 46 P.2d 562.

21. Bacciocco v. Curtis, 1938, 12 Cal.2d 109, 82 P.2d 385.

personal in nature. For example, if the lessor assigns the reversion, the duty to make a refund cannot be enforced against the assignee unless the amount of deposit was delivered to him. An assignee of the leasehold estate is not entitled to the credit in the absence of an express assignment of the right. The minority rule is that a deposit is in the nature of a "continuing security" and the security passes with an assignment of the reversion.[22]

Second: The lessee may deposit funds with the lessor as security for the faithful performance of the terms of the lease. But the understanding may be that the deposit is to be applied in satisfaction of the rent-obligation if the lessee complies with the terms of the lease. It may be agreed, for example, that it will be applied in payment of the last month's rent. In a situation of this kind, if the lessor declares a forfeiture for default on the part of the tenant he is not entitled to retain the amount deposited for payment of the last month's rent. An obligation to pay the last month's rent would not accrue because of the forfeiture.[23]

If a covenant provides that the deposit is to be used in satisfaction of the obligation to pay rent it may be enforced by and against remote parties. For example, an assignee of the reversion may be held accountable.[24] In this respect the covenant differs from one that calls for a deposit for security purposes only.

Theories Underlying Liability

By accepting a lease the lessee thereby becomes a promisee with respect to all covenants contained in the lease. The covenant to pay rent need not be expressed in formal language. It is sufficient if designated rent is expressly "payable" at stated times.[25] The existence of an express covenant has been denied in a case where the lease was made to a tenant "he yielding and paying" designated rent.[26] In view of the marked distinction between a covenant and a condition, an express covenant cannot be found in language that the lease is subject to the condition that designated rental is paid.

If the liability of a lessee is based upon an express promise to pay rent he remains liable in spite of the fact that the lease is subsequently assigned. While the assignment terminates privity of estate it does not terminate privity of contract that was created by the express covenant. Two additional points are as follows:

First: If the obligation of a lessee to pay rent is based upon an implied promise it rests upon the existence of privity of estate.[27] Accordingly, his liability as to unaccrued rent ceases with an assignment of the lease. There is no basis for implying a promise to pay after the lessee has assigned the leasehold estate. However, this result will follow only if the lessor consented to the assignment. This consent may be express or it may be implied, such as in a case where the lessor accepts rent from the assignee.[28]

Second: If a leasehold estate is assigned, privity of contract may exist as between the lessor and the assignee by force of an assump-

---

22. Moskin v. Goldstein, 1923, 225 Mich. 389, 196 N.W. 415.

23. Michaels v. Fishel, 1902, 169 N.Y. 381, 62 N.E. 425. *Cf.:* Sinclair v. Burke, 1930, 133 Or. 115, 287 P. 686, noted in 8 N.Y.Univ.Law Quarterly Rev. 144 (1930).

24. Four-G Corp. v. Ruta, 1958, 25 N.J. 503, 138 A.2d 18; Flatbush Savings Bank v. Levy, 1951, 109 N.Y.S. 2d 247.

25. Samuels v. Ottinger, 1915, 169 Cal. 209, 146 P. 638.

26. Kimpton v. Walker, 1873, 9 Vt. 191.

27. Wall v. Hinds, 1855, 70 Mass. (4 Gray) 256; Kanawha-Gauley Coal & Coke Co. v. Sharp, 1914, 73 W.Va. 427, 80 S.E. 781.

28. Nova Cesarea Harmony Lodge v. White, 1876, 30 Ohio St. 569.

tion agreement. The assignee may expressly assume the covenants in the lease. Then, as a third party beneficiary, the lessor may hold the assignee liable for breach of any covenant that may occur even after the assignee has parted with his estate by re-assignment.[29] While the re-assignment terminates privity of estate it does not terminate privity of contract. An assignment "subject to the agreements of the lessee mentioned in the lease" does not constitute an assumption agreement.[30] Such an agreement results only if the language is clear and unambiguous.[31]

In the absence of an assumption agreement the assignee's liability to the lessor rests upon privity of estate only. Except as noted, the assignee may avoid liability for breach of a covenant that occurs after the assignee has parted with his estate by re-assignment. This terminates privity of estate. While an assignee may terminate privity of estate by assigning the lease to a person who is financially irresponsible,[32] a "colorable assignment" will not accomplish this purpose. An assignment is colorable if it is made to another for the benefit of the assignor.[33] It is also colorable if made to a corporation that is considered to be the *alter ego* of the assignor.[34] However, the corporation will cease to be the *alter ego* of the assignor when the

assignor divests himself of his stock in the corporation.[35]

MODIFICATION AGREEMENTS

71. An agreement purporting to modify the terms of a lease, such as a reduction in the amount of rent, is unenforceable unless supported by consideration. It must also be in writing if the lease is in writing as required by the Statute of Frauds.

Some authorities follow the view that the lessee's obligation to pay rent is discharged to the extent that rent is actually paid in compliance with the modification. It then becomes an executed oral agreement.

Litigation relating to modification agreements usually involves two distinct issues. Generally, the lessor claims a right to recover the difference between the rent called for in the lease and the rent actually paid by the lessee. He also claims a right to abrogate the modification agreement as to future payments of rent.

In Adams Recreation Palace, Inc. v. Griffith (Ohio),[36] the lessee claimed that the rent actually paid and accepted by the lessor under the modification agreement discharged the rent obligation. The modification agreement had been made at a time when the lessee was insolvent and would have been compelled to give up the business he conducted on the leased land if compelled to pay the rent as provided for in the lease. The court held that the modification agreement was supported by consideration.[37] It was emphasized that the

29. Barde v. Portland News Publishing Co., 1935, 152 Or. 77, 52 P.2d 194.

30. Consolidated Coal Co. v. Peers, 1896, 166 Ill. 361, 46 N.E. 1105.

31. Waxenberg v. J. J. Newberry Co., 1939, 302 Ill. App. 128, 23 N.E.2d 574.

32. Johnson v. Sherman, 1860, 15 Cal. 287 (*dictum*); A. D. Juilliard & Co. v. American Woolen Co., 1943, 69 R.I. 215, 32 A.2d 800, 148 A.L.R. 187; Tibbals v. Iffland, 1895, 10 Wash. 451, 39 P. 102.

33. Century Holding Co. v. Ebling Brewing Co., 1918, 185 App.Div. 292, 173 N.Y.S. 49; Negley v. Morgan, 1863, 46 Pa. 281.

34. Shea v. Leonis, 1939, 14 Cal.2d 666, 96 P.2d 332.

35. National Bank of Commerce of Seattle v. Dunn, 1938, 194 Wash. 472, 78 P.2d 535.

36. 58 Ohio App. 216, 16 N.E.2d 489 (1937), noted in 13 Univ. of Cinn.Law Rev. 496 (1939), 5 Law Jr. Ohio St.Univ. 115 (1938).

37. *Accord:* Wm. Lindeke Land Co. v. Kalman, 1934, 190 Minn. 601, 252 N.W. 650, 93 A.L.R. 1393, noted in 32 Mich.Law Rev. 1001 (1934), 18 Minn.Law Rev. 885 (1934); Ma-Beha Co., Inc. v. Acme Realty Co., Inc., 1941, 286 Ky. 382, 150 S.W.2d 1; Liebreich original lease had been executed at a time of high prices and that the modification agreement resulted in mutual advantages. The lessor gained an advantage from the continued occupancy of his building and the tenant from the reduction in rent.

The prevailing rule is that economic conditions do not furnish a sufficient consideration to support a modification agreement. The lessor may insist that the lessee make future payments in accord with the terms of the lease, and he may also recover the difference between the amounts actually paid under the modification agreement and the rent as stipulated in the lease.[38] In an increasing number of cases the view is adopted that while the lessor may insist that his lessee make future payments according to the terms of the lease, he cannot recover the difference between the rent provided for in the lease and the rent actually paid under the modification agreement. This conclusion is supported upon the ground that there is an executed oral agreement to the extent that payments have been made.[39] In at least one state it is provided by

statute that if the modification agreement is evidenced by a writing, no consideration is necessary for its validity.[40]

Generally, if a contract is required to be in writing under provisions of the Statute of Frauds, a modification of the contract must also be in writing.[41] It has been suggested that this rule is inapplicable if the parol modification relates only to specific covenants in a lease.[42]

CLASSIFICATION OF RENT AND THE RIGHT TO DISTRAIN FOR ITS COLLECTION

72. "Rent Service" is the rent which is a concomitant of a reversionary interest. At common law, the collection of such rent could be enforced by distraint. "Rent Charge" and "Rent Seck" do not spring from or depend upon the ownership of a reversionary interest. If the right to distrain for rent is expressly reserved, the rent is "rent charge." If the right to distrain is not expressly reserved, no such right exists, and the rent is "rent seck". In the United States, the right to distrain for rent is generally regulated by statute.

Usually, the right to rent is a concomitant of a reversion and, as such, it is called "rent service." Under the common law rule, in the case of rent service, the lessor may enforce the payment of rent which is due and payable by seizing chattels located on the leased land. The right so to seize chattels is called the right to "distrain for rent."

If rent is not a concomitant of a reversion, as where one person owns the right to rent and another owns the reversion, then the rent

v. Tyler State Bank & Trust Co., Tex.Civ.App.1936, 100 S.W.2d 152, noted in 22 Wash.Univ.Law Qt. 570 (1937). A similar result was reached in Long Mercantile Co. v. Saffron, Mo.App.1937, 104 S.W.2d 770, either upon the ground of promissory estoppel or upon the ground that the new agreement operated as a surrender of the old lease. This case is followed in Stewart v. Carleton Bldg. Co., Mo.App., 1940, 138 S.W.2d 720.

38. Levine v. Blumenthal, 1936, 117 N.J.L. 23, 186 A. 457; Decker v. Richard J. Seltzer, Inc., 1935, 116 Pa.Super. 58, 176 A. 29. See Torrey v. Adams, 1925, 254 Mass. 22, 149 N.E. 618, 43 A.L.R. 1447 (promise by lessee to pay increased rent held to be unenforceable).

39. Perry v. Farmer, 1936, 47 Ariz. 185, 54 P.2d 999; Julian v. Gold, 1931, 214 Cal. 74, 3 P.2d 1009, noted in 5 So.Cal.Law Rev. 245 (1932). For a criticism of this view, see Williston on Contracts (rev.ed.) § 120; Whidden, Modification of Leases by Agreement to Reduce Rent, 15 Chicago-Kent Rev. 186 (1937).

40. Thompson's Laws of N. Y. (1939), Pers.Prop. § 33 (2), discussed in 23 Va.Law Rev. 446 (1937).

41. Robertson v. Melton, 1938, 131 Tex. 325, 115 S.W. 2d 624, 118 A.L.R. 1505; Corson Corp. v. Frontier, Inc., 1960, 55 Wash.2d 652, 349 P.2d 424.

42. See, Sutherland v. Madden, 1935, 142 Kan. 343, 46 P.2d 32; Glass v. Bryant, 1946, 302 Ky. 236, 194 S.W.2d 390; 12 Temple Law Qt. 260 (1938).

is either "rent charge" or "rent seck." If the right to rent is in a person other than the owner of the reversion there is no right to distrain for rent unless this right was expressly reserved in the rental agreement. If the right is so reserved "rent charge" is involved. If the right is not reserved the situation involves "rent seck."

A general assignment of a lease does not operate as an assignment of the reversion in the leased land.[43] The assignment, being made by the lessor, confers upon the assignee a right to the rent that may accrue under the lease. If there is compliance with recording statutes such an assignment will prevail as against a subsequent purchaser of the leased land.[44]

In the United States the right to distrain for rent is not looked upon with favor.[45] In some states the matter is regulated by statute.[46] Even in the absence of statute, the courts have recognized exceptions to the common law rule. For example, under the common law rule the one entitled to payment of rent can seize chattels located on the leased land whether the chattels belong to the lessee or to a third party.[47] However, some authorities hold that there is no right to seize the chattels of a third party if the chattels were placed upon the land for purposes of trade. In Thomas v. Spruks (Fed.),[48] the "public trade" exception was applied where the chattel consisted of coal which had been extracted from the land by the lessee and sold by him to another.

At common law a distress and an impounding are distinct things. The distress is sufficient if the lessor publicly states that designated chattels are not to be removed from the land. This distress does not carry the right to sell the goods. No precise act or form of words is essential for a distress. While at common law it is necessary to take the goods to a public pound, there is authority that goods may be impounded on the land where located, and it is usually provided by statute that the goods may be sold to satisfy the debt.[49]

OBLIGATION TO PAY RENT

73. In the absence of agreement to the contrary, rent is not payable in advance.

The obligation to pay rent is not apportionable on the basis of time.

In the absence of agreement to the contrary rent is not payable until the expiration of the lease. A provision in the lease calling for the payment of a stated amount at a designated time and for monthly payments thereafter does not require that the monthly payments be made at the beginning of each month.[50] In Bernard v. Triangle Music Co. (Wash.),[51]

43. Demarest v. Willard, 1828, 8 Cow. (N.Y.) 206.

44. Faircloth v. Flewellen, Tex.Civ.App.1939, 130 S.W. 2d 1098.

45. Langdell, A Brief Survey of Equity Jurisdiction, 10 Harv.Law Rev. 71, 84 (1896). The right to distrain for rent was denied in Gruber v. Pacific States Savings & Loan Co., 1939, 13 Cal.2d 144, 88 P.2d 137.

46. See, for example, Lovett v. Lee, 1940, 141 Fla. 395, 193 So. 538; Burnett v. Boukedes, 1962, 240 S.C. 144, 125 S.E.2d 10. For discussion of the various types of statutory provisions, see note, 6 Univ. of Chicago Law Rev. 505 (1939).

47. In re West Side Paper Co., 1908, 89 C.C.A. 110, 162 F. 110. A Pennsylvania statute exempts household goods leased or hired under a bailment, lease or conditional sales agreement (Reinhart v. Gerhardt, 1943, 152 Pa.Super. 229, 31 A.2d 737).

48. 89 F.2d 998 (3 Cir.1937), certiorari denied Philadelphia & R. C. & I. Co. v. Spruks, 302 U.S. 718, 58 S.Ct. 38, 82 L.Ed. 554, noted in 51 Harv.Law Rev. 170 (1937).

49. See, for example, Elkman v. Rovner, 1943, 133 N.J.Eq. 93, 30 A.2d 516.

50. Kistler v. McBride, 1901, 65 N.J.L. 553, 48 A. 558; Liebe v. Nicolai, 1897, 30 Or. 364, 48 P. 172.

51. 1 Wash.2d 41, 95 P.2d 43, 126 A.L.R. 558 (1939).

payments of rent during the first two years of a three year lease were expressly made payable in advance. Since a similar provision was not inserted in the lease with respect to the third year, rent for that year was not payable until the end of the year.

Except as agreed by the parties, the obligation to pay rent is not apportionable on the basis of time. In Hammond v. Thompson, (Mich.),[52] the defendant, a tenant at will, agreed to pay rent at the rate of thirty-five dollars a month, payable at the end of each month, starting September 15, 1894. On October 14, 1894, at two-thirty p. m., plaintiff lessor sold the leased land and this terminated the estate prior to the expiration of the rental period. Since the rent was not due until the last minute of the last day (midnight October 14th), the plaintiff was not entitled to recover the rent or any part thereof.[53]

The same rule applies if the lessor accepts a surrender of the leasehold estate prior to the time fixed for the payment of rent [54] or if the lessee purchases the leased land.[55] If a lessor declares a forfeiture of the lease his right to recover rent is limited to the amount due prior to the termination of the lease.[56] But statutes in some states provide that the lessor is entitled to recover for the reasonable value of use and occupation until such time as he recovers possession of the land.[57] There is also statutory authority for the rule that rent may be apportioned on the basis of time.[58]

RIGHT TO RENT

74. If rent is attached to a reversion it is payable to the owner of the reversion when it becomes due.

   a. **Assignment of reversion. The vendor of land that is subject to a lease cannot successfully claim a right to rent under an oral reservation.**

   b. **The right to rent is apportionable. The owner of rent, or of the reversion to which rent is attached, may partition his interest by granting a portion of his interest to others.**

If rent is attached to a reversion it is payable to the one who is the owner of the reversion when the rent becomes due. In Bank of Pennsylvania v. Wise (Pa.),[59] defendant purchased the reversion, the possessory estate being under lease to plaintiff, and fourteen days thereafter one-half year's rent became due. The court held that plaintiff was entitled to the full year's rent. In Rockingham v. Penrice (Eng.),[60] a life tenant had a power to execute a lease. He executed the power and died on the day fixed for the payment of rent. The court held that the rent was not due until the end of the day. At that time the estate was vested in the remainderman and, for that reason, the remainderman was entitled to all of the rent. This claim was sustained as against a right to the rent asserted

---

52. 168 Mass. 531, 47 N.E. 137 (1897).

53. *Accord*: Perry v. Aldrich, 1843, 13 N.H. 343. See In re Newark Shoe Stores, D.Md.1933, 2 F. Supp. 384, noted in 1 Univ. of Chicago Law Rev. 344 (1933).

54. Willis v. Kronendonk, 1921, 58 Utah 592, 200 P. 1025, 18 A.L.R. 917, noted in 22 Col.Law Rev. 180 (1922).

55. State ex rel. Com'rs of Land Office v. Bright, Okl.1953, 264 P.2d 725. But see, White v. Coates, 1943, 17 Wash.2d 686, 137 P.2d 113.

56. See Becker v. Rute, 1940, 228 Iowa 533, 293 N. W. 18, noted in 26 Iowa Law Rev. 151.

57. See, for example, New York Civil Practice Act, § 1434.

58. See, for example, West's Ann.Cal.Civ.Code, § 1935, as applied in Silveira v. Ohm, 1949, 33 Cal.2d 272, 201 P.2d 387. *Cf.*: Hindin v. Caine, 1951, 104 Cal. App.2d 238, 231 P.2d 83 (not apportionable as to rent paid in advance).

59. 3 Watts (Pa.) 394 (1834).

60. 1 P.Wms. 177, 24 Eng.Rep. 345 (1711).

by the executor of the estate of the life tenant.[61]

Assignment of Reversion

The right to rent will pass with a general grant of the reversion but a general grant of the rent will not result in a conveyance of the reversion.[62] The vendor of land that is subject to a lease will not be permitted to prove an oral reservation of the rent. Such evidence would violate the parol evidence rule in that it would vary the legal effect of the deed.[63]

If a lessor conveys a part of the reversion, such as in a case where he executes a lease which is to become immediately operative, but subject to a former lease, the grantee is entitled to the rent specified in the former lease.[64] However, he is not entitled to rent that is due at the time of the conveyance because the right to accrued rent is a mere chose in action.[65]

The Right to Rent is Apportionable

The owner of rent, or of the reversion to which rent is attached, may partition his interest by granting portions thereof to others. Each grantee will then be entitled to collect his proportionate share of the rent.[66] Any other view would unduly restrict the free alienation of estates in land and would be especially detrimental in cases where estates are distributed to heirs and devisees.

Apportionment of the right to rent will also result if a part of the leased land is surrendered or if a forfeiture is declared as to a part thereof.[67] In Higgins v. California Petroleum & Asphalt Co. (Cal.),[68] A and B were the owners of separate tracts of land but they executed a joint lease. Thereafter, the tenant acquired ownership of the area owned by A. The court held that the acquisition of this parcel extinguished *pro tanto* the covenant of the lessee to pay rent.

ACTUAL EVICTION

75. In case of an actual eviction the lessee is relieved of his obligation to pay rent during the period of the eviction. This is true even if the lessee remains in possession of a part of the leased land.

An actual eviction is involved if the lessor, or one acting with his consent, interferes with the possession of the land by the lessee. Acts of trespass or acts that merely interfere with the enjoyment of leased land do not constitute an actual eviction.

The obligation to pay rent is entire in nature and cannot be apportioned by the wrongful act of the lessor. Therefore, if a lessee is the victim of an actual eviction he cannot be held liable for any part of the rent even if he remains in possession of a part of the leased land.[69] However, he may not be excused from the performance of other covenants in the lease, such as a covenant to repair.[70] In the case of a deliberate and in-

---

61. *Accord*: Watson v. Penn, 1886, 108 Ind. 21, 8 N.E. 636.

62. Demarest v. Willard, 1828, 8 Cow.(N.Y.) 206.

63. McCall v. Morgan, 1943, 244 Ala. 472, 14 So.2d 374.

64. Russo v. Yuzolino, 1896, 19 Misc. 28, 42 N.Y.S. 482; Attoe v. Hemmings, [K.B.1612] 2 Bulst. 281, 80 Eng.Rep. 1123.

65. Damren v. American Light & Power Co., 1898, 91 Me. 334, 40 A. 63.

66. Reed v. Ward, 1853, 22 Pa. 144; Ards v. Watkins, [1598, 1599] Cro.Eliz. 637, 651, 78 Eng.Rep. 877, 890.

67. Ehrman v. Mayer, 1881, 57 Md. 612 (surrendered).

68. 109 Cal. 304, 41 P. 1087 (1895).

69. Skaggs v. Emerson, 1875, 50 Cal. 3; Smith v. McEnany, 1897, 170 Mass. 26, 48 N.E. 781; Ravet v. Garelick, 1922, 221 Mich. 70, 190 N.W. 637, 28 A.L.R. 1331. But see, Crossthwaite v. Caldwell, 1894, 106 Ala. 295, 18 So. 47.

70. Smith v. McEnany, 1897, 170 Mass. 26.

tentional eviction the lessee may be in a position to establish tort liability on the part of the lessor and be entitled to recover damages for mental disturbance.[71]

An actual eviction is involved if the lessor, or some person acting with his consent, interferes with the possession of the land by the lessee. This requires something more than a mere interference with the enjoyment of the leased land or acts of simple trespass.[72] In North Pacific Steamship Co. v. Terminal Investment Co. (Cal.),[73] it is held that an eviction did not result from the mere fact that a sign had been erected on the leased land. Since an actual eviction involves a disturbance of possession, interference with the use of an easement that is appurtenant to the land does not constitute an actual eviction.[74] A contrary conclusion is indicated in Edmison v. Lowry (S.D.),[75] where the lessor obstructed a street in front of the leased land. But in this case the lessee's estate extended to the center of the street and he was thus deprived of possessory rights. It is similar to a case where the lessor blocks a passageway leading to the leased land.[76] An actual eviction may be based upon the fact that the lessor caused the appointment of a receiver to manage the leased land.[77] However, an eviction is not involved if the authority of the receiver is limited to the collection of rent from sub-lessees.[78]

There cannot be an actual eviction if the lessee has not been placed in actual possession of the leased land.[79] In Illinois Central Railroad Co. v. A. H. Bowman & Co. (Ky.),[80] the lessor's failure to deliver possession of part of the leased land did not discharge the lessee from his rent obligation. He took possession of part of the land and by so doing impliedly agreed to an apportionment of the rent.[81]

CONSTRUCTIVE EVICTION

76. Liability for rent is not affected by the conduct of a lessor which merely interferes with the lessee's enjoyment of the leased land. But if the disturbance is substantial in nature the lessee may give up possession of the land and thereby avoid further liability under the lease. His defense to a rent action is constructive eviction.

The wrongful conduct of a lessor that merely results in an interference with the enjoyment of leased land does not relieve the lessee from his obligation to pay rent.[82] If this results in a breach of the lessor's covenant for quiet enjoyment the lessee may be entitled to damages but in the absence of a provision to the contrary the covenants in a lease are independent. This means that

---

71. See Richardson v. Pridmore, 1950, 97 Cal.App.2d 124, 217 P.2d 113, 17 A.L.R.2d 929.

72. Bartlett v. Farrington, 1876, 120 Mass. 284 (cutting flowers and removing a partly decayed tree).

73. 43 Cal.App. 182, 185 P. 205 (1919).

74. Duncan v. Granas, 1913, 106 Cal. 41, 134 P. 979.

75. 3 S.D. 77, 52 N.W. 583 (1892).

76. Pridgeon v. Excelsior Boat Club, 1887, 66 Mich. 326, 33 N.W. 502.

77. City Nat. Bank & Trust Co. v. Livingston, 1941, 66 Ohio App. 47, 31 N.E.2d 460, noted in 41 Col.Law Rev. 934 (1941).

78. Exeter Co. v. Holland Corp., 1933, 172 Wash. 323, 341, 20 P.2d 1, 23 P.2d 864, noted in 13 Boston Univ. Law Rev. 745 (1933).

79. McClurg v. Price, 1868, 59 Pa. 420.

80. 218 Ky. 466, 291 S.W. 711 (1927).

81. *Accord*: Kline v. Guaranty Oil Co., 1914, 167 Cal. 476, 140 P. 1. *Cf.*: Moore v. Mansfield, 1902, 182 Mass. 302, 65 N.E. 398.

82. Veysey v. Moriyama, 1921, 184 Cal. 802, 195 P. 662, 20 A.L.R. 1363; A. W. Banister Co. v. P. J. W. Moodie Lumber Corp., 1934, 286 Mass. 424, 190 N.E. 727, noted in 8 So.Cal.Law Rev. 250 (1935); Edgerton v. Page, 1859, 20 N.Y. 281; Angelo v. Deuster, Tex.Civ.App.1930, 30 S.W.2d 707, noted in 9 Tex. Law Rev. 293 (1931); Pinching v. Wurdeman, 1926, 56 App.D.C. 223, 12 F.2d 164.

the lessee cannot rely upon breach of a covenant for quiet enjoyment if an action is brought against him to recover rent. But if there is a substantial interference with the lessee's enjoyment of the leased land by the wrongful acts of the lessor the foundation is established for a constructive eviction. The final step is up to the lessee. If he sees fit to give up possession of the leased land he thereby avoids liability for rent that becomes payable after that date.[83] There is a minority rule that a lease is a contract and recovery of rent may be denied if there is a failure of consideration even if the lessee remains in possession.[84]

Usually, the claim of constructive eviction will not be sustained unless it is shown that the lessor was notified of the condition and afforded an opportunity to make the necessary corrections.[85]

There is no uniform criterion by which the type of wrongful conduct may be evaluated so as to determine whether or not it is sufficient to furnish a basis for constructive eviction. There is authority for the view that a constructive eviction may be based upon the fact that the lessor used rooms in his apartment for illegal and immoral purposes.[86] Eviction may arise out of the fact that the lessor of space for advertising erected a building which obstructed the view.[87] A constructive eviction cannot be based upon the fact that an apartment becomes "infested with insects" [88] unless, of course, this condition is brought about as a result of some default on the part of the lessor.[89]

Assuming proof of the fact that interference with enjoyment was substantial in nature, there are conflicting views as to additional requirements for a constructive eviction. In some of the early decisions it is indicated that there must be proof of the fact that the lessor intended an eviction. This means that there must be some affirmative wrongful act. The lessor's failure or even refusal to perform his covenants under the lease will not suffice.[90] But the preferred view is that importance is not attached to the question as to whether the disturbance resulted from acts of omission or commission.[91] A constructive eviction may arise out of the lessor's failure to perform covenants in the lease, such as to re-

---

83. P. J. W. Moodie Lumber Corp. v. A. W. Banister Co., 1934, 286 Mass. 424, 190 N.E. 727, noted in 8 So.Cal.Law Rev. 250 (1935). *Cf.*: Majen Realty Corp. v. Glotzer, 1946, 61 N.Y.S.2d 195.

84. Stifter v. Hartman, 1923, 225 Mich. 101, 195 N.W. 673.

85. Richards v. Dodge, Fla.1963, 150 So.2d 477. *Cf.*: Milheim v. Baxter, 1909, 46 Colo. 155, 103 P. 376.

86. Dyett v. Pendleton, 1826, 8 Cow.(N.Y.) 727. See Lloyd, The Disturbed Tenant—A Phase of Constructive Eviction, 79 Univ. of Pa.Law Rev. 707, 712 (1931).

87. Thomas Cusack Co. v. Pratt, 1925, 78 Colo. 28, 239 P. 22, 44 A.L.R. 55, noted in 24 Mich.Law Rev. 511 (1926).

88. Hopkins v. Murphy, 1919, 233 Mass. 476, 124 N. E. 252, 13 A.L.R. 816; Hughes v. Westchester Development Corp., 1935, 64 App.D.C. 292, 77 F.2d 550.

89. Hopkins v. Murphy, 1919, 233 Mass. 476, 124 N. E. 252, 13 A.L.R. 816; Ray Realty Co. v. Holtzman, 1938, 234 Mo.App. 802, 119 S.W.2d 981, noted in 24 Wash.Univ.Law Quarterly 281 (1939). See Delamater v. Foreman, 1931, 184 Minn. 428, 239 N.W. 148, noted in 17 Iowa Law Rev. 543 (1932). *Cf.*: Johnson v. Snyder, 1950, 99 Cal.App.2d 86, 221 P.2d 164 (unsanitary conditions in a market for which the lessor was apparently responsible).

90. Stewart v. Childs Co., 1914, 86 N.J.L. 648, 92 A. 392.

91. Grabenhorst v. Nicodemus, 1875, 42 Md. 236; Smith v. Tennyson, 1914, 219 Mass. 508, 107 N.E. 423 (failure of lessor to give his consent to have a new key made for the leased premises); Karpp v. Royer, 1960, 362 Mich. 64, 106 N.W.2d 244 (lessor's failure to purchase gasoline storage tanks in compliance with his covenant in the lease).

pair,[92] make basement walls water-tight,[93] furnish heat [94] or elevator services.[95]

To terminate a lease on the ground of constructive eviction the lessee must vacate the premises within a reasonable time after the wrongful acts involved.[96] Whether or not he remains in possession, he may be entitled to recover damages for breach of a covenant of quiet enjoyment. Tort liability may be involved if the acts are malicious, oppressive or wanton.[97] However, the wrongful acts of third parties, not sanctioned by the lessor, cannot be used as the basis for a constructive eviction because the lessor is not under a duty to control such acts.[98]

ACTS OF THIRD PARTIES

77. Liability for rent is not affected by the wrongful acts of third parties that are not authorized by the lessor.

Interference with the enjoyment of leased land that is caused by the wrongful act of a third party will not sustain the claim of a constructive eviction unless the lessor is directly or indirectly responsible therefor.[99] This rule is based upon the ground that a lessor is not under a duty to protect the lessee against such acts unless he covenants to do so.[1] For example, in the Oregon case of Wolf v. Eppenstein,[2] a lessee gave up possession of the leased land because another part of the building was used by other tenants for illegal and immoral purposes. This did not relieve the lessee from his obligation to pay rent. Evidence did not show that the illegal use was authorized or sanctioned by the lessor.[3] A contrary conclusion is reached in some cases upon the ground that a lessor is under a duty to evict tenants who conduct illegal activities.[4]

---

92. Piper v. Fletcher, 1901, 115 Iowa 263, 88 N.W. 380; Sewell v. Hukill, 1960, 138 Mont. 242, 356 P. 2d 39; McCardell v. Williams, 1897, 19 R.I. 701, 36 A. 719 *(dictum)*. See West's Ann.Cal.Civ.Code, § 1941.

93. Gibbons v. Hoefeld, 1921, 299 Ill. 455, 132 N.E. 425.

94. Bass v. Rollins, 1895, 63 Minn. 226, 65 N.W. 348; Russell v. Olson, 1911, 22 N.D. 410, 133 N.W. 1030; Buchanan v. Orange, 1916, 118 Va. 511, 88 S.E. 52. *Cf.*: Schaaf v. Nortman, 1963, 19 Wis.2d 540, 120 N.W.2d 654. The same result was reached in Higgins v. Whiting, 1926, 102 N.J.L. 279, 131 A. 879, noted in 39 Harv.Law Rev. 1102 (1926), where the court attempts to distinguish Stewart v. Childs Co., 1914, 86 N.J.L. 648, 92 A. 392.

95. McCall v. New York Life Ins. Co., 1909, 201 Mass. 223, 87 N.E. 582. See 18 Boston Univ.Law Rev. 244 (1938).

96. Automobile Supply Co. v. Scene-In-Action Corp., 1930, 340 Ill. 196, 172 N.E. 35, 69 A.L.R. 1085; Ellis v. McDermott, 1929, 7 N.J.Misc. 757, 147 A. 236 *(dictum)*, noted in 39 Yale Law Jr. 585 (1930); Maki v. Nikula, 1960, 224 Or. 180, 355 P.2d 770; Toy v. Olinger, 1921, 173 Wis. 277, 181 N.W. 295, 20 A.L.R. 1366; Gateway Co., Inc. v. Charlotte Theatres, Inc., 5 Cir. 1961, 297 F.2d 483.

97. Jones v. Kelly, 1929, 208 Cal. 251, 280 P. 942.

98. McCullough v. Houar, 1908, 141 Iowa 342, 117 N.W. 1110; Seaboard Realty Co. v. Fuller, 1900, 33 Misc. 109, 67 N.Y.S. 146.

99. See Case v. Minot, 1893, 158 Mass. 577, 33 N.E. 700 (lessor authorized a tenant to make repairs that interfered with the enjoyment of premises by another tenant).

1. Blomberg v. Evans, 1927, 194 N.C. 113, 138 S.E. 593, 53 A.L.R. 686; Hockersmith v. Sullivan, 1912, 71 Wash. 244, 128 P. 222.

2. 71 Or. 1, 140 P. 751 (1914).

3. *Accord*: Cougle v. Densmore, 1894, 57 Ill.App. 591; Katz v. Duffy, 1927, 261 Mass. 149, 158 N.E. 264, 58 A.L.R. 1047, noted in 8 Boston Univ.Law Rev. 62 (1928); 2 Cincinnati Law Rev. 106 (1928); Hughes v. Westchester Dev. Corp., 1935, 64 App. D.C. 292, 77 F.2d 550.

4. Keenan v. Flanigan, 1925, 157 La. 749, 103 So. 30, 38 A.L.R. 248 (nuisance); J. W. Cushman & Co. v. Thompson, 1908, 58 Misc. 539, 109 N.Y.S. 757; Bruckner v. Helfaer, 1929, 197 Wis. 582, 222 N.W. 790, noted in 29 Col.Law Rev. 530 (1929); 14 Iowa Law Rev. 487 (1929) (disorderly conduct).

The duty of a lessor may be enlarged by covenant. For example, in the Illinois case of University Club of Chicago v. Deakin,[5] a covenant provided that the leased store in a building should be used only as a jewelry and art shop. The lessor covenanted not to rent any other store in the building to any tenant making a specialty of the sale of Japanese or Chinese goods or pearls. Thereafter another store was leased subject to restrictions as stated above. But this second lessee violated the restriction and the first lessee gave up possession of the store. The court held that the lessor did not fulfill the terms of his covenant by merely inserting a restriction in the second lease. He was under a duty to see that the second lessee lived up to the terms of the restrictive covenant. Failure to perform this duty resulted in a constructive eviction.[6]

EVICTION BY TITLE PARAMOUNT

78. If a lessee is evicted by title paramount from all of the leased land the obligation to pay rent is extinguished. If he is evicted from only a part of the leased land the rent is apportioned.

If a lessee is evicted by title paramount from all of the leased land, the obligation to pay rent is extinguished. Since the consideration for the covenant to pay rent is the right to the enjoyment of the land, the lessee cannot be required to pay rent if he is deprived of that right.[7] If the lease contains a covenant for quiet enjoyment, or if such a covenant is implied, the lessee can recover

damages resulting from the eviction [8] unless, of course, he took the leasehold estate subject to the outstanding interest, such as a mortgage.[9]

If the lessee is evicted by title paramount from only a part of the leased land the rent will be apportioned.[10] According to a minority rule, the lessee is required to pay the reasonable rental value of that part of the land to which he retains possession.[11]

EMINENT DOMAIN PROCEEDINGS

79. The obligation to pay rent is extinguished if all of the leased land is taken in eminent domain proceedings. A partial taking does not impair the obligation to pay rent.

    a. **Bonus value.** A lessee is entitled to an award that represents the bonus value of his leasehold estate.

    b. **Fixtures.** Ordinarily, the valuation placed upon land in eminent domain proceedings includes the value of fixtures.

If all of the leased land is taken in eminent domain proceedings the lessee is not entitled to any compensation based upon his covenant to pay rent.[12] This follows from the fact that the obligation to pay unaccrued rent is extinguished because of the proceedings. The governmental agency acquires the reversion and also the leasehold estate and the leasehold estate is destroyed by merger.

If only part of the leased land is taken and the remaining portion is susceptible of occu-

5. 265 Ill. 257, 106 N.E. 790 (1914), noted in 28 Harv. Law Rev. 522 (1915); 10 Ill.Law Rev. 61 (1915); 13 Mich.Law Rev. 317 (1915).

6. *Accord*: People's Trust Co. v. Schultz Novelty & Sporting Goods Co., 1926, 244 N.Y. 14, 154 N.E. 649, noted in 12 Cornell Law Qt. 392 (1927). *Contra*: Lucente v. Davis, 1905, 101 Md. 526, 61 A. 622.

7. Morse v. Goddard, 1847, 54 Mass.(13 Metc.) 177.

8. Ganz v. Clark, 1929, 252 N.Y. 92, 169 N.E. 100.

9. Wagner v. Van Schaick Realty Co., 1914, 163 App. Div. 632, 148 N.Y.S. 736.

10. Cheairs v. Coats, 1900, 77 Miss. 846, 28 So. 728; Fifth Ave. Bldg. Co. v. Kernochan, 1917, 221 N.Y. 370, 117 N.E. 579, reargument denied 222 N.Y. 525, 118 N.E. 1057, noted in 18 Col.Law Rev. 89 (1918). *Cf.*: McLarren v. Spalding, 1852, 2 Cal. 510.

11. Seabrook v. Moyer, 1879, 88 Pa. 417.

12. Corrigan v. City of Chicago, 1893, 144 Ill. 537, 33 N.E. 746. *Contra*: Foote v. City of Cincinnati, 1842, 11 Ohio 408.

pation, the obligation to pay unaccrued rent according to the terms of the lease remains unimpaired.[13] There is no abatement or apportionment of rent as a result of the partial taking. The leasehold estate is not destroyed. Accordingly, the lessee is entitled to an award that will compensate him because of his obligation under the rent covenant.[14] The minority rule is that in a partial-taking situation the rent should be apportioned.[15] That is to say, the obligation to pay rent is extinguished with respect to that part of the land that is taken by the governmental agency. The main argument in support of this view is that it protects a lessor and does not relegate him to the position of an unsecured creditor with respect to rent that may subsequently accrue on the land taken by the governmental agency. This is the statutory rule in some states.[16]

13. City of Pasadena v. Porter, 1927, 201 Cal. 381, 257 P. 526, 53 A.L.R. 679, discussed in 16 Cal.Law Rev. 48, 50 (1927); Stubbings v. Village of Evanston, 1891, 136 Ill. 37, 26 N.E. 577; Gluck v. City of Baltimore, 1895, 81 Md. 315, 32 A. 515; A. W. Banister Co. v. P. J. W. Moodie Lumber Corp., 1934, 286 Mass. 424, 190 N.E. 727, noted in 8 So.Cal.Law Rev. 250 (1935); F. W. Woolworth Co. v. City of Berlin, 1925, 82 N.H. 153, 130 A. 741; Check Workman v. Mifflin, 1858, 30 Pa. 362; Elliott v. Joseph, 1961, 163 Tex. 71, 351 S.W.2d 879; Olson Land Co. v. Alki Park Co., 1911, 63 Wash. 521, 115 P. 1083.

14. See Aldrich v. R. J. Ederer Co., 1922, 302 Ill. 391, 134 N.E. 726 (under some circumstances an equitable lien may be imposed on the money awarded the tenant as security for the lessee's continuing obligation to pay rent).

15. Board of Levee Commissioners v. Johnson, 1889, 66 Misc. 248, 6 So. 199; Biddle v. Hussman, 1856, 23 Mo. 597; Uhler v. Cowen, 1899, 192 Pa. 443, 44 A. 42. Cf.: Mayor, etc. of Baltimore v. Latrobe, 1905, 101 Md. 621, 61 A. 203 (apportioned if part taken substantially impairs the usefulness of the part not taken.)

16. Hinrichs v. City of New Orleans, 1898, 50 La.Ann. 1214, 24 So. 224; Matter of Daly, 1898, 29 App.Div. 286, 51 N.Y.S. 576; Rhode Island Hospital Trust Co. v. Hayden, 1898, 20 R.I. 544, 40 A. 421. See 40 Harv. Law Rev. 1135, 1137 (1927).

There is only a "partial taking" within the meaning of the rule if all of the leased land is condemned but only for a *temporary period of time*.[17] Under such circumstances the compensation awarded to the lessee may include the cost of moving to a new location.[18]

Bonus Value

A lessee is entitled to an award that represents the bonus value of his leasehold estate.[19] For example, if all of the leased land is taken the lessee is entitled to the present market value of the unexpired term less the amount of unaccrued rent.

If only a part of the leased land is taken, and the remaining portion is susceptible of occupation, the lessee is entitled to the present market value of the leasehold estate on the part taken. The weight of authority is that there is no deduction for unaccrued rent because the lessee remains liable for the full amount of rent called for in the lease. According to the minority rule the rent is apportioned and the award to the lessee is reduced to the extent that he is discharged from the obligation to pay rent.

Fixtures

Ordinarily, the valuation placed upon land in eminent domain proceedings includes the value of fixtures. If a lessee has a right to remove the fixtures then he is entitled to

17. Leonard v. Autocar Sales & Service Co., 1946, 392 Ill. 182, 64 N.E.2d 477, 163 A.L.R. 670, certiorari denied 327 U.S. 804, 66 S.Ct. 968, 90 L.Ed. 1029, rehearing denied 328 U.S. 878, 66 S.Ct. 1118, 90 L.Ed. 1646, and 328 U.S. 879, 66 S.Ct. 1330, 90 L.Ed. 1647.

18. United States v. General Motors Corp., 1945, 323 U.S. 373, 65 S.Ct. 357, 89 L.Ed. 311, 156 A.L.R. 390.

19. Edmands v. City of Boston, 1871, 108 Mass. 535. Cf.: Los Angeles County Flood Control Dist. v. Andrews, 1921, 52 Cal.App. 788, 205 P. 1085 (leasehold estate was not, in fact, taken).

their value.[20]   This is true even though, by agreement, the lessee is not entitled to receive an award for the taking of his leasehold estate.[21]

DESTRUCTION OF FIXTURES AND FRUSTRATION OF PURPOSE

80. The common law rule is that liability for rent is not affected by the destruction of fixtures. Under some circumstances a lessee may be relieved from his obligation to pay rent by application of the contract rule as it relates to frustration of purpose.

According to the common law rule a lease involves the conveyance of an estate in land and the risk of loss is on the lessee. In the early case of Paradine v. Jane (Eng.),[22] the lessee was held liable for rent even though he had been dispossessed by an invading enemy "to the King and the kingdom." The tenant assumes the risks incident to the destruction of fixtures because such destruction does not result in a termination of the leasehold estate.[23] Exceptions to the common law rule are as follows:

First: If a lease consists of a relatively small space in a comparatively large building a destruction of the building results in a termination of the lease. It is considered that the lease relates only to the building and does not include an estate in the land.[24]

Second: If the leased land is to be used *only* for a stated purpose, such as for the sale of intoxicating liquor, and a law is passed making that use illegal, the lessee cannot be held liable for rent that subsequently becomes due and payable.[25]   His estate has come to an end because he cannot make any beneficial use of the land. A different situation is involved if the land cannot be used for the restricted purpose without a license. In such a case the lessee assumes the risk of securing the required license.[26]

If a covenant pertaining to the use of land is permissive and not restrictive, the liability of the lessee under the rent-covenant continues even if this permissive use becomes impossible whether by force of statute or otherwise.[27]   The lessee is free to use the leased land for other purposes. That is also the rule if there are two or more restrictive covenants relating to the use of the land and *some but not all* of the restrictive uses are declared to be illegal.[28]

---

20. Wingert v. Prince, Fla.1960, 123 So.2d 277; In re City of New York, 1910, 66 Misc. 488, 122 N.Y.S. 321. But see Newman v. Commonwealth, 1957, 336 Mass. 444, 146 N.E.2d 485 (where lessee terminated lease as permitted by the terms thereof).

21. In re Allen Street & First Ave., Borough of Manhattan, City of New York, 1931, 256 N.Y. 236, 176 N.E. 377, noted in 31 Col.Law Rev. 1195 (1931).

22. Style, 47, 82 Eng.Rep. 519 (K.B. 1647).

23. White v. Molyneux, 1847, 2 Ga. 124; Fowler v. Bott, 1809, 6 Mass. 63; Gibson v. Perry, 1860, 29 Mo. 245. See Bunting v. Orendorf, 1929, 152 Miss. 327, 120 So. 182, noted in 28 Mich.Law Rev. 77 (1929) (land inundated by unprecedented flood).

24. McMillan v. Solomon, 1868, 42 Ala. 356; Stockwell v. Hunter, 1846, 52 Mass. (11 Metc.) 448; Graves v. Berdan, 1863, 26 N.Y. 498; Winton, Lessor v. Cornish, 1832, 5 Ohio 477; Harrington v. Watson, 1883, 11 Or. 143, 3 P. 173.

25. Doherty v. Monroe Eckstein Brewing Co., 1921, 115 Misc. 175, 187 N.Y.S. 633, affirmed 198 App.Div. 708, 191 N.Y.S. 59; Marshall v. Smith, Ohio 1960, 174 N.E.2d 558 (waiver of restricted use by lessors not controlling); Brunswick-Balke-Collender Co. v. Seattle Brewing & Malting Co., 1917, 98 Wash. 12, 167 P. 58. *Contra:* Imbeschied v. Lerner, 1922, 241 Mass. 199, 135 N.E. 219, 22 A.L.R. 819.

26. Standard Brewing Co. v. Weil, 1916, 129 Md. 487, 99 A. 661; Teller v. Boyle, 1890, 132 Pa. 56, 18 A. 1069.

27. Lawrence v. White, 1909, 131 Ga. 840, 63 S.E. 631.

28. Grace v. Croninger, 1936, 12 Cal.App.2d 603, 55 P.2d 940; Stern Holding Co. v. O'Connor, 1938, 119 N.J.L. 291, 196 A. 432.

Third: Under some circumstances emphasis is placed upon the contractual aspects of a lease and the rights and liabilities of the parties are resolved on the basis of contract law. For example, there is authority for the view that if fixtures are destroyed through no fault on the part of the lessee he may remain in possession of the land and his duty to pay rent is proportionally reduced because of failure of consideration.[29]

The defense of impossibility of performance may be used if the parties contemplated the continued existence of fixtures. Thus, in the Oregon case of Eggen v. Wetterborg,[30] land with equipment was leased for the purpose of operating a gasoline service station. A beer tavern was operated in conjunction with the station. In addition to a flat monthly rental, the lessee was required to pay "one-half cent per gallon for each gallon of gasoline delivered to the premises." The fixtures and equipment necessary for the operation of the gasoline station were completely destroyed by fire. The court held that this resulted in a termination of the lease even though the lessee desired to remain in possession and operate the beer tavern. The continued operation of the service station was mandatory since this was essential to performance of the terms of the lease because rental was fixed on a percentage basis. Thus, the lessor and the lessee contemplated the continued existence of the service station. In view of the fact that neither party assumed responsibility for the continued existence of the necessary equipment the lease must be regarded as subject to the implied condition that if the particular thing failed the "contract" shall be dissolved and the parties excused from further performance.[31]

The general rule is that the doctrine of commercial frustration is applicable in the case of a lease.[32] However, this is true only if there is complete or nearly complete frustration.[33] Further, the doctrine is not applicable with respect to risks that were known or should have been known to the parties.[34]

Fourth: Statutes in a number of states provide that if a lessee is without fault he may terminate a lease if the leased land becomes uninhabitable or if substantial damage is caused by the destruction of fixtures.[35] In many cases the rights and liabilities of the parties are governed by covenants in the lease.[36]

ILLEGALITY

81. A lessor cannot recover rent if the land is leased for an illegal purpose. Some authori-

---

29. Wattles v. South Omaha Ice & Coal Co., 1897, 50 Neb. 251. 69 N.W. 785. *Cf.:* Whitaker v. Hawley, 1881, 25 Kan. 674, (where the lessee carried insurance for the benefit of the lessor).

30. 193 Or. 145, 237 P.2d 970 (1951).

31. *Accord:* Davis v. Shepperd, 1938, 196 Ark. 302, 117 S.W.2d 337.

32. Davis v. Shepperd, 1938, 196 Ark. 302, 117 S.W.2d 337; University Club of Chicago v. Deakin, 1914, 265 Ill. 257, 106 N.E. 790, (*dictum*), noted in 28 Harv.Law Rev. 522 (1915), 10 Ill.Law Rev. 61 (1915), 13 Mich.Law Rev. 317 (1915); Colonial Operating Corporation v. Hannon Sales & Service, Inc., Mun. Ct.1942, 178 Misc. 879, 34 N.Y.S.2d 116, noted in 42 Col.Law Rev. 1058 (1942).

33. Perry v. Champlain Oil Co., 1957, 101 N.H. 97, 134 A.2d 65; Wood v. Bartolino, 1944, 48 N.M. 175, 146 P.2d 883.

34. Essex-Lincoln Garage, Inc. v. City of Boston, 1961, 342 Mass. 719, 175 N.E.2d 466 (lease of parking lot and subsequent change in traffic pattern). But see, Jones v. Fuller-Garvey Corp., 1963, —— Alaska ——, 386 P.2d 838 (doctrine of frustration applied because building was destroyed by fire).

35. See, for example, Conn.Gen.Stats. § 47–24; N.J. R.S. 46:8–6, 7; Thompson's Laws of N.Y. (1939), Real Property Law, § 227; West's Ann.Cal.Civ.Code, § 1932(2).

36. See, for example, Egan v. Dodd, 1917, 32 Cal. App. 706, 164 P. 17; Scharbauer v. Cobean, 1938, 42 N.M. 427, 80 P.2d 785, 118 A.L.R. 102; Finnegan v. McGavock, 1939, 230 Wis. 112, 283 N.W. 321.

ties reach this same conclusion if a lessor was informed of the fact that the lessee intended to use the land for an illegal purpose and actually did use it for such purpose.

The lease of land for an illegal purpose is void and neither the lessor nor the lessee are entitled to benefits under the lease even if the land is not used for the intended purpose.[37] In Hartsin Construction Co. v. Millhauser (N.Y.),[38] land was used for a purpose that was prohibited under existing zoning laws. Recovery of rent was denied.[39]

A lessor will be denied recovery of rent if, at the time of the lease, he knew that the lessee's intention was to use the land for an illegal purpose.[40] A contrary conclusion is reached in some decisions if it does not appear that the lessor participated in the illegal use or actually intended such use to

be made.[41] In any event, mere suspicion on the part of the lessor that the leased land is to be used for an illegal purpose will not bar his recovery of rent.[42] If, after leasing his land, the lessor discovers the fact that it is being used for an illegal purpose his failure to take steps to prevent such use will not involve him in the lessee's guilt.[43] Further, if he did know of an intended illegal use he is entitled to his rent if the land was not actually used for the illegal purpose.[44]

If land is leased for a stated purpose and use for that purpose is illegal because of structural defects, the lessor is entitled to his rent if the lessee is under a contractual duty to do what is necessary to comply with the law or, according to some cases, if he has authority to do so.[45]

---

37. Auditorium Kennel Club v. Atlantic City, 1938, 16 N.J.Misc. 354, 199 A. 908 (lessee denied recovery of deposit). *Cf.:* Municipal Metallic Bed Mfg. Corp. v. Dobbs, 1930, 253 N.Y. 313, 171 N.E. 75, 68 A.L.R. 1376, noted in 7 N.Y.Univ.Law Qt.Rev. 993 (1930).

38. 136 Misc. 646, 241 N.Y.S. 428 (1930).

39. But see Warshawsky v. American Automotive Products, 1956, 12 Ill.App.2d 178, 138 N.E.2d 816.

40. Musco v. Torello, 1925, 102 Conn. 346, 128 A. 645, 42 A.L.R. 1032, noted in 11 Cornell Law Qt. 102 (1925); Upfill v. Wright, [1911] 1 K.B. 506.

41. Ashford v. Mace, 1912, 103 Ark. 114, 146 S.W. 474, noted in 26 Harv.Law Rev. 181 (1912).

42. See, Harbison v. Shirley & Silvers, 1908, 139 Iowa 605, 117 N.W. 963; Rundle-Spence Mfg. Co. v. Jakopichek, 1930, 201 Wis. 463, 229 N.W. 550.

43. Kessler v. Pearson, 1906, 126 Ga. 725, 55 S.E. 963.

44. Green v. Frahm, 1917, 176 Cal. 259, 168 P. 114 (*dictum*). *Cf.:* Mitchell v. Scott, 1883, 62 N.H. 596.

45. Plaza Amusement Co. v. Rothenberg, 1930, 159 Miss. 800, 131 So. 350, noted in 31 Col.Law Rev. 504 (1931). *Cf.:* Economy v. S. B. & L. Bldg. Corp., 1930, 138 Misc. 296, 245 N.Y.S. 352, noted in 44 Harv.Law Rev. 1299 (1931) (not a fireproof building as required by law so failure of consideration was available as a defense).

CHAPTER 15
SURRENDER OF LEASEHOLD ESTATES

Sec.
82. Surrender by Act of the Parties.
83. Surrender by Operation of Law.

SURRENDER BY ACT OF THE PARTIES

82. The surrender of a lease involves the conveyance of an estate in land. Accordingly, a surrender by act of the parties, as distinguished from a surrender by operation of law, must be executed with the formalities prescribed by the Statute of Frauds.

    a. *Interesse termini.* **The Statute of Frauds applies if a surrender involves an** *interesse termini* **to the same extent that it applies in the case of any estate.**

    b. Physical cancellation of a lease. The physical cancellation of a lease does not result in a reconveyance of the estate.

    c. Surrender to take effect in futuro. The preferred view is that an agreement to surrender all or any part of a leasehold estate, operative *in praesenti* **or** *in futuro* **involves the conveyance of an estate in land. Validity of the agreement depends upon compliance with the Statute of Frauds.**

A lease may be terminated by surrender. It consists of the relinquishment of the leasehold estate to the owner of the reversion or remainder. The English Statute of Frauds, enacted in 1677, provides that a deed or note in writing, signed by the party surrendering a leasehold estate, is essential, unless the surrender is by "act and operation of law."[1] Under the English statute the surrender of any lease, even a valid oral lease, must be in writing.[2] While this rule is followed in some of the American states,[3] exception is usually made in the case of short term leases. The general rule is that if the unexpired term of a lease could be created without the necessity of a writing a writing is not necessary for its surrender. This conclusion is reached either because of express statutory provision[4] or is based upon the interpretation of the controlling statute.[5]

Interesse Termini

Argument may be made that even though a surrender must be in writing, a parol agreement for surrender is sufficient if made before the lessee takes possession of the land. It is reasoned that prior to taking possession the lessee has a mere contract right, as distinguished from a leasehold estate. In other words, he has a mere interest in the term (an *interesse termini*). As such, the arrangement only involves the cancellation of a contract right.[6] However, modern authorities support the rule that the lessee acquires an estate at the time of the execution of his lease regardless of the time fixed for enjoyment in possession.[7]

---

1. 29 Car. II, c. 3, § 3.

2. Mollett v. Brayne, [1809] 2 Campb. 103, 170 Eng. Rep. 1095; Lord Ward v. Lumley, [1860] 5 Hurl. & N. 87, 157 Eng.Rep. 1112.

3. See, for example, T. B. Cartmell Paint & Glass Co. v. Cartmell, 1936, 7 W.W.Harr. 528, 37 Del. 528, 186 A. 897.

4. See, for example, statutes construed in Smith v. Devlin, 1861, 23 N.Y. 363; Garrick Theatre Co. v. Gimble Bros., 1914, 158 Wis. 649, 149 N.W. 385, noted in 28 Harv.Law Rev. 436 (1915). *Cf.:* Alschuler v. Schiff, 1896, 164 Ill. 298, 303, 45 N.E. 424, 425; Glass v. Bryant, 1946, 302 Ky. 236, 194 S.W.2d 390.

5. McDaniels v. Harrington, 1916, 80 Or. 628, 157 P. 1068; Whelen v. Laird, 1914, 56 Pa.Super. 489; 1 Am.Law of Property, § 3.99, p. 391, n. 7. *Contra:* Reyes v. Smith, Tex.Civ.App.1956, 288 S.W.2d 822, ref. n. r. e.

6. See Tiffany, Surrender, 3 Mich.Law Rev. 18, 20 (1904).

7. As to the nature of an *interesse termini*, see 18 Col.Law Rev. 595 (1918).

Physical Cancellation of a Lease

If the Statute of Frauds requires that a surrender by act of the parties be evidenced by a writing, the *physical cancellation* of a lease will not operate as a surrender. This is true even though the parties intended to accomplish a surrender.[8]

Surrender to take Effect in Futuro

There are two views as to the validity of an oral agreement between the lessor and the lessee that a leasehold estate will be surrendered after the expiration of a stated time or upon the happening of a designated event.

First: According to one view such an agreement does not involve the conveyance of an estate in land. Rather, it is merely an agreement to modify the terms of an existing lease as it relates to duration. The validity of such an oral modification is governed by the local law as it relates to oral modifications of written contracts. In some states it is held that a contract in writing can be modified only by a contract in writing or an executed oral agreement.[9]

In the Wisconsin case of Garrick Theatre Co. v. Gimble Bros.,[10] the plaintiff, Garrick Theatre Co., lessee under written leases executed by defendant, Gimble Bros., orally agreed to an earlier termination. The leases had been executed during the years 1906 and 1907 and were to continue until April 30, 1913. On March 19, 1912, it was orally agreed that the lessee would surrender the last year of the leasehold estates in consideration of the lessor's promise to pay the lessee

five hundred dollars. The court held that the plaintiff lessee was entitled to recover this amount. Following the authority of earlier decisions it was held that the statute providing that an agreement had to be in writing if it was not to be performed within a year applied only to transactions involving things other than land.

Second: The preferred view is that an agreement to surrender all or any part of a leasehold estate, operative *in praesenti* or *in futuro* involves the conveyance of an estate in land. Accordingly, the validity of the agreement depends upon its execution with the formalities prescribed by the Statute of Frauds.[11] In some cases it is indicated that a surrender will result if the lessee gives up possession of the land at the time of the agreement.

SURRENDER BY OPERATION OF LAW

83. Generally, statutes provide that a surrender by "act and operation of law" need not be in writing. Situations involving this type of surrender are as follows:

a. Creation of a new leasehold estate in the same tenant. An estate created in a lessee by one lease is surrendered by operation of law if a second lease creates an estate in the same tenant that is inconsistent with the first lease. However, this result is contingent upon the fact that the second lease is enforceable according to its terms.

b. Creation of a leasehold estate in a second lessee where the lessor and the first lessee intend a surrender. If a lessor, with the consent of his first lessee, creates a leasehold estate in a second lessee that is inconsistent with the existence of the

8.   Rowan v. Lytle, 1834, 11 Wend. (N.Y.) 616; Lord Ward v. Lumley, 1860, 5 Hurl. & N. 87, 157 Eng.Rep. 1112. *Cf.:* Beidler v. Fish, 1883, 14 Ill.App. 29 (intentional cancellation operates as a surrender).

9.   See Burgett v. Loeb, 1909, 43 Ind.App. 657, 88 N.E. 346; West's Ann.Cal.Civ.Code, § 1698.

10.   158 Wis. 649, 149 N.W. 385 (1914), noted in 28 Harv.Law Rev. 436 (1915).

11.   Mundy v. Warner, 1898, 61 N.J.L. 395, 39 A. 697; Allen v. Jaquish, 1839, 21 Wend. (N.Y.) 628; Cromwell v. Bissinger Candy Co., 1920, 13 Ohio App. 216. See, Schnebly, Operative Facts in Surrenders, 22 Ill.Law Rev. 22, 33 (1927). *Cf.:* Brewer v. National Union Building Ass'n, 1897, 166 Ill. 221, 46 N.E. 752; Fish v. Thompson, 1902, 129 Mich. 313, 88 N.W. 896.

first lease, the first leasehold estate is surrendered by operation of law.

This result follows only if the second lease is enforceable according to its terms.

c. Creation of a leasehold estate in a second lessee where the lessor does not intend a surrender to result. There is a surrender by operation of law if a lessee abandons the leased premises and the lessor rerents to a third party. It is immaterial whether or not the lessor intended a surrender to result.

Of course, a surrender does not result if the lessor had authority to rerent for and in behalf of the first lessee. Such authority may be implied from the fact that the lessor notifies the first lessee that he is rerenting for and in behalf of said lessee.

d. Resumption of possession by the lessor. If a lessee or an assignee abandons the leased premises, resumption of possession by the lessor results in a surrender by operation of law. The intention of the lessor or of the lessee is not of controlling importance.

A surrender will not result if the lessor takes possession merely for the purpose of making repairs that are necessary for the protection of the land from the elements.

By the terms of the English Statute of Frauds a surrender by "act and operation of law" need not be in writing.[12] A similar provision is found in the statutes enacted in a majority of the American states. The various situations involving surrender by operation of law are discussed in the following paragraphs.

Creation of a New Leasehold Estate in the Same Tenant

A surrender by operation of law may result if a lessor executes a second lease to his lessee creating an estate that is inconsistent with the estate created by the first lease.[13] Usually, this inconsistency arises because of the fact that the second lease covers a period of time that is also covered in the first lease. Even a short period of "overlap" will result in a surrender of the first lease because a lease is not apportionable on the basis of time. But a surrender does not result in the absence of inconsistency in the estates involved.[14] That is the case, for example, if the second lease is to become operative at the termination of the first lease.

It is fair to assume that the lessor and the lessee intended a surrender in order to give effect to the second lease.[15] The second lease need not be in writing if it is enforceable according to its terms.[16] Thus, a written lease for a term of years may be surrendered by an oral lease that is not within the scope of the Statute of Frauds. Since the surrender is "by operation of law" it need not be in writing. However, there is outward manifestation of the intention of the parties arising out of the fact that they executed a second lease. This tends to conform to the policy of the Statute of Frauds.

First: A surrender will not result if, during the lapse of time between the making of the first and the second leases the lessor's estate has been affected to such an extent that it is no longer possible for him to create the new estate.[17] Nor will a surrender result if the second lease is unenforceable because not

12. 29 Car II, c. 3, § 3 (1676).

13. Ive's Case, 1597, 5 Coke, 11a, 77 Eng.Rep. 64.

14. Tracy v. Albany Exchange Co., 1852, 7 N.Y. 472.

15. See Schnebly, Operative Facts in Surrenders, 22 Ill.Law Rev. 117, 118 (1927).

16. Ryan v. Kirchberg, 1885, 17 Ill.App. 132; Evans v. McKanna, 1893, 89 Iowa 362, 56 N.W. 527.

17. Van Rensselaer's Heirs v. Penniman, 1831, 6 Wend. (N.Y.) 569; Chamberlain v. Dunlop, 1891, 126 N.Y. 45, 26 N.E. 966; Davidson ex dem Bromley v. Stanley, 1768, 4 Burr. 2210, 98 Eng.Rep. 152.

executed with the requisite formalities.[18] In all such cases the intent of the lessee to surrender the first lease might be said to be on condition that the second lease created in him a new estate, one entitled to legal recognition.

In the early English case of Roe v. Archbishop of York,[19] the rule is declared that a surrender results even if the second lease is voidable as distinguished from void. But this view was not followed in later English cases.[20] However, there is authority for the view that a voidable lease does result in a surrender but the surrender itself is subject to an implied condition that in case the second lease is voided the surrender, in turn, is likewise voided.[21]

Second: An intention to modify an existing lease is to be distinguished from an intention to make a second lease. At times it is difficult to draw the distinction, such as in a case where the new agreement relates only to a change in the amount of rent to be paid. In the New York case of Coe v. Hobby,[22] the court states: "It is preposterous to say that a reduction of the rent is a surrender of an existing lease, and the granting of a new one." [23]

In the English case of Fenner v. Blake,[24] an oral agreement to surrender an existing lease at a stated future time was held to be inoperative as an express surrender because it was not in writing. However, it was held that the new oral agreement constituted a second lease and that the first lease was surrendered by operation of law. The only change in terms between the first lease and the second lease related to the duration of the term and there was no further evidence that the parties intended a new lease. In some cases the intention in this respect can be ascertained by the fact that they acted under the belief that the first lease had been abrogated at the time of the execution of the new lease.[25] Whether or not they were mistaken in this belief is not material.

Creation of a Leasehold Estate in a Second Lessee Where the Lessor and First Lessee Intend a Surrender

Whenever a lessor, with the consent of his lessee, creates a leasehold estate in a second lessee that is inconsistent with the estate created in the first lessee, that estate is surrendered by operation of law.[26] But this type of transaction is to be distinguished from one where the intention is to make an assignment of the first lease.

In addition to the fact that the co-existence of the two estates would result in an inconsistency, the right of the third party under the second lease will be enforced. The lessor

---

18. Lamont v. United States Reduction Co., 1915, 191 Ill.App. 446; Smith v. Kerr, 1888, 108 N.Y. 31, 15 N.E. 70. *Cf.:* Nachbour v. Wiener, 1889, 34 Ill.App. 237 (where rent was recovered under first lease and an additional amount for space occupied under the second lease).

19. 6 East 86, 102 Eng.Rep. 1219 (1805).

20. Doe v. Courtney, [1848] 11 Q.B. 702, 116 Eng.Rep. 636; Doe v. Poole, [1848] 11 Q.B. 713, 116 Eng.Rep. 641.

21. Zick v. London United Tramways, Ltd., L.R., [1908] 2 K.B. 126, noted in 22 Harv.Law Rev. 55 (1908).

22. 72 N.Y. 141 (1878).

23. But see Long Mercantile Co. v. Saffron, Mo.App. 1937, 104 S.W.2d 770.

24. L.R. [1900] 1 Q.B. 426, noted in 14 Harv.Law Rev. 72 (1900).

25. Evans v. McKanna, 1893, 89 Iowa 362, 56 N.W. 527; Conkling v. Tuttle, 1884, 52 Mich. 630, 18 N.W. 391. *Cf.:* Edwards v. Hale, 1892, 37 W.Va. 193, 16 S.E. 487; Ossowski v. Wiesner, 1898, 101 Wis. 238, 77 N.W. 184; Crook v. Zorn, 5 Cir. 1938, 95 F.2d 782.

26. Triest & Co. v. Goldstone, 1916, 173 Cal. 240, 159 P. 715; Hesseltine v. Seavey, 1839, 16 Me. 212; Smith v. Niver, 1848, 2 Barb. (N.Y.) 180.

and the first lessee will be estopped to deny the fact of surrender.[27] A written instrument is not necessary because the surrender takes place by act and operation of law. However, the policy of the Statute of Frauds is furthered because of the execution of the second lease and, in many cases, a taking of possession of the land by the third party under his new lease.

First: A surrender of the first lease will not result if the second lease is not enforceable according to its terms because of a change affecting the lessor's estate which took place between the time when the first lease had been executed and the time when the second lease was made.[28]

Second: The surrender of the first lease is subject to the implied condition that the second lease is enforceable according to its terms. In the New York case of Schieffelin v. Carpenter,[29] the defendant lessee covenanted to pay rent, to repair and to refrain from damaging fruit trees. In an action for breach of these covenants the defendant contended that the lease had been surrendered by operation of law before the alleged breach because, prior to the expiration of the term, the lessor, lessee and third parties orally agreed that defendant was to give up possession of the land and that a new lease would be executed to the third parties for a term of eight or ten years. Pursuant to that agreement defendant gave up possession of the land to the third parties who took possession and paid rent to the lessor for one year and thereafter abandoned the premises. The court held that defendant's lease had not been surrendered by operation of law. The new lease to the third parties was not enforceable because it was not in writing as required by the Statute of Frauds.

Third: A surrender does not result from the assignment of a lease even if the assignee executes an agreement to be personally liable for performance of the covenants in the lease (an assumption agreement). The assignee may pay rent directly to the lessor. However, a surrender results by operation of law if the lessor accepts a new tenant in the stead of the original lessee.

In Triest & Co. v. Goldstone (Cal.),[30] land was leased to a corporation. The corporate charter was forfeited and the directors divided the corporate assets. One group of directors formed a partnership and took possession of one part of the leased land. Another group formed a partnership and took possession of the remaining part of the land. Thereafter, each partnership paid $200 a month rent. The court held that the original lease had been surrendered by operation of law because the lessor accepted new tenants in the stead of the original lessee.

Creation of a Leasehold Estate in a Second Lessee Where the Lessor does not Intend a Surrender to Result

The abandonment of leased land under circumstances evidencing the lessee's intention to surrender the lease, followed by a new lease from the lessor to a second lessee, results in a surrender of the first lease by operation of law.[31] The lessor is not under a duty to rerent as a means by which to mitigate damages [32] and his intention not to bring about a surrender of the lease is immaterial.

---

27. Jenkins v. Root, 1920, 269 Pa. 229, 112 A. 153; Fenner v. Blake, L.R. [1900] 1 Q.B. 426.

28. See Zick v. London United Tramways, Ltd., L.R. [1908] 2 K.B. 126, noted in 22 Harv.Law Rev. 55 (1908).

29. 15 Wend. (N.Y.) 400 (1836).

30. 173 Cal. 240, 159 P. 715 (1916).

31. Welcome v. Hess, 1891, 90 Cal. 507, 27 P. 369.

32. Abraham v. Gheens, 1924, 205 Ky. 289, 265 S.W. 778, 40 A.L.R. 186.

The coexistence of both leases is impossible. If the lessor, in making the new lease, is merely acting as an agent for the first lessee a surrender does not result. The lessor's act is then the act of the lessee. The new agreement constitutes either an assignment or a sublease. Rules relating to the creation of an agency are as follows:

First: The power of the lessor to act as an agent may rest upon an express authorization in the original lease or upon a subsequent agreement. The existence of an express agency imposes a duty on the lessor to use reasonable diligence in attempting to rerent the premises.[33] This is also the rule if the lessee abandons the premises and the lessor accepts possession with the understanding that he will rerent.[34]

The usual agency arrangement does not authorize the lessor to enter into a new lease for a longer period than the unexpired term of the original lease. A surrender will result from the execution of such a lease.[35] Of course, the agency agreement may be broad enough to confer such authorization.

Second: Under some circumstances an agency authority may be implied. The prevailing rule is that a surrender will not result if the lessor rerents after notifying the lessee that a surrender will not be accepted and that the premises will be rerented in his be-

half.[36] But in spite of such notice a surrender will result if the lessor rerents for a period longer than the unexpired term of the original lease.[37]

The minority rule is that the above stated notice-procedure will not prevent a surrender by operation of law.[38] To prevent a surrender by operation of law there must be express consent on the part of the lessee.

Third: In some states it is held that the contract rule respecting the mitigation of damages is applicable in lease cases.[39] A surrender does not result even if the lessor rerents the premises without notice to the lessee.

Fourth: In a few cases, it is either suggested or held that covenants in a lease, includ-

---

33. John Church Co. v. Martinez, Tex.Civ.App.1918, 204 S.W. 486, error refused; International Trust Co. v. Weeks, 1906, 203 U.S. 364, 27 S.Ct. 69, 51 L.Ed. 224. *Cf.:* Robinson Seed & Plant Co., Tex. Civ.App.1914, 167 S.W. 749, error refused; In re Garment Center Capitol, 2 Cir. 1938, 93 F.2d 667, 115 A.L.R. 202.

34. In re Schomacker Piano Forte Mfg. Co., D.C.Pa. 1908, 163 F. 413.

35. In re Goldburg's Estate, 1933, 148 Misc. 607, 266 N.Y.S. 106. But see, Sallah v. Myriad Inv. Corp., 1934, 150 Misc. 722 269 N.Y.S. 63 (where the point was not raised).

36. Oldewurtel v. Wiesenfeld, 1903, 97 Md. 165, 54 A. 969; Alsup v. Banks, 1891, 68 Misc. 664, 9 So. 895. See McCormick, The Rights of the Landlord upon Abandonment of the Premises by the Tenant, 23 Mich.Law Rev. 211, 213 (1925). If an assignee abandons the premises it is sufficient if notice of intention to rerent is given to the lessee (De Hart v. Allen, 1945, 26 Cal.2d 829, 161 P.2d 453, noted in 34 Cal.Law Rev. 252 (1946).

37. Welcome v. Hess, 1891, 90 Cal. 507, 27 P. 369 (also, lessor failed to give notice to lessee); Casper Nat. Bank v. Curry, 1937, 51 Wyo. 284, 65 P.2d 1116, 110 A.L.R. 360 (also failed to give notice and included land in the lease that was not embraced within the original lease). *Contra:* Armijo v. Pettit, 1927, 32 N.M. 469, 259 P. 620, 61 A.L.R. 767.

38. Gray v. Kaufman Dairy & Ice Cream Co., 1900, 162 N.Y. 388, 56 N.E. 903.

39. Campbell v. McLaurin Inv. Co., 1917, 74 Fla. 501, 77 So. 277; Roberts v. Watson, 1923, 196 Iowa 816, 195 N.W. 211 (*dictum*), noted in 9 Iowa Law Bulletin 119 (1924), 22 Mich.Law Rev. 615 (1924); Guy v. Gould, 1928, 126 Kan. 25, 266 P. 925, 61 A.L.R. 774; Novak v. Fontaine Furniture Co., 1929, 84 N.H. 93, 146 A. 525; Carey v. Hejke, 1938, 119 N.J.L. 594, 197 A. 652 (*dictum*), noted in 3 Univ. of Newark Law Rev. 216 (1938); Selts Inv. Co. v. Promoters of the Federated Nations of the World, 1929, 197 Wis. 476, 222 N.W. 812 (*dictum*). *Cf.:* Zucker v. Dehm, 1942, 128 N.J.L. 435, 26 A.2d 564.

ing the covenant to pay rent, may survive a surrender of the leasehold estate.[40]

Resumption of Possession by the Lessor

If a lessee abandons the leased land and the lessor takes possession thereof the lease is surrendered by operation of law. Possession of the land by the lessor is inconsistent with the continuance of the lease. The change of possession is an outward manifestation of the intent of both parties and thus satisfies the policy of the Statute of Frauds. Additional rules are as follows:

First: If the assignee of a lease abandons the leased premises the lessor may resume possession of the land and thereby terminate the lease. Such a surrender may be accomplished in spite of the protests on the part of the lessee.[41] After the assignment the lessee retained no estate or interest in the land.

Second: The resumption of possession by the lessor may be evidenced by such acts as the making of repairs or alterations.[42] However, a surrender will not result if the lessor takes possession merely for the purpose of making repairs necessary to protect the land from the elements.[43]

[40.] Novak v. Fontaine Furniture Co., 1929, 84 N.H. 93, 146 A. 525; Ralph v. Deiley 1928, 293 Pa. 90, 141 A. 640, 61 A.L.R. 763. See McGrath v. Shalette, 1932, 114 Conn. 622, 159 A. 633; Whitcomb v. Brant, 1917, 90 N.J.L. 245, 100 A. 175, criticized in 30 Harv.Law Rev. 766 (1917).

[41.] Flynn v. Mikelian, 1962, 208 Cal.App.2d 305, 25 Cal.Rptr. 138. See Kandis v. Pusch, 1927, 86 Ind. App. 246, 155 N.E. 618, 619.

[42.] Meeker v. Spalsbury, 1901, 66 N.J.L. 60, 48 A. 1026; Armijo v. Pettit, 1927, 32 N.M. 469, 259 P. 620, 61 A.L.R. 767; In re Schomacker Piano Forte Mfg. Co., D.C.Pa.1908, 163 F. 413.

[43.] Baskin v. Thomas, 1926, 56 App.D.C. 310, 12 F.2d 845 (repainted and repapered and sought another tenant after giving notice that surrender would not be accepted); Davis v. Allen, 1939, 97 Utah 285, 92 P.2d 1100 (repaired water pipes).

B. FREEHOLD ESTATES

CHAPTER 16

LIFE ESTATES

TYPES OF LIFE ESTATES

84. A life estate is one where the duration is measured by the life or lives of one or more human beings and is not otherwise terminable at a fixed or computable period of time. It may be an estate for the lifetime of the grantee or an estate for the lifetime of another (an estate *pur autre vie*). The estate may be one for the lifetime of the grantee and also for the lifetime of another.

The common law rule is that if the owner of an estate *pur autre vie* should predecease the person whose life has been designated as the measuring life, the first occupant (a general occupant) acquires the life estate. To avoid this, the conveyor of the life estate, or the life tenant, may designate the person to take (special occupant). The "general occupant" rule is not followed in the United States. The estate is distributed as an asset of the deceased life tenant.

A life estate is one in which the duration is measured by the life or lives of one or more human beings and is not otherwise terminable at a fixed or computable period of time. If the conveyance is A to B at the will of C, B acquires a life estate. The maximum period of duration is the lifetime of C and the estate is not terminable at any fixed or computable period of time.[1] If the duration is measured by the lifetime of a person other than the grantee it is called an estate *pur autre vie* (for the life of another). A person may have an estate for his own life and also for the life of another or others.[2] Any number of lives may be used as a means by which the duration of the estate may be determined provided the persons so designated may be ascertained with reasonable certainty.[3] In some states statutes have been passed that place restrictions on the duration of leases. These statutes have no application in the case of life estates.[4]

The common law rule is that if the owner of an estate *pur autre vie* should predecease the person whose life had been designated as the measuring life, the first occupant, called a general occupant, acquires the life estate.[5] But if the conveying instrument designated the person entitled to take under such circumstances this person, called a special occupant, would be entitled.[6] The life tenant himself had the power to designate a special occupant.[7]

2. Utty Dale's Case, [1591] Cro.Eliz. 182, 78 Eng.Rep. 439; In re Amos, [1891] 3 Ch. 159.

3. 1 Rest. Property, § 107.

4. Parish v. Rogers, 1897, 20 App.Div. 279, 46 N.Y.S. 1058, 1059; Anderson v. Blixt, N.D.1955, 72 N.W.2d 799.

5. 2 Bl.Comm. 259.

6. 2 Bl.Comm. 259; 1 Rest. Property, § 151, *Comment a* (gift to life tenant and his heirs—heirs take as special occupants).

7. See Utty Dale's Case, [1591] Cro.Eliz. 182, 78 Eng. Rep. 439 (lessee of life tenant may take as special occupant).

1. See 1 Rest. Property, § 18(b).

The common law rule allowing a general occupant to acquire the life estate was abolished in England by a statute passed in 1677.[8] The prevailing rule in the United States is that a "general occupant" cannot acquire the life estate. It may be disposed of by will [9] or claimed by a special occupant.[10] Otherwise, it will be considered to be a part of the estate of the deceased life tenant and distributed as intestate property.[11]

LIFE ESTATES RESULTING FROM MARRIAGE

85. The common law rule is that upon marriage a husband acquires a right to the use and profits of his wife's freehold estates, an estate in right of the wife (*jure uxoris*). This estate continues only during the time of the marriage.

Upon birth of issue capable of inheriting the land, a husband acquires a life estate in land of which his wife is seised of a freehold estate of inheritance (curtesy initiate) and it replaces the husband's estate *jure uxoris*. Upon the death of the wife it becomes curtesy consummate.

If at any time during marriage a husband is seised of a freehold estate of inheritance, his surviving widow is entitled to dower (a life estate in $\frac{1}{3}$ of the land). Prior to the husband's death her interest is a mere expectancy (an inchoate right of dower).

a. Prerequisites for claims of dower and curtesy. These estates are allowed only upon proof of a legally recognized marriage.

A widow is entitled to dower if issue born of the marriage, if any, would be entitled to take the land as an heir. Curtesy is not allowed unless issue entitled to inherit the land is actually born alive.

A dower right extends only to a life estate in one-third of the land of which the husband was seised during coverture. Curtesy extends a right to a life estate in all of the land of which the wife was seised during the marriage.

b. Estates out of which dower and curtesy may be allowed. These estates are based upon ownership of freehold estates of inheritance. This does not include property held by the deceased spouse in joint tenancy because, in that event, the surviving joint tenant is entitled. These estates are also subject to the hazards of defeasance that may be attached to the estate of the deceased spouse.

c. Divorce and misconduct. The common law rule is that an absolute divorce will bar a claim of dower or curtesy. The matter is usually regulated by statute.

d. Statutory share. In many states a widow is entitled to a statutory share in her husband's estate. Unless she is required by the terms of her husband's will to make an election, her interest as an heir is in addition to her dower rights.

A husband can defeat the wife's claim of a statutory share by making an *inter vivos* conveyance of his property. Such a conveyance can be set aside only if it is a sham or a "fictitious transfer."

Upon marriage a husband acquires a right to the use and profits of his wife's freehold estates, an estate in right of the wife (*jure uxoris*).[12] The estate continues only during the marriage.[13] It ends upon the death of either spouse and upon divorce. At early common law an absolute divorce could be obtained only by Act of Parliament. Consequently, for practical purposes the husband acquired a right to the use and profit of the land during the joint lives of the parties. This estate is subject to sale or mortgage by the husband and may be reached to satisfy the claims of his creditors.[14] The estate *jure uxoris* has practically

---

8. 29 Chas. II, c. 3, § 12 (1677).

9. Folwell v. Folwell, 1903, 65 N.J.Eq. 526, 56 A. 117.

10. 1 Rest. Property, § 151(a).

11. 1 Rest. Property, § 151(b) and Special Note.

12. 2 Bl.Comm. 433.

13. Wright v. Wright's Lessee, 1852, 2 Md. 429.

14. Montgomery v. Tate, 1858, 12 Ind. 615.

disappeared with the enactment of Married Women's Acts. These acts give married women a right to manage their own separate estates.

Upon the birth of issue capable of inheriting the land, a husband acquires a life estate in land of which his wife is seised of a freehold estate of inheritance. This estate is designated as curtesy initiate and it replaces the husband's estate *jure uxoris*.[15] It may be sold or mortgaged by the husband and may be reached to satisfy the claims of his creditors.[16] Upon the death of the wife it becomes curtesy consummate. In some states it is held that by force of Married Women's Acts, birth of issue does not give the husband a vested interest in the wife's property.[17] Under this view, until the death of the wife the husband has a mere inchoate right of curtesy, an interest which cannot be subjected to the claims of his creditors.[18]

If at any time during the marriage the husband is seised of a freehold estate of inheritance, his surviving widow is entitled to dower. This consists of a life estate in one-third of the land. While a dower right arises at the time of the husband's death, it is merely a cause of action until dower has been assigned as the result of judicial proceedings.[19] Prior to the death of the husband the interest of the wife is called an inchoate right of dower. It is frequently stated that this is a mere expectancy and not an estate.[20] The law governing dower rights is the law in existence at the time of the husband's death and not the law existing at the time of the marriage.[21]

But a court of equity will protect the inchoate right of dower from fraudulent conveyances made by the husband in contemplation of marriage [22] or after the marriage.[23] Protection is also available against the claims of creditors if the claims arose after the marriage. Security may be required to protect the interest if oil, gas or other substances are removed from the land thus resulting in a depreciation in the value of the estate.[24] Decisions supporting a contrary view take the position that a wife cannot interfere with her husband's full en-

---

15. See Foster v. Marshall, 1851, 22 N.H. 491 (in the case of adverse possession the statute would not start to run against the wife until after the death of the husband).

16. Van Duzer v. Van Duzer, 1837, 6 Paige (N.Y.) 366; Mattocks v. Stearns, 1837, 9 Vt. 326.

17. See, for example, McNeer v. McNeer, 1892, 142 Ill. 388, 32 N.E. 681.

18. Bucci v. Popovich, 1921, 93 N.J.Eq. 121, 115 A. 95, affirmed 93 N.J.Eq. 511, 116 A. 923. *Cf.*: Hopper v. Gurtman, 1941, 126 N.J.L. 263, 18 A.2d 245, 133 A.L.R. 621.

19. Huffman v. Huffman, 1937, 57 Ohio App. 33, 11 N.E.2d 271.

20. Opinion of the Justices, 1958, 337 Mass. 786, 151 N.E.2d 475; Brenkworth v. Lanier, 1963, 260 N.C. 279, 132 S.E.2d 623. But see Hampton v. Hampton Holding Co., 1955, 17 N.J. 431, 111 A.2d 761, 764.

21. Sanders v. Taylor, 1937, 193 Ark. 1095, 104 S.W. 2d 797.

22. Deke v. Huenkemeier, 1913, 260 Ill. 131, 102 N.E. 1059, noted in 8 Ill.Law Rev. 500 (1914); Martin v. Martin, 1940, 282 Ky. 411, 138 S.W.2d 509, noted in 30 Ky.Law J. 124 (1941); Granger v. Granger, 1941, 296 Mich. 357, 296 N.W. 288, noted in 40 Mich.Law Rev. 300 (1941) (inadequate consideration); Breshears v. Breshears, 1950, 360 Mo. 1057, 232 S.W.2d 460. See, Bregy and Wilkinson, Antenuptial Transfers as Frauds on Marital Rights, 90 Univ. of Pa.Law Rev. 62 (1941). *Cf.*: Lill v. Lill, 1960, 18 Ill.2d 393, 164 N.E.2d 12.

23. Delaney v. Manshum, 1906, 146 Mich. 525, 109 N.W. 1051; Brown v. Brown, 1913, 94 S.C. 492, 78 S.E. 447 (sale of standing timber). See Coleman v. Davis, Fla.App.1960, 120 So.2d 56 (does not include a right to improvements erected on the land after the conveyance); Byrnes v. Owen, 1926, 243 N.Y. 211, 153 N.E. 51.

24. Tatum v. Tatum, 1927, 174 Ark. 110, 295 S.W. 720, 53 A.L.R. 306 (funds derived from the exploitation ordered impounded for the protection of the inchoate right of dower).

joyment of the land during his lifetime.[25] In Flynn v. Flynn (Mass.),[26] land owned by the husband was condemned and his wife claimed a right to share in the award because of her inchoate right of dower. Her claim was denied upon the ground that dower claims are excluded from condemnation awards.[27] In any event, a wife may relinquish her inchoate right of dower by an antenuptial contract [28] or by a release.[29]

Prerequisites for Claims of Dower and Curtesy

The claims of dower and curtesy rest upon proof of a legally recognized marriage as distinguished from a putative (good faith) or *de facto* marriage.[30] A voidable marriage will suffice for the purpose if it is not voided before the right to the estate arises.[31]

Under the common law rule the requirements for assignment of dower are not the same as those furnishing a right to curtesy.[32] A widow is entitled to dower if issue born of the marriage, if any, would be entitled to inherit the estate. Curtesy is not allowed

unless issue entitled to inherit the land is actually born alive.

The extent of the respective estates in the land are not the same. A widow is only entitled to a life estate in one-third of the husband's land. A husband is entitled to a life estate in all of the wife's freehold estates of inheritance which the issue of the marriage might inherit.

The reasons for distinction between dower and curtesy no longer exist. In a majority of the states statutes have been passed which place dower and curtesy on an equal basis, both as to requirements for allowance of the estates and as to the extent of the estates. Additional rules are as follows:

First: Neither dower nor curtesy will be allowed with respect to land which is conveyed to one spouse for the purpose of an *immediate* reconveyance.[33] In the Maryland case of Rawlings v. Lowndes,[34] land was conveyed to the husband who gave a purchase money mortgage. The mortgage did not become operative for sixteen days after the conveyance at which time it was acknowledged and delivered to the vendor. The court held that the husband was beneficially seised of the land during the interim and that dower rights attached.

Second: Neither dower nor curtesy are estates acquired by inheritance. Accordingly, the surviving spouse cannot disclaim the estate to the prejudice of creditors.[35]

Estates Out of Which Dower and Curtesy May be Allowed

Except as noted, the claim of dower or curtesy must be based upon proof of the

25. Rumsey v. Sullivan, 1914, 166 App.Div. 246, 150 N.Y.S. 287.

26. 171 Mass. 312, 50 N.E. 650 (1898).

27. *Contra:* Wheeler v. Kirtland, 1875, 27 N.J.Eq. 534; In re New York & Brooklyn Bridge, 1894, 75 Hun (N.Y.) 558, 27 N.Y.S. 597; In re Cropsey Ave. in City of New York, 1935, 268 N.Y. 183, 197 N.E. 189, 101 A.L.R. 694, noted in 49 Harv.L.Rev. 654 (1936), 20 Minn.L.Rev. 315 (1936).

28. Stilley v. Folger, 1846, 14 Ohio 610. See Kyle v. Kyle, Fla.App.1961, 128 So.2d 427.

29. Mueller v. Fidelity-Baltimore National Bank, 1961, 226 Md. 629, 174 A.2d 789. But see Pfifer v. First National Bank of Oregon, 1963, 235 Or. 561, 385 P.2d 1007.

30. 2 Bl.Comm. 127 (curtesy), 130 (dower).

31. 2 Tiffany, Real Property (3rd ed.) § 488 (dower), § 553 (curtesy).

32. See Co.Litt., § 29a (curtesy), § 31a (dower).

33. McCauley v. Grimes, 1830, 2 Gill. & J. (Md.) 318; Holbrook v. Finney, 1808, 4 Mass. 566.

34. 34 Md. 639 (1871).

35. Watson v. Watson, 1839, 13 Conn. 83.

fact that the deceased spouse was seised of a freehold estate of inheritance during coverture. Thus, these marital estates cannot be claimed out of a life estate (a freehold estate not of inheritance) [36] nor out of a term for years (not a freehold estate). [37] Since seisin requires possession, a person cannot be seised of a future interest, such as a reversion or a remainder. [38]

A widow is entitled to dower if her husband was actually or constructively seised of a freehold estate of inheritance during the marriage. [39] However, a husband is not entitled to curtesy on the basis of the wife's *constructive seisin* of a freehold estate of inheritance. [40] According to some authorities this conclusion is based upon the fact that at common law inheritable rights were based upon actual seisin of the ancestor. [41] In the absence of actual seisin of the wife issue of the marriage would not be entitled to inherit the property. Accordingly, an essential element is lacking insofar as curtesy is concerned. Some authorities attribute the rule to the fact that a husband is under a duty to protect the wife's freehold estates by establishing actual seisin in the wife. If he defaults in the performance of this duty he thereby forfeits his right to claim an estate therein.

A person cannot be seised of an equitable estate. Even if a freehold estate of inheritance is involved, the seisin is in the legal owner and not in the beneficial owner. In England it was provided by statute, passed in 1833, that both dower and curtesy claims could be based upon equitable estates. [42] Prior to that time the rule was that curtesy, but not dower, could be based upon equitable estates. Dower was not allowed for historical reasons.

The concept of seisin has never been of controlling importance in the United States. Either by force of statute or judicial decision it is now recognized in a majority of the states that dower may be assigned and curtesy allowed in the case of freehold estate of inheritance either legal or equitable. [43]

Generally, if a wife joins with her husband in the execution of a mortgage on the husband's land, her dower right will continue as to the husband's equity of redemption and it will attach as to any surplus remaining after satisfaction of the indebtedness. It has been suggested that under such circumstances the wife occupies the position of a surety for the mortgaged indebtedness and will be entitled to her full dower rights out of the mortgaged land as against the claims of the husband's unsecured creditors. [44] Additional points are as follows:

First: Rights of dower and curtesy may be sustained with respect to land claimed by the deceased spouse as an adverse possessor. [45]

---

36. Bodkin v. Wright, 1937, 266 Ky. 798, 100 S.W.2d 824. See Barr v. Howell, 1914, 85 Misc. 330, 147 N.Y.S. 483 (life estate with a power of testamentary disposition, with a gift over in default of appointment).

37. Spangler v. Stanler, 1847, 1 Md.Ch. 36 (99 year lease, renewable forever and owner could have demanded a conveyance in fee at any time). *Contra:* Ralston Steel Car Co. v. Ralston, 1925, 112 Ohio St. 306, 147 N.E. 513, 39 A.L.R. 334 (perpetual lease).

38. Butler v. Cheatham, 1872, 71 Ky. (8 Bush.) 594 (dower denied); Hess v. Hess, 1939, 162 Or. 266, 91 P.2d 850 (curtesy denied).

39. Pfaff v. Heizman, 1951, 218 Ark. 201, 235 S.W.2d 551, 23 A.L.R.2d 957.

40. But see Borland's Lessee v. Marshall, 1853, 2 Ohio St. 308 (constructive seisin of wife sufficient).

41. 2 Bl.Comm., p. 128.

42. 3 & 4 Wm. IV, c. 105, § 3 (1833).

43. 1 American Law of Property, § 5.23, p. 660.

44. Brown v. McLean, 1940, 217 N.C. 555, 8 S.E.2d 807, criticized in 19 No.Car.Law Rev. 82 (1940).

45. Randolph v. Doss, 1839, 4 Miss. (3 How.) 205 (dower); Colgan v. Pellens, 1886, 48 N.J.L. 27, 32, 2 A. 633, 636 (curtesy).

These estates are subject to defeasance if the ousted owner asserts his ownership within the time permitted under rules relating to adverse possession.

Second: If, at the time of marriage, a spouse is the owner of land as a joint tenant, with right of survivorship, the other spouse will not be entitled to dower or curtesy if that form of cotenancy is recognized at the time of the owner's death. The reason for this rule is that in the case of a joint tenancy ownership continues in the surviving joint tenant.[46] It is not an estate of inheritance for the purpose under discussion.

If the right of survivorship has been abolished, dower or curtesy are available if the joint tenancy was not terminated by partition proceedings during the lifetime of the owner.[47] Of course, the claim is limited to the undivided interest of the deceased spouse.

Third: Dower and curtesy are estates carved out of the assets of a deceased spouse. They are not derived as independent estates created by the original conveyance. From this it follows that dower and curtesy estates are subject to the hazards of defeasance that may be attached to the estate of the deceased spouse.[48] For example, if dower or curtesy is claimed out of a fee simple determinable, or a fee simple subject to a condition subsequent, the marital estate will terminate upon the happening of the event named or upon the exercise of the power of termination.

Theoretically, the defeasibility aspect of dower or curtesy exists if the primary estate is a fee simple subject to an executory limi- tation and reliable authority supports this conclusion.[49] However, a contrary conclusion was reached in the English case of Buckworth v. Thirkell,[50] and the numerical weight of American authority is in accord with the views expressed in that case.[51] The court departs from the traditional view that dower and curtesy are estates carved out of the assets of a deceased spouse and substitutes therefor the view that assignment of these estates is a "built-in right" in the case of a fee simple subject to an executory interest. The Statute of Uses, passed in 1536,[52] authorized the creation of executory interests and these new types of interests were not allowed to disturb rights of dower and curtesy as they existed prior to the enactment of that statute.

Divorce and Misconduct

The common law rule is that an absolute divorce will bar a claim of dower or curtesy.[53] A legal separation, sometimes called a divorce from bed and board (*a mensa et thoro*) does not terminate the marital relationship. In the absence of an express statute such a divorce will not bar claims of dower and curtesy. This is also true with respect to an interlocutory decree of divorce.[54]

Statutes in some states provide that these marital estates may be denied upon proof of certain types of misconduct, such as adultery, on the part of the claimant. Several states have statutes preserving dower or curtesy

---

46. Babbit v. Day, 1886, 41 N.J.Eq. 392, 5 A. 275.

47. Turner v. Turner, 1946, 185 Va. 505, 39 S.E.2d 299.

48. As for estates in fee tail, see 1 Rest. Property, Appendix, p. 13.

49. 1 Rest. Property, § 54, *Comment b*, Illust. 4.

50. Reported in a note in Doe v. Hutton, 3 Bos. & Pul. 643, 652, 127 Eng.Rep. 347, 351 (1804).

51. See authorities cited in 1 Rest. Property, Appendix 7.

52. 27 Hen. VIII, c. 10 (1536).

53. Co.Litt. § 32b.

54. Rollins v. Gould, 1923, 244 Mass. 270, 138 N. E. 815.

if a divorce [55] or legal separation [56] was obtained because of the fault of the other spouse.

Statutes have been passed in many states providing that a murderer is not entitled to property rights in the estate of his victim. Some decisions take the position that these statutes are applicable in the case of dower and curtesy.[57] In other states these interests are barred upon the equitable principle that a person will not be permitted to profit from his own wrong. Following this theory, a constructive trust will be declared in favor of the heirs or devisees of the deceased spouse.[58]

Statutory Share

In many states a widow is entitled to a statutory share in her husband's estate.[59] Unless she is required by the terms of the will to make an election, her interest as an heir is in addition to her dower rights.[60] Some statutes expressly provide that the statutory share of a surviving spouse is in lieu of dower.[61]

A statutory share is a tenuous thing because of the fact that a husband can defeat the claim of the wife by an *inter vivos* conveyance of his property.[62] In a few states the view is followed that the husband's conveyance can be avoided if he creates a voluntary trust for the purpose of depriving his wife of her statutory share. However, the weight of authority is that motive or intent of the husband is not a controlling factor. The conveyance or transfer can be set aside only if it is a sham or "fictitious transfer."

According to one view, the statutory share cannot be defeated by the creation of a trust if the husband retains substantial control over the property, such as a life estate in the property and a power to amend or revoke the trust. It is said that such a trust is "illusory in nature." [63] According to another view, the statutory share may be defeated by such a trust.[64] For all practical purposes, application of the latter view nullifies the statutes relating to statutory shares.

---

55. See 1 American Law of Property, § 5.36 (dower), § 5.72 (curtesy).

56. See, for example, Chivvis v. Chivvis, 1962, 158 Me. 354, 184 A.2d 773.

57. See 1 American Law of Property, § 5.71, p. 803.

58. See Horn v. Cole, 1941, 203 Ark. 361, 156 S.W.2d 787 (dower rights denied); Hamblin v. Marchant, 1918, 103 Kan. 508, 175 P. 678, 6 A.L.R. 1403, affirmed on rehearing 104 Kan. 689, 180 P. 811, 6 A.L.R. 1403 (1919) (dower rights denied because of statute); Estate of Kalfus v. Kalfus, 1963, 81 N.J.Super. 435, 195 A.2d 903 (curtesy rights denied on basis of a constructive trust).

59. See Sayre, Husband and Wife as Statutory Heirs, 42 Harv.Law Rev. 330 (1929); Sullivan, The Passing of Dower and Curtesy, 19 Geo.Law Jr., 306 (1931).

60. Skovborg v. Smith, 1950, 9 N.J.Super. 389, 74 A. 2d 910.

61. See, for example, N.Y.Cons.Laws, ch. 13, Decedent Estate Law, § 82.

62. Redman v. Churchill, 1918, 230 Mass. 415, 119 N. E. 953.

63. Smith v. Northern Trust Co., 1944, 322 Ill.App. 168, 54 N.E.2d 75; Ackers v. First National Bank of Topeka, 1963, 192 Kan. 319, 387 P.2d 840; Mushaw v. Mushaw, 1944, 183 Md. 511, 39 A.2d 465; Walker v. Walker, 1891, 66 N.H. 390, 31 A. 14; Newman v. Dore, 1937, 275 N.Y. 371, 9 N.E.2d 966, 112 A. L.R. 643, noted in 36 Mich.Law Rev. 496 (1938); Pengelly Estate, 1953, 374 Pa. 358, 97 A.2d 844; Norris v. Barbour, 1949, 188 Va. 723, 51 S.E.2d 334.

64. Williams v. Collier, 1935, 120 Fla. 248, 158 So. 815, 162 So. 868; DeLeuil's Executors v. DeLeuil, 1934, 255 Ky. 406, 74 S.W.2d 474; Brown v. Fidelity Trust Co., 1915, 126 Md. 175, 94 A. 523; Kerwin v. Donaghy, 1945, 317 Mass. 559, 59 N.E.2d 299; Rose v. Rose, 1942, 300 Mich. 73, 1 N.W.2d 458; Smyth v. Cleveland Trust Co., 1961, 172 Ohio St. 489, 179 N.E. 2d 60; Dunnett v. Shields & Convant, 1924, 97 Vt. 419, 123 A. 626. But see, Purcell v. Cleveland Trust Co., Ohio Prob.1964, 200 N.E.2d 602 (reaching a contrary rule on the basis of a statute).

CONSTRUCTION

86. If words of inheritance are not necessary to create an estate in fee simple, a conveyance "A to B" may create an estate in fee simple in B unless there is an express provision that he is to take a life estate.

   a. Life estate with a limited or general power. A life estate is not enlarged into a fee simple merely because of the fact that a life tenant is given a limited or a general power of disposal.

   b. Limitation over on remarriage of spouse. A conveyance to a spouse "and his heirs" so long as he remains a widower creates a fee simple determinable. If words of "absolute ownership" are not used, the estate created is a determinable life estate.

   c. Estates terminable at will. If an estate is terminable at the will of the conveyor it is also, by implication, terminable at the will of the conveyee. The result is an estate at will. However, if the estate is terminable at the will of the conveyee it is not, by implication, also terminable at the will of the conveyor. Assuming compliance with the formalities prescribed by the Statute of Frauds or the Statute of Wills, the conveyee acquires a determinable life estate.

   d. Measuring life and estates *pur autre vie*. In a conveyance "A to B for life," B acquires an estate for his own lifetime if A had the power to convey such an estate.

      If A did not have the power to convey an estate measured by the lifetime of B, but did have a power to convey an estate for his own lifetime, or for the lifetime of another, the "measuring life" is determined by reference to all of the circumstances surrounding the conveyance.

The creation of a life estate requires compliance with the formalities prescribed by the Statute of Frauds or the Statute of Wills.[65]

While it is not necessary that the conveying instrument specifically state that the estate is "for life," such a provision is highly desirable because it may avoid ambiguity. For example, statutes in many states provide that words of inheritance ("and his heirs") are not necessary to convey an estate in fee simple—a matter discussed under a separate heading.[66] Some statutes provide, in addition, that unless declared otherwise in the conveying instrument, a grantor is presumed to convey his entire estate or interest. Under such a statute, in a conveyance "A to B," the grantee presumably acquires an estate in fee simple, or absolute ownership, if A had the power to create such an estate. It may well be that A intended to convey only a life estate. In fact, there is some authority for the view that a gift of personal property "for life" results in absolute ownership if there is no limitation over and the gift is not made in trust.[67] There seems to be no basis for this rule of construction.

Assuming that a conveyor intended to create a life estate an issue may be raised as to whether the duration of the estate is to be measured by the lifetime of the one conveying the estate or the lifetime of the one to whom it is conveyed. These various construction problems are discussed in the following paragraphs.

Life Estate with a Limited or General Power

The prevailing rule is that a life estate is not enlarged into a fee simple or absolute ownership merely because of the fact that a life tenant is given a limited or a general power of disposal. For example, a conveyance A to B *for life*, with a provision that B may use

---

65. But see Cannon v. Harris, 1946, 161 Kan. 225, 166 P.2d 998.

66. See infra § 88.

67. See, for example, In re Rogers' Estate, 1914, 245 Pa. 206, 91 A. 351.

the property "as her own," and "she shall not be restricted in any manner in the use and disposal," constitutes only a life estate and a gift over of any property that may be undisposed of at the time of B's death is valid.[68] Statutes in some states provide that the creditors of a life tenant may satisfy their claims out of the property if the life tenant has a power to dispose of the property in fee simple, or absolutely.[69]

In Shoaf v. Wright (Okl.),[70] testator devised and bequeathed property to his widow to be used by her so long as "she lives and enjoys the same." The court held that the widow acquired absolute ownership.[71] The gift was not specifically made to the widow for life. The court points out, however, that if there had been a gift over after the death of the wife the interest of the widow would have been limited to a life estate.[72] This life-estate construction avoids the claim that the gift over is void for repugnancy.[73] The argument is that one who acquires ownership in fee simple, or absolutely, has a power of testamentary disposition and if he dies intestate the property forms a part of his

estate. The gift over is repugnant to these incidents of absolute ownership.[74]

Limitations Over on Remarriage of Spouse

A conveyance to a spouse may specifically provide that it is in fee simple, or absolute ownership in the case of personal property, subject to termination upon the remarriage of the spouse. That is the case, for example, if the conveyance is to the spouse "and her heirs" so long as she remains a widow, or "remains unmarried."

In the absence of a clear expression of intent, the cases are in conflict as to the nature of the estate or interest conveyed. For example, if a testator devises or bequeaths property to his spouse "so long as she remains a widow," there is authority for the view that the widow acquires an estate in fee simple, or absolute ownership, subject to termination upon remarriage.[75] It is assumed, of course, that the provision does not constitute an invalid restraint upon marriage. However, the preferred view is that the conveyance creates a determinable life estate.[76] The maximum duration of "widowhood" is the lifetime of the spouse.

Estates Terminable at Will

Lord Coke declared the rule to be that if a lease is terminable at the will of the lessor, "the law implyeth it to be at the will of the

---

68. Rock Island Bank & Trust Co. v. Rhoads, 1933, 353 Ill. 131, 187 N.E. 139; Julian v. Northwestern Trust Co., 1934, 192 Minn. 136, 255 N.W. 622; Smiles v. Daube, 1938, 130 Pa.Super. 565, 198 A. 457; Mitchell v. Edds, 1945, 143 Tex. 307, 184 S.W.2d 823, 158 A.L.R. 470.

69. See Rest. Property, 1948 Supplement, § 111, Comment *b*, Special Note.

70. 174 Okl. 87, 49 P.2d 526 (1950).

71. *Cf.*: Wise v. Wise, 1941, 109 Ind.App. 207, 34 N.E.2d 143.

72. *Accord:* In re Byrne's Estate, 1935, 320 Pa. 513, 181 A. 500. See Colburn v. Burlingame, 1923, 190 Cal. 697, 214 P. 226, 27 A.L.R. 1374.

73. See Krumm v. Cuneo, 1943, 71 Ohio App. 521, 47 N.E. 1003. *Cf.*: Ripley v. Benjamin, 1940, 111 Vt. 76, 10 A.2d 205.

74. See infra, § 194.

75. Taylor v. Farrow, Ky.App.1951, 239 S.W.2d 73, noted in Wash.Univ.Law Quarterly, Vol. 1951, No. 4, p. 595; Pomroy v. Jenkins, 1940, 151 Kan. 466, 99 P.2d 752; Anderson v. Anderson, 1930, 119 Neb. 381, 229 N.W. 124; Anderson v. Anderson, 1935, 150 Or. 476, 46 P.2d 98. *Cf.*: In re Burpee's Estate, 1951, 367 Pa. 329, 80 A.2d 721.

76. In re Reinhardt's Estate, 1887, 74 Cal. 365, 16 P. 13; Anderson v. Gifft, 1940, 229 Iowa 515, 294 N.W. 721; Blackwood v. Blackwood, 1953, 237 N.C. 726, 76 S.E.2d 122; Wetzel v. Besecker, 1945, 77 Ohio App. 235, 64 N.E.2d 602; Rest. Property, 1948 Supplement, p. 395, § 108, *Comment bb.*

lessee also; for it cannot be only at the will of the lessor, but it must be at the will of the lessee also. And so it is when the lease is made to have and to hold at the will of the lessee, this must be also at the will of the lessor." [77]

The conclusions indicated by Lord Coke are sound if the estate was not created with the formalities prescribed by the Statute of Frauds or the Statute of Wills. Otherwise, the conclusions indicated are not supported by reason. It cannot properly be said that the conclusions are necessary because of the requirements of mutuality because contractual obligations are not involved. The matter relates to the creation of estates.

In a conveyance "A to B terminable at the will of A," a construction problem may be raised as to whether or not the parties intended to create a determinable life estate in B. However, a determinable life estate is created if the conveyance is "A to B *for life,* terminable at the will of A." [78] If the conveyance is "A to B, terminable at the will of B," B acquires a determinable life estate.[79]

Measuring Life and Estates Pur Autre Vie

In a conveyance "A to B for life," B acquires an estate for his own lifetime if A had the power to convey such an estate. This conclusion is reached by applying the rule of *strict construction* against a grantor. Historically, an estate for one's own lifetime is considered to be a greater estate than an estate for the lifetime of another. It may

not be more valuable but there is assurance of enjoyment of the estate as long as the grantee lives. This same rule of construction is followed if the grantor, A, is the owner of an estate in fee tail. The owner of an estate in fee tail has a *power to convey* such an estate.

A grantor may have a limited estate, such as an estate for his own lifetime and, for that reason, is without power to create an estate for the lifetime of another. In that event the ambiguity is resolved by reference to facts surrounding the conveyance. By such means an attempt is made to ascertain the true intent of the parties. The most important factor relates to comparative values. If the consideration paid compares favorably with the value of an estate measured by the lifetime of the grantor then there is a strong argument that the parties intended the creation of such an estate. In the Restatement, Property, the proposition is stated as follows: "In such case the intent of the parties 'manifested by the transaction' is ascertained by considering facts extrinsic to the instrument, such as the consideration paid, the relative ages of the conveyor and conveyee and the relative probable durations of the estate subject to the power of disposition of the conveyor and of the life of the conveyee, and by applying canons for the construction of ambiguous instruments, such as the canon that a conveyance should be construed against the conveyor or so as to convey all that he has, and the canon that a conveyance will be construed to be lawful, if possible." [80]

PRIVILEGES AND DUTIES OF LIFE TENANT

87. While a life tenant is entitled to the beneficial use of land, unless privileged, he does not have a right to act in such a manner

77. Co.Litt., 55a.

78. 1 Rest. Property, § 113, Illustration 1.

79. Sweetser v. McKenney, 1875, 65 Me. 225; Thompson v. Baxter, 1909, 107 Minn. 122; Stalling v. Jones, 1951, 193 Tenn. 200, 245 S.W.2d 199; Newsom v. Meade, 1926, 102 W.Va. 489, 135 S.E. 604. *Contra:* Foley v. Gamester, 1930, 271 Mass. 55, 170 N.E. 799. *Cf.:* Norman v. Morehouse, Tex.Civ.App.1922, 243 S. W. 1104; Conley v. Gaylock, 1959, 144 W.Va. 457, 108 S.E.2d 675.

80. 1 Rest.Property, § 108, *Comment a.*

as to impair the value of estates and interests owned by others in the same land.

    a. **Damage caused by third party.** If a life tenant is without fault, he is not responsible for damage that may be caused to the land by others. The life tenant may recover damages from such third party but the amount of recovery is limited to the interest of the life tenant.

    b. **Insurance.** A life tenant is not under a duty to insure the property either for his own protection or for the protection of others who have an estate or interest.

    c. **Taxes and interest.** A life tenant is under a duty to pay ordinary taxes to the extent that he derives benefits from the life estate. He is also under a duty to pay interest on an indebtedness that constitutes a lien on the property.

    d. **Assessments for permanent improvements** are apportioned between the life tenant and the owners of future interests in the property.

While a life tenant is entitled to the beneficial use of the land, this means "reasonable use" in light of the fact that other owners have an interest or interests in the same land. In general, acts that cause a permanent damage to the land constitute waste, a matter discussed under a separate heading.[81]

Damage Caused by Third Party

Contrary to early authorities,[82] the present rule is that a life tenant cannot be held liable for damage caused to the land by third parties unless, of course, the life tenant participated in or induced the acts. So also, a life tenant is not liable for damage caused by accident or by an extraordinary force of nature.[83]

If a third party does cause damage to the land the life tenant is entitled to recover only to the extent of his interest in the land or to the extent that he has obligated himself to maintain and preserve the property against such damage.[84] The owner of a future interest in the land is entitled to damages only if the wrongdoer causes a condition that is permanent in nature. In that event, recovery is measured by the diminution in the market value of his estate or interest.[85]

Insurance

A life tenant is not under a duty to insure. Those who own future interests in the property can secure protection by obtaining their own insurance. If a life tenant does insure he is not under a duty to account for insurance money.[86] This rule is followed even if he collects more than the value of his life estate.[87] There is a minority rule that a life tenant is under a duty to carry insurance for the protection of the owners of future interests in the property because he is under a duty to

---

81. For discussion of Waste, see supra, § 14.

82. See, for example, Fay v. Brewer, 1825, 3 Pick. (Mass.) 203; Co.Litt. 54a.

83. See Rogers v. Atlantic, Gulf & Pacific Co., 1915, 213 N.Y. 246, 107 N.E. 661; 1 Rest. Property, § 146.

84. Brown v. Woodliff, 1892, 89 Ga. 413, 15 S.E. 491; Polk v. Haworth, 1911, 48 Ind.App. 32, 95 N.E. 332 *(dictum)*; Zimmerman v. Shreeve, 1883, 59 Md. 357; Jordan v. City of Benwood, 1896, 42 W.Va. 312, 26 S.E. 266 *(dictum)*; 1 Rest. Property, § 118, see Rest. Property, Tent.Draft No. 3, Appendix 193–236. *Contra:* Rogers v. Atlantic, Gulf & Pacific Co., 1915, 213 N.Y. 246, 107 N.E. 661 (life tenant recovered for the entire damage caused to the land).

85. Swick v. West Virginia Coal & Coke Co., 1940, 122 W.Va. 151, 7 S.E.2d 697, noted in 47 W.Va.Law Qt. 67 (1940).

86. Farmers' Mut. Fire & Lightning Ins. Co. v. Crowley, 1945, 354 Mo. 649, 190 S.W.2d 250; Stockton v. Maney, 1937, 212 N.C. 231, 193 S.E. 137.

87. Corder v. McDougall, 1932, 216 Cal. 773, 16 P.2d 740; Harrison v. Pepper, 1896, 166 Mass. 288, 44 N. E. 222; Blanchard v. Kingston, 1923, 222 Mich. 631, 193 N.W. 241; King v. King, 1932, 163 Miss. 584, 143 So. 422, noted in 19 Va.Law Rev. 282 (1933); In re Gorman's Estate, 1936, 321 Pa. 292, 184 A. 86.

"preserve and protect" the property.[88] Under this rule he is designated as a "quasi-trustee" of insurance money.

If insurance is obtained for the protection of the interests of both the life tenant and the owners of future interests, the life tenant is entitled to the income from insurance proceeds if it is not used to restore the property.[89]

Taxes and Interest

A life tenant is under a duty to pay ordinary taxes (as distinguished from taxes for permanent improvements) unless the instrument creating the estate relieves him from this obligation.[90] A provision that he takes the life estate "without cost or hindrance to him in any way" is not broad enough to relieve him from this duty.[91] So also, the obligation remains even if he is under a duty to pay rent.[92]

Although a lien for taxes may accrue, if the taxes do not become payable until after the death of the life tenant, the obligation may be apportioned between his estate and the owner of the next succeeding estate, such as the remainderman.[93] Apportionment is also indicated where the land is held in trust and the life tenant dies before the end of the tax year.[94] Apportionment is made on the basis of the tax year regardless of the time fixed for payment.[95]

The amount of taxes for which a life tenant may be held liable is limited to the value of benefits which have accrued to him by way of rents, issue and profits derived from the land, or the reasonable rental value if he occupied the land.[96] The transferee of a life estate is under a duty to pay taxes that have accumulated at the time he acquires the estate but only to the extent that the benefits derived from the land by such transferee exceed the current carrying charges.[97]

First: A life tenant who defaults in the performance of his duty to pay taxes may be held liable as for waste.[98] If he purchases the land at a tax sale his ownership will be subordinate to the interest of the reversioner or remainderman.[99] This is due to the fact that the life tenant is under a duty to pay the taxes and this duty is one owing to the owners of future interests. However, a

---

88. Clark v. Leverett, 1924, 159 Ga. 487, 126 S.E. 258, 37 A.L.R. 180; Green v. Green, 1897, 50 S.C. 514, 27 S.E. 952.

89. 1 Rest. Property, § 123(1).

90. Thayer v. Shorey, 1934, 287 Mass. 76, 191 N.E. 435, 94 A.L.R. 307.

91. Kruse v. Meissner, 1945, 136 N.J.Eq. 209, 40 A.2d 777.

92. Prettyman v. Walston, 1864, 34 Ill. 175; Morrison v. Fletcher, 1905, 119 Ky. 488, 84 S.W. 548; Falvey v. Hicks, 1926, 315 Mo. 442, 286 S.W. 385. *Cf.*: 1 Rest. Property, § 130, Illustration 2.

93. Trust Co. of Georgia v. Kenny, 1939, 188 Ga. 243, 3 S.E.2d 553.

94. In re Hone's Estate, 1934, 152 Misc. 221, 274 N.Y. S. 101, noted in 44 Yale Law Jr., 1110 (1935).

95. 1 Rest. Property, § 129, *Comment g.*

96. Calcagni v. Cirino, 1940, 62 R.I. 44, 2 A.2d 889; 65 R.I. 408, 14 A.2d 803; 1 Rest. of Property, § 130, (b).

97. Murch v. J. O. Smith Manufacturing Co., 1890, 47 N.J.Eq. 193, 20 A. 213; 1 Rest. Property, § 130, *Comment d.*

98. Thayer v. Shorey, 1934, 287 Mass. 76, 191 N.E. 435, 94 A.L.R. 307. On this basis, relief may be available in equity (Abernethy v. Orton, 1903, 42 Or. 437, 71 P. 327).

99. Higginbotham v. Harper, 1943, 206 Ark. 210, 174 S.W.2d 668; Turner v. Edwards, 1940, 207 Minn. 455, 292 N.W. 257 (where tax deed was acquired through the connivance of the life tenant); Zaring v. Lomax, 1949, 53 N.M. 273, 206 P.2d 706. *Cf.*: Federal Land Bank v. Newsom, 1936, 175 Miss. 134, 166 So. 346, noted in 50 Harv.Law Rev. 534 (1937) (where taxes paid by mortgagee of the life tenant); Bryson v. Conn. General Life Ins. Co., Tex.Civ.App. 1946, 196 S.W.2d 532.

remainderman may acquire a tax title and assert it to the prejudice of the owner of a life estate.[1]

Second: A life tenant is under a duty to pay interest on an indebtedness that constitutes a lien on the property, such as a mortgage. If he defaults in the performance of this duty, and foreclosure proceedings are instituted, redemption by the life tenant will inure to the benefit of the owner of a future interest in the property. Of course, the owner of the future interest remains liable in connection with principal indebtedness.[2]

If the owner of a future interest encumbers his interest the owner of a life estate is free to purchase that interest at foreclosure proceedings in the absence of manipulation or collusion.[3]

Assessments for Permanent Improvements

Assessments levied against land by public authority for permanent improvements are apportioned between the life tenant and the owners of future interests. The basis for this rule is that the improvements redound to the benefit of the owner of the life estate and also to the benefit of the owner of future interests.

Improvements are permanent in nature if they do not usually require replacement from time to time. For example, a change in the grade of a street is generally considered to be a permanent improvement.[4] The age or life expectancy of the life tenant, the remainderman or the reversioner does not constitute a factor in determining whether or not an improvement is to be classified as "permanent."

If an improvement is permanent in nature the assessment may be apportioned between the life tenant and the owner of a future interest on the basis of the valuation placed upon the respective estates. The life tenant is required to pay that proportion of the assessment which the value of the life estate bears to the value of the fee.[5] A different method of apportionment is usually followed if the fee is held in trust. In that event, it is generally held that the trustee must pay the assessment out of the trust estate and then charge the life tenant an appropriate rate of interest on the amount of the expenditure.[6]

---

1. Duffley v. McCaskey, 1939, 345 Mo. 550, 134 S.W.2d 62, 126 A.L.R. 853, noted in 24 Minn.Law Rev. 589 (1940).

2. In re Application of Lee, 1927, 171 Minn. 182, 213 N.W. 736.

3. Muzzy v. Muzzy, 1953, 364 Mo. 373, 261 S.W.2d 927.

4. In Reyburn v. Wallace, 1887, 93 Mo. 326, 3 S.W. 482, apportionment was denied because, primarily, the assessment was levied for the resurfacing of streets.

5. Chambers v. Chambers, 1898, 20 R.I. 370, 39 A. 243 (construction of a sewer and curbing).

6. Plympton v. Boston Dispensary, 1871, 106 Mass. 544 (special assessment for the opening of a street).

CHAPTER 17

ESTATES IN FEE

INTRODUCTION

88. The most extensive estate is a fee simple. It is an estate of potentially infinite duration. The word "fee" indicates that it is an estate of inheritance. The word "simple" signifies that there are no restrictions with respect to the inheritable characteristics of the estate.

a. Words of inheritance. According to the English common law intention to convey an estate in fee can be manifested only by the use of words of inheritance.
This rule is not applicable if a conveyance is made by will. Such words are not necessary if a conveyance is made to a trustee or in a partition between concurrent owners, except in the case of tenants in common. If the conveyance is to a corporation the appropriate word is "successors" rather than "heirs."

In practically all of the states statutes have been passed abolishing or modifying the common law rule.

b. Words of limitation and words of purchase. Usually, words such as "heirs" and "heirs of the body" are considered to be words designating the fact that the grantee acquires an estate in fee. That is to say, they are _words of limitation._

As a matter of construction, these words may indicate an intention on the part of a conveyor to convey an estate to specific persons who qualify under the description. In that event, they are designated as _words of purchase._

The most extensive estate is a fee simple.[1] It is an estate of potentially infinite duration. The word "fee" indicates that it is an estate of inheritance. The word "simple" signifies that there are no restrictions with respect to the inheritable characteristics of the estate.

As will be noted under a separate heading, in the case of an estate in fee tail inheritance may be restricted to the heirs of the body of the grantee. However, an estate in fee tail is the only type of estate in fee wherein such restrictions may be imposed. It is contrary to public policy to permit the creation of estates in fee of a type other than those that have already received judicial sanction. If the intention is to create a freehold estate of inheritance any restrictions imposed will be disregarded and the grantee or devisee will acquire a fee simple estate. It has been so held in a conveyance "A to B and her heir and C is the only heir contemplated herein."[2] So also, in a conveyance "A to B and her heirs (should she have any);[3] and "A to B and her heirs on her father's side."[4]

---

1. See supra, § 2.

2. Beeman v. Stilwell, 1922, 194 Iowa 231, 189 N.W. 969.

3. Bryant v. Britt, 1950, 216 S.C. 299, 57 S.E.2d 535, 16 A.L.R.2d 666.

4. Johnson v. Whiton, 1893, 159 Mass. 424, 34 N.E. 542.

Words of Inheritance

In the early development of the feudal system, a tenant's estate was, for practical purposes, limited to a life estate. Usually, it was the desire of the lord that upon the death of a tenant the estate should pass to his eldest son because he was the person in the best position to assume the obligations imposed under the feudal system. The conveyor could assure this continuity by a specific provision that the conveyance was A to B *and his heirs.* The rule developed that an intent to convey an hereditary estate (a fee) can be manifested *only* by naming heirs in the conveyance. Thus, the word "heirs" or the words "heirs of the body" are said to be *words of inheritance.* With exceptions to be noted, unless such words are used in a conveyance the grantee can acquire only a life estate. Thus, a conveyance "A to B forever" gives B only a life estate. Although there is some conflict on the point, a conveyance "A to B or his heirs" is the same as a conveyance A to B and his heirs." [5] The words of inheritance must be used either in the granting clause or in the habendum clause of the deed. It is not sufficient that a warranty in the deed runs to the grantee and his heirs.[6]

Words of inheritance may be incorporated by reference into the conveying instrument.[7] Situations where words of inheritance are not necessary to convey an estate in fee simple are as follows:

1. Since a corporation cannot have heirs the appropriate words of conveyance are to the corporation and its successors.

2. Words of inheritance are not necessary to convey an estate in fee simple to a trustee. This conclusion is based upon the ground that a trustee acquires the estate necessary to accomplish the purposes of the trust.

3. Words of inheritance are not necessary to devise an estate in fee simple. Historically, wills are construed according to the intention of the testator.

4. Words of inheritance are not necessary in order to release an estate in fee simple to one who has a vested estate in fee simple in the same land except in a case where the parties are tenants in common.[8]

5. In Penienskice v. Short (Del.),[9] it is held that a Receiver of Taxes, who was under a statutory duty to convey an estate in fee simple of the taxable, could convey such an estate without the use of words of inheritance.

6. In practically all of the states it is now provided by statute that words of inheritance are not necessary to convey an estate in fee simple even by deed.[10] In some states this conclusion has been reached without the aid of statute.[11] In many states it is also provided by statute that a conveyor presumably intends to convey his entire interest.

Words of Limitation and Words of Purchase

In a conveyance "A to B and his heirs," or "A to B and the heirs of his body," the word "heirs" and the words "heirs of his body," are usually considered to be words of limitation because they are used to indicate

---

5. See 1 Rest. Property, § 27, *Comment d.*

6. Grainger v. Hamilton, 1955, 228 S.C. 318, 90 S.E.2d 209.

7. Evans v. Brady, 1894, 79 Md. 142, 28 A. 1061 Lytle v. Lytle, 1840, 10 Watts. (Pa.) 259 (incorporated language of a will where words of inheritance are not necessary to convey a fee simple); 1 Rest. Property, § 28.

8. 1 Rest. Property, § 29.

9. 38 Del. 526, 194 A. 409 (1937).

10. For enumeration of statutes see Rest. Property, 1948 Supplement, § 39, Special Note.

11. See, for example, Dennen v. Searle, 1961, 149 Conn. 126, 176 A.2d 561; De Freitas v. Coke, 1963, 46 Hawaii 425, 380 P.2d 762.

the type of estate created in B.[12] In a conveyance "A to B and his children," the words "and his children" are usually considered to be words of purchase because it is indicated that the children are to take in their own right (as grantees) under the conveying instrument.

As a matter of construction, however, the word "heirs," or the words "heirs of the body," may be classified as words of purchase. It has been so held in a conveyance "A to B and her *present* heirs."[13] The word "present" restricts the meaning of the word "heirs." The word "heirs" is not used as a word of limitation unless it is used in a technical sense, *i. e.*, as describing persons entitled to inherit the property if the ancestor dies intestate.

Under some circumstances the word "children" may be construed as meaning "heirs of the body" and, as such, may be classified as a word of limitation.[14]

CONDITIONAL FEE AND ESTATE IN FEE TAIL

89. Prior to the passage of the statute *De Donis Conditionalibus* (1285), the courts held that in a conveyance "A to B and the heirs of his body" the grantee acquired a conditional fee. The condition was birth of issue capable of inheriting the estate. After such event, for all practical purposes the estate of the grantee was enlarged to a fee simple.

This construction did not conform to the intention of the conveyor. His purpose was to vest an estate in the grantee that would pass to the heirs of the body of successive owners until the line of descent should become ex-

tinct. **The Statute *De Donis Conditionalibus* required such a construction and the resulting estate is an estate in fee tail.**

a. Barring of estates in fee tail. By 1472 it was recognized that a tenant in tail could maintain a fictitious action, called a common recovery, and thereby bar the issue in tail as well as all interests "in reversion or remainder." The issue in tail could also be barred by a simplified judicial procedure called a "fine."

b. Conditional fee and fee tail in the United States. Except in a few states the conditional fee is not recognized in the United States. In a majority of the states statutes have been passed abolishing or modifying the estate in fee tail.

Prior to 1285, in a conveyance "A to B and the heirs of his body," B acquired a conditional fee. The condition was birth of issue capable of inheriting the land. Upon the birth of issue the estate in B became, for many purposes, an estate in fee simple. But if B was not survived by such issue, and he had not alienated the land prior to the time of his death, the land reverted to the grantor or his heirs.[15]

The probable intention of the grantor of such an estate was that ownership of the land should pass from B to the "heirs of his body" from generation to generation. When this line of inheritance should become extinct the ownership was to revert to the grantor or his heirs. The statute *De Donis Conditionalibus*,[16] passed in 1285, directed that a conveyance in the form under discussion should be construed according to the intention of the parties. The result was a new type of estate designated as a fee tail. The donor (conveyor) of a fee tail could restrict the inheritable characteristics of the estate so that ownership of the land would pass only to the

---

12. See Hall v. Morris, Fla.App.1959, 112 So.2d 40; Gray v. Stillman, Okl.1961, 365 P.2d 369 ("blood heirs").

13. Fountain County Coal & Mining Co. v. Beckleheimer, 1885, 102 Ind. 76, 1 N.E. 202.

14. Eubanks v. McDonald, 1955, 225 Ark. 470, 283 S.W.2d 166.

15. 2 Pollock and Maitland, History of English Law (2nd ed.) p. 17.

16. Stat. 13 Edw. I, c. 1 (1285).

heirs male of the donee's (conveyee's) body (fee tail male) or to the heirs female of his body (fee tail female). Conveyance could be made to husband and wife and the heirs of their bodies (fee tail special) or it could be made to a man or a woman and the heirs of his or her body by a designated wife or husband.

The Barring of Estates in Fee Tail

Under provisions of the statute *De Donis Conditionalibus* if the tenant in tail conveyed the land, upon his death the issue in tail could regain possession and assert ownership. To this extent the estate was inalienable. Further, estates in fee tail "were not to be forfeited for felony or treason," [17] and passed to issue free from the claims of the ancestor's creditors.[18]

Because of the "evil results of such estates," [19] they were not looked upon with favor by the courts. By 1472 it was firmly established that a tenant in tail could maintain a fictitious action, called a common recovery, and thereby bar the issue in tail as well as all interests "in reversion or remainder." [20] Estates tail might also be barred by a fictitious action called a "fine." In the case of a fine, an action brought to establish ownership of the land in fee simple was compromised by the parties, with leave of the court, and judgment entered. This would bar the issue in tail but not interests held "in remainder or reversion." Unlike a common recovery, a fine did not involve a step-by-step judicial proceedings. The action was terminated by a compromise agreement. The statute *De*

Donis Conditionalibus specifically provided that a fine should have no effect on estates tail, but this was later changed by statute.[21] The procedure involved in connection with these actions was rather complex, the details of which are not of modern importance.[22]

Conditional Fee and Fee Tail in the United States

In a few states it is held that the statute *De Donis Conditionalibus* was not adopted as a part of the local common law. Accordingly, in these states the conditional fee is recognized. This is the law in Iowa, Oregon and South Carolina.[23]

An estate in fee tail is recognized in Delaware, Maine, Massachusetts and Rhode Island (if created by deed).[24] Statutes in a majority of the states provide that an estate that would be a fee tail at common law is a fee simple.[25] Other statutes declare that the grantee of a fee tail acquires only a life estate with a remainder in fee simple to the person to whom the estate tail would pass according to the course of the common law.[26] In a few states there is statutory authorization for the creation of a fee tail for one generation. The first taker has an estate of inheritance (as distinguished from a life estate) and the potential takers have a mere expectancy. In general, they cannot main-

---

17. This was changed by statute passed in 1534 (26 Henry VIII).

18. See Mildmay's Case, [1606] 6 Coke 40, 77 Eng. Rep. 311.

19. See 2 Bl.Comm. 116.

20. Taltarum's Case, Y.B. 12 Ecw. 4, Mich. term, pl. 25 (1472).

21. 4 Hen. VII, c. 24 (1490); 32 Hen. VIII, c. 36 (1540).

22. For details, see Williams, Real Property (24th ed.) pp. 133 *et seq.*

23. See Rest. Property, 1948 Supplement, Introductory Note, p. 379, Special Notes 1, 7.

24. See Rest. Property, 1948 Supplement, Introductory Note, p. 379, Special Notes, 2, 7.

25. For classification of statutes, see Rest. Property, 1948 Supplement, Introductory Note, p. 379.

26. For construction of such a statute, see Toney v. Toney, 1951, 218 Ark. 433, 236 S.W.2d 716; Bibo v. Bibo, 1947, 397 Ill. 505, 74 N.E.2d 808.

tain an action for waste and their interests are not alienable during the lifetime of the first taker.[27]

FEE SIMPLE DETERMINABLE

90. A fee simple determinable is a fee simple created to continue until the happening of a stated event. The estate then terminates automatically. This type of estate is recognized in practically all of the American states.

    a. Possibility of reverter. The conveyor of a fee simple determinable retains a future interest described as a possibility of reverter.

    b. Reverter clause. If the intention to convey an estate in fee simple determinable is otherwise expressed it is not necessary that the conveying instrument contain a reverter clause.

    c. Purpose clause. A fee simple determinable is not created by a mere statement in the conveying instrument that the land is to be used for a stated purpose.

A fee simple determinable is a fee simple created to continue until the happening of a stated event. Historical examples include such conveyances as A to B and his heirs "so long as (the land) is used for church purposes," [28] A to B and his heirs "so long as St. Paul's (Church) shall stand," [29] and A to B and his heirs "tenants of the manor of Dale." [30] Since the duration of the estate is correlated to the happening of a named event the estate terminates automatically upon the

happening of that event.[31] The claim of termination must be supported by evidence of something more than a temporary interruption with respect to the use involved.[32]

Usually, the words of special limitation are contained in the granting clause of a deed. However, such words may also appear only in the habendum clause. In that event the habendum clause is not inconsistent with the granting clause because it merely specifies the type of estate in fee simple that is involved in the conveyance.[33]

Possibility of Reverter

The grantor of a fee simple determinable retains a future interest described as a possibility of reverter. In the case of a testamentary disposition the possibility of reverter constitutes a part of the estate of the testator.

It has been contended that the recognition of this type of an estate in fee simple is inconsistent with the provisions of the Statute Quia Emptores.[34] The alleged inconsistency arises out of the claim that the statute abolished tenure as between the grantor and the grantee of an estate in fee simple and the retention of a possibility of reverter in the conveyor is inconsistent with this concept.[35] However, in spite of this technical argument, an estate in fee simple determinable is rec-

---

27. Cook v. Hardin County Bank Co., 1945, 76 Ohio App. 203, 63 N.E.2d 686.

28. McDougall v. Palo Alto Unified School District, 1963, 212 Cal.App.2d 422, 28 Cal.Rptr. 37.

29. Plow.Comm. 349, 557. See Reed v. Lewis, 1881, 74 Ind. 433 (deed of a sawmill "until the machinery on the herein described premises shall be removed). *Cf.:* Norman v. Morehouse, Tex.Civ.App.1922, 243 S.W. 1104, error refused.

30. 2 Bl.Comm. 109.

31. Johnson v. Lane, 1940, 199 Ark. 740, 135 S.W.2d 853; Carr v. Georgia Railroad, 1884, 74 Ga. 73; Saletri v. Clark, 1961, 13 Wis.2d 325, 108 N.W.2d 548. *Cf.:* Board of Education v. Winding Gulf Collieries, 4 Cir. 1945, 152 F.2d 382, certiorari denied 328 U.S. 844, 66 S.Ct. 1023, 90 L.Ed. 1618.

32. Middlesboro Town & Land Co. v. Louisville & N. R. Co., 1938, 274 Ky. 756, 120 S.W.2d 394.

33. Board of Chosen Freeholders v. Buck, 1912, 79 N.J.Eq. 472, 82 A. 418.

34. 18 Edw. 1, cc. 1, 3 (1290).

35. Sanders, Uses and Trusts (4th ed., 1824) 200; Gray, Rule Against Perpetuities (4th ed. 1942), §§ 31, 32.

ognized in practically all of the American states.[36] Authorities frequently refer to the possibility of reverter as a "mere possibility of an estate." Retention of this type of interest is not inconsistent with the policy declared in the Statute Quia Emptores. The nature and characteristics of a possibility of reverter are discussed under a separate heading.[37]

Reverter Clause

If the intent to convey a fee simple determinable is otherwise expressed it is not necessary that the conveying instrument contain a reverter clause. The possibility of reverter is a concomitant of a fee simple determinable.[38] An oil and gas lease may provide for termination if the lessee fails to perform the covenants in the lease. In that event, the possibility of reverter, while not expressly described in the lease is "created by the lease." [39]

Purpose Clause

A provision in the conveying instrument that the property is to be used for a specific purpose will not result in the creation of a fee simple determinable.[40] Authorities support this conclusion even if there is provision that the property is to be used for a stated purpose "and for no other purpose." [41]

Under some circumstances a restriction as to use may constitute a covenant and be enforceable as such at least as between the grantor and grantee.[42] A charitable trust may be created if property is conveyed to a charitable corporation or if a conveying instrument imposes a duty to use the property for a stated charitable purpose.[43]

In City of Gering v. Jones (Neb.),[44] property was conveyed to a city, the deed providing that it was "to be used for the use and benefit of the Citizens of the said City." The court held that the City did not acquire the property in trust because the stated purpose was "the very purpose for which the municipality was created, namely, for the use and benefit of the citizens of the City." A claim of dedication was also denied because the land was not conveyed to the city for a specific use,

---

36. See Powell, Determinable Fees, 23 Col.Law Rev. 207, 234 (1923); Vance, Rights of Reverter and the Statute Quia Emptores, 36 Yale Law Jr. 593, 607 (1927); 1 Rest. Property, § 44.

37. See infra, § 139.

38. First Universalist Society of North Adams v. Boland, 1892, 155 Mass. 171, 29 N.E. 524; Board of Chosen Freeholders of Cumberland County v. Buck, 1912, 79 N.J.Eq. 472, 82 A. 418; Board of Education of Lebanon, etc. v. Hollingsworth, 1936, 56 Ohio App. 95, 10 N.E.2d 25, noted in 4 Ohio St.Univ.Law Jr. 1, p. 106 (1937). *Cf.:* In re Matter of Copps Chapel Methodist Episcopal Church, 1929, 120 Ohio St. 309, 166 N.E. 218, criticized in 9 Boston Univ. Law Rev. 291 (1929). See Editorial Note, 3 Cinn. Law Rev. 491 (1929); McCall, Estates on Condition and on Special Limitation in North Carolina, 19 No.Car.Law Rev. 334, 341 (1941); 1 Rest. Property, § 44(b).

39. Kaiser v. Love, 1962, 163 Tex. 558, 358 S.W.2d 586.

40. First Presbyterian Church of Salem v. Tarr, 1939, 63 Ohio App. 286, 26 N.E.2d 597; Carter Oil Co. v. Welker, 7 Cir. 1939, 112 F.2d 299, noted in 39 Mich. Law Rev. 477 (1941) (deed to railroad for its right-of-way).

41. Beran v. Harris, 1949, 91 Cal.App.2d 562, 205 P.2d 107; Boone Biblical College v. Forrest, 1937, 223 Iowa 1260, 275 N.W. 132, 116 A.L.R. 67 (to be used for educational and religious purposes only); Quinn v. Pere Marquette R. Co., 1931, 256 Mich. 143, 239 N.W. 376 (to be used for railroad purposes only); Williams v. Thompson, 1939, 216 N.C. 292, 4 S.E.2d 609 (to be used as a parsonage and for no other purpose); 1 Rest. Property, § 44, *Comment m. Cf.:* Slegel v. Lauer, 1892, 148 Pa. 236, 23 A. 996.

42. See Marshall v. Standard Oil Co. of California, 1936, 17 Cal.App.2d 19, 61 P.2d 520.

43. Loechel v. Columbia Borough School Dist., 1952, 369 Pa. 132, 85 A.2d 81.

44. 175 Neb. 626, 122 N.W.2d 503 (1963).

such as a use for park purposes.[45] A claim of dedication may be denied even if land is conveyed to a city for a specific public purpose. Circumstances may show that the parties did not intend a dedication.[46]

Statutes authorizing the taking of property by eminent domain proceedings usually specify the estate that may be acquired. Under some statutes, if land is condemned for a specific purpose, such as "for school purposes," a determinable fee is acquired. Only such an estate is necessary for the purpose involved.[47]

FEE SIMPLE SUBJECT TO A CONDITION SUBSEQUENT

91. A fee simple subject to a condition subsequent is a fee simple that may be terminated by the conveyor, or his successor in interest, upon the happening of a named event. The estate continues until such time as action is taken by the owner of the future interest (right of entry or power of termination).

This type of estate is recognized in a majority of the American states.

a. **Re-entry clause. While a re-entry clause is not essential to the creation of this estate, failure to insert such a clause in the conveyance may justify the conclusion that there is an ambiguity as to the true intention of the parties. In that event, extrinsic evidence is admissible to resolve the ambiguity.**

b. **Implied conditions. Ordinarily, conditions are not implied. According to some authorities exception to this rule is made**

if a conveyance is made in consideration of a promise to support the grantor.

c. **Option to repurchase distinguished from a right of entry. A provision in a deed may constitute a repurchase option rather than a right of entry for condition broken.**

d. **Equitable relief against forfeiture. Under varying circumstances a court of equity may grant relief against forfeiture.**

A fee simple subject to a condition subsequent is an estate in fee simple but it is subject to termination upon the happening of a stated event if the grantor or testator, or person who has succeeded to his interest, elects to exercise the right of entry (power of termination). This election may be manifested by an action of ejectment. The validity of an estate in fee simple subject to a condition subsequent is generally recognized in the various American states.

The characteristic which distinguishes this estate from a fee simple determinable is that the estate continues in the grantee or his successors unless and until the right of entry is exercised. The estate does not end *ipso facto* upon the happening of the named event. The reason for this is that the words which provide for termination of the estate are not regarded as a part of the original limitation of the estate but are considered as words providing for the cutting off of the estate before its normal termination. In the case of a fee simple determinable the words of contingency are regarded as a part of the limitation itself.

The future interest created in the conveyor of an estate in fee simple subject to a condition subsequent is a right of entry for condition broken, also called a power of termination. If there is a breach of the condition the conveyor may exercise the right of entry not only as against the grantee of the possessory estate but also as against the owners of future interests created by the same convey-

---

45. See Ruben v. City of Los Angeles, 1959, 51 Cal.2d 857, 337 P.2d 825, 827, n. 2, appeal dismissed, certiorari denied 361 U.S. 30, 80 S.Ct. 118, 4 L.Ed.2d 98.

46. Page v. Provines, 1937, 179 Okl. 391, 66 P.2d 7; Pearson v. Nelley, 1938, 331 Pa. 376, 200 A. 654.

47. See Thomison v. Hillcrest Athletic Ass'n, 1939, 39 Del. (9 W.W.Harr.) 590, 5 A.2d 236, noted in 25 Va.Law Rev. 986 (1939).

ance.[48] The right of entry may be created in connection with successive conveyances of the same property and may relate to the same or different conditions.[49] The characteristics of the right of entry are discussed under a separate heading.[50]

Re-entry Clause

The usual language used for the creation of a fee simple subject to a condition subsequent is "upon condition" or "provided" that the land is used for a designated purpose followed by an express clause giving the conveyor a right of entry if there is a breach of the condition.

While a "re-entry clause" is not essential to the creation of this estate, failure to insert such a clause in the conveying instrument may justify the conclusion that there is ambiguity as to the true intention of the parties. As a result, extrinsic evidence is admissible to resolve the ambiguity. This may show that the intention was merely to create contractual liability (a simple covenant), to create a trust or equitable servitudes.[51]

Implied Conditions

Ordinarily, conditions are not implied. However, there is authority for the view that a condition will be implied in equity if land is conveyed in consideration of a promise made by the grantee to support the grantor and there is default in the performance of this promise. It is considered that this type of conveyance should not be construed as in the case of commercial transactions.[52] This is the statutory rule in some states.[53] Other possible remedies are discussed in the following paragraphs.

First: In some states the grantor may be entitled to rescind the transaction for failure of consideration.[54] However, this relief may not be available in the absence of proof of the insolvency of the grantee.[55]

Second: Rescission may be allowed upon the ground of fraud—fraud being presumed from the grantee's subsequent breach of his promise to support the grantor.[56]

Third: Some authorities support the view that such a conveyance creates an equitable lien in favor of the grantor.[57] Others hold that the conveyance is executory in nature until such time as the grantee has fully performed.[58]

---

48. Lucas v. Lucas, 1931, 171 Ga. 806, 156 S.E. 680, 76 A.L.R. 737.

49. Parry v. Berkeley Hall School Foundation, 1937, 10 Cal.2d 422, 74 P.2d 738, 114 A.L.R. 562, noted in 51 Harv.Law Rev. 1113 (1938), 12 So.Cal.Law Rev. 101 (1938).

50. See infra, § 140.

51. Chouteau v. City of St. Louis, 1932, 331 Mo. 781, 55 S.W.2d 299; Post v. Weil, 1889, 115 N.Y. 361, 22 N.E. 145; Second Church of Christ, Scientist v. Le Prevost, 1941, 67 Ohio App. 101, 35 N.E.2d 1015; 1 Rest. Property, § 45, *Comments l, n,* and 1948 Supplement, Property, § 45, *Comment p. Cf.:* Young v. Cramer, 1940, 38 Cal.App.2d 64, 100 P.2d 523 (equitable servitudes created even though the deed contained a re-entry clause).

52. Kroening v. Kroening, 1936, 223 Wis. 113, 269 N.W. 536. *Contra:* Lavely v. Nonenaker, 1931, 212 Cal. 380, 298 P. 976.

53. Statute applied in Bush v. Greer, 1937, 235 Ala. 56, 177 So. 341.

54. Caldwell v. Mullin, 1937, 101 Colo. 113, 71 P.2d 415; Lowman v. Lowman, 1938, 105 Ind.App. 102, 12 N.E.2d 961; Watson v. Gilliam, 1934, 252 Ky. 762, 68 S.W.2d 399. But see Manning v. Street, 1939, 279 Ky. 253, 130 S.W.2d 735, comment, 29 Ky.Law Jr. 235 (1941).

55. Schneider v. Smith, 1940, 189 Ga. 704, 7 S.E.2d 76.

56. Stout v. Wilson, 1940, 199 Ark. 1188, 136 S.W.2d 693; Collins v. McKelvain, 1939, 138 Fla. 463, 189 So. 655.

57. Federal Land Bank v. Luckenbill, 1938, 213 Ind. 616, 13 N.E.2d 531.

58. Shook v. Bergstrasser, 1947, 356 Pa. 167, 51 A.2d 681.

Option to Repurchase Distinguished from a Right of Entry

A provision in a deed may constitute a repurchase option in the grantor rather than a right of entry. In Gange v. Hayes (Ore.),[59] the deed provided: "As a further consideration, it is understood and agreed, that if the (grantee), or its successors or assigns, should at any time or for any reason, cease operation of its lumbering or planing mill industries located on this property for the period of twenty-four consecutive months, the (grantor) at its own option to be exercised, can demand and shall receive a Warranty Deed back from the (grantee), its successors or assigns, for the above described property upon the payment of the original purchase price of Five Hundred Dollars ($500.00), less the annual rental of One Hundred Dollars ($100.00) per year." The court held that this language created a repurchase option in the grantor and not a fee simple subject to a condition subsequent in the grantee. The fact that the grantee obligated itself to execute a deed of reconveyance upon the demand of the grantor is sufficient justification for the conclusion reached. Further, this construction is aided by the fact that the grantor was under an obligation to make a money payment.[60] Since the option could be exercised at any time it was void under the rule against perpetuities.[61]

Equitable Relief against Forfeiture

Equitable relief against forfeiture will be available if the owner of the right of entry has, by words or conduct, waived his right to terminate the estate for breach of the condition.[62] Such relief may also be available if the delay in performing an act was due to unforeseen difficulties of performance.[63] Equity may also prevent the declaration of a forfeiture if the breach of condition involved default in the payment of money if the default was not substantial in nature and was not due to an intentional breach.[64]

FEE SIMPLE SUBJECT TO AN EXECUTORY INTEREST

92. A fee simple may be defeasible because of a provision that upon the happening of a named event ownership is to pass from the grantee to one other than the grantor.

The future interest created in the third party is called an executory interest.

a. Statute of Uses and the Statute of Wills. The creation of an executory interest was made possible by the passage of the Statute of Uses and the Statute of Wills.

b. Failure of an executory interest. If a fee simple determinable is followed by an executory interest the possessory estate terminates automatically upon the happening of the named event. It is not material whether or not the executory interest is void.

If the possessory estate is not of a type that terminates automatically upon the happening of a named event it becomes an estate in fee simple absolute if the executory interest is void.

A fee simple may be defeasible because of a provision in the conveying instrument that upon the happening of a stated event owner-

---

59. 193 Or. 51, 237 P.2d 196 (1951)

60. 4 Rest. Property, § 394, *Comment c.*

61. See Rest. Property, 1948 Supplement, § 394, *Comment f.*

62. Los Angeles & Arizona Land Co. v. Marr, 1921, 187 Cal. 126, 200 P. 1051; Robinson v. Cannon, 1940, 346 Mo. 1126, 145 S.W.2d 146. See note, Reentry Barred by Passage of Time, 13 Univ. of Pitt. Law Rev. 716 (1952).

63. Peek v. Woman's Home Missionary Society, 1922, 304 Ill. 427, 136 N.E. 772, 26 A.L.R. 917, noted in 36 Harv.Law Rev. 758 (1923).

64. Dodsworth v. Dodsworth, 1912, 254 Ill. 49, 98 N.E. 279.

ship is to pass from the grantee to another. For example, in a conveyance "A to B and his heirs, but if C pays B $10,000 then to C and his heirs," the estate created in B is a fee simple subject to an executory interest. The gift to C and his heirs is not a remainder because a remainder cannot be limited after an estate in fee simple. The distinction between executory interests and remainders is discussed under a separate heading.[65]

Statute of Uses and the Statute of Wills

The creation of an executory interest was made possible by the passage of the Statute of Uses[66] and the Statute of Wills.[67] Prior to the passage of these statutes a fee simple subject to an executory interest was not recognized. In those states that have not adopted the Statute of Uses there is express statutory authorization for the creation of executory interests. The characteristics of executory interests are discussed under a separate heading.[68]

Failure of an Executory Interest

The failure of an executory interest may or may not serve to enlarge a possessory estate into a fee simple absolute (an indefeasible estate). If the possessory estate is a fee simple determinable it terminates upon the happening of the named event without reference to the validity or invalidity of an executory interest. For example, in Institution for Savings in Roxbury v. Roxbury Home for Aged Women (Mass.),[69] land was conveyed to the Institution in fee simple, with a provision that if it should cease to exist the land should go to the Roxbury Home for Aged Women. This executory interest was

void because of the rule against perpetuities. The court held that upon the happening of the event the estate vested in the Institution terminated even if the executory interest was void.[70]

If the possessory estate is not of a type that terminates automatically upon the happening of a named event it may be enlarged to a fee simple absolute (an indefeasible estate) upon failure of an executory interest. In Proprietors of the Church in Brattle Square v. Grant (Mass.),[71] land was devised to the Church upon condition that if the land was not improved for use as a minister's residence it was to go to the testatrix's nephew and his heirs. The court held that since the executory interest was void under the rule against perpetuities the Church acquired an estate in fee simple absolute.[72] A right of entry was not created in the estate of the testatrix. It is reasoned that the testatrix probably would not have intended that the estate in the Church should be divested upon the happening of the event unless the executory interest was effective. The prevailing American rule favors the view that the issue is to be resolved according to the "judicially construed" intent of the conveyor.[73] There is a construction preference for the indefeasibility of prior interests.[74]

An executory interest may fail for reasons other than the rule against perpetuities.[75] In

---

65. See infra, § 141.

66. 27 Hen. VIII, c. 10 (1536).

67. 32 Hen. VIII, c. 1 (1540).

68. See infra, § 141.

69. 244 Mass. 583, 139 N.E. 301 (1923).

70. *Contra:* McMahon v. Consistory of Saint Paul's Reformed Church, 1950, 194 Md. 262, 71 A.2d 17.

71. 3 Gray (Mass.) 142 (1855).

72. *Accord:* Beverlin v. First Nat. Bank, 1940, 151 Kan. 307, 98 P.2d 200, 55 A.L.R. 688.

73. See 2 Rest. Property, § 228.

74. See 2 Rest. Property, § 229. A contrary view is expressed in Doe d. Blomfield v. Eyre, 1848, 5 Comm. Bench 713, 136 Eng.Rep. 1058. But see Jackson v. Noble, 1838, 2 Keen. 590, 48 Eng.Rep. 755.

75. For discussion of the rule against perpetuities, see infra, Chapter 36.

McGlothlin v. McElvain (Ill.),[76] testator devised land to his daughter, Rachel, providing that if she should die without leaving lawful issue surviving at the time of her death, the property was to be distributed among testator's other children then surviving. All of Rachel's brothers and sisters predeceased her and she then died without issue. The court held that the property should be distributed according to the terms of Rachel's will. Her estate became indefeasible because no one was entitled to take under the executory interests.[77]

In the case of testamentary dispositions, executory interests may fail because the devisee or legatee was dead at the time the will was executed (a void devise or bequest according to common law rules). If he was alive at the time the will was executed but predeceased the testator there would be a lapsed legacy.[78] A gift may fail because of the fact that a devisee or legatee acted as a witness in the execution of the will or he may contest the will and bring himself within the scope of a forfeiture clause.

CONSTRUCTION PROBLEMS AND ILLEGAL LIMITATIONS AND CONDITIONS

93. **Wherever possible, provisions of a conveying instrument are construed in such a manner as to avoid termination of the estate.**

a. **Type of estate created.** The language of a conveying instrument may be susceptible to the construction that it creates a determinable fee or a fee simple subject to a condition subsequent. The preferred construction is in favor of a fee simple subject to a condition subsequent.

b. **Nature and scope of the event designated.** A rule of strict construction is followed as a means by which to reach the conclusion that the conduct of the owner of a possessory estate did not come within the scope of a condition or limitation.

c. **Impossibility of performance.** Impossibility of performance with respect to the event or condition that is to terminate an estate may operate to excuse performance.

d. **Illegal limitations and conditions.** The termination of an estate cannot be based upon the happening of an event that is illegal or contrary to public policy.

In construing the provisions of an instrument conveying a determinable fee or a fee simple subject to a condition subsequent, an issue may be raised as to the nature and scope of the event that may bring about a termination of the estate. There is a construction-preference in favor of the owner of the possessory estate. This is due to the general attitude against the "forfeiture of estates" even though a true forfeiture is not involved in the case of a determinable fee.

This construction-preference is evidenced in cases where a clause in a conveying instrument is construed to be a *covenant* rather than a limitation or a condition.[79] This construction avoids the termination of an estate and default involves contractual liability. In Behlow v. Southern Pacific R. Co. (Cal.),[80] land was conveyed for railroad purposes only and there was a reverted clause. The deed also provided that "as a further consideration" for the grant the railroad would construct two stations on the land at one of which all trains would stop. The court held that the provision for reverter did

---

76. 407 Ill. 142, 95 N.E.2d 68 (1950), noted in 46 Ill. Law Rev. 776 (1951).

77. *Cf.*: South Norwalk Trust Co. v. St. John, 1917, 92 Conn. 168, 101 A. 961; Kurrie v. Kentucky Trust Co., 1946, 302 Ky. 592, 194 S.W.2d 638.

78. Drummond's Ex'r v. Drummond, 1875, 26 N.J. Eq. 234.

79. See Carruthers v. Spaulding, 1934, 242 App.Div. 412, 275 N.Y.S. 37.

80. 130 Cal. 16, 62 P. 295 (1900).

not apply as to the erection of the stations or as to the stopping of the trains. The words "as a further consideration" are indicative of the fact that the parties contemplated contractual liability only.

Even if a limitation or condition is involved, failure to comply therewith on a temporary basis cannot be used as a ground upon which to terminate the estate.[81] In some cases it is stated that termination must be based upon an intention to abandon the property insofar as the designated use is concerned.[82]

Type of Estate Created

The language of a conveying instrument may be susceptible to the construction that it creates a determinable fee or to the construction that it creates a fee simple subject to a condition subsequent. That is the case, for example, in a conveyance "A to B and his heirs upon condition that the land is used for church purposes. In the event that it is not used for this purpose the estate is to terminate and revert to A and his heirs."

There is an argument that the ambiguity should be resolved in favor of the creation of a determinable fee because a forfeiture is not involved in the termination of such an estate.[83] However, upon the happening of the event the estate may terminate or be terminated whether it is a determinable fee or a fee simple subject to a condition subsequent. Whether or not a technical forfeiture is involved is not of great importance.

Preference should be given to the construction that the instrument resulted in the creation of a fee simple subject to a condition

subsequent.[84] A rule of strict construction against the grantor—a recognized rule of construction—justifies this conclusion. Since this estate does not terminate automatically upon the happening of the event it is a more desirable estate from the possessor's point of view than a determinable fee, an estate that does terminate automatically and without the necessity of re-entry. A provision for reverter is not inconsistent with the existence of a fee simple subject to a condition subsequent.[85]

Nature and Scope of the Event Designated

In Regular Predestinarian Baptist Church of Pleasant Grove v. Parker (Ill.),[86] land was conveyed "so long as" it was used for church purposes. Although using the land for church purposes the grantee executed an oil and gas lease. The court held that this *additional use* was not inconsistent with the terms of the deed. The case is distinguished from one where the land is to be used *exclusively for church purposes*.[87]

In Flajole v. Gallaher (Mich.),[88] a deed provided: "It is understood that the land herein described is to be used for the erection of a kiln for drying chicory roots, and if not used for said purpose, then the title to said land shall revert to said first party." The grantee built the kiln shortly after the conveyance. Some thirty-four years thereafter the kiln was accidentally destroyed by fire and was not rebuilt. Plaintiff, claiming un-

---

81. See Clark v. Jones, 1943, 173 Or. 106, 144 P.2d 498.

82. See, for example, Locke v. Union Graded School District No. 6, 1939, 185 Okl. 471, 94 P.2d 547.

83. Richardson v. Holman, 1948, 160 Fla. 65, 33 So. 2d 641.

84. Storke v. Penn Mut. Life Ins., Co. 1945, 390 Ill. 619, 61 N.E.2d 552. *Cf.*: Avery v. Consumers Power Co., 1934, 265 Mich. 696, 253 N.W. 189.

85. Dyer v. Siano, 1937, 298 Mass. 537, 11 N.E.2d 451.

86. 373 Ill. 607, 27 N.E.2d 522, 137 A.L.R. 635 (1940).

87. Union Missionary Baptist Church v. Fyke, 1937, 179 Okl. 102, 64 P.2d 1203 (a case where termination of the estate was not claimed).

88. 354 Mich. 606, 93 N.W.2d 249 (1958).

der the original grantor, brought an action in ejectment to recover possession of the land claiming termination of the estate because the owner of the possessory estate did not intend to rebuild the kiln. Relief was denied upon the ground that the condition was fulfilled when the original grantee erected the kiln. The case differs from one where the condition is to erect *and maintain* a structure.[89]

It has been noted that in practically all of the American states statutes have been passed abolishing or modifying the common law rule requiring words of inheritance for the conveyance of an estate in fee. Even if words of inheritance are not necessary, there is authority for the view that if a conveyance is not made to the grantee "and his heirs," the duration of the limitation or condition may be limited to the lifetime of the grantee.[90]

Impossibility of Performance

Usually, the termination of an estate will be denied if there is impossibility of performance with respect to the event or condition involved and the owner of the possessory estate is without fault.[91] The impossibility may arise by operation of law.[92] It is not assumed that the conveyor of the estate would have intended the estate to terminate under such circumstances.

Illegal Limitations and Conditions

The termination of an estate cannot be based upon the happening of an event that is illegal or contrary to public policy. The public policy issue is most frequently presented in cases involving restraints upon alienation. Such cases are discussed under a separate heading.[93] A public policy issue may also arise in the following situations.

First: Limitations and conditions are void to the extent that they purport to restrain the proper exercise of governmental authority. For example, in Wills v. City of Los Angeles (Cal.),[94] plaintiff conveyed land to defendant City for street purposes but subject to the express condition against use of the land for the operation of streetcars. The City granted a franchise for such purpose and plaintiff claimed that such use justified his termination of the estate. This claim was denied. Since the land was conveyed for street purposes, a condition restricting its use for a proper street purpose was contrary to public policy and void.

Second: The general rule is that a restriction placing a *total* restraint upon marriage is contrary to public policy and void.[95] Some decisions support the rule that while a condition in restraint of marriage is void, a valid gift may be made until the donee remarries.[96] It is considered that such a *limitation* is not designed to prohibit marriage.[97] This is the statutory rule in some

---

89. See, for example, Rosecrans v. Pacific Electric Ry. Co., 1943, 21 Cal.2d 602, 134 P.2d 245 (to erect and maintain a railroad).

90. See Williams, Restrictions on the Use of Land, 27 Tex.Law Rev. 158, 169 (1948).

91. Keyser v. Calvary Brethren Church, 1949, 192 Md. 520, 64 A.2d 748; True v. Cook, 1948, 95 N.H. 198, 60 A.2d 138.

92. Woodville v. United States, 10 Cir. 1946, 152 F. 2d 735, certiorari denied 328 U.S. 842, 66 S.Ct. 1021, 90 L.Ed. 1617.

93. See infra, Chapter 37.

94. 209 Cal. 448, 287 P. 962, 69 A.L.R. 1044.

95. Sullivan v. Garesche, 1919, 229 Mo. 496, 129 S.W. 949. *Cf.:* Randall v. Marble, 1879, 69 Me. 310.

96. See, for example, Harbin v. Judd, 1960, 47 Tenn. App. 604, 340 S.W.2d 935.

97. For criticism of a distinction made in this situation between a condition and a limitation, see Browder, Jr., Conditions and Limitations in Restraint of Marriage, 39 Mich.Law Rev. 1288, 1313 (1941).

states.[98]

The preferred view is that partial restraints upon marriage are valid if they are reasonable, such as in a case where the restraint is limited to the minority of the subject.[99] So also, the restraint may prohibit marriage to a particular person,[1] or to a person of a particular religious faith.[2] There is also authority for the view that there may be a restraint against remarriage if a gift is made by one spouse to the other.[3]

If an otherwise valid restraint upon marriage is embodied in a will, some authorities hold that it is void unless there is a *gift over* upon breach of the condition. It is reasoned that in the absence of a gift over the testator did not intend to make a conditional gift. His purpose was merely to frighten the donee into compliance with the condition (*in terrorem doctrine*).[4]

Third: The prevailing rule is that valid restraints may be imposed respecting religious training and practices. Constitutional guarantees as to religious belief are limitations on the powers of government and do not prohibit restraints imposed by individuals.[5]

---

98. See, for example, West's Ann.Cal.Civ.Code, § 710.

99. Shackelford v. Hall, 1857, 19 Ill. 212.

1. Turner v. Evans, 1919, 134 Md. 238, 106 A. 617. *Cf.:* In re Estate of Duffill, 1919, 180 Cal. 748, 183 P. 337.

2. Gordon v. Gordon, 1955, 332 Mass. 197, 124 N.E.2d 228; United States Nat. Bank of Portland v. Snodgrass, 1954, 202 Or. 530, 275 P.2d 860, 50 A.L.R.2d 725. But see Maddox v. Maddox's Adm'r, 1854, 52 Va. (11 Grat.) 804, 814.

3. Knight v. Mahoney, 1890, 152 Mass. 523, 25 N.E. 971, 9 L.R.A. 573. But see Estate of Scott, 1915, 170 Cal. 65, 148 P. 221.

4. See Moskowitz v. Federman, 1943, 72 Ohio App. 149, 51 N.E.2d 48.

5. Delaware Trust Co. v. Fitzmaurice, 1943, 27 Del. Ch. 101, 31 A.2d 383, modified in part Crumlish v. Delaware Trust Co., 27 Del.Ch. 374, 38 A.2d 463 (1944); In re Kempf's Will, 1937, 252 App.Div. 28, 297 N.Y.S. 307, affirmed 278 N.Y. 613, 16 N.E.2d 123 (condition precedent). But see Drace v. Klinedinst, 1922, 275 Pa. 266, 118 A. 907, 25 A.L.R. 1520, noted in 26 Harv.Law Rev. 765 (1923).

C. CONCURRENT OWNERSHIP

CHAPTER 18

COMMON LAW TYPES OF CONCURRENT OWNERSHIP

JOINT TENANCY

94. Each joint tenant is considered to be the owner of the whole estate and also of an undivided part *(per my et per tout)*. This is brought about by the fact that there is unity in ownership with respect to time, title, interest and possession. The result is that upon the death of one joint tenant the surviving joint tenant or tenants continue as owners of the whole estate.

Statutes usually provide that the creation of a joint tenancy requires an express declaration that the parties are to take "as joint tenants."

   a. **Creation of a joint tenancy.** In the absence of statute, the owner of property cannot create a joint tenancy by a purported conveyance to himself and another or others.

   b. **Survival bank accounts.** Statutes frequently provide that money deposited in a bank in the names of two or more persons is payable to the survivor. Usually such deposits do not create a joint tenancy according to common law rules.

   c. **Fire insurance.** One joint tenant is entitled to insure joint-tenancy property and, in the absence of special contract, other joint tenants are not entitled to share in the proceeds derived from such insurance.

   d. **Tracing.** A sale of joint-tenancy property terminates the tenancy unless there is an express provision in the contract of sale that the consideration received is also to be held in joint tenancy.

   e. **Termination of a joint tenancy.** A joint tenancy may be terminated by the death of a joint tenant, by agreement of the parties, by the conveyance of an undivided interest, by a valid contract to convey an undivided interest, by execution levied against the interest of a joint tenant and by partition.

With exceptions to be noted, the existence of a joint tenancy depends upon proof of the fact that the parties acquired ownership at the same time (unity of time), by the same conveying instrument (unity of title), have equal interests (unity of interest) and an equal right to possession. In the case of land there must be compliance with provisions of the Statute of Frauds. Statutes in some states require a writing in the case of personal property.[1]

Concurrent ownership by an individual and a corporation cannot properly be classified as a joint tenancy because the interests are not equal.[2] The lifetime of the individual is neither fixed nor indefinite, while that of a corporation is either fixed or indefinite.

---

[1] See, for example, West's Ann.Cal.Civ.Code, § 683.

[2] American Bible Society v. Mortgage Guarantee Co., 1932, 217 Cal. 9, 17 P.2d 105 *(dictum)*. See De Witt v. San Francisco, 1852, 2 Cal. 289 (two corporations cannot hold beneficially as joint tenants).

Therefore, the interest in the right of survivorship is not equal.

At common law, a conveyance to two or more persons may result in the creation of a joint tenancy unless there is expression of a contrary intent.[3] The reason for this rule is purely historical.[4] Each joint tenant is considered to be the owner of the whole estate and also of an undivided part *(per my et per tout)*. Because of his ownership of the "whole estate" a joint tenant remains the owner of the whole estate when the interest of another joint tenant is released because of his death. Inaccurately, this is described as a right of survivorship. This characteristic of survivorship tended to keep land under a single ownership and thus facilitated the enforcement of feudal dues and incidents.

Because of the characteristic of survivorship joint tenancies have never been looked upon with favor in the United States. It is thought that upon the death of an owner his property should pass to his own estate and not to a surviving joint tenant. It is also thought that in many cases persons acquiring property as concurrent owners are not fully informed as to the right of survivorship.

Statutory rules relating to the creation of joint tenancies are to be found in practically all of the states. A usual provision is that a conveyance or transfer of property to two or more owners results in a tenancy in common "unless expressly declared to be a joint tenancy." [5] A few statutes require an express statement as to joint tenancy and also a statement that the parties are not to take as tenants in common ("to B and C as

joint tenants and not as tenants in common").[6] Other statutes either abolish joint tenancies or abolish the characteristic of survivorship.[7] This form of concurrent ownership may not be recognized in the case of personal property.[8] Under the Uniform Stock Transfer Act, the validity of joint tenancy ownership of corporate stock is determined by the law of the domicile of the owner.[9]

If for any reason a joint tenancy is not created, it does not follow that a right of survivorship is not involved. In practically all of the states it is recognized that a conveyance may be made to two or more persons for life or absolutely, with a remainder or executory interest to the survivor.[10] Such an arrangement differs from a joint tenancy in at least one important respect. A joint tenancy may be terminated by one or more of the joint tenants, a matter discussed under a

---

3. 2 Bl.Comm. 180.

4. 2 Pollock & Maitland, History of English Law (2nd ed.) p. 20.

5. But see N.J.S.A. 46:2D–1, declaring that a mortgage acquired by husband and wife is presumably held in joint tenancy. Construed in Brodzinsky v. Pulek, 1962, 75 N.J.Super. 40, 182 A.2d 149.

6. See Cookman v. Silliman, 1938, 22 Del.Ch. 303, 2 A.2d 166.

7. See Houghton v. Brantingham, 1913, 86 Conn. 630, 86 A. 664; Sergeant v. Steinberger, 1826, 2 Ohio 305; Stout v. Van Zante, 1923, 109 Or. 430, 220 P. 414 (recognized only as to property held by trustees and executors).

8. See, for example, Hart v. Hart, 1918, 201 Mich. 207, 167 N.W. 337.

9. Bellinger v. West Coast Telephone Co., 1959, 54 Wash.2d 576, 343 P.2d 189.

10. Equitable Loan & Security Co. v. Waring, 1903, 117 Ga. 599, 44 S.E. 320; Malone v. Sullivan & Williams, 1932, 136 Kan. 193, 14 P.2d 647, 85 A.L.R. 275; Lober v. Dorgan, 1921, 215 Mich. 62, 183 N.W. 942 (personal property); Anson v. Murphy, 1948, 149 Neb. 716, 32 N.W.2d 271; Burns v. Nolette, 1929, 83 N.H. 489, 144 A. 848, 67 A.L.R. 1051 (bank account); Redemptorist Fathers v. Lawler, 1903, 205 Pa. 24, 54 A. 487; Ball v. Deas, 1848, 2 Strob. Eq. (S.C.) 24 (where common law joint tenancy created by will and one of tenants died before testator, the survivor was entitled to take all); McLeroy v. McLeroy, 1931, 163 Tenn. 124, 40 S.W.2d 1027; Winchester v. Wells, 5 Cir. 1959, 265 F.2d 405; Edwards v. Comm. of Internal Revenue, 10 Cir. 1939, 102 F.2d 757.

separate heading. However, in the usual situation a remainder or executory interest to a survivor is indestructible.

In some cases a construction problem is involved as to whether a conveyance resulted in the creation of a joint tenancy or whether survivorship-rights were based upon a remainder or executory interest. In other cases an issue is raised as to whether or not appropriate words were used to create a joint tenancy in compliance with the terms of a statute. Some of the construction problems are as follows:

First: In Hunter v. Hunter (Mo.),[11] testatrix devised property to her mother B and her sister C "as joint tenants with the right of survivorship." By statute, all devises of land were presumed to be in fee simple, even though words of inheritance were not used, unless there were gifts over in fee simple or words indicating that the testator intended to create only life estates. Here the testatrix did not use words of inheritance. B conveyed her undivided interest in the property to the plaintiff. After B's death C claimed ownership of the property under the survivorship-clause. Plaintiff claimed that B and C acquired the property as joint tenants and that the conveyance by B resulted in the creation of a tenancy in common.[12]

The court held in favor of C. While the use of words of inheritance was not essential to devise an estate in fee simple, failure to use such words justified the conclusion that the testatrix intended to create a joint tenancy only for life. Thus, the estate created in the survivor was a remainder.[13]

11. 320 S.W.2d 529, 69 A.L.R.2d 1048 (1959).

12. McLeroy v. McLeroy, 1931, 163 Tenn. 124, 40 S.W.2d 1027; Weber v. Nedin, 1933, 210 Wis. 39, 242 N.W. 487, 246 N.W. 307.

13. *Accord:* Jones v. Snyder, 1922, 218 Mich. 446, 188 N.W. 505; Hannon v. Christopher, 1881, 34 N.J.

Second: A conveyance or transfer to two or more persons "jointly" is not a clear expression of an intent to create a joint tenancy.[14] Such an expression is not inconsistent with the creation of a tenancy in common. However, there is authority for the view that the use of such a word creates an ambiguity justifying the admission of evidence bearing upon the conveyor's intent as shown by surrounding circumstances. In that event, proof of intent is judged by the law of the place where the instrument was executed even though it relates to land located in another state.[15]

Third: A specific intent to create a joint tenancy is not evidenced by the fact that a note or other obligation is made payable "to B or to C."[16]

Creation of a Joint Tenancy

A joint tenancy cannot be created by a conveyance or transfer wherein the grantor names himself and another or others as joint tenants.[17] Since a grantor cannot convey to himself his title cannot properly be said to have been acquired simultaneously

Eq. 459; In re Hutchinson's Estate, 1929, 120 Ohio St. 542, 166 N.E. 687. See Johnson v. Woodard, Mo.App.1962, 356 S.W.2d 526; Rowland v. Rowland, 1885, 93 N.C. 214 (tenancy in common in fee with executory interest).

14. Albright v. Winey, 1939, 226 Iowa 222, 284 N.W. 86, noted in 37 Mich.Law Rev. 1318 (1939). *Contra:* Donahue v. Winey, 1939, 226 Iowa 222, 284 N.W. 86. See State ex rel. Ashauer v. Hostetter, 1939, 344 Mo. 665, 127 S.W.2d 697, noted in 5 Mo.Law Rev. 114 (1940). *Cf.:* In re Lewis, [1942] Ch. 424, 111 L.J.Ch. 256, noted in 59 Law Quarterly Rev. 21 (1943).

15. Taylor v. Taylor, 1945, 310 Mich. 541, 17 N.W.2d 745, 157 A.L.R. 559.

16. Konecny v. von Gunten, 1963, 151 Colo. 376, 379 P.2d 158 (notes); Engelbrecht v. Engelbrecht, 1926, 323 Ill. 208, 153 N.E. 827 (certificate of deposit).

17. Strout, Adm'r v. Burgess, 1949, 144 Me. 263, 68 A.2d 241, 12 A.L.R.2d 939.

with that of the other grantee or grantees, nor could the titles derive from one instrument. Thus, a joint tenancy does not result because there is a lack of the unities of time and title. Accordingly, a tenancy in common results. Statutes in some states specifically provide that a joint tenancy may result from such a transaction [18] and this conclusion has been reached in a number of states without the aid of statutes.[19]

Even if a statute does provide that a joint tenancy may be created by a conveyance made by one spouse to himself and the other spouse, an intention to accomplish this purpose must be shown. For example, that intention is not shown by the mere fact that a husband, the sole owner of land, conveys the land to a third party and provides that the purchase price is to be paid to the husband and wife "as vendors." It may be that the sole purpose of this arrangement was to obtain a release of the wife's dower right in the land sold.[20]

Survival Bank Accounts

Usually, the balance credited to a joint and survival bank account is awarded to the survivor if the form of the account complies with the technical requirements of the local joint-account statute.[21] This is also true with respect to United States Savings Bonds that are issued according to federal regulations. Technically, these arrangements do not involve joint tenancies. However, such accounts are frequently referred to as joint tenancy accounts because of the fact that the survivor is entitled to the proceeds. The problems involved are usually considered in the subject of personal property under the heading of gifts.

Fire Insurance

In Russell v. Williams (Cal.),[22] B and C were the owners of property as joint tenants. B insured the property against loss by fire and after a fire the amount due under the policy was paid to B. After his death C filed a claim against B's estate for the amount involved claiming that the money was "substituted for the property" and that he was entitled thereto by right of survivorship. In denying this claim it is pointed out that a policy of fire insurance does not insure the property. It is a personal contract indemnifying the insured against loss resulting from the destruction of or damage to his interest in that property. In the absence of special contract, the proceeds of a fire policy are not a substitute for the property the loss of which is the subject of indemnity.[23]

Tracing

According to one view, a sale of joint-tenancy property terminates the tenancy un-

---

18. See, for example, West's Ann.Cal.Civ.Code, § 683; Illinois, Joint Rights and Obligations Act, Ill.Rev. Stat.1963, ch. 76, § 2, as amended; Mass.Gen.Laws Ann. ch. 184, § 8; Neb.R.S.1943, § 76–118; N.J.S.A. 46:3–17.1 (R.S. 46:3–17, N.J.S.A.); Wis.Stats.Ann. § 230.45(3).

19. See, for example, Switzer v. Pratt, 1946, 237 Iowa 788, 23 N.W.2d 837; Therrien v. Therrien, 1946, 94 N.H. 66, 46 A.2d 538, 166 A.L.R. 1023; In re Horler's Estate, 1917, 180 App.Div. 608, 168 N.Y.S. 221; Lafayette v. Brinham, 1949, 363 Pa. 360, 69 A.2d 130.

20. Hendricks v. Wolf, 1937, 279 Mich. 598, 273 N.W. 282; In re Fischer's Estate, 1964, 22 Wis.2d 637, 126 N.W.2d 596. Cf.: Cantor v. Palmer, Fla.App. 1964, 163 So.2d 508 (lease of land owned by husband that described lessors as husband and wife

did not create a tenancy by the entirety in unaccrued rent).

21. In re Fenstermaker's Estate, 1964, 413 Pa. 645, 198 A.2d 857. Cf.: Northwestern Nat. Bank of Sioux Falls v. Daniel, 1964, 80 S.D. 528, 127 N.W.2d 714 (certificates of deposit).

22. 58 Cal.2d 487, 24 Cal.Rptr. 859, 374 P.2d 827 (1962).

23. Contra: Rock County Savings & Trust Co. v. London Assur. Co., 1962, 17 Wis.2d 618, 117 N.W.2d 676.

less there is an express provision that the consideration received is also to be held in joint tenancy.[24] This conclusion is consistent with the view that joint tenancies are not looked upon with favor. It also avoids complicated problems that might otherwise arise in connection with tracing the proceeds through various transmutations. However, according to another view, the joint tenancy exists as to the proceeds derived from the sale.[25] It is reasoned that if the parties intended a joint tenancy as to the property conveyed they intended a joint tenancy as to the proceeds derived from the sale. The tracing problem is minimized by the fact that evidence may show termination of the joint tenancy by course of conduct. For example, if there is a division of the proceeds derived from the sale there is sufficient proof of an intent to terminate the tenancy.

In Illinois Public Aid Commission v. Stille (Ill.),[26] the court takes the position that a sale of joint-tenancy property terminates the tenancy if the purchase price is paid in full. However, the court supports the rule that the joint tenancy continues with respect to any part of the unpaid purchase price.[27] It is stated that this conclusion avoids complications that might arise in connection with the tracing situation.

Termination of a Joint Tenancy

The death of an owner results in the termination of a joint tenancy as to the released-share. However, this result may not follow if the death resulted from the wrongful act of the surviving joint tenant. For example, in the Wisconsin case of In re King's Estate,[28] husband and wife were joint tenants. The husband murdered his wife and then committed suicide. The court held that the wife's estate was entitled to the joint tenancy property. The wrongful act of the husband prevented him from asserting the right of survivorship. Since he could not deprive the wife of her right to hold the property as a joint tenant because of his wrongful act, the right remained and became operative upon the death of the husband. The wife's position as a joint tenant continued in her administrator and heirs at law. Upon the death of the husband the right of survivorship could be asserted in behalf of her estate. In some cases the same result is reached on the theory that the husband's wrongful act resulted in the creation of a constructive trust.[29] Additional termination problems are discussed in the following paragraphs.

First: A joint tenant does not have an estate that can be devised or bequeathed.[30] A right of testamentary disposition is not a right incident to the estate or interest. Because of the right of survivorship, claims of dower or curtesy do not attach in the case of

---

24. In re Baker's Estate, 1956, 247 Iowa 1380, 78 N.W.2d 863; Buford v. Dahlke, 1954, 158 Neb. 39, 62 N.W.2d 252. *Cf.*: In re Ogier's Estate, 1963, 175 Neb. 883, 125 N.W.2d 68 (joint tenancy terminated to the extent that funds are withdrawn from a joint bank account).

25. See Fish v. Security-First Nat. Bank, 1948, 31 Cal.2d 378, 189 P.2d 10.

26. 14 Ill.2d 344, 153 N.E.2d 59 (1958).

27. See Kent v. O'Neil, Fla.1951, 53 So.2d 779; Watson v. Watson, 1955, 5 Ill.2d 526, 126 N.E.2d 220; Childs v. Childs, 1936, 293 Mass. 67, 199 N.E. 383; Simon v. Chartier, 1947, 250 Wis. 642, 27 N.W.2d 752.

28. 261 Wis. 266, 52 N.W.2d 885 (1952).

29. Vesey v. Vesey, 1952, 237 Minn. 295, 54 N.W.2d 385, 32 A.L.R.2d 1090; Estate of Cox, 1963, 141 Mont. 583, 380 P.2d 584.

30. Estate of Moy, 1963, 217 Cal.App.2d 24, 31 Cal. Rptr. 374; Wilkins v. Young, 1895, 144 Ind. 1, 41 N.E. 68; Bassler v. Rewodlinski, 1906, 130 Wis. 26, 109 N.W. 1032. See Gould v. Kemp, [1834] 2 Myl. & K. 304, 39 Eng.Rep. 959.

joint tenancy property.[31] The surviving joint tenant acquired his interest at the time the estate was created and not at the time of the death of a joint tenant.

Second: A joint tenancy may be terminated by mutual agreement of the owners. The agreement need not be in writing and may be express or implied.[32] Termination is a necessary result if the agreement destroys one of the essential unities that go to make up this form of concurrent ownership.[33] It is also a necessary result if the agreement destroys the right of survivorship, an essential characteristic of the estate.[34]

Third: A joint tenancy will survive an agreement regulating possessory rights as between the joint tenants. For example, if B and C are joint tenants they remain joint tenants in spite of an agreement that gives either B or C a right to the exclusive possession of the property either for life or a period less than life.[35] This is also the rule even if the contract relating to possession is contemporaneous with the creation of the joint tenancy.[36]

Some authorities take the position that an agreement restricting possessory rights is inconsistent with a joint tenancy because such a

tenancy requires unity of possession.[37] But the possessory right of a joint tenant is subject to his control by contract or otherwise to the extent that this does not interfere with the rights of the other joint tenants.

Fourth: A joint tenant has the power and right to make an *inter vivos* conveyance of his undivided interest in the property. This severs the conveyed interest from the joint tenancy.[38] The unities of time and title are lacking as between the grantee of this undivided interest and the other joint tenant or tenants. Accordingly, the grantee becomes a tenant in common even though a joint tenancy continues as to the other shares. If one of three or more joint tenants conveys his interest to a third person, the latter becomes a tenant in common instead of a joint tenant with the others, although the others remain joint tenants between themselves.[39] This result follows even if the conveyance is made to the other joint tenants. The joint tenancy is terminated only as to the part conveyed. The others still have unity of interest as to property covered in the original conveyance.[40]

Fifth: A joint tenant has the power and right to enter into a contract looking to the transfer or conveyance of his undivided interest in the property. A valid contract to transfer or convey results in a severance of the interest from the joint tenancy because it disrupts the "unity of interest." [41]

There is a difference of opinion as to whether or not a severance results if all of the joint tenants enter into a contract to transfer

---

31. See Babbitt v. Day, 1886, 41 N.J.Eq. 392, 5 A. 275.

32. See Brodzinsky v. Pulek, 1962, 75 N.J.Super. 40, 182 A.2d 149.

33. Carson v. Ellis, 1960, 186 Kan. 112, 348 P.2d 807 (unity of possession).

34. McDonald v. Morley, 1940, 15 Cal.2d 409, 101 P.2d 690, 129 A.L.R. 810; Greiger v. Pye, 1941, 210 Minn. 71, 297 N.W. 173 (*dictum*); In re Wilford's Estate, 1879, L.R.Ch.D. 267.

35. Hammond v. McArthur, 1947, 30 Cal.2d 512, 183 P.2d 1.

36. Toth v. Crawford, 1963, 212 Cal.App.2d 827, 28 Cal.Rptr. 343.

37. See Greiger v. Pye, 1941, 210 Minn. 71, 297 N.W. 173.

38. Shackelton v. Sherrard, Okl.1963, 385 P.2d 898.

39. Hammond v. McArthur, 1947, 30 Cal.2d 512, 183 P.2d 1 (*dictum*).

40. Jackson v. O'Connell, 1961, 23 Ill.2d 52, 177 N.E.2d 194.

41. In re Hewett, [1894] 1 Ch.Div. 362.

or convey the property. According to one view such a severance does result. It is reasoned that it "must be a natural conclusion if there is a severance where one of two joint tenants conveys an interest in property held in joint tenancy the same result must be reached where both joint tenants enter into a contract for the conveyance of all their interest even though the vendors retain legal title to the realty as security." [42]

Sixth: A joint tenant has the power and the right to execute a lease of his undivided interest. The lessee acquires the interest subject to the rights of the other joint tenants.

It may be suggested that the execution of such a lease terminates the joint tenancy to the extent of the lessor's interest.[43] In support of this contention it may be said that the execution of such a lease destroys the unity of possession, a necessary element of a joint tenancy. However, the unity of possession is not destroyed. The lessor is exercising his possessory right in the property through the lessee. If the lessor dies during the continuance of the lease the surviving joint tenant or tenants are entitled to the released interest subject to the rights of the lessee.

Seventh: According to the common law rule, a mortgage results in a transfer of ownership to the mortgagee (the title theory of a mortgage). Applying this rule, a mortgage of joint-tenancy property, given by one of the joint tenants, results in a termination of the joint tenancy because it terminates the unity of title as well as the unity of interest.[44]

In many states it is considered that a mortgage does not result in a transfer of ownership. It merely creates a lien in the mortgagee (the lien theory of a mortgage). Accordingly, the mortgage does not terminate a joint tenancy. If the lien is not satisfied during the lifetime of the debtor the surviving joint tenant will take free from the obligation.[45]

Eighth: The undivided interest of a joint tenant is subject to the claims of his creditors. However, a judgment lien cannot be asserted against a surviving joint tenant.[46] To satisfy his claim, a creditor must levy execution during the lifetime of the debtor. If this is not done the surviving joint tenant is entitled to the property free from the creditor's claim.[47]

TENANCY BY THE ENTIRETY

95. **A tenancy by the entirety is a form of concurrent ownership based upon the common law concept of unity of husband and wife.**

    a. **Personal property. The prevailing rule is that a tenancy by the entirety may exist with respect to personal property.**

    b. **Creation of a tenancy by the entirety. Unless a contrary intention is expressed, a conveyance to parties who are husband and wife creates a tenancy by the entirety. This is true even if they are to take "jointly." The preferred view is that one spouse cannot create a tenancy by the entirety by conveying property to himself and the other spouse.**

    c. **Management. The enactment of a Married Women's Act confers upon a married woman equal rights with her husband in**

---

42. In re Baker's Estate, 1956, 247 Iowa 1380, 78 N.W.2d 863, 867, 64 A.L.R.2d 902. See also, Buford v. Dahlke, 1954, 158 Neb. 39, 62 N.W.2d 252, 256.

43. See Clerk v. Clerk, [1694] 2 Vern. 323, 23 Eng. Rep. 809.

44. See Lawler v. Byrne, 1911, 252 Ill. 194, 196, 96 N.E. 892.

45. County of Fresno v. Kahn, 1962, 207 Cal.App.2d 213, 24 Cal.Rptr. 394. See also, Hamel v. Gootkin, 1962, 202 Cal.App.2d 27, 20 Cal.Rptr. 372 (deed of trust).

46. Musa v. Segelke & Kohlhaus Co., 1937, 224 Wis. 432, 272 N.W. 657, 111 A.L.R. 168.

47. Wood v. Logue, 1914, 167 Iowa 436, 149 N.W. 613.

connection with the management of property held as tenants by the entirety.

d. **Creditors.** The common law rule is that a husband has a right to possession and management of property held as tenants by the entirety. His creditors may satisfy their claims by attaching that interest. The claims may also be satisfied out of the property if the husband survives the wife. Conflicting views are followed in the various states regarding the claims of creditors.

e. **Termination.** A tenancy by the entirety may be terminated by voluntary partition. It is terminated by operation of law in case of divorce or the death of either spouse.

A tenancy by the entirety is a common law form of concurrent ownership that can exist only as between husband and wife. This "unity of person" is required in addition to the unities of time, title, interest and possession that are required in the case of a joint tenancy. As in the case of a joint tenancy, upon the death of one spouse ownership continues in the surviving spouse, a characteristic usually described as a "right of survivorship." Unlike a joint tenancy, a tenancy by the entirety is not subject to partition except by operation of law or by mutual consent.

The rule against involuntary partition results from the fact that each spouse is considered to be the owner of the whole estate. Ownership is by the whole and not by the part (*per tout et non per my*).

In many states tenancies by the entirety are not recognized. In some states it is held that this form of concurrent ownership is not consistent with local conditions and, for that reason, not valid according to the "adopted" common law.[48] In other states statutes have been enacted that enumerate the various

forms of concurrent ownership and they omit mention of tenancies by the entireties.[49] In still other states it is held that the adoption of a Married Women's Act necessarily results in the abolition of tenancies by the entirety. It is reasoned that one of the characteristics of such a tenancy is the existence of managerial rights in the husband. An act that confers an equal right of management upon the wife makes impossible the existence of the tenancy.

The preferred view is that the existence of a tenancy by the entirety is not repugnant to the provisions of a Married Women's Act.[50] Managerial rights of the husband are referable to marital property rights and not to the type of concurrent ownership that may be involved. Management by the husband is not an essential characteristic of a tenancy by the entirety.

In a few states a tenancy by the entirety is viewed as a tenancy in common with an indestructible right of survivorship. According to this view, either the husband or the wife may convey his or her interest to a third party who thereby becomes a tenant in common. The estate is subject to defeasance if the grantor fails to survive the other spouse.[51]

Personal Property

The early common law rule that a husband had management and control of his wife's personal property led to the conclusion that a tenancy by the entirety could not exist with respect to personal property. The power of the husband to dispose of the property by

---

48. Whittlesey v. Fuller, 1836, 11 Conn. 337; Kerner v. McDonald, 1900, 60 Neb. 663, 84 N.W. 92; Farmers' & Merchants' Nat. Bank v. Wallace, 1887, 45 Ohio St. 152, 12 N.E. 439.

49. See, for example, Swan v. Walden, 1909, 156 Cal. 195, 103 P. 931; Wilson v. Wilson, 1890, 43 Minn. 398, 45 N.W. 710.

50. See, for example, Bloomfield v. Brown, 1942, 67 R.I. 452, 25 A.2d 354.

51. Finnegan v. Humes, 1937, 252 App.Div. 385, 299 N.Y.S. 501.

unilateral act was inconsistent with this type of cotenancy with its right of survivorship.

Modern law does not sanction the husband's marital property rights as those rights existed at common law. Accordingly, there is no theoretical reason why a tenancy by the entirety may not be created in personal property and a majority of the decisions support this conclusion.[52] Accordingly, the rents, issue and profits of property held as tenants by the entirety follows the same classification.[53] So also, if property held as tenants by the entirety is sold the proceeds derived from the sale is also held as tenants by the entirety.[54]

Even in a jurisdiction that denies the existence of a tenancy by the entirety in personal property, there is authority supporting the view that an executory contract to sell land held as tenants by the entirety does not result in an equitable conversion. According-

ly, the interests under such a contract are held as tenants by the entirety.[55]

Creation of a Tenancy by the Entirety

If a conveyance or transfer is made to a husband and wife "as joint tenants," there is a clear expression of intent as to the form of concurrent ownership. A joint tenancy should be the result if that form of concurrent ownership is recognized in the particular jurisdiction.[56]

However, there is substantial authority for the view that husband and wife acquire title as tenants by the entirety.[57] This conclusion indicates that husband and wife cannot own property as joint tenants. As aptly pointed out in Witzel v. Witzel (Wyo.),[58] "most cases apparently favorable (to this view) are from jurisdictions which have either ignored joint tenancies and survivorship as an incident to joint tenancies, abolished joint tenancies, modified the same, or have qualified the presumption that a conveyance to husband and wife creates an estate by the entirety by limiting that presumption to instances where there is nothing more in the deed or devise which indicates a contrary intention." After a careful review of the authorities the court held that the conveyance created a joint

---

52. Rauhut v. Reinhart, 1935, 22 Del.Ch. 431, 180 A. 913; M.Lit, Inc. v. Berger, 1961, 225 Md. 241, 170 A.2d 303; Childs v. Childs, 1935, 293 Mass. 67, 199 N.E. 383; Scholten v. Scholten, 1927, 238 Mich. 679, 214 N.W. 320; Madden v. Gosztonyi Sav. & Trust Co., 1938, 331 Pa. 476, 200 A. 624, 117 A.L.R. 904; Campbell v. Campbell, 1934, 167 Tenn. 77, 66 S.W.2d 990; Oliver v. Givens, 1963, 204 Va. 123, 129 S.E.2d 661. *Contra:* Brown v. Havens, 1952, 17 N.J.Super. 235, 85 A.2d 812 (leasehold estate); In re Stebbins' Estate, 1925, 125 Misc. 150, 210 N. Y.S. 424; Hawthorne v. Hawthorne, 1963, 13 N.Y.2d 82, 242 N.Y.S.2d 50, 192 N.E.2d 20 (proceeds derived from insurance against fire on property held as tenants by the entirety). Wilson v. Ervin, 1947, 227 N.C. 396, 42 S.E.2d 468; Stout v. Van Zante, 1923, 109 Or. 430, 219 P. 804, 220 P. 414.

53. Brandt v. Hershey, 1962, 198 Pa.Super. 539, 182 A.2d 219; Ward Terry and Co. v. Hensen, 1956, 75 Wyo. 444, 297 P.2d 213.

54. Carlisle v. Parker, 1936, 38 Del. 83, 188 A. 67; Muskegon Lumber & Fuel Co. v. Johnson, 1954, 338 Mich. 655, 62 N.W.2d 619; Sterling v. Smith, 1963, 200 Pa.Super. 544, 189 A.2d 889; Oliver v. Givens, 1963, 204 Va. 123, 129 S.E.2d 661.

55. In re Maguire's Estate, 1937, 251 App.Div. 337, 296 N.Y.S. 528, motion granted Maguire's Will, Re, 252 App.Div. 752, 298 N.Y.S. 1008, affirmed 277 N.Y. 527, 13 N.E.2d 458, noted in 7 Brooklyn Law Rev. 256 (1937). *Contra:* Panushka v. Panushka, 1960, 221 Or. 145, 349 P.2d 450. *Cf.:* Central Trust Co. v. Street, 1923, 95 N.J.Eq. 278, 127 A. 82 (purchase money mortgage held as tenants in common).

56. Thornburg v. Wiggins, 1893, 135 Ind. 178, 34 N.E. 999, 22 L.R.A. 42; Witzel v. Witzel, Wyo.1963, 386 P.2d 103; 4 Thompson, Real Property, § 1787, p. 75, 1961 Replacement.

57. See, for example, Hoag v. Hoag, 1912, 213 Mass. 50, 99 N.E. 521; Settle v. Settle, 1925, 56 App.D.C. 50, 8 F.2d 911.

58. 386 P.2d 103, 105 (Wyo.1963).

tenancy that remained unchanged after a decree of divorce had been granted.

With exceptions to be noted, a tenancy by the entirety will not result if one spouse, as owner, conveys property to himself and the other spouse. Since the title of each spouse is then acquired at different times (the owner cannot convey to himself) the essential unities of time and title are lacking.[59] But even under this view, if a grantor uses one name as a grantor and another name as a grantee, he may be estopped to deny the fact that a tenancy by the entirety was created if the claim of a *bona fide* purchaser is involved.[60]

There is substantial authority for the view that one spouse can create a tenancy by the entirety by conveying property to himself and the other spouse. In some decisions this view is supported upon the ground that the intention of the grantor is the controlling factor.[61] In other cases it is held that the conveyance is made to a separate and distinct entity consisting of the husband and wife.[62]

A tenancy by the entirety cannot be created in described property by a conveyance of an undivided one-half interest in the property by one spouse to the other.[63] Additional rules are as follows:

First: Even if a conveying instrument describes the grantees as husband and wife they are not tenants by the entirety if they are not, in fact, husband and wife. The general rule is that they are tenants in common. Unity of person is an essential element of a tenancy by the entirety.[64]

If the conveyance describes the parties as "tenants by the entirety" the grantor has, by the use of such a description, evidenced his intent to create a right of survivorship because this is the important characteristic of such a tenancy. Accordingly, there is authority for the view that the parties acquire ownership as joint tenants.[65]

Second: Unless a contrary intent is expressed, a conveyance to parties who are husband and wife creates a tenancy by the

---

59. Ames v. Chandler, 1929, 265 Mass. 428, 164 N.E. 616; Michigan State Bank v. Kern, 1915, 189 Mich. 467, 155 N.W. 502; Richardson v. Richardson, 1940, 111 Vt. 140, 11 A.2d 227.

60. Stone v. Culver, 1938, 286 Mich. 263, 282 N.W. 142, 119 A.L.R. 512.

61. Kluck v. Metsger, Mo.1961, 349 S.W.2d 919. See Therrien v. Therrien, 1946, 94 N.H. 66, 46 A.2d 538, 166 A.L.R. 1023 (involving a joint tenancy).

62. Johnson v. Landefeld, 1939, 138 Fla. 511, 189 So. 666, noted in 19 Ore.Law Rev. 60 (1939); Cadgene v. Cadgene, 1939, 17 N.J.Misc. 332, 8 A.2d 858, affirmed 124 N.J.L. 566, 12 A.2d 635 (1940); Boehringer v. Schmid, 1930, 254 N.Y. 355, 173 N.E. 220; Woolard v. Smith, 1956, 244 N.C. 489, 94 S.E.2d 466; In re Vandergrift's Estate, 1932, 105 Pa.Super. 293, 161 A.2d 898. This is a statutory rule in some states. See, for example, Or.C.L.A., § 63–210.

63. Pegg v. Pegg, 1911, 165 Mich. 228, 130 N.W. 617; In re Walker's Estate, 1940, 340 Pa. 13, 16 A.2d 28, 132 A.L.R. 628, noted in 26 Cornell Law Quarterly 507 (1941), 89 Univ. of Pa.Law Rev. 681 (1941). *Cf.:* In re Farrand's Estate, 1926, 126 Misc. 590, 214 N.Y.S. 793; Dutton v. Buckley, 1926, 116 Or. 661, 242 P. 626; Runions v. Runions, 1948, 186 Tenn. 25, 207 N.W.2d 1016.

64. Loper v. Loper, Del.Super.1934, 170 A. 804 (described as "husband and wife"); Daniels v. Daniels, 1961, 362 Mich. 176, 106 N.W.2d 818; Balazinski v. Lebid, 1961, 65 N.J.Super. 483, 168 A.2d 209.

65. Lilly v. Schmock, 1941, 297 Mich. 513, 298 N.W. 116; Giudici v. Lofaso, 1951, 199 Misc. 401, 103 N.Y. S.2d 335; Thornton v. Pierce, 1937, 328 Pa. 11, 194 A. 897; Coleman v. Jackson, 1960, 109 U.S.App.D.C. 242, 286 F.2d 98, 83 A.L.R.2d 1043, certiorari denied 366 U.S. 933, 81 S.Ct. 1656, 6 L.Ed.2d 391. See Mitchell v. Frederick, 1934, 166 Md. 42, 170 A. 733, 92 A.L.R. 1412. *Contra:* State ex rel. Ashauer v. Hostetter, 1939, 344 Mo. 665, 127 S.W.2d 697 (because not "expressly declared" to be a joint tenancy as required by statute). See Kepner, The Effect of an Attempted Creation of an Estate by the Entirety in an Unmarried Grantee, 6 Rutgers Law Rev. 550 (1952).

entirety.[66] This is true even if the grantees are not described as husband and wife in the conveying instrument. A conveyance to husband and wife "jointly" is consistent with the creation of a tenancy by the entirety.[67] The use of the word "jointly," standing alone, does not evidence an intention to create a joint tenancy.

Third: In a conveyance to a named person and to a husband and wife (to B and C and D, husband and wife), the husband and wife acquire an undivided one-half interest as tenants by the entirety.[68] But an intention to create a tenancy in common may be evidenced by a direction that the grantees are to "share and share alike" or that the property is to be "equally divided." In that event, B, C and D would each acquire an undivided one-third interest.[69]

Fourth: If property is conveyed to husband and wife for the purpose of conducting a business or commercial enterprise they may hold as tenants in partnership rather than as tenants by the entirety.[70]

Fifth: In Tingle v. Hornsby (Fla),[71] the husband, owner of land, entered into a con-

tract to sell the property. In the contract of sale he and his wife were both named as "sellers." The court held that the interests created in the contract in behalf of the "sellers" were created at the same time and resulted in a tenancy by the entirety in the absence of proof that such was not the intention of the husband.[72]

Management

The prevailing rule is that the enactment of a Married Women's Act confers upon a married woman equal rights with her husband in connection with the management of property held as tenants by the entirety.[73] The husband is under a duty to account for rents and profits. Neither husband nor wife has a right to sell or encumber the property without the consent of the other spouse.[74] The tort liability of a married woman with respect to the condition of the property held under this form of ownership is the same as that of any other owner.[75]

In a few states it is held that the husband has complete managerial rights according to the common law rule.[76] It is even held that

---

66. Eilts v. Moore, 1946, 117 Ind.App. 27, 68 N.E.2d 795; Marburg v. Cole, 1878, 49 Md. 402; Sterrett v. Sterrett, 1960, 401 Pa. 583, 166 A.2d 1. *Contra:* Carver v. Gilbert, 1963, —— Alaska ——, 387 P.2d 928 (tenancy by the entirety viewed as a species of joint tenancy); Bader v. Dyer, 1898, 106 Iowa 715, 77 N.W. 469 (statutory preference in favor of a tenancy in common).

67. Curtis v. Patrick, 1963, 237 Ark. 124, 371 S.W.2d 622; Lauderdale v. Lauderdale, Fla.App.1957, 96 So. 2d 663; Milligan v. Bing, 1937, 341 Mo. 648, 108 S. W.2d 108.

68. Heatter v. Lucas, 1951, 367 Pa. 296, 80 A.2d 749.

69. Dixon v. Davis, Fla.App.1963, 155 So.2d 189. *Cf.:* Mosser v. Dolsay, 1942, 132 N.J.Eq. 121, 72 A.2d 155.

70. Northampton Brewery Corp. v. Lande, 1939, 138 Pa.Super. 235, 10 A.2d 583, noted in 44 Dickinson Law Rev. 232 (1940). *Cf.:* M. Lit, Inc. v. Berger, 1961, 225 Md. 241, 170 A.2d 303.

71. 111 So.2d 274 (Fla.App.1959).

Burby Real Prop. 3rd Ed. HB—15

72. See Jordan v. Jordan, 1950, 217 Ark. 30, 228 S. W.2d 636.

73. French v. National Refining Co., 1940, 217 Ind. 127, 26 N.E.2d 47 (lease); Zanzonico v. Zanzonico, 1938, 124 N.J.Eq. 477, 2 A.2d 597; **Finnegan v.** Humes, 1937, 252 App.Div. 385, 299 N.Y.S. 501, affirmed 277 N.Y. 682, 14 N.E.2d 389 (1938), noted in 23 Cornell Law Quarterly 598 (1938), 15 N.Y.Univ. Law Quarterly Rev. 292 (1938); Kennedy v. Erkman, 1957, 389 Pa. 651, 133 A.2d 550.

74. Carlisle v. Parker, 1936, 38 Del. 83, 188 A. 67; M. Lit, Inc. v. Berger, 1961, 225 Md. 241, 170 A.2d 303, 306; Austin & Bass Builders, Inc. v. Lewis, Mo.1962, 359 S.W.2d 711.

75. Fung v. Chang, 1963, 47 Hawaii 149, 384 P.2d 303.

76. Page v. Donnelly, 1963, 346 Mass. 768, 193 N.E.2d 682; Arrand v. Graham, 1941, 297 Mich. 559, 298 N.W. 281, 136 A.L.R. 1206, rehearing denied 297 Mich. 559, 300 N.W. 16, 136 A.L.R. 1210; Nesbitt

he has a right to convey the property subject to a right in the wife to claim ownership in the event that she survives the husband.

The fact that a husband may have management and control of the property does not mean that he is the "owner" of the property. In Huber v. Penn Mutual Fire Insurance Co. (Del.),[77] a husband obtained a fire insurance policy on described property. The policy provided that it was to be void if the interest of the insured was otherwise than unconditional sole ownership. The court held that the policy was void because the insured and his wife owned the property as tenants by the entirety.[78]

Creditors

Under the common law rule, the husband has a right to possession and management of property held as tenants by the entirety. Under this view, the *possessory rights* of the husband can be reached to satisfy the claims of his creditors.[79] So also, their claims may be satisfied out of the property if the husband survives the wife. However, if the wife survives the husband she will continue as owner free from the claims of the husband's creditors. Creditors of the wife can claim no possessory rights.[80] Their claims can be satisfied out of the property only in the event that the wife survives the husband.

In a majority of the states that recognize tenancies by the entirety, Married Women's

Acts have been passed that confer upon the wife a right to manage and control her own separate property. The prevailing rule is that this applies to property held as tenants by the entirety. While creditors of both the husband and the wife can satisfy their claims out of the property, the individual creditors are excluded.[81] It is considered that this rule is necessary to preserve the rights of the non-debtor spouse. It follows from this thinking that property held as tenants by the entirety, both as to income and the contingent right of survivorship, becomes immune to the claims of the separate creditors of either spouse.[82]

In Wharton v. Citizens' Bank (Mo.),[83] a joint obligation was incurred by the husband and wife. The obligation of the husband was discharged in bankruptcy. The court held that since a joint judgment could not then be secured against the husband and wife, the land held by them as tenants by the entirety could not be reached by the creditor.[84] If separate bankruptcy proceedings are instituted against both the husband and the wife, the proceedings may be consolidated with the result that property held as tenants by the entirety may be held liable for the joint obligations of both bankrupts.[85]

Even if the property cannot be subjected to the payment of individual debts, there is

v. Fairview Farms, Inc., 1954, 239 N.C. 481, 80 S. E.2d 472.

77.   42 Del. (3 Terry) 369, 33 A.2d 729 (1943).

78.   *Contra:* Connecticut Fire Ins. Co. v. McNeil, 6 Cir.1929, 35 F.2d 675.

79.   Raptes v. Cheros, 1927, 259 Mass. 37, 155 N.E. 787. *Contra:* Bankers Trust Co. v. Humber, 1933, 264 Mich. 71, 249 N.W. 454; Grabenhofer v. Garrett, 1963, 260 N.C. 118, 131 S.E.2d 675.

80.   Licker v. Gluskin, 1929, 265 Mass. 403, 164 N.E. 613, 63 A.L.R. 231.

81.   Carlisle v. Parker, 1936, 38 Del. 83, 188 A. 67; Ohio Butterine Co. v. Hargrave, 1920, 79 Fla. 458, 84 So. 376; Chandler v. Chaney, 1871, 37 Ind. 391; Bloomfield v. Brown, 1942, 67 R.I. 452, 25 A.2d 354, 141 A.L.R. 170. See M. Lit, Inc. v. Berger, 1961, 225 Md. 241, 170 A.2d 303, 306.

82.   4 Powell, Real Property, § 623, p. 663.

83.   223 Mo.App. 236, 15 S.W.2d 860 (1929).

84.   *Contra:* First Nat. Bank of Goodland v. Pothuisje, 1940, 217 Ind. 1, 25 N.E.2d 436, 130 A.L.R. 1238, noted in 6 Mo.Law Rev. 207 (1941)—the obligation was that of the entity and only the husband's individual liability was discharged by the bankruptcy proceedings.

85.   Reid v. Richardson, 4 Cir.1962, 304 F.2d 351.

authority for the view that the individual creditor of one spouse may subject the interest of his debtor to the payment of the claim if the debtor acquires the exclusive right to the property by force of the death of the other spouse.[86] However, the claim of the creditor to an interest in the property will be defeated if the debtor-spouse does not survive the non-debtor spouse or if the debtor and the non-debtor spouse terminate the tenancy by a conveyance of the land to a third person. A conveyance by the debtor-spouse is not a fraudulent conveyance because the conveyance is by the entity and not by the individuals composing that entity.[87] Further, at the time of the conveyance the creditor did not have a claim that could then be asserted against the property.

In a number of states a tenancy by the entirety is considered to be in the nature of a tenancy in common but without a right to compel partition. There is a remainder or executory interest in the survivor. These interests are alienable and may be subjected to the claims of the individual creditors of the husband or wife.[88]

Termination

A tenancy by the entirety may be terminated by *voluntary* partition.[89] A divorce de-

stroys the unity of person that is essential to the existence of the tenancy. After the decree the parties are tenants in common.[90] The court may have statutory authority to award more than half of the property to one of the spouses.[91]

The tenancy is also terminated by the death of either spouse. Because of the required unity of person, each spouse is considered to be the owner of the entire estate. Consequently, upon the death of either spouse the ownership continues in the survivor.[92] Frequently, this is erroneously referred to as a right of survivorship. This continuity of ownership renders inapplicable the statutory rule declared in many states that a person who feloniously causes the death of another is deprived of inheritable rights. However, the prevailing rule is that if one spouse feloniously causes the death of the other spouse, the wrongful act is a sufficient basis upon which to declare a constructive trust of property held as tenants by the entirety. Constitutional provisions against the forfeiture of estates does not prevent a court of equity from adjusting the interests of a

86. See, for example, Hoffman v. Newell, 1932, 249 Ky. 270, 60 S.W.2d 607, 89 A.L.R. 489.

87. C. I. T. Corp. v. Flint, 1939, 333 Pa. 350, 5 A.2d 126, 121 A.L.R. 1022. See Murphey v. C. I. T. Corp., 1943, 347 Pa. 591, 33 A.2d 16.

88. See King v. Greene, 1959, 30 N.J. 395, 153 A.2d 49, 75 A.L.R.2d 1153; Hiles v. Fisher, 1895, 144 N. Y. 306, 39 N.E. 337, 30 L.R.A. 305; Lopez v. Mc-Quade, 1934, 151 Misc. 390, 273 N.Y.S. 34; Finnegan v. Humes, 1937, 252 App.Div. 385, 299 N.Y.S. 501, affirmed 277 N.Y. 682, 14 N.E.2d 389 (1938), noted in 23 Corn.Law Quarterly 598 (1938), 15 N.Y.Univ. Law Quarterly Rev. 292 (1938); Ganoe v. Ohmart, 1927, 121 Or. 116, 254 P. 203.

89. See Ash v. Ash, 1937, 280 Mich. 198, 273 N.W. 446 (release by one spouse to the other).

90. Bernatavicius v. Bernatavicius, 1927, 259 Mass. 486, 156 N.E. 685, 52 A.L.R. 886; Wilhelm v. Wilhelm, 1928, 126 Or. 388, 270 P. 516, noted in 10 Or. Law Rev. 206 (1931); Stewart v. Bleau's Estate, 1929, 102 Vt. 273, 147 A. 692, noted in 14 Minn.Law Rev. 562 (1930), 39 Yale Law Jr. 912 (1930). This is the statutory rule in Arkansas (Ark.Stat.Ann. (1949) § 34–1215, applicable to tenancies by the entireties created after 1947); Michigan (Comp.Laws Mich. (1929) § 12767); Pennsylvania (68 Pa.Stat. § 501 (Purdon), applicable to tenancies by the entireties created since 1949). *Contra:* In re Cochran's Real Estate, 1949, 31 Del.Ch. 545, 66 A.2d 497.

91. See Brownley v. Lincoln County, 1959, 218 Or. 7, 343 P.2d 529. *Cf.:* Schafer v. Schafer, 1927, 122 Or. 620, 260 P. 206, 59 A.L.R. 707, noted in 76 Univ. of Pa.Law Rev. 469 (1928).

92. Lang v. Commissioner of Internal Revenue, 1933, 289 U.S. 109, 53 S.Ct. 534, 77 L.Ed. 1066.

wrongdoer and his victim in property held in co-ownership.[93]

According to one view, an equitable division is accomplished by treating the wrongful act as terminating the tenancy by the entirety and converting it into a tenancy in common.[94] The preferred view is that ownership continues in the survivor but it is held in trust for the benefit of the estate of the victim except that the survivor is entitled to the rents and profits during his lifetime (a life estate).[95] Additional points are as follows:

First: An offer of an agreement to terminate an estate by the entirety may be implied from the fact that one tenant by the entirety wrongfully uses part of the property for his own purposes. Acceptance may be indicated by an action for an accounting or an action by the other spouse for a division.[96]

Second: The execution of a joint will by the husband and wife will not result in the termination of a tenancy by the entirety.[97] There is some basis for an argument that if the husband and wife *enter into an agreement* providing that upon the death of either spouse the property is not to go to the sur-

vivor the tenancy by entirety is thereby terminated by mutual consent.

TENANCY IN COMMON

96. A tenancy in common is a "sole and several" tenancy without the right of survivorship.

The prevailing rule is that if two or more persons own undivided possessory estates or interests in property they are presumably tenants in common. It is said to be a "sole and several" tenancy. This means that ownership extends only to an *undivided interest.* In this respect the tenancy is distinguished from a joint tenancy, a form of tenancy discussed under a separate heading. Tenants in common have an equal right to possession. Upon the death of one tenant his estate or interest passes to his estate or as directed in his will.

At common law, persons taking an estate by descent are described as coparceners.[98] At the present time such concurrent owners are classified as tenants in common.

TAXES, REPAIRS AND IMPROVEMENTS

97. The general rule is that a cotenant is entitled to contribution from the other owners if he pays more than his proportionate share of the taxes.

   a. **Repairs.** In general, even if a cotenant makes necessary repairs, he is not entitled to contribution from the other concurrent owners.

   b. **Improvements.** In general, a share-the-cost right does not exist with respect to the cost of improvements erected by a concurrent owner.

With exceptions to be noted, a cotenant who pays more than his proportionate share of taxes assessed against the property is entitled to contribution from his cotenants.[99] Such a payment is not made as a volunteer.

93. See Hargrove v. Taylor, 1964, 236 Or. 451, 389 P.2d 36, 39.

94. Ashwood v. Patterson, Fla.1951, 49 So.2d 848; Bradley v. Fox, 1955, 7 Ill.2d 106, 129 N.E.2d 699; Grose v. Holland, 1948, 357 Mo. 874, 211 S.W.2d 464, noted in 1 Ala.Law Rev. 100 (1948); 13 Mo.Law Rev. 463 (1948).

95. Colton v. Wade, 1951, 32 Del.Ch. 122, 80 A.2d 923; Bryant v. Bryant, 1927, 193 N.C. 372, 137 S.E. 188, 51 A.L.R. 1100; Neiman v. Hurff, 1952, 11 N.J. 55, 93 A.2d 345; Hargrove v. Taylor, 1964, 236 Or. 451, 389 P.2d 36; In re King's Estate, 1952, 261 Wis. 266, 52 N.W.2d 885; 20 Pa.Stat. § 3445. For discussion of the problem, see Bogert, Trusts & Trustees, (2nd ed.) § 478; 4 Scott, Trusts, (2d ed.) § 493.

96. See Reifschneider v. Reifschneider, 1964, 413 Pa. 342, 196 A.2d 324.

97. In re Richichi's Estate, 1938, 3 N.Y.S.2d 722, 167 Misc. 191.

98. Holdsworth's History of English Law, p. 126.

99. Putty v. Putty, Tex.Civ.App.1928, 6 S.W.2d 136.

It is an expenditure that is necessary to protect the interest of the one making the payment. In addition, authorities support the rule that a cotenant is under a duty to protect the property and this duty includes the obligation to pay taxes.[1] Variations and exceptions to the rule are as follows:

First: A cotenant in the exclusive possession of property is not entitled to contribution arising out of expenditures made for ordinary taxes assessed against the property.

Second: Statutes in some states provide that a cotenant may pay his share of the taxes assessed against the property and, by so doing, protect his undivided interest. According to one view, if he pays more than his share he acts as a volunteer and is not entitled to contribution.[2] According to another view the right to contribution is not lost. It is considered that procedure under the statute is optional.[3]

Third: In some states separate assessments are levied against the interests of cotenants. This is especially true with respect to mineral rights.[4] Under such a procedure a cotenant acts as a volunteer if he pays taxes in excess of his individual assessment and he will not be entitled to reimbursement under a contribution rule.

Fourth: Some decisions follow a rule that because of the nature of a tenancy by the entirety, a spouse who pays taxes assessed against the property is not entitled to contribution.[5]

Repairs

The general rule is that a cotenant who makes even necessary repairs is not entitled to contribution. However, there is authority for the view that if repairs become necessary during the absence of a cotenant he may be compelled to share in the expense.[6]

According to the common law rule a cotenant, *before making repairs,* might secure a court order that would impose an obligation on other owners to share in the cost.[7] This remedy (by a writ *de reparatione facienda*) [8] was available only if such owners refused to join in making the repairs.[9] Relief affecting a like result is available under the general American rule. Some authorities take the position that the common law remedy is obsolete and that contribution may be demanded in connection with necessary and reasonable repairs.[10]

If a cotenant is compelled to account for rents and profits from the land he is usually allowed credit for expenditures made in connection with repairs.[11] On the other hand, if he enjoys exclusive possession he is under a duty to keep the premises in repair without the benefit of contribution.[12] In some states

---

1. Kirsch v. Scandia American Bank, 1924, 160 Minn. 269, 199 N.W. 881; Wheeler v. Handy, 1924, 123 Misc. 775, 206 N.Y.S. 148.

2. In re Lohr's Estate, 1938, 132 Pa.Super. 125, 200 A. 135.

3. Olson v. Chapman, 1940, 4 Wash.2d 522, 104 P.2d 344, noted in 54 Harv.Law Rev. 521 (1941), 16 Wash. Law Rev. 165 (1941).

4. See Todd v. Bruner, 1963, —— Tex. ——, 365 S.W. 2d 155.

5. In re Cochran's Real Estate, 1949, 31 Del.Ch. 545, 66 A.2d 497.

6. Haven v. Mehlgarten, 1857, 19 Ill. 91.

7. Calvert v. Aldrich, 1868, 99 Mass. 74.

8. Co.Litt. 200.b.

9. Woodbury v. Stetson, 1936, 108 Vt. 110, 183 A. 490.

10. See, for example, Fowler v. Fowler, 1882, 50 Conn. 256.

11. Pickering v. Pickering, 1885, 63 N.H. 468, 3 A. 744.

12. Calvert v. Aldrich, 1868, 99 Mass. 74; Mastbaum v. Mastbaum, 1939, 126 N.J.Eq. 366, 9 A.2d 51.

statutes provide that failure to perform this duty constitutes waste.[13]

Improvements

A share-the-cost right does not exist with respect to the cost of improvements erected by a concurrent owner.[14] This rule is founded upon the ground that, in general, a person who so erects improvements without an agreement as to costs acts as a mere volunteer. Reimbursement may be available, however, under the following circumstances:

First: If the improver is held accountable for "rents and profits," he is entitled to credit for that proportion of the rents and profits attributable to the improvements.[15]

Second: If partition proceedings are instituted it may be judicially determined that a physical division of the land can be made without prejudice. In that event, the improved area of the land may be awarded to the cotenant who expended the money or effort involved.[16]

Third: If partition proceedings are instituted and the land is sold, the improver may be entitled to credit to the extent that his expenditures enhanced the value of the land.[17] The cost or appraised value of the improvements are not controlling factors.[18]

ACCOUNTING ARISING OUT OF POSSESSION

98. The general rule is that a cotenant is not under a duty to account for use and occupation of the common property. However, an accounting duty exists with respect to rents and profits received from a stranger to the title.

With exceptions to be noted, and in the absence of an agreement to the contrary, a cotenant may occupy the property without charge. One of the characteristics of concurrent ownership is an equal right to possession. A charge cannot be made for the enjoyment of this right.[19] However, the cotenant in possession is ordinarily liable for the payment of carrying charges, such as ordinary taxes and interest on encumbrances. He is also under a duty to make ordinary repairs.[20] Additional rules are as follows:

First: If an owner of land dies intestate his heirs acquire title as tenants in common. An heir in possession of the property at the time of the death of the ancestor may be held accountable for the reasonable rental value in an action brought by the representative of the estate.[21] The exemption-rule is applicable only as between the concurrent owners.

Second: If one cotenant is dispossessed or excluded from possession by another cotenant, he may be restored to possession in an ejectment action.[22] In addition, because of

---

13. Stimson, Am.St.Law, § 1377.

14. Woodbury v. Stetson, 1936, 108 Vt. 110, 183 A. 490; Ward v. Ward's Heirs, 1895, 40 W.Va. 611, 21 S.E. 746.

15. Cain v. Cain, 1898, 53 S.C. 350, 31 S.E. 278.

16. Appeal of Kelsey, 1886, 113 Pa. 119, 5 A. 447.

17. Wallis v. McGuire, 1962, 234 Ark. 491, 352 S.W.2d 940; Fenton v. Miller, 1898, 116 Mich. 45, 74 N.W. 384.

18. See Mahon v. Nelson, 1963, 254 Iowa 1349, 121 N.W.2d 103; Summers v. Satterfield, 1938, 120 W. Va. 1, 196 S.E. 159, 122 A.L.R. 229.

19. Pico v. Columbet, 1859, 12 Cal. 414; Mastbaum v. Mastbaum, 1939, 126 N.J.Eq. 366, 9 A.2d 51; Petrone v. Petrone, 1936, 248 App.Div. 908, 290 N.Y.S. 707; Kahnovsky v. Kahnovsky, 1941, 67 R.I. 208, 21 A.2d 569. *Contra:* Everly v. Shannopin Coal Co., 1940, 139 Pa.Super. 165, 11 A.2d 700 (statutory rule); McKnight v. Basilides, 1943, 19 Wash.2d 391, 143 P.2d 307.

20. See Roberts v. Roberts, 1941, 136 Tex. 255, 150 S.W.2d 236, 136 A.L.R. 1019.

21. Limberg v. Limberg, 1939, 256 A.D. 721, 11 N.Y.S. 2d 690, affirmed 281 N.Y. 821, 24 N.E.2d 488.

22. Trustees of the Church & Society of North Greig v. Johnson, 1867, 66 Barb. (N.Y.) 119.

the ouster, he is entitled to recover damages for use and occupation of the land.[23]

Third: In England the Statute of Anne was enacted in 1705.[24] It provides that a cotenant who receives more than his just share of the rents and profits from the land may be compelled to account to the other owners. The statute does not compel an accounting for the enjoyment of possessory rights.

In some of the American states the Statute of Anne is considered to be a part of the local common law.[25] In a majority of the states statutes have been enacted requiring an accounting under similar circumstances.[26]

The prevailing rule is that the Statute of Anne imposes a duty to account if the tenant receives rent from a third party or if he profits from use of the land for such purposes as farming or mining operations. Money received by a tenant in possession from a roomer is not classified as "rent" within the meaning of the rule.[27]

The tenant is under a duty to account only for net profits. In other words, he is entitled to credit for necessary operating expenses.[28] In the absence of an agreement to the contrary, he is not entitled to compensation for his services.[29]

There is authority for the view that the accounting-duty does not exist in the case of tenants by the entirety. This is said to be due to the fact that in such a tenancy there is but one owner (unity of husband and wife).[30]

ACQUISITION OF OUTSTANDING TITLE BY ONE CONCURRENT OWNER

99. If a cotenant redeems the property from a tax sale or sale made to foreclose a lien, his cotenants are entitled to their respective interest in the redeemed property.

Technically, neither a fiduciary nor a confidential relationship arises out of the concurrent ownership of property. This is true whether the ownership is under one title, as in the case of joint tenants, or under separate titles, as may be the case if the parties are tenants in common. Of course, such a relationship may arise for other reasons, such as a close family relationship.[31] But even in the absence of a fiduciary or confidential relationship, it does not follow that there is not a "guide of conduct" that regulates transactions by and between cotenants that relates to ownership of the property.[32]

If a cotenant redeems the property from a tax sale, or sale made to foreclose a lien, his cotenants are entitled to their respective interests in the redeemed property.[33] Such

---

23. Sons v. Sons, 1922, 151 Minn. 360, 186 N.W. 811; Mastbaum v. Mastbaum, 1939, 126 N.J.Eq. 366, 9 A.2d 51. *Cf.:* In re Elsinger's Estate, 1961, 12 Wis. 2d 471, 107 N.W.2d 580 (surviving tenant in common liable for reasonable rental value after demand for rent made by executrix of estate of deceased tenant in common).

24. 4 Anne, c. 16, § 27 (1705).

25. See Howard v. Throckmorton, 1881, 59 Cal. 79.

26. See 4 Powell, Real Property, § 604, fn. 51.

27. Schell v. Schell, 1946, 74 Cal.App.2d 785, 169 P.2d 654.

28. Price v. Andrew, 1937, 104 Ind.App. 619, 10 N.E.2d 436; Dewing v. Dewing, 1896, 165 Mass. 230, 42 N.E. 1128; Edsall v. Merrill, 1883, 37 N.J.Eq. 114 (mining); Buckelew v. Snedeker, 1876, 27 N.J.Eq. 82 (farming).

29. See In re Cochran's Real Estate, 1949, 31 Del. Ch. 545, 66 A.2d 497.

30. See Kahnovsky v. Kahnovsky, 1941, 67 R.I. 208, 21 A.2d 569.

31. See 4 Powell, Real Property, § 605.

32. See Dolan v. Cummings, 1907, 116 App.Div. 787, 102 N.Y.S. 91 (1907).

33. Kievman v. Grevers, 1937, 122 Conn. 406, 189 A. 609 (sale resulting from foreclosure of an outstanding lien); Hayden v. Hughes, 1938, 147 Kan. 511, 77 P.2d 938 (sale resulting from foreclosure of outstanding lien); Page v. Webster, 1860, 8

right will be lost, however, if they do not pay or tender their proportionate share of the redemption price within a reasonable time.[34] The redemption was within the cotenant's line of duty. There is a mutual obligation to pay taxes and other carrying charges.[35] In addition, the "community of interest" in the property and "good faith" justifies this conclusion.[36] Special situations are as follows:

First: According to some authorities, if a purchase is made at a public sale the cotenant is entitled to retain the benefits if he acted without fraud or collusion.[37]

Second: Some decisions support the conclusion that, in the absence of fraud or collusion, a new title is created if the property is purchased by a person other than a cotenant. In that event, a cotenant may acquire beneficial ownership from the third party.[38]

Third: In many states fractional mineral interests are separately assessed and separately taxed. If such an interest is sold for taxes a tenant in common may acquire beneficial ownership if he acted in good faith and without collusion. It is not material that he was also the owner of surface rights.[39]

Fourth: A tax title acquired by a cotenant is not void; it is merely voidable. A *bona fide* purchaser for value and without notice from the cotenant will acquire an indefeasible title.[40]

ADVERSE POSSESSION

100. In the absence of an ouster the rules relating to acquisition of title by adverse possession are not applicable as between the concurrent owners of property.

Presumably, the possession of land by a cotenant is referable to a right and is not adverse to cotenants.[41] The possession may become adverse if the cotenants are excluded from possession (ouster) or if the cotenants are specifically notified of the adverse claim or can be charged with notice because of the acts of the possessor. Usually, notorious and hostile acts will be sufficient for this purpose if they are of such a nature that a man of ordinary prudence would be put on his guard. Knowledge of an adverse claim may be imputed to a cotenant because of the open and notorious nature of the claim asserted.[42]

PARTITION

101. A voluntary partition of land can be accomplished only by compliance with the provisions of the Statute of Frauds.

Except in the case of a tenancy by the entirety, and in the case of community property, judicial proceedings may be instituted to compel partition.

Mich. 263 (sale resulting from default in payment of taxes); Clausell v. Riley, 1940, 188 Miss. 647, 196 So. 245 (tax default).

34. See Arends v. Fresichs, 1921, 192 Iowa 285, 184 N.W. 650.

35. See Hurley v. Burley, 1889, 148 Mass. 444, 19 N.E. 545.

36. Page v. Webster, 1860, 8 Mich. 263. See Elston v. Piggott, 1883, 94 Ind. 14 ("quasi trustee").

37. See Bragg v. Ross, 1942, 349 Mo. 511, 162 S.W.2d 263; Ammann v. Foster, 1937, 179 Okl. 44, 64 P.2d 653; Vaughan v. Kiesling, Tex.Civ.App.1941, 150 S.W.2d 435; Starkweather v. Jenner, 1909, 216 U.S. 524, 30 S.Ct. 382, 54 L.Ed. 602.

38. Pease v. Snyder, 1950, 169 Kan. 628, 220 P.2d 151; Kirkpatrick v. Mathiot, 1842, 4 Watts & S. (Pa.) 251.

39. Jesberg v. Klinger, 1961, 187 Kan. 582, 358 P.2d 770.

40. Lund v. Heinrich, 1963, 410 Pa. 341, 189 A.2d 581.

41. Dimmick v. Dimmick, 1962, 58 Cal.2d 417, 24 Cal. Rptr. 856, 374 P.2d 824; Todd v. Bruner, 1963, — Tex. —, 365 S.W.2d 155.

42. Unick v. St. Joseph Loan & Trust Co., 1946, 146 Neb. 789, 21 N.W.2d 752; Vaughan v. Kiesling, Tex. Civ.App.1941, 150 S.W.2d 435. See Johns v. Scobie, 1939, 12 Cal.2d 618, 86 P.2d 820 (recordation of defective deed executed by the owner).

Partition cannot be accomplished by the unilateral act of one cotenant in attempting to convey a specific part of the common property.

Reasonably restrictions can properly be placed upon the right of partition.

According to the common law rule partition could only be accomplished with the consent of all the cotenants.[43] An exception was made in the case of coparceners. Since that type of concurrent estate was created by operation of law, compulsory partition was sanctioned. An English statute, passed in 1539, authorized compulsory partition in the case of joint tenants and tenants in common if this could be accomplished by a physical division of the land.[44] By statute passed in 1868 it was provided that if physical division was impracticable, a court order could be issued authorizing a sale of the land and division of the proceeds.[45] Except in the case of a tenancy by the entireties, and in the case of community property, that is the statutory rule declared in the various American states. The reason why a cotenant desires partition is not of controlling importance.[46]

Partition proceedings are under the jurisdiction of a court of equity. Applying the maxim that one who seeks equity must do equity, the court is free to adjust accounts between the parties in a fair and equitable manner. One concurrent owner may be charged for use and occupation of the property (reasonable rental value) and he may be given credit for the value of improvements erected, repairs made and taxes paid.[47] In

dividing the proceeds it may appear that one of the concurrent owners contributed more to the purchase price than the other or others and, for that reason, claims a greater share in the proceeds. For example, if husband and wife acquire property as joint tenants, in partition proceedings the husband may claim that he contributed more to the purchase price than the wife and that he is entitled to a greater share in the proceeds derived from a sale. In answer to this it may be said that the husband, by acquiring title with his wife as a joint tenant, thereby made a gift to her of an undivided one-half interest even if she made no contribution to the purchase price. Accordingly, the proceeds derived from the sale should be equally divided.[48] However, an unequal distribution may be some evidence of the fact that the parties did not intend to create a joint tenancy.[49]

Additional rules relating to partition are as follows:

First: A voluntary partition of land can be accomplished only by compliance with the provisions of the Statute of Frauds.[50] There may be an exchange of deeds or a partition agreement. An oral agreement may be specifically enforceable in equity under the part performance doctrine.[51] There is authority that an oral partition is valid in the case of joint tenants if this is followed by

43. 2 Bl.Comm. 185.

44. 31 Hen. VIII, c. 1 (1539).

45. 31 & 32 Vict. c. 40 (1867–8).

46. Heldt v. Heldt, 1963, 29 Ill.2d 61, 193 N.E.2d 7; Willard v. Willard, 1892, 145 U.S. 116, 12 S.Ct. 818, 36 L.Ed. 644.

47. See Fundaburk v. Cody, 1954, 261 Ala. 25, 72 So.2d 710, 48 A.L.R.2d 1295; Thomas v. Thomas,

1960, 143 Colo. 1130, 352 P.2d 279; Webb v. Mitchell, Tex.Civ.App.1963, 371 S.W.2d 754.

48. See In re Holmes' Estate, 1964, 414 Pa. 403, 200 A.2d 745 (tenancy by the entirety).

49. Jezo v. Jezo, 1964, 23 Wis.2d 399, 129 N.W.2d 195.

50. See Boyers v. Boyers, 1949, 310 Ky. 727, 221 S.W. 2d 657; Williams v. Robertson, 1952, 235 N.C. 478, 70 S.E.2d 692; 4 Powell, Real Property, § 610, p. 624, n. 46.

51. Drumm v. Pavlick, 1948, 141 N.J.Eq. 375, 57 A.2d 662. But see, Meacham v. Meacham, 1892, 91 Tenn. 532, 19 S.W. 757.

a several possession.[52] It is reasoned that each joint tenant is, in fact, an owner of the entire estate and the agreement merely operates as a means by which to "locate the interests."

If words of limitation ("and his heirs" or "heirs of the body") are necessary to convey an estate in fee simple, such words must be used if the partition deeds relate to estate in fee.[53] However, if the partition relates to an estate in fee held by joint tenants or tenants by the entirety, such words are not necessary. This follows from the fact that each joint tenant or tenant by the entirety is the owner of the "whole estate."

Second: A lease executed by one cotenant does not result in a partition. The other cotenants are entitled to share possessory rights with the lessee.[54]

Third: While a tenant in common or a joint tenant has a right to convey his undivided interest, he does not have a right to convey a specific part of the property (conveyance by metes and bounds). A partition cannot be brought about by such unilateral action. However, a partition may result if the other cotenants recognize the validity of the conveyance. Otherwise, the grantee may elect to take the estate which the grantor had a right to convey—an undivided interest.[55] The minority rule is that such a conveyance is void against the other cotenants.[56]

Under the doctrine of "equitable partition", if a physical division of the property is approved in partition proceedings, the area described in the conveyance will be set aside to the grantee if this can be done without prejudice to the other cotenants.[57]

Fourth: The general rule is that cotenants may enter into a valid agreement against partition, voluntary or involuntary, if it is limited to a reasonable time.[58] A similar restriction may be embodied in the instrument creating the concurrent estates. If land is involved there is authority for the view that an oral agreement against partition cannot be enforced because of the Statute of Frauds.[59]

An agreement against partition, as such, does not constitute a direct restraint against alienation because it does not prohibit the alienation of the estate owned by the concurrent owners. Of course, there is an argument that an agreement against partition does impair the alienability of the property involved because of the fact that a purchaser from a concurrent owner is bound by the restriction. It involves a covenant "running with the land" in equity and equity jurisdiction is involved in partition proceedings.

Fifth: The filing of a complaint for partition does not result in a severance of a joint tenancy. The complaint may be withdrawn at any time until issue has been joined by the other cotenant. The right of survivorship

---

52. Tomlin v. Hilyard, 1867, 43 Ill. 300; Glovier v. Dingus, 1939, 173 Va. 268, 4 S.E.2d 551, 133 A.L.R. 468.

53. Rector v. Waugh, 1852, 17 Mo. 13.

54. Swartzbaugh v. Sampson, 1936, 11 Cal.App.2d 451, 54 P.2d 73, Comment, 25 Cal.Law Rev. 203 (1937).

55. Stark v. Barrett, 1860, 15 Cal. 361.

56. Starr v. Leavitt, 1817, 2 Conn. 243; Bartlet v. Harlow, 1815, 12 Mass. 348; Mauzy v. Nelson, 1963, —— W.Va. ——, 131 S.E.2d 389, 97 A.L.R.2d 732 (testamentary disposition).

57. Lasater v. Ramirez, Tex.Com.App.1919, 212 S.W. 935. See Larrison v. Walker, Tex.Civ.App.1941, 149 S.W.2d 172.

58. Rowland v. Clark, 1949, 91 Cal.App.2d 880, 206 P.2d 59; Rosenberg v. Rosenberg, 1952, 413 Ill. 343, 108 N.E.2d 766; 4 Powell, Real Property, § 611, p. 626, n. 55. See Valley v. Valley, 1964, 105 N.H. 297, 199 A.2d 93.

59. Cottom v. Bennett, 1963, 214 Cal.App.2d 709, 29 Cal.Rptr. 715; Drumm v. Pavlick, 1948, 141 N.J. Eq. 375, 57 A.2d 662. See also Casolo v. Nardella, 1948, 193 Misc. 378, 84 N.Y.S.2d 178 (bases upon parol evidence rule).

will attach if a cotenant dies prior to that time.[60]

Sixth: In Rostan v. Huggins (N.C.),[61] it is held that the mortgagee of an undivided interest of a concurrent owner is bound by partition proceedings even though he had not been made a party to the proceedings. This conclusion is based upon the ground that the right to partition is one of the rights incident to a cotenancy and the mortgagee's interest is acquired subject to that right.[62]

Seventh: Usually, in partition proceedings, a physical division of the land will not be ordered if this would result in substantial prejudice to the defendant cotenants. This may be shown by proof of the fact that the share of each owner will be materially less than his share of the money equivalent that could probably be obtained from a sale.[63] Generally, prejudice exists if physical division would result in a depreciation of the aggregate value of the land.[64]

60. Sheridan v. Lucey, 1959, 395 Pa. 305, 149 A.2d 444.

61. 216 N.C. 386, 5 S.E.2d 162, 126 A.L.R. 410, noted in 24 Minn.Law Rev. 707 (1940).

62. *Contra:* Jackman v. Beck, 1881, 37 Ark. 125.

63. Williams v. Wells Fargo Bank & Union Trust Co., 1943, 56 Cal.App.2d 645, 133 P.2d 73.

64. See Murphy v. Bates, 1937, 224 Iowa 389, 276 N.W. 29.

CHAPTER 19

COMMUNITY PROPERTY

INTRODUCTION

102. The community property theory with respect to marital property rights is followed in Arizona, California, Idaho, Louisiana, Nevada, New Mexico, Texas and the State of Washington. The wife has a vested interest in each item of community property as distinguished from a mere expectancy. Each spouse has a legal interest in the property regardless of the state of the title.

a. **Putative marriage.** According to the civil law rule, even if a purported marriage is absolutely void, a person who enters into the relationship in good faith is entitled to demand community rights. As to such person the relationship is designated as a putative marriage.

b. **Conventional community.** Husband and wife may enter into an agreement classifying subsequent property acquisitions in a manner other than that declared by statute. Such an agreement results in the creation of a conventional community.

c. **Community property defined.** Separate property is all property owned at the time of marriage and property acquired after marriage by gift, devise, bequest and descent. All other acquisitions are classified as community property.

An increase in the intrinsic value of separate property will not result in a change in its classification.

A change in the form of property does not result in a change in its classification.

d. **Presumptions as to status of property.** There is a rebuttable presumption that property acquired after marriage is community. In some states it is provided by statute that property acquired by a married woman by an instrument in writing is presumably a part of her separate estate.

In Louisiana, if land is purchased in the name of the husband it is conclusively presumed to be community unless it is expressly provided in the deed that it was acquired with the husband's separate property and as a part of his separate estate.

There is a rebuttable presumption that property possessed by either spouse at the time of the dissolution of a marriage is community property.

e. **Conflict of laws.** The respective interests of husband and wife in land are determined by the law of the state in which the land is situated. The interests in personal property are determined by reference to the law of the domicile of the spouse at the time the property is acquired.

The community property theory with respect to marital property is of ancient origin. With variations as to form, it was recognized by custom in various Germanic tribes as early as the seventh century.[1] It became established in France and Spain and was transplanted to their colonies in the new world, including Louisiana. In a number of states the immediate background is Mexico. The system is now a part of the law in Arizona, California, Idaho, Louisiana, Nevada, New Mexico, Texas and the State of Washington.

In all of the community property states the wife has a vested interest in *each item* of community property as distinguished from a mere expectancy.[2] It is a *legal interest* even if legal title is taken in the name of the husband.[3] However, the Texas rule is that the legal title is in the spouse to whom a conveyance or transfer is made and the other spouse has an equitable interest in the property.[4] The concept that ownership is in a "legal entity" consisting of the husband and wife has, in general, been repudiated.[5] In Mercury Fire Insurance Co. v. Dunaway (Tex.),[6] ownership of community property stood in the name of the husband but a fire insurance policy was issued to the wife. The court held that the policy could not be avoided because of a clause that it was to be void if the insured was not the sole and unconditional owner of the property. It is held that the rights of husband and wife in community property are unified and equal. However, it is questionable that there is "sole ownership" in each spouse. In some states the conclusion reached in this case is authorized by statute.[7]

Putative Marriage

According to the civil law, even if a purported marriage is absolutely void, a person who enters into the relationship in good faith is entitled to demand community rights.[8] As to such person the relationship is designated as a putative marriage.[9] The test of good faith is subjective in nature.[10] A putative marriage may result as to the innocent spouse even though a *marriage ceremony* was not performed as required by local law in connection with the creation of a marriage relationship.[11] In some states it is stated that community property rights depend upon proof of a legally recognized marriage. However, it is held that property acquired during a putative relationship will be distributed on an equitable basis. A putative spouse may also be entitled to a judgment on a quasi-contractual basis,[12] a recognized remedy in many com-

---

1. See Lobingier, An Historical Introduction to Community Property Law, 8 National Univ.Law Rev. 45 (1928); Oppenheim, The Significance of Recent Louisiana Legislation Concerning the Marital Community—Louisiana Acts 49 and 286 of 1944, 19 Tulane Law Rev. 200 (1944).

2. See discussion in Yiatchos v. Yiatchos, 1964, 376 U.S. 306, 84 S.Ct. 742, 745, 11 L.Ed.2d 724.

3. See, for example, McDaniel v. McDaniel, 1933, 134 Cal.App. 597, 25 P.2d 843; In re Wilson's Estate, 1935, 56 Nev. 353, 53 P.2d 339, rehearing denied 56 Nev. 500, 56 P.2d 1207.

4. Edwards v. Brown, 1887, 68 Tex. 329, 4 S.W. 380, rehearing denied 68 Tex. 329, 5 S.W. 87.

5. Mortensen v. Knight, 1956, 81 Ariz. 325, 305 P.2d 463; Bortle v. Osborne, 1930, 155 Wash. 585, 285 P. 425, 67 A.L.R. 1152.

6. 74 S.W.2d 418, error refused (Tex.Civ.App.1934), noted in 13 Tex.Law Rev. 236 (1935).

7. See, for example, La.Act 158 of 1936, discussed in 12 Tulane Law Rev. 131 (1937).

8. See LSA–Civil Code, Art. 117, as construed in Succession of Primus, La.App.1961, 131 So.2d 319.

9. Scott v. Brown Paper Mill Co., La.App.1937, 174 So. 212.

10. Figoni v. Figoni, 1931, 211 Cal. 354, 295 P. 339, noted in 20 Cal.Law Rev. 453 (1932); 4 So.Cal. Law Rev. 159, 244 (1931); Knoll v. Knoll, 1918, 104 Wash. 110, 176 P. 22, 11 A.L.R. 1391.

11. Succession of Marinoni, 1935, 183 La. 776, 164 So. 797, noted in 10 Tulane Law Rev. 435 (1936); Whaley v. Peat, Tex.Civ.App.1964, 377 S.W.2d 855. *Contra:* In re Greathouse's Estate, Tex.Civ.App. 1944, 184 S.W.2d 317, noted in 24 Tex.Law Rev. 92 (1945).

12. Sanguinetti v. Sanguinetti, 1937, 9 Cal.2d 95, 69 P.2d 845. See Jones v. Jones, 1956, 48 Wash.2d 862,

mon law jurisdictions in the case of a *de facto* marriage.[13]

As a matter of statutory interpretation, a putative spouse may be classified as an "heir" [14] of the other party to the relationship or even as a "surviving spouse." [15] However, in the interpretation of federal statutes these terms are usually restricted to a legally recognized spouse.[16]

A putative spouse does not have a claim to property acquired by the other party to the relationship either prior to or after the termination of the relationship. However, the "community share" must be satisfied as to property acquired during the continuance of the relationship.[17] After this claim is satisfied, a legally recognized spouse may assert rights with respect to the balance of the property.[18]

As a matter of public policy, a claim of property rights will be denied if the claim is founded upon a meretricious relationship.[19]

Conventional Community

If a married person is domiciled in a community property state, and in the absence of an agreement with his spouse to the contrary, he is governed by the law as it relates to community property. The situation involves a "legal community." If the husband and wife enter into an agreement relating to future acquisitions of property, that differs from the local law, the agreement results in the creation of a "conventional community." Such an agreement is to be distinguished from one that merely relates to the classification of presently owned property as being separate or community. The validity of a classification-agreement is recognized in all of the community property states.

An agreement creating a conventional community is recognized in all of the community property states except Texas. In that state the Constitution defines community property. Such a constitutional provision is inconsistent with the creation of a conventional community.[20]

Statutes generally prescribe the formalities required for the creation of a conventional community.[21] It is usually provided that the agreement must be executed with the formalities prescribed for the conveyance of a freehold estate in land. It is probable that statutes relating to "marriage settlements" are

296 P.2d 1010, 54 A.L.R.2d 1403 (award of alimony sustained); McGhee v. McGhee, 1960, 82 Idaho 367, 253 P.2d 760 (award of damages on basis of "constructive fraud" made payable on a monthly basis).

13. See, Fung Dai Kim Ah Leong v. Lau Ah Leong, 9 Cir.1928, 27 F.2d 582, certiorari denied 278 U.S. 636, 49 S.Ct. 33, 73 L.Ed. 552, noted in 2 So.Cal. Law Rev. 293 (1929); 76 Univ. of Pa. Law Rev. 439 (1928).

14. Kunakoff v. Woods, 1958, 166 Cal.App.2d 59, 332 P.2d 773 (putative wife qualified as an "heir" under a wrongful death statute). In Jackson v. Lindlom, La.App.1955, 84 So.2d 101, recovery under wrongful death statute was denied because a putative wife did not qualify as a "widow" within the meaning of the act.

15. Estate of Krone, 1948, 83 Cal.App.2d 766, 189 P. 2d 741; Estate of Ricci, 1962, 201 Cal.App.2d 146, 19 Cal.Rptr. 739 (the putative spouse as well as the legal wife was entitled to take as a "surviving spouse").

16. United States v. Robinson, 5 Cir.1930, 40 F.2d 14; Beebe v. Moormack Gulf Lines, Inc., 5 Cir.1932, 59 F.2d 319, certiorari denied 287 U.S. 597, 53 S.Ct. 22, 77 L.Ed. 520.

17. Hubbell v. Inkstein, 1852, 7 La.Ann. 252; Morgan v. Morgan, 1892, 1 Tex.Civ.App. 315, 21 S.W. 154.

18. But see, Prince v. Hopson, 1956, 230 La. 575, 89 So.2d 128.

19. Stevens v. Anderson, 1953, 75 Ariz. 331, 256 P.2d 712; Keene v. Keene, 1962, 57 Cal.2d 657, 21 Cal. Rptr. 593, 371 P.2d 329; In re Sloan's Estate, 1908, 50 Wash. 86, 96 P. 684. Cf.: Fernandez v. Garza, 1960, 88 Ariz. 214, 354 P.2d 260; Iredell v. Iredell, 1957, 49 Wash.2d 627, 305 P.2d 805.

20. Burton v. Bell, 1964, —— Tex. ——, 380 S.W.2d 561.

21. See Corker v. Corker, 1891, 87 Cal. 643, 25 P. 922, for a definition of a marriage settlement.

also applicable to agreements resulting in the creation of conventional communities.[22] In Arizona the agreement is valid only if executed prior to marriage.[23] That is also the rule in Louisiana except that those establishing a domicile in that state after marriage may enter into such an agreement within a reasonable time after moving into the state.[24]

According to one view, the validity of an antenuptial contract is determined by the law of the place where the agreement is made. However, well reasoned decisions take the position that the law of the matrimonial domicile applies either because that place has the most significant contacts with the matters involved ("center of gravity" theory) or because of the presumed intention of the parties.[25]

Community Property Defined

Separate property is all property owned at the time of marriage and property acquired after marriage by gift, devise, bequest and descent. All other acquisitions are classified as community property. An increase in the intrinsic value of separate property will not result in a change in its classification. However, the owner of this property may be under a duty to reimburse the community to the extent that the increase was due to the use of community funds or the effort and skill of the husband or wife.[26] Reimbursement is not indicated if the spouse received a reasonable and fair compensation for services rendered.

The payments so received constitute community property.[27]

A change in the form of property does not result in a change in its classification. Property acquired with community funds is classified as community property. If a husband or wife participates in a company pension or retirement plan, the benefits flowing from the plan constitute community property to the extent that the community contributes to the fund involved.[28] It is not material whether the contribution is in the form of payroll deductions or a "fringe benefit" where the cost is paid by the employer. If there are successive marriages the benefits should be apportioned according to the contributions made during each successive marriage.[29] The employer may be protected if payments are made to a named beneficiary other than the spouse entitled thereto. However, the one to whom payment is made should be held accountable.[30]

If, during marriage, separate funds are commingled with community funds so that they cannot be traced or identified, the commingled funds or assets acquired by the use of such funds constitute community property.[31]

22. See, for example, In re Wittman's Estate, 1961, 58 Wash.2d 841, 365 P.2d 17, construing RCW 26.16.-120.

23. Ariz.R.S. § 25–201.

24. La.Stat.Ann.–C.C. art. 2329.

25. See, for example, In re Knippel's Estate, 1959, 7 Wis.2d 335, 96 N.W.2d 514.

26. Abraham v. Abraham, 1956, 230 La. 78, 87 So.2d 735.

27. See Van Camp v. Van Camp, 1921, 53 Cal.App. 17, 199 P. 885 (increase in the intrinsic value of corporate stock); Beals v. Fontenot, D.La.1939, 29 F. Supp. 602 (increase in the intrinsic value of corporate stock).

28. See Neeley v. Lockton, 1964, 63 Wash.2d 929, 389 P.2d 909.

29. But see, Benson v. City of Los Angeles, 1963, 60 Cal.2d 355, 384 P.2d 649.

30. Messersmith v. Messersmith, 1956, 229 La. 495, 86 So.2d 169.

31. Buehler v. Buehler, 1946, 73 Cal.App.2d 472, 166 P.2d 608; Mumm v. Mumm, 1963, 63 Wash.2d 349, 387 P.2d 547. See Rose v. Rose, 1960, 82 Idaho 395, 353 P.2d 1089.

Presumptions as to Status of Property

Except as noted, there is a rebuttable presumption that property acquired after marriage is community property. However, in some states it is provided by statute that property acquired by a married woman by an instrument in writing is presumed to be her separate estate. This presumption is conclusive in favor of a *bona fide* purchaser for value and without notice. If the property is acquired by a married woman and her husband by an instrument in which they are described as such the property is presumed to be community.[32] This presumption is not rebutted by proof of the fact that the consideration was paid with separate property unless it is also shown that there was lack of gift intent.[33] Also, if the parties are living separate the earnings and accumulations may constitute separate property. In that event the presumption under discussion has no application.[34] Additional presumptions are as follows:

First: In Louisiana if land is purchased in the name of the husband it is conclusively presumed to be community property unless it is expressly provided in the deed that it was acquired with the separate property of the husband and for his separate estate.[35] If the deed contains such recitals the property constitutes a part of the husband's separate estate unless it is shown that the recitals are false.

If land is acquired in the name of the wife she may rebut the presumption that it constitutes community property by proof that payment was made with her separate property that was under her administration.[36] Recital of these facts need not be set forth in the deed.[37] Even in the face of recitals it may be shown that they are false.[38] However, a husband who has been a party to a deed that contains such recitals is thereafter estopped to contradict the deed.[39]

Second: There is a rebuttable presumption that property possessed by either the husband or the wife at the time of the dissolution of marriage is community property.[40] The probative value of this presumption is insignificant if the marriage is one of short duration.

Third: By statute in California there is a presumption that property owned at the time of death by a person who has been divorced from his or her spouse more than four years prior thereto was not community property acquired during marriage with such divorced spouse, but it is his or her separate property.[41]

32. See, for example, West's Ann.Cal.Civ.Code, § 164. For construction of a similar statute see August v. Tillian, 1947, 51 N.M. 74, 178 P.2d 590. *Cf.:* Fidelity & Casualty Co. v. Mahoney, 1945, 71 Cal.App. 2d 65, 161 P.2d 944 (the presumption applies only after there is proof that the property in question was, in fact, acquired after marriage).

33. Williams v. Williams, 1960, 178 Cal.App.2d 522, 3 Cal.Rptr. 59. *Cf.:* August v. Tillian, 1947, 51 N. M. 74, 178 P.2d 590.

34. See, In re Armstrong's Estate, 1949, 33 Wash.2d 118, 204 P.2d 500, noted in 25 Wash.Law Rev. 284 (1950); In re Hewett's Estate, Alaska, 1961, 358 P.2d 579.

35. Succession of Hemenway, 1955, 228 La. 572, 83 So.2d 377.

36. Prince v. Hopson, 1956, 230 La. 575, 582, 89 So.2d 128, 130.

37. See, Succession of Blades, La.App.1961, 127 So.2d 263.

38. Monk v. Monk, 1962, 243 La. 429, 144 So.2d 384.

39. Rousseau v. Rousseau, 1946, 209 La. 428, 24 So.2d 676. See also, Hodge v. Ellis, 1955, 154 Tex. 341, 277 S.W.2d 900.

40. Caswell v. Caswell, 1930, 105 Cal.App. 475, 288 P. 102; Bruyninckx v. Woodward, 1950, 217 La. 736, 47 So.2d 478; Marshall v. Superior Court, 1922, 119 Wash. 631, 206 P. 362.

41. West's Ann.Cal.Code Civ.Proc. § 1963(40).

Conflict of Laws

The respective interests of husband and wife in land are determined by the law of the state wherein the land is situated. The interests in personal property are determined by reference to the law of the domicile of the spouse at the time of acquisition.[42] However, if land is the separate property of one spouse the status of the rent from that land, as being separate or community property, is determined by the law of the situs. This conclusion is reached even though the rent would be community property according to the law of the domicile of the owner.[43] The right to rent is an incorporeal hereditament. Being an interest in land it is separate or community property according to the law of the state wherein the land is located. This is also true with respect to accrued rent because a change in the form of property does not change its status.

The rule that a change in the form of property does not result in a change in its classification, is applicable in other situations. For example, if the parties are domiciled in a non-community property state, and the earnings of the husband or wife are invested in land in a community property state, the land remains the separate estate of the spouse.[44] It is not material that the investment was made with the earnings that would have been community property if acquired while domiciled in a community property state.[45]

In Depas v. Mayo (Mo.),[46] while husband and wife were domiciled in Louisiana certain community property was acquired that the husband subsequently used to purchase land in Missouri. The Missouri court held that the community interest of the wife could be protected by impressing a trust upon the land.[47]

The general rule is that a change of domicile by an owner will not result in a change in the character of property as being separate or community. In Estate of Thornton (Cal.),[48] husband and wife were domiciled in Montana and the husband's earnings constituted a part of his separate estate. Thereafter they established a domicile in California. After the husband's death his widow claimed that the money acquired by the husband while domiciled in Montana constituted community property. A California statute then provided that property acquired while domiciled elsewhere would constitute community property if it would have been community property if acquired while domiciled in California. In denying the claim of the widow it is held that the statute violated the Privileges and Immunities Clauses of the United States Constitution as well as the Due Process Clause of the Fourteenth Amendment.

It is now provided by statute in California that property of the type involved in Estate of

---

42. People v. Bejarano, 1961, 145 Colo. 304, 358 P.2d 866 (nature of wife's interest in community property); Choate v. Ransom, 1958, 700 Nev. 100, 323 P.2d 700 (cause of action for personal injuries); Reeves v. Schulmeier, 5 Cir.1962, 303 F.2d 802 (cause of action for personal injuries). But see, Matney v. Blue Ribbon, Inc., 1942, 202 La. 505, 12 So.2d 253, noted in 18 Tulane Law Rev. 319 (1943); Mounsey v. Stahl, 1956, 62 N.M. 135, 306 P.2d 258.

43. In re Clark's Estate, 1955, 59 N.M. 433, 285 P.2d 795; Comm'r of Internal Revenue v. Skaggs, 5 Cir. 1941, 122 F.2d 721, certiorari denied 315 U.S. 811, 62 S.Ct. 796, 86 L.Ed. 1210 (1942).

44. But see, Hammonds v. Comm'r of Internal Revenue, 10 Cir.1939, 106 F.2d 420.

Burby Real Prop. 3rd Ed. HB—16

45. Huston v. Colonial Trust Co., Tex.Civ.App.1954, 266 S.W.2d 231, ref. n. r. e.; Brookman v. Durkee, 1907, 46 Wash. 578, 90 P. 914. But see, La.Stat. Ann.–C.C. art. 2400; Neuner, Marital Property and the Conflict of Laws, 5 La.Law Rev. 167, 169 (1943).

46. 11 Mo. 314 (1848).

47. See Rozan v. Rozan, N.D.1964, 129 N.W.2d 694.

48. 1 Cal.2d 1, 33 P.2d 1, 92 A.L.R. 1343 (1934).

Thornton is *quasi*-community property (a form of separate property). That is to say, if a husband or wife acquires property while domiciled in another state that would have been community property if acquired while domiciled in California, and they subsequently establish a domicile in California, that property is classified as *quasi*-community property if it consists of land in California or personal property wherever situated.[49]

For some purposes, *quasi*-community property has the same characteristics as community property if the marriage is dissolved by divorce or death. In divorce proceedings it may be distributed between the husband and wife as in the case of community property.[50] Upon the death of the *owner* the surviving spouse is entitled to a community share in spite of a testamentary provision to the contrary (a one-half interest) and is entitled to all of the property in case of an intestacy.[51] It is to be observed, however, that the non-owner spouse is not given testamentary rights with respect to the property and can assert no rights to the property during the lifetime of the owner-spouse except in connection with a decree or divorce or separate maintenance.

CLASSIFICATION OF PROPERTY ON THE BASIS OF TIME OF ACQUISITION

103. **Property acquired before marriage, or after the dissolution of a marriage constitutes separate property.**

a. **Executory contracts.** According to one view, property acquired by force of an executory contract is classified as community property only if the contracting party was married at the time of the agreement. A second view is that the acquisition is community if the party was married at the time of performance of the agreement. Still a third view is that the property will be apportioned as community or separate according to contributions made to its acquisition.

b. **Land grants under homestead statutes.** If a homesteader is married at the time he receives a patent the land may be classified as community property. However, if a federal land grant is involved this classification may be in conflict with federal statutes.

c. **Adverse possession.** Title acquired by adverse possession is classified as community property only if the adverse possessor is married at the expiration of the full statutory period.

Since property acquired before marriage, or after the dissolution of marriage, constitutes separate property, the time of acquisition is of controlling importance in determining whether property is to be classified as separate or community. Various situations are considered in the following paragraphs.

Executory Contracts

There is a lack of uniformity in the decisions as to the proper classification of property acquired in connection with the performance of an executory contract. It is to be noted, however, that if separate or community property contributes to the acquisition, reimbursement may be required regardless of the conclusion reached as to the proper classification of the property. The important rules respecting classification are as follows:

First: An acquisition is classified as community property if the contracting party was married at the time of the inception of the right—the date upon which the contract was

---

49. West's Ann.Cal.Civ.Code, § 140.5 (added in 1961).

50. West's Ann.Cal.Civ.Code, § 146 (as amended in 1961). The constitutionality of this statute has been sustained (Addison v. Addison, 1965, —— Cal.2d ——, 43 Cal.Rptr. 97, 399 P.2d 897.

51. West's Ann.Cal.Prob.Code, § 201.5 (as amended in 1961).

made.[52] Otherwise, the classification is that of separate property. For example, in Mc-Curdy v. McCurdy (Tex.),[53] a life insurance policy was issued to decedent prior to the time of his marriage. After his marriage premiums were paid with community funds. The court held that proceeds derived from the policy constitute a part of the separate estate of the insured.[54]

Second: Regardless of marital status at the time of contracting, an acquisition is classified as community if the contracting party was married at the time of performance according to the terms of the contract—at the time of the acquisition of ownership.[55] Otherwise, separate property is involved.

Third: The property will be apportioned as community or separate according to contributions made to its acquisition.[56]

Land Grants under Homestead Statutes

If a homesteader is married at the time he receives a patent the land may be classified as community property. Title is acquired after marriage other than by gift, devise, bequest or descent. However, classification as separate property has received some judicial approval upon the ground that the acquisition constitutes a gift.[57]

In the case of federal land grants classification as community property may be in conflict with provisions of the federal statutes. For example, the federal statute specifically provides that if a homesteader dies his widow is entitled to the patent. The title acquired by the widow is a part of her separate estate even though a classification as community property would be in accord with state law.[58] However, a classification as community property is not in conflict with federal law if the parties were married at the time of entry upon the land and if the marriage relationship continued until the granting of a patent.[59]

Adverse Possession

An adverse possessor does not acquire ownership until the expiration of the full statutory period. Accordingly, if he is married at that time the acquisition is classified as community property.[60]

CLASSIFICATION OF PROPERTY ON THE BASIS OF SOURCE OF ACQUISITION

104. **With exceptions to be noted, all property acquired after marriage other than by gift, devise, bequest and descent is classified as community property.**

    a. **Rents, issues and profits of separate property. The civil law rule is that rents, issues and profits of separate property constitute community property. In some states this rule has been changed by statute.**

    b. **Earnings. Generally, earnings of either the husband or wife are classified as community property. Statutes frequently pro-**

52. Bishop v. Williams, Tex.Civ.App.1920, 223 S.W. 512, error refused. See In re Miller's Estate, 1940, 44 N.M. 214, 100 P.2d 908.

53. 372 S.W.2d 381 (Tex.Civ.App.1963).

54. *Accord:* In re Moseman's Estate, 1886, 38 La. Ann. 219.

55. In re Monaghan's Estate, 1943, 60 Ariz. 342, 137 P.2d 393; Succession of Siverd, 1928, 167 La. 383, 119 So. 399.

56. Vieux v. Vieux, 1926, 80 Cal.App. 222, 251 P. 640. See In re Kuhn's Estate, 1925, 132 Wash. 678, 233 P. 293.

57. See Ellis v. Ellis, 1950, 97 Cal.App.2d 808, 218 P.2d 823.

58. McCune v. Essig, 1905, 199 U.S. 382, 26 S.Ct. 78, 50 L.Ed. 237.

59. Buchser v. Buchser, 1913, 231 U.S. 157, 34 S.Ct. 46, 58 L.Ed. 166.

60. Crouch v. Richardson, 1925, 158 La. 822, 104 So. 728; Sauvage v. Wauhop, Tex.Civ.App.1912, 143 S.W. 259, error dismissed. *Cf.:* Estate of Hill, 1914, 167 Cal. 59, 138 P. 690.

vide that earnings and accumulations constitute separate property if the parties are not living together as husband and wife.

c. Credit acquisitions. Property acquired on the basis of community credit is classified as community property. The use of separate credit results in the acquisition of separate property.

d. Damages for personal injuries. In the absence of a statute to the contrary, damages recovered for personal injuries suffered by either the husband or the wife constitute community property.

e. Industrial accident awards. Industrial accident awards to either husband or wife constitute community property.

f. Recovery in wrongful death action. Damages awarded to husband or wife in a wrongful death action arising out of the death of a child of the marriage constitutes community property.

With exceptions to be noted, all property acquired after marriage other than by gift, devise, bequest and descent is classified as community property. Special problems involving methods of acquisition are discussed in the following paragraphs.

Rents, Issues and Profits of Separate Property

According to the civil law rule, the rents, issues and profits of separate property fall into the community. With some variations, this rule is followed in Idaho,[61] Louisiana [62] and Texas.[63] However, things severed from the land, such as minerals, oil and gas, gravel, etc., follow the classification of the land.[64]

61. Idaho Code, § 32–906.

62. Fertel v. Fertel, La.App.1962, 148 So.2d 853.

63. Arnold v. Leonard, 1925, 114 Tex. 535, 273 S.W. 799.

64. Gulf Refining Co. v. Garrett, 1946, 209 La. 674, 25 So.2d 329; Commissioner of Internal Revenue v. Wilson, 5 Cir. 1935, 76 F.2d 766; Welder v. Commissioner of Internal Revenue, 5 Cir. 1945, 148 F.2d 583.

Unlike crops, such items are not considered to be "rents, issues and profits." In Louisiana, the fruits of the wife's separate property, wherever situated and however administered, fall into the community unless the wife by written instrument declares that she reserves all such fruits for her separate estate. This declaration must be notarized, witnessed and recorded.[65]

In a number of community property states it is provided by statute that the rents, issues and profits of separate property constitute separate property.[66]

Earnings

Generally, earnings of either the husband or the wife constitute community property. A Nevada statute provides that when the husband has allowed the wife to appropriate her earnings to her own use, the same, with the issues and profits thereof, is deemed a gift from him to her and is her separate estate.[67] In some states it is also provided by statute that under rather limited conditions a wife may obtain a court order allowing her to conduct a business as a "sole trader." In that event the earnings are classified as a part of the wife's separate estate.[68]

Statutes frequently provide that the earnings and accumulations of the wife while living separate from her husband constitute a part of her separate estate.[69] This may also

65. La.Stat.Ann.–C.C. art. 2386, as amended in 1944. See Slater v. Culpepper, La.App.1961, 129 So.2d 499.

66. See, for example, In re Torrey's Estate, 1939, 54 Ariz. 369, 95 P.2d 990; Estate of Gold, 1915, 170 Cal. 621, 151 P. 12; Laughlin v. Laughlin, 1944, 49 N.M. 20, 155 P.2d 1010.

67. See, In re Wilson's Estate, 1935, 56 Nev. 353, 53 P.2d 339.

68. See, for example, Gray v. Perlis, 1926, 76 Cal. App. 511, 245 P. 221; Youngworth v. Jewell, 1880, 15 Nev. 45.

69. See, for example, Makeig v. United Security Bank & Trust Co., 1931, 112 Cal.App. 138, 296 P. 673

be true as to the earnings of the husband after a decree of separate maintenance or an interlocutory decree of divorce.[70] Even without the aid of statute, there is authority for the view that the earnings of the husband while living separate from his wife constitute a part of his separate estate if the wife has abandoned him without justification.[71]

An apportionment problem may arise in those states recognizing the rule that rents, issues and profits of separate property constitute separate property. The Arizona case of In re Torrey's Estate [72] furnishes an example. At the time of his marriage the husband owned two restaurants valued at $3,035. His widow claimed that the income from these restaurants that accrued after marriage constituted community property. The community contribution arose because of the effort and skill of the husband in his management of the restaurants. In sustaining the widow's contention it is pointed out that the income was due primarily to the effort and skill of the husband.[73] A reasonable rate of return on the value of the investment measures the contribution of the separate estate.[74] Of course there may be proof of the fact that the separate contribution was in

excess of the "reasonable rate of return." [75] The profits of a business could be apportioned as in the case of a commercial partnership. The community contribution consists of the reasonable value of the services involved. The separate contribution consists of a reasonable rate of return on the investment, or the reasonable rental value of the separate property. This method of apportionment has been approved for purposes of taxation.[76]

Apportionment is also indicated in a case where the separate contribution consists of land used for agricultural purposes and the community contribution consists of farming operations. The separate estate is entitled to the reasonable rental value of the land. Balance of the income belongs to the community.[77] Any increase in the value of the land that is due to the "community contribution" is also community property.[78]

Credit Acquisitions

Credit is a form of property. Accordingly, property acquired on the basis of community credit is classified as community property.[79] The use of separate credit results in the acquisition of separate property.

It is frequently stated in the cases that whether community credit or separate credit is involved in a given transaction depends

---

(construing West's Cal.Civ.Code, § 169); Lorang v. Hays, 1949, 69 Idaho 440, 209 P.2d 733 (construing § 32–909 I.C.); Personal Finance, Inc. v. Simms, La.App.1962, 148 So.2d 176 (construing art. 2334, LSA–R.C.C.).

70. See, for example, West's Ann.Cal.Civ.Code, § 169.1 (separate maintenance) and § 169.2 (interlocutory decree of divorce).

71. Pendleton v. Brown, 1923, 25 Ariz. 604, 221 P. 213.

72. 54 Ariz. 369, 95 P.2d 990 (1939).

73. *Accord:* Estate of Gold, 1915, 170 Cal. 621, 151 P. 12; In re Bing's Estate, 1940, 5 Wash.2d 466, 105 P. 689.

74. Pereira v. Pereira, 1909, 156 Cal. 1, 103 P. 488.

75. See Gilmore v. Gilmore, 1955, 45 Cal.2d 142, 287 P.2d 769; Tassi v. Tassi, 1958, 160 Cal.App.2d 680, 325 P.2d 872.

76. Todd v. Comm'r, 9 Cir. 1945, 153 F.2d 553; Todd v. McColgan, 1949, 89 Cal.App.2d 509, 201 P.2d 414. See LeSourd, Community Property Status of Income from Business Involving Personal Services and Separate Capital, 22 Wash.Law Rev. 19 (1947).

77. Estate of Neilson, 1962, 57 Cal.2d 733, 22 Cal.Rptr. 1, 371 P.2d 745; Laughlin v. Laughlin, 1944, 49 N.M. 20, 155 P.2d 1010.

78. Mayhood v. La Rosa, 1962, 58 Cal.2d 498, 24 Cal. Rptr. 837, 374 P.2d 805.

79. Gleich v. Bonzio, 1937, 128 Tex. 606, 99 S.W.2d 881.

upon "the intention of the creditor." For example, separate credit is indicated if separate property is used as security.[80] That is also the case if a husband or wife has an established credit on the basis of his or her separate property.[81] In other situations it may be assumed that credit was extended on the basis of community credit.[82] There is authority for the view that the intention of the creditor is not a controlling factor. It is held that community credit is used if community property can be held liable for the obligation involved.[83] This legal-liability rule dispenses with the necessity of speculation regarding the presumed intention of the creditor.

Property acquired on credit is classified as community or separate as of the time of acquisition. This classification is not changed by the fact that the debt is subsequently paid by the use of community property or by the use of separate property.

Damages for Personal Injuries

Usually, damages recovered for personal injuries suffered by either the husband or the wife are not defined as separate property.[84] Accordingly, they fall into the community. As a result, even if a defendant's negligence caused the injuries, he cannot be held liable if the spouse of the injured party was guilty of contributory negligence.[85] This negligence is imputed to the injured spouse as a means by which to prevent benefits flowing to the negligent spouse. However, it may be provided by statute that a cause of action accruing to the wife for personal injuries while she is living separate from her husband constitutes a part of her separate estate.[86]

In Fredrickson & Watson Construction Co. v. Boyd (Nev.),[87] a wife was allowed to recover damages for personal injuries in spite of contributory negligence by the husband. In classifying the acquisition as separate property of the wife it is recognized that all property acquired after marriage other than by gift, devise, bequest and descent constitutes community property. However, it is considered that the property in question was not "acquired" within the meaning of the statute. The word "acquired" is limited to acquisitions resulting from personal effort such as in the case of wages, salary or other earnings.[88] This is the statutory rule in a number of states where it is declared that damages awarded a married person for personal injuries constitutes a part of his or her separate estate.[89] The Louisiana statute provides that all claims for personal injuries suffered by a wife are the exclusive property of the wife and recoverable by her alone.

---

80. But see Finley v. Finley, 1955, 47 Wash.2d 307, 287 P.2d 475 (where both husband and wife signed the note).

81. See Dyment v. Nelson, 1913, 166 Cal. 38, 134 P. 988.

82. See Succession of Franek, 1953, 224 La. 747, 70 So.2d 670 (community credit because wife did not have sufficient separate property to justify the loan made to her).

83. Morris v. Waring, 1916, 22 N.M. 175, 159 P. 1002; Dillard v. Dillard, Tex.Civ.App.1960, 341 S.W.2d 668. *Cf.:* McElyea v. McElyea, 1945, 49 N.M. 322, 163 P.2d 635.

84. Swager v. Peterson, 1930, 49 Idaho 785, 291 P. 1049.

85. Tinker v. Hobbs, 1956, 80 Ariz. 166, 294 P.2d 659; Bell v. Phillips Petroleum Co., Tex.Civ.App.1954, 278 S.W.2d 407; Chase v. Beard, 1959, 55 Wash.2d 58, 346 P.2d 315.

86. See, for example, Lorang v. Hays, 1949, 69 Idaho 440, 209 P.2d 733.

87. 60 Nev. 117, 102 P.2d 627 (1940).

88. *Accord:* Soto v. Vandeventer, 1952, 56 N.M. 483, 245 P.2d 826, 35 A.L.R.2d 1150.

89. See, for example, West's Ann.Cal.Civ.Code, § 163.5.

However, claims for the wife's loss of earnings and of her services as a housewife belong to the community and contributory negligence of the husband may bar recovery.[90]

Industrial Accident Awards

Compensation benefits, authorized by Workmen's Compensation Acts payable to either the husband or the wife, are classified as community property. It is reasoned that such compensation is awarded in lieu of wages.[91]

Recovery in Wrongful Death Action

Damages recovered by either husband or wife in a wrongful death action arising out of the death of a child of the marriage is classified as community property. It is property acquired after marriage other than by gift, devise, bequest or descent.[92] However, some authorities follow the view that such an acquisition constitutes separate property. It is considered that the property is not *acquired* within the meaning of the law as it relates to community property because it is not referable to the use of effort or skill of the spouse.[93]

TRANSMUTATION OF PROPERTY FROM COMMUNITY TO SEPARATE AND VICE VERSA

105. **The general rule is that husband and wife may transmute separate property to community property and *vice versa*.**

a. **Separate property to community property. In the absence of a statute to the contrary, there is authority for the rule that separate property can be transmuted to community property by oral agreement, express or implied.**

b. **Community property to separate property. This type of transmutation may be accomplished by a partition agreement or by a gift of community property by one spouse to the other. They may, for example, create a joint tenancy or one spouse may name the other spouse as beneficiary under a life insurance policy and pay the premiums with community funds. The gift becomes operative upon the death of the insured. A transmutation also takes place if community funds are used to erect improvements upon the separate of either the husband or the wife.**

The general rule is that husband and wife may transmute separate property to community property and *vice versa*. A Washington statute specifically provides that this can be accomplished by agreement.[94]

An agreement of this type does not result in the creation of a conventional community because a conventional community looks to the classification of subsequently acquired property as distinguished from presently owned property. The Texas Constitution defines community property. While this provision prohibits the creation of a conventional community[95] it does not prohibit agreements between husband and wife that relate to a change in the status of presently owned

---

90. Kientz v. Charles Dennery, Inc., La.App.1944, 17 So.2d 506, noted in 19 Tulane Law Rev. 141 (1944). *Cf.:* McHenry v. American Employer's Insurance Co., 1944, 206 La. 70, 18 So.2d 656, noted in 19 Tulane Law Rev. 456 (1945).

91. Dawson v. McNaney, 1950, 71 Ariz. 79, 223 P.2d 907; Northwestern Redwood Co. v. Industrial Accident Commission, 1921, 184 Cal. 484, 194 P. 31; Glens Falls Ins. Co. v. Yarbrough, Tex.Civ.App.1963, 369 S.W.2d 640. *Contra:* Richards v. Richards, 1955, 59 N.M. 308, 283 P.2d 881.

92. Cervantes v. Maco Gas Co., 1960, 177 Cal.App.2d 246, 2 Cal.Rptr. 75; Ostheller v. Spokane & Inland Empire R. Co., 1919, 107 Wash. 678, 182 P. 630. See Sutton v. Champagine, 1917, 141 La. 469, 75 So. 209.

93. Baca v. Baca, 1963, 71 N.M. 468, 379 P.2d 765; Los Angeles & S. L. R. R. v. Umbaugh, 1942, 61 Nev. 214, 123 P.2d 224.

94. See Neeley v. Lockton, 1964, 63 Wash.2d 929, 389 P.2d 909.

95. Gorman v. Gause, Tex.Com.App.1933, 56 S.W.2d 855.

property.[96] Specific problems are discussed in the following paragraphs.

Separate Property to Community Property

A spouse may transmute his or her separate property into community property. It may be contended that such an acquisition is by *gift* and property acquired by gift is, by definition, separate property. This technical argument has received some judicial approval.[97] However, the preferred view is that property acquired by gift is separate property *unless the donor has evidenced a contrary intention.*[98]

Assuming that such a transmutation can be made, a question is raised as to required formalities. Argument may be made that if land is involved the transmutation requires a deed as prescribed by the Statute of Frauds. If a chattel is involved there must be delivery in compliance with the law as it relates to gifts. If the transmutation is accomplished by "statutory agreement" the agreement must be executed as prescribed by statute. In some states the community is considered to be a *quasi* legal entity. On this hypothesis, if the husband is the owner of land as a part of his separate estate he may deliver a deed to the *community* and thereby accomplish a transmutation of separate property to community property.[99]

There is authority for the rule that, in the absence of statute, a transmutation of property from separate to community can be accomplished by word of mouth[1] or even by conduct.[2] This conclusion is based upon the concept that the title to community property may be in the name of the husband or in the name of the wife. This concept is inconsistent with the view that if a spouse desires to transmute his separate property to community property he must transfer title to the other spouse.

Community Property to Separate Property

Husband and wife may make valid gifts *inter sese* of their interests in community property and thereby transmute it to separate property.[3] Except as noted, if the transaction involves real property there must be compliance with the provisions of the Statute of Frauds. In the case of chattels there must be compliance with the law as it relates to delivery in the case of a gift. This follows from the fact that ownership must pass from one spouse to the other in order to consummate the transaction. However, if the legal title to the property is held in the *name of the donee* spouse no purpose would be accomplished by a purported transfer of ownership by the donor spouse. Accordingly, the transmutation may be accomplished by an oral declaration.[4]

In Paudler v. Paudler,[5] community funds were used in the purchase of land. At the direction of the husband, the wife was named as grantee and the deed recited that

---

96. See Robbins v. Robbins, Tex.Civ.App.1939, 125 S.W.2d 666.

97. See Burlingham v. Burlingham, 1963, 72 N.M. 433, 384 P.2d 699, 707.

98. See Tittle v. Tittle, 1949, 148 Tex. 102, 220 S.W.2d 637.

99. See, for example, In re Shea's Estate, 1962, 60 Wash.2d 810, 376 P.2d 147.

1. Woods v. Security First National Bank, 1956, 46 Cal.2d 697, 299 P.2d 657. *Contra:* Davies v. Metropolitan Life Ins. Co., 1937, 191 Wash. 459, 71 P.2d 552.

2. Long v. Long, 1948, 88 Cal.App.2d 544, 199 P.2d 47.

3. Schwartz v. Schwartz, 1938, 52 Ariz. 105, 79 P.2d 501.

4. Estate of Wieling, 1951, 37 Cal.2d 106, 230 P.2d 808.

5. 210 F.2d 765 (5 Cir. 1954).

the property was her "separate property and estate." The court held that, in the absence of fraud, the husband was estopped to deny the truth of the recital. If such a recital is contained in a deed executed by the husband the parol evidence rule prevents the admission of evidence that would change the "nature of the transaction." However, the husband is not foreclosed from introducing evidence of the fact that the deed was a sham and not intended to be an instrument of conveyance.[6]

But an intention on the part of the husband to transmute community property to the separate property of the wife must be "clear and unequivocal". The mere establishment of a joint bank account by the husband with community funds to enable the wife to pay community debts without any intention to make a gift will not suffice for the purpose.[7]

Important methods of transmutation are as follows:

First: Community property and joint tenancy are inconsistent forms of concurrent ownership. If community funds are used in the acquisition of property as joint tenants a transmutation to separate property results.[8] But such a transmutation cannot be accomplished in the absence of consent on the part of both the husband and the wife.[9] For example, one spouse cannot create a joint tenancy by the use of community funds if the other spouse has no knowledge of the transaction.

In a number of decisions it is held that even if property is acquired by husband and wife described as "joint tenants" the property may retain its status as community property. Extrinsic evidence is admissible to prove that the husband and wife did not intend a transmutation from community to separate.[10] It is considered that transmutation is a matter of intention and the parol evidence rule does not exclude evidence offered to prove the "true nature" of the written instrument. Even assuming that a transmutation does take place, the rule is followed in some states that the property may be transmutation back to community property by oral agreement.

A Texas statute provides that a transmutation of community property to separate property *by partition* can be accomplished only by a written instrument subscribed and acknowledged by the husband and wife.[11] But it is also provided by statute that a husband and wife may, by written agreement, create a joint estate out of their community property, with right of survivorship.[12] Even in the absence of such a statute, a transmutation may be accomplished by the purchase of United States Savings Bonds. Because of the supremacy clause of the United States Constitution state restrictions regarding such transmutations are not applicable.[13]

---

6. Salveter v. Salveter, 1929, 206 Cal. 657, 275 P. 801.

7. Geo. L. Ducros Tile Co. v. Ruth, La.App.1962, 137 So.2d 484.

8. Siberell v. Siberell, 1932, 214 Cal. 767, 7 P.2d 1003; Chavez v. Chavez, 1952, 56 N.M. 393, 244 P.2d 781. See also, Mullikin v. Jones, 1955, 71 Nev. 14, 278 P.2d 876.

9. Blankenship v. Blankenship, 1963, 212 Cal.App.2d 736, 28 Cal.Rptr. 176. *Cf.:* Socal v. King, 1950, 36 Cal.2d 342, 223 P.2d 627.

10. Tomaier v. Tomaier, 1944, 23 Cal.2d 754, 146 P.2d 905.

11. See Brunson v. Brunson, Tex.Civ.App.1963, 372 S.W.2d 761 (construing § 46 of the Probate Code, Vernon's Ann.Tex.Stats.).

12. Art. 4624a, Vernon's Ann.Tex.Civ.Stats. (construed in Hilley v. Hilley, 1961, 161 Tex. 569, 342 S.W.2d 565, overruling Ricks v. Smith, 1958, 159 Tex. 280, 318 S.W.2d 439).

13. Free v. Bland, 1962, 369 U.S. 663, 82 S.Ct. 1089, 8 L.Ed.2d 180.

Second: If a husband or wife obtains a policy of life insurance and names the other spouse as beneficiary, the proceeds derived from the policy constitute separate property. This is true even though premiums were paid with community funds.[14] The transmutation is accomplished by gift from the insured to the beneficiary. If the estate of the insured is named as beneficiary the proceeds constitute community property.[15]

Third: If a husband uses community funds to erect improvements upon his separate estate, the improvements become a part of the husband's separate estate. This transmutation is brought about because of the general rules relating to accession and fixtures. However, the husband is under a duty to reimburse the community because he does not have a right to enrich his own estate by the use of community funds.[16] The prevailing rule is that the extent of reimbursement is measured by the increase in the value of the land that resulted from the expenditure.[17] The increase, if any, is determined as of the date of the dissolution of the community.[18] It is obvious that the increase in value might not equal the costs of the improvements.[19] In that event there is a resultant loss to the community. It would seem that the only way to protect the interest of the wife is to require reimbursement of the funds expended by the husband plus interest.[20]

If a husband uses community funds to erect improvements upon the wife's separate property it is presumed that he thereby intended to make a gift to the wife to the extent of the expenditures involved.[21] However, the husband is not foreclosed from proving that he did not intend to make such a gift. In that event the community is entitled to reimbursement to the extent that funds were used for the purpose, plus interest.

MANAGEMENT AND CONTROL OF COMMUNITY PROPERTY

106. In general, a husband has management and control of community property but this right may be forfeited if he abandons his wife without justification. It is frequently provided by statute that a conveyance or encumbrance of community real property requires the written consent of the wife. In some states a wife has managerial rights as to some types of community property, such as her earnings.

The general rule is that mutual consent is necessary if a transaction involves the gift of community property. Otherwise, such a gift may be set aside. In some states the gift will be sustained to the extent of one-half if proceedings to set it aside are not started until after the dissolution of the community by death or divorce.

With exceptions to be noted, management and control of community property is placed

14. Davis v. Magnolia Petroleum Co., Tex.Civ.App. 1937, 105 S.W.2d 695.

15. Succession of Budding, 1902, 108 La. 406, 32 So. 361.

16. *Cf.:* Estate of Turner, 1939, 35 Cal.App.2d 576, 96 P.2d 363 (where husband expended community funds to pay taxes and assessments levied against his separate estate). *Cf.:* Mayhood v. La Rosa, 1962, 58 Cal.2d 498, 24 Cal.Rptr. 837, 374 P.2d 805 (apparently community acquired an estate in the land).

17. Lawson v. Ridgeway, 1951, 72 Ariz. 253, 233 P.2d 459; Provost v. Provost, 1929, 102 Cal.App. 775, 283 P. 842; Tilton v. Tilton, 1963, 85 Idaho 245, 378 P.2d 191; Dakan v. Dakan, 1935, 125 Tex. 305, 83 S.W.2d 620; In re Cormack's Estate, 1925, 133 Wash. 374, 233 P. 942.

18. Giamanco v. Giamanco, La.App.1961, 131 So.2d 159. See Lawson v. Ridgeway, 1951, 72 Ariz. 253, 233 P.2d 459. But see, Succession of McClelland, 1859, 14 La.Ann. 762, 763 (actual cost).

19. See Abunza v. Olivier, 1956, 230 La. 445, 88 So.2d 815.

20. See Kingsbery v. Kingsbery, 1963, 93 Ariz. 217, 379 P.2d 893 (reimbursement required).

21. Shaw v. Bernal, 1912, 163 Cal. 262, 124 P. 1012. *Cf.:* Chrisentery v. Chrisentery, La.App.1960, 124 So.2d 426.

in the hands of the husband.[22] This right of management is not absolute. Statutory restrictions have been imposed looking to the protection of the wife's interest. In addition, there is authority for the view that the husband is a *"quasi* trustee" and may be held personally accountable for an abuse of the power of management that is conferred upon him.[23] Criminal liability may follow intentional acts that result in damage to or destruction of community property by the husband.[24]

In a number of states it is provided by statute that even though the husband has general managerial rights with respect to community personal property, it is not without limitation. He cannot "sell, convey, or encumber the furniture, furnishings, or fittings of the home, or the clothing or wearing apparel of the wife or minor children that is community, without the written consent of the wife." [25] Household goods do not cease to be furnishings of the home merely because they are stored in a warehouse.[26] A conveyance or encumbrance by the husband in violation of the statute is void even against a *bona fide* purchaser or mortgagee for value and without notice.[27]

If a husband abandons his wife without justification he may thereby lose his right of management with respect to community personal property.[28] A married woman's status as an abandoned wife authorizes her to sue for the recovery of community property.[29] In some states it is provided by statute that a wife has a right to manage and control her earnings even though this involves management of community property.[30]

To the extent that community property can be held liable for debts incurred by the husband to that extent community real property can be attached to obtain satisfaction. The consent of the wife is not necessary to a sale on execution.[31] However, two important theories relating to voluntary conveyances of community real property are as follows:

First: In some of the states the husband has the power and the right to convey community real property and the conveyance may be made without the consent of the wife. With exceptions to be noted, the wife does not have the power to make such a conveyance.

A Texas statute provides that community real property "may be disposed of by the husband alone." [32] The rule followed in that state is that the legal title vests in the spouse named as grantee and the title of the other spouse is equitable.[33] Even if community

---

22. Sanders v. P. & S. Insurance Co., La.App.1960, 125 So.2d 24 (husband is proper party to prosecute a suit for restitution of community asset); Ellis v. City of San Antonio, Tex.Civ.App.1961, 341 S.W. 2d 508 (husband is proper party to give notice of injuries suffered by the wife—a preliminary step in establishing municipal liability).

23. See, for example, Fields v. Michael, 1949, 91 Cal. App.2d 443, 205 P.2d 402.

24. People v. Schlette, 1956, 139 Cal.App.2d 165, 293 P.2d 79, certiorari denied 352 U.S. 1012, 77 S.Ct. 556, 1 L.Ed.2d 559.

25. See, for example, West's Ann.Cal.Civ.Code, § 172.

26. Matthews v. Hamburger, 1939, 36 Cal.App.2d 182, 97 P.2d 465.

27. Dynan v. Gallinatti, 1948, 87 Cal.App.2d 553, 197 P.2d 391.

28. Wampler v. Beinert, 1923, 125 Wash. 494, 216 P. 855.

29. Rogers v. Winters, 1960, 161 Tex. 451, 341 S.W.2d 417.

30. See, for example, West's Ann.Cal.Civ.Code, § 171c.

31. Holt v. Empey, 1919, 32 Idaho 106, 178 P. 703.

32. Seydler v. Herder, Tex.Civ.App.1962, 361 S.W.2d 411. See art. 4619, Vernon's Ann.Civ.Stats.

33. Edwards v. Brown, 1887, 68 Tex. 329, 4 S.W. 380.

real property is taken in the name of the wife she does not have capacity to make a conveyance without the consent of the husband.[34] However, oral consent will suffice for this purpose.[35]

In Louisiana a husband may convey community real property unless it stands of record in the name of the wife alone.[36] This rule is designed as a means by which to protect the separate property of the wife. The underlying theory is that if property is acquired in the name of the wife it is presumably a part of her separate estate. A conveyance of community real property by the husband without "a real consideration" is designated as a "simulated sale" and may be set aside by the wife.[37] If there is a consideration, even though it may not be an adequate consideration, the remedy of the wife is against the husband to recover damages for fraud.[38]

Second: In a majority of the states it is provided by statute that, except in the case of short term leases, a conveyance or encumbrance[39] of community real property by the husband requires the written consent of the wife.[40] A lease is an "encumbrance"

within the meaning of such a statute.[41] The wife of a lessee must consent to a modification[42] or a surrender[43] of a lease (unless a short term lease is involved).[44]

Usually, there is a statutory rule that if the wife is incompetent a judicial order may be obtained authorizing a sale by the husband subject to conditions looking to the protection of the wife in the proceeds derived from the sale.[45]

A conveyance made by the husband without the written consent of the wife is not void. It is merely voidable. Accordingly, if a wife is informed of the facts and accepts benefits of the transaction she may be estopped to deny the validity of the transaction.[46] Some statutes provide that if the husband is the owner of record, a conveyance by him alone is presumed to be valid. The wife must institute proceedings to set the conveyance aside within a stated period after recordation of the conveying instrument.[47] If a *bona fide* purchaser for value and without notice is involved there is authority for the view that the transaction can be avoided

---

34. Daniels v. Mason, 1896, 90 Tex. 240, 38 S.W. 161.

35. Lockhart v. Garner, 1957, 156 Tex. 580, 298 S.W. 2d 108.

36. Young v. Arkansas-Louisiana Gas Co., 1936, 184 La. 460, 166 So. 139. See Succession of Franek, 1953, 224 La. 747, 70 So.2d 670, construing La. art. 2334, LSA.

37. Azar v. Azar, 1960, 239 La. 941, 120 So.2d 485. See Thigpen v. Thigpen, 1956, 231 La. 206, 91 So.2d 12.

38. See Brooke v. Brooke, La.App.1961, 132 So.2d 685.

39. Batts v. Greer, 1963, 71 N.M. 454, 379 P.2d 443 (grant of an easement).

40. See, for example, Ariz.R.S., §§ 33–451, 33–452 (conveyance or encumbrance shall not be valid unless executed and acknowledged by both husband

and wife—except in the case of a mining lease); West's Ann.Cal.Civ.Code, § 172a; Idaho Code, § 32–912; New Mexico—1941 Comp. § 65–403; Wash. RCW 26.16.040.

41. Fargo v. Bennett, 1922, 35 Idaho 359, 206 P. 692.

42. Intermountain Realty Co. v. Allen, 1939, 60 Idaho 228, 90 P.2d 704.

43. But see, First National Bank v. Brashear, 1927, 200 Cal. 389, 253 P. 143.

44. *Cf.:* Tibbals v. Iffland, 1895, 10 Wash. 451, 39 P. 102 (husband may assign a leasehold estate without the wife joining therein).

45. See Estate of Risse, 1957, 156 Cal.App.2d 412, 319 P.2d 789.

46. Rice v. McCarthy, 1925, 73 Cal.App. 655, 239 P. 56; Wilson v. Beck, Tex.Civ.App.1926, 286 S.W. 315. *Cf.:* Bowman v. Hardgrove, 1939, 200 Wash. 78, 93 P.2d 303.

47. See, for example, West's Ann.Cal.Civ.Code, § 172a.

only if there is restoration of the consideration paid.[48]

A California statute provides that if title is of record in the name of the wife, a conveyance or mortgage by the wife is conclusively presumed to be valid in favor of a *bona fide* purchaser or encumbrancer.[49]

Gifts

While the general rule is that one spouse has a right to make a gift of community property to the other spouse,[50] mutual consent is necessary if the gift is made to a third party.[51] Some statutes provide that the consent must be expressed in writing.[52] In at least one state it is held that a gift by the husband to a third party will be sustained if it is reasonable in light of "total worth" of the community and is not made for the purpose of defrauding the wife.[53] In Louisiana a gift may be sustained if it is made for the establishment of the children of the marriage.[54]

The rule against unauthorized gifts of community property cannot be circumvented under the guise of an exercise of "contractual power" by the husband or wife. As aptly stated in Neeley v. Lockton (Wash.),[55] it

"may, however, be stated that the general rule in Washington is that contracts, and particularly beneficiary designations, will control only to the extent that they are not inconsistent with the community property law." [56]

A donor who makes an unauthorized gift is not in a position to attack its validity.[57] Relief is available only to the injured spouse. However, a cause of action for the violation of such a property right survives the owner of the right. For example, if a wife has a right to set aside a gift of community property made by her husband, the executor of the wife's estate may assert that right.[58]

The general rule is that if one spouse makes an unauthorized gift of community property the other spouse can set it aside in its entirety [59] unless he is estopped to do so by electing to take benefits under the gift (doctrine of election).[60]

There is authority for the rule that the gift can be set aside only to the extent of one-half if proceedings are not instituted until after the dissolution of the community.[61]

---

48. Mark v. Title Guarantee & Trust Co., 1932, 122 Cal.App. 301, 9 P.2d 839. See Fairchild v. Wiggins, 1963, 85 Idaho 402, 380 P.2d 6.

49. See West's Ann.Cal.Civ.Code, § 164.

50. Estate of Miller, 1937, 23 Cal.App.2d 16, 71 P.2d 1117; Davis v. Magnolia Petroleum Co., Tex.Civ. App.1937, 105 S.W.2d 695.

51. Nimey v. Nimey, 1935, 182 Wash. 194, 45 P.2d 949. *Cf.:* In re McCoy's Estate, 1937, 189 Wash. 103, 63 P.2d 522.

52. See, for example, West's Ann.Cal.Civ.Code, §§ 172, 172a.

53. Nixon v. Brown, 1923, 46 Nev. 493, 214 P. 524.

54. Melady v. Succession of Bonnegent, 1917, 142 La. 534, 77 So. 143. See Thompson v. Societe Catholique D'Education, 1925, 157 La. 875, 103 So. 247.

55. 63 Wash.2d 929, 389 P.2d 909, 911 (1964).

56. *Accord:* Tyre v. Aetna Life Ins. Co., 1960, 54 Cal. 2d 399, 6 Cal.Rptr. 13, 353 P.2d 725. But see, Benson v. City of Los Angeles, 1963, 60 Cal.2d 355, 33 Cal.Rptr. 257, 384 P.2d 649; In re Webb's Estate, 1956, 49 Wash.2d 6, 297 P.2d 948; Free v. Bland, 1962, 369 U.S. 663, 82 S.Ct. 1089, 8 L.Ed.2d 180.

57. Brandt v. Brandt, 1939, 32 Cal.App.2d 99, 89 P.2d 171.

58. Harris v. Harris, 1962, 57 Cal.2d 367, 19 Cal.Rptr. 793, 369 P.2d 481.

59. Britton v. Hammell, 1935, 4 Cal.2d 690, 52 P.2d 221; Novo v. Hotel Del Rio, 1956, 141 Cal.App.2d 304, 295 P.2d 576 (gambling losses sustained by husband classified as "gifts").

60. See Lahaney v. Lahaney, 1929, 208 Cal. 323, 281 P. 67.

61. Trimble v. Trimble, 1933, 219 Cal. 340, 26 P.2d 477 (death); Rubenstein v. Solk, 1935, 5 Cal.App.2d 426, 43 P.2d 324 (interlocutory decree of divorce); Anderson v. Idaho Mutual Benefit Ass'n, 1956, 77 Idaho 373, 292 P.2d 760. But see Occidental Life Ins. Co. v. Powers, 1937, 192 Wash. 475, 74 P.2d

This conclusion is in recognition of the fact that the donor spouse does have a vested interest in community property. Under the circumstances it is proper to consider the gift as a partition of interests.

LIABILITY FOR DEBTS

107. In a majority of the states it is provided by statute that married women have capacity to contract.

a. Separate property of the wife. In general, a married woman is liable for her own debts but she is not liable for the debts of her husband. Under varying circumstances, statutes in a number of states impose a "family-expense" liability upon the wife.

b. Separate property of the husband. The husband cannot be held liable for the torts committed by the wife if there is no participation on his part.

> In general, the separate property of the husband cannot be held liable for contractual obligations incurred by the wife. However, if he fails to provide her with the necessaries of life, and if she has not abandoned him without justification, a third person who supplies these necessaries may recover the reasonable value thereof from the husband.

> In some states a judgment may be obtained against the husband for a "community debt" incurred by the wife.

c. Community property. According to one theory, community property may be held liable only for the debts of the spouse entrusted with its management.

> In a number of states the view is followed that community property can be held liable only for community debts. However, a debtor's share of community property can be held to satisfy a debt imposed by law if it accrued prior to the time of the marriage.

27, 114 A.L.R. 531, noted in 19 Ore.Law Rev. 384 (1940). *Cf.:* In re Towey's Estate, 1945, 22 Wash.2d 212, 155 P.2d 273, noted in 20 Wash.Law Rev. 167 (1945).

If liability depends upon whether or not a community debt is involved, the issue should be determined by reference to the law of the domicile of the debtor at the time the debt was incurred.

Separate Property of the Wife

For a married woman to be held personally liable *on a community debt,* such as a debt incurred for necessaries, the proof of her intention to bind herself personally must be clear and convincing.[62] It is reasoned that if the wife does enter into a contract for necessaries she is presumably acting as an agent for her husband. Under such circumstances, the agent's intention to incur personal liability must be shown.

If an action is brought to establish contractual liability in connection with a transaction arising after marriage, a married woman may rely upon the defense of coverture to the extent that ancient rules regarding her incapacity have not been removed by statute. In a majority of the states such incapacity has been removed by the enactment of Married Women's Acts and a married woman's separate estate may be reached to satisfy the claims of creditors.

Early Louisiana authorities declare the rule that a married woman cannot be held personally liable on an obligation that arose out of the assumption of a debt of her husband or on a community debt. This incapacity has been removed by the Louisiana Married Woman's Emancipation Act which provides:[63] "They (married women) may make contracts of all kinds, and assume or stipulate for obligations of all kinds, and in any form or manner now permitted, or which may hereafter be permitted, by law

62. Rouchon v. Rocamora, La.App.1956, 84 So.2d 873 (rent); Smith v. Viser, La.App.1960, 117 So.2d 673 (mdse.).

63. LSA–R.S. 9–101.

for any person, married or unmarried, of either sex, and in no case shall any act, contract, or obligation of a married woman require, for the validity or effectiveness thereof, the authority of her husband or of the judge." Problems relating to liability of husband and wife are discussed in the following paragraphs.

According to the view followed in Texas, the capacity of a married woman to contract in such manner as to bind her separate estate is restricted to cases where the contract is for the benefit of her separate estate.[64] However, the court has repudiated the common law rule that, except as authorized by statute, the contract of a married woman is void. It is held that such a contract is merely voidable.[65] Accordingly, an unauthorized contract may be ratified by conduct that takes place after the disability of coverture has been removed.[66] Further, a married woman may be bound by a representation that a contract is made for the benefit of her separate estate [67] and if she contracts as a *feme sole* she will be estopped to assert the incapacities respecting contracts that arise from marriage.[68]

In the Texas case of Panhandle Construction Co. v. Lindsey,[69] it is held that a married woman cannot be held liable for breach of an express or an implied warranty even though she does sign a deed involving the conveyance of community real property. The claimed obligations were not related to the preservation of her separate estate. In those states following the view that the capacity of a married woman to contract is unrestricted, a married woman who signs a deed as a vendor may be held liable for breach of covenants, express or implied.[70] Additional rules are as follows:

First: A married woman may be held personally liable for her torts. However, in a few states the view is followed that the community is a *quasi* legal entity. Under this theory it is held that if the tort occurred in connection with a community activity the wife cannot be held personally liable. Only the community property can be reached to satisfy the claim.[71]

Second: Except as noted, a wife cannot be held liable for debts incurred by the husband. However, in some states it is provided by statute that the separate property of the wife may be charged for the support of the husband if he has not deserted her and, because of infirmity, he is unable to support himself.[72]

A Washington statute provides that the expenses of the family and the expense incident to the education of the children are chargeable against the property of either the husband or the wife.[73] A similar but more

---

64. Borders v. Moran, Tex.Civ.App.1932, 51 S.W.2d 434. See Wyner v. Express Publishing Co., Tex.Civ. App.1956, 288 S.W.2d 583.

65. But see, Teas v. Kimball, 5 Cir. 1958, 257 F.2d 817 (a married woman who has not had her disabilities of coverture removed is incapable of entering into a mercantile partnership).

66. Leake v. Saunders, 1935, 126 Tex. 69, 84 S.W.2d 993 (1935).

67. Willson v. Manasco, Tex.Civ.App.1933, 63 S.W. 2d 910.

68. Hale v. Realty Acceptance Corp., Tex.Civ.App. 1938, 122 S.W.2d 334, noted in 17 Tex.Law Rev. 376 (1939). See Podolnick v. Hamilton, Tex.Civ.App. 1961, 349 S.W.2d 715.

69. 123 Tex. 613, 72 S.W.2d 1068 (1934).

70. See, for example, Platner v. Vincent, 1924, 194 Cal. 436, 229 P. 24.

71. See, for example, Ellis v. White, La.App.1954, 71 So.2d 640.

72. See, for example, West's Ann.Cal.Civ.Code, § 176; 2 Idaho Code Ann. (1932) 31–916; 2 Nev.Hillyer Comp.Laws (1929), § 3378; N.Mex.Ann.Stats. (1929), § 68–105.

73. RCW 26.20.010.

restricted type of family expense statute has been enacted in California.[74] It is provided that while the general rule is that the separate estate of the wife cannot be held liable for debts incurred by the husband, certain types of the wife's separate property may be held liable for debts incurred by the husband while the parties were living together as husband and wife if the debt was incurred for necessaries. In that event, the separate estate of the wife can be reached to satisfy the debt to the extent that the property consists of gifts from the husband after marriage, earnings and accumulations of the wife and of her minor children living under her custody during a period of separation from her husband, money earned by her as a sole trader [75] and money received by her as damages for her personal injuries.

Third: A wife may be held liable for obligations incurred by her husband while he is acting as the wife's agent.[76]

Separate Property of the Husband

The general rule is that the husband cannot be held liable for the torts of his wife. In those states having a common law background this conclusion has been reached because of the enactment of Married Women's Acts.[77] In some states this rule is based upon specific statutory provision.[78]

With exceptions to be noted, the separate estate of the husband is not liable for contractual obligations incurred by the wife either before or after marriage. This conclusion conforms to provisions of Married Women's Acts that confer upon married women a right to manage their own separate estates. Important exceptions are as follows:

First: A husband is under a duty to support his wife. If he fails to make adequate provision for her support a third person who supplies the wife with necessaries may recover the reasonable value thereof from the husband.[79]

A person claiming a right to recover under the rule must allege and prove not only that the husband failed to provide but that the articles for which recovery is sought constituted necessaries as determined by the "mode of living" to which the parties were accustomed.[80] Liability cannot be based upon transactions taking place after the wife abandons the husband without justification. Further, a wife is not entitled to reimbursement if she expends her own funds for necessaries.[81]

In Washington it is provided by statute that family expenses are chargeable against the property of both husband and wife or either of them. However, this responsibility ceases to exist insofar as the support of the wife is concerned if the parties are separated and living apart by "mutual consent" and the wife, by her conduct, evidenced her unwillingness to fulfill her marital obligations.[82]

Second: In some of the states the view is followed that the husband may be held liable for "a community debt" incurred by the

---

74. West's Ann.Cal.Civ.Code, § 171. See Ackley v. Maggi, 1927, 86 Cal.App. 631, 261 P. 311.

75. See West's Ann.Cal.Code Civ.Proc. §§ 1819, 1820.

76. Ransford v. Ainsworth, 1925, 196 Cal. 279, 237 P. 747; Powell v. First Nat. Bank of Harlingen, Tex. Civ.App. 1934, 75 S.W.2d 471.

77. See, for example, Hageman v. Vanderdoes, 1914, 15 Ariz. 312, 138 P. 1053.

78. See, for example, West's Ann.Cal.Civ.Code, § 171a.

79. Tricketts, Inc. v. Viser, La.App. 1962, 137 So.2d 424 (art. 120, LSA–C.C.).

80. See Allied Finance Co. v. Butaud, Tex.Civ.App. 1961, 347 S.W.2d 366.

81. Gonzales v. Gonzales, 1927, 117 Tex. 183, 300 S. W. 20.

82. Yates v. Dohring, 1946, 24 Wash. 877, 168 P.2d 404.

wife. For example, in the Louisiana case of Breaux v. Decuir,[83] the wife incurred an obligation in the amount of $148.45 for groceries. In an action against the husband for this amount judgment went in favor of the creditor. The court held that it was not material that the husband had supplied the wife with sufficient funds for the purpose. The obligation constituted a "community debt" for which the husband could be held liable.[84]

Third: A husband may be held liable on a debt incurred by his wife if it can be shown that the wife incurred the obligation while acting as the husband's agent.[85]

In the Louisiana case of King v. Dearman,[86] action was brought against defendant husbands to recover rent under a commercial lease. The wives of defendants leased space for the operation of an ice-cream store. The court sustained a judgment against defendants upon the ground that the rent involved a community obligation for which the husbands were liable. This conclusion is based upon the ground that a wife's earnings from a separate trade or business as a public merchant or otherwise, fall within the community if she is living in community with the husband at the time.[87] The liability of the husband does not depend upon his permission, authorization or consent. A community obligation is involved because of the fact that profits from the business fall into the community.[88]

Community Property

According to one theory, community property may be held liable only for the debts incurred by the spouse entrusted with its management. This means that, in general, community property may be held liable only for the debts of the husband because he has a right to manage and control community property. Some of the variations and exceptions to this rule are as follows:

First: According to Art. 1409, Code Napoleon, the community property is liable for all personal debts of the spouses incurred prior to marriage. This rule has been followed in a number of community property states, including California.[89] However, a California statute provides that "earnings" of the husband are not liable for the debts of the wife contracted before marriage.[90] It is also provided that the earnings of the wife are exempt from the debts of the husband incurred prior to marriage.[91]

Second: In some states the managerial rights of the husband are restricted by statute. For example, it is provided by statute in California that a married woman has a right to manage and control "community property money earned by her until it is commingled with other community property." [92] Such "money earned by her" is not liable for debts incurred by the husband except "for the necessaries of life" furnished while the parties are living together.[93]

A Texas statute provides that the wife's earnings and revenues from her separate property are not liable for debts incurred by

---

83. 49 So.2d 495 (La.App.1950).

84. *Accord:* Jones v. Davis, La.App.1934, 155 So. 269 (medical expenses).

85. Hulsman v. Ireland, 1928, 205 Cal. 345, 270 P. 948.

86. 105 So.2d 293 (La.App.1958).

87. See, LSA–Civil Code, arts. 131, 2402, 2403.

88. *Contra:* Coats v. Bockstein, Tex.Civ.App. 1943, 176 S.W.2d 968.

89. See, for example, Van Maren v. Johnson, 1860, 15 Cal. 308.

90. West's Ann.Cal.Civ.Code, § 170.

91. See West's Ann.Cal.Civ.Code, § 168.

92. West's Ann.Cal.Civ.Code, § 171c.

93. West's Ann.Cal.Civ.Code, § 168.

the husband.[94] The exemption of this "special community property" continues *only until it is converted into other property.* It then becomes liable for debts incurred by the husband.[95]

Third: In the Texas case of Campbell v. Johnson,[96] an issue was raised as to liability for damages resulting from the negligence of defendant's wife in connection with the operation of an automobile. The court held that the community property could be held liable. It is reasoned that according to the common law rule a husband is liable for torts committed by his wife. While a statute provided that the husband's separate estate could not be held liable for such an obligation the common law rule remained unchanged in other respects.[97]

A California statute provides that for civil injuries committed by a married woman, "damages may be recovered from her alone, and her husband shall not be liable therefor, except in cases where he would be jointly liable with her if the marriage did not exist." [98] The statute is ambiguous as to the liability of community property. However, a rule of non-liability is declared in McClain v. Tufts.[99] The decision is based in part upon the ground that if the community property could be held liable for the torts of the wife the result would encroach upon the right of the husband to manage and control such property.

Fourth: Community property may be held liable for obligations of the wife if such obli-gations are incurred by her while acting as an agent for the husband.[1]

Community Debt Rule

In a number of states the view is followed that community property can be held liable only for community debts. In general, this rule exempts community property from liability for debts incurred by either the husband or the wife prior to marriage.[2] A Louisiana statute specifically provides that "the debts contracted during the marriage enter into the partnership or community of gains, and must be acquitted out of the common fund, whilst the debts of both husband and wife, anterior to the marriage, must be acquitted out of their own personal individual effects." [3]

The statute declares a community-debt rule but is interpreted in the light of the Spanish law from which it was adopted. According to that law, while the community is not responsible for the separate debts of either spouse, or contracts or debts incurred prior to marriage, a *spouse's share* in the community is responsible for an obligation imposed upon him by law. Accordingly, the payment of money necessary for the support of children of a former marriage may be a proper charge against the community property of a second marriage.[4]

---

94. Art. 4616, Vernon's Ann.Civ.Stats.

95. Moss v. Gibbs, 1963, —— Tex. ——, 370 S.W.2d 452.

96. 284 S.W. 261 (Tex.Civ.App.1926).

97. See also, McDonald v. Senn, 1949, 53 N.M. 198, 204 P.2d 990 (interest of wife may be reached to satisfy the indebtedness).

98. West's Ann.Cal.Civ.Code, § 171a.

99. 83 Cal.App.2d 140, 187 P.2d 818 (1947).

1. Hulsman v. Ireland, 1928, 205 Cal. 345, 270 P. 948.

2. Katz v. Judd, 1919, 108 Wash. 557, 185 P. 613. *Cf.:* Hirales v. Boegen, 1944, 61 Ariz. 210, 146 P.2d 352.

3. LSA-C.C. art. 2403. See Keyser v. James, La.App. 1963, 153 So.2d 97.

4. Gardner v Gardner, 1964, 95 Ariz. 202, 388 P.2d 417; Fazzio v. Kreiger, 1954, 226 La. 511, 76 So. 2d 713; Fisch v. Marler, 1939, 1 Wash.2d 698, 97 P.2d 147 (husband's earnings); Greear v. Greear, 9 Cir.1962, 303 F.2d 893. But see, Stafford v. Stafford, 1941, 10 Wash.2d 649, 117 P.2d 753 (real property exempt).

An obligation may be classified as a community debt as well as an individual debt. Additional rules are as follows:

First: An obligation may be incurred by the wife in connection with a community activity. In that event it qualifies as a "community debt" and the community property may be held liable for its satisfaction.[5] The debt may arise as a result of a recreational activity. Recreational activities on the part of either spouse promotes and advances the general welfare of the community and inures to its benefit.[6]

In Louisiana it is provided by statute that if "the wife is a public merchant, she may, without being empowered by her husband, obligate herself in anything relating to her trade; and in such case, her husband is bound also, if there exists a community of property between them."[7] Interpreting this statute, there is authority for the rule that the community property may be held for commercial debts incurred by the wife in connection with such business even if the husband did not give his consent to the wife's activities.[8] This is the price that must be paid for the economic advantage resulting to the community. The profits, if any, constitute community property.[9]

Second: A husband's debt is presumably a community debt. The controlling question to be determined from the evidence is whether or not the transaction was intended to benefit the community. If such was the intention then a community debt is involved. A community debt may be involved, for example, if a husband executes a note for the benefit of a corporation in which he is a stockholder.[10] A debt incurred in connection with a business activity may be a community debt even though the husband and wife were living apart at the time of the transaction.[11]

Third: Community liability cannot be avoided merely because of the fact that the claim is based upon an intentional or even a malicious act. It is sufficient if the liability is based upon an act incident to the management or the protection of community property.[12] Liability may also be imposed because of a wrongful act that takes place in the course of one's employment. It is no defense that the employment is that of a public official.[13]

Conflict of Laws

In those states where creditors can reach community property only if the debt was incurred for the benefit of the community (community debt), an issue is raised as to choice of law.

In Achilles v. Hoopes (Wash.),[14] H and W, husband and wife, were domiciled in the

---

5. Werker v. Knox, 1938, 197 Wash. 453, 85 P.2d 1041, noted in 14 Wash.Law Rev. 228 (1939).

6. Brantley v. Clarkson, 1950, 217 La. 425, 46 So.2d 614 (modifying Adams v. Golson, 1937, 187 La. 363, 174 So. 876); Moffitt v. Krueger, 1941, 11 Wash.2d 658, 120 P.2d 512. *Cf.:* MacKenzie v. Sellner, 1961, 58 Wash.2d 101, 361 P.2d 165 (at time of automobile accident the husband and wife were living separate).

7. LSA–C.C. art. 131.

8. King v. Dearman, La.App.1958, 105 So.2d 293. *Cf.:* Charles Lob's Sons v. Karnofsky, 1933, 177 La. 229, 148 So. 34.

9. See Colagrossi v. Hendrickson, 1957, 50 Wash.2d 266, 310 P.2d 1072.

10. Donato v. Fishburn, 1961, 90 Ariz. 210, 367 P.2d 245; E. I. Dupont de Nemours & Co., Inc. v. Garrison, 1942, 13 Wash.2d 170, 124 P.2d 939.

11. Dizard & Getty v. Damson, 1964, 63 Wash.2d 526, 387 P.2d 964.

12. Hansen v. Blevins, 1962, 48 Idaho 49, 367 P.2d 758; McHenry v. Short, 1947, 29 Wash.2d 263, 186 P.2d 900. *Cf.:* Verstraelen v. Kellog, 1962, 60 Wash. 2d 115, 372 P.2d 543.

13. Kilcup v. McManus, 1964, 64 Wash.2d ——, 394 P.2d 375. See Shaw v. Greer, 1948, 67 Ariz. 223, 194 P.2d 430.

14. 40 Wash.2d 664, 245 P.2d 1005 (1952).

State of Washington. H, while employed in Oregon, purchased stock in a corporation and gave his note in payment. The note was not paid and this action was brought in Washington to recover the amount thereof. An issue was raised as to whether or not the community property of H and W could be reached to satisfy the obligation. The court held that the community property could not be held liable for payment.[15] It is pointed out that while the note was payable in Minnesota, there was no proof as to the Minnesota law on the question so it would be presumed to be the same as the Oregon law.

In reaching the conclusion indicated it is reasoned that (a) according to Washington law community property cannot be reached to satisfy the separate debt of either the husband of the wife, and (b) this debt was incurred in a state following the rule that all debts are, of necessity, separate debts because the rule as to community debts is not followed, and (c) the character of the debt as a separate or community debt is determined by *reference to the law of the place fixed for performance*. In the case of a tort reference is made to the place where the event occurred.[16]

Contrary to the rule declared in Achilles v. Hoopes, if a judgment is rendered against either the husband or the wife, and it is claimed that community property cannot be reached to satisfy that indebtedness, the community character of the debt should be determined by reference to the law of the domicile of the debtor as it existed

when the debt was incurred.[17] In the first place, this suggested rule would prevent a husband from avoiding community liability by merely crossing a state line and conducting his business in a state that does not follow the community-debt rule. In the second place, the issue is one of particular interest to the state of domicile and can be resolved only by reference to the law of that state.

DIVORCE

108. There is a lack of uniformity in the statutes as to the manner in which community property is to be distributed in divorce proceedings.

a. Property settlement agreement. Upon separation, husband and wife may enter into a property settlement agreement.

> **Fraudulent concealment is involved if the husband fails to disclose the nature and extent of community property. A property settlement agreement may be set aside upon proof of fraudulent concealment and this may justify a collateral attack on a judgment that purports to adjust property rights.**

b. *Res judicata* as to type of property. Divorce proceedings may result in an adjudication as to the nature and extent of community ownership.

Statutes in some states authorize actions for separate maintenance. By this means an award may be made for support and maintenance without the necessity of divorce. There may also be authorization for division of community property in such an action.[18]

In divorce proceedings, while the court may not have jursdiction to award the sepa-

---

15. *Accord:* Escrow Service Co., Inc. v. Cressler, 1961, 59 Wash.2d 38, 365 P.2d 760.

16. Mountain v. Price, 1944, 20 Wash.2d 129, 146 P. 2d 327; Maag v. Voykovich, 1955, 46 Wash.2d 302, 280 P.2d 680.

17. See Babcock v. Tam, 9 Cir.1946, 156 F.2d 116. *Cf.:* Durian v. Curl, Tex.Civ.App.1955, 279 S.W.2d 616.

18. See, for example, Ariz.R.S. § 25–333; West's Ann. Cal.Civ.Code § 137. *Cf.:* Cummings v. Cummings, 1944, 20 Wash.2d 703, 149 P.2d 155 (only a lien may be imposed to secure payment of judgment).

rate property of one spouse to the other,[19] it does have jurisdiction to partition community property.[20] A Texas statute provides: "Nothing herein shall be construed to compel either party to divest himself or herself of the title to real estate." [21] But this does not apply to an order making partition of community real property.[22]

Statutes in some states direct that community property is to be divided as the court deems just.[23] In others the property is to be equally divided.[24] However, some statutes provide that an equal division need not be made if a divorce is granted upon the ground of adultery or extreme cruelty.[25] In that event division is made according to the discretion of the court. In other words, more than half may be awarded to the innocent spouse. If a divorce is granted to *both parties* the equal-division rule applies because neither litigant can qualify as an *innocent*

spouse.[26] In divorce proceedings the husband may be restrained from disposing of or incumbering community property until such time as partition is made.[27] If a divorce is granted without adjudication of property rights, and in the absence of a property settlement agreement, the parties own the property as tenant in common.[28]

According to the civil law rule, a divorce nullifies all "advantages or donations" conferred by the marriage contract or during the marriage insofar as the offending spouse is concerned. However, this is not true if a divorce is granted upon the ground of voluntary separation.[29]

Property Settlement Agreement

Upon separation, husband and wife may enter into a property settlement agreement.[30] The fact of separation need not be set forth in the agreement.[31] A distinction is made between a property settlement agreement and an agreement for support and maintenance. A support and maintenance agreement is not discharged in bankruptcy [32] and may be enforced by contempt proceedings.[33]

---

19. Hailey v. Hailey, 1960, 160 Tex. 372, 331 S.W.2d 299.

20. Schwartz v. Schwartz, 1938, 52 Ariz. 105, 79 P.2d 501, 116 A.L.R. 633; Barba v. Barba, 1951, 103 Cal. App.2d 395, 229 P.2d 465 (but division may be made of quasi community property, see West's Ann.Cal. Civ.Code, § 148). The constitutionality of this statute has been sustained (Addison v. Addison, 1965, —— Cal.2d ——, 43 Cal.Rptr. 97, 399 P.2d 897).

21. Art. 4638, Vernon's Ann.Civ.Stats.

22. See Tipton v. Tipton, 1930, 209 Cal. 443, 288 P. 65 (more than half must be given to the innocent spouse); Nichols v. Nichols, 1962, 84 Idaho 379, 372 P.2d 758 (half need not be awarded to the innocent spouse).

23. See Hanner v. Hanner, 1964, 95 Ariz. 191, 388 P. 2d 239; Freeman v. Freeman, 1963, 79 Nev. 33, 378 P.2d 264; Clark v. Clark, Tex.Civ.App.1962, 362 S. W.2d 655.

24. See, for example, Fitzgerald v. Fitzgerald, 1962, 70 N.M. 11, 369 P.2d 398; West's Ann.Cal.Civ.Code, § 146.

25. West's Ann.Cal.Civ.Code, § 146 (also enumerates incurable insanity); Idaho Code, § 32–712.

26. De Burgh v. De Burgh, 1952, 39 Cal.2d 858, 250 P.2d 598; Davis v. Davis, 1960, 82 Idaho 351, 353 P.2d 1079.

27. Moffitt v. Lloyd, Tex.Civ.App.1936, 98 S.W.2d 860.

28. Lang v. Lang, 1920, 182 Cal. 765, 190 P. 181; Manning v. Benham, Tex.Civ.App.1962, 359 S.W.2d 927; Ambrose v. Moore, 1907, 46 Wash. 463, 90 P. 588. See Brown v. Brown, 1915, 170 Cal. 1, 147 P. 1168. *Cf.:* Daigre v. Daigre, 1956, 230 La. 472, 89 So.2d 41 (partial partition not permitted).

29. Roy v. Florane, 1960, 239 La. 749, 119 So.2d 849.

30. But see, Russo v. Russo, 1945, 208 La. 17, 22 So. 2d 671, noted in 20 Tulane Law Rev. 442 (1946).

31. Boland v. Boland, 1935, 7 Cal.App.2d 401, 46 P.2d 238.

32. See, Remondino v. Remondino, 1940, 41 Cal.App.2d 208, 106 P.2d 437.

33. See, Lazar v. Superior Court, 1940, 16 Cal.2d 617, 107 P.2d 249.

Classification as an agreement for support and maintenance is aided by the fact that it is incorporated in the divorce decree and it appears that the intention of the parties was primarily to reach agreement on amounts to be paid for support and maintenance and not to adjust property rights. A property settlement agreement may be involved even though it contains a provision for payment of support.[34]

There is authority for the view that a reconciliation abrogates a separation agreement to the extent that it remains executory unless the contract contains an express provision to the contrary.[35] However, this is an issue that should be resolved according to the intention of the parties.

To the extent that the husband has management and control of community property his position demands that he make full disclosure to the wife as to the nature and extent of the holdings. Fraudulent concealment is involved if he fails to perform this duty during negotiations for a property settlement agreement or if property rights are litigated during the course of divorce proceedings. A property settlement agreement may be set aside upon proof of fraudulent concealment.[36] There is authority for the view that this constitutes "extrinsic fraud" and justifies a collateral attack on a judg-

Res Judicata as to Type of Property

Divorce proceedings afford a proper forum wherein an issue may be resolved as to

ment purporting to adjust property rights.[37] whether or not designated property constitutes community property.[38] Assuming that the property is subject to the jurisdiction of the court[39] there is finality to the judgment. In other words, it constitutes *res judicata*[40] that the property is or is not community property. Of course, a final adjudication is not involved even if the issue is raised by the pleadings if the judgment is silent regarding the matter.[41] Usually, if the pleadings contain an allegation that there is no community property, there is a final adjudication of the matter if the judgment is silent as to property rights. It is not expected that the court will render a negative judgment.[42]

If the pleadings contain an allegation that designated property is community property, a judgment in the affirmative constitutes *res judicata* that there is no other community property. If the parties desire to adjudicate property rights it must be done in one action. It would be intolerable if a separate action could be maintained for the purpose of adjudicating the status of individual items of property that might go to compose the total of community wealth.

34. See, Ettlinger v. Ettlinger, 1935, 3 Cal.2d 172, 44 P.2d 540.

35. Mundt v. Conn. Gen. Life Ins. Co., 1939, 35 Cal. App.2d 416, 95 P.2d 966.

36. Val v. Bank of America, 1961, 56 Cal.2d 329, 364 P.2d 247, 15 Cal.Rptr. 71; Luquette v. Floyd, La. App.1963, 147 So.2d 894.

37. Flores v. Arroyo, 1961, 56 Cal.2d 492, 15 Cal.Rptr. 87, 364 P.2d 263.

38. See Krier v. Krier, 1946, 28 Cal.2d 841, 172 P.2d 681 (this is also true in an action for separate maintenance).

39. See Taylor v. Taylor, 1923, 192 Cal. 71, 218 P. 756, 51 A.L.R. 1074; Wayne v. Reynolds, La.App. 1960, 125 So.2d 223; McElreath v. McElreath, 1961, 162 Tex. 190, 345 S.W.2d 722.

40. Klebora v. Klebora, 1931, 118 Cal.App. 613, 5 P. 2d 965.

41. Tabler v. Peverill, 1906, 4 Cal.App. 671, 88 P. 994.

42. Champion v. Woods, 1889, 79 Cal. 17, 21 P. 534. But see, Metropolitan Life Ins. Co. v. Skov, D.Or. 1943, 51 F.Supp. 470.

DEATH

109. There is a lack of uniformity in the statutes relating to the power of testamentary disposition of community property and the share to which a surviving spouse is entitled.

a. **Simultaneous death.** Under the Uniform Simultaneous Death Act, if husband and wife die in a common disaster, and there is no sufficient evidence that they died otherwise than simultaneously, the estate of each spouse is entitled to administration as to one-half of the community property.

b. **Source of title doctrine.** Special rules of intestate succession may be applicable as to property that was formerly the separate property of a predeceased spouse or was community property of the decedent and the predeceased spouse.

c. **Doctrine of election.** A person cannot take benefits under a will and at the same time reject its adverse or onerous provisions. He must elect to take under the will or disavow its provisions.

d. **Administration.** The prevailing rule is that funeral expenses and expenses of last illness are debts primarily payable out of the estate of the deceased spouse.

In a few of the community property states it is provided that upon the death of the wife all of the community property passes to the surviving husband.[43] However, upon the death of the husband one-half of the property passes to the surviving spouse and the other half is subject to his testamentary disposition. In a majority of the states both the husband and the wife have a power of testamentary disposition as to one-half of the property.[44] If this power is not exercised one-half of the property passes to the issue,

heirs at law and distributees of the decedent.[45] In a few states the property passes to the surviving spouse.[46]

Simultaneous Death

According to the provisions of the Uniform Simultaneous Death Act,[47] where a husband and wife have died, leaving community property and there is no sufficient evidence that they have died otherwise than simultaneously, one-half of all the community property shall be administered upon, distributed, or otherwise dealt with, as if the husband had survived and as if said one-half were his separate property and the other one-half thereof shall be administered upon, distributed, or otherwise dealt with, as if the wife had survived and as if said one-half were her separate property.

As originally enacted, a separate clause provided that where the insured and the beneficiary in a policy of life or accident insurance have died and there is no sufficient evidence that they have died otherwise than simultaneously the proceeds of the policy shall be distributed as if the insured had survived the beneficiary.[48] This section applies even if a policy of life insurance is paid for with community funds. For example, if a policy is obtained on the life of the husband, the proceeds constitute a part of his estate

---

43. Nev., 2 Hillyer Comp.Laws (1929) §§ 3364, 3365; New Mexico Stats.Ann. (1941) §§ 31–108, 31–109. See, In re Wilson's Estate, 1935, 56 Nev. 353, 53 P. 2d 339.

44. Ariz.R.S. § 14–203; West's Ann.Cal.Prob.Code, § 201; 1 Idaho Code Ann. (1932) § 14–113 (with some limitations); LSA–C.C. arts. 915, 916 (with some limitations); Wash.—RCW 11.04.050.

45. See, Ariz.R.S. § 14–201 (if no descendants then to surviving spouse); LSA–C.C. art. 915 (if no descendants, one-half of the deceased spouse's share goes to his parents and the other half to the surviving spouse; Tex.Vernon's Ann.Civ.St. art. 3662 (descendants take one-half and the surviving spouse one-half); Wash.—RCW 11.04.052. In Louisiana the surviving spouse is entitled to the use of the property for life (Succession of Bonnette, 1937, 188 La. 297, 176 So. 397).

46. West's Ann.Cal.Prob.Code, § 201; Idaho Code Ann. (1932) § 14–113.

47. § 4.

48. § 4.

(he being the insured) to the exclusion of the estate of the wife.[49] The Uniform Simultaneous Death Act was amended in 1953 to provide that the proceeds of such a community asset should be divided between the estate of the husband and the estate of the wife.[50] This does not mean that a similar change has been made in the various estates that have adopted the Act in its original form.

Source of Title Doctrine

Statutes in some states provided for a special rule of *intestate succession* depending upon the origin or source of the title.[51] The rule applies only if the decedent died intestate, without issue and without a surviving spouse. It is applicable only if the property in question was formerly the separate property of a predeceased spouse or was formerly the community property of the decedent and a predeceased spouse. It may be that the property was acquired from the predeceased spouse by gift, inheritance or by right of survivorship in the case of a joint tenancy.[52] The rules may be applicable as to property originally acquired in a non-community property state.[53] Distribution is made as follows:

First: Issue of the predeceased spouse is entitled to the property whether it was formerly the separate property of the predeceased spouse or the community property of the predeceased spouse and the deceased spouse.[54]

Second: If the property was formerly the separate property of the predeceased spouse, and there is no issue entitled to distribution, the property is distributed to his father and mother or the survivor of them. If they are both deceased then the property is distributed to his brothers and sisters. It is considered that since the property had its source in the separate property of the predeceased spouse it should be returned to his or her branch of the family.

Third: If the property was formerly the community property of the predeceased spouse and the deceased spouse, and there is no issue of the predeceased spouse, one-half of the property is distributed to the father and mother of the predeceased spouse or, if none, to his brothers and sisters. The other half is distributed in like manner to the family of the deceased spouse. It is considered that since the property had its source in the community property of the parties it should be distributed to the families of each spouse.

Doctrine of Election

A person cannot take benefits under a will and at the same time reject its adverse or onerous provisions. He must elect either to take under the will or disavow its provisions. For example, assume that a husband has a power of testamentary disposition as to one-half of the community property and that he is also the owner of separate property. He may direct in his will that his separate property is to be distributed to his widow and that all of the community property (not just his undivided half) is to be distributed to

---

49. Estate of Wedemeyer, 1952, 109 Cal.App.2d 67, 240 P.2d 8; Brown v. Lee, Tex.Civ.App.1963, 371 S.W.2d 694; In re Clise's Estate, 1964, 64 Wash.2d —, 391 P.2d 547.

50. Uniform Simultaneous Death Act, § 5.

51. West's Ann.Cal.Prob.Code, §§ 228, 229; 2 Idaho Code Ann. 14–103(8); New Mexico, 1941 Comp. § 31–116.

52. Estate of Abdale, 1946, 28 Cal.2d 587, 170 P.2d 918.

53. Estate of Krey, 1960, 183 Cal.App.2d 312, 6 Cal. Rptr. 804.

54. An adopted child qualifies as "issue" within the meaning of the statute (Estate of Mercer, 1928, 205 Cal. 506, 217 P. 1067).

his children. The widow may elect to take against the will. That is to say, she may claim her undivided interest in the community property. However, in that event she will not be entitled to take the separate estate under the will.

Before the doctrine of election can be applied it must be clear that the testator intended to put the surviving spouse to her election. In Estate of Rossi (Cal.),[55] testator's will left one-half of his "property or possessions" to his widow and the other one-half to his children. The court held that the will did not evidence the fact that the testator intended to require an election on the part of his widow. As such, she was entitled to one-half of the community property as a surviving member of the community. She was also entitled to one-half of her husband's interest because of the will. It is not clear that the husband intended to dispose of *all* of the community property. He intended to dispose of only *his property or possessions* and the extent of that interest was one-half of the property.[56] This conclusion is aided by the fact that the testator presumably intended his widow to take some interest under the will. She was entitled to one-half of the community property without the aid of the will.

Administration

In a number of states it is provided by statute that upon the death of either spouse all of the community property is subject to administration. While the share of the surviving spouse is not considered to be a part of the estate of the decedent, administration is necessary to ascertain the share of the surviving spouse. The extent of that interest

is made to depend upon the indebtedness to be satisfied out of community property.[57]

A California statute provides that community property passing from the control of the husband, either by reason of his death or by virtue of testamentary disposition by the wife, is subject to his debts and to administration and disposal. In the event of testamentary disposition by the wife, the husband, pending administration, retains the same power to sell, manage and deal with the community personal property as he had in her lifetime. His possession and control of the community property is not transferred to the personal representative of the wife except to the extent necessary to carry her will into effect.[58] A Nevada statute provides that upon the death of the wife the entire community belongs to the surviving husband and no administration of the estate is required.[59] In Texas the rule is followed that a surviving husband or wife may sell community property for the payment of community debts and convey the interest of the children. This may be done without administration.[60] Additional problems are as follows:

First: A California statute provides that funeral expenses and expenses of last illness shall be deemed debts primarily payable out of the estate of the deceased spouse, whether or not the surviving spouse is financially able to pay such expenses and whether or not

---

55.　169 Cal. 148, 146 P. 430 (1915).

56.　See La Tourette v. La Tourette, 1914, 15 Ariz. 200, 137 P. 426. *Cf.:* Estate of Wolfe, 1957, 48 Cal.2d 570, 311 P.2d 476.

57.　Ariz.R.S. §§ 14–531, 14–533, 14–514; Vernon's Ann. Tex.Civ.Stats.(1936) arts. 3627–3631, 3661–3681 (but no administration where the surviving spouse takes all of the community property by right of survivorship); Wash.—RCW 11.04.050, 11.28.030.

58.　West's Ann.Cal.Prob.Code, §§ 202, 203.

59.　See In re Wilson's Estate, 1935, 56 Nev. 353, 53 P. 2d 339.

60.　Turner v. Sawyer, Tex.Civ.App.1954, 271 S.W.2d 119. *Cf.:* Ewald v. Hufton, 1918, 31 Idaho 373, 173 P. 247 (not conveyed for the purpose of paying debts).

the surviving spouse or any other person is also liable therefor.[61] This same rule is followed in a number of other states.[62] Its application results in a tax advantage in that the expenses involved are deductible from the gross estate of the decedent.

Second: If community property is subject to administration, it is proper to allocate the expense of administration between the community property and the separate property. This allocation is made on the basis of values.[63]

61. West's Ann.Cal.Prob.Code, § 951.1.

62. See Womack v. McCook Bros. Funeral Home, Inc., 1940, 194 La. 296, 193 So. 652; Langhurst v. Langhurst, 1945, 49 N.M. 329, 164 P.2d 204.

63. Estate of Hart, 1962, 206 Cal.App.2d 82, 23 Cal. Rptr. 495.

PART 4

TITLES

A. ORIGINAL TITLE

CHAPTER 20

ACQUISITION OF OWNERSHIP BY ADVERSE POSSESSION

INTRODUCTION

110. According to the English rule, the function of the Statute of Limitations is to bar stale claims. The prevailing American rule is that the purpose of the statute is not only to bar stale claims but is to confer ownership upon the adverse possessor.

a. **Presumption of a lost grant.** Without reference to adverse possession, a claimant may establish his right to property on the theory of a "lost grant." Long continued possession of land coupled with acts of ownership may raise a presumption of a grant.

b. **Conveyance by legal owner.** In the absence of statute to the contrary, the legal owner cannot convey land that is held adversely.

c. **Relation back doctrine.** Under some circumstances it is considered that title acquired by adverse possession relates back to the time when the possession had its inception.

d. **Rights of an adverse possessor.** Like any possessor of land, an adverse possessor is entitled to crops that he may harvest. He may maintain possessory actions against persons who wrongfully invade his legally protected interest and cannot be defeated by the claim that a third party (the legal owner) has superior rights to those of plaintiff.

Under the feudal system emphasis was placed on the possession of land rather than on its ownership. This is evidenced in the law as it related to disseisin that resulted from a wrongful entry upon land and the ouster of the one in possession. A disseisor acquired all the rights of ownership, and the disseisee lost those rights. The ousted owner had a mere cause of action to redress the wrong as distinguished from a proprietary interest. He could recover possession by appropriate legal proceedings (a real action) or by resort to self-help. The right of self-help was lost by the death of the disseisor. The law "cast the land upon the heir" of the disseisor (descent cast) and "tolled" the real owner's right to enter, so that he could only recover the land by an action. This doctrine of descent cast was based upon the ground that a drastic remedy such as self-help should not be visited upon the innocent heirs of the disseisor.[1]

---

1. In England the doctrine of descent cast was abolished by St. 3 & 4 Wm. IV c. 27 (1833).

While the right of action to recover possession was transmissible upon the death of the disseisee, and could be released to the disseisor, it was not otherwise assignable.[2] Statute Westminster I,[3] passed in 1275, limited the time within which the disseisee could maintain an action to recover possession of the land. It then became necessary for him to prove that he, or his ancestor, was seised of the land after the time of Richard I (1189). Thus, the time during which the disseisee could prove seisin became longer and longer. The date was moved ahead by subsequent legislation. Finally, in 1623, a statute was passed that adopted a fixed-time rule.[4] With exceptions relating to possible disabilities on the part of the disseisee, his action to recover possession of the land would fail unless he could prove that he or his ancestor was seised of the land within a period of twenty years prior to the time he filed his action. This statute furnishes the pattern for the statutes adopted in the various states. The time declared in these statutes varies from a minimum of four years to a maximum of twenty-one years.[5]

It is also to be observed that the old doctrine of disseisin has been discarded and replaced by the doctrine of adverse possession. As stated by Professor Bordwell, the "old disseisin was a doctrine of change of title which might be revested as from the beginning by the re-entry of the disseisee. The modern adverse possession is a doctrine of inchoate title which might ripen into perfect title by the lapse of time." [6]

According to the English rule, the function of the Statute of Limitations is to bar stale claims. Thus, action by the legal owner may be barred by lapse of time regardless of the claim asserted by the possessor of land.[7] But the prevailing American rule is to the contrary. Even if a statute purports to bar the claim of a legal owner after the lapse of a stated period, it is operative only in favor of one in possession claiming a freehold estate. The purpose of the statute is to confer ownership upon such a possessor and not merely to bar stale claims. It is not considered to be appropriate to confer such a benefit upon a mere squatter. In addition to asserting a claim of freehold, to qualify as an adverse possessor the possession of the claimant must be actual, open, hostile, notorious, continuous and exclusive. These various factors are discussed under separate headings.

If an owner cannot recover possession of his land because of the Statute of Limitations, he cannot recover possession by resort to self-help. For all practical purposes the adverse possessor is the owner of the property in question.[8] Statutes in some states specifically provide that compliance with the requirements prescribed for adverse possession results in vesting of title in the adverse claimant.

---

2. Bingham, Legal Possession, 13 Mich.Law Rev. 535, 563 (1915).

3. 3 Edw. I, c. 39 (1275).

4. 21 James I, c. 16, §§ 1, 2 (1623).

5. For a compilation of the statutes, see Taylor, Titles to Land by Adverse Possession, 20 Iowa Law Rev. 551 (1935).

6. Bordwell, Property in Chattels, 29 Harv.Law Rev. 374, 378 (1916).

7. See Bordwell, Disseisin and Adverse Possession, 33 Yale Law Journal 141 (1923); Walsh, Title by Adverse Possession, 16 N.Y.Univ.Law Quarterly Review 532, 547 (1939); Warren, A Problem in "Tacking," 88 Univ. of Pa.Law Rev. 897, 905 (1940).

8. See Hushaw v. Kansas Farmers' Union Royalty Co., 1939, 149 Kan. 64, 86 P.2d 559.

Presumption of a Lost Grant

Without reference to adverse possession, a claimant may establish his right to property on the theory of a "lost grant." As an evidentiary matter, long continued possession of land, coupled with acts of ownership, may raise a presumption of a grant.[9] Failure to produce the grant may be explained upon the ground that it has been lost or destroyed. In some instances it seems that the presumption is fictitious in nature.

In the absence of statute the claim of adverse possession cannot be sustained against the United States, the state or a subdivision thereof. However, a claim may be sustained upon the theory of a lost grant.[10] The presumption is not mandatory. It is one that may or may not be drawn by the trier of facts.[11]

Conveyance by Legal Owner

Even if the interest of an "ousted owner" cannot properly be classified as a "mere right," the common law rule is followed in many states that if land is held adversely a deed of the land by the legal owner is champertous and void.[12] A purported grant of minerals by the ousted owner is void[13] and the land cannot be sold to satisfy the claims of his creditors.[14] However, a deed delivered to the adverse possessor is operative as a release of the rights of the legal owner.[15]

The rule that a legal owner cannot convey land while it is in the adverse possession of another was changed in England by statute passed in 1845[16] and the rule has been changed by statute in a number of American states.[17]

Relation Back Doctrine

Under some circumstances the ownership of one who acquires title by adverse possession relates back to the time when the adverse possession had its inception. This is a means by which to protect the adverse possessor from liability for acts committed during the period of possession. For example, in Counce v. Yount-Lee Oil Co. (Fed.),[18] it is held that an adverse possessor could not be held liable for the value of oil taken from the land during the period of adverse possession. One who acquires title by adverse possession is also entitled to land formed by accretion during the statutory period.[19]

Rights of an Adverse Possessor

Like any possessor of land, an adverse possessor has rights that are based upon posses-

9. Trustees of Schools v. Lilly, 1940, 373 Ill. 431, 26 N.E.2d 489, noted in 25 Minn.Law Rev. 100 (1940).

10. See United States v. Fullard-Leo, 1947, 331 U.S. 256, 67 S.Ct. 1287, 91 L.Ed. 1474, noted in 33 Cornell Law Quarterly 437 (1948); 46 Mich.Law Rev. 572 (1948); 95 Univ. of Pa.Law Rev. 406 (1947).

11. Bordages v. Stanolind Oil & Gas Co., Tex.Civ. App.1939, 129 S.W.2d 786, noted in 19 Tex.Law Rev. 87 (1940).

12. See, for example, Florida Power Corp. v. McNeely, Fla.1961, 329 S.W.2d 366 (rule not applicable because land was not held adversely because only a prescriptive right was claimed); Sohier v. Coffin, 1869, 101 Mass. 179; Knowlton v. Coye, 1949, 76 N.D. 478, 37 N.W.2d 343; Blair v. Gwosdof, 1959, 46 Tenn.App. 314, 329 S.W.2d 366.

13. Kentucky West Virginia Gas Co. v. Woods, 5 Cir., 1940, 110 F.2d 94.

14. McConnell v. Brown, 1827, 21 Ky. (5 T.B.Mon.) 478.

15. Williams v. Thomas, 1941, 285 Ky. 776, 149 S.W. 2d 525; Dever v. Hagerty, 1902, 169 N.Y. 481, 62 N. E. 586.

16. 8 & 9 Vict. c. 106, § 6 (1845).

17. See Ames, The Disseisin of Chattels, 3 Harv.Law Rev. 23, 25 (1889).

18. 87 F.2d 572 (5 Cir.1937), certiorari denied Wilkinson v. Yount-Lee Oil Co., 1937, 302 U.S. 693, 58 S.Ct. 12, 82 L.Ed. 536, noted in 51 Harv.Law Rev. 160 (1937).

19. Schmidt v. Marschel, 1942, 211 Minn. 539, 2 N.W. 2d 121.

sion alone. For example, he is the owner of crops that he may harvest during the period of his possession.[20] The legal owner of the land may hold the adverse possessor liable for the *mesne profits*, an amount equivalent to the reasonable rental value of the land.[21]

Cases where the legal owner of land seeks to recover timber or other substances severed from the land during the period of adverse possession are beset by procedural difficulties. He may seek specific recovery or damages. His right to a judgment depends upon his proof of ownership of the land at the time of severance. The action is transitory in nature and "title to land" is not usually determined in such an action. Recovery will be denied unless the issue of ownership is only incidentally involved.[22] That is the situation if the severance was caused by a trespasser, or by one in possession of the land without color of title. In Halleck v. Mixer (Cal.),[23] a distinction is drawn between a case where severance was caused by one in possession of land under color of title and by one in possession without color of title. The legal owner recovered timber that had been severed by an adverse possessor who did not have any basis for his claim of ownership to the land.[24]

Since trespass *quare clausum fregit* is a possessory action, an adverse possessor is en-titled to a judgment in such an action against a person who invades the legally protected interest. The defendant cannot successfully defend the action by proof of the fact that a third party (the legal owner) has superior rights to those of the plaintiff. In other words, the defense of *jus tertii* (the right or interest of a third party) is not available unless the defendant is claiming under such party.

There is a difference of opinion as to the measure of damages. The preferred view is that the amount of recovery depends upon the extent of the plaintiff's interest in the land. He is not entitled to recover for permanent damage caused to the land if he has a mere possessory right terminable at the will of the legal owner.[25] The minority rule is that the possessor of land is entitled to recover to the full extent of the damage caused to the land without regard to the extent of his interest.[26] This is the rule followed in the case of personal property.

In eminent domain proceedings an adverse possessor is entitled to an award to the extent that his possessory interest is involved and to the extent that the interest can be evaluated. In Perry v. Clissold (Eng.),[27] an adverse possessor was awarded the value of the land taken even though the statutory pe-

---

20. See, Rector v. Lewis, 1920, 46 Cal.App. 168, 188 P. 1018, noted in 8 Cal.Law Rev. 247 (1920) (simple possessor); Stockwell v. Phelps, 1866, 34 N.Y. 363 (adverse possessor); Brothers v. Hurdle, 1849, 32 N.C. 490 (simple possessor).

21. Page v. Fowler, 1870, 39 Cal. 412.

22. Ducros v. St. Bernard Cypress Co., 1918, 145 La. 691, 82 So. 841, comment 29 Yale Law Jr. 539 (1920); Mather v. Ministers of Trinity Church, 1817, 3 Serg. & R. (Pa.) 509; Clarke v. Clyde, 1901, 25 Wash. 661, 66 P. 46, noted in 15 Harv.Law Rev. 486 (1902).

23. 16 Cal. 574 (1860).

24. *Cf.*: Kimball v. Lonmas, 1866, 31 Cal. 154.

25. La Salle County Coal Co. v. Sanitary District, 1913, 260 Ill. 423, 103 N.E. 175; Wattemeyer v. Wis., Iowa & Neb. Ry. Co., 1887, 71 Iowa 626, 33 N.W. 140; Anderson v. Thunder Bay River Boom Co., 1885, 59 Mich. 216, 23 N.W. 776; Winchester v. City of Stevens Point, 1883, 58 Wis. 350, 17 N.W. 3, 547.

26. North v. Cates, 1812, 2 Bibb.(Ky.) 591; Todd v. Jackson, 1857, 26 N.J.L. 525; Beaumont Lumber Co. v. Ballard, Tex.Civ.App.1893, 23 S.W. 920 (express finding that plaintiff was not an adverse possessor). See Roberts, A Possessor's Right to Damages for Permanent Injuries to Realty, 28 Ill.Law Rev. 919 (1934).

27. L.R. [1907] A.C. 73, 95 L.T.R. 890, noted in 20 Harvard Law Rev. 563 (1907).

riod had not expired at the time the proceedings were instituted. At the time of the award the claim of the original owners was barred by the statute. Under such circumstances the value of the possessory right was equal to the value of the land.[28]

PHYSICAL ASPECTS OF POSSESSION

111. **One who exercises dominion over land acquires the status of a possessor.** The acts of dominion that may be sufficient to constitute actual possession vary with the conditions involved, such as the size of the area, its normal use etc.

    a. **Color of title.** Generally, color of title is not required for the acquisition of title by adverse possession. However, it is an important factor in a situation involving constructive adverse possession.

    b. **Constructive adverse possession.** Actual possession of a part of a larger tract may carry constructive possession of the entire area if it is claimed in good faith and under color of title.

    c. **Possession must be exclusive.** Possession shared by the legal owner or the public generally is not adverse.

    d. **Possession must be open and notorious.** Acquisition of title by adverse possession depends upon a possession that is open and notorious during the statutory period.

    e. **Possession must be continuous.** A break in the continuity of possession places the constructive possession of the land in the legal owner. This interrupts the running of the Statute of Limitations.

One who exercises dominion over land acquires the status of a possessor. If there is a lack of permanency in connection with the unauthorized use of land the actor is a trespasser and not a possessor.[29]

The dominion required for possession may be evidenced by the fact that the land is fenced or otherwise enclosed.[30] A usual statutory provision is that for the purpose of constituting an adverse possession by a person claiming title, not founded upon some written instrument or some judgment or decree, land shall be deemed to have been possessed and occupied when it has been protected by a substantial enclosure or when it has been usually cultivated or improved.[31] If the possession is under a written instrument or some judgment or decree, actual possession of only a part of the area may give constructive possession of the remaining part. This doctrine of constructive adverse possession is discussed under a separate heading.[32] The acts of dominion that may be sufficient to constitute possession vary with the conditions involved, such as the size of the area, its location and normal use.[33]

According to one view, the use of land for grazing purposes may result in the acquisition of title by adverse possession.[34] This is

---

28. See Campbell v. City of New Haven, 1924, 101 Conn. 173, 125 A. 650, noted in 23 Mich.Law Rev. 180 (1924) (severance damages denied); Costello v. Burke, 1884, 63 Iowa 361, 19 N.W. 247 (award denied); Andrew v. Nantasket Beach R. Co., 1890, 152 Mass. 506, 25 N.E. 966; Robbins v. Milwaukee & Horicon R. Co., 1858, 6 Wis. 636.

29. Huling v. Seccombe, 1928, 88 Cal.App. 238, 263 P. 362 (occasional cutting of grass); Doctor v. Turner, 1930, 251 Mich. 175, 231 N.W. 115.

30. De Las Fuentes v. Macdonnel, 1892, 85 Tex. 132, 20 S.W. 43. But see, Orsborn v. Deep Rock Oil Corp., 1954, 153 Tex. 281, 267 S.W.2d 781 (fencing alone does not constitute possession). See also, West Production Co. v. Kahanek, 1938, 132 Tex. 153, 121 S.W.2d 328, noted in 17 Tex.Law Rev. 360 (1939).

31. See, for example, West's Ann.Cal.Code Civ.Proc. § 325; Wis.S.A. 330.09(1).

32. See infra, note 45 and text.

33. Brumagim v. Bradshaw, 1870, 39 Cal. 23. As to open, wild and unfenced land, see Sherman v. Goloskie, 1963, —— R.I. ——, 188 A.2d 79, rehearing denied —— R.I. ——, 188 A.2d 370; Mullis v. Winchester, 1961, 237 S.C. 487, 118 S.E.2d 61.

34. Kellogg v. Huffman, 1934, 137 Cal.App. 278, 30 P.2d 593; McRae v. Ketchum, 1939, 138 Fla. 610, 189 So. 853; Northwoods Development Corp. v. Kle-

assuming that grazing constitutes a normal use of the land in question. According to another view, this conclusion will be reached only if the land is fenced or otherwise enclosed. This rule is followed out of deference to the local policy of permitting unrestricted grazing upon uninclosed land.[35]

Except as noted, possession of the surface of land carries with it possession of minerals beneath the surface and the area above the surface. If land is held adversely the claim extends not only to the surface but to the area beneath the surface, including minerals.[36] If the record owner does not have a right to convey the surface during the period of adverse possession he does not have a right to convey the minerals beneath the surface.[37] But the adverse possessor of the surface is not in adverse possession of the minerals beneath the surface if there was a severance prior to the time of adverse possession.[38] A severance results if the record owner conveys the minerals in place or creates a profit that includes a right to take minerals, retaining title to the surface, or *vice versa*.

It is not necessary that the adverse possessor be in actual possession of the land claimed adversely. The possession may be in one claiming under the adverse possessor,

such as a tenant.[39] According to some authorities this rule does not apply in the case of a written lease unless the land in question is included in the terms of the lease.[40]

Color of Title

An adverse possessor who claims under color of title is one who claims under a written instrument that he believes in good faith to be a conveyance of the land in question. The instrument does not constitute color of title unless it is fair on its face and contains a description of the land in question.[41]

While color of title is not generally required for the acquisition of title by adverse possession, it is of importance in various situations. Statutes in some states provide that one claiming under color of title may acquire title in a shorter period of time than one not claiming under color of title.[42] Color of title is essential if a claim is based on constructive adverse possession.[43] According to some decisions it may aid the claimant in proving the fact of possession. For example, in Knight v. Denman (Neb.),[44] it is held that the use of land for grazing purposes alone does not constitute adverse possession. However, it is indicated that a different conclusion would

ment, 1964, 24 Wis.2d 387, 129 N.W.2d 121; Young v. Newbro, 1948, 32 Wash.2d 141, 200 P.2d 975.

35. De Las Fuentes v. Macdonell, 1892, 84 Tex. 132, 20 S.W. 43.

36. See Tennessee Coal, Iron & R. Co. v. Brewer, 5 Cir.1937, 92 F.2d 804, noted in 37 Mich.Law Rev. 308 (1938).

37. Kentucky West Virginia Gas Co. v. Woods, 6 Cir. 1940, 110 F.2d 94.

38. Failoni v. Chicago and North Western Ry. Co., 1964, 30 Ill.2d 258, 195 N.E.2d 619; Smith v. Pittston, 1962, 203 Va. 408, 124 S.E.2d 1; United Fuel Gas Co. v. Dyer, 4 Cir.1950, 185 F.2d 99, noted in 14 Univ. of Detroit Law Jr., 153 (1951). See Buckner v. Wright, 1951, 218 Ark. 448, 236 S.W.2d 720.

39. Kellogg v. Huffman, 1934, 137 Cal.App. 278, 30 P. 2d 593; Dean v. Goddard, 1893, 55 Minn. 290, 56 N.W. 1060; Sanders v. Worthington, 1964, —— Tex. ——, 382 S.W.2d 910.

40. Holmes v. Turner's Falls Lumber Co., 1890, 150 Mass. 535, 23 N.E. 305; Williams v. Fuerstenberg, Tex.Com.App., 1930, 23 S.W.2d 305, criticized in 8 Tex.Law Rev. 574 (1930). *Contra:* Capps v. Merrifield, 1924, 227 Mich. 194, 198 N.W. 918 (sufficient if parties understood that the area constituted a part of the leased land).

41. Sanchez v. Garcia, 1963, 72 N.M. 406, 384 P.2d 681.

42. See Taylor, Title to Land by Adverse Possession, 20 Iowa Law Rev. 551, 553 (1935).

43. See Jackson ex dem. Gilliland v. Woodruff, 1823, 1 Cow. (N.Y.) 276.

44. 64 Neb. 814, 90 N.W. 863 (1902), affirmed 68 Neb. 383, 94 N.W. 622 (1903).

be reached if the claimant acted under color of title.

Constructive Adverse Possession

Under the doctrine of constructive adverse possession a claimant may acquire title by adverse possession even though he does not take actual possession of all the land in question.[45] His actual possession of a part of the land claimed adversely affords constructive possession of the remaining area.[46] However, this doctrine is applicable only if claim to the entire area is made by one who acts in good faith and under color of title. That is to say, his claim must be based upon a written instrument that purports to be a conveyance. This instrument must contain a description of the land in question.[47] Some authorities take the position that color of title is not necessary if the extent of the area in question is apparent from the physical condition of the land.[48]

As has been stated, the adverse claimant must prove actual possession of a part of the land claimed adversely for the full statutory period.[49] It is not sufficient if the claimant is the owner in fact of the land actually occupied by him. In that event the possession gives no warning of adverse claim to the owner of other land in the area. Some decisions support the rule that as to size and use, the land actually occupied must bear a reasonable relationship to the entire tract.[50]

A claim of constructive possession fails with respect to land that is in the actual possession of another. If the owner in fact is in actual possession of a part of the area in question he is considered to be in constructive possession of the remaining part to the extent that it is not in the actual possession of the adverse claimant.[51]

Possession Must be Exclusive

The acquisition of title by adverse possession must be supported by a possession that is exclusive of the legal owner and exclusive of the public generally. However, two or more persons may be in possession of the land and thereby acquire a joint interest by adverse possession.[52]

Possession Must be Open and Notorious

Acquisition of title by adverse possession depends upon a possession that is open and notorious during the statutory period. This assures actual or constructive notice to the landowner that an adverse claim is asserted.[53] In Marengo Cave Co. v. Ross,[54] A and B were the owners of adjoining land. The opening to a subterranean cavity, known as Marengo Cave, was located on A's land. The cave extended under land owned by B. A maintained exclusive possession of the cave for

45. Murphy v. Doyle, 1887, 37 Minn. 113, 33 N.W. 220.

46. But see Brown v. Berman, 1962, 203 Cal.App.2d 327, 21 Cal.Rptr. 401.

47. Jackson v. Woodruff, 1823, 1 Cow.(N.Y.) 276.

48. Nelson v. Johnson, 1920, 189 Ky. 815, 226 S.W. 94, noted in 19 Mich.Law Rev. 645 (1921).

49. Bailey v. Martin, 1951, 218 Ark. 513, 237 S.W.2d 16; Wheatley v. San Pedro, L.A. & S.L.R. Co., 1915, 169 Cal. 505, 147 P. 135; Bailey v. Carleton, 1841, 12 N.H. 9; Mullis v. Winchester, 1961, 237 S.C. 487, 118 S.E.2d 61.

50. Bailey v. Martin, 1951, 218 Ark. 513, 237 S.W.2d 16; Jackson v. Woodruff, 1823, 1 Cow.(N.Y.) 276. See Brumagim v. Bradshaw, 1870, 39 Cal. 24.

51. Bishop v. Gilmer Co., Tex.Civ.App.1939, 131 S.W. 2d 173.

52. See Philbin v. Carr, 1921, 75 Ind.App. 560, 129 N. E. 19, 706.

53. See La Chance v. Rubashe, 1938, 301 Mass. 488, 17 N.E.2d 685 (actual knowledge is not necessary).

54. 212 Ind. 624, 10 N.E.2d 917 (1937), noted in 37 Mich.Law Rev. 307 (1938), 13 Notre Dame Lawyer 147 (1938).

the statutory period. However, no physical evidence existed that would indicate the encroachment on B's land. A's claim of adverse possession was denied. The possession was not open and notorious.

A somewhat similar situation exists where land is used by a railroad as a right of way. The landowner is justified in assuming that the claim is limited to an easement and not to a possessory estate.[55]

Possession must be Continuous

A break in the continuity of possession places constructive possession of the land in the legal owner. This interrupts the running of the Statute of Limitations.[56] In Kellogg v. Huffman (Cal.),[57] an adverse possessor used land for grazing purposes during the entire grazing season of each year. While this did not include every day of each year the possession was held to be continuous within the meaning of the rule. The land was reasonably adapted for the use under discussion. So also, in Britt v. Houser (Ky.),[58] the continuity of possession was not broken by the fact that at times each year actual use of the land was not possible because of flood conditions of the Ohio River.

The continuity of possession is not interrupted by the fact that the adverse possessor offers to purchase the estate from the true owner. Such an offer does not necessarily indicate that the claimant recognizes another as the owner and that the subsequent possession is in recognition of that ownership. The offer may be motivated by a desire to avoid litigation.[59] The institution of an action against an adverse claimant to recover possession of the land or to determine ownership merely suspends the operation of the statute during the time of such proceedings.[60] However, the continuity of possession is interrupted if the true owner obtains a final judgment confirming his ownership as against the claim of the adverse possessor.[61]

Under some circumstances one adverse possessor may use the time of occupancy by a prior adverse possessor in computing the statutory period. While unconnected possessions cannot be tacked,[62] tacking is permitted if privity of estate exists between the successive adverse claimants. Privity of estate exists if the parties occupy the relationship of grantor and grantee, devisor and devisee, ancestor and heir or if possession passed by judicial decree. There is also authority for the view that the period of possession by a life tenant claiming under a void will may be tacked to the period of possession of the remainderman claiming under the same will.[63]

Privity of estate exists if it is understood by a grantor and grantee that the area in question was included within the terms of a conveyance. It is not necessary that the land in question be described in the conveying in-

---

55. Mich. Central R. Co. v. Garfield Petroleum Corp., 1940, 292 Mich. 373, 290 N.W. 833, 127 A.L.R. 507, comment, 39 Mich.Law Rev. 297 (1940). See Hoffman v. Zollman, 1912, 49 Ind.App. 664, 97 N.E. 1015.

56. Agency Co. v. Short, 1888, L.R. 13 App.Cas. 793.

57. 137 Cal.App. 278, 30 P.2d 593 (1934).

58. 171 Ky. 494, 188 S.W. 628 (1916).

59. Nechtow v. Brown, 1963, 369 Mich. 460, 120 N.W. 2d 251; Meaders v. Moore, 1939, 134 Tex. 127, 132 S.W.2d 256, 125 A.L.R. 817. See Deponte v. Ulupalakua Ranch, Ltd., 1964, —— Hawaii ——, 395 P.2d 273 (quitclaim deed), rehearing denied, 396 P.2d 826. *Cf.*: Segelke v. Atkins, 1960, 144 Colo. 558, 357 P.2d 636.

60. See Taylor, Continuity in Adverse Possession of Land, 27 Iowa Law Rev. 396, 406 (1942).

61. Creech v. Jenkins, 1938, 276 Ky. 163, 123 S.W.2d 267, comment, 28 Ky.Law. Journal 95 (1939). See Shepherd v. Lyle, Okl.1964, 395 P.2d 641.

62. Doe ex dem. Harlan v. Brown, 1853, 4 Ind. 143. But see, Doe ex dem. Goody v. Carter, [1847] 9 Q.B. 863 (following the rule that the main purpose of the statute is to bar *stale claims*).

63. Hanson v. Johnson, 1884, 62 Md. 25.

strument. For example, in Gregory v. Thorrez (Mich.),[64] a hedge was grown along a line that was considered by the two adjoining owners, A and B, as the true boundary line. In fact, the hedge encroached some seven feet upon B's land. A occupied the land up to the hedge for a period less than that prescribed by the Statute of Limitations and then sold the lot to C. At the time of the sale A and C understood that the land conveyed extended to the hedge. The land described in the deed, however, did not include the seven-foot strip. A question arose as to whether or not the period of adverse possession by A could be tacked to the period of adverse possession by C in computing the statutory period. The court answered this question in the affirmative.[65] There is a minority rule to the contrary. It is reasoned that an adverse possessor does not have an estate that can be conveyed.[66]

MENTAL ASPECTS OF POSSESSION

112. Benefits under the Statute of Limitations are limited to the possessor of land who claims a freehold estate either in himself or one under whom he claims. This requirement is satisfied if his possession is not in subordination to the rights of the legal owner.

    a. Claim of right. A claim of right is not required for the acquisition of title by adverse possession.

64. 277 Mich. 197, 269 N.W. 142 (1936).

65. *Accord:* Sorensen v. Costa, 1948, 32 Cal.2d 453, 196 P.2d 900; Cooper v. Tarpley, 1942, 112 Ind. App. 1, 41 N.E.2d 640; McNeely v. Langan, 1871, 22 Ohio St. 32; El Cerrito, Inc. v. Ryndak, 1962, 60 Wash.2d 847, 376 P.2d 528.

66. Ramsey v. Ramsey, 1948, 229 N.C. 270, 49 S.E. 2d 476; Masters v. Local Union No. 472, United Mine Workers, 1941, 146 Pa.Super. 143, 22 A.2d 70, criticized in 46 Dick.Law Rev. 202 (1942); Adams v. Adams, 1951, 220 S.C. 131, 66 S.E.2d 809, noted in 23 Miss.Law Rev. 291 (1952). For discussion of the view that tacking should be permitted where there is only "privity of claim" see Warren, A Problem in Tacking, 88 Univ. of Pa.Law Rev. 897, 911 (1940).

    b. Mistake as to ownership. A person who occupies land under the mistaken belief that he is the owner may acquire title by adverse possession.

Benefits under the Statute of Limitations are limited to the possessor of land who claims a freehold estate either in himself or one under whom he claims.

In Maas v. Burdetzke (Minn.),[67] defendant took possession of land under the mistaken belief that ownership was in the United States and he claimed benefits under the federal homestead law. In fact, plaintiff was the owner of the land and he denied defendant's claim of title by adverse possession. He contended that defendant did not claim title "as against the whole world" because he did not claim title adversely against the United States. In sustaining defendant's claim of title by adverse possession it is pointed out that a claim of title against the United States is not necessary.[68] Such a claim, even if made, would be ineffectual.

It was sufficient that the defendant claimed a freehold estate as against the legal owner of the land.[69] This means that he did not possess the land in subordination to the right of the true owner. Such a possession may also be described as "hostile." In Harrelson v. Reaves (S.C.),[70] the adverse claimant acquired possession of the land in question under an oral gift from the owner. In sustaining the claim of adverse possession the court states: "An entry under a parol gift, though permissive and friendly in the popular sense, is hostile to and adverse to the paper title in the legal sense, because there is an assertion of

67. 93 Minn. 295, 101 N.W. 182 (1904).

68. But see Hunnewell v. Burchett, 1899, 152 Mo. 611, 54 S.W. 487.

69. *Cf.:* Patterson v. Reigle, 1846, 4 Pa. 201.

70. 219 S.C. 394, 65 S.E.2d 478, 481 (1951), noted in 4 So.Carolina Law Quarterly 320 (1951).

ownership in the occupant." The possession of the claimant was not in subordination to the rights of the legal owner. There is some authority for the view that a possession cannot be described as "hostile" unless the claimant is aware of the fact that the land belongs to another.[71]

Claim of Right

A claim of right, as distinguished from the claim of a freehold estate, is not essential for adverse possession.[72] Statutes in some states provide that possession under a *bona fide* claim will result in the acquisition of title in a shorter period than that fixed for the acquisition of title in other cases.[73] The minority rule is that claim of right is essential for the acquisition of title by adverse possession. The benefits under the Statute of Limitations are not available to an intentional wrongdoer.[74]

Mistake as to Ownership

It is indicated in some decisions that one cannot qualify as an adverse possessor unless he is aware of the fact that the land occupied is the property of another.[75] But the weight of authority is to the contrary. A person need not be an intentional wrongdoer in order to claim the benefit of the statute.

According to the preferred view, a person who occupies land under the mistaken belief that he is the owner may qualify as an adverse possessor.[76] There seems to be no doubt about this if he testifies that his purpose was to claim title whether or not he was, in fact, the owner.

Some authorities take the position that there is a disclaimer of adverse possession if the claimant testifies that he did not intend to claim title to land that he did not own. For example, in Ennis v. Stanley (Mich.),[77] plaintiff claimed title to a six acre tract on the basis of adverse possession. He testified as follows:

"Q. Have you intended all these years to claim something that you did not own as your own? A. Why, no.

"Q. You intended only to claim what was your own, and you thought it was to that line? A. That's right."

The court held that the plaintiff did not occupy the land under sufficient claim to acquire title by adverse possession. It is obvious that plaintiff entertained a claim of title under the mistaken belief that he was the owner. It is not sound to say that he did not qualify as an adverse possessor because of a purely hypothetical matter relating to a supposed state of mind. The question is immaterial to the matter under inquiry.[78]

---

71. See Predham v. Holfester, 1954, 32 N.J.Super. 419, 108 A.2d 458.

72. Rupley v. Fraser, 1916, 132 Minn. 311, 156 N.W. 350.

73. Usually, the shorter period is applicable to possessors claiming under color of title (Ga.Code, §§ 85–406, 85–407; Vernon's Tex.Ann.Civ.St. arts. 5507, 5508, 5509).

74. Creel v. Hammans, 1944, 234 Iowa 532, 13 N.W.2d 305; Riebold v. Smith, Mo.App.1941, 150 S.W.2d 599; Jasperson v. Scharnikow, 9 Cir.1907, 150 F. 571.

75. Preble v. Maine Cent. R. Co., 1893, 85 Me. 260, 27 A. 149; Gibson v. Dudley, 1951, 233 N.C. 255, 63 S.E.2d 630; Predham v. Holfester, 1954, 32 N.J. Super. 419, 108 A.2d 458; Babb v. Harrison, 1951, 220 S.C. 20, 66 S.E.2d 457. See Wagner v. Thompson, 1947, 163 Kan. 662, 186 P.2d 278; Vlachos v. Witherow, 1955, 383 Pa. 173, 118 A.2d 174.

76. Sorensen v. Costa, 1948, 32 Cal.2d 453, 196 P.2d 900; French v. Pearce, 1831, 8 Conn. 439; Johnson v. Thomas, 1904, 23 App.D.C. 141, appeal dismissed 197 U.S. 619, 25 S.Ct. 797, 49 L.Ed. 909.

77. 346 Mich. 296, 78 N.W.2d 114 (1956).

78. Norgard v. Busher, 1960, 220 Or. 297, 349 P.2d 490; Northwoods Development Corp. v. Klement, 1964, 24 Wis.2d 387, 129 N.W.2d 121. See also, Hedgpeth v. Maddux, Mo.1963, 366 S.W.2d 314.

DISABILITY OF OWNER OF RECORD AND SPECIAL RELATIONSHIPS

113. The claim of title by adverse possession may be denied because of disabilities of the owner of record, the fact that future interests are involved or because of the relationship of the parties.

a. Disabilities. The operation of the Statute of Limitations may be postponed if the owner of property is under a disability, such as minority or insanity, when the cause of action first accrues.

b. Special relationships. In general, the Statute of Limitations will not operate in favor of a tenant, a co-owner of property, a grantor or vendee under an executory contract until such time as there is a disclaimer.

c. Future interests. In general, future interests cannot be acquired by adverse possession.

There are situations where the running of the statute may be postponed for one of three reasons.

First: The record owner may be under a disability that justifies indulgence in his behalf. Those usually mentioned in the statutes are minority, coverture, insanity and imprisonment.[79]

Second: Because of the nature of his estate the owner of that estate may not have a cause of action.

Third: Because of the relationship of the parties there may be legal justification on the part of the owner in assuming that the possession involved is not adverse.

Disabilities

The exemption clause is applicable only as to the disability, or disabilities, existing when the cause of action accrued. If land was held adversely when the owner died the disability of one who succeeds to the estate will not interrupt the running of the statute.[80] If the owner was under a disability at the time of his death the statute will start to run regardless of a disability in the new owner. There can be no "tacking of disabilities" either with respect to successive disabilities in the same owner[81] or with respect to disabilities in successive owners.[82] However, if an owner is under two or more disabilities when the cause of action first accrues, the disability of longest duration will control.[83]

If land is held in trust the disability of a beneficiary is not controlling because the statute runs against the legal owner.[84] This is also true with respect to an executor or administrator if he is considered to be the legal owner of the property. However, if he merely has possession of the land for purpose of administration the statute will not operate to bar the claim of an heir or devisee under a disability at the time of the death of the ancestor.

Some statutes provided that the record owner may maintain his action within a stated period of time after the disability has been removed. Other statutes provide that

---

79. See Statute 21 James I, c. 16, §§ 1, 2 (1623).

80. Alvarado v. Nordholt, 1892, 95 Cal. 116, 30 P. 211; Burdette v. May, 1890, 100 Mo. 13, 12 S.W. 1056; Lyons v. Carr, 1906, 77 Neb. 883, 110 N.W. 705; Fore v. Berry, 1913, 94 S.C. 71, 78 S.E. 706; Lion Oil Refining Co. v. White, Tex.Civ.App.1940, 138 S.W.2d 290, as modified White v. Glengarry Oil Co., Sup., 156 S.W.2d 523. *Contra:* Everett's Ex'rs v. Whitfield's Adm'rs, 1859, 27 Ga. 133.

81. Milton v. Pace, 1916, 85 S.C. 373, 67 S.E. 458.

82. Griswold v. Butler, 1820, 3 Conn. 227; De Hatre v. Edmunds, 1906, 200 Mo. 246, 98 S.W. 744; Field v. Turner, 1952, 56 N.M. 31, 239 P.2d 723; Doe d. George v. Jesson, [1805] 6 East. 80, 102 Eng.Rep. 1217.

83. Jackson v. Johnson, 1825, 5 Cow. (N.Y.) 74.

84. Cameron v. Hicks, 1906, 141 N.C. 21, 53 S.E. 728, (even though some, but not all, of the trustees were under a disability); Milton v. Pace, 1910, 85 S.C. 373, 67 S.E. 458 (statute operated to bar equitable remainders).

the duration of disability is not computed as a part of the statutory period. Statutes frequently provide a maximum time during which the disability exemption will be allowed.[85]

Special Relationships

The relationship between the legal owner of land and the occupant may have an important bearing upon the application of the Statute of Limitations. This is true in the following situations:

First: A disclaimer is necessary to start the Statute of Limitations operating in favor of a tenant. According to the English common law a written disclaimer is necessary in the case of an estate for years,[86] and a disclaimer results in forfeiture of the estate.

Statutes in many of the American states abolish forfeiture of a leasehold estate as the result of a disclaimer. It is usually provided that insofar as adverse possession is concerned, the relationship of landlord and tenant continues for a stated period after the actual termination of a tenancy.[87]

Possession under a mistaken belief that a privilege has been granted which authorizes the occupation is not adverse. Usually, such an occupant becomes a tenant at will.[88]

Acceptance of a lease by one who qualifies as an adverse possessor will not necessarily interrupt the running of the statute. If the legal owner is lessor it may be shown that the adverse possessor acted under the mistaken belief that the land held adversely was not included within the terms of the lease.[89] If one other than the legal owner is the purported lessor, the continued adverse possession would result in acquisition of title by the lessor.[90]

Second: A disclaimer is also essential for the acquisition of title by adverse possession if the claim is made by one co-owner of land as against another.[91] Each owner has a legal right to possession of the land and possession is referable to the enjoyment of this legal right unless there is notice to the contrary. In the absence of a direct communication to the co-owners that the claimant is holding adversely, the adverse claimant's possession must be of such a nature as to evidence his intention, and the acts incident to possession must be open and notorious.[92] A purported conveyance of the entire area by one co-owner constitutes a disclaimer if the other co-owners have knowledge of the conveyance or can be charged with notice. The purchaser qualifies as an adverse possessor if his possession is exclusive.[93]

Third: After a conveyance of land the continued possession of the grantor is presumed

---

[85]. See, for example, West's Ann.Cal.Code Civ.Proc. § 328; Ky.R.S. 413.030; Mo.Rev.Stats., § 516.030 (1959).

[86]. Doe d. Graves v. Wells, [1839] 10 A. & E. 427, 113 Eng.Rep. 162.

[87]. See, for example, West's Ann.Cal.Code Civ.Proc. § 326.

[88]. Bond v. O'Gara, 1900, 177 Mass. 139, 58 N.E. 275; Johns v. Johns, 1914, 244 Pa. 48, 90 A. 535.

[89]. See Mitchell v. McShane Lumber Co., 5 Cir.1915, 220 F. 878.

[90]. See Valley National Bank of Phoenix v. Fulton, 1954, 77 Ariz. 11, 266 P.2d 397. *Cf.:* Ellis v. White, La.App.1954, 71 So.2d 640.

[91]. See West v. Evans, 1946, 29 Cal.2d 414, 175 P.2d 219 (the recordation of a deed from one tenant in common does not constitute an ouster).

[92]. Johns v. Scobie, 1939, 12 Cal.2d 618, 86 P.2d 820, 121 A.L.R. 1404; Ramey v. Ramey, Ky.App.1962, 353 S.W.2d 191; Poenisch v. Quarnstrom, 1962, —— Tex. ——, 361 S.W.2d 367. *Cf.:* Johnson v. James, 1964, Ark., 377 S.W.2d 44. See also, Meaders v. Moore, 1939, 134 Tex. 127, 132 S.W.2d 256, 125 A.L.R. 817.

[93]. See Monesson v. Alsofrom, 1964, 82 N.J.Super. 587, 198 A.2d 783; Coleman v. Buttram, Tex.Civ. App.1931, 40 S.W.2d 977, noted in 10 Tex.Law Rev. 336 (1932).

to be permissive.[94]   Accordingly, the statute
will start to run in his favor only when the
grantee is informed as to the adverse claim.[95]
There must be some unequivocal act of hos-
tility.[96]

Fourth: The possession of a vendee under
an executory contract of sale is considered
to be in subordination to the rights of the
vendor.   This situation continues until the
vendee performs all of the conditions under
his contract, surrenders possession of the
land or expressly repudiates the vendor's
ownership.[97]   If the vendor is not the legal
owner of the land he may claim adverse possession through his vendee unless the vendor's possession was permissive at the time
of the sale.[98]

Future interests

A life tenant or those claiming under him
cannot acquire title by adverse possession as
against the owner of a future interest for two
reasons.   In the first place, the possession is
lawful and the claim of adverse possession
cannot arise out of a lawful possession.   In
the second place, the owner of a future interest does not have a cause of action to recover
possession until the termination of the life
estate.[99]   This is true even if a local statute

provides that the owner of a future interest
may proceed against an adverse possessor
and have his rights judicially declared.   According to some authorities, this remedy affords a sufficient basis for holding that the
statute will start to run immediately.[1]   It is
assumed, of course, that there are sufficient
facts to charge the owner of the future interest with knowledge of the fact that an adverse
claim is being asserted.[2]   The same conclusion is indicated if the owner of the future
interest can protect his interest by paying
the taxes.[3]   Additional rules are as follows:

First: Adverse possession may extinguish
an estate tail, including the interest of the
creator of the estate.[4]   This result is based
upon the ground that the interest of the conveyor is a mere expectance.

Second: It is indicated in some decisions
that contingent remainders will be destroyed
if a life estate is extinguished by adverse possession.   This is in accord with the doctrine
of destructibility of contingent remainders.[5]

Third: If a claimant was in adverse possession at the time the future interests were created, the creation of the interests will not interrupt the running of the statute.[6]

---

94.   Williams v. Thomas, 1941, 285 Ky. 776, 149 S.W.
2d 525; Owens v. Peters, 1937, 126 Pa.Super. 501,
191 A. 399.

95.   Parrish v. Minturn, 1963, 234 Or. 475, 382 P.2d
861; Vlachos v. Witherow, 1955, 383 Pa. 173, 118 A.
2d 174.

96.   Fort Wayne Smelting & Refining Works v. City
of Fort Wayne, 1938, 214 Ind. 454, 14 N.E.2d 556.

97.   Bell v. Bell, 1955, 151 Me. 207, 116 A.2d 921 (oral
contract); Gramann v. Beatty, 1938, 134 Neb. 568,
279 N.W. 204.

98.   Gioscio v. Lautenschlager, 1937, 23 Cal.App.2d
616, 73 P.2d 1230.

99.   Thompson v. Pacific Electric Ry. Co., 1928, 203
Cal. 578, 265 P. 220, noted in 16 Cal.Law Rev. 348
(1928); McDonald v. Burke, Ky.1956, 288 S.W.2d

363 (in the absence of estoppel); Callison v. Wabash
Ry. Co., 1925, 219 Mo.App. 271, 275 S.W. 965 (contingent remainder).

1.   Murray v. Quigley, 1902, 119 Iowa 6, 92 N.W. 869;
Howth v. Farrar, 5 Cir.1938, 94 F.2d 654.   *Contra:*
Unick v. St. Joseph Loan & Trust Co., 1946, 146
Neb. 789, 21 N.W.2d 752 (this remedy is optional
only).   See Ward v. Meredith, 1919, 186 Iowa 1108,
173 N.W. 246.

2.   Gibbs v. Bates, 1949, 215 Ark. 646, 222 S.W.2d
805, noted in 4 Okl.Law Rev. 505 (1951).

3.   Nelson v. Davidson, 1896, 160 Ill. 254, 43 N.E.
361.

4.   Baldridge v. McFarland, 1855, 26 Pa. 338.

5.   Baldridge v. McFarland, 1855, 26 Pa. 338 *(dictum)*.

6.   2 Rest. Property, § 226.

PAYMENT OF TAXES

114. In the absence of statute, the payment of taxes by an adverse claimant is not essential to the acquisition of title by adverse possession.

In the absence of statute, the payment of taxes on the land in question is not a prerequisite to the acquisition of title by adverse possession. However, the payment of taxes is some evidence of the assertion of an adverse claim.

Statutes in a number of states provide that title cannot be acquired by adverse possession unless the claimant pays all taxes that are assessed against the land during the statutory period. Apparently, these statutes have been enacted for the benefit of the land-owner. By an examination of the tax record he can ascertain the existence of adverse claims. An adverse possessor can perfect his claim if he pays the taxes even if the record owner also pays all taxes assessed against the land.[7] According to one view, the adverse possessor must pay the taxes as they accrue.[8] According to another view there is sufficient compliance with this requirement if taxes are eventually paid even though not paid on an accrual basis.[9] In some of the statutes the tax-requirement is not applicable in cases where the land in dispute forms a part of a boundary line.[10] Under such circumstances it is unlikely that the disputed area will be assessed as a part of the land of the adverse claimant.

Statutes in some states provide that title by adverse possession may be acquired under a "short-time" statute if taxes are paid by the adverse claimant.[11]

---

7. Cavanaugh v. Jackson, 1893, 99 Cal. 672, 34 P. 509. *Cf.:* Williams v. Stillwell, 1933, 217 Cal. 487, 19 P. 2d 773, noted in 22 Cal.Law Rev. 111 (1933).

8. Aggelos v. Zella Mining Co., 1940, 99 Utah 417, 107 P.2d 170, 132 A.L.R. 213; Brownstin v. Brelle, 1938, 193 Wash. 553, 76 P.2d 613.

9. Gray v. Walker, 1910, 157 Cal. 881, 108 P. 278; Laas v. All Persons, etc., 1948, 121 Mont. 43, 189 P.2d 670.

10. See, for example, Mellenthin v. Brantman, 1941, 211 Minn. 336, 1 N.W.2d 141.

11. See Taylor, Titles To Land by Adverse Possession, 20 Iowa Law Rev. 551, 553 (1935).

B. DERIVATIVE TITLE

CHAPTER 21

MODE OF CONVEYANCE

CONVEYANCES AT COMMON LAW

115. **Feoffment was the most important common law method of conveying freehold estates. It involved a symbolic delivery of the land by "livery of seisin." Other methods included exchange, partition, fine and common recovery, lease and release, surrender and dedication.**

Prior to the passage of the Statute of Uses in 1536 feoffment was the most important common law method of conveying possessory estate of freehold. This involved a symbolic delivery of the land by the feoffor to the feoffee (livery of seisin).

According to Maitland, the physical acts involved in a feoffment grew out of a "mental incapacity, an inability to conceive that mere rights can be transferred." This is referred to as the "materialistic attitude." [1] But the procedure served a useful purpose. At a time when recording acts were unknown, the notoriety attending a feoffment resulted in notice respecting the ownership of land.

In the usual case the ceremony took place upon the land itself. The feoffor would hand a symbol of the land to the feoffee, such as a lump of earth or a twig, and would accompany the act with words of transfer. This was called livery in deed. If the parties did not actually go upon the land and make a symbolic delivery, but did purport to make a transfer while within view of the land, the transaction was considered to be a livery in law. This constituted a conveyance if the feoffee took possession of the land prior to the death of the feoffor, or if he was prevented from taking possession by the wrongful act of the feoffor. [2]

A feoffment could be made by any person who was in possession of the land. If the feoffor was not in possession under a claim of ownership, or if he purported to transfer an estate greater than his own, the feoffment was tortious. This would be the case, for instance, if the feoffor owned only an estate for life and purported to convey an estate in fee. A tortious feoffment operated to destroy the life estate in the feoffor, thus giving the owner of the remainder or reversion an immediate right of entry.

Since livery of seisin contemplated an immediate transfer, this method could not be used to create an estate to become possessory at a future date. This rule is usually expressed by the statement that estates could not be created to take effect *in futuro*. [3] So also, non-possessory estates in land could not be conveyed by feoffment because livery of seisin would not be possible. Such interests

---

1. See Maitland, The Mystery of Seisin, 2 Law Quarterly Review 489 (1886).

2. Co.Litt., § 59; 2 Bl.Comm. *316. See Thorne, Livery of Seisin, 52 Law Quarterly Rev. 345 (1936).

3. 3 Bl.Comm. 314.

were conveyed by grant (an instrument under seal).[4]

Livery of seisin that resulted in the creation of an estate tail was called a gift (*donatio*).[5]

Exchange

An exchange consisted of mutual grants of land, equal in quality but not necessarily equal in value, such as a fee for a fee, life estate for a life estate, etc. Livery of seisin was not necessary. The important element of notoriety was supplied by the requirement that the parties had to enter upon the land so acquired before the exchange was considered to be complete. If one died before entry the transfer failed.[6]

Partition

Partition involved the division of land in the case of concurrent ownership. The division had to be accompanied by livery of seisin and, except in the case of coparceners, the division had to be by deed. Since coparceners were compelled to make partition the division could be by parol. A writing was required by the Statute of Frauds even in the case of coparceners.[7]

Fine and Common Recovery

A conveyance by fine or common recovery was accomplished by legal proceedings. In the case of a fine the transfer was made by a settlement or compromise entered upon the court records.[8] In a common recovery, however, each and every step in the proceedings was taken and final judgment entered.[9] In many situations the proceedings were fictitious in nature and were used as a means by which to destroy contingent interests. This was especially true in the case of an estate tail.

Lease and Release

A freehold estate could be conveyed by a lease and release. The first step involved the making of a lease of the property to the intended grantee. This was consummated when the lessee took possession of the land. Prior to that time he had a mere interest in the term (an *interesse termini*) and not an estate.[10] The second step was a grant of the reversion to the tenant, accomplished by grant (a sealed instrument).

According to the common law rule, a release involved the transfer of an estate in reversion or in remainder to one having an interest in possession. It could operate to enlarge the possessory estate. That was the case if one having an estate in remainder released his estate to a life tenant. Likewise, if a tenant was actually in possession under his lease the owner of the fee subject to the lease could release his interest to the tenant. So also, a release could operate as a transfer. For example, one coparcener could release all of his interest to another coparcener, and a disseisee could release his right of re-entry to the disseisor.[11]

At the present time a release may be used to convey ownership to one who has no previous right to the land and is, in most states, equivalent to the word "quitclaim."[12]

---

4. 2 Bl.Comm. 317. See Boardwell, The Common Law Scheme of Estates, 18 Iowa Law Rev. 425, 440 (1933).

5. 2 Bl.Comm. 316.

6. 2 Bl.Comm. 323.

7. 2 Bl.Comm. 324.

8. 2 Pollock & Maitland, History of English Law (2d ed.) 94.

9. Cheshire's Modern Real Property (4th ed.) p. 340.

10. 2 Bl.Comm. 317.

11. 2 Bl.Comm. 324. See Samuels, History and Development of the Modern Real Estate Deed, 16 Univ. of Cinn.Law Rev. 219, 235 (1942).

12. See Moss v. Gibbs, 1963, —— Tex. ——, 370 S.W.2d 452.

Surrender

A surrender involved the giving up of an estate for life or for years to the owner of the reversion or remainder.[13] As the result of a surrender the estate for life or years was destroyed by merger. There was privity of estate between the parties. Therefore, livery of seisin was not necessary even in the case of a life estate.[14] It was necessary that the estate surrendered be a smaller estate than the estate owned by the person to whom the surrender was made.[15] At the present time this method of conveying property is of particular importance in the case of leasehold estates. A further discussion of the problems involved will be found under that heading.

Dedication

At an early date the English courts recognized the rule that an indefinite body of persons, such as the inhabitants of a town, could, by custom, acquire rights in land held under private ownership. A custom which had existed from time immemorial, without interruption, if reasonable, acquired the force of law. Thus, it was recognized that the inhabitants of a town could acquire the right to go upon land for the purpose of drying their fishing nets, holding fairs or taking water.[16]

In general, a customary right could not be acquired to take the soil or a substance of the soil because such a use was considered to be unreasonable.[17] For example, a customary right to pasture cattle was denied.[18] However, a customary right to take gravel for ballasting ships was recognized. It was considered that since the custom was for the maintenance of navigation it was for the public good.[19] According to Blackstone, the recognition of customary rights arose out of "the necessities of the public."[20] Such rights could not be acquired by prescription because a prescriptive right presupposes the existence of a definite grantee while a customary right may vest only in an undefined body of persons.

In order the more adequately to meet modern conditions with respect to "necessities of the public," particularly with reference to the public right to use roads and bridges, there was developed the doctrine of dedication.[21] Under this doctrine there was no requirement that public use "from time immemorial" be established. A public right could be established upon proof that the owner of the land intended that his land be used for a public purpose, and actual use by the public for that purpose. This resulted in a common law dedication. In the case of a common law dedication, as in the case of customary rights, the public right may exist even though there is no corporate or individual grantee and even though the right is not evidenced by a writing. The doctrine is not governed by the requirements of the Statute of Frauds.

The doctrine of customary rights has never received extensive recognition in the United

---

13. Co.Litt. 338a.

14. 2 Bl.Comm. 326.

15. A life tenant cannot surrender to a tenant for years (2 Bl.Comm. 326).

16. See, for example, Abbot v. Weekley, [1665] 1 Lev. 176, 83 Eng.Rep. 357 (right to go upon land to dance).

17. Digby, History of the Law of Real Property (5th ed.), p. 184 n. 1.

18. Smith v. Gatewood, [1607] Cro.Jac. 152, 79 Eng. Rep. 133.

19. Linn-Regis v. Taylor, [1684] 3 Lev. 160, 83 Eng. Rep. 629.

20. 2 Bl.Comm. 33.

21. See Chaplin, Dedication and Trust Legislation, 16 Harv.Law Rev. 329, 332 (1903).

States.[22] However, the doctrine of dedication is recognized in all of the states. It is generally considered that common law, or implied, dedication is based upon estoppel.[23] If a landowner evidences an intention that his land be used for a public purpose, and this is followed by public use, he is estopped to deny the existence of the public right.[24] The intention to dedicate may be found from long continued public use.[25] A public right may be acquired to use land for street purposes, parks, bridges, burial places and, according to some decisions, church purposes. Statutes usually provide that an offer to dedicate results if a landowner records a map or plat depicting streets, parks, etc.[26]

In the case of statutory dedication acceptance may be accomplished by official action or by public use. But if the acceptance is by public use it does not necessarily follow that a municipality may be held liable for injuries resulting from a defective condition of the land involved. Some authorities follow the rule that public liability can be imposed only if the acceptance resulted from official action.[27]

In Yuba City v. Consolidated Mausoleum Syndicate (Cal.),[28] a period of thirty-one years expired between the filing of a map indicating an intention to dedicate land for street purposes and an acceptance by the city. Since the offer had not been withdrawn at the time of acceptance the dedication was held to be operative.

CONVEYANCE UNDER THE STATUTE OF USES

116. The enactment of the Statute of Uses made possible a new method of conveying freehold estates. A use could be raised by bargain and sale, or by covenant to stand seised. By force of the statute, the use thus created, if within the provisions of the statute, would be converted into a legal estate.

The passage of the Statute of Uses [29] in 1536 made possible a new method of conveying freehold estates that has been adopted in modern conveyancing.

It has been noted that the purpose of the statute was to abolish the practice of separating the legal ownership of freehold estates from the beneficial interest or use.[30] This was sought to be accomplished by legislative enactment that the person who had the use would also have the legal title. If a freeholder desired to convey his estate he could accept payment from the purchaser. This payment "raised a use" (by bargain and sale) in the purchaser who thereby acquired the legal title by force of the Statute of Uses. The conveyance was thus accomplished without the necessity of a feoffment, with its attendant notoriety and without even a change of possession. The Statute of Enrollments [31] was passed immediately after the passage of the Statute of Uses. It required that such a use raised by bargain and sale had to be enrolled.

---

22. Ackerman v. Shelp, 1825, 8 N.J.L. 125; Gillies v. Orienta Beach Club, 1935, 159 Misc. 675, 289 N.Y.S. 733, noted in 21 Minn.Law Rev. 107 (1936). But see, Knowles v. Dow, 1851, 22 N.H. 387.

23. 4 McQuillin, Municipal Corporations (2nd ed.) § 1664, p. 476. See comment, 10 Cal.Law Rev. 419 (1922).

24. 4 McQuillin, Municipal Corporations (2nd ed.) § 1668. See City of Cincinnati v. White's Lessee, 1832, 31 U.S. (6 Pet.) 431, 8 L.Ed. 452.

25. Keiter v. Berge, 1945, 219 Minn. 374, 18 N.W.2d 35.

26. See Parks, The Law of Dedication in Oregon, 20 Ore.Law Rev. 111, 157 (1941).

27. Cox v. Board of Comm'rs, 1943, 181 Md. 428, 31 A.2d 179.

28. 207 Cal. 587, 279 P. 427 (1929).

29. 27 Hen. VIII, c. 10 (1536).

30. See supra, Chapter 2.

31. 27 Hen. VIII, c. 16 (1536).

After the passage of the Statute of Uses a new method of creating a use was recognized. A landowner could create a use by executing a sealed instrument covenanting to stand seised to the use of covenantee. The validity of such a use was affirmed in Sharington v. Strotton [32] provided the covenantee was related to the covenantor either by blood or marriage.

CONVEYANCING IN THE UNITED STATES

117. **Statutes usually provide that freehold estates can be conveyed by deed. But this statutory method may not exclude other methods recognized at common law or under the Statute of Uses.**

A writing which evidences an intention to convey an estate will be sustained as a conveyance even if the language is informal in nature.

Statutes have been enacted in all of the states providing that freehold estates in land can be conveyed by deed. The technique established by statute is referable to the method that had its origin in the Statute of Uses.

There is authority for the view that the statutory method is not exclusive of other methods of conveyancing recognized at common law. For example, in French v. French (N.H.),[33] a father conveyed land to his son and then the son executed a deed purporting to convey a life estate to the father. The son's deed was not executed with the formalities required by the local statute in that it was not witnessed. But the conveyance of a life estate to the father was sustained. Because of the relationship of the parties the deed constituted a covenant to stand seised. The Statute of Uses was considered to be a part of the adopted common law of the state.

It operated to place the legal title in the father according to the terms of the covenant.[34]

The validity of a feoffment was sustained in Perry v. Price (Mo.).[35] A recorded deed was inoperative because the conveyance was not supported by consideration. However, the validity of the transaction was sustained as a common law feoffment. The recordation of the deed acted as a substitute for livery of seisin. It is also noted that a transfer of title will be sustained if there is compliance with any recognized method of conveyancing even if there is a failure to comply with the formalities prescribed for the method selected by the parties.[36]

An informal writing may be sufficient to convey an estate or interest in land.[37] In New Home Building Supply Co., Inc. v. Nations (N.C.),[38] a deed conveying merchantable timber contained the following endorsement signed by the grantee: "I, A. E. Lundy, do hereby transfer this deed in its entirety to New Home Bldg., Supply Co., Inc., with the exception of pulpwood." The court held that ownership passed according to the terms of the endorsement.

A similar situation is presented in Metzger v. Miller (Fed.).[39] Plaintiff's mother sent a letter to him stating that she would give him described land if he would look after matters

---

32. 1 Plow. 298, 75 Eng.Rep. 454 (1565).

33. 3 N.H. 234 (1825).

34. *Accord:* Murray v. Kerney, 1911, 115 Md. 514, 81 A. 6. *Contra:* Gorham v. Daniels, 1851, 23 Vt. 600 (it was held that the Statute of Uses was not a part of the adopted common law).

35. 1 Mo. 553 (1835).

36. Roe ex dem. Wilkinson v. Tranmer, 1757, 2 Wils. 75, 95 Eng.Rep. 694.

37. See Webb v. Den ex dem. Weatherhead, 1854, 58 U.S. (17 How.) 576, 15 L.Ed. 35; Operative Words of Conveyance, 35 Yale Law Jr., 732 (1926).

38. 259 N.C. 681, 131 S.E.2d 425 (1963).

39. 291 F. 780 (D.Cal.1923), noted in 22 Mich.Law Rev. 373 (1924).

incident to the probate of an estate. In a subsequent letter to the son the mother indicated that she considered him to be the owner of the land. The court held that the letter constituted a valid conveyance.[40] However, such a conclusion cannot be sustained if the writing does not purport to be a present conveyance but merely indicates an intention to make a conveyance at some time in the future. Language was so construed in McGarrigle v. Roman Catholic Orphan Asylum of San Francisco (Cal.).[41] After conveying a life estate the deed provided: "It is the purpose (of grantor) that after the death (of the life tenant) the (land) shall become and be (the property of the orphanage)." [42]

40. See Barnes v. Banks, 1906, 223 Ill. 352, 79 N.E. 117.

41. 145 Cal. 694, 79 P. 447 (1905).

42. *Accord:* Litten v. Warren, 1936, 11 Cal.App.2d 635, 54 P.2d 39, criticized in 24 Cal.Law Rev. 468 (1936).

CHAPTER 22

CONVEYANCE BY DEED AND BOUNDARY LINE AGREEMENTS

ESSENTIAL FORMALITIES IN THE EXECUTION OF A DEED

118. The Statute of Frauds provides that the conveyance of a freehold estate can be accomplished only by a written instrument signed by the grantor or his duly authorized agent. A similar requirement is declared in connection with the execution of a contract for the sale of land or a memorandum thereof. Under some circumstances an oral contract may be specifically enforceable in equity under the part performance doctrine.

a. Seal. In a majority of the states a seal is not necessary in connection with the conveyance of a possessory estate.

b. Signature. Statutes usually provide that the due execution of a deed requires the signature of the grantor. Signature by the grantee is not required. His acceptance makes him a party to the deed.

c. Attestation and acknowledgement. Usually, the due execution of a deed does not require attestation or acknowledgement. Statutes frequently require acknowledgement as a prerequisite to recordation.

d. Consideration. A consideration is necessary to raise a use by bargain and sale. However, the recital of a consideration will suffice. Even if a consideration is not recited in a deed, a conveyance will be sustained if a consideration was, in fact, paid.

Statutes in the various states usually provide that the conveyance of a freehold estate can be accomplished only by a written instrument signed by the grantor or by his duly authorized agent. It is also generally provided that "no action shall be brought" upon a contract for the sale of such an estate unless the contract "or some memorandum or note thereof" shall be in writing and signed by the party sought to be charged or by his duly authorized agent.[1] These statutes are patterned after the English Statute of Frauds, enacted in 1676.[2] In some states it is also provided by statute that if an agent is authorized to buy or sell "real estate" for a compensation or commission, he cannot recover the compensation or commission unless the agency agreement is evidenced by a writing.[3] There can be no recovery for the reasonable value of services rendered even if the owner

1. *Cf.:* Feusner v. Farley, 1959, 80 Wyo. 124, 338 P.2d 835 (a "grubstake contract" is not within the scope of the statute. There is also authority for the view that an executory contract to convey land can be rescinded by a parole agreement (Niernberg v. Feld, 1955, 131 Colo. 508, 283 P.2d 640). See also, Carter v. McCall, 1940, 193 S.C. 456, 8 S.E.2d 844, 151 A.L.R. 641 (conveyance of land not involved in agreement that gave a real estate broker one-half the value of described land for services rendered).

2. 29 Car. 11, c. 16 (1676).

3. See, for example, West's Ann.Cal.Civ.Code, § 1624 (5). There must be written evidence of the *employment contract* (Franklin v. Hansen, 1963, 59 Cal.2d 570, 30 Cal.Rptr. 530, 381 P.2d 386.

accepts the benefits or an oral authorization.[4] However, a subsequent promise in writing to pay a commission can be enforced.[5] It is also to be noted that an agreement between brokers to share a commission is not within the scope of the statute.[6]

Even if a contract is not executed with the formalities prescribed by the Statute of Frauds it may be specifically enforceable in equity under the part performance doctrine.[7] However, there is a difference of opinion as to the type of conduct that will take the case out of the operation of the statute. For example, it is generally agreed that this relief is available if the purchaser takes possession of the land with the consent of the vendor, pays the full consideration and erects improvements upon the land that are of a substantial nature. These acts furnish outward manifestations of the intention of the parties and this satisfies the policy of the Statute of Frauds. In addition, the change of possession and erection of improvements indicate that a serious hardship to the purchaser will result if the contract is not enforced. The remedy at law to recover money paid by the purchaser is not an adequate remedy.

But many authorities follow the view that something less than the conduct as outlined above will justify a decree of specific performance. Relief may be granted because of a change of possession or because of hardship indicated if equitable relief is denied. The

Restatement of Contracts provides that where, acting under an oral contract for the transfer of an interest in land, the purchaser with the assent of the vendor

(a) makes valuable improvements on the land, or

(b) takes possession thereof or retains a possession thereof existing at the time of the bargain, and also pays a portion or all of the purchase price,

the purchaser or the vendor may specifically enforce the contract.[8]

First: Some authorities follow the rule that retention of a possession existing at the time of the contract is not sufficient part performance to take a case out of the operation of the Statute of Frauds.[9] Further, the possession must be actual as distinguished from constructive.[10] This is a strict application of the rule that the part performance doctrine is not applicable if the possession is not referable to the contract.

Second: In some decisions it is indicated that the primary basis for application of the part performance doctrine is the hardship to the purchaser that would follow the denial of such relief. While this hardship may result from a taking of possession, specific performance may be granted upon proof of irreparable injury even if the purchaser does not take possession of the land.[11] So also, even if the purchaser does take possession, specific performance may be denied if the possession was beneficial to the purchaser.[12] While a purchaser may be entitled

---

4. Gould v. Otto, 1927, 81 Cal.App. 409, 254 P. 272.

5. Coulter v. Howard, 1927, 203 Cal. 17, 262 P. 751, noted in 16 Cal.Law Rev. 442 (1928).

6. Howard v. D. W. Hobson Co., 1918, 38 Cal.App. 445, 176 P. 715.

7. But see, Dean v. Cassiday, 1889, 88 Ky. 572, 11 S. W. 601; Box v. Stanford, 1849, 21 Miss. (13 Smedes & M.) 93; Barnes v. Brown, 1874, 71 N.C. 507; Goodloe v. Goodloe, 1905, 116 Tenn. 252, 92 S.W. 767.

8. Rest. Contracts, § 197.

9. See Cauthron v. Goodwin, Okl.1955, 287 P.2d 893 (the case involved the validity of an oral lease).

10. See Hambey v. Wood, 1919, 181 Cal. 286, 184 P. 9.

11. Orlando v. Ottaviani, 1958, 337 Mass. 157, 148 N.E. 2d 373.

12. Burns v. Daggett, 1886, 141 Mass. 368, 6 N.E. 727.

to specific performance on the basis of hardship, it does not follow that such relief would also be available to the vendor.[13]

Third: The weight of authority is that payment of consideration alone does not constitute sufficient part performance to take a case out of the operation of the Statute of Frauds. The act of payment is not definitely referable to a buy and sell agreement. Further, an action at law to recover the consideration paid is an adequate remedy.[14]

There is a minority rule that payment of the purchase price in whole or in part is sufficient part performance to justify equitable relief by way of specific performance. This is especially true if payment is evidenced by a receipt.[15]

Fourth: The validity of an oral gift of land will be sustained if the donee takes possession and erects improvements upon the land that are substantial in nature.[16] It must be shown that the intent was to make a gift *in praesenti*[17] and evidence pertaining to the transaction must be "clear and convincing."[18]

The general rule is that equity will not aid a volunteer. Accordingly, it may be contended that equity will not grant specific performance in an oral-gift situation. However, this is either an exception to the general

rule[19] or, as indicated in some cases, justifies application of the rules relating to promissory estoppel.[20]

Seal

The use of a sealed instrument or grant is not included in the list of English common law methods of conveying possessory estates. However, the conveyance of a possessory estate by lease and release did require the use of such a grant. Of course, a grant was not necessary insofar as the lease was concerned. But the reversion could be released to the tenant in possession only by grant, the method used for the transfer of incorporeal interests.

Except in a conveyance by lease and release, the English common law, as adopted in the several states, does not require the use of a sealed instrument in connection with the conveyance of a possessory estate.[21] It is true, the English Statute of Enrollments[22] required the use of a sealed instrument for the creation of a use by bargain and sale, but this statute was local in nature and is not considered to be a part of the common law as adopted in the states. The English Statute of Frauds,[23] passed in 1677, does not include a seal as a required formality for the conveyance of possessory estates.

With various exceptions, such as in the case of corporations, statutes in a majority of the states have abolished the distinction between sealed and unsealed instruments.[24]

---

13. Palumbo v. James, 1929, 266 Mass. 1, 164 N.E. 466.

14. Taylor v. Clark, 1944, 143 Neb. 552, 13 N.W.2d 621.

15. Hamilton v. Traub, 1947, 29 Del.Ch. 475, 51 A.2d 581; Stasi v. Nigro, 1947, 135 N.J.L. 473, 52 A.2d 527.

16. Anson v. Townsend, 1887, 73 Cal. 415, 15 P. 49. See Lehman v. Barry, Tex.Civ.App.1939, 126 S.W.2d 499.

17. Reinhardt v. Fleming, 1943, 18 Wash.2d 637, 140 P.2d 504, 155 A.L.R. 73.

18. Poka v. Holi, 1960, 44 Hawaii 582, 358 P.2d 53; Aiello v. Knoll Golf Club, 1960, 64 N.J.Super. 156, 165 A.2d 531.

19. See Pound, Consideration in Equity, 13 Ill.Law Rev. 667, 672 (1919).

20. Greiner v. Greiner, 1930, 131 Kan. 760, 293 P. 759, noted in 15 Minn.Law Rev. 825 (1931).

21. But see, Jackson ex dem. Gouch v. Wood, 1815, 12 Johns.(N.Y.) 73.

22. 27 Hen. VIII, c. 16 (1536).

23. 29 Car. 11, c. 3 (1677).

24. The seal-requirement is retained in some states. See, for example, Conn.Gen.Stat.1949, § 7085; Gen.

Signature

According to the English common law the due execution of a deed required the seal but not the signature of the grantor.[25] An acknowledgement by the grantor that an instrument is his deed is not an acknowledgement that he signed it. It could be his deed without his signature.[26] But the name of the grantor had to appear in the deed for identification purposes.

Statutes usually provide that a deed must be signed by the grantor. Thus, there is no reason for applying the common law rule that the name of the grantor appear in the body of the deed. The signature serves the dual purpose of due execution and identification. Yet, according to some authorities, a deed must contain the name of the grantor as well as his signature.[27]

Statutes generally provide that if a grantor is unable to write his signature may be by mark, authenticated by witnesses. The place of signature is not of controlling importance unless the statute specifically requires that the writing be "subscribed." While it is generally held that "subscription" requires signature at the end of the writing,[28] some authorities hold that the word "subscribe" means "to attest by writing." According to

this view the location of the signature is not of controlling importance.[29]

It is not necessary that the grantee sign the deed. His acceptance of the document is sufficient to make it mutually binding. A covenant in such a deed poll may create an encumbrance binding upon an owner claiming title under the original grantee.[30] This is also the case with respect to leases that are signed only by the lessor but accepted by the lessee.[31]

Attestation and Acknowledgement

Usually, the due execution of a deed does not require attestation or acknowledgement.[32] Statutes have been passed in many states providing that a deed must be acknowledged as a prerequisite to recordation.

Consideration

The theory underlying a conveyance by deed is that a use may be raised by bargain and sale (a valuable consideration) or by "a covenant to stand seised" which is based upon relationship by blood or marriage (good consideration).

A recital of consideration such as "for value received" is sufficient to raise a use

---

Laws Vt. (1917), § 2739 and a Virginia statute construed in Smith v. Plaster, 1928, 151 Va. 252, 258, 144 S.E. 417, 419.

25. See, Must a Deed Be Signed as Well as Sealed? 88 L.T. 41 (1889).

26. Osborne v. Tunis, 1856, 25 N.J.L. 633.

27. Cordano v. Wright, 1911, 159 Cal. 610, 115 P. 227. *Contra:* Sterling v. Park, 1907, 129 Ga. 309, 58 S. E. 828.

28. See Gentry's Guardian v. Gentry, 1927, 219 Ky. 569, 293 S.W. 1094 (1927), noted in 14 Va.Law Rev. 66 (1927).

29. See California Canneries Co. v. Scatena, 1897, 117 Cal. 447, 450, 49 P. 462 (dealing with a bill of sale).

30. Burbank v. Pillsbury, 1869, 48 N.H. 475. See Druecker v. McLaughlin, 1908, 235 Ill. 367, 374, 85 N.E. 647, 649, comment, 3 Ill.Law Rev. 458 (1909) (covenant created equitable servitudes binding on grantee); Finley v. Simpson, 1850, 22 N.J.L. 311 (grantee bound by covenant to pay a mortgage).

31. Chandler v. Hart, 1911, 161 Cal. 405, 119 P. 516; Starwich v. Washington Cut Glass Co., 1911, 64 Wash. 42, 116 P. 459.

32. But see Winsted Sav. Bank & B. Ass'n v. Spencer, 1857, 26 Conn. 195; Langmede v. Weaver, 1901, 65 Ohio St. 17, 60 N.E. 992. An acknowledgement may be necessary for the conveyance of a homestead interest. See, for example, West's Ann.Cal.Civ.Code, § 1242.

because the grantor is estopped to deny the truth of a recital in his deed.[33] In Catlin Coal Co. v. Lloyd (Ill.),[34] the recited consideration in a deed had been erased except for the word "dollars." In holding the deed to be inoperative the court considered that this was not intended to be a recital of consideration. Even if a consideration is not recited in the deed the conveyance will be sustained if there is proof that a consideration was, in fact, paid.[35] In a number of states it is provided by statute that a valid conveyance can be made by deed without consideration. For example, a California statute provides that a "vountary transfer is an executed contract, subject to all rules of law concerning contracts in general; except that a consideration is not necessary to its validity."[36]

CAPACITY OF GRANTOR

119. **Even though civil rights may be impaired because of conviction of a crime, this does not usually deprive the convicted person of capacity to convey land.**

  a. **Infancy.** A deed executed by a minor is voidable and not void.

  b. **Insanity.** The deed of an insane person, if executed prior to an adjudication of insanity, is voidable and not void.

  c. **Married women.** Married Women's Acts have generally removed the common law disabilities of married women with respect to the conveyance of their separate property.

Even though civil rights may be impaired because of conviction of a crime, this does not usually deprive the convicted person of capacity to convey land. Other capacity situations are discussed in the following paragraphs.

Infancy

An *inter vivos* conveyance of land or any interest therein made by a grantor at a time when he is under the incapacity of minority is voidable.[37] Such a grantor may bring suit to set aside the conveyance within a reasonable time *after* he reaches majority.[38] Contrary to the general rule applied in the case of chattels, a minor cannot disaffirm a conveyance of an estate in land until after he has attained majority.[39] The conveyance may be set aside even as against a purchaser from the grantee who qualifies as a *bona fide* purchaser for value and without notice.[40] The prevailing rule is that a minor will not be estopped to set a conveyance aside because of his misrepresentation as to age.[41]

The right to avoid a conveyance may be lost if the minor does not proceed with due diligence after reaching his majority.[42] This is especially true if, in addition to delay, there is knowledge on the part of the grantor that valuable improvements were being erected upon the land and steps were not taken to assert his rights.

Insanity

A grantor has sufficient mental capacity to execute a deed if he comprehends the

---

33. Jackson ex dem. Hudson v. Alexander, 1908, 3 Johns. (N.Y.) 484.

34. 180 Ill. 398, 54 N.E. 214 (1899).

35. Mildmay's Case [1582–1584] 1 Co.Rep. 175a, 76 Eng.Rep. 379 (*dictum*).

36. West's Ann.Cal.Civ.Code, § 1040.

37. *Cf.*: West's Ann.Cal.Civ.Code, § 33 (void if minor is under the age of 18).

38. No disaffirmance is necessary if the conveyance is void as distinguished from voidable (Hakes Inv. Co. v. Lyons, 1913, 166 Cal. 557, 137 Cal. 911).

39. See 1 Williston on Contracts (rev.ed.) § 235.

40. 1 Williston on Contracts (rev.ed.) § 233.

41. 5 Tiffany, Real Property (3rd ed.) § 1362.

42. Merritt v. Jowers, 1937, 184 Ga. 762, 193 S.E. 238; Spencer v. Lyman Falls Power Co., 1938, 109 Vt. 294, 196 A. 276.

nature and extent of the property involved and is aware of the circumstances surrounding the transactions, such as the fact that a present conveyance is made of the property, the consideration involved, if any is intended and the name of the grantee.[43] Intoxication is usually considered as a form of insanity.[44] A finding as to sanity or insanity by a board of commissioners, while entitled to some weight, is not a judgment as to mental status.[45]

The prevailing rule is that a deed executed by an insane person is voidable and not void.[46] This is true unless the insane person is under the care of a court appointed guardian.[47] In that event the deed is void as to the guardian. Also, a deed executed by a person who is entirely without understanding is void.[48] This is the statutory rule in some states.[49]

The claim of incapacity may be asserted in an action at law if the possession or ownership of land is in issue.[50] The minority rule is that the claim can be asserted only in an equity action brought to rescind the deed.[51]

Married Women

According to the common law rule, a married woman does not have the capacity to convey land unless her husband joins in the conveyance or gives his written consent to the conveyance.[52]

Married Women's Acts, adopted in many states, provide that a married woman has a right to manage her separate property as if she were a *feme sole*. Under such statutes it is not necessary that the husband consent to a conveyance made by the wife.

GRANTEE

120. A deed is void unless the grantee is identified with reasonable certainty. However, a person to whom a deed is delivered may have express or implied authority to fill in the name of the grantee if *bona fide* purchasers or mortgagees are involved.

A deed is not operative if the grantee is not designated with reasonable certainty.[53] For example, a conveyance to an unincorporated group or association will fail unless the membership is relatively small and readily ascertainable.[54] In Rixford v. Zeigler (Cal.),[55] the grantee was named as the "Community styling itself the German Roman Catholic St. Bonifazieus Church Community." The conveyance was on condition that the land be used for church and school purposes. Since the church was unincorpo-

---

43. Richard v. Smith, 1962, 235 Ark. 752, 361 S.W.2d 741; Broat v. Broat, Sup.1940, 18 N.Y.S.2d 709.

44. 1 Williston on Contracts (rev.ed.) § 259. See Comment, Competency of a Habitual Drunkard to Execute a Deed, 13 Rocky Mountain Law Rev. 71 (1940).

45. Channell v. Jones, 1939, 184 Okl. 644, 89 P.2d 769.

46. Hassey v. Williams, 1937, 127 Fla. 734, 174 So. 9; Brown v. Khoury, 1956, 346 Mich. 97, 77 N.W. 2d 336; Free v. Owen, 1938, 131 Tex. 281, 113 S.W. 2d 1221.

47. See 15 Tex.Law Rev. 518 (1937).

48. Channell v. Jones, 1939, 184 Okl. 644, 89 P.2d 769.

49. See, for example, West's Ann.Cal.Civ.Code, § 38.

50. Moran v. Moran, 1895, 106 Mich. 8, 63 N.W. 989.

51. See, May the Deed of an Insane Grantor be Avoided at Law as Well as in Equity? 28 Ky.Law Jr. 479 (1940).

52. See Bryan v. Dennis, 1852, 4 Fla. 445; Howard v. Turner, Ky.App.1941, 152 S.W.2d 589; Cruthis v. Steele, 1963, 259 N.C. 701, 131 S.E.2d 344.

53. A memorandum for the sale of land does not satisfy the Statute of Frauds if it fails to identify the purchaser. See Randazzo v. Kroenke, 1964, 373 Mich. 61, 127 N.W.2d 880.

54. Under the Uniform Partnership Act a conveyance may be made to a partnership in the partnership name (Uniform Laws Ann. p. 16, § 8(4).

55. 150 Cal. 435, 88 P. 1092 (1907).

rated the deed failed.[56] In Mayo v. Wood (Cal.),[57] the grantees were designated as "the present and future owners of town lots and town property in Sacramento City." At the time of the conveyance the town was not incorporated. While the court expresses the view that the grantees were ascertained with reasonable certainty, the conveyance could be sustained upon the ground that the land was dedicated for public use.[58]

While a purported conveyance to the "heirs" of a living person will fail for lack of a grantee because a living person cannot have "heirs," [59] it may be sustained if the word "heirs" was used as meaning "children" and if there are grantees qualifying under that description.[60]

Uncertainty may arise because of the fact that the grantees are designated in the alternative. In Rowerdink v. Carothers (Mich.),[61] the conveyance was to A and B "or the survivor of them." As a matter of construction, the court held that the deed created a life estate in A and B and a remainder in fee to the survivor. In Schade v. Stewart (Cal.),[62] the grantees were described as "the heirs or devisees of Jennie C. Hurd, deceased." The court held that ownership passed to the persons designated by the probate court as those entitled to the estate of Jennie C. Hurd.

A deed without a named grantee is null and void. While the owner may authorize another to fill in the name of the grantee that authority would have to be created by a written instrument because of the Statute of Frauds.[63] However, if a *bona fide* purchaser or mortgagee is involved, the owner may be estopped to set up the Statute of Frauds.[64] Further, authority to fill in the name of a grantee may be implied.[65] Estoppel also applies if an agent has express authority to fill in the name of a grantee and he wrongfully fills in his own name and conveys to a *bona fide* purchaser or mortgagee.[66]

DELIVERY OF DEEDS

121. **An effective delivery depends upon the intention of the grantor and can be accomplished even in the absence of a physical transfer of the deed. Once a deed has been delivered a cancellation of the instrument will not revest ownership in the grantor. A presumption of delivery arises from the fact that the possession of a deed is in the grantee. A similar presumption arises if the grantor causes the recordation of a deed.**

a. **Reservation of a power of revocation. The claim that a deed has been delivered will fail if the grantor retained a power to recall the deed at any time he might choose.**

56. *Cf.*: Barnhart v. Bowers, 1936, 143 Kan. 866, 57 P.2d 60, noted in 35 Mich.Law Rev. 656 (1937) (validity sustained upon the ground that the conveyance was for a charitable purpose and a trustee was appointed to take the legal title).

57. 50 Cal. 171 (1875).

58. Futterer v. City of Sacramento, 1925, 196 Cal. 248, 237 P. 48.

59. Booker v. Tarwater, 1894, 138 Ind. 385, 37 N.E. 979; Hall v. Leonard, 1822, 18 Mass. (1 Pick.) 27.

60. Tharp v. Yarbrough, 1887, 79 Ga. 382, 4 S.E. 915; Seymour v. Bowles, 1898, 172 Ill. 521, 50 N.E. 122; Tinder v. Tinder, 1891, 131 Ind. 381, 30 N.E. 1077; Heath v. Hewitt, 1891, 127 N.Y. 166, 27 N.E. 959; Huss v. Stephens, 1865, 51 Pa. 282, subsequent hearing 54 Pa. 20 (1866).

61. 334 Mich. 454, 54 N.W.2d 715 (1952).

62. 205 Cal. 658, 272 P. 567 (1928).

63. Curlee v. Morris, 1938, 196 Ark. 779, 120 S.W.2d 10.

64. Hanson v. Hulett, 1946, 74 N.D. 300, 22 N.W.2d 209.

65. Hall v. Kary, 1907, 133 Iowa 465, 110 N.W. 930. *Contra:* Bryce v. O'Brien, 1936, 5 Cal.2d 615, 55 P.2d 488, noted in 25 Cal.Law Rev. 106 (unless there is proof of negligence). See also, Gilbert v. Plowman, 1935, 218 Iowa 1345, 256 N.W. 746, noted in 34 Mich. Law Rev. 132 (1935).

66. Handelman v. Mandel, 1921, 70 Colo. 136, 197 P. 1021; Wright v. Sconyers, 1931, 150 Okl. 3, 300 P. 672, 75 A.L.R. 1098.

However, he may properly retain the power of revocation with respect to an estate conveyed.

b. **Delivery by estoppel.** If a grantor prepares a deed that is complete as a conveying instrument he may be estopped to deny the fact of delivery if the named grantee acquires possession thereof and creates rights in a *bona fide* purchaser or mortgagee.

c. **Death cases.** A grantor may deliver a deed to a third party and direct that it be delivered to the grantee after the death of the grantor. The prevailing rule is that this may create a present estate in the grantee subject to a life estate in the grantor.

d. **Conditional delivery of deeds.** An escrow involves the deposit of a properly executed deed by the grantor with a stranger to the instrument. It is to be delivered by this custodian to the named grantee upon the happening of a named event or upon the performance of stated conditions.

e. **Status of the depositary.** At the outset the depositary is a mere custodian of property relating to the escrow. However, after substantial performance of the conditions, or the happening of the event, he becomes an agent of the grantee with respect to the deed and an agent of the grantor with respect to the consideration.

f. **"Passing of title" in an escrow transaction.** Ownership passes to the escrow grantee upon the happening of the event or performance of the conditions. The custodian need not deliver the deed to the grantee. In the absence of estoppel, even if the escrow grantee wrongfully obtains possession of the deed he cannot create rights in a third party that are superior to those of the escrow grantor.

Once ownership has passed to the escrow grantee, by applying the fiction of "relation back" his ownership may relate back to the inception of the escrow. This fiction is applied as a means by which to adjust the equities of the parties.

g. **Conditional delivery to the grantee.** If a deed is delivered directly to the grantee he acquires ownership free from conditions that are not specifically stated in the deed. However, extrinsic evidence is admissible to prove that there was a condition precedent to delivery as distinguished from a condition subsequent.

While the delivery of a deed is usually accompanied by an actual physical transfer of the instrument this is not essential. It will suffice if the grantor evidences by word or conduct an intention that the deed be operative. He may even retain possession of the deed.[67] Since delivery depends upon the intention of the grantor, acts done or statements made by the grantor subsequent to the signing of a deed may evidence an intention on his part to have the deed operative as a conveying instrument.[68]

Once a deed has been delivered, and ownership has passed to the grantee, a re-delivery of the deed to the grantor will not revest the ownership in him. This is true even if there is an intentional cancellation of the deed.[69] The deed itself is merely evidence of ownership. In order to divest himself of ownership the grantee must execute a new deed and deliver it as required by law. There is authority for the view that if a deed is cancelled or destroyed by mutual consent the grantee or persons claiming under him will be estopped to prove the provisions of the deed so cancelled or destroyed. Other authorities

67. Goodman v. Goodman, 1931, 212 Cal. 730, 300 P. 449; McKemey v. Ketchum, 1920, 188 Iowa 1081, 175 N.W. 325; Smith v. Dolman, 1926, 120 Kan. 283, 243 P. 323; Lessee of Mitchell v. Ryan, 1854, 3 Ohio St. 377; Kanawell v. Miller, 1918, 262 Pa. 9, 104 A. 861; Matson v. Johnson, 1908, 48 Wash. 256, 93 P. 324; Doe ex dem. Garnons v. Knight, [1826] 5 B. & C. 671, 108 Eng.Rep. 250; Shep. Touch., p. 57.

68. Phelps v. Pratt, 1907, 225 Ill. 85, 80 N.E. 69.

69. Tabor v. Tabor, 1904, 136 Mich. 255, 99 N.W. 4 (*dictum*).

take the position that secondary evidence cannot be used for this purpose.[70] In Lee v. Beagell (N. Y.),[71] it is held that a deed redelivered to the grantor to secure an indebtedness resulted in the creation of an equitable mortgage.

Statements and occasional decisions are to be found to the effect that to constitute delivery the grantor must part with possession of the deed.[72] In some cases reliance is had upon the rule that the valid gift of a chattel requires an actual delivery of the object of the gift. But this rule is not applicable in a situation involving the delivery of a deed. Statements that in order to effectuate a valid delivery the grantor "must part with control" of the deed refer to "legal control." [73]

The mere physical transfer of a deed by the grantor to the grantee will not result in a conveyance if it is shown that the grantor did not intend it to be operative as his deed. That is the case, for example, if the grantor hands the deed to the grantee with instructions to take care of it for the grantor.[74] That is also the situation if a deed is handed to the grantee at a time when the grantor was under the mistaken belief that the deed would not be operative until it was recorded,[75] or

acknowledged.[76] Delivery is not accomplished if a deed is handed to the named grantee to facilitate the transfer of title if the grantee finds a purchaser for the land,[77] or if the grantee promises to return the deed (as distinguished from reconvey the title) at any time on demand.[78] Of course there is no delivery if the deed is taken without the consent of the grantor.[79]

If the fact of delivery is equivocal, acts and statements of the grantor, both before and after the alleged delivery, are admissible to prove his intention.[80] Presumptions relating to delivery are as follows:

First: The physical transfer of a deed by the grantor to the grantee raises a presumption of intention to deliver the instrument.[81]

Second: Based upon the hypothesis that a person owns things that are in his possession, a deed in the possession of a grantor presumably remains undelivered.[82] A presump-

70. See 9 Miss.Law Jr. 376, 379 (1937).

71. 174 Misc. 6, 19 N.Y.S.2d 613 (1940).

72. Griffith v. Sands, 1928, 84 Colo. 456, 271 P. 191; Murray v. Kerney, 1911, 115 Md. 514, 81 A. 6; Barnes v. Barnes, 1894, 161 Mass. 381, 37 N.E. 379; Barnes v. Aycock, 1941, 219 N.C. 360, 13 S.E.2d 611; Witham v. Witham, 1937, 156 Or. 59, 66 P.2d 281, 110 A.L.R. 253, noted in 16 Or.Law Rev. 420 (1937).

73. See Platt v. Platt, 1930, 110 Cal.App. 327, 294 P. 73.

74. Ball v. Sandlin, 1917, 176 Ky. 537, 195 S.W. 1089. *Cf.:* Curry v. Colburn, 1898, 99 Wis. 319, 74 N.W. 778 (handed to grantee for purpose of examination).

75. Hotaling v. Hotaling, 1924, 193 Cal. 368, 224 P. 455, 56 A.L.R. 734.

76. Kimbro v. Kimbro, 1926, 199 Cal. 344, 249 P. 180, noted in 15 Cal.Law Rev. 156 (1927).

77. Phillips v. Farmers' Mutual Fire Insurance Co., 1919, 208 Mich. 84, 175 N.W. 144, 7 A.L.R. 1606.

78. Gaylord v. Gaylord, 1909, 150 N.C. 222, 63 S.E. 1028.

79. Stanton v. Chamberlain [1588] Owen, 95, 74 Eng. Rep. 925.

80. Crenshaw v. Crenshaw, 1948, 68 Idaho 470, 199 P. 2d 264; Resh v. Fox, 1961, 365 Mich. 288, 112 N.W. 2d 486; Johndrow v. Johndrow, 1947, 199 Okl. 363, 186 P.2d 325; Leiser v. Hartel, 1916, 315 Pa. 537, 174 A. 106. *Cf.:* Witham v. Witham, 1937, 156 Or. 59, 66 P.2d 281, 110 A.L.R. 253 (statement in grantor's will that he had previously conveyed the land to the named grantee not sufficient to overcome the presumption of non-delivery arising out of retention of possession of the deed by the grantor).

81. Coombs v. Fessenden, 1917, 116 Me. 304, 101 A. 465.

82. Donahue v. Sweeney, 1915, 171 Cal. 388, 153 P. 708; Butts v. Richards, 1913, 152 Wis. 318, 140 N. W. 1.

tion of delivery arises out of the fact that a deed is in the possession of the grantee.[83]

Third: A presumption of delivery arises from the fact that the grantor recorded the deed.[84] This presumption is of greater probative value than the presumption of non-delivery arising out of the fact that the grantor retained possession of the deed.[85] This is especially true if evidence indicates the fact that the grantor intended to reserve a life estate.[86] Statutes in some states provide that the recordation of a deed shall be conclusive evidence of the delivery of the instrument in favor of purchasers for value and without notice.[87] Recordation of a deed by a grantor has no probative value in proving an acceptance by the grantee. Accordingly, in a jurisdiction following the rule that acceptance is an essential part of delivery the recordation of a deed by the grantor does not raise a presumption of delivery.[88]

Fourth: A presumption of delivery does not arise from the fact that the deed was acknowledged by the grantor.[89] In some states it is provided by statute that a "grant duly executed is presumed to have been delivered at its date." There must be proof of the fact that delivery before such a statute is applicable.[90] Once that fact is established then the presumption arises as to the date of delivery.

Reservation of a Power of Revocation

The requirements of delivery are satisfied if a deed vests an estate in the grantee during the lifetime of the grantor. A power in the grantor to withdraw or recall a deed at any time he may choose is inconsistent with the creation of such an estate. However, a grantor may properly retain the power to terminate an estate that has been created by the delivery of his deed. For example, in Tennant v. John Tennant Memorial Home (Cal.),[91] a deed was delivered by the grantor that vested an estate in the grantee to become possessory at the death of the grantor. The delivery of the deed was complete in spite of the fact that the grantor retained the power to revoke the conveyance at any time during his lifetime.[92] Such a deed is not testamentary in nature because it vested an estate in the grantee during the lifetime of the grantor.

83. Reynolds v. Dryer, 1931, 112 Cal.App. 712, 297 P. 563; Smith v. Dolman, 1936, 120 Kan. 283, 243 P. 323; see Tiffany, Delivery and Acceptance of Deeds, 17 Mich.Law Rev. 103, 111 (1918); 20th Cent.Law Jr. 44 (1885). But a deed in the possession of a third party does not raise a presumption of delivery (Chambley v. Rumbaugh, 1939, 333 Pa. 319, 5 A.2d 171).

84. Lawson v. Boo, 1939, 227 Iowa 100, 287 N.W. 282; Pentico v. Hays, 1907, 75 Kan. 76, 88 P. 738; *contra:* Barnes v. Barnes, 1894, 161 Mass. 381, 37 N.E. 379.

85. Pentico v. Hays, 1907, 75 Kan. 76, 88 P. 738; Lessee of Mitchell v. Ryan, 1854, 3 Ohio St. 377. *Contra:* Clowers v. Clemons, 1938, 185 Ga. 567, 196 S.E. 28 (where grantor also continued in possession of the land).

86. Hill v. Kreiger, 1911, 250 Ill. 408, 95 N.E. 468.

87. See, for example, M.G.L.A. c. 183 § 5.

88. See Maynard v. Maynard, 1813, 10 Mass. 456 (no evidence of acceptance).

89. Fisher v. Hall, 1869, 41 N.Y. 416; Mumpower v. Castle, 1920, 128 Va. 1, 104 S.E. 706, noted in 19 Mich.Law Rev. 440 (1921). But see Moore v. Hazelton, 1864, 9 Allen (Mass.) 102; Butts v. Richards, 1913, 152 Wis. 318, 140 N.W. 1.

90. Boyd v. Slayback, 1883, 63 Cal. 493; Springhorn v. Springer, 1926, 75 Mont. 294, 243 P. 803.

91. 167 Cal. 570, 140 P. 242 (1914).

92. *Accord:* Ricker v. Brown, 1903, 183 Mass. 424, 67 N.E. 353 (grantor reserved the power to dispose of the land). *Contra:* Goins v. Melton, 1939, 343 Mo. 413, 121 S.W.2d 821, noted in 23 Minn.Law Rev. 683 (1939) upon the ground that the deed is testamentary in nature. See also, Yordy v. Yordy, 1950, 169 Kan. 211, 217 P.2d 912. *Cf.:* Sims v. Brown, 1913, 252 Mo. 58, 158 S.W. 624.

Delivery by Estoppel

Even though a grantor has no intention to deliver a deed, under varying circumstances he may be estopped to deny the fact of delivery.

This rule of estoppel applies if the deed is complete as a conveying instrument and the grantor, or his possessory agent, allows the named grantee to obtain possession of the deed and he conveys to a *bona fide* purchaser or mortgagee for value and without notice. It is not necessary to prove negligence on the part of the grantor. The rule is based upon the principle that, as between two innocent parties, the one who has made it possible to perpetrate a fraud should suffer the loss. In Tutt v. Smith (Iowa),[93] the grantors handed the deed to their agent with directions to take it to a named party who was to hold it in escrow. Prior to the creation of an escrow the named grantee obtained possession of the deed (the manner of acquisition is not indicated) and purported to convey the property to an innocent purchaser. The innocent purchaser was protected. Although the grantors were in possession of the land at the time the fraudulent grantee purported to convey the land, this possession was not constructive notice of their claim. This case is to be distinguished from one where the named grantee secures possession of a deed from a custodian in an escrow transaction. In that event estoppel does not apply because the custodian is not the "possessory agent" of the grantor.[94]

An estoppel may arise because of negligence on the part of a grantor.[95] In McNeil v. Jordan (Kan.),[96] plaintiff, desiring to convey her land to McNeil, instructed her attorney, Payson, to prepare a proper deed. This was done. Without the knowledge or consent of plaintiff, Payson substituted another deed in which he, Payson was named as grantee. This substituted deed was signed by plaintiff before a notary, recorded by Payson and conveyed by him to an innocent third party. The court held that the conduct of plaintiff was such as to estop her from denying the validity of the deed. In addition, Payson acted as plaintiff's agent and the grantor was bound by his acts.

The charge of "delivery by estoppel" usually cannot be sustained with respect to a deed that is incomplete. A grantor is not under a duty to anticipate that one who acquires wrongful possession of the deed will commit forgery by filling in blank spaces. This is true even if the named grantee acquires such possession.[97] The case differs from one where the grantor does, in fact, deliver an incomplete deed. In that event there is some basis for the argument that he has conferred implied authority to fill in blank spaces and may be estopped to set up the defense of the Statute of Frauds.[98]

Death Cases

The fact of delivery is not consistent with an intention on the part of a grantor to retain legal control (as distinguished from physical control) of a deed until the time of his death.[99] In that event the deed is said to be

---

Gould v. Wise, 1893, 97 Cal. 532, 32 P. 576, 33 P. 323 (negligence not shown).

93. 201 Iowa 107, 204 N.W. 294, 48 A.L.R. 394 (1925).

94. Clevenger v. Moore, 1931, 148 Okl. 162, 298 P. 248. *Cf.:* Micklethwait v. Fulton, 1935, 129 Ohio St. 488, 196 N.E. 166, noted in 13 N.Y.Univ.Law Qt.Rev. 131 (1935).

95. Merck v. Merck, 1909, 83 S.C. 329, 65 S.E. 347 (error to omit instruction on this theory). See

96. 28 Kan. 7 (1882).

97. Tisher v. Beckwith, 1872, 30 Wis. 55.

98. See supra, § 120.

99. Orris v. Whipple, 1938, 224 Iowa 1157, 280 N.W. 617, 129 A.L.R. 1, noted in 24 Iowa Law Rev. 167 (1938)—grantor placed deed in her safe deposit box where it was found after her death; Hynes v. Hal-

testamentary in nature. This means that the purpose of the grantor is to have the deed operate to transfer ownership at the time of the death of the grantor. That purpose can be accomplished only by means of a properly executed will. In Parrott v. Avery (Mass.),[1] the grantor executed a deed in which he named his grandson as grantee. The deed was placed in a chest owned by the grantor. The will bequeathed the chest and its contents to the grantee. The court held that the deed was inoperative because it had not been delivered during the lifetime of the grantor.[2] Ownership did not pass under the will because the deed formed no part of the will.[3] Under some circumstances such a document may be probated as a part of the will under the doctrine of incorporation by reference. If a deed is executed with the formalities prescribed by the Statute of Wills it may be probated as a will upon proof of testamentary intent.[4]

The invalidity of a deed for lack of delivery is also evidenced in a case where the grantor hands the deed to a third part with directions to deliver the deed after the death of the grantor. If the third part is a *"possessory agent"* of the grantor the deed remains under

his control until the time of his death.[5] Of course, if there is proof of the fact that the grantor intended to create an estate in the named grantee *when he executed the deed* the situation does not involve a testamentary transaction and the validity of the conveyance should be sustained regardless of the physical location of the deed.[6]

There are conflicting views as to the rights created under a deed if the grantor hands it to a person who is not his possessory agent and directs him to hand it to the named grantee after the death of the grantor.

The prevailing rule is that the validity of the deed will be sustained, if possible, upon the theory that it vests an immediate estate in the grantee subject to a life estate in the grantor.[7] But, at time of the death of the

---

stead, 1937, 282 Mich. 627, 276 N.W. 578. *Cf.:* Ferrell v. Stinson, 1943, 233 Iowa 1131, 11 N.W.2d 701, noted in 29 Iowa Law Rev. 500 (1944).

1. 159 Mass. 594, 35 N.E. 94 (1893).

2. See, for example, Estate of Skerrett, 1885, 67 Cal. 585, 8 P. 181.

3. *Accord:* In re Young's Estate, 1899, 123 Cal. 337, 55 P. 1011. See Griffith v. Sands, 1928, 84 Colo. 456, 271 P. 191 (direction in deed that it be delivered after his death); Hynes v. Halstead, 1937, 282 Mich. 627, 276 N.W. 578 (deed handed to third party with understanding that it would be returned to the grantor on demand).

4. In re Wawrzyniak's Estate, 1941, 297 Mich. 520, 298 N.W. 118. But see Noble v. Fickes, 1907, 230 Ill. 594, 82 N.E. 950, noted in 21 Harv.Law Rev. 451 (1908).

5. Brown v. Brown, 1876, 66 Me. 316; Felt v. Felt, 1908, 155 Mich. 237, 118 N.W. 953; Cook v. Brown, 1857, 34 N.H. 460; Johnson v. Johnson, 1903, 24 R. I. 571, 54 A. 378; Fischer v. Gorman, 1937, 65 S.D. 453, 274 N.W. 866. *Contra:* Belden v. Carter, 1809, 4 Day (Conn.) 66, questioned in Grilley v. Atkins, 1905, 78 Conn. 380, 385, 62 A. 337; Davis v. John E. Brown College, 1929, 208 Iowa 480, 222 N.W. 858, *cf.:* Orris v. Whipple, 1938, 224 Iowa 1157, 280 N.W. 617, noted in 24 Iowa Law Rev. 167 (1938); Ruggles v. Lawson, 1816, 13 Johns. (N.Y.) 285; Morse v. Slason, 1841, 13 Vt. 296; Henry v. Phillips, 1912, 105 Tex. 459, 151 S.W. 533.

6. Dry v. Adams, 1937, 367 Ill. 400, 11 N.E.2d 607, noted in 3 John Marshall Law Quarterly 454 (1938). *Cf.:* Fischer v. Gorman, 1937, 65 S.D. 453, 274 N.W. 866 (incapacity of the grantor at the time his agent purported to deliver the deed).

7. Bury v. Young, 1893, 98 Cal. 446, 33 P. 338; Klosterboer v. Engelkes, 1963, 255 Iowa 1076, 125 N.W.2d 115; In re Loper's Estate, 1962, 189 Kan. 205, 368 P.2d 39; White v. Wester, 1934, 170 Okl. 250, 39 P.2d 22; Maxwell v. Harper, 1909, 51 Wash. 351, 98 P. 756. Some authorities indicate that the interest created in the grantor remains an estate in fee simple but is subject to an executory interest created in the grantee. See Sutton v. Sutton, 1919, 141 Ark. 93, 216 S.W. 1052, noted in 18 Mich.Law Rev. 564 (1920); Abbott v. Holway, 1891, 72 Me. 298; Murray v. Kerney, 1911, 115 Md. 514, 81 A. 6; Stonehill v. Hastings, 1911, 202 N.Y.

grantor the property may constitute a part of his estate for taxation purposes.[8]

Of course, this life estate rule is not applicable if the grantor has evidenced an intention to the contrary.[9] For example, a grantor in fear or peril of death may instruct that the deed be delivered to the named grantee "after," "upon" or "in case of" the grantor's death. It is true, these expressions may be construed to mean that delivery is to be made to the grantee "when" the grantor dies, regardless of time or cause.[10] But that construction is not possible if there is an instruction to return the deed to the grantor if he should survive the particular peril. An instruction that the deed is to be returned to the grantor is inconsistent with the creation of an estate in the grantee at the time of the alleged delivery.[11]

In Long v. Ryan (Cal.),[12] the grantor deposited a deed with a trust company with instructions to hold it until a specified date. If the grantor was alive at that time the deed was to be returned to her. If she was dead at the date fixed the deed was to be delivered to the grantee. The grantor died prior to the stated time and the grantee claimed ownership under the deed. The court held that the deed failed for lack of delivery. The instructions given by the grantor were inconsistent with the view that the intention was to vest immediate ownership in the grantee with the reservation of a life estate.[13]

In Dunlap v. Marnell (Neb.),[14] a husband prepared a deed of his land naming his wife as grantee. At the same time the wife prepared a deed of her land naming her husband as grantee. Both deeds were deposited with a third party with instructions not to return either deed except upon the written order of both grantors. Upon the death of either grantor both deeds were to be returned to the survivor. The wife died first and her deed was delivered to the husband. The validity of the deed was sustained.[15] The contention that a transaction is testamentary in nature and void is open to question if it is based upon the terms and conditions of a legally recognized contract.[16] The execution of a contract creates *inter vivos* rights.

Problems pertaining to the admissibility of evidence to prove the intention of a grantor are as follows:

First: An intention on the part of the grantor to create an immediate estate in the grantee, and thus establish a valid delivery, may be implied. The implication may come from the fact that the deed was handed to a

---

115, 94 N.E. 1068; Jones v. Caird, 1913, 153 Wis. 384, 141 N.W. 228.

8. In re Hubbs, 1933, 41 Ariz. 466, 19 P.2d 672; In re Estate of Ogden, 1932, 209 Wis. 162, 244 N.W. 571.

9. See, for example, Obranovich v. Stiller, 1963, 220 Cal.App.2d 205, 34 Cal.Rptr. 923; Wilcox v. Wilcox, 1938, 283 Mich. 313, 278 N.W. 79; Wheeler v. Rines, Mo.1964, 375 S.W.2d 48 (provision in deed: "THIS DEED, IS NOT TO TAKE EFFECT till after The Death of (grantor))."

10. Owings v. First Nat. Bank, 1014, 97 Neb. 257, 149 N.W. 777. But see, Williams v. Kidd, 1915, 170 Cal. 631, 151 P. 1.

11. But a deed cannot be delivered to the grantee subject to a condition subsequent that is not expressed in the deed itself (Hojnacki v. Hojnacki, 1937, 281 Mich. 636, 275 N.W. 659; Benson v. Carroll, 1939, 257 App.Div. 1051, 14 N.Y.S.2d 51, affirmed 282 N.Y. 776, 27 N.E.2d 49.

12. 166 Cal. 442, 137 P. 29 (1913).

13. *Accord:* Masquart v. Dick, 1957, 210 Or. 459, 310 P.2d 742.

14. 95 Neb. 535, 145 N.W. 1017 (1914).

15. *Contra:* Kenney v. Parks, 1899, 125 Cal. 146, 57 P. 772.

16. See McCarthy v. Pieret, 1939, 281 N.Y. 407, 24 N.E.2d 102, noted in 38 Mich.Law Rev. 900 (1940); Jackson v. Jackson, 1913, 67 Or. 44, 135 P. 201; In re Murphy's Estate, 1938, 193 Wash. 400, 75 P.2d 916, criticized in 37 Mich.Law Rev. 167 (1938).

third party with directions to deliver it to the named grantee after the death of the grantor.

There is a difference of opinion as to whether or not subsequent acts and statements of the grantor are admissible in evidence to prove that he did not intend to create a present estate in the grantee and that the deed is testamentary in nature and void. In support of the rule that such evidence is not admissible it may be contended that subsequent acts and statements should not be admitted to prove prior intention.[17] It would give a grantor a means of escape from the transaction if he should see fit to change his mind. However, it is believed that the evidence should be admissible.[18] In the usual situation the grantee is a mere volunteer and there is an ambiguity with respect to the intention of the grantor. These considerations indicate that a liberal rule should be followed with respect to the admissibility of evidence.

Second: In O'Brien v. O'Brien (N. D.),[19] the custodian returned the deed to the grantor when requested to do so. This was considered to be important evidence to prove the fact that the grantor did not intend to convey an irrevocable estate at the time the deed was deposited. In Loomis v. Loomis (Mich.),[20] the custodian testified that if the grantor had called for the deed during her lifetime he would probably have surrendered it to her. Since the attitude on the part of the custodian was not based on anything that the grantor had said at the time the deed was deposited, the court held that the testimony would have no bearing on the issue as to whether or not the deed had been delivered. Such evidence would have probative value if the attitude of the custodian was based upon instructions given to him by the grantor at the time of the alleged delivery.[21]

Conditional Delivery of Deeds

An escrow involves the deposit of a properly executed deed by the grantor with a stranger to the instrument. It is to be delivered by him to the named grantee upon the happening of a named event or upon the performance of stated conditions. The deposit places the deed beyond recall by the grantor for the time agreed upon. It is then to be returned to him if there is default in the happening of the event or the performance of the conditions. It is obvious that a deed is not placed beyond recall if it is deposited with the grantor's possessory agent or if the happening of the event or the performance of the conditions are under the control of the grantor. Accordingly, the deposit of a deed under such circumstances properly cannot be classified as an escrow.

In a number of states it is considered that the mere deposit of a deed with a third party results in a *continuing offer to convey* upon the performance of named conditions. Under this view the deed can be placed beyond recall by the grantor only by the execution of a binding contract to convey.[22] However, if the

---

17. Napier v. Elliott, 1909, 162 Ala. 129, 50 So. 148; Pentico v. Hays, 1907, 75 Kan. 76, 88 P. 738; Coombs v. Fessenden, 1917, 116 Me. 304, 101 A. 465; Chase v. Woodruff, 1907, 133 Wis. 555, 113 N.W. 973 (see a later appeal involving the same matter, 138 Wis. 641, 120 N.W. 499 (1909)).

18. Williams v. Kidd, 1915, 170 Cal. 631, 151 P. 1; Linn v. Linn, 1914, 261 Ill. 606, 616, 104 N.E. 229; Hynes v. Halstead, 1937, 282 Mich. 627, 276 N.E. 578. See also, Landry v. Landry, 1928, 265 Mass. 265, 163 N.E. 851; Mower v. Mower, 1924, 64 Utah 260, 228 P. 911.

19. 19 N.D. 713, 125 N.W. 307 (1910).

20. 178 Mich. 221, 144 N.W. 552 (1913).

21. Hynes v. Halstead, 1937, 282 Mich. 627, 276 N.W. 578; Johnson v. Johnson, 1903, 24 R.I. 571, 54 A. 378.

22. Fitch v. Bunch, 1866, 30 Cal. 208; Main v. Pratt, 1916, 276 Ill. 218, 114 N.E. 576; Freeland v. Charnley, 1881, 80 Ind. 132; Foulkes v. Sengstacken, 1917,

stated conditions are performed prior to revocation ownership of the land passes to the named grantee because this constitutes an acceptance of the offer. If the grantor and the grantee execute identical escrow instructions these instruments will be construed together as constituting a binding contract.[23] So also, if the deed, as delivered, embodies the terms of a contract to convey the grantee can enforce the contract. The Statute of Frauds merely requires the agreement to be signed by the party sought to be charged.[24] If the grantor allows the grantee to take possession of the land an oral contract to convey may be enforceable under the part performance doctrine.[25]

Status of the Depositary

Prior to substantial performance of the conditions specified in the escrow transaction, or the happening of the event involved, the depositary is a mere *custodian* of the deed and other documents or property placed in his possession. He is not a trustee because he does not acquire legal title to the property in question. He is not an agent of either party, individually, because his only duty is to perform the acts directed in the escrow instructions.[26] This he is under a duty to do even though he is directed otherwise by one of the

parties to the escrow.[27] Although the parties to an escrow transaction may, by mutual agreement, modify the escrow instructions, the depositary is not an agent of such parties. For example, if the depositary absconds with property deposited in escrow, such as the purchase price, the one who made the deposit must suffer the loss unless the escrow transaction was substantially performed at the time of the defalcation.[28] If the depositary were the agent of those participating in the transaction the loss would be shared on an equal basis. However, there is authority for the view that knowledge possessed by the depositary with respect to the transaction will be imputed to the escrow parties.[29]

After the conditions specified in the escrow transaction have been substantially performed, or after the named event has come to pass, the depositary becomes the possessory agent of the grantee with respect to the deed and the agent of the grantor with respect to property deposited by the grantee or in his behalf.

"Passing of Title" in an Escrow Transaction

In compliance with the intention of the grantor, ownership passes to the escrow grantee upon the happening of the named event or the performance of the named conditions.[30] Delivery of the deed by the custo-

83 Or. 118, 158 P. 952, 163 P. 311; McLain v. Healy, 1917, 98 Wash. 489, 168 P. 1; Campbell v. Thomas, 1877, 42 Wis. 437. For criticism of this view, see Aigler, Is a Contract Necessary to Create an Effective Escrow?, 16 Mich.Law Rev. 569 (1918); Tiffany, Conditional Delivery of Deeds, 14 Col.Law Rev. 389, 399 (1914).

23. Tuso v. Green, 1924, 194 Cal. 574, 229 P. 327, noted in 13 Cal.Law Rev. 361 (1925).

24. See Clay v. Reynolds, 1934, 169 Okl. 416, 37 P.2d 244, 100 A.L.R. 192.

25. Conner v. Helvik, 1937, 105 Mont. 437, 73 P.2d 541. See also, Cannon v. Handley, 1887, 72 Cal. 133, 13 P. 315.

26. See Bell, Conditional Delivery of Deeds in Oregon, 9 Or.Law Rev. 152, 155 (1930).

27. See Southern v. Chase State Bank, 1936, 144 Kan. 472, 61 P.2d 1340, 107 A.L.R. 944 (the construction placed upon the escrow agreement by either of the parties to the escrow is not binding upon the depositary).

28. See Shreeves v. Pearson, 1924, 194 Cal. 699, 230 P. 448.

29. Early v. Owens, 1930, 109 Cal.App. 489, 293 P. 136.

30. Newport Bay Dredging Co. v. Helm, 1932, 120 Cal. App. 127, 7 P.2d 1039; Val Verde Hotel Co. v. Ross, 1924, 30 N.M. 270, 231 P. 702; Bogelow, Conditional Delivery of Deeds of Land, 26 Harv.Law Rev. 565, 568 (1913). Cf.: Baker v. Snavely, 1911, 84 Kan. 179, 114 P. 370 (an escrow grantee will not be pro-

dian, sometimes referred to as "the second delivery", is not essential. The grantee is entitled to the deed, however, and may maintain an appropriate action for its recovery. If the custodian absconds before ownership passes to the grantee the loss must be sustained by the one who deposited the property involved.[31] If the custodian absconds after the happening of the event or the performance of the conditions the escrow grantee will be protected in his ownership of the land.[32]

Prior to the happening of the event, or the performance of the conditions, the escrow grantor remains the owner of the land. He is the proper person to sign a petition of landowners.[33] He is the "sole and unconditional" owner of the property within the meaning of a provision in a fire insurance policy.[34] In the absence of special circumstances or agreement to the contrary he is liable for taxes that accrue during the escrow period.[35] A warranty against taxes "at the time of delivery" refers to the time when ownership passes to the grantee.[36]

In Everts v. Agnes (Wis.),[37] a landowner, Everts, executed a deed naming Agnes as grantee. The deed was deposited with Zettler who was instructed to deliver it to Agnes when Agnes should execute certain notes and mortgages. Without having performed the conditions Agnes secured possession of the deed, caused it to be recorded, and purported to convey the land to Swift, an alleged *bona fide* purchaser. It is held that Swift did not have a valid claim of ownership under his deed from Agnes. Agnes did not acquire ownership because he did not perform the conditions.[38] Of course, an innocent purchaser will be protected if a grantor entrusts the deed to an agent of the grantee and this agent permits the grantee to gain possession.[39] A grantor may also be estopped to deny delivery if the escrow grantee takes possession of the land with the consent of the grantor and subsequently acquires wrongful possession of the deed and conveys to a *bona fide* purchaser or mortgagee for value and without notice.[40] Armed with a deed and possession of the land the escrow grantee has *indicia* of ownership. The grantor participated in the creation of this condition. A grantor may be denied relief if he knows or should know that his deed has been

tected as to prior equities if he has notice thereof at the time he performs the conditions).

31. Lieb v. Webster, 1948, 30 Wash.2d 43, 190 P.2d 701.

32. Lechner v. Halling, 1950, 35 Wash.2d 903, 216 P. 2d 179.

33. Hull v. Sangamon River Drainage District, 1906, 219 Ill. 454, 76 N.E. 701.

34. American Central Fire Ins. Co. v. Arndt, 1917, 129 Ark. 309, 195 S.W. 1075; Pomeroy v. Aetna Ins. Co., 1912, 86 Kan. 214, 120 P. 344 (even though the escrow grantee was in possession of the land).

35. Mohr v. Joslin, 1913, 162 Iowa 34, 142 N.W. 981. *Cf.:* Wood v. Morath, 1921, 128 Miss. 143, 156, 90 So. 714 (adjustment made if escrow grantee occupies the land during tax period).

36. McMurtrey v. Bridges, 1913, 41 Okl. 264, 137 P. 721.

37. 4 Wis. 343 (1855).

38. *Accord:* Promise v. Duke, 1929, 208 Cal. 420, 281 P. 613; Dixon v. Bristol Savings Bank, 1897, 102 Ga. 461, 31 S.E. 96; Merchants' & Farmers' State Bank v. Olson, 1933, 189 Minn. 528, 250 N.W. 366, 89 A.L.R. 1289; Smith v. South Royalton Bank, 1859, 32 Vt. 341. See 37 Yale Law Journal 357 (1928).

39. Hubbard v. Greeley, 1892, 84 Me. 340, 24 A. 799. *Cf.:* Micklethwait v. Fulton, 1935, 129 Ohio St. 488, 196 N.E. 166, noted in 13 N.Y.Univ.Law Quarterly 131 (1935) (entrustment of deed to agent of grantor and the loss resulted from the agent's negligence). See also, Clevenger v. Moore, 1927, 126 Okl. 246, 259 P. 219, 54 A.L.R. 1237.

40. Quick v. Milligan, 1886, 108 Ind. 419, 9 N.E. 392; Schurtz v. Colvin, 1896, 55 Ohio St. 274, 45 N.E. 527. *Contra:* Houston v. Forman, 1926, 92 Fla. 1, 109 So. 297, 48 A.L.R. 401. See White, Escrows and Conditional Delivery of Deeds in Ohio, 2 Univ. of Cinn.Law Rev. 28, 46 (1928).

acquired by the escrow grantee without right and steps are not taken to recover possession of the deed or to have it cancelled.[41]

Once ownership has passed to the escrow grantee because of his performance of the conditions, circumstances may warrant the conclusion that conflicting rights should be adjusted on the hypothesis that ownership passed to the grantee when the grantor delivered the deed in escrow. This result is accomplished by resort to the fiction of "relation back." It is considered that "title passed as of the time of the first delivery. It will be called into play when necessary to adjust the equities that are inherent in the transaction. Situations that involve an application of this fiction are as follows:

First: The fiction of relation back is applied in a case where a grantor becomes incapacitated between the date when a deed is delivered into escrow and the date upon which the conditions are performed. That is the case, for example, if the grantor dies or becomes mentally incompetent or otherwise without capacity to make the conveyance.[42]

Second: The fiction of relation back will be applied if necessary to protect the escrow grantee against the claims of an intervening third party unless that party qualifies as a *bona fide* purchaser or mortgagee.

Since the legal title remains in the grantor during the escrow period, a conveyance or mortgage by him to a person who has no actual or constructive notice of the rights of the escrow grantee, and who pays the full consideration and takes in the legal title before receiving notice will cut off the prior equity of the escrow grantee.[43] There is authority for the view that a purchaser at an execution sale may qualify as a *bona fide* purchaser.[44]

The general rule is that creditors of the grantor are not classified as *bona fide* purchasers.[45] This is also true with respect to judgment creditors. In Hall v. Harris (N. C.),[46] creditors of the grantor levied execution after his deed had been deposited in escrow. Three days after the levy the escrow grantee complied with the conditions. The escrow grantee prevailed as against the judgment creditors.

Third: The relation-back doctrine is applied not only where rights of intervening parties are involved but also when there are conflicting claims as between the grantor and grantee. In Scott v. Stone (Kan.),[47] it is held that the escrow grantor is not entitled to both the rent paid by tenants during the escrow period and also to interest on the purchase price. In the absence of an agreement to the contrary the ownership of the escrow grantee will relate back to the time when the deed

---

41. See Mays v. Shields, 1903, 117 Ga. 814, 45 S.E. 68; Haven v. Kramer, 1875, 41 Iowa 382; Bales v. Roberts, 1905, 189 Mo. 49, 87 S.W. 914; Matteson v. Smith, 1901, 61 Neb. 761, 86 N.W. 472.

42. Davis v. Clark, 1897, 58 Kan. 100, 48 P. 563; Tharaldson v. Everts, 1902, 87 Minn. 168, 91 N.W. 467; Webster v. Kings County Trust Co., 1895, 145 N.Y. 275, 39 N.E. 964 (no conveyance from heirs of the deceased grantor would be necessary); Jackson v. Jackson, 1913, 67 Or. 44, 135 P. 201; Gammon v. Bunnell, 1900, 22 Utah 421, 64 P. 958; Bronx Inv. Co. v. National Bank of Commerce, 1907, 47 Wash. 566, 92 P. 380.

43. Waldock v. Frisco Lumber Co., 1918, 71 Okl. 200, 176 P. 218.

44. Cady v. Purser, 1901, 131 Cal. 552, 63 P. 844.

45. Tiffany, Conditional Delivery of Deeds, 14 Col. Law Rev. 389, 402 (1914). *Contra:* Rathmell v. Shirey, 1899, 60 Ohio St. 187, 53 N.E. 1098 (creditors of grantor protected against escrow grantee who was a mere volunteer); May v. Emerson, 1908, 52 Or. 262, 96 P. 454, 1065 (construing an Oregon statute).

46. 40 N.C. 303 (1848).

47. 72 Kan. 545, 84 P. 117 (1906).

was delivered into escrow. Accordingly, he is entitled to the rents involved.[48]

Conditional Delivery to the Grantee

If a deed is delivered directly to the grantee he acquires ownership free from conditions that are not specifically stated in the deed. This rule is declared in Whyddon's Case (Eng.),[49] and is generally followed in the United States.[50]

As a matter of policy, application of this rule lends stability to titles in the area of conveyancing. However, the reason given for application of the rule is open to question. It is usually stated that the provisions of a deed cannot be altered by extrinsic evidence because of the parol evidence rule.[51] But matters relating to the delivery of a deed do not find expression in the language of a deed. It is well recognized that extrinsic evidence is proper to prove that a deed was delivered to a third party on condition. It is also recognized that extrinsic evidence is admissible to prove that the physical transfer of a deed to the grantee did not constitute delivery because of some *condition precedent*. That is the situation, for example, if there was an understanding that the deed was not to be operative until such time as the grantee paid

the consideration [52] or until its recordation.[53] In Blades v. Wilmington Trust Co. (N. C.),[54] upon the death of a grantee the deed was found in her safe deposit box. It was contained in an envelope upon which the deceased grantee had written the following notation: "Deed from Florence to me, to be used should I survive her. Should I die first, it remains hers to do as she desires, to sell it if she desires . . ." The grantor survived the grantee. The court held that the grantee did not acquire ownership under the deed because it had not been delivered. At the time the grantor handed the deed to the grantee it was not intended that it should be operative as a conveyance.[55]

ACCEPTANCE BY THE GRANTEE

122. Conveyance by deed requires acceptance by the grantee. The general rule is that acceptance will be presumed if the conveyance is beneficial to the grantee.

A conveyance by deed requires the consent of the grantor as well as that of the grantee. The consent of the grantor is manifested by delivery of the deed. The consent of the grantee is manifested by his acceptance.

In some decisions it is stated that a conveyance is a contract and, like other contracts, requires an offer and acceptance. But the transaction does not necessarily involve a contractual relationship and it is not helpful

---

48. *Accord:* Price v. Pittsburg, etc., Ry. Co., 1864, 34 Ill. 13. See also, Hawi Mill & Plantation Co. v. Finn, 1927, 82 Cal.App. 255, 255 P. 543 (to regulate right to crops); Cowden v. Broderick & Calvert, 1938, 131 Tex. 434, 114 S.W.2d 1166, 117 A.L.R. 61 (to prevent forfeiture of an oil and gas lease).

49. Cro.Eliz. 520, 78 Eng.Rep. 769 (1596).

50. But see, Whitaker v. Lane, 1920, 128 Va. 317, 104 S.E. 252, 11 A.L.R. 1157, discussed in Simonton, Transferring Title to Land by Deeds, 36 W.Va. Law Quarterly, 343, 351 (1930). For criticism of the rule, see Tiffany, Conditional Delivery of Deed, 14 Col. Law Rev. 389, 390 (1914). Whyddon's Case was not followed in Hawksland v. Gatchel, [1601] Cro.Eliz. 835, 78 Eng.Rep. 1062.

51. See Lawton v. Sager, 1851, 11 Barb. (N.Y.) 349.

52. Inman v. Quirey, 1917, 128 Ark. 605, 194 S.W. 858; Lee v. Richmond, 1894, 90 Iowa 695, 57 N.W. 613; Burnett v. Rhudy, 1923, 137 Va. 67, 72, 119 S.E. 97, noted in 22 Mich.Law Rev. 479 (1924).

53. Hotaling v. Hotaling, 1924, 193 Cal. 368, 224 P. 455, 56 A.L.R. 734. But see, Wipfler v. Wipfler, 1908, 153 Mich. 18, 116 N.W. 544; Loughran v. Kummer, 1929, 297 Pa. 179, 146 A. 534.

54. 207 N.C. 771, 178 S.E. 565 (1935).

55. *Accord:* Buckwald v. Buckwald, 1938, 175 Md. 115, 199 A. 800. *Contra:* Sweeney v. Sweeney, 1940, 126 Conn. 391, 11 A.2d 806; Tabor v. Tabor, 1904, 136 Mich. 255, 99 N.W. 4.

to apply this contractual concept.[56] According to the Massachusetts rule, the acceptance of a deed is an essential part of the act of delivery.[57] It is considered that an effective delivery requires an acceptance. This conclusion is inconsistent with the generally accepted view that delivery is a unilateral manifestation of intention on the part of the grantor to transfer ownership.

The general rule is that acceptance will be presumed if the conveyance is beneficial to the grantee.[58] However, he may reject the conveyance within a reasonable time after he acquires knowledge of the facts. In Lessee of Mitchell v. Ryan (Ohio),[59] the grantor, Shannon, executed and recorded a deed that named his daughter as grantee. She died before being informed of the grant. The court held that the ownership passed to the daughter at the time of delivery. In some states it is held that this acceptance will be presumed only if the conveyance is made to a minor, an incompetent or to a competent adult who is informed of the conveyance and makes no objection thereto.[60] If a competent adult is not informed of a conveyance until after the death of the grantor, consent then given may relate back to the date of delivery. However, this fiction of relation back may not be applicable if this would be prejudicial to the rights of an intervening third party, such as the right of a surviving joint tenant.[61]

DESCRIPTION OF LAND

123. **A description is sufficient if the land can be identified from the provisions in a contract or deed. A description can be incorporated by reference. It may be based upon a private or governmental survey.**

a. **Conveyance of a part of a larger tract. If the purpose is to convey, except or mortgage a specific part of a larger tract, as distinguished from an undivided interest, there must be sufficient description to identify the area involved.**

b. **Ambiguous description. If a contract to convey land or a deed contains conflicting measurements, priority is given to the description concerning which the parties are least likely to be mistaken.**

c. **Presumptively title passes to the center of a monument. If land is bounded by a monument, such as a street or a body of water, a conveyance or mortgage of the land presumably extends to the center of the monument if the grantor or mortgagor is the owner of that area. However, actual measurement of the area conveyed is made from the side of the monument.**

The Statute of Frauds requires that the subject matter of a contract to convey freehold estates, or a deed conveying such an estate, be identified in the written instrument.[62] It must furnish some link or key to extrinsic testimony which identifies the property.[63] Exception is found in situations where equitable relief is available under the part performance doctrine.[64]

---

56. See Tiffany, Delivery and Acceptance of Deeds, 17 Mich.Law Rev. 103, 122 (1918).

57. Maynard v. Maynard, 1813, 10 Mass. 456.

58. Klingaman v. Burch, 1940, 216 Ind. 695, 25 N.E.2d 996; Kyle v. Kyle, 1916, 175 Iowa 734, 157 N.W. 248; Miller v. Miller, 1913, 91 Kan. 1, 136 P. 953; Fryer v. Fryer, 1906, 77 Neb. 298, 109 N.W. 175 (mortgage); Thompson v. Leach, [1691] 2 Vent. 198, 86 Eng.Rep. 391.

59. 3 Ohio St. 377 (1854).

60. See Turner v. Turner, 1916, 173 Cal. 782, 161 P. 980; Hill v. Kreiger, 1911, 250 Ill. 408, 95 N.E. 468.

61. Green v. Skinner, 1921, 185 Cal. 435, 197 P. 60, noted in 9 Cal.Law Rev. 499 (1921). *Cf.:* Aigler, 25 Mich.Law Rev. 171 (1926).

62. See Roberts v. Lebrain, 1952, 113 Cal.App.2d 712, 248 P.2d 810.

63. Stuesser v. Ebel, 1963, 19 Wis.2d 591, 120 N.W. 2d 679.

64. See also, Oatman v. Niemeyer, 1929, 207 Cal. 424, 278 P. 1043 (involving reformation of a deed).

A description is adequate if the land can be identified by reference to the contract or deed.[65] The description need not be in the instrument itself. There may be reference therein to some other instrument, such as a plat, map or survey. This reference-document need not be an official one and it is not necessary that it be acknowledged or recorded. It is sufficient if it identifies the land in question even though it may be incomplete or even inaccurate in some respects.[66]

A valid description may be in general terms, such as "all of my land wherever situated." Such a deed conveys all of the land owned by the grantor at the time of the conveyance.[67] Similarly, a conveyance of all of the grantor's land in a designated state or subdivision of that state is sufficiently certain as a description.[68]

The conveyance of specific land requires a specific description. In the first place, it must be located geographically. That is to say, there must be reference to the state in which the land is located and the place within the state must be designated, such as by county, city, etc.[69] However, these description-deficiencies may be supplied by a recording officer's notations.[70] In Hertel v. Woodard (Or.),[71] the seller signed a receipt for the sale of a lot and house "number 960 Union Street." The writing did not mention the city, county or state in which the land was located. In seeking enforcement of the contract the purchaser alleged that a lot in Salem, Oregon was "the only real premises whatsoever owned by defendant." In denying enforcement of the contract the court points out that the receipt is not necessarily limited to a sale of property owned by the seller.[72] In this respect the case differs from one wherein the property is described as "my farm" or "my property." Under such circumstances it is possible to identify the property and the validity of the contract may be sustained.[73] However, the validity of a deed containing such a description is open to question. Less certainty is required in a description of land in the case of a contract to convey than is required in the case of a deed.[74] Technical methods of description are as follows:

First: Land may be described by metes and bounds. This contemplates a delineation of the exterior lines of the area in question. Use may be made of natural or artificial monuments. The monument, such as a body of water or a street, may constitute the boundary. If not, it may be used for measurement purposes. The measurements (courses and

---

65. Robinson v. Black, 1963, 73 N.M. 116, 385 P.2d 971 (memorandum "real estate purchased as auction from Ray Robinson Estate in Carlsbad, N.M. on August 17, 1961). See 4 Tiffany, Real Property (3rd ed.) § 992. But see, Martin v. Seigel, 1949, 35 Wash.2d 223, 212 P.2d 107, 23 A.L.R.2d 1 (description of land by street and number is not sufficient even if accompanied by a statement as to the state and city in which the land is situated).

66. Hughes v. Meem, 1962, 70 N.M. 122, 371 P.2d 235.

67. Pettigrew v. Dobbelaar, 1883, 63 Cal. 396.

68. See Crocker v. Smith, 1937, 366 Ill. 535, 9 N.E. 2d 309.

69. Saterstrom v. Glick Bros. Sash, etc., Co., 1931, 118 Cal.App. 379, 5 P.2d 21; Hertel v. Woodard, 1948, 183 Or. 99, 191 P.2d 400 (earnest money receipt).

70. Boyd v. McElroy, 1940, 105 Colo. 527, 100 P.2d 624; Holley's Executor v. Curry, 1905, 58 W.Va. 70, 51 S.E. 135. See Montgomery v. Graves, 1945, 301 Ky. 260, 191 S.W.2d 399 (description augmented by notorized O.P.A. document).

71. 183 Or. 99, 191 P.2d 400 (1948).

72. But see, Sanders v. McNutt, 1947, 147 Ohio St. 408, 72 N.E.2d 72.

73. Cramer v. Ballard, 1946, 315 Mich. 496, 24 N.W.2d 80; Henderson v. Lemke, 1911, 60 Or. 363, 119 P. 482.

74. Wright v. L. W. Wilson Co., Inc., 1931, 212 Cal. 569, 299 P. 521.

distances) are run from an identified starting place to a monument or at a stated angle (direction) for a stated distance.

Urban property is usually surveyed and divided into lots that are numbered on a recorded map or plat. A lot may then be conveyed and described by referring to the plat and lot number.

Second: In compliance with congressional authority that dates back to 1796, the United States government has surveyed lands in the public domain. In conveying large tracts of this land that has since passed into private ownership areas are described by reference to the survey.

The key to the survey is the division of the land into areas that are six miles square, called townships. Each township is divided into thirty-six sections, each section being one mile square. These sections within the township are numbered consecutively from one to thirty-six. The numbering starts in the northeast corner of a section and proceeds from east to west. The next row is numbered from west to east. Each section may be divided into halves and quarters and the quarters may, in turn, be further divided. The description starts with the location of the land in the quarter section.

The townships are located and numbered by reference to a base line that runs east and west on a parallel of latitude, and a principal meridian running along a longitude. At every six miles along the base line and the meridian, perpendicular lines are run. These lines intersect to form townships. A line of townships running north and south is called a range, and the ranges are numbered east and west from the meridian. Each township in a range is also numbered north and south from the base line.[75]

Conveyance of a Part of a Larger Tract

If the purpose is to convey, except or mortgage a specific part of a larger tract, as distinguished from an undivided interest, the part involved must be described. In Harris v. Woodard (N. C.),[76] a mortgage was given on three acres of a forty acre tract. Since there was no means by which to identify the three specific acres from the terms of the mortgage, the mortgagee was denied priority as against a subsequent mortgagee of the entire tract.[77]

A different situation is presented if the specific area can be identified from language found in the conveying instrument. For example, in Honey v. Gambriel (Ill.),[78] a deed conveying a described tract of 49½ acres provided "except the ½ acre where the graveyard is not situated." This description furnished a means by which the ½ acre could be identified.[79] In the absence of a provision to the contrary, the area conveyed or excepted will be made as nearly square as possible in order to maintain symmetry in the descriptions of land. If it appears that the purpose was not to convey or except a specific part of a larger tract the conveyance may transfer an undivided interest.[80]

Ambiguous Description

Descriptions of land in a contract to convey or in a deed may result in an ambiguity if

75. For a general discussion of the problems involved, see 3 Am.Law of Property, § 1299, et seq.

76. 130 N.C. 580, 41 S.E. 790 (1902).

77. *Accord:* Matney v. Odom, 1948, 147 Tex. 26, 210 S.W.2d 980 ("four (4) acres out of the East end of a ten-acre block (described)").

78. 303 Ill. 74, 135 N.E. 25 (1922).

79. *Accord:* Lego v. Medley, 1891, 79 Wis. 211, 48 N. W. 375.

80. Morehead v. Hall, 1900, 126 N.C. 213, 35 S.E. 428; Seguin v. Maloney-Chambers Lumber Co., 1953, 198 Or. 272, 253 P.2d 252, rehearing denied 256 P.2d 514 (conveyance of standing timber). *Cf.:* W. T. Carter & Bro. v. Ewers, 1939, 133 Tex. 616, 131 S.W.2d 86, 123 A.L.R. 908.

reference is made to specific monuments (description by metes and bounds) and also by reference to courses and distances. The ambiguity results if these two methods of description are in conflict. There may also be an ambiguity in connection with the identification of a monument. This ambiguity may be resolved by the use of extrinsic evidence.[81]

In resolving ambiguities relating to descriptions priority is usually given to the description concerning which the parties are least likely to be mistaken. For example, there may be a call for a direction (an angle) to a monument, such as a street. It may be found that the given direction does not lead to the monument. The description relating to the monument will prevail and the call for direction will be disregarded.[82] Specification of a distance to a monument will be disregarded if it is not the correct distance.[83] Conflicting calls for a natural monument and an artificial monument will be resolved in favor of the natural monument.[84] A call for a direction will prevail over a call for a distance. The fact that acreage is stated incorrectly does not lessen the certainty of the description in a deed.[85] The call for acreage is the least reliable of all the calls in a deed.[86] Mention of the quantity of land may aid in defining the area [87] but it does not control the rest of the description unless, of course, there is an express warranty.

An ambiguity may be resolved by course of conduct. If a grantee takes possession of the land and the grantor and the grantee act in reliance upon one of two or more interpretations of the language in the deed, that interpretation will prevail.[88]

Presumptively Title Passes to the Center of a Monument

A deed may describe the land conveyed by reference to a monument, such as a street or a body of water. If the grantor owns the land to the center of the monument that area presumably passes to the grantee by operation of law. This result follows unless an intention to the contrary is expressed in the deed.[89]

This rule is based upon the presumed intention of the grantor as well as upon public policy. If this presumption were not applied the grantor would retain an estate in land that, in many instances, would be of nuisance value only. The grantee might be deprived of valuable incidents of ownership with respect to the use and enjoyment of the street or stream.

According to some authorities, rather indefinite language in a description is sufficient to overcome this presumption. In Berton v. All Persons (Cal.),[90] the description was "to the northerly line of Frank Place and easterly along said line . . .". It is held that this language was sufficient to overcome the presumption that title passed to the center of Frank Place. And in Woolf v. Pierce (N. Y.),[91] the description was as follows: "Begin-

---

81. Claremont v. Carlton, 1821, 2 N.H. 369.

82. Hall v. Eaton, 1885, 139 Mass. 217, 29 N.E. 660.

83. Stefanick v. Fortona, 1915, 222 Mass. 83, 109 N.E. 878. See also, Hoban v. Cable, 1894, 102 Mich. 206, 60 N.W. 466.

84. See Whitehead v. Ragan, 1891, 106 Mo. 231, 17 S. W. 307.

85. Wyatt v. Wycough, 1960, 232 Ark. 760, 341 S.W.2d 18.

86. Texas Pacific Coal & Oil Co. v. Masterson, 1960, 160 Tex. 548, 334 S.W.2d 436.

87. Spooner v. Menard, 1963, 124 Vt. 61, 196 A.2d 510.

88. Davies v. Wickstrom, 1909, 56 Wash. 154, 105 P. 454.

89. Kassner v. Alexander Drug Co., 1943, 194 Okl. 36, 147 P.2d 979. But see, Suburban Land Co., Inc. v. Town of Billerica, 1943, 314 Mass. 184, 49 N.E.2d 1012, 147 A.L.R. 660.

90. 176 Cal. 610, 170 P. 151 (1917).

91. 209 N.Y. 344, 103 N.E. 508, 2 A.L.R. 1 (1913).

ning on the northwest corner of Walnut and Second, and then west along said street . . .". The fact that the starting point was at the *side of the monument* was held to be sufficient evidence to overcome the presumption that title passed to the center of the street. However, a description referring to a stake or monument placed upon the side of a street is not necessarily controlling in determining whether or not the starting point is on the side of the street instead of the center thereof.[92]

A contrary and it is believed a more desirable policy is followed in Salter v. Jonas (N. J.).[93] In that case the area was described as beginning at and running along the easterly line of Roland Street. In reaching the conclusion that the grantee acquired ownership to the center of the street it is held that nothing less than express words to the contrary will be sufficient to overcome the presumption.[94] Other situations are as follows:

First: In Chicago & E. I. R. Co. v. Willard (Ill.),[95] in the grant of a right of way the area was described as fifty feet on each side of an established survey line. This description included four feet of an existing highway. The court held that including a part of the highway in the description carried the implication that the balance of the highway was excluded from the terms of the grant.

Second: Even if a description makes no mention of a monument, the presumption is that ownership extends to the center of a monument that actually forms a part of the boundary.[96] That is also the case if reference is made to a plat or map which indicates a monument, such as a street. The plat or map then becomes a part of the description.[97]

Third: The presumption that ownership passes to the center of a monument applies whether the monument is a public or a private way,[98] and whether or not the way is actually opened at the time of the conveyance.[99] In Gould v. Wagner (Mass.),[1] a mortgage described the land as abutting upon a five-foot private passageway. While the mortgagor was the owner of the entire passageway he did not own any land on the opposite side of the passageway. The court held that the mortgage only included the land to the center of the monument. There is authority for the view that in a case of this type there is a presumption that a deed or mortgage includes the entire monument[2] unless there is evi-

---

92. Van Winkle v. Van Winkle, 1906, 95 App.Div. 605, 89 N.Y.S. 26, affirmed 184 N.Y. 193, 77 N.E. 33, noted in 6 Col.Law Rev. 536 (1906).

93. 39 N.J.L. 469 (1877).

94. *Accord:* 823 Broad St. v. Marcus, 1939, 17 N.J. Misc. 25, 3 A.2d 589 (land described as running "along the side line" of a street); City of Nashville v. Lawrence, 1925, 153 Tenn. 606, 284 S.W. 882, 47 A.L.R. 1266; McPherson v. Monegan, 1947, 120 Mont. 454, 187 P.2d 542. See Aigler, Boundaries on Highways, 24 Mich.Law Rev. 170 (1925).

95. 245 Ill. 391, 92 N.E. 271 (1910).

96. Bowers v. Atchison, T. & S. F. Ry. Co., 1925, 119 Kan. 202, 237 P. 913, 42 A.L.R. 228.

97. Suburban Land Co., Inc. v. Town of Billerica, 1943, 314 Mass. 184, 49 N.E.2d 1012, 147 A.L.R. 660; Sizer v. Devereux, 1853, 16 Barb.(N.Y.) 160.

98. Saccone v. West End Trust Co., 1909, 224 Pa. 554, 73 A. 971.

99. Schneider v. Jacob, 1887, 86 Ky. 101, 5 S.W. 350, 9 Ky.Law Rep. 382; Loud v. Brooks, 1928, 241 Mich. 452, 217 N.W. 34, noted in 13 Iowa Law Rev. 346 (1928), 26 Mich.Law Rev. 690 (1928). *Contra:* Elliott v. McIntosh, 1919, 41 Cal.App. 763, 183 P. 692; Bangor House Proprietary v. Brown, 1851, 33 Me. 309; Hopkinson v. McKnight, 1866, 31 N.J.L. 422. *Cf.:* Anderson v. Citizens' Sav. & Trust Co., 1921, 185 Cal. 386, 197 P. 113.

1. 196 Mass. 270, 82 N.E. 10 (1907).

2. Saccone v. West End Trust Co., 1909, 224 Pa. 554, 73 A. 971. See also, Johnson v. Grenell, 1907, 188 N.Y. 407, 81 N.E. 161 (where it appeared that unless the grantee acquired ownership of the entire

dence that the other half of the area would be of substantial value to the grantor or mortgagor.[3]

Fourth: The rules under discussion apply to both public and private grants. In Brunswig Drug Co. v. O'Donnell (Cal.),[4] the grantee of land from a city claimed ownership to the center of a street that formed a part of the boundary line. The city contended that the general rule applicable to private grants should not be applied because public grants are to be construed strictly against the grantee. In holding that ownership did pass to the center of the monument the court follows the view that the rule of strict construction against the grantee applies only in case of an ambiguity. An ambiguity did not exist with respect to the deed from the city.

Fifth: In the absence of a provision to the contrary, measurements of land conveyed are made from the side of a monument such as a street or a body of water. This is true even though ownership may pass to the center of the monument. Such ownership passes by operation of law and not from the description in the conveying instrument.[5] This rule has its origin in the assumption that the parties intend to describe the full extent of the area set apart for the exclusive use and occupancy of the grantee.

BOUNDARY LINE AGREEMENTS

124. Under varying circumstances, judicial recognition is extended to boundary line agreements even if not executed with the formalities prescribed by the Statute of Frauds. Application of the doctrine usually requires proof that the parties were not informed as to the true boundary line, that there was an express or implied agreement as to its location and possession that conformed to the agreement.

Under varying circumstances, judicial recognition is extended to boundary line agreements even if not executed with the formalities prescribed by the Statute of Frauds. In some decisions it is held that this can be accomplished only by express agreement.[6] However, the weight of authority is that the agreement may be implied by acquiescence.[7] Recognition of a fixed boundary line is an important means by which to avoid vexatious litigation relating to property lines and, for that reason, the conclusion is favored as a matter of public policy.

Usually, the validity of an oral agreement fixing a boundary line is questioned upon the ground that it constitutes a conveyance in violation of the Statute of Frauds. A conveyance is not involved if the agreement relates to a variable boundary line, such as in a case where land is described as bordering upon a body of water.[8] An agreement establishing a fixed boundary line merely makes certain what had theretofore been uncertain and variable.

If the boundary line is not ascertainable by reference to the descriptions contained in deeds, an agreement fixing the boundary line is not properly classified as a conveyance. It is merely an expression of agreement as to the proper construction to be placed upon the

---

street he would be deprived of valuable riparian rights).

3. Geddes Coarse Salt Co. v. Niagara, etc., Power Co., 1913, 207 N.Y. 500, 101 N.E. 456.

4. 6 Cal.App.2d 1, 43 P.2d 873 (1935).

5. Dodd v. Witt, 1885, 139 Mass. 63, 29 N.E. 475. *Contra:* Rossi v. Sophia, 1931, 163 Wash. 173, 300 P. 522, criticized in 6 Wash.Law Rev. 178 (1931). See Joens v. Baumbach, 1924, 193 Cal. 567, 226 P. 400.

6. See, for example, Thomas v. Harlan, 1947, 27 Wash.2d 512, 178 P.2d 965, 170 A.L.R. 1138.

7. Moniz v. Peterman, 1934, 220 Cal. 429, 31 P.2d 353; Nelson v. Da Rouch, 1935, 87 Utah 457, 50 P.2d 273.

8. Muchenberger v. City of Santa Monica, 1929, 206 Cal. 635, 275 P. 803, 62 A.L.R. 219.

language in the conveying instruments.[9] This is also true in the case of ambiguous descriptions.[10]

But a boundary line agreement may be sustained in a case where the true boundary line could be ascertained by a survey. In that event a fiction is called into play. It is said that the agreement does not result in a conveyance of the land which lies between the agreed line and the true line, but it does fix the line itself and the description carries title up to the agreed line regardless of its accuracy.[11] The intention of the parties not to claim ownership except in accordance with the true line is consistent with the doctrine of agreed boundaries.[12]

There is authority for the view that since a husband has a right to manage community real property he has a right to enter into a boundary line agreement that involves community property. This is true even though he does not have a right to convey community real property without the written consent of the wife.[13] It is doubted that the fiction should be applied in a situation that does, in fact, relate to ownership.

Circumstances under which the doctrine is applied are as follows:

First: The establishment of a boundary line that does not conform to the true location depends upon proof of the fact that the parties involved were uniformed as to the true location.[14] It is not material that the true boundary line could have been determined by a survey.[15]

Second: Usually, there is proof of the fact that the adjoining property owners entered into an oral agreement fixing the boundary line. However, such an agreement may be implied "by long acquiescence" in an existing boundary line condition.[16] But acquiescence in the existence of a fence as a barrier is not acquiescence in the existency of a boundary line.[17]

Third: The validity of a boundary line agreement does not depend upon occupancy of land for any prescribed period of time,[18] such as the time fixed for the acquisition of title by adverse possession. However, occupancy for this statutory period may be required if a party relies upon an implied agreement.[19] It may also be the basis upon which to imply that there was uncertainty as to the true boundary line. Of course, if occupancy does

---

9. As for the rights of a subsequent *bona fide* purchaser for value and without notice of the agreement, see Steele v. Shuler, 1963, 211 Cal.App.2d 698, 27 Cal.Rptr. 569.

10. Davies v. Wickstrom, 1909, 56 Wash. 154, 105 P. 454.

11. French v. Brinkman, 1963, 60 Cal.2d 547, 35 Cal. Rptr. 289, 293, 387 P.2d 1 ; Harris v. Backus, 1958, 212 Or. 695, 321 P.2d 315.

12. Martin v. Lopes, 1946, 28 Cal.2d 618, 170 P.2d 881.

13. See Janes v. LeDeit, 1964, —— Cal.App.2d ——, 39 Cal.Rptr. 559. See also, Nesbitt v. Fairview Farms, Inc., 1954, 239 N.C. 481, 80 S.E.2d 472 (tenancy by the entireties).

14. Tripp v. Bagley, 1928, 74 Utah 57, 276 P. 912, 69 A.L.R. 1417.

15. Mello v. Weaver, 1950, 36 Cal.2d 456, 224 P.2d 691; Sobol v. Gulinson, 1933, 94 Colo. 92, 28 P.2d 810; Ekberg v. Bates, 1951, 121 Utah 123, 239 P.2d 205.

16. Stewart v. Bittle, 1963, 236 Ark. 716, 370 S.W.2d 132; Ernie v. Trinity Lutheran Church, 1959, 51 Cal.2d 702, 336 P.2d 525; Daley v. Gruber, 1960, 361 Mich. 358, 104 N.W.2d 807. But see, Haklits v. Oldenburg, 1964, 124 Vt. 199, 201 A.2d 690.

17. Mahrenholz v. Alff, 1962, 253 Iowa 446, 112 N.W.2d 847. See also, Drury v. Pekar, 1960, 224 Or. 37, 355 P.2d 598.

18. Spencer v. Supernois, 1954, 176 Kan. 135, 268 P.2d 946.

19. See Woll v. Costella, 1938, 59 Idaho 569, 85 P.2d 679; Kinkade v. Simpson, 1948, 200 Okl. 507, 197 P.2d 968.

continue for the statutory period rights may be determined by applying the law as it relates to adverse possession.[20]

There is authority for the view that rights cannot be successfully asserted under a boundary line agreement unless occupancy does continue for the period fixed for the acquisition of title by adverse possession. But this period of time is applied only by way of analogy. It is considered that fulfillment of this requirement satisfies the policy of the Statute of Frauds. It may be that the occupancy involved does not satisfy the requirements for the acquisition of title by adverse possession. For example, in some states a claim of title by adverse possession will fail unless the claimant paid taxes on the property for the statutory period. However, a claim may be based on a boundary line agreement without reference to the payment of taxes.

20. See Jackson v. Deemar, 1964, 373 Mich. 22, 127 N.W.2d 856.

CHAPTER 23

COVENANTS IN DEEDS RESPECTING TITLE

TYPES OF COVENANTS

125. The "usual covenants for title" include the covenant of seisin, right to convey, against encumbrances, quiet enjoyment and warranty. The covenant of further assurance is not in general use.

a. Covenants of seisin and right to convey. A covenant of seisin is a covenant that the grantor has an estate, or the right to convey an estate, in quality and quantity, which he purports to convey. It is more comprehensive than a covenant of right to convey because to satisfy the covenant the grantor must deliver possession of the land.

b. Covenant against encumbrances. Some authorities support the rule that a breach of covenant against encumbrances cannot be based upon the existence of an easement or profit that was known to the grantee or which was open, obvious and notorious.

The weight of authority is that the existence of a public way does not constitute a breach of a covenant against encumbrances.

c. Covenants of warranty and quiet enjoyment. These covenants obligate the covenantor to protect the estate against lawful claims of ownership. A cause of action does not arise until there is an eviction, actual or constructive.

d. Further assurance. A covenant for further assurance imposes an obligation upon the covenantor to perform whatever acts may be reasonably demanded by the covenantee for the purpose of perfecting title.

An agreement to convey land by a deed containing the "usual covenants for title" con-templates that the deed shall contain the covenant of seisin, right to convey, against encumbrances, quiet enjoyment and warranty.[1] In Funk v. Baird (N. D.),[2] A contracted to sell land to B and convenanted to convey "by deed of warranty." Before the conveyance had been made A died and his estate passed to his heirs. The heirs brought suit for specific performance of the contract. Relief was denied upon the ground that the vendee was entitled to a deed which contained the usual covenants of title under which the personal liability of A could be established. The deed tendered by A's heirs, while it fixed the liability of the heirs did not fix liability as contracted by A. As against the vendee, the heirs did not have a right to insist upon substituting their personal covenants for those of the original contracting party.

There are two views as to the effect of express covenants for title in what would otherwise be a quitclaim deed. According to one view such covenants have a limited operation. They operate merely with respect to the estate that is conveyed by the deed.[3] According to another view the covenants change the nature of the instrument to a

1. Wilson v. Wood, 1865, 17 N.J.Eq. 216. See also, Holzworth v. Roth, 1960, 78 S.D. 287, 101 N.W.2d 393 (implied in a standard form warranty deed).

2. 70 N.D. 396, 295 N.W. 87, criticized in 26 Cornell Law Qt. 722 (1941).

3. White & Corbitt v. W. W. Stewart & Co., 1908, 131 Ga. 460, 62 S.E. 590; Coble v. Barringer, 1916, 171 N.C. 445, 88 S.E. 518.

warranty deed. Otherwise, it is argued that the covenants for title would be valueless.[4]

The various types of covenants for title are discussed in the following paragraphs.

Covenants of Seisin and Right to Convey

Seisin is generally understood to mean possession of land coupled with a claim of ownership in fee.[5] According to one view, a covenant of seisin is not breached even if the covenantor was in possession of the land wrongfully asserting a claim of ownership in fee.[6] However, the preferred view is that a covenant of seisin is not satisfied by such a wrongful possession. It is a covenant that the grantor has an estate, or the right to convey an estate, in quality and quantity, which he purports to convey.[7] The existence of a servitude, such as an easement, which does not affect the actual and lawful seisin of the land by the grantor does not constitute a breach of this covenant.[8]

A covenant of seisin is more comprehensive than a covenant of right to convey. Both ownership and possession by the grantor are necessary to satisfy a covenant of seisin.[9] Ownership alone will satisfy a covenant of right to convey. That covenant is not breached even if the land is in the adverse possession of another. This is true unless the local rule

nullifies a conveyance by an owner of land that is held adversely. Some decisions support the rule that a covenant of seisin and a covenant of right to convey are synonymous.[10]

Covenant against Encumbrances

A lien, such as a mortgage, is an encumbrance that affects ownership but does not interfere with the use of the land. Encumbrances such as easements, profits and equitable servitudes affect ownership and also interfere with the use of land.[11]

An encumbrance that affects ownership but does not interfere with the use of land constitutes a breach of a covenant against encumbrances.[12] This is true even if the grantee knew of the existence of the encumbrance at the time he acquired ownership. Since this type of encumbrance may be removed by payment of the obligation it is assumed that the parties understood that payment would be made by the grantor.

If the encumbrance consists of a burden that cannot be lifted simply by the payment of money—it is necessary to obtain the consent of the owner of the interest—and the encumbrance affects both ownership and use, the authorities are divided on the question of breach. According to one view, the grantor may be compelled to pay damages for breach

---

4. Loomis v. Bedel, 1840, 11 N.H. 74; Kimbro v. Harper, 1925, 113 Okl. 46, 238 P. 840, noted in 24 Mich.Law Rev. 303 (1926).

5. Lockwood v. Sturdevant, 1827, 6 Conn. 373.

6. Wilson v. Widenham, 1863, 51 Me. 566; Raymond v. Raymond, 1852, 64 Mass. (10 Cush.) 134; Yow v. Armstrong, 1963, 260 N.C. 287, 132 S.E.2d 620.

7. See Lockwood v. Sturdevant, 1827, 6 Conn. 373; Parker v. Brown, 1844, 15 N.H. 176. This is the statutory rule in some states. See 3 Neb.Law Bulletin 462 (1925).

8. Moore v. Johnston, 1888, 87 Ala. 220, 6 So. 50.

9. Stearns v. Jewel, 1915, 27 Colo.App. 390, 149 P. 846.

10. Bernklau v. Stevens, 1962, 150 Colo. 1187, 371 P.2d 765; Schiff v. Dixon, 1951, 204 Okl. 1112, 227 P.2d 639.

11. Even if an easement does not exist because of lack of formalities in the creating instrument, the equitable right to enforce the servitude will constitute an encumbrance (City of New York v. New York & S. B. Ferry & S. Transp. Co., 1921, 231 N.Y. 18, 131 N.E. 554, 16 A.L.R. 1059).

12. Thomas v. St. Paul's M. E. Church, 1889, 86 Ala. 138, 5 So. 508 (vendor's lien); Kelsey v. Remer, 1875, 43 Conn. 129 (attachment lien); Campbell v. McClure, 1895, 45 Neb. 608, 63 N.W. 920 (*dictum*), (tax lien); Corbett v. Wrenn, 1894, 25 Or. 305, 35 P. 658 (mortgage).

of covenant if the land conveyed is burdened by an easement or profit even if the condition was known to the grantee or was visible to him.[13] According to another view, a breach of a covenant against encumbrances cannot be based upon the existence of an easement or profit that was known to the grantee or which is open, obvious and notorious.[14] It is reasoned that since burdens of this type cannot be removed simply by a money payment it may be assumed that the grantee did not acquire ownership with a tacit understanding that the grantor would remove the encumbrance.

Whether or not the existence of a private profit or easement will constitute a breach of covenant against encumbrances, according to some cases the existence of a public way does not constitute a breach.[15] In support of this conclusion it is reasoned that a public way constitutes a benefit to the land conveyed and not a burden. This reasoning seems to be fallacious. A public way does, in fact, constitute an encumbrance. Whether it constitutes a benefit or a burden should only be a factor to be considered in the assessment of damages recoverable for breach of the covenant.

Covenants of Warranty and for Quiet Enjoyment

A covenant of warranty is an assurance or guaranty of title. This covenant and the covenant for quiet enjoyment obligate the covenantor to protect the estate against lawful claims of ownership.[16] Such duty does not exist with respect to unfounded claims.[17] In some states the extent of the warranty may be restricted by the execution of a "special warranty deed. In that event the scope of the warranty is limited to claims arising by, through or under the grantor.[18] Such a restricted warranty may also be implied in the case of a "grant deed." [19]

According to the English common law doctrine of warranty, a breach of warranty imposes an obligation on the grantor (feoffer) to substitute other land of like kind and value for the land which he purported to convey. Such an obligation does not attach for breach of the modern covenant of warranty. Instead, the grantor may be compelled to respond in damages.

---

13. Mitchell v. Warner, 1825, 5 Conn. 497 (right to take water); Lavey v. Graessle, 1929, 245 Mich. 681, 224 N.W. 436, 64 A.L.R. 1477 (right of way); Huyck v. Andrews, 1889, 113 N.Y. 81, 20 N.E. 581 (easement to extend a dam and raise the height thereof). See Estep v. Bailey, 1919, 94 Or. 59, 185 P. 227 (the encumbrance was the right of a tenant to harvest a crop).

14. Schurger v. Moorman, 1911, 20 Idaho 97, 117 P. 122; Memmert v. McKeen, 1886, 112 Pa. 315, 4 A. 542; Taxman v. McMahan, 1963, 21 Wis.2d 215, 124 N.W.2d 68. The encumbrance must be visible at the time of the contract of purchase (Wood v. Evanitzsky, 1951, 369 Pa. 123, 85 A.2d 24).

15. Desvergers v. Willis, 1876, 56 Ga. 515; Scribner v. Holmes, 1861, 16 Ind. 142; Holmes v. Danforth, 1891, 83 Me. 139, 21 A. 845 (if the land conveyed is described with reference to the public highway); Sandum v. Johnson, 1913, 122 Minn. 368, 142 N.W. 878 (public road had been legally established but had not been opened for public travel at the time of conveyance); Huyck v. Andrews, 1889, 113 N.Y. 81, 20 N.E. 581 (*dictum*); Missouri State Life Ins. Co. v. Whisman, 1937, 181 Okl. 168, 73 P.2d 130.

16. But see, H. Weston Lumber Co. v. Lacey Lumber Co., 1920, 123 Miss. 208, 85 So. 193, 10 A.L.R. 436 (an estate that is vested in the grantee does not constitute a breach of this covenant).

17. Chestnut v. Tyson, 1894, 105 Ala. 149, 16 So. 723; Reed v. Stevens, 1919, 93 Conn. 659, 107 A. 459, 5 A.L.R. 1081. See Eggers v. Mitchem, 1949, 240 Iowa 1199, 38 N.W.2d 591 (a grantee is not entitled to reimbursement for expense incident to an action that established his title).

18. See, for example, Harris v. Sklarew, Fla.1964, 166 So. 164.

19. See, for example, West's Ann.Cal.Civ.Code, § 1113. See also, Silverblatt v. Livadas, 1960, 340 Mass. 474, 164 N.E.2d 875 (statutory covenants in a quitclaim deed).

If a third party institutes proceedings that question the validity of the title, the grantee may so inform the grantor and give him an opportunity to appear and defend the action (voucher to warranty). If the grantor does not appear he cannot question the validity of a judgment that may be entered against the grantee.[20] However, the grantee is not required to give such notice to the grantor. Failure to do so merely means that in an action for breach of warranty the grantor has a right to prove that the title is not defective in spite of the prior judgment to the contrary.[21]

A breach of these covenants does not occur until the possession of the grantee, or those claiming through him, is disturbed by an eviction;[22] and the Statute of Limitations does not start to run until that time.[23] But a constructive eviction may suffice for this purpose. That is the case, for example, if the one asserting the paramount title is in possession of the land. The assertion of a paramount title may constitute a constructive eviction if the conveyance involves unimproved and unoccupied land.[24]

Further Assurance

A covenant for further assurance imposes an obligation upon the covenantor to perform whatever acts may be reasonably demanded by the covenantee for the purpose of perfecting title. This form of covenant is not of general use in the United States.

REMOTE PARTIES AND TYPES OF COVENANTS THAT "RUN WITH THE LAND"

126. It is generally stated that certain types of covenants respecting title that are contained in deeds may be enforced by remote parties on the basis of "privity of estate."

Covenants such as warranty, quiet enjoyment and further assurance are continuous in nature and may be enforced by a remote party. Other covenants, such as seisin right to convey and against encumbrances are not continuous in nature and do not "run with the land".

Remote Parties

A claim for damages arising out of a breach of covenant pertaining to title is enforceable in an action for breach of contract. Traditionally, the basis for such liability must be founded upon "privity of contract." If A purports to convey Blackacre to B and his heirs, and the deed contains a covenant of warranty, and then B conveys Blackacre to C and his heirs, there is *privity of contract* as between A and B. But that privity does not exist as between A and C, the "remote party." A question is raised as to whether or not the remote party can recover damages from A for breach of the covenant.

The problem is not as simple as the one presented in connection with covenants contained in leases, a matter discussed under a separate heading.[25] The lessor has a reversion in the leased land. The remote party, an assignee of the leased land, has a possessory estate incident to the reversion. Thus, there is a tenural relationship between the lessor and the remote party. This relation-

20. Elliott v. Thompson, 1941, 63 Idaho 395, 120 P.2d 1014. See Smith v. Peoples Bank & Trust Co., 1961, 254 N.C. 588, 119 S.E.2d 623, 627.

21. See Holzworth v. Roth, 1960, 78 S.D. 287, 101 N.W.2d 393; 3 American Law of Property, § 12.131.

22. Ward v. Johnson, 1938, 272 Ky. 234, 113 S.W.2d 1132; Johnson v. Nyce's Ex'rs, 1848, 17 Ohio 66. But see, Elliott v. Thompson, 1941, 63 Idaho 395, 120 P.2d 1014 (eviction not necessary if the outstanding title is in the United States).

23. Wilder v. Wilhite, 1962, 190 Kan. 564, 376 P.2d 797.

24. St. John v. Palmer, 1843, 5 Hill. (N.Y.) 599; Compton v. Trico Oil Co., Tex.Civ.App.1938, 120 S.W.2d 534, error refused, noted in 17 Tex.Law Rev. 368 (1939).

25. See supra, § 58.

ship is described as "privity of estate" and is used as a substitute for "privity of contract." Covenants in the lease may be enforced on this basis.

But if A conveys Blackacre to B and his heirs, and the deed contains a covenant of title, and then B conveys Blackacre to C and his heirs, there is a complete lack of tenure as between A and C, the remote party. This has been the law since the enactment of the Statute Quia Emptores in 1290.[26] This is all the more true in a case where A did not, in fact, have an estate in Blackacre to convey and C seeks to hold him liable for breach of warranty.[27]

There is no doubt about the desirability of allowing the remote party redress for breach of covenant of title but it is reckless to base that liability on the concept of "privity of estate." This is also true with respect to other types of covenants that are contained in deeds, as pointed out under a separate heading.[28] However, while recovery is usually stated to be on the theory of "privity of estate," such privity is not necessary to establish liability. As a rule of property law,

certain types of covenants of title may be enforced by remote parties. This is the statutory rule in some states.[29] In a few decisions liability is declared on some theory of implied assignment of a cause of action.

Types of Covenants that "Run With the Land"

Some covenants impose an obligation on a covenantor to render performance whenever required to give effect to representations made by him concerning title. Such covenants are "covenants running with the land," and include covenants of warranty, quiet enjoyment and further assurance. The covenants of warranty and for quiet enjoyment require performance by the covenantor whenever possession is disturbed by the owner of a paramount title.[30] However, a covenant of general warranty does not run with the land after a cause of action for breach has accrued.[31] A covenant for further assurance imposes an obligation upon the covenantor to furnish further assurance of title whenever demanded if the demand is considered to be reasonable.

Those covenants which relate to a presently existing fact respecting the title do not run with the land. These covenants can be broken only at the instant that they are made. For example, covenants of seisin and right to convey relate to a presently exist-

---

26. 18 Edw. 1, cc. 1, 3 (1290).

27. Some cases hold that a transfer of possession is sufficient (Slater v. Rawson, 1843, 47 Mass. (6 Metc.) 439; Libby v. Hutchinson, 1903, 72 N.H. 190, 55 A. 547; Beddoe's Ex'r v. Wadsworth, 1839, 21 Wend. (N.Y.) 120). Other cases take the position that it is sufficient if the purported grantee takes possession of the land even if the possession does not come from the grantor (Wead v. Larkin, 1870, 54 Ill. 489; Tillotson v. Prichard, 1888, 60 Vt. 94, 14 A. 302). Other decisions indicate that even possession is not necessary (Rockafellor v. Gray, 1922, 104 Iowa 1280, 191 N.W. 107, noted in 8 Iowa Law Bulletin 259 (1923), 21 Mich.Law Rev. 801 (1923), 7 Minn.Law Rev. 489 (1923); Solberg v. Robinson, 1914, 34 S.D. 55, 147 N.W. 87. *Contra:* Slater v. Rawson, 1840, 42 Mass. (1 Metc.) 450; Bull v. Beiseker, 1907, 16 N.D. 290, 113 N.W. 870; Wallace v. Pereles, 1901, 109 Wis. 316, 85 N.W. 371).

28. See supra, § 40.

29. See, for example, West's Ann.Cal.Civ.Code, §§ 1462, 1463 (covenants for the direct benefit of the land conveyed); Bernklau v. Stevens, 1962, 150 Colo. 1187, 371 P.2d 765 (construing C.R.S. '53, 118–1–21).

30. See Smith v. Peoples Bank & Trust Co., 1961, 254 N.C. 588, 119 S.E.2d 623, 627.

31. Ell v. Trent, 1922, 195 Ky. 26, 241 S.W. 324; Compton v. Trico Oil Co., Tex.Civ.App.1938, 120 S.W.2d 534, error refused, noted in 17 Tex.Law Rev. 368 (1939).

ing fact.[32] If the covenantor is not seised, or if he does not have a right to convey, there is a breach of covenant the instant the covenant is made. This is also true with respect to a covenant against encumbrances.[33] Obviously, these covenants, lacking as they do in the quality of continuousness, do not run with the land because the breach leaves nothing of the covenants. The only redress is recovery of damages by the immediate grantee, a remedy that does not extend to a remote grantee. According to some authorities a remote grantee may recover for breach of a covenant that is not continuous in nature. One theory is that, even if a covenant is broken when made it may also be broken at a later date when possession of the land is disturbed.[34] Another theory is that a broken covenant may "run with the land" the same as do covenants that are continuous in nature.[35] Still a third theory is that the benefit of such a covenant may pass to a remote grantee by way of an implied assignment.[36]

DAMAGES

127. The measure of damages for breach of a covenant of warranty or seisin is the value of the consideration received by the covenantor, plus interest.

The breach of a covenant against encumbrances may consist of a lien, such as a mortgage. In case of eviction or removal of the lien the covenantor may be held liable for amounts paid by the covenantee, not exceeding the consideration received by the covenantor.

The breach of a covenant against encumbrances may consist of a servitude, such as a profit or an easement. The measure of damages for breach is the difference between the value of the land without the encumbrance and its value subject to the encumbrance.

The measure of damages for breach of a covenant of warranty [37] or seisin [38] is the value of the consideration received by the covenantor, plus interest. If the covenant is breached only with respect to a part of the estate conveyed the recovery is limited to a proportionate part of the consideration received by the covenantor.[39] It is not material whether the value of the estate has increased or decreased.[40] However, some authorities follow the rule that if an action is brought for breach of warranty the covenantee is entitled to recover according to the value of the estate at the time of eviction.[41] If a remote grantee claims damages for breach of warranty his recovery is limited to the consideration paid by him even though the covenantor

32. Simons v. Diamond Match Co., 1909, 159 Mich. 241, 123 N.W. 1132; Kuntzman v. Smith, 1910, 77 N.J.Eq. 30, 75 A. 1009; Smith v. Peoples Bank & Trust Co., 1961, 254 N.C. 588, 119 S.E.2d 623; Solberg v. Robinson, 1914, 34 S.D. 55, 147 N.W. 87.

33. Abstract Company of Sarasota v. Roberts, Fla. 1962, 144 So.2d 3.

34. Kingdon v. Nottle, [1813] 1 M. & S. 355, 105 Eng. Rep. 133 (covenant of seisin).

35. Richard v. Bent, 1871, 59 Ill. 38 (covenant against encumbrances).

36. Rockafellor v. Gray, 1922, 194 Iowa 1280, 191 N.W. 107 (covenant of seisin), noted in 8 Iowa Law Bulletin 259 (1923), 21 Mich.Law Rev. 801 (1923), 7 Minn.Law Rev. 489 (1923).

37. Swafford v. Whipple, 1851, 3 G. Greene (Iowa) 261; Campbell v. Gallentine, 1927, 115 Neb. 789, 215 N.W. 111, 61 A.L.R. 1; Elliott v. Thompson, 1843, 23 Tenn. (4 Humph.) 99.

38. Marston v. Hobbs, 1807, 2 Mass. 433. Cf.: Logan v. Moulder, 1839, 1 Ark. 313 (entitled to recover the value of the land at the time the covenant was executed).

39. Gilbert v. Bulkley, 1824, 5 Conn. 262; Campbell v. Gallentine, 1927, 115 Neb. 789, 215 N.W. 111, 61 A.L.R. 1; Newbern v. Hinton, 1925, 190 N.C. 108, 129 S.E. 181.

40. Weber v. Anderson, 1874, 73 Ill. 439; Bennet v. Jenkins, 1816, 13 Johns. (N.Y.) 50.

41. Horsford v. Wright, 1786, Kirby (Conn.) 3; Cecconi v. Rodden, 1883, 147 Mass. 164, 16 N.E. 749; Park v. Bates, 1840, 12 Vt. 381.

received more for the land than was paid by the remote grantee.[42]

The breach may involve a covenant against encumbrances. If the encumbrance consists of a lien, such as a mortgage, only nominal damages can be recovered if the action is brought prior to the time of eviction or the removal of the encumbrance.[43] If the action is brought after the happening of one or the other of these events the plaintiff is entitled to substantial damages. The damage award is the price paid for the clearance of title [44] but not exceeding the consideration received by the covenantor.[45] Even if an intermediate grantor is liable on his covenant against a lien-type of encumbrance, he is not entitled to recover substantial damages against his grantor until the intermediate grantor is compelled to pay damages. Otherwise, any payments made by him are made as a mere volunteer.[46]

If the encumbrance consists of a servitude, such as a profit or an easement, the covenantee is entitled to recover substantial damages without reference to eviction or clearing title. The measure of damages is the difference between the value of the land without the encumbrance and its value subject to the encumbrance.[47] If an intermediate grantor makes payment to clear the title it is not considered that he is acting as a mere volunteer. He is entitled to recover the amount involved from his grantor.[48]

---

42. See, Liability of a Grantor to a Remote Grantee on His Covenants For Title, 25 Iowa Law Rev. 340, 345 (1940).

43. Reed v. Pierce, 1853, 36 Me. 455; Simon v. Williams, 1925, 140 Miss. 854, 105 So. 487, 44 A.L.R. 402, noted in 39 Harv.Law Rev. 505 (1926); Delavergne v. Norris, 1811, 7 Johns.(N.Y.) 358; Perkins v. Good, 1937, 179 Okl. 405, 65 P.2d 1218; Woodward v. Harlin, 1931, 121 Tex. 46, 39 S.W.2d 8.

44. McDowell v. Milroy, 1873, 69 Ill. 498.

45. Guthrie v. Russell, 1877, 46 Iowa 269; Foote v. Burnet, 1840, 10 Ohio 317. *Cf.:* Johnson v. Collins, 1874, 116 Mass. 392; Hartshorn v. Cleveland, 1890, 52 N.J.L. 473, 19 A. 974.

46. Thompson v. Richmond, 1906, 102 Me. 335, 66 A. 649. The same rule is applied in the case of a covenant of warranty (Booth v. Starr, 1814, 1 Conn. 244).

47. Mitchell v. Stanley, 1877, 44 Conn. 312, Morgan v. Smith, 1849, 11 Ill. 194; Wetherbee v. Bennett, 1861, 84 Mass. (2 Allen) 428; Turner v. Moon, [1901] 2 Ch. 825, 70 L.J.Ch. 822, 85 L.T. 90, 50 W.R. 237. See Simonton, Observations on Covenants for Title, 34 W.Va.Law Qt. 257, 262 (1928).

48. Lyons v. Chapman, 1931, 40 Ohio App. 1, 178 N.E. 24, noted in 10 Tenn.Law Rev. 133 (1932).

CHAPTER 24

ESTOPPEL BY DEED

INTRODUCTORY STATEMENT

128. The modern doctrine of estoppel by deed is an outgrowth of common law rules relating to warranty of title. Application of the doctrine is based upon the concept that a grantor, and persons claiming ownership through him, are bound by representations made concerning the state of the title.

According to one view, the title acquired by the grantor passes to the grantee by operation of law. According to another view, rules relating to true estoppel are applicable.

In the early development of the law a "warranty" was usually involved if a freehold estate was conveyed by feoffment. This imposed an obligation upon the feudal lord and his heirs to protect the feoffee tenant in the estate conveyed. The protection took the form of restoring the tenant with a like estate of equal value in case of his eviction by title paramount.[1] Ultimately, the restoration-concept was discontinued and the warranty was considered to be more in the nature of a personal covenant with an award of damages available in case of breach. This is the rule followed in the United States.

The doctrine of estoppel by deed is an outgrowth of the common law doctrine of warranty.[2] If a grantor purports to convey a freehold estate but, in fact, is not the owner of such an estate, the estate subsequently acquired by him will inure to the benefit of the grantee.

Application of the doctrine may avoid the necessity of an action at law to recover damages for breach of warranty but it may be applied in a case where such an action could not be maintained. So also, it is not necessary to prove estoppel in the sense of reliance upon representations of ownership made by a grantor. Application of the doctrine is based upon the concept that a grantor, and persons claiming ownership through him, should be bound by representations made concerning the state of the title. In Ayer v. Philadelphia & Boston Face Brick Co. (Mass.),[3] the doctrine was applied even though the truth respecting ownership appeared on the face of the deed. There was a recital that the land was subject to a mortgage.[4]

A grantor is estopped from asserting an after-acquired title as against his grantee under a warranty deed regardless of what conduit or circuity of conveyance the title may pass through in returning to the grantor. In Hanlon v. McLain (Okl.),[5] A, the owner of land, executed a mortgage to B. Thereafter A executed mineral deeds to C that contained warranties of title. C had knowledge of the prior mortgage. The mortgage was foreclosed and the purchaser at foreclosure sale subsequently conveyed to A. It is held that this after-acquired title inured to the benefit

---

1. See Co.Litt. 365a.

2. See 22 Harv.Law Rev. 136 (1908).

3. 159 Mass. 84, 34 N.E. 177 (1893).

4. See also, Born v. Bentley, 1952, 207 Okl. 21, 246 P.2d 738.

5. 206 Okl. 227, 242 P.2d 732 (1952).

of C.[6] Some authorities reach a contrary conclusion upon the ground that the estate acquired by such a grantor is a "new and independent title." [7]

According to the preferred view, the after-acquired title passes to the grantee by operation of law. This grantee will prevail even against an intervening *bona fide* purchaser for value and without notice.[8] However, there is authority for the view that the situation is one that calls for an application of the rules relating to a true estoppel. That is to say, the original grantor is estopped to set up his newly acquired title as against his grantee or mortgagee. However, that estoppel will not operate as against a *bona fide* purchaser or mortgagee.[9] Under this view, the original grantee may maintain an action against the grantor for breach of covenant or, at the election of the grantee, rely upon the doctrine of estoppel.[10] This right of election is not available under the "title rule."

---

6. See Barberi v. Rotchild, 1936, 7 Cal.2d 537, 61 P.2d 760.

7. Schultz v. Cities Service Oil Co., 1939, 149 Kan. 148, 86 P.2d 533; Rowell v. Rowell, 1946, 119 Mont. 201, 174 P.2d 223, 168 A.L.R. 1141.

8. Doe d. Potts v. Dowdall, 1866, 3 Houst. (Del.) 369; Perkins v. Coleman, 1890, 90 Ky. 611, 14 S.W. 640; White v. Patten, 1837, 24 Pick.(Mass.) 324; Hagensick v. Castor, 1898, 53 Neb. 495, 73 N.W. 932, criticized in 11 Harv.Law Rev. 555 (1898); Scott v. Cohen, 5 Cir., 1940, 115 F.2d 704 (*dictum*) (the court held that the recording of the instrument, which formed the basis of estoppel by deed, gave constructive notice to the person subsequently acquiring the estate from the grantor).

9. Builders Sash & Door Co. v. Joyner, 1921, 182 N.C. 518, 109 S.E. 259, 25 A.L.R. 81 (*dictum*); Gallagher v. Stern, 1915, 250 Pa. 292, 95 A. 518, noted in 29 Harv.Law Rev. 457 (1916). See Lawler, Estoppel to Assert an After Acquired Title in Pennsylvania, 3 Univ. of Pitt. Law Rev. 165, 177 (1937).

10. Blanchard v. Ellis, 1854, 1 Gray (Mass.) 195 (damages recoverable if the grantee was evicted); Resser v. Carney, 1893, 52 Minn. 397, 54 N.W. 89; Jones v. Gallagher, 1916, 54 Okl. 611, 154 P. 552.

Under this rule the breach of covenant is cured by passage of the estate to the grantee by operation of law.[11]

TYPE OF DEED REQUIRED

129. Application of the doctrine of estoppel by deed is not determined by the type of deed involved. It is applicable if there is a representation respecting title expressed in the form of a warranty or otherwise.

An after-acquired title will not inure to the benefit of a grantee under a deed that merely purports to release or quitclaim the grantor's then existing interest in the land.[12] A warranty of title in what would otherwise be a quitclaim deed will not necessarily render the instrument a warranty deed.[13] The warranty may be referable to the grantor's interest in the property rather than to a specific estate that he may or may not have.

If by recital or affirmation in a deed it appears that a designated estate was intended to be conveyed, a subsequently acquired estate by the grantor will inure to the benefit of the grantee. This is true even though covenants of title are not contained in the deed.[14] A representation that a designated estate was intended to be conveyed may be

---

11. Baxter v. Bradbury, 1841, 20 Me. 260; Reese v. Smith, 1849, 12 Mo. 344.

12. Holmes v. Countiss, 1938, 195 Ark. 1014, 115 S.W.2d 553; Morrison v. Whiteside, 1902, 116 Ga. 459, 42 S.E. 729; Lodge v. Thorpe, 1947, 120 Mont. 226, 181 P.2d 598; Selsor-Bradley v. Reed, 1924, 97 Okl. 204, 223 P. 651; United States National Bank of La Grande v. Miller, 1927, 122 Or. 285, 258 P. 205, 58 A.L.R. 339; Dowse v. Kammerman, 1952, 122 Utah 85, 246 P.2d 881.

13. Brown v. Harvey Coal Corp., D.Ky.1931, 49 F.2d 434. *Contra:* Bayley v. McCoy, 1880, 8 Or. 259.

14. Hannon v. Christopher, 1881, 34 N.J.Eq. 459; Keady v. Martin, 1914, 69 Or. 299, 137 P. 856. See Weegens v. Karels, 1940, 374 Ill. 273, 29 N.E.2d 248; Van Rensselaer v. Kearney, 1850, 52 U.S. (11 How.) 297, 13 L.Ed. 703. *Contra:* Jackson ex dem. McCrackin v. Wright, 1817, 14 Johns.(N.Y.) 193.

found even though words of quitclaim are used.[15] The doctrine may be applicable if a deed contains any covenant for title the breach of which would be cured by an after-acquired title, such as a covenant for quiet enjoyment.[16] According to one view, a covenant of seisin is satisfied by delivery of possession. Under this interpretation of the covenant its use will not justify application of the doctrine of estoppel by deed.[17]

A covenant for title, although promissory in terms, is usually interpreted as an affirma-tion of intention to convey a specific estate. This justifies an application of the doctrine of estoppel by deed. In Ayer v. Philadelphia & Boston Face Brick Co. (Mass.),[18] Justice Holmes points out that since a deed is to be construed as a whole, the claim of estoppel will not be sustained if it is based upon an ordinary statement in the deed and the truth respecting the title appears elsewhere in the deed. But if the affirmation takes the form of an express covenant of title, the grantor will be bound by the affirmation even though elsewhere in the deed expressions are to be found showing the truth respecting the title. He states: "In short, if a man by a deed says, I hereby estop myself to deny a fact, it does not matter that he recites as a preliminary that the fact is not true."

---

15. Henningsen v. Stromberg, 1950, 124 Mont. 185, 221 P.2d 438, noted in 37 Va.Law Rev. 142 (1951); Hagensick v. Castor, 1898, 53 Neb. 495, 73 N.W. 932, criticized in 11 Harv.Law Rev. 555 (1898). See Lawler, Estoppel To Assert an After-Acquired Title in Pennsylvania, 3 Pitt.Law Rev. 165, 170 (1937).

16. Smith v. Williams, 1880, 44 Mich. 240, 6 N.W. 662.

17. Allen v. Sayward, 1828, 5 Greenl.(Me.) 227.

18. 159 Mass. 84, 86, 34 N.E. 177 (1893).

CHAPTER 25

THE RECORDING SYSTEM

INTRODUCTORY STATEMENT

130. According to the prevailing American rule, recording statutes afford a means of giving constructive notice of ownership with respect to estates or interests disclosed in a recorded instrument.

An unrecorded instrument is valid as between the immediate parties and those who do not qualify as *bona fide* purchasers for value and without notice.

If a conveying instrument is void for such reasons as forgery or lack of delivery, it does not gain efficacy by recordation even in favor of an alleged *bona fide* purchaser or mortgagee for value and without notice.

Recording statutes are not applicable with respect to title acquired by adverse possession.

According to the English common law, the estate which a grantor conveys cannot be affected by a subsequent purported conveyance of the same estate made to another by the same grantor. The first conveyance leaves no ownership in the grantor which he can convey to another.[1] Notice or lack of notice of the first conveyance is of no significance. The same rule applies as between successive transferees of equitable estates. Priority of right is determined upon the basis of priority in time of acquisition.

This common law rule was modified by the enactment of the Statute of Anne in 1708.[2] It provides that the common law rule of priority on the basis of time of acquisition applies only if the grantee who is entitled to priority on that basis records his conveyance before the subsequent purported conveyance. Recordation does not operate to give constructive notice of the prior conveyance. Recordation is a means by which the first grantee can retain his priority. For example, the recordation of a conveyance creating an equitable interest in B does not prevent a subsequent purchaser from qualifying as a *bona fide* purchaser for value of the legal estate.[3] According to the rule followed as to equitable estates, a *bona fide* purchaser of the legal estate, if he takes in good faith and for value, will prevail as against those claiming prior equitable estates. If the recordation of the instrument operated to give constructive notice a subsequent purchaser could not qualify as a *bona fide* purchaser.

The prevailing American rule is that recording statutes afford a means of maintain-

---

1. Aigler, The Operation of the Recording Acts, 22 Mich.Law Rev. 405 (1924).

2. St. 7 Anne, c. 20 (1708) (applicable only in the County of Middlesex). See Bordwell, English Property Reform and its American Aspects, 37 Yale Law Journal 179, 201 (1927).

3. Bedford v. Bacchus, [1730] 2 Eq.Cas.Ab. 615, pl. 12, 22 Eng.Rep. 516.

ing priority and also furnish a means of giving constructive notice of interests created by the recorded instrument.[4] This prevents a subsequent purchaser or mortgagee from qualifying as a *bona fide* purchaser for value and without notice.[5] Under some statutes priority is made to depend upon priority of time of recording. For example, if A conveys land to B who does not then record his deed and subsequently A conveys the same land to C who purchases in good faith and for value and without notice of the prior deed, B will still prevail if he records his deed prior to recordation by C.[6]

Instruments pertaining to real property that are usually included within the scope of recording statutes include deeds, mortgages, executory contracts of sale and leases of specified duration. But an unrecorded deed or other conveying instrument is valid as between the immediate parties and those who cannot qualify as *bona fide* purchasers or mortgagees for value and without notice.[7] Further, if a conveying instrument is void for such reasons as forgery or lack of delivery it does not gain efficacy by recordation even in favor of an alleged party taking in good faith, for value and without notice.[8] The

usual recording statute applies to derivative titles and not to an original title such as that acquired by adverse possession. Accordingly, even a *bona fide* purchaser for value and without notice from the owner of record will acquire the ownership subject to the rights of one who has acquired title by adverse possession.[9]

By failing to record a deed the grantee creates a power in the grantor to divest the estate conveyed by a subsequent conveyance of the same property to a *bona fide* purchaser for value and without notice. This is also true with respect to other conveying instruments, such as mortgages and leases. An improper exercise of this power may subject the grantor etc., to civil liability to the grantee under the unrecorded instrument.[10] The grantor's act in making the second conveyance may constitute a breach of the warranty contained in his first deed.[11] An action may also be maintained against him on the theory of money had and received.[12]

PROFITS, EASEMENTS AND EQUITABLE SERVITUDES

131. Recording statutes have no application if a profit or easement is acquired by prescription. Even if a servitude is created by an unrecorded deed, one who acquires the servient estate may be charged with notice because of the physical condition of the land.

Recording statutes have no application if a profit or easement is created by prescrip-

4. Stroud v. Lockart, 1797, 4 Dall.(Pa.) 153, 1 L.Ed. 779. See Beale, The Origin of the System of Recording Deeds in America, 19 Green Bag 335 (1907); Haskins, The Beginnings of the Recording System in Massachusetts, 21 Boston Univ.Law Rev. 281 (1941).

5. Parkist v. Alexander, 1815, 1 Johns.Ch.(N.Y.) 394. But see Lynch v. Johnson, 1915, 170 N.C. 110, 86 S.E. 995, rehearing denied 171 N.C. 611, 89 S.E. 61; Mayham v. Coombs, 1846, 14 Ohio 428.

6. See, for example, West's Ann.Cal.Civ.Code, § 1107. For a contrary rule, see Rouse v. Craig Realty Co., 1924, 203 Ky. 697, 262 S.W. 1083; Craig v. Osborn, 1923, 134 Miss. 323, 98 So. 598, noted in 37 Harv.Law Rev. 1141 (1924).

7. Dole v. Thurlow, 1846, 12 Metc.(Mass.) 157.

8. Stone v. French, 1887, 37 Kan. 145, 14 P. 530 (lack of delivery).

9. Winters v. Powell, 1912, 180 Ala. 425, 61 So. 96; Schall v. Williams Valley Railroad Co., 1860, 35 Pa. 191. For discussion of this problem, see Ferrier, The Recording Acts and Titles by Adverse Possession and Prescription, 14 Cal.Law Rev. 287 (1926).

10. Hilligas v. Kuns, 1910, 86 Neb. 68, 124 N.W. 925. See Aigler, The Operation of Recording Acts, 22 Mich.Law Rev. 405, 415 (1924).

11. See Curtis v. Deering, 1835, 12 Me. 499.

12. See Wade v. Comstock, 1860, 11 Ohio St. 71.

tion.[13] Accordingly, the purchaser or mortgagee of the servient estate acquires his interest subject to the prescriptive right even though he may qualify as a *bona fide* purchaser for value and without notice. Recording statutes apply only in the case of derivative titles as distinguished from original titles.

A derivative title is involved if profits, easements or equitable servitudes are acquired by grant.[14] Unless recorded, a *bona fide* purchaser for value without actual notice will acquire the servient estate free from the servitude.[15] The creation of a profit or easement by implied grant or implied reservation is referable to a deed. This is also the case with respect to the creation of a profit or easement by necessity. However, if the servitude is created by implication or by necessity the recordation of the deed may not result in constructive notice.[16] There is a difference of opinion as to whether or not an estate created by a "collateral instrument" is in the chain of title.[17]

Even if an instrument creating a servitude is not recorded a person acquiring the servient estate will take subject to the servitude unless he qualifies as a *bona fide* purchaser for value and without notice. An heir or devisee cannot so qualify because he does not take for value.[18] Also, one who acquires the estate may be charged with notice because of the physical condition of the land.[19] This may be the case even if the use of the profit or easement is not continuous.[20] It is sufficient if the physical condition of the land indicates the existence of the servitude whether or not the condition is actually observed by the purchaser or mortgagee.[21] A person cannot qualify as a *bona fide* purchaser for value and without notice if facts could have been ascertained by the exercise of reasonable diligence.[22]

ERRORS IN RECORDING

132. **A person who causes the recordation of an instrument is under a duty to see that proper entries have been made.**

A person who files an instrument for record is under a duty to examine the record and see that proper entries have been made.[23] The recordation is for his protection and he is in the best position to detect errors. For example, if A mortgages land to B to secure a debt of $3,000, and the recording officer erroneously enters the amount in the record as $300,

13. Jones v. Harmon, 1959, 175 Cal.App.2d 869, 1 Cal. Rptr. 192.

14. See Jobling v. Tuttle, 1907, 75 Kan. 351, 89 P. 699 (executed oral agreement).

15. Wayt v. Patee, 1928, 205 Cal. 46, 269 P. 660 (equitable servitudes); Sharp v. Matthews, 1883, 4 Ky.Law Rep. 827 (agreement for an easement); Wills v. Reid, 1905, 86 Miss. 446, 38 So. 793 (unrecorded bond for title to passageway).

16. See Mesmer v. Uharriet, 1916, 174 Cal. 110, 162 P. 104; Hawley v. McCabe, 1933, 117 Conn. 558, 169 A. 192, noted in 14 Boston Univ.Law Rev. 432 (1934); Backhausen v. Mayer, 1931, 204 Wis. 286, 234 N.W. 904, 74 A.L.R. 1245, noted in 7 Wis.Law Rev. 42 (1931).

17. See infra, § 133.

18. Riddle v. Jones, 1921, 191 Ky. 763, 231 S.W. 503.

19. Sprenzel v. Windmueller, 1918, 286 Ill. 411, 121 N.E. 805; Douglas v. Jordan, 1925, 232 Mich. 283 205 N.W. 52, 41 A.L.R. 1437.

20. Bird v. Smith, 1839, 8 Watts.(Pa.) 434.

21. Calhoun v. Ozburn, 1938, 186 Ga. 569, 198 S.E. 706; Rollo v. Nelson, 1908, 34 Utah 116, 96 P. 263.

22. Berlin v. Robbins, 1934, 180 Wash. 176, 38 P.2d 1047.

23. Cady v. Purser, 1901, 131 Cal. 552, 63 P. 844 (upon the questionable ground that the recording officer is the agent of the one who files an instrument for record); Terrell v. Andrew County, 1869, 44 Mo. 309; Frost v. Beekman, 1814, 1 Johns.Ch.(N.Y.) 288; Prouty v. Marshall, 1909, 225 Pa. 570, 74 A. 550 (error pertained to the initials of the mortgagor).

a subsequent *bona fide* purchaser or mortgagee is entitled to rely on the $300 entry. However, if an error in recordation results in an ambiguity that is disclosed on the record, a person who relies upon the record is under a duty to investigate the matter.[24] He is entitled to rely upon the record only if he has been misled thereby. The minority rule protects the person who files the instrument for record.[25] It is considered that he has fulfilled his duty under the recording act when he files the instrument for record with the proper recording official. Generally, recording statutes provide that the index is a part of the record. In that event, an error in indexing may prevent the claim of constructive notice.[26] Under some statutes the index is not considered to be a part of the record.[27]

CHAIN OF TITLE

133. **The recordation of an instrument results in constructive notice only if the instrument is in the chain of title.**

     a.   **Collateral instruments. A valid claim of constructive notice cannot be based upon provisions in a collateral instrument even if executed by a grantor who is in the chain of title.**

     b.   **Recitals. A claim of constructive notice may be sustained because of recitals contained in recorded instruments that are in the chain of title or that pertain to the title.**

     c.   **Ancestor and heir. A purchaser or mortgagee from an heir or devisee is entitled to rely upon the fact that the record title is in the name of the ancestor.**

The effectiveness of recordation depends upon whether or not the recorded instrument constitutes a link in the chain of title.[28] For example, assume that A conveys land to B by a deed that is not recorded. Thereafter, B conveys the land to C by a deed that is recorded. The recordation of the deed from B to C is not in the chain of title. There is nothing to connect B with the title that is of record in A. Accordingly, a person who acquires the estate from A is not charged with constructive notice and takes free from the claims of B and C.[29]

In Morse v. Curtis (Mass.),[30] A mortgaged land to B and later mortgaged the same land to C, who had notice of the prior mortgage. C recorded his mortgage and then B recorded. C assigned his mortgage to D who took in good faith, for value and without notice. B's mortgage was not in D's chain of title and, for that reason, he did not have constructive notice of B's interest. D was not under a duty to examine the records to determine whether or not a deed or mortgage from the common grantor (A) that was earlier in date than the one under which he claimed was recorded *after* the instrument in his chain of title.[31]

A similar situation is presented if estoppel by deed is involved. For example, assume

24.   Chapman & Co. v. Johnson, 1905, 142 Ala. 633, 30 So. 797.

25.   Mangold v. Barlow, 1884, 61 Miss. 593.

26.   Parry v. Reinertson, 1929, 208 Iowa 739, 224 N.W. 489, 63 A.L.R. 1051; Woodley v. Gregory, 1933, 205 N.C. 280, 171 S.E. 65; Dorman v. Goodman, 1938, 213 N.C. 406, 196 S.E. 352, noted in 52 Harv.Law Rev. 170 (1938); 19 No.Car.Law Rev. 77 (1940)—index gave the wrong middle initial of the grantor; Ritchie v. Griffiths & Metcalfe, 1890, 1 Wash. 429, 25 P. 341.

27.   Mutual Insurance Co. v. Dake, 1881, 87 N.Y. 257; Green v. Garrington, 1866, 16 Ohio St. 548; Curtis v. Lyman, 1852, 24 Vt. 338.

28.   See Capper v. Poulsen, 1926, 321 Ill. 480, 152 N.E. 587.

29.   Board of Education v. Hughes, 1912, 118 Minn. 404, 136 N.W. 1095.

30.   140 Mass. 112, 2 N.E. 929 (1885).

31.   *Contra:* Woods v. Garnett, 1894, 72 Miss. 78, 16 So. 390; Van Rensselaer v. Clark, 1837, 17 Wend. (N.Y.) 25. A contrary conclusion was also reached in Parrish v. Mahany, 1899, 12 S.D. 278, 81 N.W. 295, but in that case a different type of recording statute was involved.

that A, who does not have an estate, purports to convey the land to B by warranty deed and that this deed is recorded by B. An estate that A may later acquire will inure to the benefit of B. The recordation of the warranty deed, not being in the chain of title, is not effective to charge constructive notice to one who may take an estate from A after A has, in fact, acquired the estate. A burden is not cast upon such a purchaser or mortgagee to ascertain whether or not his grantor or mortgagor (A), purported to convey or mortgage the property prior to the time that he acquired ownership.[32]

Collateral Instruments

In Glorieux v. Lighthipe (N. J.),[33] A was the owner of two adjoining lots, numbers one and two. A sold lot #1 to B. This deed contained a covenant creating building restrictions mutually enforceable by and between the owners of lot #1 and lot #2. Thereafter, A conveyed lot #2 to C. This deed was silent as to building restrictions and C had no knowledge as to their existence. Even though the deed of lot #1 from A to B was recorded, the court held that C could not be charged with constructive notice of the provisions therein relating to restrictions. This deed was not in C's chain of title.[34] Due diligence does not require an examination of such collateral instruments even if executed by a grantor who is in the chain of title.[35] Of course, a claim of constructive notice may be sustained if a conveyance is made by reference to a map or plat wherein restrictions are designated.

Recitals

A charge of constructive notice may be based upon recitals in a recorded instrument that is in the chain of title or that pertains to the title.[36] For example, a lessee is charged with constructive notice of a recital in a deed under which his lessor acquired ownership of the leased land.[37]

In Guerin v. Sunburst Oil & Gas Co. (Mont.),[38] a recorded option contained a recital that it was subject to an outstanding lease. A purchaser of the land was charged with constructive notice of the lease even though he did not acquire ownership under the option. While the option was not in the purchaser's chain of title it was a recorded instrument that pertained to the title.

Ancestor and Heir

In Youngblood v. Vastine (Mo.),[39] A executed a deed of trust to B that had not been re-

32. Wack v. Collingswood Extension Realty Co., 1933, 114 N.J.Eq. 253, 168 A. 639; Richardson v. Atlantic Coast Lumber Corp., 1912, 93 S.C. 254, 75 S.E. 371. *Contra:* McCusker v. McEvey, 1870, 9 R.I. 528; Jarvis v. Aikens, 1853, 25 Vt. 635. A contrary conclusion was also reached in Balch v. Arnold, 1899, 9 Wyo. 17, 59 P. 434, but in that case the local recording statute would justify that conclusion because it required the register of deeds to enter an abstract of all documents affecting title under a legal description of the land involved.

33. 88 N.J.L. 199, 96 A. 94 (1915).

34. *Accord:* Judd v. Robinson, 1907, 41 Colo. 222, 92 P. 724; Hancock v. Gumm, 1921, 151 Ga. 667, 107 S.E. 872, 16 A.L.R. 1003, noted in 21 Col.Law Rev. 826 (1921); Buffalo Academy of the Sacred Heart

v. Boehm Bros., 1935, 267 N.Y. 242, 196 N.E. 42; King v. James, 1950, 88 Ohio App. 213, 97 N.E.2d 235. *Contra:* Lowes v. Carter, 1915, 124 Md. 678, 93 A. 216; McQuade v. Wilcox, 1921, 215 Mich. 302, 183 N.W. 771, 16 A.L.R. 997, noted in 20 Mich.Law Rev. 344 (1922); Finley v. Glenn, 1931, 303 Pa. 131, 154 A. 299; Moore v. Center, 1964, — Vt. —, 204 A.2d 164.

35. *Cf.:* Camp Clearwater, Inc. v. Plock, 1958, 52 N.J. Super. 583, 146 A.2d 527.

36. Baker v. Mather, 1872, 25 Mich. 51 (recital in deed that the land is subject to a mortgage gives constructive notice of the mortgage even if the mortgage is not recorded).

37. Moore v. Bennett, [1678] 2 Ch. 246, 22 Eng.Rep. 928.

38. 68 Mont. 365, 218 P. 949 (1923).

39. 46 Mo. 239 (1870).

corded at the time of A's death. Thereafter, the heirs of A executed a warranty deed of the land to C. The court held that a *bona fide* purchaser for value and without notice from an heir or devisee is entitled to rely upon the record title the same as any other purchaser.[40]

BONA FIDE PURCHASERS

134. **The protection afforded by a recording statute is available only to** *bona fide* **purchasers or mortgagees or to a person claiming from or through such a party.**

a. **Value. The payment of nominal consideration will not support the claim that a person is a** *bona fide* **purchaser. Otherwise, inquiry is not made as to the adequacy of consideration. In general, if only part of the consideration has been paid at the time of notice, the purchaser will be protected** *pro tanto.*

b. **Improperly recorded instrument. A usual statutory provision is that only acknowledged instruments may be recorded. Constructive notice does not arise from the fact that an instrument has been recorded if it was not executed with prescribed formalities.**

c. **Possession that is consistent with the record. Notice will not be implied from possession if that possession is consistent with the title as disclosed by the record.**

d. **Possession by a grantor. The temporary possession of a grantor does not constitute constructive notice of an interest claimed by the grantor.**

The prevailing rule is that an unrecorded instrument is valid as against subsequent purchasers, mortgagees etc., who have notice

of the prior conveyance.[41] Even the protection afforded by a recording statute is available only to *bona fide* purchasers or mortgagees or to a person claiming from or through such a party.[42] To qualify as a *bona fide* purchaser one must take in good faith, for value and without notice, actual or constructive. In the absence of a statute to the contrary,[43] creditors are not considered to be *bona fide* purchasers.[44] The burden of proof is on the person claiming to be a *bona fide* purchaser.[45]

The general rule is that a grantee under a quitclaim deed may qualify as a *bona fide* purchaser. This follows from the fact that a quitclaim deed is in general use as a conveying instrument.[46] Some decisions are to the contrary. It is reasoned that the function of such a deed is to release whatever right, title or interest was vested in the grantor.[47]

---

40. *Accord:* Meikel v. Borders, 1891, 129 Ind. 529, 29 N.E. 29; Earle v. Fiske, 1870, 103 Mass. 491; Burns v. Berry, 1879, 42 Mich. 176, 3 N.W. 924. *Contra:* Hill v. Meeker, 1855, 24 Conn. 211; Webb v. Doe ex dem. Wilcher, 1863, 33 Ga. 565; Harris v. Williford, 1942, 179 Tenn. 299, 165 S.W.2d 582 (subsequently changed by statute (Tenn.Code § 7668)).

41. Jackson ex dem. Gilbert v. Burgott, 1813, 10 Johns. (N.Y.) 457.

42. Mingus v. Bell, 1947, 148 Neb. 735, 29 N.W.2d 332; Brown v. Sheets, 1929, 197 N.C. 268, 148 S.E. 233, 63 A.L.R. 1357.

43. For a collection of these statutes see Note, Rights of Creditors of the Mortgagor Against the Holder of an Unrecorded Mortgage, 13 Col.Law Rev. 539, n. 11, 12 (1913).

44. Holden v. Garrett, 1879, 23 Kan. 98, Reprint Ed. 66 (judgment creditor).

45. Kindred v. Crosby, 1959, 251 Iowa 198, 100 N.W. 2d 20.

46. Phoenix Title & Trust Co. v. Old Dominion Co., 1927, 31 Ariz. 324, 253 P. 435, 59 A.L.R. 625; Beach v. Faust, 1935, 2 Cal.2d 290, 40 P.2d 822; Boynton v. Haggart, 8 Cir. 1903, 120 F. 819, 57 C.C.A. 301 (*dictum*).

47. Smith's Heirs v. Branch Bank at Mobile, 1852, 21 Ala. 125; Marshall v. Roberts, 1872, 18 Minn. 405 (but the rule in this case was changed by statute, see Strong v. Lynn, 1888, 38 Minn. 315, 37 N.W. 448); Fowler v. Will, 1905, 19 S.D. 131, 102 N.W. 598.

It is usually provided by statute that to qualify as a *bona fide* purchaser or mortgagee the estate or interest must be acquired without notice. Some statutes provide that the acquisition must be without "actual notice." But "actual notice" does not mean "actual knowledge." [48] And knowledge of the existence of a prior conveying instrument is not necessarily knowledge of a prior conveyance.[49] And a purchaser or mortgagee is not charged with notice of a prior interest because of common reputation in the community that such an interest exists.[50]

Notice of an outstanding interest may be implied if a person is in possession of the land by force of an unrecorded instrument. While this possession does not constitute constructive notice of the possessor's interest, it is sufficient to put a subsequent purchaser, mortgagee etc., on inquiry and he is charged with notice of facts that such an inquiry would have disclosed.[51] This notice-rule applies even though the one charged with notice was not aware of the possession [52] and even though he was a non-resident of the state wherein the land is located.[53] Reasonable diligence requires an inspection of the land.[54]

Value

The payment of a "nominal" consideration will not support the claim that a person is a *bona fide* purchaser for value.[55] Otherwise, inquiry is not made as to the adequacy of the consideration unless there is a claim of bad faith or fraud.[56] The cancellation of a pre-existing debt constitutes value.[57] For example, a purchaser at an execution sale may qualify as a *bona fide* purchaser although the consideration consists of the satisfaction of the judgment.[58]

A mere promise to pay the consideration involved in the transaction does not constitute value.[59] This follows from the fact that the promisor can defend an action brought to recover the consideration if he did not receive the estate or interest as contemplated. However a different rule applies if the promise is in the form required for a negotiable instrument and is in the hands of a holder in due course.[60] Such a holder may be entitled to enforce the promise in spite of the defense of failure of consideration or fraud in the inducement.

---

48. Brinkman v. Jones, 1878, 44 Wis. 498. But see, South Street Inn, Inc. v. Muehsam, 1948, 323 Mass. 310, 81 N.E.2d 821.

49. Nordman v. Rau, 1911, 86 Kan. 19, 119 P. 351. *Contra:* Parkside Realty Co. v. MacDonald, 1913, 166 Cal. 426, 137 P. 21.

50. Strong v. Strong, 1936, 128 Tex. 470, 98 S.W.2d 346, 109 A.L.R. 739.

51. Martinique Realty Corp. v. Hull, 1960, 64 N.J. Super. 599, 166 A.2d 803. *Cf.:* High Fidelity Enterprises, Inc. v. Hull, 1962, 210 Cal.App.2d 279, 26 Cal. Rptr. 654 (possession must be open, notorious, exclusive and visible).

52. Galley v. Ward, 1880, 60 N.H. 331.

53. Meagher v. Dean, 1939, 97 Utah 173, 91 P.2d 454.

54. *Cf.:* Mishawaka St. Joseph Loan & Trust Co. v. Neu, 1935, 209 Ind. 433, 196 N.E. 85, 105 A.L.R. 881, noted in 2 Univ. of Pitt.Law Rev. 89 (1935).

55. Morris v. Wicks, 1910, 81 Kan. 790, 106 P. 1048 ($1.00); Payton v. Norris, 1931, 240 Ky. 555, 42 S.W. 2d 723, noted in 10 Tex.Law Rev. 378 (1932) ($1.00).

56. Strong v. Whybark, 1907, 204 Mo. 341, 102 S.W. 968.

57. Adams v. Vanderbeck, 1896, 148 Ind. 92, 45 N.E. 645, rehearing denied 148 Ind. 92, 47 N.E. 24; Noe v. Smith, 1917, 67 Okl. 211, 169 P. 1108, L.R.A.1918C 435 (*dictum*). *Cf.:* Cary v. White, 1873, 52 N.Y. 138 (value is not involved if a person takes a mortgage merely as security for a pre-existing debt). *Contra:* Western Grocer Co. v. Alleman, 1910, 81 Kan. 543, 106 P. 460, rehearing denied 81 Kan. 900, 106 P. 997.

58. Sternberger & Willard v. Ragland, 1897, 57 Ohio St. 148, 48 N.E. 811. *Contra:* McCalla v. Knight Investment Co., 1908, 77 Kan. 770, 94 P. 126.

59. Thomas v. Stone & Graham, 1843, Walker Ch. (Mich.) 117.

60. Davis v. Ward, 1895, 109 Cal. 186, 41 P. 1010.

If only part of the consideration has been paid at the time of notice, the purchaser will be protected *pro tanto*.[61] The owner of the interest under the unrecorded conveyance will be entitled to the land upon condition that he restore the amounts paid by the subsequent purchaser. It has been stated, however, that if the purchaser has erected substantial improvements and would, therefore, be subjected to undue hardship if he were required to give up the land, his ownership will be protected even though he has made only partial payments at the time of notice.[62]

Improperly Recorded Instrument

A usual statutory provision is that only acknowledged instruments may be recorded. In that event, the recordation of an unacknowledged instrument does not result in constructive notice.[63] However, one who has knowledge as to the existence of such an instrument may have difficulty in establishing a claim of good faith.[64] Curative statutes have been enacted in a number of states. It is provided that in cases where an instrument is, in fact, recorded, even though it should not have been recorded because of some defect in its execution, it will constitute constructive notice after the expiration of a stated period.

Possession that is Consistent with the Record

Notice will not be implied from possession if that possession is consistent with the title as disclosed by the record. For example,

if the record shows that two or more persons are concurrent owners of the land, the possession of one is consistent with the record and will not give constructive notice of an enlarged claim.[65] However, there is authority for the rule that there is a duty to make inquiry as to the rights of a tenant even though the tenant's possession is consistent with the record.[66] This rule is in deference to the known fact that unrecorded supplemental agreements are quite common as between landlords and tenants.

If the grantor and the grantee in an unrecorded deed are members of the same family group, such as parent and child or husband and wife, continued occupancy of the land by the grantee will not be sufficient to charge a subsequent purchaser with notice of his interest under the prior conveyance.[67] The possession of the grantee, not being exclusive, is not inconsistent with the record title in the grantor.

Possession by a Grantor

The temporary possession by a grantor does not constitute constructive notice of a claimed interest. For example, if A conveys land to B, takes back a purchase money mortgage and remains in possession of the

61. Durst v. Daugherty, 1891, 81 Tex. 650, 17 S.W. 388.

62. Henry v. Phillips, 1912, 163 Cal. 135, 124 P. 837 (*dictum*).

63. Sigourney v. Larned, 1830, 10 Pick.(Mass.) 72.

64. Parkside Realty Co. v. MacDonald, 1913, 166 Cal. 426, 137 P. 21; Woods v. Garnett, 1894, 72 Miss. 78, 16 So. 390; Phillis v. Gross, 1913, 32 S.D. 438, 143 N.W. 373; Perrin v. Reed, 1861, 35 Vt. 2. *Contra:* Nordman v. Rau, 1911, 86 Kan. 19, 119 P. 351.

65. Ildvedsen v. First State Bank of Bowbells, 1912, 24 N.D. 227, 139 N.W. 105.

66. Basch v. Tide Water Associated Oil Co., 1942, 49 Cal.App.2d 743, 121 P.2d 545; Brinser v. Anderson, 1888, 129 Pa. 376, 11 A. 809, 18 A. 520. By a divided court, a contrary conclusion was reached in Hull v. Gafill Oil Co., 1933, 263 Mich. 650, 249 N.W. 24, noted in 47 Harv.Law Rev. 359. A contrary conclusion was also reached in Red River Valley Land & Inv. Co. v. Smith, 1898, 7 N.D. 236, 74 N.W. 194 and Hamilton v. Ingram, 1896, 13 Tex.Civ.App. 604, 35 S.W. 748.

67. Atwood v. Bearss, 1881, 47 Mich. 72, 10 N.W. 112 (conveyance by wife to husband); Rankin v. Coar, 1890, 46 N.J.Eq. 566, 22 A. 177 (mother to son); Strong v. Strong, 1936, 128 Tex. 470, 98 S.W.2d 346, 109 A.L.R. 739 (parent and child).

land, a subsequent purchaser of the land from B may qualify as a *bona fide* purchaser for value and without notice. It is proper to assume that A's possession is that of a tenant at will. As such, it is not inconsistent with the record showing ownership to be in B.[68] But if the possession of A has continued

for a substantial period of time, due diligence would compel an inquiry.[69]

[68.] Handelman v. Mandel, 1921, 70 Colo. 136, 197 P. 1021 (less than three weeks); Tutt v. Smith, 1925, 201 Iowa 107, 204 N.W. 294, 48 A.L.R. 394, noted in 10 Minn.Law Rev. 359 (1926) (possession for ap-

proximately one month). But see, Pell v. McElroy, 1868, 36 Cal. 268; Ostergard v. Norker, 1918, 102 Neb. 675, 169 N.W. 5 (continued possession of tenant considered to be possession of the landlord).

[69.] Turman v. Bell, 1891, 54 Ark. 273, 15 S.W. 886 (approximately six months); O'Toole v. Omlie, 1899, 8 N.D. 444, 79 N.W. 849 (eight years). *Cf.:* Morgan v. McCuin, 1910, 96 Ark. 512, 132 S.W. 459 (possession of a small part of the area conveyed).

CHAPTER 26

TITLE REGISTRATION AND LIS PENDENS

TITLE REGISTRATION—THE TORRENS SYSTEM

135. **Under the Torrens System of title registration the certificate of title is designed to reveal all outstanding estates and interests in the land. However, under some circumstances unregistered interests may be given priority.**

a. **Registration procedure. Registration is accomplished by judicial proceedings similar to proceedings in a quiet title action.**

b. **Transfer of ownership. A transfer of ownership is accomplished through a surrender of the old certificate of title to the registrar and his issuance of a new certificate.**

c. **Withdrawal of registration. Usually, statutory procedure is available as a means by which to withdraw from this system of title registration.**

The Torrens System of land-title registration, fashioned after the system of registering titles to ships, was introduced in Australia in 1858 by Sir Robert Torrens.[1] Theoretically, all estates and interests in land are set forth in a certificate of title. This system of registration is used extensively in the United States in the case of motor vehicles and is used in many states as an optional means of registering land-titles.[2]

Under the recording system a buyer or encumbrancer is required to make a detailed examination of all records in the chain of title and what may appear to be a perfect title of record may, in fact, be a defective title. Under the Torrens System the certificate of title is, in theory, conclusive as to the state of the title.[3] But some unregistered claims may be given priority.[4] This may be true with respect to short term leases, tax claims[5] or claims arising under the laws of the United States.[6] So also, those who have an estate or interest in the land who are not properly served with process in connection with the registration proceedings will not be bound by the judgment. The certificate is not conclusive if the registration itself was procured by fraud or forgery if the registered owner was free from fault. In Eliason v. Wilborn (U. S.),[7] A had been the holder of a certificate of title under the Torrens Act of Illinois. As the result of negotiations he entrusted the certificate to B who presented it to the Registrar of Titles together with a forged conveyance to himself. He was successful in securing a new

---

1. Systems of registration of title were used in Europe as early as 1836. See 8 Thompson, Real Property (perm. ed.) § 4405.

2. For an enumeration of the various statutes, see 8 Thompson, Real Property (perm. ed.) § 4405, p. 246.

3. For discussion of the advantages of this system, see McDougal and Brabner-Smith, Land Title Transfer: A Regression, 48 Yale Law Journal 1125 (1939); Rood, 12 Mich.Law Rev. 379, 393 (1914). For discussion of the disadvantages, see Boardwell, The Resurrection of Registration of Title, 7 Univ. of Chicago Law Rev. 470, 488 (1940).

4. See Staples, The Conclusiveness of a Torrens Certificate of Title, 8 Minn.Law Rev. 200 (1924).

5. Harrison v. Darden, 1943, 223 N.C. 364, 26 S.E.2d 860.

6. Shevlin-Mathieu Co. v. Fogarty, 1915, 130 Minn. 456, 153 N.W. 871 (ownership was in the United States).

7. 281 U.S. 457, 50 S.Ct. 382, 74 L.Ed. 962 (1930).

certificate of title naming B as the registered owner. A few days later B purported to convey to C who purchased for value and in good faith. Before a new certificate was issued to C he was informed of A's claim. The court held that the claim of C was superior to the claim of A. Having acquired title to registered land A knew that transfer of ownership depended upon the provisions of the Torrens Act. The statute required the production of the outstanding certificate as a condition to the issuance of a new certificate. A entrusted his certificate to B and thus assumed the risk incident to the possible issuance of a new certificate.

Registration is usually limited to estates in fee simple, legal or equitable. This may include long term leases, such as an estate for 99 years, renewable forever.[8] Statutes generally provide that rules relating to adverse possession are not applicable to registered titles. Registration statutes also provide for the establishment of an assurance fund for the indemnity of persons having any interest in land who may sustain damage by the decree of registration. This fund is augmented by assessments against those who make application for title registration.

Registration Procedure

Registration of title under the Torrens System is accomplished by judicial proceedings similar to proceedings in a quiet title action. Upon application for the registration of title, the court appoints an examiner of titles to investigate the pertinent facts respecting the title. The proceedings before the court are judicial in nature. The court does not act as a mere administrative tribunal. A statute making the preliminary report of the examiner as to the state of the title *prima facie*

evidence of the contents thereof is in compliance with due process.[9]

When the examiner files his report a summons is issued by which all claimants of any estate or interest in the land are made parties defendant. Where possible, there is actual service of process. Otherwise, as in the case of unknown claimants, substituted service may be used. All of those served are bound by the decree because the proceedings are *in rem*.

If, after a hearing, the court determines that the claimant is entitled to registration a decree is so entered confirming the title and ordering registration. While statutes in some states provide for a jury trial on controversial issues respecting title, this is not an essential element of due process because the proceedings are equitable in nature.[10] The particulars of all estates, interests and encumbrances are entered upon the record and upon the certificate of title. The original of the certificate of title is kept in a register by the registrar of titles, and a copy is delivered to the applicant.

Transfer of Ownership

The execution of a deed is construed to be merely a contract to convey and as authority to the registrar to transfer ownership. The transfer is affected by the issuance of a new certificate to the transferee upon surrender of the transferor's certificate. If the transfer is to be of less than the entire estate or interest of the transferor, a new certificate is issued evidencing the remaining interest. Transfers by descent, devise or by judicial

---

8. See, for example, Vinewood Realty Co. v. Village of Willowick, 1940, 136 Ohio St. 257, 25 N.E.2d 345.

9. Crowell v. Akin, 1921, 152 Ga. 126, 108 S.E. 791, 19 A.L.R. 51.

10. Crowell v. Akin, 1921, 152 Ga. 126, 108 S.E. 791, 19 A.L.R. 51.

decree are made by the registrar in accordance with orders and decrees of the court.[11]

Withdrawal of Registration

In Application of Carns (N. Y.),[12] land was registered under the Torrens Title Act. Petitioners, representing the estate of the deceased owner, made application to the court to withdraw the registration. A statute provided that withdrawal would be permitted if it appeared that registration was no longer expedient and practical because of peculiar and unusual circumstances or exigencies involving the title itself. Withdrawal was sought upon the ground that the mortgagee of the land was willing to accept a deed in satisfaction of the indebtedness. Otherwise, it was claimed, he would foreclose and secure a deficiency judgment.

Application of withdrawal was granted upon the ground that the statute, being remedial in nature, should be given a liberal construction. It is pointed out that the difficulties incident to withdrawal have been a prime objection to this method of registration.

In the absence of statute, registration is considered to be an "agreement running with the land" and the land, once registered, shall remain so forever. Withdrawal by special legislative act is too expensive a process to be practical.

LIS PENDENS

136. **A party to litigation involving ownership of land may protect his interest against subsequent purchasers or mortgagees of the land by filing a notice as to the pending action (*lis pendens*).**

According to the English common law one who acquires an estate or interest in land acquires it subject to the rights that may evolve out of pending litigation pertaining to the land. In other words, he acquires his interest with notice of such rights. To constitute *lis pendens* (a pending suit) there must be an action pending in a court of competent jurisdiction that involves the title to the particular land. In addition, the land must be particularly described in the pleadings so that it can be identified by reasonable inquiry.

Under modern conditions it is not reasonable that one should be charged with notice of claims respecting land merely because of the fact that it is involved in pending litigation. Accordingly, statutes in many states provide for the recordation of notice that such an action is pending.[13] If a litigant desires to protect his rights as against purchasers, mortgagees etc., he must file notice that there is a pending suit (*lis pendens*).

While the owner of land may be entitled to maintain an action for malicious prosecution, he cannot maintain an action for disparagement of title based upon the filing of a *lis pendens*. It is usually provided by statute that publications made in the course of judicial proceedings are absolutely privileged. This is the rule in defamation cases and is applicable in an action for disparagement of title. The filing of a *lis pendens* is, in effect, a "republication of the pleadings" that involves an absolute privilege.[14]

11. See Patton, The Torrens System of Land Title Registration, 19 Minn.Law Rev. 519, 525 (1935).

12. 181 Misc. 1047, 43 N.Y.S.2d 497 (1943).

13. See, for example, West's Ann.Cal.Code Civ.Proc. § 408.

14. Albertson v. Raboff, 1956, 46 Cal.2d 375, 295 P.2d 405.

PART 5

FUTURE INTERESTS

CHAPTER 27

VARIOUS TYPES OF FUTURE INTERESTS AND THEIR CHARACTERISTICS

REVERSIONS

137. A reversion is the estate remaining in a grantor, or the estate of a testator, who has conveyed an estate that is considered to be a "lesser estate" than that owned by the conveyor.

   a. **Freehold estate subject to a lease.** While the owner of a freehold estate has a reversion if there is an outstanding lease, there are some situations where it is considered that he has a possessory estate rather than a reversion. That is the rule if matters relate to dower or curtesy or if the right to partition is involved.

   b. **Worthier Title Doctrine.** An *inter vivos* conveyance of a possessory estate followed by a gift to the heirs or next of kin of the conveyor presumably leaves a reversion in the conveyor. However, such a gift in favor of heirs or next of kin will be sustained if evidence establishes the fact that such was the intention of the conveyor.

It has been noted that estates are classified on the basis of potential duration. If the owner of a "greater estate" conveys a "lesser estate" he has a reversion by operation of law. Historically, a fee tail is classified as a lessor estate than a fee simple. Therefore, if the owner of an estate in fee simple conveys an estate in fee tail he has a reversion.[1] A life tenant has a reversion if he conveys a non-freehold estate, such as an estate for years. There is a reversion if the owner of an estate for his own life conveys an estate for the lifetime of another.[2] The owner of a non-freehold estate has a reversion if he conveys an estate that is potentially of shorter duration than the estate owned by the one making the conveyance. If the purpose of a trust does not require an application of the entire trust estate there is a reversion in the trustor or in his estate.[3]

Since a reversion arises from the conveyance of an estate that is considered to be a "lesser estate" than that owned by the conveyor, the reversion is created by operation of law—express words of creation are not required. A reversion is not an estate that "reverts." It is an estate that "remains" in a grantor or the estate of a testator.

The creation of a contingent estate, such as a contingent remainder, results in the

---

1. Simes & Smith, Future Interests (2nd Ed.), § 83.

2. 2 Rest.Property, § 154, *Comment d, Illust. 9.*

3. Beal v. Higgins, 1922, 303 Ill. 370, 135 N.E. 759. But see, Van Der Volgen v. Yates, 1853, 9 N.Y. 219.

creation of a reversion.[4] According to common law rules, contingent remainders are destructible.[5] Accordingly, there is a reversion in a grantor who creates alternative contingent remainders that would result in the disposition of the entire estate if the remainders were not destroyed. For example, in Loddington v. Kime (Eng.),[6] the devise was A to B for life (without impeachment for waste), and in case he have any issue male, then to such issue male and his heirs; and if he die without issue male, then to C and his heirs. A reversion existed in the estate of the testator. This interest would become possessory if the remainders were destroyed, such as by premature termination of the life estate. In a case such as this a reversion would not exist in a state where the doctrine of destructibility has been abolished by statute. In that event no vestige of an interest would be left in the grantor or the estate of a testator.[7]

The owner of a reversion has an estate that may be disposed of by *inter vivos* conveyance or by will. In the absence of a testamentary disposition the estate will pass as in the case of intestacy.[8]

Freehold Estate Subject to a Lease

The owner of a freehold estate has a reversion if there is an outstanding lease. However, there are some situations where it is considered that the freeholder has a possessory estate rather than a reversion. Under such circumstances his estate might more properly be described as a freehold estate subject to a lease. The freeholder is considered to be the owner of a possessory estate in connection with an application of the law as it relates to dower and curtesy.[9] That is also the rule if matters relating to partition are involved.[10]

Worthier Title Doctrine

According to the English common law, the owner of an estate in fee could not make an *inter vivos* conveyance to his own right heirs. For example, if A, the owner of an estate in fee simple, conveyed to B for life, remainder to the heirs or heirs of the body of A, the purported remainder failed. As a result of the conveyance B acquired a life estate and A retained the reversion. A's heirs would acquire the estate, if at all, by inheritance. This was considered to be a "worthier title." The testamentary aspect of this doctrine found expression in the rule that a purported devise of an estate to heirs is inoperative if it is the identical estate that they are entitled to take in case of intestacy.[11] In that event the acquisition is by intestate succession rather than by the devise. Under the feudal system an application of these rules was advantageous to the overlord in connection with the preservation of feudal incidents.[12]

---

4. Fidelity-Philadelphia Trust Co. v. Harloff, 1943, 133 N.J.Eq. 44, 30 A.2d 57. See Spiegel's Estate v. Comm'r of Internal Revenue, 1949, 335 U.S. 701, 69 S.Ct. 301, 93 L.Ed. 330 (it is immaterial that it is extremely improbable that the reversion will ever become possessory).

5. See infra, § 138.

6. 1 Salk. 224, 91 Eng.Rep. 198 [1695].

7. See Simes & Smith, Future Interests (2nd Ed.), § 85, p. 73.

8. Parks v. Kimes, 1884, 100 Ind. 148. For discussion of the English common law rule, see 2 Rest. Property, § 164, *Comment c.*

9. Carter v. Williams, 1851, 43 N.C. 177.

10. Brinn v. Slawson & Hobbs, 1947, 273 App.Div. 1, 74 N.Y.S.2d 825; Rawson v. Brown, 1922, 104 Ohio St. 537, 136 N.E. 209.

11. Co.Litt., 12b; 4 Kent's Comm. 506. See Harper and Heckel, The Doctrine of Worthier Title, 24 Ill. Law Rev. 627, 635 (1930). In England this doctrine was abolished by Stats. 3 & 4 Wm. IV, c. 106, § 3 (1833).

12. See Simes & Smith, Future Interests (2nd Ed.), § 1601, p. 493.

While the testamentary aspect of the Worthier Title Doctrine is not generally followed in the United States, there are a few cases in which it has been applied.[13] In the leading case of Doctor v. Hughes (N. Y.),[14] the *inter vivos* aspect of the Worthier Title Doctrine is applied as a rule of construction and this conclusion is in accord with the present weight of authority in the United States.[15] Some decisions indicate the rule to be an expression of policy.[16] It permits the settlor of an *inter vivos* trust to revoke the trust insofar as it purports to make a gift to his heirs or the heirs of his body. To that extent the *inter vivos* trust is, like a will, ambulatory in nature. The doctrine is applicable to *inter vivos* gifts in trust of land and both chattels real and chattels personal.

The doctrine is applicable only if an *inter vivos* gift is followed by a gift to the conveyor's "heirs" or "next of kin," and only if these words are used in a technical sense, and not as meaning "children," etc. As a rule of construction, there is a presumption that the conveyor did not intend to create a future interest in those who would eventually qualify as his "heirs" or "next of kin." In other words, presumptively there is a reversion in the conveyor. As stated in Doctor v. Hughes,[17] "to transform into a remainder what would ordinarily be a reversion, the intention to work the transformation must be clearly expressed."

An intention to create a remainder may be gathered from the fact that the trust purports to make a full and complete disposition of the trust property.[18] This would also seem to be true if the trustor reserves a limited power, such as a power of testamentary disposition.[19] The reservation of such a power would be meaningless except on the hypothesis that the conveyor intended to create a future interest in his heirs or next of kin.[20] This argument may also be made with respect to the reservation of a power of revocation. However, the insertion of a power of revocation does not necessarily carry that implication. It is the clear expression of an intention not to create interests in the heirs or next of kin.

---

13. See Herring v. Herring, 1919, 187 Iowa 593, 174 N.W. 364; Ellis v. Page, 1851, 61 Mass.(7 Cush.) 161; Cordon v. Gregg, 1940, 164 Or. 306, 97 P.2d 732, 101 P.2d 414, noted in 20 Ore.Law Rev. 164 (1941). *Cf.:* In re Everett's Estate, 1947, 238 Iowa 564, 28 N.W.2d 21.

14. 225 N.Y. 305, 122 N.E. 221 (1919), noted in 4 Cornell Law Quarterly 83 (1919), 28 Yale Law Journal 713 (1919).

15. However, the doctrine has been rejected in one state (Phoenix State Bank & Trust Co. v. Buckalew, 1947, 15 Conn.Sup. 149) and has been abolished by statute in a few states. See, for example, West's Ann.Cal.Civ.Code, § 1073; Neb.Rev.Stat.(1943), §§ 76–114, 76–115. See also, Shaw v. Arnett, 1948, 226 Minn. 425, 33 N.W.2d 609. Without reference to the Worthier Title Doctrine, a California statute provides that a voluntary trust may be revoked at any time unless the power of revocation is expressly granted away (West's Ann.Cal.Civ.Code, § 2280). A statute abolishing the Rule in Shelley's Case will not result in an abolition of the Worthier Title Doctrine (Wilcoxen v. Owen, 1938, 237 Ala. 169, 185 So. 897; Fidelity & Columbia Trust Co. v. Williams, 1937, 268 Ky. 671, 105 S.W.2d 814; Doctor v. Hughes, 1919, 225 N.Y. 305, 122 N.E. 221, noted in 4 Cornell Law Quarterly 83 (1919), 28 Yale Law Jr. 713 (1919); Robinson v. Blankenship, 1906, 116 Tenn. 394, 92 S. W. 854).

16. See, for example, Brolasky's Estate, 1931, 302 Pa. 439, 153 A. 739; Robinson v. Blankinship, 1906, 116 Tenn. 394, 92 S.W. 854.

17. 225 N.Y. 305, 122 N.E. 221, 222 (1919).

18. Richardson v. Richardson, 1948, 298 N.Y. 135, 81 N.E.2d 54.

19. See Simes & Smith, Future Interests (2nd Ed.), § 1608, p. 509.

20. *Cf.:* Clark v. Judge, 1964, 84 N.J.Super. 35, 200 A. 2d 801.

REMAINDERS

138. A remainder is an estate that is granted over to a third party after the expiration of a particular estate of freehold—a life estate or an estate in fee tail.

    a. **Rule in Shelley's case.** According to this rule, if land is conveyed to a person for life, remainder to his heirs, the person acquires an estate in fee simple. It is an estate in fee tail if the purported remainder is to the heirs of the body.

        The rule applies only if the life estate and purported remainder are created by the same instrument, the word "heirs" or the words "heirs of the body" are used in a technical sense, and both estates are of the same quality.

        This rule has been abolished in a majority of the American states.

    b. **Classification of remainders.** A remainder is vested if there is no possibility of a break in the continuity of the seisin at the time of the termination of the supporting particular estate. If there is a possibility of a gap a contingent remainder is involved. A remainder may be vested subject to being divested in whole or in part.

    c. **Destructibility of contingent remainders.** According to the English common law the recognition of a contingent remainder depends upon the continued existence of the supporting freehold estate. There may be a natural termination of that estate or there may be termination by forfeiture or merger. In any event, if the remainder is contingent at the time of termination it is destroyed.

        In England the doctrine of destructibility has been abolished by statute and it has limited recognition in the United States.

    d. **Alienation of remainders.** Vested remainders are freely alienable. This is also the general rule respecting contingent remainders except that a contingent remainder is not transmissible at death if survivorship is the contingency involved. One acquiring a contingent remainder takes it subject to defeasance upon the happening of the event involved.

In a conveyance A to B for life remainder to C and his heirs the estate conveyed to C and his heirs is a remainder. It is an estate granted over to a third party after the expiration of a particular estate of freehold—an estate for life or an estate in fee tail.

A remainder is not involved if the estates are created by separate conveying instruments. There must be a simultaneous conveyance.[21] If A conveys a life estate to B there is a reversion in A. If this interest is subsequently conveyed to C and his heirs C is the grantee of a reversion and not a remainderman. But if a life estate is devised to B a remainder may be created in C by a codicil to the will. The will and the codicil are construed together as constituting one conveying instrument.[22]

Rule in Shelley's Case

The rule in Shelley's case (Eng.),[23] applies if land is conveyed to a person for life and a remainder is limited to that person's heirs or the heirs of his body. According to the rule, instead of acquiring a life estate the person acquires an estate in fee simple or an estate in fee tail. For example, in a conveyance A to B for life, remainder to the heirs of B, B acquires an estate in fee simple. It is construed that the conveyance is to B for life with a remainder to B and his heirs. Then, by rules relating to merger, the entire estate is considered to be vested in B.[24] This merger may be postponed to satisfy any estate in-

---

21. 2 Rest.Property, § 156(1).

22. Simes & Smith, Future Interests (2nd Ed.), § 108, p. 86.

23. Wolfe v. Shelley, [1581] 1 Coke Rep. 93b, 76 Eng. Rep. 206.

24. See Hayes, Conveyancing (5th ed., 1840) 542, discussed in Martin v. Knowles, 1928, 195 N.C. 427, 142 S.E. 313.

tervening between the life estate in the ancestor and the remainder to his heirs or the heirs of his body.[25] In view of the fact that the heirs do not take an estate in their own right to words "heirs" or "heirs of the body" are words of limitation and not words of purchase.

From an historical point of view it is probable that the rule was designed for the protection of the landed nobility. Under the feudal system the overlord was entitled to certain pecuniary benefits which flowed from tenure.[26] If the "heir" or the "heirs of the body" of the designated life tenant were to take as "purchasers" under the conveyance (take in their own right), the overlord would be deprived of such feudal incidents as wardship and marriage that might otherwise be available upon the death of the person designated as life tenant. In Provost of Beverley's Case (Eng.),[27] a conveyance was made to B for life, remainder to his heirs. After B's death his son entered upon the land. The court held that he succeeded to the estate by descent from B and was, therefore, liable for relief (a money payment exacted from an heir upon succeeding to ownership acquired by descent). The rule in Shelley's case has been either abolished or modified by statute in a majority of the American states.[28] Under such circumstances, a conveyance of the type under consideration creates a life estate, as directed, with a remainder to the "heirs" or the "heirs of the body" of the life tenant.

The rule in Shelley's case is applicable only in connection with the conveyance of freehold estates in land [29] and is applied as a rule of law as distinguished from a rule of construction. In other words, it will be applied even if a conveyor specifically directs that it is not to be applied.[30] However, it is not applicable if the gift following the life estate is an executory interest as distinguished from a remainder.[31] Other requirements for application of the rule are discussed in the following paragraphs.

First: The limitation of a life estate to the ancestor and the purported remainder to his heirs or heirs of his body must be created by the same conveying instrument. The rule is applicable if the devise of a life estate is contained in a will and the remainder is devised by a codicil. The will and codicil are construed together as constituting one instrument. The rule is also applicable if a life estate is given to the ancestor and, by the same instrument, a power of appointment is given to another who, in exercising the power, appoints to the heirs or heirs of the body of the person named as ancestor. Those taking upon the exercise of a power of appointment take from the donor of the power and not from the donee. Accordingly, rights under the power derive from the will.[32]

Second: The rule is applicable only if the words "heirs" or "heirs of the body" are used in a technical sense.[33] In First National Bank

25. Simes & Smith, Future Interests (2nd Ed.), § 1556, p. 463.

26. For discussion of the feudal incidents, see supra, § 1.

27. Y.B. 40 Edw. 111, 9 (1366).

28. For a compilation of statutes, see 3 Rest. Property, § 313, *Comment a*, Special Note. It was abolished in England by the Law of Property Act of 1925, § 131.

29. 3 Rest. Property, § 312, *Comment b.*

30. Jesson v. Wright, [1820] 2 Bligh. 1, 4 Eng.Rep. 230. *Cf.:* Sybert v. Sybert, Tex.1953, 254 S.W.2d 999; Taylor v. Cleary, 1877, 29 Grat.(Va.) 448.

31. See Simes & Smith, Future Interests (2nd Ed.), § 192, p. 214.

32. Van Grutten v. Foxwell, [1897] A.C. 658; 3 Rest. Property, § 312, *Comment i.*

33. Farrell v. Faries, 1941, 25 Del.Ch. 404, 22 A.2d 380; Conger v. Lowe, 1890, 124 Ind. 368, 24 N.E. 889, 9 L.R.A. 165 (possible application of the rule

of Fort Smith v. Graham (Ark.),[34] the conveyance was to B for life "and at her death to descend and go to her children and heirs at law in fee simple." In applying the rule it is pointed out that since those taking in remainder were to take by descent the gift was to the heirs of the life tenant.

According to the English common law the word "heirs" is not used in a technical sense unless it is used to describe all the lineal heirs, or heirs of the body, of the ancestor, from generation to generation, *ad infinitum* —an indefinite line of succession.[35] For example, the rule is not applicable in a conveyance to B for life, then in fee to the heirs of the body of B living at the time of his death. This refers to heirs living at a particular time and not to heirs as meaning an indefinite line of succession. At the present time this interpretation of the meaning of the word "heirs" or "heirs of the body" would practically nullify an application of the rule in Shelley's case.[36] The prevailing American rule is that the words "heirs" or "heirs of the body" are used in a technical sense if used to describe persons entitled to succeed to the estate at the time of the death of the person named as ancestor.[37] The "indefinite line of succession" concept has been discarded.

Third: The rule does not apply unless the life estate in the ancestor and the purported remainder to his heirs are both legal or both equitable.[38] That is to say, they must be of the same quality.

This requirement is of particular importance if a conveyance is made in trust. If a trust is created with respect to the life estate of the ancestor, and the trust is to continue for the benefit of his heirs, then both estates are equitable and the rule applies. If the trust is to terminate upon the death of the ancestor then the rule does not apply. This follows from the fact that there is an equitable life estate and a legal remainder.[39]

Classification of Remainders

The feudal concept of seisin left a deep impression in the law as it relates to the classification of remainders, especially the rule that "seisin cannot be in abeyance." The successful operation of the feudal system depended upon the fact that at all times an identified person was in possession of the land claiming a freehold estate. Such a person was seised of the land and responsible for the rendition of the feudal dues and the performance of all obligations required according to the form of tenure involved.

In a conveyance A to B for life, remainder to C and his heirs, B is seised of the land in his own behalf and in behalf of C. The seisin of inheritance is held by B as a bailiff for C. Thus, upon the termination of B's life estate, whether by the death of B or by "premature termination" such as by forfeiture in case of a tortious feoffment, the seisin passes to C. Because of the fact that

---

not discussed); Hopkins v. Hopkins, 1909, 103 Tex. 15, 122 S.W. 15.

34. 195 Ark. 586, 113 S.W.2d 497 (1938).

35. Archer's Case, [1597] 1 Co. 66b, 76 Eng.Rep. 146. See English's Estate, 1921, 270 Pa. 1, 112 A. 913; Aetna Life Ins. Co. v. Hoppin, 7 Cir., 1914, 214 F. 928.

36. See Jonas v. Jones, 1941, 153 Kan. 108, 109 P.2d 211 (the rule in Shelley's case was not abolished until after the effective date of this decision); Donald v. Troxell, Tex.Civ.App.1961, 346 S.W.2d 398; Crawford v. Barber, Wyo.1963, 385 P.2d 655.

37. See 3 Rest. Property, § 312, *Comment f.*

38. In re Walton's Estate, 1962, 409 Pa. 225, 186 A.2d 32.

39. In re Johnson's Estate, 1937, 192 Wash. 439, 73 P.2d 755. See 1 Bogert, Trusts and Trustees, § 207; 3 Rest. Property, § 312, *Comment h.*

there is no possibility of a break in the continuity of seisin (no possibility of a gap), the estate in C is described as a *vested remainder*.[40]

In the early development of the law only vested remainders were recognized. If there was a *possibility* of a break in the continuity of seisin the remainder was described as contingent and void. However, sometime between 1388 and 1453 the validity of a contingent remainder was established.[41] Of course, if a gap actually occurred the remainder was destroyed.[42]

Recognition was first extended in the case of a conveyance A to B for life, remainder to the heirs of C, a living person. The remainder to C is contingent because there is a possibility of a gap. For example, there would be a gap if the life estate in B terminated prior to the time of C's death. This follows from the fact that the identity of C's heirs cannot be ascertained until the time of C's death. Later, recognition was extended to other types of contingent remainders.

Technical difficulties were encountered in connection with the recognition of contingent remainders. Primarily, difficulty was encountered in determining where the "seisin of inheritance" was pending the happening of the event. It did not remain in the conveyor because further act was not required on his part to place the estate in the remainderman. Because of the contingency the life tenant did not have the seisin of inheritance as a bailiff for the remainderman. The difficulty was resolved by resort to the fiction that

pending the happening of the event the seisin was in a state of suspended animation.[43]

The historical classification of remainders is followed at the present time and both vested and contingent remainders are recognized. A remainder is vested if there is no possibility of a gap or break in the continuity of seisin. A contingent remainder is indicated if there is a possibility of a gap.

In classifying remainders consideration is given to the ancient rule that a life estate may be terminated by forfeiture even though this method of termination is not recognized at the present time. For example, in a conveyance A to B for life, remainder to the heirs of B, the heirs of B acquire a contingent remainder if the rule in Shelley's case has been abolished.[44] This is true even though, in fact, there is no possibility of a gap or break in the continuity of the seisin. The heirs of B will be ascertained at the instant of his death. However, considering the fact that the life estate may be terminated otherwise than by the death of B the remainder is contingent.

Of necessity, a remainder must be classified as contingent if the remainderman cannot be identified. That is the case, for example, in a conveyance A to B for life, remainder to the heirs of C, a living person. The remainderman cannot be identified until the death of C and the remainder must, of necessity, continue to be contingent until that time. That is also the situation in the case of a gift A to B for life, remainder to the children of B "who shall attain the age of twenty-one years." Attainment of the stated

---

40. In connection with the classification of remainders, see 2 Rest. Property, § 157.

41. See Gulliver, Cases and Materials on Future Interests, p. 59.

42. See infra, note 49.

43. See Gulliver, Cases and Materials on Future Interests, p. 197.

44. But see Moore v. Littel, 1869, 41 N.Y. 66 (decided under a statutory definition of vested remainders).

age is a part of the description of the remainderman.[45]

A classification problem may be presented even if the remainderman is identified. A contingency may be attached to the gift. A contingent remainder is involved in a conveyance A to B for life remainder to C if he reaches the age of twenty-one. However, the remainder is not contingent in a conveyance A to B for life, remainder to C and his heirs, but if C fails to attain the age of twenty-one then to D and his heirs. The remainder in C is vested subject to being divested if he fails to reach the stated age. A combination of these provisions is found in the conveyance before the court for construction in the early English case of Edwards v. Hammond.[46] The language is A to B for life, remainder to C and his heirs "if he live to the age of 21 years; provided, and upon condition, that if he dies before 21," then to D and his heirs. The court held that "taking all the words together, this was not a condition precedent, but a present devise * * * subject to and defeasible by the condition subsequent, scil. his not attaining the age of 21 * * *." A further discussion of problems relating to the classification of remainders is to be found under various headings, such as remedies available to the owners of future interests, requirements of survivorship, class gifts and the Rule against Perpetuities.

There are situations where a future interest created in one other than a conveyor cannot be classified as a remainder. That is the case, for example, if there is absolute certainty of a gap or break in the continuity of seisin. Such a situation exists in a conveyance A to B for life and one day after the death of B then to C and his heirs. Another

example is presented in a case where the future interest follows an estate in fee simple. According to common law rules, a remainder cannot be limited after an estate in fee simple. Still a third example exists in a case where the future interest is to take effect in defeasance of a prior estate. These future interests that cannot be classified as remainders are recognized as executory interests made possible by the passage of the Statute of Uses [47] and are discussed under a separate heading.[48]

Destructibility of Contingent Remainders

According to the English common law the recognition of a contingent remainder depends upon the continued existence of the supporting freehold estate (the particular estate of freehold). In a conveyance A to B for life, remainder to the heirs of C (a living person), the remainder is destroyed if the life estate terminates prior to the death of C. Otherwise there would be a break in the continuity of seisin (seisin would be in abeyance) from the time of the termination of the life estate until the death of C when the remainderman could be ascertained.

The termination of a life estate does not depend upon the death of the life tenant. In addition to such a natural termination of the life estate, a premature termination may be brought about in either of two ways. In the first place, the life estate may be terminated by a tortious feoffment. Under the feudal system a life tenant was under a duty of loyalty to the overlord. A tortious feoffment involved a breach of this duty with a resultant forfeiture of the life estate. While the life tenant may have a right to convey the life estate he does not have a right to convey the estate in fee. This rule of pre-

---

45. Festing v. Allen, [1843] 12 Mees. & W. 279, 152 Eng.Rep. 1204.

46. 3 Lev. 132, 83 Eng.Rep. 614 (1683).

47. 27 Hen. VIII, c. 10 (1536).

48. See infra, § 141.

mature termination was followed even after the concept of loyalty ceased to be a factor.[49] In the second place, a premature termination of a life estate may be brought about by surrender. That is to say, the life estate may be surrendered to the owner of the reversion.[50]

The common law recognizes a means by which a conveyor may prevent the destruction of a contingent remainder by the premature termination of a life estate. The conveyor may provide that if the life estate is terminated prematurely the property is to vest in a trustee or trustees until the death of the life tenant. This may be designated as a trust to preserve contingent remainders.[51] If the legal title is held by a trustee a break in the seisin does not result even if there is a gap in connection with the equitable estate. This is also the case if the subject matter of a conveyance is an equitable interest, such as land that is subject to a mortgage.[52] According to common law rules the legal title to mortgaged property is in the mortgagee. It is also to be noted that the doctrine of destructibility has no application if the remainder relates to chattels real or chattels personal. The concept of seisin is not associated with such interests.

The passage of the Statute of Uses in 1536 made possible the creation of a new type of future estate designated as an executory interest. The doctrine of destructibility is not applicable to such an interest. However, the Statute of Uses did not put an end to the destructibility rule. The courts declared that if a future interest could be construed to be a remainder, as distinguished from an executory interest, the remainder-construction was to be followed.[53] In other words, destructibility could not be avoided by the simple device of construing a gift to be an executory interest.

In England the doctrine of destructibility of contingent remainders has been abolished by statute. Destructibility by premature termination was abolished in 1844[54] and destructibility by natural termination of the particular estate was abolished in 1877.[55]

The doctrine of destructibility has been abolished by statute in a majority of the American states. In a few states the doctrine has been repudiated by judicial decision.[56] However, decisions recognizing the doctrine are to be found in Florida, Oregon, Pennsylvania and Tennessee.[57]

Alienation of Remainders

A vested remainder is transmissible at death and is alienable *inter vivos*.[58] At one time it was considered that a contingent remainder was a "mere possibility" and inalienable. There was also fear that to permit alienation would encourage champerty and maintenance. Gradually, exceptions to the rule against alienation were recognized. The

---

49. Chudleigh's Case, [1590] 1 Co.Rep. 120a, 76 Eng. Rep. 270; Archer's Case, [1598] 1 Co.Rep. 66b, 76 Eng.Rep. 146.

50. For a discussion of merger see Gulliver, Cases and Materials on Future Interests, p. 204.

51. Abbis v. Burney, [1881] 17 Ch.Div. 211.

52. Astley v. Micklethwait, [1880] 15 Ch.Div. 59; In re Freme, [1891] 3 Ch.Div. 167.

53. See Purefoy v. Rogers, [1670] 2 Wm. Saunders, 380, 2 Lev. 39, 85 Eng.Rep. 1181; White v. Summers, [1908] 2 Ch. 256. *Cf.:* In re Lechmere and Lloyd, [1881] 18 Ch.Div. 524.

54. 8 & 9 Vict., c. 106, § 8 (1844).

55. 40, 41 Vict., c. 33 (1877).

56. Indiana, Kansas, New Hampshire, Oklahoma and Hawaii.

57. See Simes and Smith, Future Interests (2nd Ed.) § 209, p. 244.

58. Bishop v. Horney, 1939, 177 Md. 353, 9 A.2d 597 (vested subject to being divested). For an enumeration of statutes declaring this to be the rule, see 2 Rest. Property, § 162, *Comment a.*

interest was considered to be sufficiently substantial in nature to be transmissible at death
if survivorship was not the contingency involved.[59]   One conveying a contingent remainder by warranty deed was estopped to
deny the validity of the transaction.[60] It was
also recognized that a contingent remainder
may be release to a person in interest.[61]

Either by statute or otherwise it is now
generally recognized that contingent remainders are freely alienable either by will, intestate succession or by *inter vivos* conveyance.[62] Of course, the estate is not transmissible at death if survivorship is the contingency involved. In some jurisdictions it is
held that a remainder is not alienable *inter
vivos* if the contingency pertains to the identity of the remainderman.[63] In any event, a
person to whom the remainder is conveyed
takes it subject to defeasance as expressed in
the instrument that created the remainder.[64]

Vested remainders may be reached to satisfy the claims of creditors. That is also true
as to contingent remainders that are freely alienable *inter vivos*.[65] In some decisions
a contrary conclusion is reached with respect
to contingent remainders that are alienable
only by a warranty deed or by release to a
person in interest.[66] In In re Landis (Fed.),[67]
a question is raised as to the rights of a
trustee in bankruptcy with respect to a contingent remainder owned by the bankrupt.
A federal statute provided that the trustee
shall be vested by operation of law with the
title of the bankrupt to all property which,
prior to the filing of the petition, he could
by any means have transferred or which
might have been levied upon and sold under
judicial process against him.[68] The court
held that since the interest was transferable
under local law (Illinois) by estoppel, contract of sale or equitable assignment, it passed
to the trustee. Contrary to the rule declared
in this case, there is authority for the view
that the statute is applicable only if the
interest is alienable by quitclaim deed to one
having no other interest in the land.[69]

POSSIBILITY OF REVERTER

**139. A possibility of reverter is the interest
retained by one who conveys a determinable
estate or a fee simple conditional. The possibility of reverter ripens into a possessory estate
upon the happening of the named event. If the
event pertains to land use it may be nullified
because of changed conditions in the area.**

**a. Alienation. The general rule is that the
possibility of reverter is alienable *inter
vivos* and is subject to general rules relating to testate and intestate succession.**

---

59. Loring v. Arnold, 1887, 15 R.I. 428, 8 A. 335.

60. Robertson v. Wilson, 1859, 38 N.H. 48.

61. Jeffers v. Lampson, 1859, 10 Ohio St. 101. *Cf.:*
De Bois v. Judy, 1920, 291 Ill. 340, 126 N.E. 104
(the life tenant is not a "person in interest" within
the meaning of the rule).

62. Putnam v. Story, 1882, 132 Mass. 205; Grimes
v. Rush, 1946, 355 Mo. 573, 197 S.W.2d 310; 2 Rest.
Property, § 162 (*inter vivos*), § 165 (testate succession).

63. Todd v. Williford, 1929, 169 Ga. 543, 150 S.E.
912; Prince v. Barham, 1920, 127 Va. 462, 103 S.E.
626. See Suskin & Berry v. Rumley, 4 Cir., 1930, 37
F.2d 304, 68 A.L.R. 768. For a criticism of this
view, see note 21 Ore.Law Rev. 81 (1941).

64. Hall v. Wright, 1911, 17 Cal.App. 502, 120 P. 429.

65. *Cf.:* Anglo California Nat. Bank v. Kidd, 1943, 58
Cal.App.2d 651, 137 P.2d 460 (involving an equitable
estate).

66. Plumlee v. Bounds, 1915, 118 Ark. 274, 176 S.W.
140; Caples v. Ward, 1915, 107 Tex. 341, 179 S.W.
856 (*dictum*).

67. 41 F.2d 700 (7 Cir., 1930), certiorari denied Farmers' Bank of Mount Pulaski, Ill. v. Bickenbach, 282
U.S. 872, 51 S.Ct. 77, 75 L.Ed. 770.

68. 11 U.S.C.A. § 110(a) (5).

69. 2 Rest. Property, § 166. See Suskin & Berry, Inc.
v. Rumley, 4 Cir., 1930, 37 F.2d 304, 68 A.L.R. 768.

b. Condemnation award. In general, the owner of a possibility of reverter is not entitled to share in a condemnation award if the proceedings involve a fee simple determinable.

If the owner of an estate in fee simple absolute conveys a determinable fee [70] the interest retained is a possibility of reverter.[71] That is also the interest retained after the conveyance of a fee simple conditional.[72] The possibility of reverter ripens into a possessory estate immediately upon the happening of the named event. In this respect it differs from a power of termination (right of entry) that arises upon the conveyance of an estate subject to a condition subsequent.[73] The power of termination must be asserted in order to terminate the possessory estate.

As in the case of a power of termination, equitable relief may be available to prevent alleged termination of a determinable estate.[74] There may be a waiver of rights that would otherwise arise upon the happening of the named event. There is also authority indicating the view that if the event involves restrictions respecting the use of land the restrictions may be nullified by changed conditions in the area.[75]

Alienation

There is substantial authority for the rule that a possibility of reverter is not alienable

inter vivos.[76] This is the statutory rule in some states.[77] However, the interest may be released to the owner of the possessory estate.[78] It is frequently stated that the interest is not alienable because it is in the nature of a mere expectancy. A rule against alienation *inter vivos* reduces the value and importance of the interest insofar as "clearing title" is concerned. But the preferred view is that a possibility of reverter is freely alienable *inter vivos.*[79] In this respect a distinction is not made between a possibility of reverter and a reversion.[80] This is the statutory rule in a number of states.[81]

The general rule is that a possibility of reverter is subject to testamentary disposition and in the absence thereof passes according to the rules of intestate succession.[82]

Condemnation Award

In general, the owner of a possibility of reverter is not entitled to share in a condem-

---

70. For discussion of a fee simple determinable, see supra, § 90.

71. See Simes & Smith, Future Interests (2nd Ed.), § 281, p. 327.

72. For discussion of a fee simple conditional estate, see supra, § 89.

73. See infra, § 140.

74. See infra, § 140.

75. See Wedum-Aldahl Co. v. Miller, 1937, 18 Cal. App.2d 745, 64 P.2d 762; Cole v. Colorado Springs Co., 1963, 152 Colo. 162, 381 P.2d 13.

76. Lynch v. Bunting, 1942, 47 Del. 171, 29 A.2d 155 (*dictum*); Pond v. Douglas, 1910, 106 Me. 85, 75 A. 320 (*dictum*); Magness v. Kerr, 1927, 121 Or. 373, 254 P. 1012, 51 A.L.R. 1466; Purvis v. McElveen, 1959, 234 S.C. 94, 106 S.E.2d 913.

77. See, for example, Ill.—S.H.A. ch. 30, § 37b.

78. Atkins v. Gillespie, 1927, 156 Tenn. 137, 299 S.W. 776.

79. See, for example, Richardson v. Holman, 1948, 160 Fla. 65, 33 So.2d 641, noted in 1 Univ. of Florida Law Rev. 309 (1948); Collette v. Town of Charlotte, 1946, 114 Vt. 357, 45 A.2d 203. See also, Jensen v. Wilkinson, Tex.Civ.App.1939, 133 S.W.2d 982, error dismissed, judgment correct, noted in 18 Tex. Law Rev. 344 (1940) (subject to sale on execution).

80. See 2 Rest. Property, § 159, *Comment a.*

81. See, for example, Pavkovich v. Southern Pacific Ry. Co., 1906, 150 Cal. 39, 87 P. 1097; Battistone v. Banulski, 1929, 110 Conn. 267, 147 A. 820, noted in 39 Yale Law Jr. 910 (1930); Application of Mareck v. Hoffman, 1960, 257 Minn. 222, 100 N.W.2d 758 (construing Minn.Stat.Ann. § 500.16, as amended 1937).

82. 2 Rest. Property, §§ 164, 165. But see Purvis v. McElveen, 1959, 234 S.C. 94, 106 S.E.2d 913.

nation award if the proceedings involve a fee simple determinable.[83] There is no reasonable means by which to evaluate the interest. Further, compliance with the terms of the conveyance by the owner of the possessory estate is prevented by operation of law. However these objections are not present in a case where the event terminating the possessory estate occurred prior to the institution of the proceedings. In that event the possibility of reverter has ripened into a possessory estate in fee simple.[84] Further, the owner of a possibility of reverter may be entitled to share in the award if it appears reasonably certain that the event terminating the estate will occur within a comparatively short period of time.[85]

POWER OF TERMINATION

140. Upon the conveyance of an estate subject to a condition subsequent a power of termination (right of entry) is created in the conveyor. Under some circumstances equitable relief may be available to prevent forfeiture.

The usual method of exercising a power of termination is by instituting legal proceedings to recover possession of the land.

   a. Alienability of the power of termination. According to the English common law a power of termination is transmissible at death but is not alienable *inter vivos*. However, it may be released to the owner of the possessory estate. An English statute,

passed in 1540, provides that a power of termination contained in a lease may be enforced by one who acquires the reversion. This is a part of the adopted common law in practically all of the American states. Statutes in many states provide that the power of termination is alienable under all circumstances.

   b. Condemnation award. In general, the owner of a power of termination is not entitled to share in an award resulting from condemnation proceedings that involve an estate subject to a condition subsequent.

Upon the conveyance of an estate subject to a condition subsequent a power of termination (right of entry) is created in the conveyor.[86] Even if there is a breach of the condition the estate continues in the grantee or devisee until such time as the power of termination is exercised. Because of the fact that a breach of condition may result in a forfeiture of the estate a rule of strict construction is followed in determining the scope of a stated condition.[87] If possible, language in a conveying instrument will be construed as promissory rather than conditional.[88]

Equitable relief against forfeiture may be available if delay in the performance of a condition is caused by unforeseen difficulties.[89] This may also be true in a case where the condition involves the payment of money and failure to make timely payment was unintentional and, without unreasonable delay, proper tender is made.[90] There may be a

83. People v. City of Fresno, 1962, 210 Cal.App.2d 500, 26 Cal.Rptr. 853; First Reformed Dutch Church v. Croswell, 1924, 210 App.Div. 294, 206 N.Y.S. 132, noted in 25 Col.Law Rev. 101 (1925), 9 Minn.Law Rev. 293. *Cf.:* State v. Federal Square Corp., 1938, 89 N.H. 538, 3 A.2d 109 (the conveying instrument provided that the estate was to terminate if the land should be condemned).

84. Romero v. Dept. of Public Works, 1941, 17 Cal.2d 189, 109 P.2d 662, noted in 29 Cal.Law Rev. 525 (1941).

85. United States v. 2,184.81 Acres of Land, D.Ark. 1942, 45 F.Supp. 681, noted in 43 Col.Law Rev. 137 (1943); 1 Rest. Property, § 53, *Comments b, c.*

86. 2 Rest. Property, § 155.

87. See Central Land Co. v. City of Grand Rapids, 1942, 302 Mich. 105, 4 N.W.2d 485.

88. See supra, § 93.

89. Peek v. Woman's Home Missionary Society, 1922, 304 Ill. 427, 136 N.E. 772, 26 A.L.R. 917, noted in 36 Harv.Law Rev. 758 (1923).

90. Dodsworth v. Dodsworth, 1912, 254 Ill. 49, 98 N.E. 279.

waiver with respect to the breach of a condition.[91] There is also authority for the view that forfeiture will be denied if the condition relates to the use of land and a change in the character of the locality would make enforcement inequitable and unjust.[92] The applicable rules are similar to those applied in a situation involving a possibility of reverter.[93] There is no prescribed time within which a power of termination must be exercised. However, in a few states statutes have been enacted limiting the time for the duration of such a power.[94] Even in the absence of statute a waiver may result if there is an unreasonable delay in asserting the power after breach of the condition.[95]

At one time the exercise of a power of termination required actual entry upon the land. In modern times this is not required. In fact, actual entry upon the land without a court order would probably result in liability. The usual method of exercising a power of termination is by instituting legal proceedings to recover possession of the land. According to some decisions it is indicated that the owner of the possessory estate is entitled to some notice of termination prior to such an action.[96]

Alienability of the Power of Termination

Except as noted, the English common law rule is that a power of termination is not alienable *inter vivos*. This is also a part of the adopted common law in a majority of the American states. There is early authority for the view that this estate is not transmissible at death, the heir being entitled to the benefit because he is the "continuing personality" of the ancestor.[97]

This conclusion conforms to the early concept that a power of termination is a "mere possibility" and not an estate or interest of any kind. Even a cause of action (a right) was not then transferable for reasons of policy, it being considered that sanction would encourage champerty and maintenance. So strong was the policy against alienation that authority developed that an attempt to alienate a power of termination by *inter vivos* transfer resulted in its destruction.[98] This conclusion grew out of a misapprehension of an early English statute that imposed criminal sanction in cases of attempted transfer and does not represent the prevailing rule in the United States.[99] A power of termination may also be released to the owner of the possessory estate. Additional rules relating to

---

91. Los Angeles, etc., Land Co. v. Marr, 1921, 187 Cal. 126, 200 P. 1051 (accepting payment with knowledge of an existing breach of condition).

92. Cole v. Colorado Springs Co., 1963, 152 Colo. 162, 381 P.2d 13. *Cf.:* Strong v. Shatto, 1919, 45 Cal. App. 29, 187 P. 159.

93. See supra, § 139.

94. For discussion of the statutory rules, see Simes & Smith, Future Interests (2nd Ed.), § 1994.

95. Robinson v. Cannon, 1940, 346 Mo. 1126, 145 S.W. 2d 146. See note, Re-entry Barred by Passage of Time, 13 Univ. of Pittsburgh Law Rev. 716 (1952).

96. See Simes & Smith, Future Interests (2nd Ed.) § 255.

97. Upington v. Corrigan, 1896, 151 N.Y. 143, 45 N.E. 359.

98. Rice v. Boston & Worcester Railroad, 1866, 94 Mass. (12 Allen) 141; Dolby v. Dillman, 1938, 283 Mich. 609, 278 N.W. 694, 117 A.L.R. 538 (changed by statute passed in 1931, see Mich.Comp.Laws 1948, § 554.111); Wagner v. Wallowa County, 1915, 76 Or. 453, 148 P. 1140. *Cf.:* New York City v. Coney Island Fire Dept., 1939, 170 Misc. 787, 10 N.Y.S.2d 164 (corporate merger or consolidation); Union Colony Co. v. Gallie, 1939, 104 Colo. 46, 88 P.2d 120. Rest. of the Law, 1948 Supplement, p. 714, § 160, *Comment e* (dissolution of a partnership).

99. Jones v. Oklahoma City, 1943, 193 Okl. 637, 145 P.2d 971; Restatement of the Law, 1948 Supplement, p. 415, § 160, where additional authorities are discussed.

alienation are discussed in the following paragraphs:

First: A power of termination may pass by inheritance and may be devised.[1] Also, it may be released to the owner of the possessory estate.[2]

In Bouvier v. Baltimore & N. Y. Ry. Co., (N. J.),[3] it is held that the power of termination can be alienated *inter vivos* after there has been a breach of the condition. Under such circumstances the interest has ceased to be a mere possibility and, being an existing right, it is assignable and transferable.[4]

Second: By Statute 32 Hen. VIII,[5] passed in 1540, a power of termination is declared to be alienable *inter vivos* if it is attached to a reversion and if the alienation includes an assignment of the reversion. This rule is a part of the adopted common law in practically all of the American states. The power of termination gives a lessor a means by which to enforce covenants in a lease, such as a covenant to pay rent. The statute makes it possible for the lessor to transfer a means of enforcement to one who acquires the reversion and the right to the benefit of covenants in the lease.

Third: Statutes have been enacted in many states making a power of termination freely alienable under all circumstances.[6]

There is also authority for the view that an undivided interest in a power of termination may be conveyed. This procedure may be used as a means by which to give property owners in a subdivision a means by which to enforce restrictions.[7]

Condemnation Award

In general, the owner of a power of termination is not entitled to share in an award resulting from condemnation proceedings that involve an estate subject to a condition subsequent.[8] There is no reasonable means by which to evaluate the interest. In addition, the owner of the possessory estate is not a free actor with respect to the use of the land after it has been condemned.[9] However, these factors cease to be of controlling importance if the condition has been breached at the time condemnation proceedings are instituted or if it appears reasonably certain that the condition would have been breached within a comparatively short period of time. Under such circumstances the owner of the power of termination is entitled to share in the award.[10]

EXECUTORY INTERESTS

141. According to the English common law, a remainder is the only type of future interest that can be created by a transferor in favor of

---

1.   2 Rest. Property, §§ 164, 165, *Comment a*, Illust. 5. See Roberts, Assignability of Possibilities of Reverter and Rights of Re-Entry, 22 Bost.Univ.Law Rev. 43, 45 (1942).

2.   Calvary Presbyterian Church v. Putnam, 1928, 249 N.Y. 111, 162 N.E. 601, noted in 27 Mich.Law Rev. 346 (1929), 8 Ore.Law Rev. 86 (1928), 37 Yale Law Jr. 530 (1928).

3.   67 N.J.L. 281, 51 A. 781 (1902).

4.   Alienability before breach was apparently permitted by statute.

5.   32 Hen. VIII, c. 34, § 1 (1540).

6.   For a compilation of statutory provisions, see 2 Rest. Property, § 160, *Comment (d)*.

7.   Shields v. Bank of America Nat. Trust & Savings Ass'n, 1964, 225 Cal.App.2d 330, 37 Cal.Rptr. 360.

8.   United States v. 2,086 Acres of Land, D.S.Car.1942, 46 F.Supp. 411. Award may be proper if there is proof of special damages. See Romero v. Dept. of Public Works, 1941, 17 Cal.2d 189, 109 P.2d 662 (apparently the case involves a fee simple determinable).

9.   See Board of Com'rs of Mahoning County v. Young, 6 Cir. 1893, 59 F. 96 (where use of land for purpose stated was prohibited by law).

10.   See 1 Rest. Property, § 53, *Comments c and d*. But see, In re Coney Island Fire Dept., Inc., 1927, 222 App.Div. 678, 224 N.Y.S. 776, discussed in City of New York v. Coney Island Fire Dept., 1940, 259 App.Div. 286, 18 N.Y.S.2d 923.

another. However, the Statute of Uses, passed in 1536, made possible the creation of a new type of future interest, called an executory interest. Such an interest could also be created by will after the passage of the Statute of Wills in 1540. Executory interests are recognized in all of the American states.

According to the English common law, a remainder is the only type of future interest that can be created by a transferor in favor of another. However, the creation of a new type of future interest, called an executory interest, was made possible by the passage of the Statute of Uses in 1536.[11] Unlike contingent remainders, an executory interest is not destructible.[12] It is also to be noted that the historical classification of remainders as being vested or contingent is not followed as to executory interests. An executory interest is not considered to be vested until the time that it becomes possessory. Executory interests are recognized in all of the American states either because of the adopted common law or because of express statutory authorization.

In the early English case of Purefoy v. Rogers,[13] the rule is declared that if an interest can be construed to be a remainder that construction will be followed rather than a construction that it is an executory interest.[14] This perpetuated the law as it related to the destruction of contingent remainders. How-

ever, some interests cannot be classified as remainders. Examples are as follows:

First: A remainder cannot be limited after an estate in fee simple. It is considered that nothing remains that would furnish substance to such a future interest. In Bryan v. Spires (Pa.),[15] in consideration of $1,000 A conveyed an undivided one-half interest in a farm to his son, James, and his heirs. The deed provided that if James died without children and possessed of the property the estate was to vest in his brother Hannibal and his heirs. James died while still "possessed of the title" and Hannibal claimed ownership under the deed. In sustaining this view it is pointed out that the conveyance created a use in Hannibal that was executed under the Statute of Uses. Thus, even though the interest could not be classified as a remainder it could be sustained as an executory interest.

Second: A future interest cannot be classified as a remainder if there is absolute certainty of a gap or break in the continuity of seisin at the time of the termination of the preceding estate of freehold. That is the case, for example, in a conveyance A to B for life and one year after the death of B to C and his heirs.[16] Accordingly, such a conveyance creates an executory interest in C.

Third: An interest cannot properly be classified as a remainder if it is to take effect in *defeasance* of the supporting life estate. Under such circumstances it cannot be said that the life tenant is a bailiff of the seisin for the remainderman. In the English case of Blackman v. Fysh,[17] A devised land to his son for life and then to the children of the son "whether now or hereafter to be born who shall live to attain the age of twenty-one

---

11. 27 Hen. VIII, c. 10 (1536). For discussion of this statute see supra, § 3. An executory interest, called an executory devise, could also be created by will after the passage of the Statute of Wills in 1540 (32 Henn. VIII, c. 1).

12. Pells v. Brown, [1620] Cro.Jac. 590, 79 Eng.Rep. 504.

13. 2 Wm.Saund. 380, 85 Eng.Rep. 1181 (1670).

14. White v. Summers, [1908] 2 Ch. 256. *Cf.:* In re Lechmere & Lloyd, [1881] 18 Ch.Div. 524. See also, Hayward v. Spaulding, 1908, 75 N.H. 92, 71 A. 219.

15. 3 Brewst.(Pa.) 580 (1869).

16. See Roe d. Wilkinson v. Tranmer, [1757] 2 Wils. 75, 95 Eng.Rep. 694.

17. 2 Ch.Div. 209, 67 L.T. 802 (1892).

years, or who, being a daughter, shall marry under that age * * * " Up to this point the interest created in the children would be a remainder and only those who qualified under the gift prior to the death of the son would be entitled to take because of the destructibility rule.[18] However, the will further provided that in the event the son attempted to sell or encumber his estate it was to terminate. Thus, under this contingency the gift over was not to take effect at the natural termination of the life estate but was to take effect in defeasance of the estate in the life tenant. Accordingly, the court held that the children acquired an executory interest.

PARTITION AND JUDICIAL SALE

142. **In judicial proceedings involving the ownership of property unborn children may be represented by identified persons who have the same interest as the unborn child. This doctrine of virtual representation applies only if there are no conflicting interests as between the "representative" and the "represented."**

    a. **Partition. In general, compulsory partition is available only in the case of concurrent owners of a possessory estate. In a substantial number of states it is now provided by statute that compulsory partition is available to concurrent owners of future interests.**

    b. **Judicial sale. A court of equity may order the sale of land in fee simple absolute if this is necessary to preserve interests in the property. It is not controlling that such a sale results in the extinguishment of future interests or that the owner of an interest in the property objects to such sale. In many states this matter is regulated by statute.**

All persons having an interest in property have a right to receive notice of pending judicial proceedings pertaining to that property. They also have a right to appear and defend their interests. These are the basic requirements of due process. Problems relating to notice etc., frequently arise in proceedings that relate to the construction of a conveying instrument, such as a deed or a will. They are also of importance in proceedings that involve partition or the judicial sale of property.

Procedural difficulties are encountered in proceedings that involve the rights of unborn children. For example, in a conveyance A to B for life, remainder to B's children, those eventually entitled to the property cannot be ascertained until the time of B's death. However, unborn children may be bound by a decree relating to construction, partition or sale of the property. This may be accomplished under the doctrine of virtual representation. Living members of the class, if any, may be said to represent those yet unborn. This rule is applicable if there are no conflicting interests as between the "representatives" and the "represented." [19] If there are no living members of the class there is authority for the view that the life tenant, B, may represent her unborn children.[20] Application of the doctrine of virtual representation will be denied if there is evidence of fraud. In some states it is provided by statute that a court appointed guardian may represent unborn children.[21]

Partition

In general, compulsory partition is available only in the case of concurrent owners of

---

18. Assuming that the doctrine of destructibility had not been abolished at the time the interests were created. See Festing v. Allen, [1843] 12 M. & W. 279, 152 Eng.Rep. 1204.

19. See Weberpals v. Jenny, 1921, 300 Ill. 145, 133 N.E. 62. See infra, § 151.

20. See 2 Rest. Property, § 184(d).

21. See, for example, West's Ann.Cal.Code Civ.Proc., § 373.5.

a possessory estate.[22] For this purpose, a "possessory estate" is involved even if it is subject to a lease.[23] Future interests are not disturbed by such proceedings. It would seem, however, that if A and B are concurrent owners of an estate in fee simple, A cannot be denied his right to compulsory partition by the act of B in creating a future interest with respect to his undivided interest.

In a substantial number of states it is now provided by statute that, under varying circumstances, compulsory partition is available to concurrent owners of future interests. This is usually true only with respect to interests that are absolutely vested. Partition of future interests does not necessarily effect the owner of a possessory estate, such as a life tenant. Of course, if the owner of a particular estate consents, the estate may be sold in fee simple absolute. Failure of a life tenant to object to a sale of the estate in fee may be construed as tacit approval of the sale on his part.[24]

Judicial Sale

In Gavin v. Curtin (Ill.),[25] testator devised a one-fourth interest in land to each of his three sons. The remaining one-fourth interest was devised to his daughter for life followed by contingent remainders. The daughter filed a bill in equity seeking a court order authorizing a sale of the land in fee simple. It is alleged that because of the existence of a mortgage on part of the property and lack of income derived from the land there was a danger that the land would be sold for taxes. In authorizing the sale the court follows the general rule that such relief is available if

this "is necessary" to preserve interests in the property.[26] In some cases it is stated that a sale may be ordered if this is for the "best interests" of the parties.[27] It is not controlling that the sale will result in an extinguishment of future interests in the land or that some of the interested parties object to the sale. Similar relief may be granted at the instance of the owner of a future interest, such as a remainderman, over objection of the life tenant.[28]

Statutes have been enacted in a substantial number of states authorizing the sale of land even though it is subject to designated future interests.[29] The statutes vary in type from one that restricts such sale in various ways to one that authorizes a sale and reinvestment of funds at the instance of either the owner of a possessory estate or the owner of even a contingent future interest.[30]

REMEDIES

143. Usually, the owner of a reversion or a vested remainder may maintain an action at law to recover damages for unauthorized acts that impair the value of the estate. Injunctive relief may also be available to prevent threatened acts. Injunctive relief is the only remedy available in the case of contingent remainders, possibilities of reverter and powers of termination. This is also generally true with respect to executory interests.

The owner of a reversion or a vested remainder may maintain an action to recover

22. Weddingfeld v. Weddingfeld, 1923, 109 Neb. 729, 192 N.W. 227.

23. See supra, § 137.

24. Baskins v. Krepcik, 1950, 153 Neb. 36, 43 N.W.2d 624.

25. 171 Ill. 640, 49 N.E. 523, 40 L.R.A. 776 (1898).

26. See Traversy v. Bell, 1923, 195 Iowa 1243, 193 N.W. 439; Rekovsky v. Glisczinski, 1928, 175 Minn. 531, 221 N.W. 906; 2 Rest. Property, § 179; Schnebly, Power of Life Tenant or Remainderman to Extinguish Other Interests by Judicial Process, 42 Harv.Law Rev. 30 (1928).

27. Wing v. Wing, 1948, 212 Ark. 960, 208 S.W.2d 776.

28. Beliveau v. Beliveau, 1944, 217 Minn. 225, 14 N.W. 2d 360.

29. See Simes & Smith, Future Interests (2nd Ed.), § 1946.

30. See West's Ann.Cal.Code Civ.Proc., §§ 752, 781.

damages for wrongful acts that cause a permanent damage to the land. However, recovery is limited to the damage caused to the plaintiff's interest.[31] Usually, the owner of a vested interest may maintain a suit in equity to enjoin threatened acts involving permanent damage to the land. However, an injunction may be denied if the probability of the reversioner acquiring a possessory estate is remote.[32]

An action to recover damages is not available to the owner of a contingent remainder[33] or an executory interest. The traditional remedy of the owner of a contingent interest is a suit in equity to enjoin the threatened acts.[34] In such proceedings, and upon proper motion, a judgment may be entered against the defendant for the payment of damages and the amount thereof may be held in a "court trust" for the benefit of the person who subsequently establishes a right thereto.[35] However the probability of vesting may be so remote that an injunction will be denied.[36]

Even if the owner of a contingent interest does have a remedy by way of an injunction, this will not bar an action at law to recover damages. The Statute of Limitations will not start to run against the owner of the contingent interest until his interest becomes vested. Until that time he does not have such a cause of action.[37]

The owner of a possibility of reverter or the power of termination may proceed in equity for an injunction to prevent acts that might reasonably cause damage to his interest.[38] Of course, it must be shown that the acts are not authorized by the nature of the defendant's estate or the terms of the conveyance.[39] Injunctive relief is also the usual remedy to protect the owner of an executory interest.

---

31. See Miller v. Edison Electric Illuminating Co., 1906, 184 N.Y. 17.

32. Hooper v. Barnes, 1896, 113 Cal. 636.

33. Latham v. Roanoke Ry. & Lumber Co., 1905, 139 N.C. 9, 51 S.E.2d 780.

34. Ohio Oil Co. v. Daughetee, 1909, 240 Ill. 361, 88 N.E. 818.

35. Watson v. Wolff-Goldman Realty Co., 1910, 95 Ark. 18, 128 S.W. 581.

36. Brown v. Brown, 1921, 89 W.Va. 339, 109 S.E. 815.

37. Rhoda v. Alameda County, 1933, 134 Cal.App. 726, 26 P.2d 691.

38. Union Missionary Baptist Church v. Fyke, 1937, 179 Okl. 102, 64 P.2d 1203 (possibility of reverter); Pavkovich v. Southern Pacific Ry. Co., 1906, 150 Cal. 39, 87 P. 1097 (power of termination).

39. See Regular Predestinarian Baptist Church v. Parker, 1940, 373 Ill. 607, 27 N.E.2d 522, 137 A.L.R. 635.

CHAPTER 28

FUTURE INTERESTS IN CHATTELS

Sec.
144. Chattels Real.
145. Chattels Personal.

CHATTELS REAL

144. Reversions, remainders, possibilities of reverter, powers of termination and executory interests may be created with respect to chattels real.

Leasehold estates formed no part of the feudal plan. While reversions resulting from subleases were recognized, there was lack of interest in the creation of other types of future interests in such estates. After the passage of the Statute *De Donis* in 1285 the fee tail estate was a convenient means by which property owners could avoid feudal obligations and assure retention of ownership of land within the family (heirs of the body) for an indefinite period of time.

But the tranquility of the "landed aristocracy" was disturbed in 1472 as a result of the decision in Taltarum's Case.[1] Judicial sanction was given to collusive legal proceedings (common recovery) as a means by which a fee tail could be converted into a fee simple absolute. The estate planners of the day directed their attention to the possible use of long term leases as a means by which to create workable family settlements.

This new technique by means of which to "tie up estates" received a cool judicial reception. In one of the early cases (1536),[2] the owner of a 40 years lease devised it to his eldest daughter, B, "and the heirs of her body." If she should die without issue "with-

in the term" it was to go to a second daughter, C, "in tail." The eldest daughter married but died during the term. Her surviving husband purported to assign the term and the question was raised as to the remedy, if any, available to the second daughter, C. In denying the existence of a remedy it is stated that "it is contrary to law that a term may be limited in remainder any more than other chattel personal, as a cup or other chattel."

An explanation is not given as to why the remainder was considered to be "contrary to law" but it is obvious that the court had no desire to encourage the creation of such future interests that might be used as an effective means of creating indestructible settlements. Estates tail were not involved because the Statute *De Donis* applied only with respect to estates in fee.

The invalidity of a remainder after a life estate in a term was based upon the false premise that a life estate is a "greater" estate than a term for years. Consequently, a gift of a life estate in the term leaves no estate that can be the subject matter of a remainder. It is true, in legal contemplation a *freehold life estate* is a greater estate than an estate for years. But a life estate in a term for years is not a freehold life estate. It is also obvious that a life estate in a term for years is not a greater estate in the sense that it is a "longer" estate. But this "technical" bar to the creation of a remainder after a life estate in a term was easily avoided by giving a determinable life estate. In that event the devise is not "of the entire estate."

1. Y.B. 12 Edw. 4, Mich. Term, pl. 25 (1472).

2. Anonymous, K.B., [1536] 1 Dyer 7a, 73 Eng.Rep. 17.

Under such circumstances a remainder was sustained in Welcden v. Elkington (Eng.),[3] where the owner of a term devised it to his wife "for as many of the years as she shall live," with remainder over to the testator's son.

It became the established rule in England that the owner of a term could devise a life estate in the term, followed by an executory devise as to the portion of the term remaining at the time of the death of the life tenant.[4] Not only was the executory interest held to be valid but it was also held to be indestructible. Successive life estates could also be created by will, the personal representative of the testator having an interest designated as a possibility of reverter.[5] There is lack of authority as to whether or not these future interests, could be created by deed. While chancery jurisdiction existed in connection with the interpretation of wills thus assuring a liberal interpretation as a means by which to carry out the intention of the testator, there is nothing to indicate that the same conclusions would not have been reached by the courts of law in the interpretation of *inter vivos* conveyances.

The prevailing American rule is that valid future interests in a chattel real may be created by deed or will. A valid life estate may be created in a chattel real and there may be a valid limitation in remainder.[6]

CHATTELS PERSONAL

145. **Reversions, remainders, possibilities of reverter, powers of termination and executory interests may be created with respect to chattels personal that are not consumable by use.**

     a. **Chattels consumable by use. Some authorities support the view that future interests can be created with respect to chattels consumable by use if the gift involves stock in trade or is embodied in a residuary clause.**

     b. **Presence or absence of a gift over. In some decisions it is held that the gift of a life estate in chattels personal is a gift of absolute ownership unless there is a gift over after the life estate.**

     c. *Inter vivos* **gift. The validity of an** *inter vivos* **gift of chattels personal depends upon proof of actual, constructive or symbolic delivery. This is also true if the purpose is to make a gift of a future interest in such property.**

     d. **Security requirement. The owner of a possessory interest in personal property may be required to give security for the protection of owners of future interests in the same property.**

     e. **Construction. Many of the technical rules of construction relating to conveyances of freehold estates are not applicable in the case of chattels personal. That is the case with respect to the rule in Shelley's case. And a conveyance that would create an estate tail in land will create absolute ownership in the case of chattels personal.**

In 1641 an English court was called upon to determine the validity of a bequest of goods by a husband to his wife for life, with remainder over to a third party.[7] In denying the validity of the purported remainder the theory is advanced that personal property is not susceptible to "successive ownership." It is pointed out, however, that if

---

3.   2 Plowd. 516, 75 Eng.Rep. 763 (1578).

4.   Manning's Case, [1609] 8 Co. 94b, 77 Eng.Rep. 618; Lampet's Case, [1612] 10 Co.Rep. 46b, 77 Eng.Rep. 994; Cotton v. Heath, [1638] Poll. 26, 86 Eng.Rep. 500.

5.   Eyres v. Faulkland, [1697] 1 Salk. 231, 91 Eng.Rep. 204.

6.   Culbreth v. Smith, 1888, 69 Md. 450, 16 A. 112, 1 L.R.A. 538.

7.   Anonymous, Com.Pl. 1641, March 106, pl. 183, 82 Eng.Rep. 432.

the testator had directed that his wife was to have only the "use and occupation" of the property for a limited time, such as for life, the gift to the third party could be sustained. This is consistent with the concept of a bailment that involves a separation of ownership from possession. Eventually, it was implied that the purpose of such a bequest was to confer "use and occupation" on the life tenant.

Some differences of opinion are to be found as to the nature of the future interest that follows the life estate. In some cases it is designated as a remainder.[8] In other cases it is designated as an executory interest.[9] Suggestions are also to be found that the first taker is a trustee of the property for the benefit of the "remainderman."

The prevailing American rule is that future interests of personal property may be created either by deed or by will. This is the statutory rule in some states.[10] The type of future interest is not limited to a remainder. In general, the same types of future interests may be created with respect to personal property that may be created in the case of real property. These include the remainder,[11] reversion,[12] possibility of reverter,[13] power of termination[14] and executory interest.[15]

Chattels Consumable by Use

With exceptions to be noted, the gift of a life interest in a chattel that is consumable by use vests absolute ownership in the donee. Any attempt to create a future interest in the chattel will fail. Livestock and farm equipment are not considered to be "consumable by use" within the meaning of this rule.[16] Future interests may also be created with respect to fixtures, such as barber shop equipment.[17] However, the "depreciation factor" may justify the classification of machinery as "consumable by use." It has been so held with respect to printing press equipment.[18]

Even if chattels are classified as consumable by use there is authority for the view that future interests may be created if the subject matter of the gift is stock in trade.[19] This is also the rule if the property is included within the residuary clause of a will.[20] In both of these cases there is a duty to convert the property into money and the gifts are, in effect, gifts of the proceeds to be derived from a sale of the property.

Presence or Absence of a Gift Over

In a few states the rule is followed that the gift of a life estate in chattels personal is a gift of absolute ownership unless a con-

---

8. Hide v. Parrat, [1697] 2 Vern. 331, 23 Eng.Rep. 813; Evans v. Walker, 3 Ch.Div. 211, 1876.

9. Findlay v. Backhouse, [1921] 2 Ch. 51.

10. See, for example, 1953 Session Laws of North Carolina, Sec. 1, Ch. 198, codified as G.S. § 39–6.2.

11. Underwood v. Underwood, 1909, 162 Ala. 553, 50 So. 305.

12. Johnson's Adm'r v. Johnson, 1898, 104 Ky. 714, 47 S.W. 883.

13. In re Terry's Estate, 1916, 218 N.Y. 218, 112 N.E. 931 (dictum); In re Burpee's Estate, 1951, 367 Pa. 329, 80 A.2d 721; Palmer v. Pres. of Union Bank, 1892, 17 R.I. 627, 24 A. 109; Hinton v. Bowen, 1950, 190 Tenn. 463, 230 S.W.2d 965.

14. Green v. Old People's Home, 1915, 269 Ill. 134, 109 N.E. 701.

15. Innes v. Potter, 1915, 130 Minn. 320, 153 N.W. 604, 3 A.L.R. 896; Moffat's Ex'rs v. Strong, 1813, 10 Johns.(N.Y.) 12.

16. Davison's Adm'r v. Davison's Adm'x, 1912, 149 Ky. 571, 149 S.W. 982; Specht's Estate, 1941, 34 Ohio Law Abstracts 201, 36 N.E.2d 865.

17. First Nat. Bank of Valdosta v. Geiger, 1940, 61 Ga.App. 865, 7 S.E.2d 756.

18. Seabrook v. Grimes, 1908, 107 Md. 410, 68 A. 883.

19. Phillips v. Beal, [1862] 32 Beav. 25, 55 Eng.Rep. 10.

20. Blakely v. Blakely, 1924, 115 Kan. 644, 224 P. 65; Healey v. Toppan, 1864, 45 N.H. 243.

trary intention is evidenced by the fact that there is a gift over.[21]

Inter Vivos Gift

The validity of an *inter vivos* gift of chattels personal depends upon proof of actual, constructive or symbolic delivery by the donor to the donee. This requirement raises a problem as to required formalities if the purpose is to make a gift of a future interest.[22] In the usual case the donor is the owner of property, such as corporate stock, and he desires to give the stock to the donee but he also desires to retain the income for life. In other words, the purpose is to make a gift of a future interest.

In view of the fact that the subject matter of such a gift makes actual delivery impossible a "deed of gift" should serve as a worthy substitute for actual delivery.[23] Certainly, if the donor expresses his desire in a signed written statement and delivers the writing to the donee there is an adequate safeguard against fraud. If the subject matter of the gift is represented by a written instrument, such as a promissory note or a stock certificate, delivery may be accomplished by a transfer of the instrument itself to the intended donee.[24] In view of the fact that the donee acquires his interest during the lifetime of the donee the transaction

cannot be avoided upon the ground that it is testamentary in nature.[25]

Security Requirement

The owner of a possessory interest in personal property may be required to give security for the protection of the owners of future interests. While security may not be required from the owner of a corresponding interest in land, chattels personal, unlike land, are perishable in nature and capable of concealment.

According to one view, there is a duty to post a bond if there is a life estate in personal property such as money or stocks and bonds.[26] Where the instrument creating a life estate in personal property is reasonably susceptible to a construction that a trust was intended, the security aspect, and the duties of the life tenant as trustee, will depend upon the law of trusts.[27] As to whether or not an instrument is "reasonably susceptible" to a trust construction depends upon such factors as the wording of the instrument, the subject matter involved and the relationship of the parties.[28]

The prevailing rule is that if an instrument creates successive legal estates as distinguished from a trust, the requirement of security is a matter that is discretionary with the court.[29] The danger of loss of the prop-

---

21. Williams, Adm'x v. Floyd, Adm'r, 1920, 12 Del.Ch. 256, 112 A. 377; McNabb v. Cruze, 1939, 132 Tex. 476, 125 S.W.2d 288.

22. See Mowry v. Thompson, 1933, 189 Minn. 479, 250 N.W. 52, noted in 18 Minn.Law Rev. 232 (1934); Williams v. Thornton, 1930, 160 Tenn. 229, 22 S.W.2d 1041.

23. Smith v. Acorn, D.C.Mun.App.1943, 32 A.2d 252; Haskell v. Art Inst. of Chicago, 1940, 304 Ill.App. 393, 26 N.E.2d 736. *Contra:* Daws v. Drusilla Home, 1948, 118 Ind.App. 639, 79 N.E.2d 420.

24. Parry v. Parry, 1963, 231 Md. 584, 191 A.2d 439.

25. But see, Zimmerman v. Fawkes, 1950, 70 Idaho 389, 219 P.2d 951.

26. See 2 Rest.Property, § 202.

27. Abbott v. Wagner, 1922, 108 Neb. 359, 188 N.W. 113; Evans v. Adams, 1936, 180 S.C. 214, 185 S.E. 57.

28. See 2 Rest.Property, § 200, *Comment (b)*.

29. Scott v. Scott, 1908, 137 Iowa 239, 114 N.W. 881 *(dictum)*; In re Merritt's Estate, 1944, 182 Misc. 1026, 46 N.Y.S.2d 497; Long v. Lea, 1935, 177 S.C. 231, 181 S.E. 6, 101 A.L.R. 266. For discussion of New York legislation on the subject see Comment, 40 Col.Law Rev. 1457 (1940); 26 Corn.Law.Qt. 457 (1941).

erty and the fact that the life tenant resides outside the jurisdiction of the court are important factors to be considered in resolving the issue.[30] Security may not be demanded of a life tenant who has an unlimited right to dispose of the property for his own benefit.[31] Ordinarily, security will not be required if one has a life interest in personal property such as furniture, pictures etc., where the retention of possession of the property is essential for beneficial enjoyment.[32] In any event, an executor is not ordinarily under a duty to ask the court for an order requiring a bond from the life tenant at the time the property is delivered to the life tenant.[33]

Construction

As has been stated, American decisions generally apply the common law classification of estates in land to equivalent interests in chattels real and chattels personal. However, it does not follow that the same rules of construction are applied or that all of the "equivalent estates" may be created.

Many of the technical rules of construction relating to freehold estates owe their origin to the feudal system. That is the case, for example, with respect to the rule in Shelley's case. That rule is not applicable if a transfer is made of a chattel.[34] Contingent

remainders in chattels, unlike such remainders in land, are not within the doctrine of the destructibility of contingent remainders. The owner of a life estate in land is not under a duty to post a bond as a means by which to protect future interests. Such a bond may be required if the interest is a life estate in chattels personal.

The Statute *De Donis* [35] made possible the creation of an estate tail. However, that statute applied only with respect to estates in land. An equivalent interest is not recognized in the case of either chattels real or chattels personal.[36] Under provisions of the Statute *De Donis,* if land is conveyed to B and the heirs of his body, B acquires an estate tail. If the transfer involves chattels real or chattels personal B acquires absolute ownership. If land is conveyed to B and his heirs, but if B dies without issue then to C and his heirs, B acquires an estate tail and C has a valid remainder. The words "dies without issue" is construed to contemplate indefinite failure of issue. If such a transfer involves a chattel real or a chattel personal, and the words "die without issue" are construed to contemplate "indefinite failure of issue" B acquires absolute ownership [37] and the gift over to C fails because of the rule against perpetuities. However, if the words "die without issue" are construed to mean "definite failure of issue" then B acquires only a life interest and C acquires a valid remainder contingent upon the death of B without issue living at that time.

---

30. Scott v. Scott, 1908, 13? Iowa 239, 114 N.W. 881.

31. Colburn v. Burlingame, 1923, 190 Cal. 697, 214 P. 226, 27 A.L.R. 1374 (power in life tenant to encroach upon the subject matter of the gift for her own individual benefit and support).

32. See 2 Rest.Property, § 203.

33. Buckman's Trustees v. Ohio Valley Trust Co., 1941, 288 Ky. 114, 155 S.W.2d 749, 138 A.L.R. 436; Collins v. Hartford Accident & Indemnity Co., 1941, 178 Va. 501, 17 S.E.2d 413, 137 A.L.R. 1046. See Lapham v. Martin, 1877, 33 Ohio St. 99.

34. 3 Rest.Property, § 312, *Comment (b).*

35. 13 Edw. I. c. 1 (1285).

36. The English Law of Property Act of 1925, ch. 29, sec. 130(1), authorizes the creation of an equitable estate tail and a corresponding interest in personal property.

37. Albee, Admr v. Carpenter, 1853, 66 Mass. (12 Cush.) 382; Seeger v. Leakin, 1893, 76 Md. 500, 25 A. 862.

CHAPTER 29

THE CREATION OF FUTURE INTERESTS
BY IMPLICATION

IMPLIED GIFTS, IN GENERAL

146. While a conveying instrument, such as a deed or will, may not contain language of direct gift, it may contain directions that can be carried out only by the implication of such a gift.

A person who claims benefits under a will as a devisee or legatee must sustain that claim on the basis of language found in the will. While the will may not contain language of direct gift it may contain language indicating a clear intent of the testator that can be carried out only by recognizing the fact that testamentary intent included a gift that is not made in specific terms. Under such circumstances there is said to be a gift by implication. Gifts by construction may be sustained in the case of a deed as well as in the case of a will.[1]

In aid of construction importance is attached to the expressed purpose or purposes of the conveyor and the relationship of the parties. In construing a will there is a presumption that a testator did not intend to die intestate with respect to any part of his estate. There is also a presumption that he did not intend to disinherit a person qualifying as a natural object of his bounty.

INTERIM GIFT BY IMPLICATION

147. A testamentary gift to the *only* persons who would have been entitled to inherit testator's property had he died intestate, but postponed until the death of one not an heir, results in a gift for life, by implication, to this named person.

A testamentary gift to the only persons who would have been entitled to inherit the testator's property had he died intestate, but postponed until the death of one not classified as such an heir, results in a gift for life, by implication, to this named person.[2] The testator clearly expressed his intention to exclude his heirs from enjoyment of the property until the death of the non-heir. This intention can be carried out only by implying an *interim* gift.

In view of the fact that this gift by implication rests upon the basis of testator's expressed intention to exclude his heirs more than it does upon his intention to make an *interim* gift, a gift by implication will not be recognized in the following situations:

First: A testamentary gift to the only persons who would have been entitled to inherit the testator's property had he died intestate, but postponed as to some but not as to all

---

1. Brock v. Hall, 1949, 33 Cal.2d 885, 206 P.2d 360, 11 A.L.R.2d 672. See 1 Rest.Property, § 115 and Appendix, p. 16.

2. Porter v. Union Trust Co., 1915, 182 Ind. 637, 108 N.E. 117; In re Keehn's Will, 1935, 156 Misc. 259, 281 N.Y.S. 591, affirmed 248 App.Div. 697, 289 N.Y.S. 819 (1936); 1 Rest.Property, § 116.

the "heirs" until the death of a non-heir, will not result in a gift by implication to the non-heir.[3] There is, of course, an intestacy of the *interim* interest but it will pass to *all of the heirs* equally. It may reasonably be said that the purpose of the testator was to prevent *exclusive enjoyment* of the *interim* interest by the heir or heirs involved in the postponed gift.

Second: A gift by implication will not arise if there is a residuary clause broad enough to include the interest in question. An *interim* gift by implication is not then necessary to accomplish the purpose of the testator.[4]

Third: A postponed gift to non-heirs does not result in a gift by implication. This does not show a purpose to exclude the heirs from enjoyment of the *interim* interest.

IMPLICATION OF CROSS REMAINDERS

148. If a life estate is created in two or more parties, followed by a gift over of the property after the deal of *all the* life tenants, the survivor of such life tenants is entitled to a gift, by implication, of *all* the property for life.

In a conveyance to B and C as tenants in common for life, and upon the death of *both* B and C to D and his heirs, B will be entitled to a life estate in all of the property if he survives C. Similarly, C will be entitled to a life estate in all of the property if he survives B.[5] A cross remainder arises by implication because of the fact that the gift

over to D cannot take effect until the death of *both* B and C. In the case of a will this conclusion is aided by the presumption against intestacy. If a cross remainder is not implied, upon the death of one of the life tenants there is a released interest that is not disposed of by will. A cross remainder may also be implied under similar circumstances in the case of a deed.[6] The language of the deed creates an ambiguity and there is a strict construction in favor of the grantee.

Cross remainders will not be implied if the conveying instrument does not create concurrent interests in the life tenants.[7] Neither will there be such an implication if specific provision is made for disposition of the property upon the death of the individual life tenants.

The fact that a conveying instrument expressly provides for cross remainders as to certain property is some evidence of the fact that cross remainders should not be implied as to other property. The argument is that if the conveyor intended to create cross remainders he knew how that purpose could be accomplished and he failed to follow that procedure. However, even under such circumstances the facts may be sufficiently compelling to warrant the conclusion that cross remainders were created by implication.[8]

GIFT OVER UPON FAILURE OF ISSUE, CHILDREN ETC.

149. A gift by implication may arise in favor of issue, children etc., if there is a gift over upon the death of a *life tenant* without issue or children.

---

3. Ralph v. Carrick, [1879] 11 Ch.Div. 873.

4. In re Vreeland's Estate, 1907, 72 N.J.Eq. 851, 65 A. 902.

5. Kramer v. Sangamon Loan & Trust Co., 1920, 293 Ill. 553, 127 N.E. 877; Addicks v. Addicks, 1914, 266 Ill. 349, 107 N.E. 580; Henry v. Henderson, 1912, 103 Miss. 48, 60 So. 33, noted in 11 Mich.Law Rev. 474 (1913); Purdy v. Hayt, 1883, 92 N.Y. 446. See Hartford Nat. Bank & Trust Co. v. Harvey, 1956, 143 Conn. 233, 121 A.2d 276.

6. Green v. Brown, 1951, 37 Cal.2d 391, 232 P.2d 487; 1 Rest.Property, § 115, *Comment a.*

7. Union National Bank of Pasadena v. Hunter, 1949, 93 Cal.App.2d 669, 209 P.2d 621 (deed); Hunt v. Mitchell, 1951, 409 Ill. 321, 99 N.E.2d 347 (will).

8. In re Hudson, 1882, 20 Ch.Div. 406.

A gift to a person for life, with a gift over if he dies without issue or without children, results in a gift by implication in favor of the issue or children surviving him.[9] It is quite clear from the language that the conveyor intended to benefit the issue or children if they survived the life tenant. Frequently, this conclusion is aided by the presumptions against intestacy or disherison. According to some authorities a gift by implication is held to arise in order to maintain the testator's apparent intention to maintain equality in the distribution of his estate among various members of his family.[10]

A gift by implication arises only where the primary estate or interest is a life estate or otherwise of restricted duration.[11] For example, if land is conveyed to B in fee simple with a gift over to C if B should die without issue, even if B should die with issue such issue cannot claim an estate by implication. Recognition of such an estate in the issue would, in effect, result in a reduction of B's interest to a life estate, a result inconsistent with the terms of the conveyance. However, the primary estate may be restricted within the meaning of the rule even though it is not limited to a life estate. In Estate of Blake (Cal.),[12] a testamentary gift was made in equal shares to B, C and D. Income was to be

paid to them and as a donee reached the age of thirty he had the right to "demand and receive" his proportionate share of the corpus. If one should die without issue before attaining that age his share was to go to the survivors. B died survived by issue but before reaching the age of thirty. First of all, the court held that the gift to B was subject to the condition of survivorship. This conclusion was reached because of the specific language used and some importance is attached to the fact that there was a gift over. It was then determined that the survivors were not entitled to take because B did not die without issue. However, an intestacy did not result because B's issue took a gift by implication.

GENERAL PLAN INCOMPLETELY EXPRESSED

150. If the provisions of a deed or will indicate the fact that the conveyor entertained a general plan with respect to the disposition of his property but failed to provide for all contingencies, omitted portions may be supplied by implication.

In some cases a study of a deed or will leads to the firm conviction that the conveyor entertained a general plan with respect to the disposition of his property but failed to provide for all of the possible contingencies that might arise. Some decisions assume judicial power to "fill in the gaps" and, at the same time, purport to follow the generally recognized rule that a court is without power to add provisions to a will.[13] Of course, the implication of a gift may avoid intestacy but frequently it is difficult to ac-

9. Estate of Heard, 1944, 25 Cal.2d 322, 153 P.2d 553; Du Pont v. Equitable Security Trust Co., 1956, 35 Del.Ch. 514, 122 A.2d 429 (deed of trust); Close v. Farmers' Loan & Trust Co., 1909, 195 N.Y. 92, 87 N.E. 1005 (reliance placed on presumptions against intestacy and disherison); Lippincott's Estate, 1923, 276 Pa. 283, 120 A. 136; Rhode Island Hospital Trust Co. v. Huntoon, 1962, — R.I. —, 181 A.2d 614; 3 Rest.Property, § 272. *Contra:* Bond v. Moore, 1908, 236 Ill. 576, 86 N.E. 386, noted in 3 Ill.Law Rev. 590 (1909).

10. See, for example, Kendall v. Kendall, 1882, 36 N.J.Eq. 91.

11. See 3 Rest.Property, § 272, *Comment c.*

12. 157 Cal. 448, 108 P. 287 (1910).

13. Brock v. Hall, 1949, 33 Cal.2d 885, 206 P.2d 360, 11 A.L.R. 672 (deed); Williams v. Jones, 1901, 166 N.Y.S. 522, 60 N.E. 240; In re Wainwright's Estate, 1954, 376 Pa. 161, 101 A.2d 724. *Cf.:* Bailey v. Bailey, 1920, 236 Mass. 244, 128 N.E. 29.

cept this reason as a justification for the conclusion reached.

An extreme case is that of Akeley's Estate (Cal.).[14] A residuary clause directed distribution of 25% to charity A, 25% to charity B and 25% to charity C. The court held that each charity was entitled to 33⅓% rather than to 25%. This was accomplished in the name of gifts by implication. Importance is attached to the fact that the will was not prepared by an attorney and that the decedent left no heirs and if the gifts could not be implied the property would escheat to the state. These matters are not of controlling importance in resolving such an issue.

14.   35 Cal.2d 26, 215 P.2d 921, 17 A.L.R.2d 647 (1950).

CHAPTER 30

CONTINGENCIES ATTACHED TO ESTATES (VESTING)

DOCTRINE OF VIRTUAL REPRESENTATION

151. In litigation involving matters of title a judgment may fix the rights of unknown or unborn parties if these parties are "represented in interest" by those who participate in the proceedings.

In litigation involving the construction of deeds or wills compliance with due process requires notice to those whose interests may be affected and they must have an opportunity to be heard. An interest may involve persons who are yet to be born or persons who cannot be presently ascertained. As a matter of pure necessity the interests of such persons must be protected by some person who can truly be said to represent the one who cannot represent himself. This necessity has resulted in the doctrine of virtual representation.[1]

One aspect of virtual representation is to be found in the case of a class gift. If a claim is asserted against the validity of a gift to a class the living and ascertained members of the class may be said to represent other potential but unascertained class members assuming, of course, that there is a *common*

interest and good faith. For example, if there is a class gift to "children" and litigation raises a question as to whether or not grandchildren are included within the class, living grandchildren may litigate the matter in behalf of unborn grandchildren, assuming identity of interest. Even if a class gift is not involved, this identity of interest may be found in connection with the various types of future interests. In some states, it is expressly provided by statute that the court may appoint a guardian *ad litem* to represent the interests of persons who are not in being or who cannot be ascertained at the time of the litigation.[2]

THE FORCE OF A CONTINGENCY WHICH MERELY AFFECTS THE QUANTITY OF A GIFT

152. A gift may be classified as vested even though some contingency exists which may affect the quantity that will eventuate in possession.

A contingency may relate to the amount of a gift as distinguished from a contingency relating to the gift itself.[3] For example, a future interest may be subject to a contingency as to the amount of the gift because of the

---

1. See Perry v. Bassenger, 1941, 219 N.C. 838, 15 S.E. 2d 365, noted in 19 N.Y.Univ.Law Quarterly Review 85 (1941); Bradley v. Henry, Tex.Civ.App.1951, 239 S.W.2d 404; See also, supra, § 142.

2. See, for example, West's Ann.Cal.Code Civ.Proc. § 373.5.

3. See 3 Rest.Property, § 276.

fact that a life tenant has a power of appointment with respect to the subject matter of the gift [4] or a power to use some part or all of the property if this is necessary for support and maintenance.[5] Such a future interest is frequently described as vested subject to being divested by an exercise of the power.

PSEUDO CONTINGENCY

153. Even though words of condition are used, circumstances may justify the conclusion that the conveyor did not intend to make a conditional gift.

Even though words of condition are used in a deed or will, circumstances may justify the conclusion that the conveyor did not intend to make a conditional gift.[6] For example, if a gift is made to B for life, then to C for life, and after the death of C, "if B is dead," then to D absolutely, D does not take a conditional gift. The words "if B is dead" add nothing to the conveyance. This follows from the fact that the life estate in C can arise only after the death of B. The conveyor, out of an excess of caution, probably made this superfluous provision to make sure that D and his heirs could not enjoy the estate in possession until after the death of B.[7]

In Kern v. Kern (Ill.),[8] land was devised to B "during her widowhood," and in case of her remarriage it was to go to named children.

4. Caples v. Ward, 1915, 107 Tex. 341, 179 S.W. 856; Doe d. Willis v. Martin, [1790] 4 D. & E. 39, 100 Eng. Rep. 882.

5. Ducker v. Burnham, 1893, 146 Ill. 9, 34 N.E. 558; Roberts v. Roberts, 1905, 102 Md. 131, 62 A. 161.

6. Baley v. Strahan, 1924, 314 Ill. 213, 145 N.E. 359 (A to B to have and take possession of after the death of C).

7. Maddison v. Chapman, [1858] 4 K. & J. 709, 719, 70 Eng.Rep. 294, 298. See 2 Rest.Property, § 157, *Comment j.*

8. 293 Ill. 238, 127 N.E. 396 (1920).

Contingency was not attached to the gift over. It was to take effect whenever and by whatever means the life estate was terminated.[9]

IDENTIFICATION OF PERSON TO TAKE

154. Contingency is attached to a gift until such time as the person or persons to take can be identified.

Contingency is attached to a gift until such time as the person to take can be identified. The identification of persons described as "heirs," or "heirs of the body," must await the death of the one named as ancestor.[10] This follows from the fact that these words describe the persons who are entitled to inherit an estate if the ancestor dies intestate. As a matter of construction, it may appear that words of the type under discussion were used to describe "children." [11] Two additional situations are as follows:

First: Until the death of a person it is not possible to identify that person's "widow" or "widower." However, a conveying instrument may be susceptible to the construction that these words were used to describe the *present spouse* of a person.[12]

Second: In the English case of Festing v. Allen,[13] a testamentary trust directed that the income be paid to testator's widow for life, or during her widowhood, then to his granddaughter for life, with remainder to the children of the granddaughter "who shall attain the age of twenty-one years." There was a gift over if the granddaughter died without issue. The widow predeceased the granddaughter and the granddaughter died

9. See In re Shuckburgh's Settlement, [1901] 2 Ch. 794.

10. See 3 Rest.Property, § 249.

11. Conger v. Lowe, 1890, 124 Ind. 368, 24 N.E. 889; Azarch v. Smith, 1928, 222 Ky. 566, 1 S.W.2d 968.

12. Easton v. Hall, 1929, 323 Ill. 397, 154 N.E. 216.

13. 12 M. & W. 279, 152 Eng.Rep. 1204 (1843).

and was survived by three infant children. The court held that the persons described as takers could not be identified at the time of the granddaughter's death because the living children did not fit the description of children "who shall attain the age of twenty-one." [14] The gift is described as a "contingent remainder" and it was destroyed under the then existing doctrine of the destructibility of contingent remainders. [15]

IMPLIED CONDITION OF SURVIVORSHIP

155. A condition of survivorship is not implied from the fact that a gift embodies an express condition not relating to survivorship.

   a. Words of present gift. A requirement of survivorship is not implied if words of present gift are used even if there is a postponement as to time of payment.

   b. Gift to donee "at," "when" or "if" he reaches a stated age. In general, a gift to a donee "at," "when" or "if" he reaches a stated age is subject to an implied condition of survivorship.

   c. Divide and pay over rule. According to some authorities a condition of survivorship may be implied from a direction that property be divided and paid over at a future time. This rule is not generally followed at the present time.

   d. Limitations in the alternative. There is an implied condition of survivorship if limitations are in the alternative and the identification of the primary taker is postponed until the happening of a named event.

A condition of survivorship is not implied from the fact that a devise or bequest embodies express conditions not relating to survivorship. For example, in a devise to B for

life and then to B's children, but if B should die without leaving children surviving to C, it is not required that C survive B in order to take the property. [16] It is true, the gift to C is subject to the condition that B die without leaving children. But the existence of that condition is not a sufficient basis upon which to imply that C must survive B in order to acquire a transmissible interest. If B should die without leaving children surviving him the property will pass to C or, if he is deceased at the time, it will pass under the terms of his will [17] or as a part of his estate to those entitled to take in the case of an intestacy. [18]

There are several reasons for this rule. In the first place, it may be assumed that the testator did not have C's survivorship in mind otherwise he would have made express provision for such a contingency. In the second place, a construction is favored that gifts are free from contingencies ("the law favors the early vesting of estates"). In the third place, there is a presumption against intestacy. If a requirement of survivorship is implied there would be an intestacy because no provision is made in the will for a gift over in the event that B should die without children and in the event that C should predecease B. Additional situations are discussed in the following paragraphs.

[14] *Cf.*: Edwards v. Hammong, [1683] 3 Lev. 132, 83 Eng.Rep. 614. (where the gift was to a named person "if he lived to the age of 21 years").

[15] See supra, § 138.

[16] Hofing v. Willis, 1964, 3 Ill.2d 365, 201 N.E.2d 852 (disapproving Drury v. Drury, 1915, 271 Ill. 336, 111 N.E. 140); Black v. Todd, 1922, 121 S.C. 243, 113 S.E. 793; 3 Rest.Property, § 261. But see Demill v. Reid, 1889, 71 Md. 175, 17 A. 1014, discussed in Second Bank-State Street Trust Co., 1961, 342 Mass. 630, 174 N.E.2d 763.

[17] Bedyk v. Bank of Delaware, 1961, 40 Del.Ch. 140,

[18] See, for example, Mich.Pub.Acts No. 211 (1931), Mich.Comp.Laws 1948, § 554.101, Mich.Stat.Ann. § 26.47.

Words of Present Gift

A requirement of survivorship is not involved if there are words of present gift, such as in a case where a will provides, "I hereby bequeath $5,000 to B, payable at twenty-one." [19] However, according to early English authorities, a gift of money, payable upon the happening of an event, involves an implied condition of survivorship if the gift is made a *charge on land*.[20] Application of this rule resulted in an advantage to the heirs of the testator and was followed because the heirs occupied a favored position. The prevailing American rule is that the creation of such a lien on land will not justify the implication of a condition of survivorship.[21]

If survivorship is not involved, the representatives of the donee's estate can demand immediate delivery of the property even if the donee dies before attaining the stated age. However, a different rule applies if the *interim income* is given to a third party. In that event, the estate of the donee is not entitled to the property until such time as he would have reached the stated age had he lived.[22]

Gift to Donee "at," "When" or "If" he Reaches a Stated Age

If a gift is made to a person "at," "when" or "if" he attains a stated age, such as the age of twenty-one, there is an implication that the gift is conditioned upon attaining the stated age (a condition of survivor-

ship).[23] Words of present gift are not used. The operative date of the gift is postponed until the donee attains the stated age. It is usually considered that the gift is subject to a condition precedent to vesting.[24] However, provisions in a conveying instrument may justify the conclusion that the gift is not subject to an implied condition of survivorship. Further, even if there is a requirement of survivorship, it may be found that the conveyor intended a *present gift* that would be subject to defeasance if the donee failed to attain the stated age. In that event, it is frequently stated that the gift is vested subject to being divested. Some of the important factors bearing upon the construction of such a gift are as follows:

First: The gift to the donee of the interim income is persuasive evidence that the donor intended to make a present gift.[25] In fact, under such circumstances the donee enjoys the rights incident to ownership from the time of the gift.

There is a gift of interim income for the purpose in question if all of the income is to be used for the support and maintenance of the donee.[26] That is also the case if part of the income is to be used for support and maintenance and the balance of the income is to be accumulated for his benefit.[27] In

19. Wardwell v. Hale, 1894, 161 Mass. 396, 37 N.E. 196; Roden v. Smith, [1744] Amb. 588, 27 Eng.Rep. 383; 3 Rest.Property, § 257, *Comment d.*

20. Chandos v. Talbot, [1731] 2 P.Wms. 601, 24 Eng. Rep. 877.

21. 3 Rest.Property, § 262. *Contra:* In re Lawrence's Estate, 1964, 22 Wis.2d 624, 126 N.W.2d 517.

22. Roden v. Smith, [1744] Amb. 588, 27 Eng.Rep. 383.

23. 3 Rest.Property, § 257, *Comment e;* Smell v. Dee, [1707] 2 Salk. 415, 91 Eng.Rep. 360. But see, Estate of Budd, 1913, 166 Cal. 286, 135 P. 1131 and West's Ann.Cal.Civ.Code, § 1341.

24. See 3 Rest.Property, § 249, *Comment k.*

25. Equitable Guarantee & Trust Co. v. Bowe, 1912, 9 Del.Ch. 336, 82 A. 693; Bush v. Hamill, 1916, 273 Ill. 132, 112 N.E.2d 375; Clobberie's Case, [1677] 2 Vent. 342, 86 Eng.Rep. 467. See Simes & Smith, Future Interests (2nd ed.), § 586; 3 Rest.Property, § 259. But see In re Walker's Trust, 1962, 17 Wis. 2d 181, 116 N.W.2d 106.

26. Hanson v. Grahan, [1801] 6 Ves. 239, 31 Eng. Rep. 1030; 3 Rest.Property, § 258, *Comment f.*

27. In re Williams, 1907, L.R. 1 Ch. 180.

Steinway v. Steinway (N. Y.),[28] the interim income rule is applied even though the trustees were entitled to retain part of the income as compensation for their services.[29]

But a direction to pay the donee stated sums (as distinguished from income) at certain intervals does not constitute a gift of interim income.[30] Further, interim income is not involved if there are two or more donees and the income is not to be apportioned according to their respective shares of the corpus.[31]

If a will makes no express disposition of the interim income, a gift of income may be implied in favor of the person named to receive the corpus upon reaching the stated age. This implication is justified in the case of a gift by a parent to his child or in a case where the testator stood in the place of a parent (*loco parentis*). Such a relationship negatives a presumption that survivorship was a condition attached to the gift.[32]

If the income is payable to the donee and he dies prior to attaining the stated age, the representatives of his estate may demand immediate payment of the legacy. Payment will not be postponed until the time when the donee would have reached the stated age had he lived. There is no longer any reason for postponement of payment.[33]

Second: In construing a will importance is attached to the presumption against intestacy. For example, assume a testamentary gift to B "at," "when" or "if" he attains the age of twenty-one. Assume further that the will does not contain a residuary clause or otherwise dispose of the property in the event that B does fail to attain the stated age. The presumption against intestacy and the absence of a gift over justifies the conclusion that the testator did not intend to make a conditional gift to B.[34] His purpose was merely to place a restriction with respect to time of possession.

Third: There is an express requirement of survivorship in the case of a gift to B "at," "when" or "if" he attains a stated age, if there is a gift over to C if B fails to attain that age (a supplanting limitation). However, it may be contended that a present gift was made to B, subject to defeasance if he failed to attain that age. In other words, it may be claimed that the gift was vested subject to being divested rather than being subject to a condition precedent to vesting. Under such a construction, B's estate would be entitled to the property if the gift over failed even if B died without having attained the stated age. Also, B would be entitled to the interim income unless other disposition is made by the conveyor.

Divide and Pay Over Rule

According to the divide and pay over rule, if a will directs that at a stated time, such as five years after the death of testator, property is to be divided and paid over to described donees, such as testator's brothers and sisters, only those surviving at that time are entitled to take.[35] It is conceived that the testator intended to make a gift to take effect *in futuro*.

---

28. 163 N.Y. 183, 57 N.E. 312 (1900).

29. See In re Ussher, 1922, 2 Ch. 321.

30. See Atkins v. Hiccocks, [1737] 1 Atk. 500, 26 Eng. Rep. 316 (where donee was to receive the corpus at time of marriage).

31. In re Parker, 1880, 16 Ch.Div. 44.

32. See Savin v. Webb, 1903, 96 Md. 504, 54 A. 64.

33. Equitable Guarantee & Trust Co. v. Bowe, 1912, 9 Del.Ch. 336, 82 A. 693.

34. See Estate of Blake, 1910, 157 Cal. 448, 108 P. 287; Furness v. Fox, 1884, 1 Cush. (Mass.) 134; Appeal of Schick, 1951, 169 Pa.Super. 226, 82 A.2d 262.

35. See Gluck, The "Divide and Pay Over" Rule in New York, 24 Col.Law Rev. 8 (1924).

The leading case espousing this rule is Matter of Crane, a New York decision.[36] The soundness of the rule has been challenged in many states. The majority rule is that a requirement of survivorship is not to be implied from a mere direction to "divide and pay over" property at a stated future time.[37] One making such a direction may well be thinking in terms of "possession" rather than "ownership." Even in states that purport to follow the rule, exceptions to its application are recognized that, for practical purposes, nullify the rule itself. The more important exceptions are as follows:

First: The rule does not apply if words of present gift are found in a will. For example, survivorship is not implied if a will provides: "I hereby give (described property) to my brothers and sisters to be divided and paid over five years after my death."

Second: If the postponement of payment is for the purpose of letting in an intermediate estate there is no reason to imply that testator intended to postpone the operative date of his gift. For example, if property is left to the testator's widow for life and at her death it is to be divided and paid over to his brothers and sisters a requirement of survivorship is not implied.[38] It is not clear why this exception was not followed in Matter of Crane.

Third: In some states it is stated that the rule does not apply if the beneficiaries are designated by name. This limits application of the rule to situations involving class gifts.

Fourth: In some decisions it is indicated that the rule does not apply if the subject matter of the gift is severed from the estate with direction that the "severed portion" is to be divided and paid over to the beneficiaries at a future time.[39] Such a direction indicates an intent to make a present gift.

Limitations in the Alternative

If the word "or" is not used as meaning "and," [40] a gift in the alternative is indicated in a conveyance to B for life, remainder to C "or" his issue, heirs, children, brothers and sisters, etc. The language clearly indicates an intention on the part of the conveyor to postpone identification of the person or persons to take until the death of B.[41] These future interests are described as alternative contingent remainders or a contingent remainder with a double aspect.[42] The contingency arises because of the fact that there is an implied condition of survivorship. The primary taker cannot be identified until the time fixed for distribution.

A different situation is presented if a problem of identification is not involved. For example, the conveyance may be to B for life, remainder to C and his heirs (the primary taker) but if C dies before B then to D and his heirs. Since the primary taker is identified, and the gift to him is unconditional in form, he acquires ownership subject to di-

---

36. 164 N.Y. 71, 58 N.E. 47 (1900).

37. 3 Rest. Property, § 260 and authorities discussed in Tent. Draft No. 9, Explanatory Note, Appendix, p. 181; Barker v. Monks, 1944, 315 Mass. 620, 53 N.E. 2d 696. See note, The "Divide and Pay Over" Rule To-day, 25 Va.Law Rev. 599 (1939).

38. Atchison v. Francis, 1917, 182 Iowa 37, 165 N.W. 587.

39. See Warner v. Durant, 1879, 76 N.Y. 133. *Cf.:* In re Walker's Trust, 1962, 17 Wis.2d 181, 116 N.W. 2d 106.

40. Greer v. Parker, 1946, 209 Ark. 553, 191 S.W.2d 584. See 1 Rest. Property, § 27, *Comment e.*

41. Robertson v. Robertson, 1943, 313 Mass. 520, 48 N.E.2d 29; Wyman v. Kinney, 1940, 111 Vt. 94, 10 A.2d 191, 128 A.L.R. 298; 3 Rest. Property, § 252 (b). *Contra:* Kneer's Estate, 1938, 130 Pa.Super. 383, 197 A. 528.

42. Festing v. Allen, [1843] 12 M. & W. 279, 152 Eng. Rep. 1204. *Cf.:* Edwards v. Hammond, [1683] 3 Lev. 132, 83 Eng.Rep. 614.

vestment if he fails to survive the time fixed in the conveyance.[43] The interest may be described as vested subject to being divested. This conclusion conforms to the rule of construction that favors the early vesting of estates. The gift to D (under the alternative limitation) is an executory interest. It does not qualify as a contingent remainder because, historically, it is not possible to have a contingent remainder after a vested remainder in fee.

SUPPLANTING LIMITATION

156. The use of a supplanting limitation in a conveyance indicates that the primary taker has an estate that is vested subject to being divested.

A supplanting limitation is involved in a gift to B for life, remainder to C and his heirs, but if C dies before B, then to D and his heirs. Upon the happening of the named contingency the estate in C is to be replaced or supplanted by the estate in D. Unlike the situation presented in an alternative limitation, the identity of the taker is made clear from the date of the gift. It is not a gift to C "or" to D. Accordingly, C acquires an immediate estate subject to defeasance if he fails to survive B. The estate is usually described as one that is vested subject to being divested.[44] Additional situations are as follows:

First: Assume a gift to B for life and then to C absolutely, but if C dies before B leaving issue surviving, then to such issue. The supplanting limitation is subject to only one contingency, *i.e.,* the death of C prior to the death of B *leaving issue.* Accordingly, if C predeceases B *without leaving issue* the property forms a part of C's estate. "The reason for this is that setting out a specific contingency, while failing to provide for an equally plausible one, leads to the conclusion that the gift is only divested at the happening of the events specified." [45] Of course there may be an express provision requiring survivorship to a stated time.[46]

Second: In Bank of Delaware v. Goldey (Cal.),[47] testator directed payment of trust income to his widow for life and then to his daughter for life, with remainder to his nephew and nieces, B, C and D, with a provision that if "either of my said nieces or my nephew should be deceased at the time of the death of my daughter, I give devise and bequeath the share of the one so dying unto the survivor or survivors, in equal shares." B, C and D predeceased the daughter, D being the last to die. The court held that there were two contingencies attached to the gifts to B, C and D. The first contingency involved death during the lifetime of the daughter. The second contingency involved survivorship by one or both of the other remaindermen. As to D, this last named contingency did not occur. Accordingly, the property constituted a part of D's estate.[48]

---

43. 3 Rest. Property, § 277, Illustration 1.

44. Hoblit v. Howser, 1930, 338 Ill. 328, 170 N.E. 257, 71 A.L.R. 1046.

45. Scott v. Powell, 1950, 86 U.S.App.D.C., 277, 281, 182 F.2d 75, 79; Episcopal Eye, Ear and Throat Hospital v. Goodwin, 1960, 107 U.S.App.D.C. 375, 278 F.2d 255. See Nicodemus Nat. Bank v. Snyder, 1940, 178 Md. 140, 12 A.2d 518; In re Rickenbach's Estate, 1943, 348 Pa. 121, 34 A.2d 527.

46. See 3 Rest. Property, § 251.

47. 40 Del.Ch. 146, 176 A.2d 199 (1961).

48. *Accord:* Leahy v. Murray, 1959, 16 Ill.2d 350, 158 N.E.2d 30.

CHAPTER 31

ACCELERATION

IN GENERAL

157. The failure of a prior interest may hasten or accelerate the time when the owner of a future interest will be entitled to assert possessory rights.

The failure of a prior interest may hasten or accelerate the time when the owner of a future interest will be entitled to assert possessory rights. As a matter of fact, the ineffectiveness of a purported "prior interest" may prevent the creation of a future interest and, in that event, acceleration is not involved. For example, if a testamentary gift is made to "B for life, remainder to C and his heirs," and B predeceases the testator, C is entitled to immediate distribution.[1] The purported future interest in C never materialized.

The elimination of a future interest may also result from the renunciation of a testamentary gift. This calls for a "reconstruction" of the will in the light of an event that occurred after the death of the testator. For example, in a testamentary gift to B for life, remainder to C and his heirs, if B survives the testator and then renounces the life estate, the life estate is eliminated from the will.[2] It is said that C's "remainder" is accelerated.[3] Of course, this conclusion will be reached only in cases where the will does not express an intention to the contrary.

A true acceleration may result if a prior interest is effectively created but terminates prior to the time of its normal expiration.[4] This termination may be caused by merger, forfeiture etc.[5] The doctrine is applicable with respect to interests created by deed as well as to interests created by will.[6]

CONTINGENCIES ATTACHED TO ESTATE

158. Acceleration will not necessarily be denied merely because apparent contingencies are attached to the accelerated estate.

In general, a future interest is not accelerated if it is subject to a condition precedent to vesting.[7] In Crossan v. Crossan (Mo.),[8] testator devised land to his wife for life, remainder to his two daughters, B and C, "provided they shall well and tenderly care for my said wife . . . during her declining years." Otherwise, the land was to go to all of the testator's living children, share and share alike. The widow renounced her life estate, and the daughters claimed that their

1. Trust Company of New Jersey v. Lange, 1938, 123 N.J.Eq. 1, 195 A. 859.

2. See 2 Rest.Property, § 231.

3. *Cf.:* West's Ann.Cal.Civ.Code, § 733, as construed in Estate of LeFranc, 1952, 28 Cal.2d 289, 239 P.2d 617.

4. Simpkins v. Simpkins, 1942, 131 N.J.Eq. 227, 24 A.2d 821. But see, Cummings v. Hamilton, 1906, 220 Ill. 480, 77 N.E. 264.

5. See Rest. of the Law, 1948 Supplement, § 238, *Comment d.*

6. Singleton v. Gordon, 1943, 60 Wyo. 26, 144 P.2d 138 (1943).

7. 2 Rest. Property, § 233.

8. 303 Mo. 572, 262 S.W. 701 (1924).

interest was accelerated. Acceleration was denied upon the ground that the result would defeat the intention of the testator. His apparent intention was that B and C should personally care for and comfort his wife during her lifetime. This condition was attached to the gift.

But what appears to be a condition precedent to the vesting of a future interest may not be considered as such if the will is construed in the light of a renunciation.[9] For example, in a case where testator devised land to his wife, remainder to his children living at the time of the wife's death, it appears that the remainder is subject to a condition precedent to vesting (identification of takers at the death of the wife). However, if the will is construed in the light of the widow's renunciation, it is reasonable to assume that the testator would not have desired to postpone identification of remaindermen until her death. A reasonable construction of the will may lead to the conclusion that the remaindermen are to be ascertained upon the failure of the life estate rather than upon the death of the life tenant. There is authority that in such a case the future interest will be accelerated.[10] But if the gift is to B for life, remainder to testator's children who reach the age of twenty-one, a renunciation of the prior interest will not accelerate the succeeding interest if children under the stated age would thus be permitted to share in the gift.[11] The testator's expressed intention was to limit the gift to children who attained twenty-one. So also, where distribution is postponed until the testator's youngest child attains the age of twenty-one.[12]

A future interest that is vested subject to being divested may be accelerated by renunciation of the prior interest. In Cockey v. Cockey (Md.),[13] a testator devised land to his wife for life, remainder to his son, S, absolutely "should he be then living." It was further provided that if S should fail to survive the life tenant the property was to be distributed to S's surviving descendants and, in default thereof, to B. The life tenant renounced. This accelerated S's estate.[14] Though the gift to S appeared to be vested subject to being divested if he predeceased the life tenant, because of the renunciation it is reasonable to assume that the testator had intended S's estate to be defeasible only during the continuance of the life estate. A like result is usually reached where the succeeding gift is to a class. For example, in a conveyance to B for life, remainder to the children of C "then living," if B renounces the children of C living at the time of the renunciation acquire indefeasible estates and children born after that time will not share in the gift.[15] However, it may be indicated that the testator intended that the class remain open until the normal termination of the life estate. In that

---

9. 2 Rest. Property, § 233, *Comment (c)*.

10. Scotten v. Moore, 1914, 5 Boyce (28 Del.) 545, 93 A. 373, Ann.Cas.1918C, 409; American National Bank v. Chapin, 1921, 130 Va. 1, 107 S.E. 636, 17 A.L.R. 304. See, 2 Rest. Property, Appendix, pg. 55, n. 10. *Contra:* Rose v. Rose, 1921, 126 Miss. 114, 88 So. 513; Ajax Electrothermic Corp. v. First Nat. Bank, 1951, 7 N.J. 82, 80 A.2d 559.

11. 2 Rest. Property, § 233, Illustration 1.

12. Compton v. Rixey's Ex'rs, 1919, 124 Va. 548, 98 S.E. 651, 5 A.L.R. 465.

13. 141 Md. 373, 118 A. 850 (1922).

14. *Accord:* Danz v. Danz, 1940, 373 Ill. 482, 26 N.E. 2d 872; Thomsen v. Thomsen, 1946, 196 Okl. 539, 166 P.2d 417, 164 A.L.R. 1426; 2 Rest.Property, 231, *Comments (h), (i)*. But see, Foreman Trust & Savings Bank v. Seelenfreund, 1928, 329 Ill. 546, 161 N.E. 88, 62 A.L.R. 201 (beneficial interests under a trust). See also, 2 Rest.Property, § 232. *Contra:* Rose v. Rose, 1921, 126 Miss. 114, 88 So. 513; Maier v. Wyandt, 1945, 78 Ohio App. 33, 69 N.E.2d 70.

15. Tomb v. Bardo, 1941, 153 Kan. 766, 114 P.2d 320, noted in 40 Mich.Law Rev. 464 (1942).

event, the succeeding interests will be accelerated but will remain subject to being divested in part.[16]

SEQUESTRATION OF RENOUNCED INTEREST

159. A renounced interest may be sequestered for the benefit of devisees or legatees who suffer a loss due to the depletion of the estate.

Frequently, an interest is renounced by a surviving spouse because the statutory share made available by the renunciation is greater than that provided in the will. This enlarged distribution to the surviving spouse may strip the estate of sufficient assets to satisfy specific devises and bequests. In that event the renounced share may be sequestered for the benefit of disappointed devisees and legatees. If so, those who have a future interest in the sequestered property will have to await the time fixed for the normal termination of the prior interest.

In Sellick v. Sellick (Mich.),[17] the testator's estate consisted of land valued at $8,500 and chattels valued at $176,000. He bequeathed $25,000 to his wife for life, remainder to B and C equally. After making other bequests aggregating $25,000 the testator gave the residue of his estate to his son, S. The widow renounced the life estate and elected to take her statutory share in the husband's estate. This greatly diminished the residue of the estate given to S. B and C claimed that the renunciation accelerated their succeeding interest and that they were entitled to immediate distribution of the $25,000. This claim

was denied. The $25,000 was sequestered and held in trust during the lifetime of the widow.[18] During that time the income was paid to the son. In some instances an interest may be accelerated subject to a charge or lien in favor of other distributees who would otherwise suffer a loss.[19] Sequestration is usually denied if the renunciation does not cause a "substantial distortion" of other testamentary gifts.[20]

According to a minority rule a renounced interest will not be sequestered for the benefit of a residuary devisee or legatee.[21] It is reasoned that a testator intends such a party to take only that portion of the estate which remains after other bequests have been satisfied. In some decisions this view is followed unless it is shown that the residuary donee is the chief object of the testator's bounty.[22] The prevailing rule is that sequestration will not be denied merely because it will benefit a residuary donee.[23]

16. Askey v. Askey, 1923, 111 Neb. 406, 196 N.W. 891; Neill v. Bach, 1950, 231 N.C. 391, 57 S.E.2d 385 (the court states this to be the general rule in class gift cases).

17. 207 Mich. 194, 173 N.W. 609, 5 A.L.R. 1621 (1919).

18. *Accord:* Dowell v. Dowell, 1939, 177 Md. 370, 9 A.2d 593, 125 A.L.R. 1008.

19. Tomb v. Bardo, 1941, 153 Kan. 766, 114 P.2d 320; Restatement of the Law, 1948 Supplement, § 234, *Comment aa*, p. 459.

20. In re Nixon's Estate, 1962, 71 N.J.Super. 450, 177 A.2d 292; 3 Rest.Property, § 234, Comment k. But see, Dowell v. Dowell, 1939, 177 Md. 370, 9 A.2d 593, 125 A.L.R. 1008.

21. Union Trust Co. v. Rossi, 1929, 180 Ark. 552, 22 S.W.2d 370.

22. Trustees Church Home v. Morris, 1896, 99 Ky. 317, 36 S.W. 2. See also, Trustees of Kenyon College v. Cleveland Trust Co., 1935, 130 Ohio St. 107, 196 N.E. 784, 99 A.L.R. 224, noted in 9 Cinn.Law Rev. 520 (1935), 30 Ill.Law Rev. 405 (1935), 84 Pa.Law Rev. 115 (1935).

23. Sellick v. Sellick, 1919, 207 Mich. 194, 173 N.W. 609, 5 A.L.R. 1621; In re Lonergan's Estate, 1931, 303 Pa. 142, 154 A. 387, noted in 80 Pa.Law Rev. 454 (1932); 2 Rest.Property, § 234.

CHAPTER 32

GIFTS OVER IN CASE OF DEATH OR DEATH WITHOUT ISSUE

GIFT OVER "IN CASE OF THE DEATH" OF THE FIRST DONEE

160. In general, if a testamentary gift is made to B and his heirs but in case of the death of B to C and his heirs an indefeasible estate vests in B if he survives the testator. If there is an intervening life estate there is a requirement that B survive the life tenant.

In a testamentary gift to B and his heirs, but in case of the death of B to C and his heirs, B takes an indefeasible interest if the survives the testator.[1] The conveyance involves a substitutional gift. The gift to C is substituted for the gift to B if B does not survive the testator. The words "in case of the death of B" connotes a contingency. Since death alone is not a contingency the contingency must relate to the time of B's death. And since time, generally, would not qualify as a contingency, because B must die sometime, the phrase must be read to mean "in case of B's death before the death of the testator." Variations of this rule are as follows:

First: The time of death may qualify as a contingency if an intermediate estate is involved. For example, in a gift to B for life, and then to C absolutely, but "in case of the death of C to D and his heirs," C will not take an indefeasible estate even if he does survive the testator. In such a case it is possible to fix the crucial date as the time of the death of the life tenant, B. Unless C

survives the death of B the estate will pass to D.[2]

Second: In a testamentary gift the language may be susceptible to the construction that the word "and" was used as meaning "or." For example, in a gift to B for life, remainder to C, D and E "and their several descendants *per stirpes,* the word "and" may be construed as meaning "or." In that event, if C, D or E fail to survive the life tenant the "descendants" are entitled to the property upon the ground that the language created an alternative remainder.[3]

Third: If a testamentary gift is made to B absolutely but "in case of B's death" to C, the will may be susceptible to the construction that the words "in case of B's death" meant "upon B's death." In that event, B acquires only a life estate.[4]

GIFT OVER IF A PERSON SHOULD "DIE WITHOUT ISSUE"

161. The modern rule is that definite failure of issue is contemplated in a conveyance A to B and his heirs but if B dies without issue then to C and his heirs.

  a. **Essentiality of time in "die without issue," "children" etc.** In a conveyance to B and his heirs but if B dies without issue to

---

1. Steinhart v. Wolf, 1923, 95 N.J.Eq. 132, 122 A. 886; Renner v. German, Tex.Civ.App.1947, 207 S.W.2d 671; 3 Rest.Property, § 263.

2. In re Gulbenkian's Will, 1961, 9 N.Y.2d 363, 174 N.E.2d 481; 3 Rest.Property, § 264.

3. In re Gulbenkian's Will, 1961, 9 N.Y.2d 363, 174 N.E.2d 481.

4. In re Thompson's Estate, 1946, 161 Kan. 641, 171 P.2d 294; Roberts v. Roberts, 1946, 147 Neb. 494, 23 N.W.2d 774. See Griffin v. Griffin, 1963, 29 Ill. 2d 354, 194 N.E.2d 641.

C and his heirs, C takes if B dies without issue at any time. However, if distribution
to B is postponed, C takes only if B dies
without issue prior to the date of distribution.

b. **Illegitimate and adopted children.** In a
conveyance to B and his heirs but if B
dies without issue to C and his heirs, the
birth of an illegitimate child to B will not
bar the claim of C unless the child qualifies
as B's heir. In the absence of an adoption-
statute to the contrary, the adoption of
a child by B will not bar C's claim.

c. **Survival of issue, descendants or children.** In a conveyance to B for life, remainder to B's issue etc., but if B dies without issue to C, C is not entitled to take if
B has issue even if the issue does not
survive the time of B's death. However,
in the absence of such a direct gift to issue,
children etc., C is entitled to take if the
issue does not survive B.

d. **Presumption as to possibility of issue.**
There is authority for the view that in determining property rights evidence is admissible to prove that a person is incapable
of having issue.

In a gift to B and his heirs, but if B dies
without issue, then to C and his heirs, the
event upon which the gift over to C is to take
effect is susceptible to either one of two interpretations.

According to one view the gift over will
not take effect until such time as the inheritable line of succession (heirs of the body)
of B becomes extinct. Under this view, if
the gift involves a freehold estate, B takes
an estate tail. If the gift involves chattels
B takes absolute ownership because there
can be no estate tail in chattels.

According to the second view, the phrase
"die without issue" may be taken to mean
that the event must occur, if at all, at a stated
time, such as at the time of the death of B.
This means that "definite failure of issue"
is contemplated. If there is failure of issue

at that time the gift over takes effect as an
executory interest. Under this view, if the
conveyance consists of a freehold estate, as
in the example given above, B acquires a fee
simple subject to an executory interest. In
the case of chattels B acquires ownership
subject to an executory interest in C.

The early English cases construed the
phrase "die without issue" as meaning indefinite failure of issue. In a conveyance to
B and his heirs, but if B died without issue
to C and his heirs, B acquired a fee tail estate.[5] This was a forced construction. It
was the only means by which the gift to C
and his heirs could be sustained. It was
valid as a remainder after an estate tail. It
could not be sustained as an executory interest because such interests were not recognized until after the passage of the Statute
of Uses in 1536.[6] The same rule of construction (indefinite failure of issue) was followed
in the case of chattels real and chattels personal. But since an estate tail could not be
created in chattels the transfer vested absolute ownership in B.

The English courts followed the same rule
of construction after the creation of executory interests was made possible by the
passage of the Statute of Uses in 1536 [7] and
the Statute of Wills in 1540.[8] This continued
until the rule as to wills was changed by the
Wills Act of 1837.[9] Accordingly, in the case
of land a conveyance to B and his heirs, but
if B died without issue to C and his heirs,
B acquired a fee tail estate and C acquired
a contingent remainder. Again, this was a
forced construction. If the gift over to C

5. Jarman on Wills (5th ed.) p. 296.

6. 27 Hen. VIII, c. 10 (1536).

7. 27 Hen. VIII, c. 10 (1536).

8. 32 Hen. VIII, c. 1 (1540).

9. Wills Act of 1837 (1 Vict. c. 26, § 29).

and his heirs had been classified as an executory interest it would have been void under the rule against perpetuities. However, it was valid as a remainder after an estate in fee tail. The same rule of construction was followed if chattels were involved. But since a fee tail estate could not be created in chattels, the transfer vested absolute ownership in B. The purported gift over to C failed as an executory interest because of the rule against perpetuities. However, in the case of chattels, there was an inclination to relax the rule, language in the conveying instrument permitting. By reaching a definite-failure-of-issue construction the gift over could be sustained because the requirements of the rule against perpetuities would be satisfied. The gift over to C would either "vest or fail" at the time of B's death (a life in being at the time of the death of the testator). That was the situation, for example, in the case of a transfer of a chattel to B, but if B should die "without *leaving* issue," then to C. The word "leaving" fixed the crucial date as the time of the death of B. At that time B either would or would not "leave" issue.[10]

In the early leading English case of Forth v. Chapman,[11] the "without-leaving-issue" language was used both with reference to land and as to chattels. The court held that definite failure of issue was contemplated as to the chattels but that indefinite failure of issue was contemplated as to the freehold estates. By this process all of the gifts over were salvaged.

But a definite-failure-of-issue construction may be required even in the case of freehold estates because of specific language. For example, in Pells v. Brown (Eng.),[12] the conveyance of a freehold estate was to B and his heirs and if B should die without issue "living his brother" C, then to C and his heirs. Since failure of issue had to occur, if at all, during the lifetime of C, the disposition involved definite failure of issue. B did not acquire a fee tail estate. Rather, he acquired an estate in fee simple with an executory interest in C.

In the United States, either by force of statute or judicial decision, "die without issue" is generally held to contemplate definite failure of issue.[13] However, some authorities follow the early English view that in the conveyance of a freehold estate in land the phrase presumptively means indefinite failure of issue.[14]

If indefinite failure of issue is not contemplated, construction problems involved in a transfer with a gift over on failure of issue, descendants, children and words of similar import, are considered in the following paragraphs.

Essentiality of Time in "Die Without Issue," "Children" etc.

In the absence of specific language, a construction problem is involved in a testamentary gift to B and his heirs (or absolute

---

10. Gordon v. Adolphus, [1769] 3 Brown 306, 1 Eng. Rep. 1335.

11. 1 P.Wms. 663, 24 Eng.Rep. 559 (1720).

12. Cro.Jac. 590, 79 Eng.Rep. 504 (1620).

13. Rest.Property, § 266; Warren, Gifts Over on Death Without Issue, 39 Yale Law Jr., 332 (1929); Editorial Note, 15 Iowa Law Rev. 361 (1930); Comment, Construction of "Die Without Issue" in Devises of Realty, 20 Tex.Law Rev. 212, 214 (1941). See, Redmond v. New Jersey Historical Society, 1942, 132 N.J.Eq. 464, 28 A.2d 189 (chattels); Steinbrenner v. Dreher, 1942, 140 Ohio St. 305, 43 N.E. 2d 283 (chattels).

14. Caccamo v. Banning, 1950, 6 Terry (Del.) 394; McCarthy v. Walsh, 1923, 123 Me. 157, 122 A. 406, noted in 37 Harv.Law Rev. 512 (1924); Hall v. Priest, 1856, 6 Gray (72 Mass.) 18. See Johnson v. Currin, 1849, 10 Pa. 498.

ownership in the case of chattels) but if B dies without issue, descendants, children etc., to C and his heirs. The problem is complicated if there is a postponed distribution, such as in a case where the gift is to B for life, remainder to C and his heirs, but if C dies without issue, children etc., to D and his heirs. Two important rules of construction are as follows:

First: The preferred view is that in a testamentary gift to B and his heirs but if B dies without issue, children etc., to C and his heirs, C is entitled to the property if B dies without issue etc., *at any time.*[15] The real contingency is "death without issue," children etc. A time restriction is not indicated. Successive estates are created in B and in C. The minority view is that the gift to C is subject to the contingency that B "die without issue," children etc., prior to the death of the testator. It is considered that the time of death and not death without issue, children etc., is the essence of the contingency.[16] But this substitutional gift construction will yield to slight evidence indicating a contrary intent.[17]

Second: A postponed distribution is involved in a gift such as to B for life, remainder to C and his heirs, but if C dies without issue, descendants etc., to D and his heirs. The date for the death of C without issue, descendants etc., may be designated as the date of B's death. If C survives that date his estate becomes indefeasible. The selection of such an "intermediate date" is supported by the weight of authority.[18] The estate acquired by C is thus released from the contingency prior to the time of his death and thus conforms to the policy favoring the "early vesting of estates." Further, the result conforms to the direction embodied in the will. An intermediate date may also be selected if a will directs that the property is to be held in trust until a designated time or if the distribution is otherwise postponed.[19]

Illegitimate and Adopted Children

In the case of a gift to B in fee (or absolutely in the case of chattels) but if B dies without "issue" or without "children" to C, the birth of an illegitimate child to B will not

---

15. Ahlfield v. Curtis, 1907, 229 Ill. 139, 82 N.E. 276 (*dictum*); Wilson v. Wilson, 1937, 270 Ky. 245, 109 S.W.2d 607; Rogers v. Baily, 1909, 76 N.J.Eq. 29, 73 A. 243; Briggs v. Hopkins, 1921, 103 Ohio St. 321, 132 N.E. 843; 3 Rest.Property, § 267.

16. Quilliam v. Union Trust Co., 1924, 194 Ind. 521, 142 N.E. 214; Pullen v. Pullen, 1950, 120 Ind.App. 284, 91 N.E.2d 856; Ballance v. Garner, 1946, 161 Kan. 371, 168 P.2d 533; Owens v. Men and Millions Movement, 1922, 296 Mo. 110, 246 S.W. 172, questioned in Humphreys v. Welling, 1937, 341 Mo. 1198, 111 S.W.2d 123, but reaffirmed in Kindred v. Anderson, 1948, 357 Mo. 564, 209 S.W.2d 912; Washbon v. Cope, 1895, 144 N.Y. 287, 39 N.E. 388; Mickley's Appeal, 1880, 92 Pa. 514; In re Gulstine's Estate, 1932, 166 Wash. 325, 6 P.2d 628.

17. Kindred v. Anderson, 1948, 357 Mo. 564, 209 S.W. 2d 912; Lawrence v. Calam, 1923, 236 N.Y. 168, 140 N.E. 232, reargument denied 292 N.Y. 618, 55 N.E.2d 378; Davenport v. Graham, 1942, 343 Pa. 497, 23 A.2d 482, noted in 8 Univ.of Pitt.Law Rev.

146 (1942); Eckhardt v. Phillips, 1940, 176 Tenn. 34, 137 S.W.2d 301, noted in 16 Tenn.Law Rev. 479 (1940).

18. Smith v. Shepard, 1939, 370 Ill. 491, 19 N.E.2d 368; Hall v. Spencer, 1950, 312 Ky. 274, 227 S.W.2d 196; Bowdle v. Hanks, 1962, 229 Md. 352, 182 A.2d 790; Davis v. Scharf, 1926, 99 N.J.Eq. 88, 133 A. 197; Payne v. Payne, 1946, 81 U.S.App.D.C. 11, 154 F.2d 297; 3 Rest. Property, § 269.

Contra: Estate of Carothers, 1911, 161 Cal. 588, 119 P. 926 (death at any time); McCulloch v. Yost, 1947, 148 Ohio St. 675, 76 N.E.2d 707 (*dictum*, death at any time); Schenck v. Schenck, 1939, 106 Ind. App. 179, 18 N.E.2d 941 (substitutional construction —death of testator); Smith v. Glen Alden Coal Co., 1943, 347 Pa. 290, 32 A.2d 227 (substitutional construction—death of testator).

19. Deering v. Skidmore, 1940, 282 Ky. 292, 138 S.W. 2d 471 (until attainment of a stated age); 3 Rest. Property, § 268. Cf.: Howell v. Deady, D.Or.1939, 48 F.Supp. 104.

bar C's claim to the property. If a statute provides that an illegitimate child is entitled to inherit from the named ancestor then the gift over is not operative.[20] This would also follow if, under local statutory rules, an illegitimate child is legitimated.

Ordinarily, an adopted child is not considered to be the "child" or the "issue" of the adopting parent.[21] Accordingly, the adoption of a child will not prevent the operation of a gift over in the event that a person dies without "issue" or without "children." [22] However, even if a child is adopted, he remains the "child" or "issue" of his natural parents to the extent that the adoption proceedings do not, under local statute, interfere with the right of that child to inherit from his natural parents, or from the child's more remote ancestors.

In a substantial number of states it is provided by statute that adopted children have all the rights of natural children. Thus, an adopted child qualifies as the "child" or "issue" of the adopting parents. In that event, the adoption prevents the operation of the gift-over clause.[23]

Survival of Issue, Descendants or Children

In Treharne v. Layton (Eng.),[24] land was devised to a granddaughter for life with remainder to her children. There was a gift over if the granddaughter died without issue.

After the death of the testator a son was born to the granddaughter but he died a few hours after birth. Heirs of the son were entitled to the land as against those claiming under the gift over. In view of the fact that there was a direct gift to issue the gift over failed. Under such circumstances the words "die without issue," descendants or children necessarily means die without ever having had issue etc.

But a different rule is followed in the *absence of a direct gift* to issue, descendants or children. A person dies without issue etc., if such issue, descendant or child fails to survive the time of the death of the named ancestor. Under such circumstances "die without issue," descendants or children does not mean die without ever having had issue etc.[25] A contrary view is expressed in a few decisions.[26] But even under this minority rule there is a requirement of survivorship if the conveying instrument provides that a gift over is to take effect if the named ancestor dies *without leaving issue* etc.[27] Some decisions support a similar conclusion if language is susceptible to the construction that the condition is satisfied by the birth of issue, such as in a case where there is a gift over if B died "without his having a child or children." [28]

Presumption as to Possibility of Issue

Regardless of age or physical condition, there is a conclusive presumption that a person is capable of having issue. Insofar as age

20.   3 Rest. Property, § 265, *Comment c.*

21.   Fletcher v. Flanary, 1946, 185 Va. 409, 38 S.E.2d 433; Wyeth v. Merchant, D.Mo.1940, 34 F.Supp. 785, affirmed 120 F.2d 242 (1941); 3 Rest. Property, § 265, *Comment d.*

22.   See Merson v. Wood, 1961, 202 Va. 485, 117 S.E.2d 661 (gift over if primary taker died "without heirs").

23.   See, for example, In re Holden's Trust, 1940, 207 Minn. 211, 291 N.W. 104; Kindred v. Anderson, 1948, 357 Mo. 564, 209 S.W.2d 912.

24.   L.R. 10 Q.B. 459 (1875).

25.   Wurts' Ex'rs v. Page, 1869, 19 N.J.Eq. 365; Briggs v. Hopkins, 1921, 103 Ohio St. 321, 132 N.E. 843.

26.   Bullock v. Seymour, 1866, 33 Conn. 289; Tolley v. Wilson, 1939, 371 Ill. 124, 20 N.E.2d 68.

27.   Trabue v. Gillham, 1951, 408 Ill. 508, 97 N.E.2d 341.

28.   Walker v. Trollinger, 1926, 192 N.C. 744, 135 S.E. 871.

is concerned, the basis for this rule is the probative value of evidence to the contrary. This is especially true with respect to persons that may be placed in the "questionable-age bracket." This is also a factor if impossibility of issue is claimed because of the physical condition of a person. In addition, there is a problem relating to public policy. The admissibility of such evidence for the purpose in question might be an encouragement to those who would submit to unnecessary operations merely for the purpose of establishing the fact that there was no longer possibility of issue. This would result in the devolution of ownership in a manner contrary to the intention of the conveyor.

The possibility-of-issue rule is applied relentlessly in situations involving an application of the rule against perpetuities.[29] However, there is authority supporting the position that in matters of taxation proof as to the probability of issue is admissible for the purpose of proving the value of an estate that is contingent upon death without issue, chil-

dren etc.[30] It is also admissible in litigation involving a right to the possession of property or a claim of equitable waste where the quantum of the estate of defendant is of controlling importance.[31]

The prevailing rule is that a final adjudication of ownership of property will have to await the death of a person if contingencies of ownership hinge upon death with or without issue.[32] However, the possibility of issue is a question of fact and the judicial process contemplates a determination of conflicting claims based upon alleged facts. Under some circumstances it seems ridiculous to apply a conclusive presumption that a living person is capable of having issue. There is authority that a final adjudication of property rights may be made on the basis of a determination that a living person cannot give birth to a child.[33]

29. Lovering v. Lovering, 1880, 129 Mass. 97; Loud v. St. Louis Union Trust Co., 1923, 298 Mo. 148, 249 S.W. 629; Jee v. Audley, [1787] 1 Cox 324, 29 Eng. Rep. 1186; In re Dawson, 1888, 39 Ch.Div. 155. *Contra:* Exham v. Beamish, 1939, Ir.R. 336.

30. Ninth Bank & Trust Co. v. U. S., D.Pa.1936, 15 F.Supp. 951.

31. See Gannon v. Peterson, 1901, 193 Ill. 372, 62 N.E. 210, 55 L.R.A. 701.

32. See Simes and Smith, Future Interests (2nd ed.), § 777, p. 258.

33. In re Bassett's Estate, 1963, 104 N.H. 504, 190 A.2d 415; Hicks v. Unborn Children, 1963, 259 N.C. 387, 130 S.E.2d 666. See also, Greer v. Parker, 1946, 209 Ark. 553, 191 S.W.2d 584 (a specific performance case).

CHAPTER 33

CLASS GIFTS

CLASS GIFT DEFINED

162. A class gift results from a disposition to a group of persons, the share of each member depending upon the number of persons who may qualify for membership.

a. Gift to a named person and to a group. A gift to a named person and to a group may constitute a class gift.

b. Devise of land to B and his children— rule in Wild's case. The first resolution in Wild's case is that if B does not have children at the time of the devise he acquires an estate in fee tail. The preferred view at the present time is that B acquires a life estate and a contingent remainder is created in children.

The second resolution is that if B does have children at the time of the devise it creates a class gift. This conclusion represents the prevailing rule at the present time.

While it is not possible to give an all-purpose definition of a class gift, fundamental concepts are embodied in the statement found in Jarman on Wills.[1] A class gift is defined as a gift by deed or will of "an aggregate sum to a body of persons uncertain in number at the time of the gift, to be ascertained at a future time, and who are all to take in equal or in some other definite proportion, the

share of each being dependent for its amount upon the ultimate number of persons." [2]

It is not necessary that the "body of persons" be capable of both increasing and decreasing in number. In determining whether or not there may be group-fluctuation in the case of a will, the situation is viewed from the time of the execution of the will. For example, in the case of a testamentary gift "to the children of B" a class gift is involved even though B is deceased at the time of the execution of the will. The class may decrease in number if one of the children then living predeceases the testator.[3] This common law rule may not be applicable if a local lapse statute operates in the case of a class gift.[4]

A single conveyance may result in the creation of two or more primary class gifts. That is the situation, for example, if there is a direction that property is to be divided "between" the testator's nephews and nieces and his wife's nephews and nieces. Each class is entitled to one-half of the property. The use of the word "between" as distinguished from

---

1. Jarman, Wills (7th ed. 1930), p. 309.

2. For a criticism of this definition see Cooley, What Constitutes a Class Gift, 49 Harv.Law Rev. 903, 925 (1936).

3. Viner v. Francis, [1789] 2 Cox. 190, 30 Eng.Rep. 88; Simes & Smith, The Law of Future Interests (2nd ed.) § 661; 3 Rest. Property, § 279, *Comment d*, Illust. 1.

4. See Rest. Property, § 298.

the word "among" facilitates this construction.[5]

The creation of a class gift depends upon proof of the fact that the conveyor intended to make a conveyance to a *group* and not to individuals. From this it follows that a class gift construction is not indicated in a conveyance made to named individuals even though susceptible to designation as a group (nephews and nieces, brothers and sisters, children etc.).[6] In the absence of evidence tending to show a contrary intention, a class gift construction will not be applied if a conveyance is made to a group wherein the members are also described by name, such as in a testamentary gift "to my brothers and sisters, namely, A, B, C and D."[7] In some cases, under the guise of construction, a class gift is said to arise as a means by which the obvious purpose of a testator can be accomplished.[8] These are not true class gift dispositions. In some situations it would seem more appropriate for the court to hold that the purpose of the testator was to create a joint tenancy rather than a class gift. This would justify a decree that a survivor is entitled to take.

Gift to a Named Person and to a Group

In the absence of evidence indicating a contrary intention, a gift to a named person and a group qualifies as a class gift.[9] In Estate of Rauschenplat (Cal.),[10] testator devised land to his sister, B, to all of the living children of his deceased half-brother, C, and to D, "share and share alike." The court held that this resulted in a class gift and that the property should be distributed on a *per capita* basis (an equal amount to each member of the class).[11] This conclusion was facilitated by the fact that distribution was directed to be made on a "share and share alike" basis. As in the case of any class gift, the death of a member of the class (D) prior to the death of the testator did not result in a lapsed legacy. Assuming that a lapse legacy statute is not applicable, this merely decreased the size of the class and resulted in a larger share for each qualifying member of the class.[12] Similarly, if all members of the "group" predeceased the testator, the named person of the class would be entitled to the entire gift if he survived the testator.[13]

In Lefeavre v. Pennington (Ark.),[14] testator's will directed that his property was to be "divided equally between all of our nephews and nieces on my wife's side and my niece." There were twenty-two nephews and nieces on the wife's side. The court held that the

5.   In re Moore's Estate, 1945, 157 Pa.Super. 296, 43 A.2d 359.

6.   Damron v. Mast, 1937, 121 N.J.Eq. 489, 191 A. 467; Matter of Kimberly, 1896, 150 N.Y. 90, 44 N.E. 945; In re Pearsall's Estate, 1915, 91 Misc. 212, 155 N.Y.S. 59; In re Griffiths' Estate, 1920, 172 Wis. 630, 179 N.W. 768; Re Bloch's Estate, 1938, 227 Wis. 468, 278 N.W. 875.

7.   Estate of Murphy, 1909, 157 Cal. 63, 106 P. 230; Blackstone v. Althouse, 1917, 278 Ill. 481, 116 N.E. 154, L.R.A.1918B, 230; 3 Rest. Property, § 280. But see, In re Heller's Estate, 1951, 14 N.J.Super. 152, 81 A.2d 418.

8.   See, for example, Bolles v. Smith, 1872, 39 Conn. 217; In re Stebbins's Estate, 1925, 125 Misc. 150, 210 N.Y.S. 424; Chase v. Peckham, 1891, 17 R.I. 385, 22 A. 285; Krog v. Hafka, 1952, 413 Ill. 290, 109 N.E.2d 213.

9.   3 Rest. Property, § 284.

10. 212 Cal. 33, 297 P. 882, 78 A.L.R. 1380 (1931).

11. Accord: In re Scheffler's Estate, 1958, 3 Wis.2d 421, 88 N.W.2d 370.

12. Manier v. Phelps, 1884, 15 Abb.N.C.(N.Y.) 123; Kingsbury v. Walter [1899] 2 Ch. 314. *Contra:* In re Pierce's Estate, 1922, 177 Wis. 104, 188 N.W. 78.

13. Davis v. Sanders, 1905, 123 Ga. 177, 51 So. 298; In re Moss: Kingsbury v. Walter, [1899] 2 Ch. 314 (*dictum*).

14. 217 Ark. 397, 230 S.W.2d 46 (1950).

testator's niece was not a member of the class and that she was entitled to one-half of the property. Some importance is attached to the fact that the property was to be divided *between* the wife's nephews and nieces and the testator's niece and that the word *between* as distinguished from the word "among," contemplates two objects only.[15]

Devise of land to B and his Children—Rule in Wild's Case

Two important resolutions are set forth in Wild's Case (Eng.),[16] decided in 1599. The case involves a testamentary disposition of land and the resolutions *(dicta)* relate to the appropriate construction of a limitation to a person "and his children" or in words construed to mean "children." These resolutions are as follows:

First: The first resolution is that if land is devised to B and his children, if B does not have children at the time of the devise he acquires a fee tail estate. Thus, it was conceived that the obvious purpose of the testator to benefit children could be accomplished by rules relating to inheritance. This was, of course, a doubtful benefit because of the then recognized procedure by means of which the owner of a fee tail could institute fictitious legal proceedings (common recovery) and defeat the claims of the heirs of his body by making a conveyance in fee simple.[17]

The purpose of the testator could have been assured of accomplishment by a construction that B acquired a life estate with a contingent remainder to his children. This alternative construction was followed in the case of a conveyance by deed where technical

words, such as to B and the heirs of his body, were required for the conveyance of a fee tail.[18] This was also the case if the transfer involved chattel interests where the creation of an estate tail was not possible.

While there are modern authorities expressing approval of the first resolution in Wild's case,[19] the preferred view is that such a conveyance creates a life estate with a contingent remainder.[20]

Second: The second resolution in Wild's Case is that if land is devised to B and his children, and if B does have children at the time of the testator's death "the parent and children take equal and concurrent estates." [21] Unless an intent to the contrary is established, this class-gift construction is followed whether the transfer is by will or *inter vivos* conveyance and whether the transfer involves land or chattels.

This resolution in Wild's Case is generally followed in the United States.[22] However,

---

15. *Cf.*: Estate of Carroll, 1944, 62 Cal.App.2d 798, 145 P.2d 644.

16. 6 Co.Rep. 16b, 77 Eng.Rep. 277 (1599).

17. Taltarum's Case, 1472, 12 Edw. IV, 19, pl. 25.

18. But a conveyance by deed may result in a fee-tail construction if words of inheritance have been abolished by statute. See Ewing v. Ewing, 1945, 198 Miss. 304, 22 So.2d 225, 161 A.L.R. 606, noted in 46 Col.Law Rev. 306 (1946); James v. James, 1939, 189 S.C. 414, 1 S.E.2d 494, noted in 25 Va. Law Rev. 988 (1939). *Cf.*: Herrick v. Lain, 1941, 375 Ill. 569, 32 N.E.2d 154.

19. See, for example, Boggs v. Baxter, Ky.App.1953, 261 S.W.2d 684; Ewing v. Ewing, 1945, 198 Miss. 304, 22 So.2d 225, 161 A.L.R. 606, noted in 46 Col. Law Rev. 306 (1946); Larew v. Larew, 1926, 146 Va. 134, 135 S.E. 819.

20. See, for example, Ellingrod v. Trombla, 1959, 116 Neb. 264, 95 N.W.2d 635 (under provisions of the Uniform Property Act); 3 Rest. Property, § 283(a).

21. 3 Rest. Property, § 283, *Comment a.*

22. Albers v. Donovan, 1939, 371 Ill. 458, 21 N.E.2d 563 (conveyance to "B and the heirs born of her body" construed to be a conveyance to "B and her children"). Strawhacker v. Strawhacker, 1937, 132 Neb. 614, 272 N.W. 772; Gordon v. Jackson, 1899, 58 N.J.Eq. 166, 43 A. 98; Wills v. Foltz, 1907, 61 W.Va. 262, 56 S.E. 473; 3 Rest. Property, § 283(a).

there is authority for a construction that would give B a life estate with a contingent remainder to his children.[23] Under this view, children born after the death of the testator qualify as class members and are entitled to share in the gift.[24]

GIFTS TO CHILDREN

163. In the absence of language indicating a contrary intention, a gift to "children" is limited to immediate offspring.

    a. Illegitimate children. Ordinarily, an illegitimate child is not entitled to share in a gift to children.

    b. Adopted children. If an adoptive parent makes a gift to his children an adopted child qualifies as a member of the class. If a gift is made by one other than the adoptive parent an adopted child does not qualify as a member of the class. However, the conveying instrument may expressly provide that adopted children are to be included as class members and such an intention may be implied. In many states there is a statutory rule that adopted children have all the rights of a natural child, including the right to share in such a gift.

    c. Children or issue of two or more life tenants. A gift to two or more life tenants with a gift over to their children may be susceptible to the construction that there are as many separate class gifts as there are life tenants.

In the absence of language indicating a contrary intent, a gift to "children" is limited

to immediate offspring.[25] However, grandchildren may derive an indirect benefit from a testamentary gift to children. If the parent dies before the death of the testator, the parent's children (grandchildren of the testator) may be entitled to take under a lapse statute. So also, if the parent acquires a transmissible interest this may pass to his children at the time of the parent's death. Variations as to the scope of a gift to "children" are as follows:

First: Even if a gift is made to children, circumstances may show that the testator's intent was to make a gift to grandchildren. For example, if a testamentary gift is made to "the children of B," and the testator was aware of the fact that B had died at the time the will was executed and was survived only by grandchildren, it is obvious that the word "children" was used as meaning "grandchildren." [26] In some cases the plan of testamentary disposition evidenced by a will may justify the conclusion that grandchildren were included in a disposition made to children.[27]

Second: A testamentary disposition to "children and grandchildren," may be construed to be a gift to "descendants." [28] In that event, great-grandchildren are entitled to share in the gift. A construction may be warranted that a gift to "children" was intended to be a gift to "issue." [29]

---

23. Schlemeyer v. Mellencamp, 1945, 159 Kan. 544, 156 P.2d 879 (statutory rule); Rummerfield v. Mason, 1944, 352 Mo. 865, 179 S.W.2d 732; Gordon v. Jackson, 1899, 58 N.J.Eq. 166, 43 A. 98; Elliott v. Diamond Coal & Coke Co., 1911, 230 P. 423, 79 A. 708. See Kuhn v. Kuhn, 1902, 68 S.W.2d 16, 24 Ky.Law Rep. 112.

24. Noyes v. Parker, 1937, 68 App.D.C. 13, 92 F.2d 562; U. S. v. 654.8 Acres of Land, D.Tenn.1952, 102 F.Supp. 937.

25. In re Estate of Schuette, 1940, 138 Neb. 568, 293 N.W. 421; In re Bennett's Estate, 1935, 282 N.Y.S. 645. *Cf.:* Steward v. Knight, 1901, 62 N.J.Eq. 232, 49 A. 535.

26. See Casner, Class Gifts—Definitional Aspects, 41 Col.Law Rev. 1, 5 (1941).

27. Davis Trust Co. v. Elkins, 1934, 114 W.Va. 742, 175 S.E. 611.

28. Estate of Brown, 1962, 199 Cal.App.2d 274, 18 Cal. Rptr. 435.

29. In re Clark's Estate, 1948, 359 Pa. 411, 59 A.2d 109.

Third: Unless a conveyor has evidenced a contrary intent, equal distribution is made to those who qualify as "children," "grandchildren," "nephews and nieces," "uncles and aunts," etc. If there is a gift to the children of named persons, such as the children of B, C and D, all of the children share equally. In other words, the distribution is made on a *per capita* basis.[30]

Illegitimate Children

Ordinarily, an illegitimate child is not entitled to share in a gift to children,[31] there are exceptions to this rule. In the first place, since an illegitimate child inherits from its natural mother, a gift by that mother to her children includes her illegitimate children. In the second place, statutes of inheritance in many states provide that, under varying circumstances, an illegitimate child may inherit from its natural parents. Therefore, the fact that a donee had an illegitimate child capable of inheriting at the effective date of the conveying instrument tends to establish the fact that the conveyor intended the child to be a class member.[32] However, there is authority for the view that such knowledge, standing alone, is not a sufficient basis upon which to base such a conclusion. In addition to proof of knowledge there must be proof of the fact that the illegitimate child was a part of the family circle, or was otherwise recognized as the object of the

testator's natural bounty.[33] In the third place, a child legitimated under statutory provisions, prior to the effective date of the conveying instrument, qualifies as a child for the purpose under discussion.[34]

Adopted Children

Adoption was not recognized in England until the passage of an adoption statute in 1926. The concept is one borrowed from the Roman law and is prescribed by statute in practically all of the American states. In legal contemplation, the person adopted becomes the "child" of the adoptive parent or parents with resultant rights and liabilities as in the case of a natural child.[35]

If an adoptive parent makes a gift to his "children" an adopted child qualifies as a member of the class.[36] However, if such a gift comes from a third party there is a presumption that only natural children were intended to take.[37] However, an ambiguity arises if it is shown that the conveyor knew of the fact that the named parent had, in fact, adopted a child.[38] This fact may be sufficient to establish the right of an adopted

---

30. Simes & Smith, Future Interests (2nd Ed.), § 740; 3 Rest. Property, § 300. See In re England's Estate, 1964, 414 Pa. 115, 200 A.2d 897 (construing language in will).

31. Marsh v. Field, 1921, 297 Ill. 251, 256, 130 N.E. 753, 755.

32. See In re Estate of Ellis, 1938, 225 Iowa 1279, 282 N.W. 758, 120 A.L.R. 975, noted in 87 Univ. of Pa.Law Rev. 752 (1939), 25 Va.Law Rev. 634 (1939); 3 Rest. Property, § 286(2) (c).

33. In re Trust of Bohnsack, 1963, 20 Wis.2d 448, 122 N.W.2d 443 (modifying rule declared in Will of Kaufer, 1931, 203 Wis. 299, 234 N.W. 504).

34. 3 Rest. Property, § 286(1) (b).

35. See In re McDonald's Estate, 1963, 20 Wis.2d 63, 121 N.W.2d 245 (testamentary gift to the children of testator included his natural child even though the child had been adopted by another).

36. Corr's Estate, 1940, 338 Pa. 337, 12 A.2d 76. See In re Tower's Estate, 1963, 410 Pa. 389, 189 A.2d 870 (testamentary gift to children of a grandchild restricted to natural children where will used such words as "blood" descendants).

37. Perkins v. New England Trust Co., 1962, 344 Mass. 287, 182 N.E.2d 308; Cutrer v. Cutrer, 1961, 162 Tex. 166, 345 S.W.2d 513, 86 A.L.R.2d 105.

38. But see Peirce v. Farmers State Bank, 1943, 222 Ind. 116, 51 N.E.2d 480.

child to share in the gift.[39] Even in the absence of such knowledge there is authority for the view that the statutory rule fixing the rights of an adopted child facilitates a finding that the use of the word "child" in a gift presumably includes an adopted child.[40] There is some indication that such a conclusion is warranted as a matter of public policy.[41] In some states it is provided by statute that an adopted child shall be deemed lawful issue of the adopting parent unless a conveying instrument shall otherwise provide.[42]

Children or Issue of Two or More Life Tenants

A gift to two or more life tenants with a gift over to their children or issue may be susceptible to the construction that there are as many separate gifts as there are life tenants. This negatives the conclusion that *all* of the property is to be distributed to *all* of the children or issue on a *per capita* basis. Upon the death of a life tenant there is a gift over of the fractional share to the deceased tenant's children or issue. A gift over to "their children" is a gift over to "their respective" children. The children receive the parent's share only.[43] This conclusion

may be justified even if the direction is that the children are to share "equally" or to "share and share alike." This equality requirement is satisfied if there is an equal distribution with respect to the various classes.[44]

GIFTS TO "ISSUE" AND "DESCENDANTS"

164. Generally, a gift to "issue" is a gift to descendants of every degree, including children, grandchildren etc. It is broader than the word "descendants" because the word "issue" may include children, grandchildren etc., of a living parent.

An illegitimate child qualifies as "issue" if such child would be entitled to inherit the property involved in case of an intestacy.

In the absence of statute, or direction to the contrary, an adopted child does not qualify as "issue" if the conveyor is not the adoptive parent.

a. As meaning children. Language in a conveying instrument may show that the conveyor used the word "issue" as meaning "children."

b. Manner of distribution. The preferred construction is that in a gift to "issue" the distribution is to be made on a *per stirpes* basis. This is the statutory rule in some states.

Absent language to the contrary, a gift to "issue" is a gift to descendants of every degree, children, grandchildren etc. It is broader that the word "descendants" [45] because the word "issue" may include children, grandchildren etc., of a *living parent*. An illegitimate child qualifies as "issue" if such

---

39. Mesecher v. Leir, 1950, 241 Iowa 818, 43 N.W.2d 149; 3 Rest. Property, § 287(2) (b). *Contra:* In re Woodcock, 1907, 103 Me. 214, 68 A. 821.

40. Estate of Stanford, 1957, 49 Cal.2d 120, 315 P.2d 681; In re Trusteeship Agreement with Nash, 1963, 265 Minn. 412, 122 N.W.2d 104 (adoption took place 19 years after creation of *inter vivos* trust).

41. Estate of Heard, 1957, 49 Cal.2d 514, 319 P.2d 637; In re Patrick's Will, 1960, 259 Minn. 193, 106 N.W.2d 888 (*de facto* adoption); Delaney v. First National Bank, 1963, 73 N.M. 192, 386 P.2d 711.

42. See, for example, In re Coe, 1964, 42 N.J. 485, 201 A.2d 571.

43. Dills v. Deavors, Ky.1954, 266 S.W.2d 788; Gaughen v. Gaughen, 1961, 172 Neb. 740, 112 N.W.2d 285; Horne v. Horne, 1943, 181 Va. 685, 26 S.E.2d 80; Arrow v. Mellish, [1847] 1 De G. & Sm. 355, 63 Eng.Rep. 1102; 3 Rest. Property, § 301. *Cf.:* Smith

v. Thayer, 1963, 28 Ill.2d 363, 192 N.E.2d 375 (where property went over as a unit); Dole v. Keyes, 1887, 143 Mass. 237, 9 N.E. 625 (where property went over as a unit).

44. 3 Page on Wills (Lifetime Ed.), § 1082, p. 291.

45. See definition of "descendant" in Reilly v. Huff, Tex.Civ.App.1960, 335 S.W.2d 275.

a child would be entitled to inherit the property involved in a case of intestacy.[46]

Since adoption procedure was unknown to the common law, claims could not arise out of adoption. However, adoption procedure is now generally recognized in the various states. Absent an expression of intent to the contrary, it may be assumed that a conveyor intends his adopted child to take under a gift to issue.[47] The preferred view is that an adopted child will not qualify as "issue" if the conveyor is not the adoptive parent.[48] But a different conclusion may be reached if it is shown that the conveyor knew of the adoption at the time of the conveyance.[49] An increasing number of cases take the position that an adopted child is entitled to take as "issue" of the adoptive parent if there is a statute providing, in effect, that such a child has all the rights of a natural child.[50] Some statutes specifically provide that an adopted child shall be deemed a descendant of one who has adopted him, the same as a natural child, for all purposes of succession by, from or through adopting parent.[51]

As Meaning Children

Language in a conveying instrument may show that the conveyor used the word "issue" as meaning "children". That may appear from the fact that the word "issue" and the word "children" were used interchangeably.

According to English authority, a conveyance containing a provision that "issue" are to take a *parent's* share is construed as one to children only.[52] The use of the word "parent," "mother" or "father" qualifies and restricts the meaning of the word "issue" to the first generation (children). While this conclusion finds some support in American decisions the prevailing rule is to the contrary.[53] It is considered that a provision giving "issue" a "parent's" share is a gift to descendants of every degree.

Manner of Distribution

According to the English rule, as declared in the leading case of Freeman v. Parsley,[54] a gift to "issue" contemplates distribution on a *per capita* basis. In other words, an equal distribution is made as between children, grandchildren, great-grandchildren etc. All of these distributees qualify as issue. For example, if a testamentary gift is made by T to his issue and, at the time of his death, he leaves surviving two children, B and C, and C has five children, these five children and B and C each receive distribution of a one-seventh interest in the estate. In other words, children take the same share as their living parents. This may not be what the testator intended but it is in compliance with his direction. Applying the same rule of

46. Eaton v. Eaton, 1914, 88 Conn. 286, 91 A. 196 (an illegitimate child of an illegitimate child); Palmer v. Horn, 1881, 84 N.Y. 516; 3 Rest. Property, § 292, *Comment (a)*.

47. See Gannett v. Old Colony Trust Co., 1959, 155 Me. 248, 153 A.2d 122 (gift by testator to *his* issue construed to include the children of his adopted son).

48. But see Estate of Breese, 1959, 7 Wis.2d 422, 96 N.W.2d 712.

49. 3 Rest. Property, §§ 287(2b), 292, *Comment (a)*.

50. Walker v. O'Brien, 9 Cir., 1940, 115 F.2d 956, certiorari denied 312 U.S. 707, 61 S.Ct. 829, 85 L.Ed. 1139 (1941), noted in 39 Mich.Law Rev. 1221 (1941).

51. See, for example, West's Ann.Cal.Probate Code, § 257.

52. Sibley v. Perry, [1802] 7 Ves. 522, 32 Eng.Rep. 211. For a discussion favoring this rule see Kales, Meaning of the Word "Issue" in Gifts to "Issue," 6 Ill.Law Rev. 217 (1911).

53. See, for example, Dolbeare v. Dolbeare, 1938, 124 Conn. 286, 199 A. 555, 117 A.L.R. 687, noted in 37 Mich.Law Rev. 630 (1939). See also, Schnebly, Testamentary Gifts to "Issue," 35 Yale Law Jr., 571, 589 (1926); 3 Rest. Property, § 292, *Comment (f)*.

54. 3 Ves. 421, 30 Eng.Rep. 1085 (1797).

construction, issue of deceased children or grandchildren would take on an equal basis with living children. If a testator desires issue of deceased children or grandchildren to take only the share to which the parent would be entitled if he were alive his purpose can be accomplished by the simple process of directing distribution on a *per stirpes* basis. This means that children are not entitled to take in competition with their living parent. They are entitled to take only if the parent is deceased and, in that event, they take by right of representation. That is, they take only the share to which the parent would have been entitled were he alive at the time fixed for distribution.

In the absence of statute the English rule finds support in American decisions. However, there is a judicial preference in favor of a *per stirpes* distribution and "slight evidence" will be sufficient to justify departure from a conclusion that would lead to a *per capita* distribution.[55] In some states statutes provide for a *per stirpes* distribution unless the testator has clearly expressed an intent that distribution be made on a *per capita* basis.[56] According to some cases such an intent may be inferred from a direction that distribution is to be made to the issue "equally" or that the donees are to "share and share alike." Some statutes provide that in the absence of an expression of such intent, distribution is to be made by reference to the local statute as it relates to intestate succes-

sion. These statutes usually provide for distribution on a *per stirpes* basis.[57]

In some states, even in the absence of statute, it is construed that a gift to "issue" includes all lineal descendants in the order in which they would be entitled to take under the law of intestate succession. This means that distribution is made on a *per stirpes* basis. Some authorities hold that a contrary intent is not evidenced by a direction that the property is to be distributed to issue "share and share alike." [58] However, a specific direction that distribution is to be made on a *per capita* basis will be respected.[59]

MAXIMUM CLASS MEMBERSHIP

165. In general, maximum class membership is determined at the time fixed for the first distribution. However, there may be a decrease in the class membership because of provisions relating to such matters as survivorship.

a. Immediate gift. In the case of an *immediate gift* to a class, membership is limited to persons born or conceived at the effective date of the gift.

> **If there are no qualified class members at the time of the effective date of the gift, and the gift involves *specific property, or an aggregate sum*, the class will include all persons who subsequently qualify as class members.**

55. In re Thompson's Estate, 1938, 202 Minn. 648, 279 N.W. 574, noted in 37 Mich.Law Rev. 630 (1939); In re Mayhew's Estate, 1932, 307 Pa. 84, 160 A. 724, 83 A.L.R. 149.

56. See, for example, Merrow v. Merrow, 1963, 105 N.H. 103, 193 A.2d 19; Rembert v. Vetoe, 1911, 89 S.C. 198, 71 S.E. 959, 2 A.L.R. 918; N.J.S. 3A:3A-1 and 2 (L.1952, c. 221) N.J.S.A.; 3 Rest. Property, § 303.

57. See, for example, McKinney's N.Y.Decedent Estate Law, § 47a. But the determination of class membership may be postponed until the termination of an intermediate estate. For example, in Murray v. Sullivan, 1962, 158 Me. 98, 179 A.2d 307, a testamentary gift was to "all of my lineal descendants", if any, then living (after death of named children of T). The court held the class was composed of grandchildren living at the time of the death of the last surviving child and they took *per capita*.

58. Warren v. First New Haven Nat. Bank, 1962, 150 Conn. 120, 186 A.2d 794. See 3 Rest. Property, § 303(1).

59. Welch v. Phinney, 1958, 337 Mass. 594, 150 N.E.2d 723.

If there are no qualified **class members** at the effective date of the gift, and the gift involves the payment of *a stated amount* to each class member, the gift will fail in its entirety unless the donor expressed an intention to the contrary. To keep the class open for all those who might subsequently qualify would thereby postpone any distribution with respect to the donor's estate. It would not be possible to ascertain what portion of the estate would be required to satisfy the demand.

b. **Postponed gift. In general, if distribution under a class gift is postponed, the maximum membership of the class is determined on the date fixed for the first distribution.**

If there are no qualified members at that time, and the gift involves specific property, or an aggregate sum, the class will include all persons who subsequently qualify as class members. If the gift involves payment of a specified amount to each class member it will fail unless the donor has expressed a contrary intention.

If the owner of property directs its distribution to persons described as children, grandchildren, brothers and sisters, nephews and nieces etc., it is proper to assume a general intent on his part to confer a benefit upon all persons answering the description. But if this direction is accompanied by another direction that the property is to be distributed at a stated time the class, of necessity, must close at that time. This means that no additional members will be admitted to the class. To admit new members would frustrate the direction as to distribution. This does not mean, of course, that all persons answering the description at the time fixed for distribution will be entitled to share in the gift. There may be a decrease in the size of the class. This may result because

of expressed conditions. For example, there may be a requirement of survivorship.[60]

Immediate Gift

In the case of an immediate gift to a class, membership is limited to persons born or conceived [61] (if subsequently born alive) answering the general description prescribed for class membership at the time of the death of the testator or on the date of an *inter vivos* trust. It is necessary that the maximum membership in the class be ascertained at that time in order to fix the share that can be distributed to each qualified class member.

In Landwehr's Estate (Pa.),[62] T's will involved a class gift to the children of his son, B. B had seven children living at the time of T's death. The court held that the class closed at the time of T's death. Membership was limited to the seven children born at that time. Two children subsequently born to B were excluded from benefits.[63] A conveyor may evidence an intent to keep the class open by an express direction, such as by a provision that the gift is to children of B "that he now has, or may hereafter have," or words of similar import.[64]

The rule of construction that a class will include only persons born at the effective date of a conveyance is not suited to a situation where there are no class members living

---

60. See infra, § 166.

61. 3 Rest. Property, § 294(a).

62. 147 Pa. 121, 23 A. 848 (1892).

63. See Warren, Devises to "Children," 35 Yale Law Jr. 785, 786 (1926); 3 Rest. Property, § 294(a). *Cf.*: Azarch v. Smith, 1928, 222 Ky. 566, 1 S.W.2d 968.

64. Pickett v. Southerland, 1864, 60 N.C. 615; De Santo v. Haug, 1961, 65 N.J.Super. 206, 167 A.2d 428; 3 Rest. Property, § 294, *Comment (p)*.

at that time. Rules applicable under such circumstances are as follows:

First: If the gift involves specific property or an aggregate sum, the class will include all persons answering the description whenever born. Weld v. Bradbury (Eng.),[65] is a leading case. Testator directed that one-half of the proceeds derived from the sale of specific property should be paid to "the children of J. S. and J. N." Neither J. S. nor J. N. had a child living either when the will was executed or when the testator died. The court held that the gift to children, taking effect as an executory interest, would include all children of J. S. and J. N. whenever born.[66]

In a situation such as that involved in Weld v. Bradbury, it is not clear that the testator intended an immediate, as distinguished from a postponed, gift to children. Certainly, if he knew at the time of his death that there were no children born who could qualify as class members he could not have intended an immediate gift. His intention to benefit children can be accomplished only by including subsequently born children as members of the class and this can be accomplished without inconvenience in connection with the administration of his estate.

Second: In Rogers v. Mutch (Eng.),[67] testatrix directed that one hundred pounds should be paid to each of the children of B who attained the age of twenty-one. At the time of her death B was without children. The court held that the attempted gift to children failed. Children born to B after the death of testatrix were not entitled to the gift.[68]

If the children born to B after the death of testatrix were allowed to take, the portion of testatrix's estate that would be required for the purpose could not be ascertained until the time of B's death. Thus, distribution of testatrix's entire estate would have to be postponed until that time. This inconvenience incident to the administration of the estate is sufficient justification for the rule that if there are no immediate takers, and the will does not clearly express a contrary intent, the attempted gift to the class will fail.[69]

This rule of convenience is only a rule of construction. Accordingly, subsequently born children will be included as class members if the testator clearly expressed his intent that they should share in the gift.[70] In Parker v. Leach,[71] after-born children were considered to be members of such a class. The intent of the testator was found in this language, "unto the sons of David R. Leach, begotten by him during his natural life, the sum of $1,000 each." Such an intention is not "clearly expressed" by such language as a gift to the children of B "now born or who may hereafter be born." This may be construed as referring to children born before or after the making of the will and not to children born after the death of the testator.[72] As has been noted, however, this language is sufficient expression of an intention to include children born after the death of the testator if the gift involves specific property or an aggregate sum.[73] Under such circumstances the admission of after-born children

---

65. 2 Vern. 705, 23 Eng.Rep. 1058 (1715).

66. *Accord:* Male v. Williams, 1891, 48 N.J.Eq. 33, 21 A. 854; 3 Rest. Property, § 294(b).

67. 10 Ch.Div. 25 (1878).

68. *Accord:* 3 Rest. Property, § 294, *Comment (o).*

69. *Cf.:* Simes & Smith, Future Interests (2nd Ed.), § 648, p. 98.

70. In re Earle's Estate, 1951, 369 Pa. 52, 85 A.2d 90, noted in 100 Univ. of Pa.Law Rev., 908 (1952).

71. 66 N.H. 416, 31 A. 19 (1890).

72. See 3 Rest. Property, § 294, *Comment (q).*

73. 3 Rest. Property, § 294, *Comment (p).*

will not necessitate the postponement of probate proceedings. Accordingly, a more liberal rule of construction is justified.

Postponed Gift

In the absence of language expressing a contrary intent, if a gift to a class is *not immediate,* the maximum membership of the class will be determined on the date fixed for distribution.[74] In other words, the class will close on that date. The class will consist of persons answering the general description at the time of the testator's death, if a will is involved, or at the time of delivery in the case of a deed.[75] It will also include those born after these dates and prior to the time fixed for distribution. Presumably, this complies with the intention of the conveyor. If there are no conditions attached to the gift, such as a condition of survivorship, the interest of each member of the class is usually described as vested subject to being divested in part to accommodate those who subsequently qualify for class membership.[76]

The period fixed for distribution is the time when a member of the class is entitled to demand possession of his share in the subject matter of the gift.[77] In the case of a gift to B for life, remainder to the children of C, the distribution of the gift to the children of C takes place at the time of the death of B. There is also a postponed gift to a class if the gift is to the children of B who

attain the age of twenty-one. If the gift consists of an aggregate amount to be distributed to the children of B, to be paid when they reach the age of twenty-one, the class will close when the first child attains that age.[78] The maximum class membership must be ascertained at that time in order to fix the proportionate share that is to be paid to the class member demanding distribution.

In Baylies v. Hamilton (N. Y.),[79] a testamentary disposition created a class gift. The subject matter of the gift was land that involved a prior life estate and other property not subject to such a prior gift. The court held that class membership was determined at the time of the testator's death as to all the property. It was considered that the gift of all the property was immediate and not postponed. A similar situation was involved in Britton v. Miller (N. C.),[80] where the subject matter of the gift was segregated. As to the property subject to immediate distribution, the class closed at the time of testator's death. As to the property subject to a life estate, the class did not close until the time fixed for distribution.

If there are no qualified class members at the postponed date for distribution, and if the gift consists of specific property, or an aggregate sum, the class will include all persons who subsequently qualify for membership.[81] However, if the gift consists of a

---

74. Devisme v. Mello, [1782] 1 Bro.C.C. 537, 28 Eng. Rep. 1285; 3 Rest. Property, § 295(a). See Warren, Devises to "Children", 35 Yale Law Jr., 785, 791 (1926).

75. Strawhacker v. Strawhacker, 1937, 132 Neb. 614, 272 N.W. 772 (deed).

76. See, for example, Steele v. Robinson, 1952, 221 Ark. 58, 251 S.W.2d 1001; In re Brown, 1897, 154 N.Y. 313, 48 N.E. 537.

77. See Casner, Class Gifts to others than "Heirs" or "Next of kin"—Increase in the Class Membership, 51 Harv.Law Rev. 254, 260 (1937).

78. Thomas v. Thomas, 1899, 149 Mo. 426, 51 S.W. 111; Heisse v. Markland, 1830, 2 Rawle (Pa.) 274; 3 Rest. Property, § 295, *Comment (j).* For a criticism of this view, see Ascertainment of Class at Majority, 11 Temp.Law Qt., 91 (1936).

79. 36 App.Div. 133, 55 N.Y.S. 390, affirmed 165 N.Y. 641, 59 N.E. 1118 (1901).

80. 63 N.C. 268 (1869).

81. See In re Emmet's Estate, 1880, 13 Ch.Div. 484 (in a gift to the children of C attaining the age of twenty-one, the class closed when a child attained that age).

designated amount to each member of the class, the gift will fail unless the donor evidenced an intention to the contrary.[82]

MINIMUM CLASS MEMBERSHIP (REQUIREMENT OF SURVIVORSHIP)

166. **Ascertainment of minimum class membership involves a determination as to whether or not participation in the gift requires survivorship.**

    a. **Conditions other than those relating to survivorship. A condition of survivorship is not implied from the fact that conditions other than survivorship are attached to a class gift.**

    b. **Express condition of survivorship as to one class. If there is an express condition of survivorship as to one class a condition of survivorship will not be implied as to a sub-class.**

    c. **Express condition of survivorship as to some members of class. Survivorship may be required as to some members of a class and not as to others.**

    d. **Alternative limitations. An implied condition of survivorship may arise if a limitation creates a remainder or an executory limitation that is expressed in the alternative.**

    e. **Express words of survivorship. The preferred view is that express words of survivorship relate to the time fixed for the distribution of the estate. Under some circumstances the word "survivors" is used as meaning "others."**

Ascertainment of minimum class membership involves a determination as to whether or not participation in the gift requires survival of class members to a stated period of time. Rules involving survivorship as they relate to individual gifts are, in general, applicable in the case of a class gift.[83] The mere fact that a gift is "payable" at a future time does not necessarily make survivorship a condition attached to the gift. The divide-and-pay-over rule is applicable in the case of class gifts to the same extent that it is applicable in the case of individual gifts.[84] Additional rules are discussed in the following paragraphs.

Conditions Other Than Those Relating to Survivorship

There is no implied condition that a class member must survive the time fixed for distribution.[85] As in the case of individual gifts, a condition of survivorship is not implied from the fact that conditions other than survivorship are attached to the gift.[86] For example, in a gift to B for life, remainder to his children, but if he is not survived by children then to the children of C, the gift to the children of C is conditioned upon B's death without children. But this does not mean that the children of C must survive the time of B's death.[87]

Express Condition of Survivorship as to One Class

If there is an express condition of survivorship as to one class a condition of survivorship will not be implied as to a sub-class. For example, in a testamentary gift to B for life, remainder to the children of B, but if a child predeceases B then to that

---

82. See 3 Rest. Property, § 295, *Comment r.*

83. See supra, § 155.

84. See In re Schmidt's Will, 1959, 256 Minn. 64, 97 N.W.2d 441.

85. Strawhacker v. Strawhacker, 1937, 132 Neb. 614, 272 N.W. 772; In re Brown, 1897, 154 N.Y. 313, 48 N.E. 537; Middleton v. Messenger, [1799] 5 Ves.Jr. 136, 31 Eng.Rep. 511.

86. See supra, § 155.

87. But see, Baker v. Baylies, 1963, 231 Md. 287, 189 A.2d 820 (applying a requirement of survivorship where the gift over after life estates was to the testator's heirs).

child's issue, it is not implied that "issue" must survive the death of the life tenant.[88]

Express Condition of Survivorship as to Some Members of Class

Survivorship may be required as to some members of a class and not as to others. In re Haradon's Estate (N. Y.),[89] involved a testamentary gift to B "so long as she remains unmarried. If she marries, or at the time of her death, divide and pay to C and her children then living, as a class, share and share alike." B remained unmarried and died without issue in 1938. C died in 1933 and her only children predeceased B. It is held that the provision as to survivorship applied only as to the children of C and not as to C herself. Consequently, the subject matter of the gift passed to the estate of C.

Alternative Limitations

An implied condition of survivorship may arise if a limitation, declared by deed or will, creates a remainder or an executory limitation expressed in the alternative. Thus, if a will creates a life estate in B with a remainder to B's "children or their issue," the preferred view is that only those children surviving B will be entitled to take.[90] This survivorship-requirement does not apply to those taking in the alternative.

A choice is indicated by the use of the word "or". The logical time for making the choice is at the expiration of the intervening interest—in this case a life estate. Some authorities fix the time of choice as the date upon which the interests are created, in this case the death of the testator.[91] In the absence of a lapse statute, such a choice would be meaningless because there is a lapsed legacy as to persons who predecease the testator.

A third view is that an alternative limitation is not involved. This is true, of course, if there is a basis upon which the word "or" can be construed to mean "and." Even this construction would be strained in any case where the limitation is to persons other than "heirs," "issue" or the children of the first taker.

Express Words of Survivorship

If express words of survivorship are used in a testamentary gift to individuals or to a class, the following construction problems may arise:

First: An issue may be involved as to the "time of survivorship" intended by the testator. For example, in a gift to B for life, remainder to the testator's surviving children, there are two possibilities. The minority rule is that survivorship refers to the time of the testator's death.[92] This conclusion is aided by a general presumption in favor of a construction that releases estates from contingencies at the earliest date possible (a presumption in favor of the early "vesting" of estates). But express words of survivorship are not necessary to require survivorship of the testator. In the absence of a controlling lapse statute a gift fails if the devisee or lega-

---

88. Porter v. Porter, 1917, 226 Mass. 204, 115 N.E. 407; In re Coleman's Will, 1948, 253 Wis. 91, 33 N. W.2d 237. But see, Maingault's Adm'r v. Carrithers, 1943, 295 Ky. 654, 175 App.Div. 591, affirmed 167 N. Y. 579, 60 N.E. 1109 (1901).

89. 173 Misc. 993, 19 N.Y.S.2d 364 (1940).

90. 3 Rest. Property, § 252. See Simes and Smith (2nd ed.), § 581.

91. See, for example, American Nat. Bank & Trust Co. v. Herndon, 1943, 181 Va. 17, 23 S.E.2d 768.

92. Alsman v. Walters, 1916, 184 Ind. 565, 111 N.E. 921; In re Patterson's Estate, 1924, 227 Mich. 486, 198 N.W. 958; In re Montgomery's Estate, 1939, 258 App.Div. 64, 15 N.Y.S.2d 729; Ross v. Drake, 1860, 37 Pa. 373; American Nat. Bank & Trust Co. v. Herndon, 1943, 181 Va. 17, 23 S.E.2d 768. *Cf.*: Johnson v. Atchinson, 1961, 362 Mich. 296, 106 N.W.2d 748.

tee fails to survive the time of the testator's death.

A second possibility is that the expression of survivorship refers to the time fixed for the distribution of the estate (the time of the death of the life tenant). While a majority of the decisions follow this view,[93] a will may contain language justifying a construction that the testator intended survivorship to refer to the time of his death.[94]

Second: A construction problem may be involved as to the meaning of the word "survivors." Assume a testamentary gift by T to his children, with a provision that if a child should die without issue, his share should go to the "survivors." Assume, further, that T was survived by two children B and C, and that B predeceased C survived by issue. Subsequently, C died without issue.[95] There is authority for the view that B's issue would be entitled to C's share. This conclusion is reached upon the ground that the word "survivors" was used as meaning "others."[96] It is a reasonable interpretation of the disposition. It is obvious that the testator intended to benefit the issue of the primary takers and this conclusion avoids any claim of an intestacy. If this interpretation is re-

jected there are two possibilities. It may be concluded that since C was the last to die he could not have "survivors;" and his interest was indefeasible because of the failure of the gift over.[97] Another possibility is that the property must be administered as a part of T's estate. An intestacy results in the absence of a residuary clause.[98]

LAPSE STATUTES

167. The general rule is that lapse statutes are applicable in the case of class gifts.

There are conflicting views regarding application of lapse statutes in testamentary dispositions creating class gifts. The enactment of these statutes is an outgrowth of common law rules relating to void bequests and lapsed legacies.

In the absence of statute a testamentary gift is void if the devisee or legatee is dead at the time of the execution of a will. If the devisee or legatee is alive at that time but predeceases the testator the gift fails—there is a "lapsed legacy." Lapse statutes have been enacted in practically all of the American states. A usual provision is that a gift does not lapse if the devisee or legatee was related to the testator and predeceased him leaving descendants. These descendants take in the stead of the named devisee or legatee. There are variations in the statutes with respect to the relationship-requirements. While the application of some statutes is limited to the lapsed legacy situation others are also applicable in the case of a bequest that would be void according to common law rules.[99]

---

93. Estate of Winters, 1896, 114 Cal. 186; Brown v. Potter, 114 Conn. 441, 159 A. 275; Hawke v. Lodge, 1910, 9 Del.Ch. 146, 77 A. 1090; Horton v. Ferris, 1962, 24 Ill.2d 32, 179 N.E.2d 680; Smith v. Harris, 1939, 227 Iowa 127, 287 N.W. 255; Covey v. McLaughlin, 1889, 148 Mass. 576, 20 N.E. 165; Van Nest v. Van Nest, 1939, 126 N.J.Eq. 234, 8 A.2d 558; Roundtree v. Roundtree, 1887, 26 S.C. 450, 2 S.E. 474. This is the statutory rule in some states, see, for example, West's Ann.Cal.Prob.Code, § 122. See Lawler, Remainder Conditioned upon Survivorship, 15 Temp.Univ.Law Quarterly 107, 110 (1940).

94. See, for example, Comisky v. Moore, 1963, 26 Ill. 2d 494, 187 N.E.2d 256.

95. See Simes and Smith, Future Interests (2nd ed), § 774.

96. See In re Fox's Estate, 1908, 222 Pa. 108, 70 A. 954; In re Cary's Estate, 1908, 81 Vt. 112, 69 A. 736.

97. McGlothlin v. McElvain, 1950, 407 Ill. 142, 95 N.E. 2d 68.

98. Marbury v. Bouse, 1946, 187 Md. 106, 48 A.2d 582, 166 A.L.R. 1272.

99. For enumeration and discussion of the various types of statutes, see 3 Rest. Property, § 298, *Comment c*, and Special Note 1.

While the broad purpose of these statutes is to prevent the failure of testamentary gifts there is a difference of opinion as to whether the legislative purpose is merely to prevent intestacy or whether it is to confer benefits upon the substituted party.

This difference relating to purpose is of particular importance if a class gift is involved. In Campbell v. Clark (N. H.),[1] a bequest was made to the testator's "nieces and nephews." One niece and one nephew died prior to the execution of the will and another niece died after the execution of the will but prior to the death of the testator. There were other nieces and nephews who survived the testator. The issue of the predeceased nephews and nieces claimed as substituted takers under the lapse statute. It is held that only the nieces and nephews who survived the testator could take under the will.[2] It is reasoned that the purpose of the lapse statute is to prevent lapsed legacies. In this case a lapsed legacy was not involved because the surviving members of the class were entitled to the entire gift.[3] It is considered that the purpose of the statute was to prevent lapsed legacies even though the word "lapse" is not used in the statute under consideration.[4]

The prevailing rule is that if the statute does not use the word "lapse" it is reasonable to assume that the legislative purpose is not only to prevent lapsed legacies but also to confer benefits upon the substituted taker.[5] The distinction between a statute that uses the word "lapse" and one that does not use that word is highly artificial. It is unlikely that a legislative body, in enacting a lapse statute, intended any such distinction to be made. A lapse statute should be given a liberal construction and should be applied in class gift situations whether or not the word "lapse" is used.[6] Of course, such a statute is not applicable if a testator expressly provides that only those devisees or legatees who survive him are entitled to benefits.[7] In some instances the application of a lapse statute has enlarged upon the description of class membership. For instance, if a gift is made to "all my first cousins" second cousins may be allowed to take under the lapse statute.[8]

Many lapse statutes provide for substituted takers only if the devisee or legatee was alive when the will was executed.[9] However, if the statute is also applicable in a "void bequest" situation its application is extended to cases involving class gifts.

---

[1]. 64 N.H. 328, 10 A. 702 (1887).

[2]. *Accord:* Lacy v. Murdock, 1946, 147 Neb. 242, 22 N.W.2d 713.

[3]. If all the potential takers under a class gift predecease the testator the statute will be applied to prevent a lapsed legacy (Harvey v. Gillow, 1893, 1 Ch. 567).

[4]. See also, Trenton Trust Co. v. Sibbits, 1901, 62 N.J.Eq. 131, 49 A. 530 (where the statute does use the word "lapse").

[5]. See Cooley, "Lapse Statutes" and Their Effect on Gifts to Classes, 22 Va.Law Rev. 373, 377 (1936). See also, Moore v. Dimond, 1858, 5 R.I. 121 (without reference to the specific wording of the statute it is considered that the legislative purpose was to confer benefits upon the substituted takers).

[6]. 3 Rest. Property, § 298(a).

[7]. Eberts v. Eberts, 1880, 42 Mich. 404, 4 N.W. 172.

[8]. Howland v. Slade, 1892, 155 Mass. 415, 29 N.E. 631. See also, Estate of Steidl, 1948, 89 Cal.App.2d 488, 201 P.2d 58 (gift was to testator's brothers and sisters. A brother predeceased testator and his children were entitled to his share under the lapse statute).

[9]. See, for example, Howland v. Slade, 1892, 155 Mass. 415, 29 N.E. 631; In re Estate of Schuette, 1940, 138 Neb. 568, 293 N.W. 421. *Contra:* Kehl v. Taylor, 1916, 275 Ill. 346, 114 N.E. 125.

CHAPTER 34

GIFTS TO "HEIRS," "ISSUE" AND "DESCENDANTS"

IN GENERAL

168. Except in situations where the worthier title doctrine is applicable, or the rule in Shelley's case is controlling, a class gift is involved in a conveyance to persons described by such terms as "heirs," "issue" and "descendants."

Except in situations where the worthier title doctrine is applicable, or the rule in Shelley's case is controlling, a gift to heirs, heirs of the body or next of kin constitutes a class gift. These terms are usually used to describe persons who are entitled to distribution of property if the owner dies intestate.

An intent to use the words "heirs" or "heirs of the body" as meaning "children" or "issue" may be gathered from the fact that the conveyor used these terms interchangeably.[1] This may also appear from the fact that direction was made for the "heir" to take the share "his parent" would have taken had he lived.[2] It has been held that the word "heirs" should be construed to mean "children" in a testamentary gift to B and his heirs "now living or born subsequent to the (execution of the will)."[3] In a few states it is provided by statute that the word

"heirs" means "children" in the absence of an expression of intent to the contrary.[4]

Technically, the word "heirs" includes only those entitled to succeed to the ownership of a freehold estate upon the death of the owner intestate. Collaterals who are entitled to take chattels real or personal are designated as "next of kin."[5] However, where the subject matter of a gift to "heirs" is a chattel real or personal, the word "heirs" may be construed to mean "next of kin."[6] In many states the distinction between "heirs" and "next of kin" has now been abolished by statute.

TIME WHEN CLASS MEMBERSHIP IS ASCERTAINED

169. Unless a contrary intention is expressed, persons described by such terms as "heirs," "issue," and "descendants" are ascertained at the time of the death of the person named as ancestor.

Unless the conveyor has evidenced a contrary intention, the membership in a class described by such words as "heirs," "issue," "descendants" etc., is ascertained at the time of the death of the person named as ances-

---

1. 3 Rest. Property, § 305, *Comment p.*

2. 3 Rest. Property, § 305, *Comment q.*

3. Hutton v. Hutton, 1936, 120 N.J.Eq. 21, 183 A. 714.

4. Ga.Code Ann. (1945) § 85–504; N.C.Gen.Stat. (1945) § 41–6. See Rest.Property, 1948 Supplement, § 305. *Cf.:* Whitley v. Arenson, 1941, 219 N.C. 121, 12 S.E.2d 906.

5. 3 Rest.Property, § 307.

6. Scudder's Ex'rs v. Vanarsdale, 1860, 13 N.J.Eq. 109.

tor.[7] However, if that person predeceased the conveyor then the class membership is determined as of the time of the conveyance.[8]

In the case of a testamentary gift to B for life, remainder to the heirs of the testator, the heirs are ascertained at the time of the testator's death. This conforms with the technical meaning of the words used. Of course, a testator may direct that the ascertainment-process take place at a later date. For example, a will may make a gift of a life estate with remainder to the heirs of the testator in accordance with the laws of succession *then* in force. The word "then" is used as an adverb of time and not merely to denote an event. Such a direction will postpone the ascertainment of the "heirs" until the expiration of the life estate.[9] This deferment disregards the technical meaning of the words "heirs" or "next of kin." Additional rules of construction are as follows:

First: There are situations where it may be assumed that a word such as "heirs" was not used in a technical sense and that *presumptive* heirs qualify as class members. That is the case, for example, if there is an immediate gift to the heirs of a living person [10] or a gift to the *present* heirs of a living person.[11] Authorities also support the rule that if a gift is made to B for life, remainder to the heirs of C, a living person, if C is alive at the time of B's death C's presumptive heirs will take.[12]

Second: If a testator makes a gift to his own "heirs," under some circumstances there is justification for an assumption that he intended the "heirs" to be determined at a time subsequent to the time of his death. For example, assume a testamentary gift by A to B and his heirs, but if B dies without issue then to A's heirs. Assume further that B was the *sole heir* at the time of A's death. It is not reasonable to assume that A intended B to take absolute ownership in the property, that this ownership should be divested if B died without issue and that B (the sole heir) was to be revested with ownership if he should die without issue. It is much more reasonable to assume that if B died without issue A intended the property to go to A's heirs determined at the time of B's death.[13]

A similar situation is involved if the primary gift is of a life estate. For example, in a gift A to B for life, but if B should die without issue, children etc., then to A's heirs. If B was the *sole heir* at the time of A's death it is not reasonable to assume that A intended to convey a limited estate to B (a life estate) and also absolute ownership in remainder. A more reasonable assumption is that A intended "heirs" to be determined at

---

7. Old Colony Trust Co. v. Stephens, 1963, 346 Mass. 94, 190 N.E.2d 110; Matter of Bump, 1922, 234 N.Y. 60, 136 N.E. 295; Holt v. Miller, 1938, 133 Ohio St. 418, 14 N.E.2d 409; Wallace v. Peoples, Tex.Civ.App.1935, 89 S.W.2d 1030; Holloway v. Holloway, [1800] 5 Ves. 399, 31 Eng.Rep. 649; 3 Rest.Property, § 308. In Pennsylvania it is provided by statute that heirs etc., are determined at the time of the termination of the intervening estate (20 P.S. §§ 180.14, 301.14 and 21 P.S. § 11).

8. Flanagan v. Spalti, 1938, 225 Iowa 1231, 282 N.W. 347.

9. Estate of Miner, 1963, 214 Cal.App.2d 533, 29 Cal. Rptr. 601; Welch v. Howard, 1917, 227 Mass. 242, 116 N.E. 492; Lemmon v. Wilson, 1944, 204 S.C. 50, 28 S.E.2d 792. See 3 Powell on Real Property, § 375, pp. 223–224.

10. Casner, Gifts to "Heirs," 53 Harv.Law Rev. 207, 230; 3 Rest.Property, § 308, *Comment h.*

11. 3 Rest.Property, § 308, *Comment j.*

12. 3 Rest.Property, § 308, *Comment t. Contra:* Bass River Savings Bank v. Nickerson, 1939, 303 Mass. 332, 21 N.E.2d 717.

13. Welch v. Brimmer, 1897, 169 Mass. 204, 47 N.E. 699, noted in 11 Harv.Law Rev. 346 (1897).

the time of B's death.[14] However, some authorities take the position that even in a case of this type, A's heirs are to be determined at the time of his death.[15] However, a minimum of evidence is sufficient to postpone the date to the time of B's death.[16]

The above discussion relates to the "sole-heir" situation. It is generally agreed that "heirs" will be determined at the time of the testator's death if the primary estate is given to some as distinguished from all of the testator's heirs.[17]

14. Jones v. Petrie, 1943, 156 Kan. 241, 132 P.2d 396; In re Ecclestone's Estate, 1954, 339 Mich. 15, 62 N.W.2d 606; Wheeling Dollar Savings & Trust Co. v. Stewart, 1946, 128 W.Va. 703, 37 S.E.2d 563; Central Dispensary & Emergency Hospital v. Saunders, 1948, 83 U.S.App.D.C. 52, 165 F.2d 626; 3 Rest.Property, § 308, *Comment k.* See Dailey v. Houston, 1962, 246 Miss. 667, 151 So.2d 919 (testator's will provided for a life estate in his widow with remainder ½ to his "heirs" and ½ to his widow's "heirs". The widow was testator's sole heir at the time of his death. The court held that the testator's heirs should be determined at the time of the widow's death. Thus, his sister and nephews and nieces were entitled to share in the gift).

15. Himmel v. Himmel, 1920, 294 Ill. 557, 128 N.E. 641, 13 A.L.R. 608; Hull v. Adams, 1948, 399 Ill. 347, 77 N.E.2d 706 (immaterial whether "such heirs" are living or dead when the period of distribution arrives); Gilman v. Congregational Home Missionary Society, 1932, 276 Mass. 580, 177 N.E. 621, noted in 45 Harv.Law Rev. 1121 (1932); First Safe Deposit Nat. Bank v. Westgate, 1963, 444 Mass. 346, 193 N.E.2d 683 (next of kin).

16. Estate of Wilson, 1920, 184 Cal. 63, 193 P. 581; Delaware Trust Co. v. Delaware Trust Co., Del.Ch. 1952, 91 A.2d 44; Boston Safe Deposit & Trust Co. v. Waite, 1932, 278 Mass. 244, 179 N.E. 624; National Bank of Fairmont v. Kenney, 1933, 113 W.Va. 890, 170 S.E. 177, noted in 18 Minn.Law Rev. 486 (1934). A gift over to "heirs then living" is a sufficient expression of intention to postpone the time for ascertaining class membership (In re Hoover's Estate, 1936, 16 Cal.App.2d 529, 60 P.2d 1010).

17. In re Cowley's Will, 1904, 120 Wis. 263, 97 N.W. 930, 98 N.W. 28. But see In re Churchill's Estate, 1925, 230 Mich. 148, 203 N.W. 118.

MAXIMUM CLASS MEMBERSHIP

170. Unless a contrary intention is expressed, in a gift to "heirs," "heirs of the body," and "next of kin," membership in the class is determined by reference to the local statute relating to intestate succession. Membership is usually ascertained as of the time of the death of the person named as ancestor.

Usually, a surviving spouse and an adopted child are included in a gift to "heirs." However, this is not the case if the gift is to "heirs of the body" or "bodily heirs."

An illegitimate child may qualify as an "heir" or "heirs of the body" if he is qualified to inherit from his natural parent according to the terms of the local statute relating to intestate succession.

Unless a conveyor evidences an intention to the contrary, class membership in a gift to persons described by such terms as "heirs," "heirs of the body" and "next of kin," is determined by reference to the applicable statute relating to intestate succession. Membership is determined on the hypothesis that the person *named as ancestor* was the owner of the property at the time of his death.[18] Thus, the applicable law is the law existing at the time of the ancestor's death. If land is involved the controlling law is the law of the situs. Otherwise, it is the law of the ancestor's domicile.[19]

If there is a gift to the "heirs" or "next of kin" of a person who died prior to the effective date of the conveyance, membership in the class is ascertained as of the date of the conveyance and not as of the time of the

18. Casner, Gifts to "Heirs," 53 Harv.Law Rev. 207, 213, 214 (1939); 3 Rest.Property, § 305, *Comment e. Contra:* In re Battell's Will, 1941, 286 N.Y. 97, 35 N.E.2d 913, noted in 19 N.Y.Univ.Law Quarterly Rev. 216 (1942) (reference made to the law of the testator's domicile as it existed at the time of his death).

19. See Second Bank-State Street Trust Co. v. Weston, 1961, 342 Mass. 630, 174 N.E.2d 763.

death of the person named as ancestor.[20] If the gift is to the "heirs" or "next of kin" of a person living at the effective date of the conveyance, class membership is ascertained on the date of the death of the named ancestor. A person who fails to survive that date cannot qualify as an "heir" or "next of kin." Additional rules are as follows:

First: If a conveying instrument does not express a contrary intent, the surviving spouse of the named ancestor qualifies as an heir if the applicable statute relating to intestate succession makes provision for a surviving spouse.[21] The preferred view is that a gift to "next of kin" includes those entitled to inherit personalty if the designated ancestor had died intestate.[22] In some states a more restricted meaning is applied. For example, there is authority for the view that a gift to "next of kin" includes only "blood relatives" of the named ancestor. This would exclude a surviving spouse.[23]

Second: Statutes usually provided that an adopted child is entitled to share in the estate of the adopting parent in case of an intestacy. As such, an adopted child qualifies as an heir of the adopting parent.[24] However, an adopted child may be excluded from class membership if the conveyor evidenced an intent to limit the gift to blood relatives.[25]

Third: An adopted child is not an "heir of the body" or a "bodily heir" of an adopting parent. Accordingly, unless a conveyor expresses a contrary intent, an adopted child cannot qualify as a member of a class so described.[26] This is also true if the gift is to "descendants" of the adopting parent.[27]

Fourth: Even if a child is illegitimate at birth, statutes usually provide that such a child may be legitimated by certain procedures, such as by the subsequent marriage of his parents. In case of legitimation the child is deemed to be legitimate from birth and qualifies as an heir of his natural parents and their ancestors.[28]

In any event, an illegitimate child may qualify as an "heir" or "heir of the body" if he is entitled to inherit from his natural parent according to the terms of the local statute relating to intestate succession.[29]

---

20. Estate of Page, 1919, 181 Cal. 537, 185 P. 383; In re Fordham's Will, 1923, 235 N.Y. 384, 139 N.E. 548; Simes and Smith, Future Interests (2nd ed), § 732, fn 93.

21. In re Schnee's Estate, 1938, 7 N.Y.S.2d 791 (included surviving spouse); 3 Rest.Property, § 307.

22. First Safe Deposit Nat. Bank v. Westgate, 1963, 346 Mass. 444, 193 N.E.2d 683; In re Stoler's Estate, 1928, 293 Pa. 433, 143 A. 121, 59 A.L.R. 1402.

23. Hartford-Connecticut Trust Co. v. Lawrence, 1927, 106 Conn. 178, 138 A. 159, noted in 37 Yale Law Jr., 272 (1927); In re Wagar's Estate, 1940, 295 Mich. 463, 295 N.W. 227; Holt v. Miller, 1938, 133 Ohio St. 418, 14 N.E.2d 409; White v. White, 1962, 241 S.C. 181, 127 S.E.2d 627; 3 Rest.Property, § 305, Comment *j*. But see, Stites v. Gray, 1955, 4 Ill.2d 510, 123 N.E.2d 483; Theen v. Miller, 1959, 250 Iowa 1144, 96 N.W.2d 734. In National Shawmut Bank of Boston v. Zink, 1964, 347 Mass. 194, 196 N.E.2d 917, the testator devised land to his widow for life but his will made no disposition of the remainder. It is held that the wife's estate was entitled to share in the property because she was authorized to take in case of an intestacy.

24. 3 Rest.Property, § 305, Comment *k*. But see Hall v. Crandall, 1941, 25 Del.Ch. 339, 20 A.2d 545.

25. Woods v. Crump, 1940, 283 Ky. 675, 142 S.W.2d 680, noted in 29 Ky.Law Journal 481 (1941).

26. Tea v. Millen, 1913, 257 Ill. 624, 101 N.E. 209, 45 L.R.A.,N.S., 1163 ("natural heirs"); 3 Rest.Property, § 306, Comment *g*. But see Gannett v. Old Colony Trust Co., 1959, 155 Me. 248, 153 A.2d 122 (testator intended to include children of his adopted son in class gift to testator's "issue").

27. Wheeling Dollar Savings & Trust Co. v. Stewart, 1946, 128 W.Va. 703, 37 S.E.2d 563.

28. Rhode Island Hospital Trust Co. v. Hopkins, 1961, 93 R.I. 173, 172 A.2d 345 (lineal heir).

29. 3 Rest.Property, § 306, Comment *h*.

MINIMUM CLASS MEMBERSHIP (REQUIREMENT OF SURVIVORSHIP)

171. A condition is not implied that a class member must survive the time fixed for distribution.

If class membership is described as including "heirs," "issue," "descendants" etc., once a person has qualified as a member of the class it is not implied that he must survive the time fixed for distribution. For example, in a gift to B for life, remainder to the heirs of C, class membership is determined at the time of C's death. The interest of such a class member is not contingent upon survival to the time of B's death.[30]

MANNER OF DISTRIBUTION

172. In the absence of a direction to the contrary, the intestacy statute furnishes the basis for determining class membership and also the manner of distribution. Statutes usually provide that distribution is to be made on a *per stirpes* basis. A direction to make distribution "equally" usually requires distribution on a *per capita* basis.

In the absence of evidence in a will indicating a contrary intent, the intestacy statute furnishes the basis for determining class membership and also furnishes the basis for determining the share that each member is entitled to take. The statutes usually provide that distribution is to be made on a *per stirpes* basis.[31]

A direction to make distribution "equally" usually requires distribution on a *per capita* basis. Thus, in Coppedge v. Coppedge (N. C.),[32] a testamentary gift provided: "The remainder of my estate is to be divided among my legal heirs * * * equally, share and share alike as provided by laws of North Carolina." The court held that while the persons to take were to be ascertained by reference to the laws of intestacy, the statute was not to be used for the purpose of determining the share that each member is entitled to take. The words "equally" and "share and share alike" required distribution on a *per capita* basis.[33] However, some authorities support the view that words of equality do not necessarily require a *per capita* distribution if the devisees and legatees are in unequal degrees of relationship. It is considered that the direction as to equality may be applied with respect to equality within each particular group.[34]

30. Estate of Liddle, 1958, 162 Cal.App.2d 7, 328 P.2d 35; Daniel v. Donohue, 1959, 215 Or. 373, 333 P.2d 1109; 3 Rest.Property, § 309, Illustration 1.

31. 3 Rest.Property, § 310.

32. 234 N.C. 173, 66 S.E.2d 777 (1951), rehearing denied 234 N.C. 747, 67 S.E.2d 463.

33. *Accord:* Lyons v. Brown, Ky.1962, 352 S.W.2d 549; Kramer v. Larson, 1954, 158 Neb. 404, 63 N.W.2d 349; Scudder's Ex'rs v. Vanarsdale, 1860, 13 N.J.Eq. 109; Ramsey v. Stephenson, 1899, 34 Or. 408, 56 P. 195; In re Bray's Will, 1951, 260 Wis. 9, 49 N.W.2d 716.

34. Allen v. Boardman, 1906, 193 Mass. 284, 79 N.E. 260; In re Burleigh's Estate, 1961, 405 Pa. 373, 175 A.2d 838.

CHAPTER 35

POWERS OF APPOINTMENT

DEFINITION AND CLASSIFICATION OF POWERS

173. A power of appointment is an authorization given to one who is not the owner of property by the terms of which he may designate the transferees of property or designate the shares in which it is to be received by the appointees.

A general power of appointment confers authority upon the donee to appoint the property to himself or to his estate. A special power restricts appointment to a person other than the donee or his estate.

a. **Appendant or appurtenant powers.** According to the English common law a person could own an estate in land and, at the same time, have a power of appointment with respect to that estate. In that event it is an appendant or appurtenant power. The prevailing American rule is that an appendant or appurtenant power is destroyed by merger.

b. **Collateral powers and powers in gross.** A power is in gross if the donee has an interest in the subject matter of the power. Otherwise, it is a collateral power. This classification is not of modern importance.

c. **Mandatory powers (powers in trust).** A special power is mandatory (in trust) if the donor has expressed his will that it be exercised. This intention may be express or it may be implied.

d. **Exclusive and non-exclusive powers and illusory appointments.** A power is exclusive if the donee has authority to appoint to one or more of the appointees and exclude others. It is non-exclusive if appointment must be made to all of the appointees.

If a power is non-exclusive an appointment is null and void if a substantial share is not given to each appointee.

The Restatement of Property [1] defines a power of appointment as a power "created or reserved by a person (the donor) having property subject to his disposition enabling the donee of the power to designate, within such limits as the donor may prescribe, the transferees of the property or the shares in which it shall be received." [2] There are many other types of powers, such as a power of sale, [3] a power of attorney, a power of revoca-

---

1. 3 Rest.Property, § 318.

2. A writing executed with the formalities prescribed by the Statute of Wills may be probated as a will if it creates a power of appointment. It is not necessary that it make any disposition of property (Delaney v. First Peoples Bank, 1964, —— Tenn. ——, 380 S.W.2d 65).

3. See Pan American Petroleum Corp. v. Cain, 1962, 163 Tex. 323, 355 S.W.2d 506 (the power to lease reserved in a deed conveying an undivided mineral interest—called an executive right).

tion, a power to cause a gift of income to be augmented out of principal, a power to designate charities, a charitable trust, a discretionary trust or an honorary trust.

A general power of appointment is one that may be exercised wholly in favor of the donee or his estate.[4] For some purposes a general power is considered to be tantamount to ownership. This is especially true if it may be exercised by deed. A special power restricts appointment to persons other than the donee or his estate. A testamentary power is one that may be exercised only by will. A power to appoint may be exercised either by deed or by will in the absence of restrictions or limitations to the contrary. There is authority for the view that the creation of a power to appoint during the lifetime of the donee does not necessarily exclude an exercise of the power by will.[5]

A power to appoint is personal in nature. In the absence of a direction to the contrary it is not assignable or transferable.[6] However, it is provided by a federal statute that a power of appointment which a bankrupt could have exercised for his own gain passes to his trustee in bankruptcy.[7]

"Appendant" or "Appurtenant" Powers

According to the early English cases a person could be the owner of an estate in land and, at the same time, have a power of appointment with respect to that estate.[8] This is designated as a power appendant or appurtenant. In the English case of Ray v. Pung,[9] land was conveyed to such persons as James Ray might appoint and until such appointment should be made, or in default of appointment, the estate was vested in James Ray and his heirs. The court held that an exercise of the power defeated dower rights that would otherwise be available to the wife of James Ray. Claims of the donee's creditors could also be defeated by an exercise of the power.[10] However, if the donee conveyed the estate the power was extinguished because of the doctrine that a conveyor cannot derogate from his own grant.[11] The prevailing American rule is that an appendant or appurtenant power is destroyed by merger.[12]

Collateral Powers and Powers in Gross

Usually, the donee of a power also has an estate or interest in the subject matter of the power, such as in a case where a person has a life estate in land and a power of appointment of the fee. This is a power in gross. If a donee does not have such an estate or interest the power is "simple collateral." While this classification is of historical interest it is not of modern importance.

Mandatory Powers (Powers in Trust)

A special power is mandatory (power in trust) if the donor has expressed his will that it be exercised. This may be found in express

---

4. 3 Rest.Property, § 320. See Gold, The Classification of Some Powers of Appointment, 40 Mich.Law Rev. 337 (1942).

5. Washington Trust Co. v. Dyer, 1964, —— R.I. ——, 200 A.2d 1.

6. Hazard v. Bacon, 1920, 42 R.I. 415, 108 A. 499.

7. Fed.Bankruptcy Act, § 70a (1898), 11 U.S.C.A. c. 7, § 110(a).

8. Sir Edward Clere's Case, [1599], 6 Co.Rep. 17b, 77 Eng.Rep. 279 (power of appointment could be exercise by will even though there were restrictions

with respect to testamentary disposition of the estate).

9. 5 B. & Ald. 561, 106 Eng.Rep. 1296 (1822).

10. Doe d. Wigan v. Jones, [1830] 10 B. & C. 459, 109 Eng.Rep. 521.

11. See Smith v. Death, [1820] 5 Madd. 371, 56 Eng. Rep. 937.

12. Browning v. Bluegrass Hardware Co., 1929, 153 Va. 20, 149 S.E. 497. See 3 Rest.Property, § 325; Note, Appendant Powers of Appointment in the United States, 50 Harv.Law Rev. 1284 (1937).

language contained in the document creating the power or it may be implied. Of course, this implication cannot be made if provision is made for persons who are to take in default of appointment (takers in default).[13]

There is a difference of opinion as to the circumstances under which an implication will be drawn that a special power is mandatory. According to the Restatement of Trusts,[14] an implication that a special power is mandatory is not to be drawn from the mere fact that provision is not made for takers in default. According to the Restatement of Property,[15] the absence of a provision for takers in default raises a presumption that a special power is mandatory. There is also a difference of opinion as to the basis for distribution of property if a special power is mandatory and the power is not exercised.[16] According to the Restatement of Trusts, a trust is created in favor of the designated appointees.[17] According to the Restatement of Property, the subject matter of the power "passes to those living objects to whom the donee could have appointed at the time of expiration of the power (gift by implication)".[18] The subject matter of the power will pass only to those living appointees to whom the donee could have appointed.[19] If a non-mandatory special power is

not exercised, the subject matter of the power constitutes a part of the estate of the donor.[20]

Exclusive and Non-exclusive Powers and Illusory Appointments

A special power may authorize appointment to one or more of the appointees (persons among whom the donee is given power to appoint) and the exclusion of others. This is an "exclusive power." It is "non-exclusive" if appointment must be made to *all* of the appointees.

The preferred view is that a power is exclusive unless the donor manifests a contrary intention.[21] If the power is non-exclusive, all living appointees of the power must be given a *substantial share* of the property. Otherwise, the appointment is illusory and void in its entirety.[22] In England the illusory appointment doctrine was abolished by statute passed in 1830 and it has been repudiated in a number of American states.[23]

Assuming that a power is non-exclusive, appointment of even a nominal share to each appointee is proof of the fact that the donee

---

13. Lambert v. Thwaites, 1866, L.R. 2 Eq. 151.

14. Rest.Trusts, § 27.

15. 3 Rest.Property, § 367(2).

16. See Simes, Powers in Trust and the Termination of Powers by the Donee, 37 Yale Law Jr., 63, 70 (1927).

17. *Accord:* See Harding v. Glyn, [1739] 1 Atk. 469, 26 Eng.Rep. 299.

18. See Gray, Powers in Trust and Gift Implied in Default of Appointment, 25 Harv.Law Rev. 1, 8 (1911).

19. American Brass Co. v. Hauser, 1938, 284 Mich. 194, 278 N.W. 816, 115 A.L.R. 1464; Daniel v. Brown, 1931, 156 Va. 563, 159 S.E. 209, 75 A.L.R.

1377. See Bridgewater v. Turner, 1930, 161 Tenn. 111, 29 S.W.2d 659; Parker v. MacBryde, 4 Cir., 1942, 132 F.2d 932, certiorari denied 318 U.S. 779, 63 S.Ct. 859, 87 L.Ed. 1147.

20. In re Combe, 1925, Ch. 210, noted in 35 Yale Law Jr., 505 (1926).

21. National State Bank of Newark v. Morrison, 1949, 7 N.J.Super. 333, 70 A.2d 888; Parker v. MacBryde, 4 Cir. 1942, 132 F.2d 932, certiorari denied 63 S.Ct. 859, 318 U.S. 779; 3 Rest.Property, § 360. *Contra:* Estate of Sloan, 1935, 7 Cal.App.2d 319, 46 P.2d 1007; Barret's Executor v. Barret, 1915, 166 Ky. 411, 179 S.W. 396, L.R.A.1016D, 493; Hopkins v. Dimock, 1946, 138 N.J.Eq. 434, 48 A.2d 204, affirmed 140 N.J.Eq. 182, 52 A.2d 853.

22. Hopkins v. Dimock, 1946, 138 N.J.Eq. 434, 48 A.2d 204, affirmed 140 N.J.Eq. 182, 52 A.2d 853: 3 Rest.Property, § 361. But see Young v. Waterpark, [1842], 13 Sim. 199, 60 Eng.Rep. 77.

23. 11 Geo. IV and 1 Wm. IV, c. 46 (1830).

had all of the appointees in mind at the time when he exercised the power. It is reasonable to assume that such was the only purpose of the donor in creating a non-exclusive power. An intention that a substantial share be given to each appointee should be clearly expressed.[24]

DEFINITENESS AS TO APPOINTEES

174. The validity of a general power of appointment does not depend upon definiteness as to the appointees. In general, this is also true as to a special power. However, in the case of a special power that is mandatory (a power in trust) the appointees must be ascertained with reasonable certainty.

Since the donee of a general power of appointment has complete freedom of action in exercising the power insofar as appointees are concerned, the validity of the power does not depend upon whether or not the potential recipients of benefits (appointees) are designated in the instrument creating the power.

With respect to a special power the Restatement of Property provides as follows:[25] " . . . a power to appoint to a group of whatever size is not for that reason invalid; and if the power is exercised in favor of one or more members of the group such members are entitled to receive the property. The fact that the group is so large that its members could not be the beneficiaries of a trust . . . does not prevent them from being the objects of a power." It is further provided: "If the group of objects, regardless of its size, is so indefinitely described by the donor that it is impossible to select anyone who could reasonably be said to answer the description, the power is void."

Definiteness is required if a special power is mandatory (a power in trust). The validity of such a power depends upon a sufficient description of the appointees. In Clark v. Campbell (N.H.),[26] testator's will provided that certain articles were to be held in trust "to make disposal by the way of a memento from myself, of such articles to such of my friends as they, my trustees, shall select." The proposed gift failed.[27] It could not be sustained either as a trust or as a special power of appointment because the beneficiaries or appointees were not described with sufficient certainty. It is clear that the testator did not intend to create a general power of appointment and it is also clear that he did not intend to make a beneficial gift to his named trustees. The case differs from one where the appointees are described in general terms, such as "relatives." In that event identification can be established by reference to the intestacy statutes.[28] It also differs from a case where a conveyor intends to create a mandatory power (power in trust) in favor of a charity. In that event the recipients of the charity are, of necessity, indefinite.

DEVOLUTION OF TITLE AND TAXATION

175. From the very nature of a power of appointment, ownership of the property is derived from the donor of the power and not from the donee. However, for some purposes the donee is considered to be the owner. This is especially true with respect to matters of taxation.

24. See, for example, Hawthorn v. Ulrich, 1904, 207 Ill. 430, 69 N.E. 885; Hodges v. Stegall, 1935, 169 Tenn. 202, 83 S.W.2d 901, 100 A.L.R. 339.

25. 3 Rest.Property, § 323, *Comment h.*

26. 82 N.H. 281, 133 A. 166, 45 A.L.R. 1433 (1926).

27. *Cf.*: In re Rowlands' Estate, 1952, 73 Ariz. 337, 241 P.2d 781; Moss v. Axford, 1929, 246 Mich. 288, 224 N.W. 425.

28. Harding v. Glyn, [1793] 1 Atk. 469, 26 Eng.Rep. 299; 3 Rest.Property, § 367(3). See In re Lawrence's Estate, 1963, 104 N.H. 457, 189 A.2d 491 ("relatives" not restricted to "heirs at law").

In general, the distinction between a power and ownership of the subject matter of a power is maintained. The donee is not the owner of the property. Accordingly, the appointees, or persons taking in default of appointment (if any) acquire ownership of the property from the donor of the power and not from the donee.[29] The statutory rule in some states is that the amount of a succession tax depends upon the degree of relationship between the decedent and the recipient of the gift. The donor of the power is the "decedent" within the meaning of these statutes.[30] However, special situations are as follows:

First: The donee of a general power of appointment has such unlimited control over the property that for some purposes he may be considered to be the owner of the property itself. This is especially true in situations that involve the claims of the creditors of the donee, a situation discussed under a separate heading.[31]

Second: Statutes have been enacted in many states providing that the donee of a power of appointment is to be considered as the owner of property in applying succession tax statutes. In other words, for this limited purpose one who acquires property as the result of an exercise of a power of appointment or takes in default of appointment takes from the donee of the power.[32] Similarly, estate tax statutes frequently provide that where there is a testamentary exercise of a general power of appointment the subject matter of the power shall be included as a part of the gross estate of the donee of the power. A power may be treated as a general power within the meaning of the Federal Estate Tax even though it is considered to be a special power according to state law.[33]

CAPACITY OF DONEE

176. A power of appointment cannot be exercised by a donee who is under the disability of infancy or insanity.

The exercise of a power of appointment is considered to be an event that results in a shift of ownership with respect to the property involved. It is not a conveyance from the donee of the power to the appointee. Accordingly, a married woman has capacity to exercise a power of appointment even though she might not have capacity to make a conveyance of similar property owned by her.[34] However, the "event" concept is not applicable if the donee is under an incapacity of minority[35] or insanity. These incapacities will nullify a purported appointment.[36]

There is justification for the distinction made between the incapacity of a married woman and the incapacity of a minor or an insane person. The rule that a married woman is without capacity to convey is a rule designed to protect the property rights of her husband and not for the purpose of protecting the property rights of the married woman. An exercise of a power of appointment conferred upon her would not be inconsistent with the purpose of the rule. But

29. 3 Rest.Property, § 333(a).

30. Emmons v. Shaw, State Treasurer, 1898, 171 Mass. 410, 50 N.E. 1033; Commonwealth v. Williams' Ex'rs, 1850, 13 Pa. 29.

31. See infra, § 181.

32. For a compilation of such statutes, see 3 Rest. Property, § 333, *Comment (c)*, Statutory Note.

33. Morgan v. Com'r of Internal Revenue, 1940, 309 U.S. 78, 626, 60 S.Ct. 424, 84 L.Ed. 585, 1035, noted in 24 Minn.Law Rev. 886 (1940).

34. Young v. Sheldon, 1903, 139 Ala. 444, 36 So. 27; 3 Rest.Property, § 345(a). See Thompson v. Lyon, 1854, 20 Mo. 155 (power appendant).

35. Thompson v. Lyon, 1854, 20 Mo. 155; Sewell v. Sewell, 1892, 92 Ky. 500, 18 S.W. 162, 17 Ky.Law Rep. 1069.

36. See 3 Rest.Property, § 345(1).

the rule that a minor or an insane person is without capacity to convey is a rule designed for the protection of the property interests of the incompetent. One under the disability of minority or insanity is considered to be in need of protection because such individual is lacking in discretionary power. Since the exercise of a power of appointment requires discretion, the power could not be effectively exercised by one who is under these disabilities.

RELEASE OF POWERS

177. A general power of appointment may be released. This is also true with respect to a special power of appointment that is not mandatory.

Authorities support the rule that a general power of appointment may be released.[37] This follows from the fact that the interest of the donee is tantamount to ownership and a release violates no fiduciary duty that he owes to the donor of the power. There is some criticism of this rule if the general power may be exercised by will only.[38] A release makes it operative *inter vivos*. In spite of this criticism such a release is generally sustained.

The general rule is that if the donee of a special power has an interest in the subject matter of the power (a power in gross), and if the power is not mandatory (in trust), it

may be released.[39] Such a power is not mandatory if provision is made for persons to take in default of appointment (takers in default). A release means that the subject matter of the power will pass to the takers in default.

There is a difference of opinion as to whether or not a special power purely collateral (one in which the donee does not have an interest in the subject matter of the power) may be released if it is not mandatory (in trust). A leading authority on the subject expresses the view that "there is no good reason of policy for denying the donee of such a power the power to extinguish it."[40] Statutes have been enacted in many states declaring rules favorable to the release of special powers, especially powers that are not mandatory.[41]

CONTRACT TO APPOINT AND FRAUDULENT APPOINTMENTS

178. If a general power of appointment is exercisable by will only, the donee cannot make an enforceable contract to exercise the power in a particular way. However, an appointment is valid even if it is made in accord with the terms of a contract.

The donee of a special power cannot enter into a valid contract to exercise the power in a particular way. Accordingly, liability against the donee or his estate cannot be based upon the breach of such a contract. An appointment made in pursuance of an agreement that would benefit non-objects is void in its entirety.

If a general power of appointment is exercisable by either deed or will, a contract to

---

37. McLaughlin v. Industrial Trust Co., 1945, 12 Del.Ch. 275, 42 A.2d 12; Voncannon v. Hudson Belk Co., 1953, 236 N.C. 709, 73 S.E.2d 875 (exercisable by will); Lyon v. Alexander, 1931, 304 Pa. 288, 156 A. 84, 76 A.L.R. 1427. See Botzum v. Havana Nat. Bank, 1937, 367 Ill. 539, 12 N.E.2d 203; O'Hara v. O'Hara, 1945, 185 Md. 321, 44 A.2d 813, 163 A.L.R. 1414 (a contract not to exercise a general testamentary power cannot be specifically enforced).

38. Gray, Release and Discharge of Powers, 24 Harv. Law Rev. 511 (1911). See 3 Rest.Property, Topic 4, Introductory Note, p. 1884.

39. Thorington v. Thorington, 1887, 82 Ala. 489, 1 So. 716; Columbia Trust Co. v. Christopher, 1909, 133 Ky. 335, 117 S.W. 943.

40. See Simes & Smith, Future Interests (2nd Ed.) § 1065, p. 523.

41. See Restatement of the Law, 1948 Supplement, § 335, *Comment e*. In England the statutory rule is that all powers that are not mandatory (in trust) may be released (In re Mills, 1930, 1 Ch. 654).

exercise the power in a particular way is valid and enforceable. For this purpose, such a power is tantamount to ownership. However, this type of contract is not enforceable even in the case of a general power if the power is exercisable only by will.[42] To allow specific performance of the contract or to allow damages for its breach would convert the testamentary power into a power exercisable by deed. However, the promisee may obtain restitution to the extent that consideration was paid by him.[43] It is also recognized that the validity of an appointment will be sustained even if it is made in pursuance of contract.[44] Also, a contract to appoint may constitute a release of the power and thus cause the interest of the takers in default of appointment to become indefeasible.[45]

The donee of a special power of appointment cannot enter into a valid contract to exercise the power in a manner that would benefit a non-object (a person not within the class of potential appointees). Even if the contract is to exercise the power for the benefit of an object, a breach of the contract cannot be used as a basis upon which to recover damages from the donee or his estate.[46] This follows from the fact that the donee of a special power is a fiduciary and, as such, cannot bind himself to deal with the subject matter of a power in any particular way. His power must remain unfettered until the time fixed for its exercise. According to the English rule, a contract to appoint a designated amount to one of the appointees may be sustained as a release of the power to the extent that the appointee would be entitled to take in default of appointment.[47]

A special power of appointment is created by the donor with the understanding that the donee will not become a party to an agreement to appoint in such a manner as to benefit a non-object of the power. Such a fraudulent appointment is void in its entirety. For example, in In re Carroll's Will (N.Y.),[48] testator gave his daughter a power to appoint to her children or kindred. It was shown that the daughter desired to appoint one hundred and fifty thousand dollars to her cousin and his son. However, she appointed two hundred and fifty thousand dollars to the cousin upon the latter's agreement to pay one hundred thousand dollars to the donee's husband —a person to whom appointment could not properly be made. It is held that the appointment failed in its entirety.[49] However, there is authority for the view that a fraudulent appointment is void only to the extent of the benefit that might have accrued to a non-object.[50]

The prevailing rule is that there may be a fraudulent exercise of a power even in the ab-

---

42. Northern Trust Co. v. Porter, 1938, 368 Ill. 256, 15 N.E.2d 487 (damages denied); O'Hara v. O'Hara, 1945, 185 Md. 321, 44 A.2d 813, 163 A.L.R. 1444 (specific performance denied). See also, United States Trust Co. v. Montclair Trust Co., 1943, 133 N.J.Eq. 579, 33 A.2d 901 (where contract was made with the donee's creditor).

43. 3 Rest.Property, § 340.

44. In re Rogers' Estate, 1938, 168 Misc. 633, 6 N.Y. S.2d 255.

45. 3 Rest.Property, § 334. But see, O'Hara v. O'Hara, 1945, 185 Md. 321, 44 A.2d 813, 163 A.L.R. 1444.

46. In re Bradshaw, 1902, 1 Ch. 436.

47. Coffin v. Cooper, [1865] 2 Drew & S. 365, 62 Eng. Rep. 660.

48. 274 N.Y. 288, 8 N.E.2d 864, 115 A.L.R. 923 (1937), reargument denied 275 N.Y. 536, 11 N.E.2d 737, noted in 36 Col.Law Rev. 1407 (1937), 51 Harv.Law Rev. 171 (1937), 46 Yale Law Jr. 344 (1936)—lower court decision.

49. Accord: Chenoweth v. Bullitt, 1928, 224 Ky. 698, 6 S.W.2d 1061; In re Cohen, 1911, 1 Ch. 37. See Eblen, Fraud on Special Powers of Appointments, 25 Ky.Law Jr. 3, 8 (1936).

50. 3 Rest.Property, § 353.

sence of an agreement to appoint if the donee is motivated by the purpose to confer a benefit upon a non-object.[51]

EXERCISE OF POWER

179. **Insofar as the exercise of a power is concerned, it is considered that a conveyance is involved. Accordingly, a deed or will purporting to exercise a power must be executed with the formalities prescribed by law.**

　　a. **Intention to exercise power.** The donee of a power may evidence his intention to exercise the power by making reference to the power or to the property that is subject to the power. Such an intention may be implied by the fact that a conveyance by the donee would be a "nullity" unless it included powered property. Statute in a number of states provide that a residuary clause in a will may result in the exercise of a general power of appointment.

　　b. **Interests which may be created.** Unless restricted by a provision in the instrument creating a power, the donee may exercise the power by appointing an estate or interest less than that authorized by the power.

　　c. **Creation of a new power.** A general power of appointment may be exercised by the creation of a new power. Unless the authority is restricted, the donee of a special power can properly exercise the power by creating a general power in the donee. He may also confer a limited estate upon the donee with a special power to appoint to persons who qualify as appointees under the original power.

　　d. **Lapse statutes.** In the absence of statute the exercise of a testamentary power fails if the appointee predeceases the donee. In a majority of American states lapse statutes have been enacted that are applicable to testamentary gifts. Usually, these statutes are also applicable in the case of a general power of appointment.

A deed or will purporting to exercise a power of appointment must be executed with the formalities prescribed by law. For this purpose, the exercise of the power is considered to be a conveyance and not a mere event that causes a shift of ownership. However, failure to comply with formalities additionally prescribed by the donor may not be fatal to the validity of the appointment. Substantial compliance with these formalities may be sufficient for the purpose if the appointee parted with value in reliance upon the appointment or if the appointee is a charity or the wife, child or creditor of the donee of the power.[52] Additional rules relating to the formalities prescribed by law are as follows:

First: The proper exercise of a power of appointment relating to land requires that the deed or will be executed with the formalities prescribed by the law of the place where the land is situated.[53]

Second: A power to appoint chattels by deed requires that the deed be exercised with the formalities prescribed by the law of the place where the chattels are located at the time the power is exercised.[54]

Third: A testamentary power with respect to chattels is properly exercised if the will is executed with the formalities prescribed by the law of the domicile of the donor of the power at the time the power was created.[55] There is also authority for the rule that such a power is properly exercised if the will complies with the formalities prescribed by the

---

51. Horne v. Title Insurance & Trust Co., D.Cal.1948, 79 F.Supp. 91; 3 Rest.Property, § 354. But see, In re Nicholson's Settlement, 1939, 1 Ch. 11, noted in 53 Harv.Law Rev. 1058 (1940).

52. 3 Rest.Property, § 347.

53. Rest., Conflict of Laws, § 234.

54. Rest., Conflict of Laws, § 286.

55. See Estate of Sloan, 1935, 7 Cal.App.2d 319, 46 P.2d 1007; Hogarth-Swann v. Weed, 1931, 274 Mass. 125, 174 N.E. 314; Rest., Conflict of Laws, § 287.

law of the domicile of the donee of the power.[56] The will is construed according to the law of the domicile of the donor.[57]

Intention to Exercise Power

Usually, the intention to exercise a power is manifested by the fact that the donee makes reference to the power. Additional methods of evidencing an intention are as follows:

First: If the donee conveys the property that is subject to the power he thereby indicates his intention to exercise the power. But if he has a limited interest in the property the conveying instrument may be treated as applicable to this limited interest rather than as applicable to an exercise of the power.[58] If a donee has only a life estate, this "limited estate" rule is not applicable and the power is exercised by a will purporting to dispose of the property.[59] So also, if the donee has only a life estate, he exercises the power if a conveyance is made in fee (or absolute ownership in the case of chattels). Under the circumstances mentioned reference to the power is not necessary.[60] However, a quitclaim deed will convey only the life estate.[61]

Second: An intention to exercise a power may be implied from the fact that bequests made by the donee would be a nullity unless satisfied out of the property that is subject to the power. That is the case if the personal estate of the donee is substantially insufficient to satisfy bequests made in a will and the insufficiency was known to the donee at the time he executed the will.[62]

Third: A power of appointment is not exercised merely because of the fact that the donee inserted a residuary clause in his will. Such a clause ("all the rest and residue of my property") is operative only as to property *owned* by the testator.[63] The fine distinction between absolute ownership and a general power of appointment has resulted in some decisions to the effect that a general power of appointment is exercised by a residuary clause.[64] But even under this view, a special power of appointment is not exercised by such a clause.[65]

In a number of states it is now provided by statute that a power of appointment may be exercised by a residuary clause.[66] It is believed that these statutes have application

---

56. See, for example, Guaranty Trust Co. of N. Y. v. Stevens, 1958, 28 N.J. 243, 146 A.2d 97; Rest., Conflict of Laws, § 287.

57. In re Phelps' Estate, Sur.1943, 45 N.Y.S.2d 621.

58. Dunning v. Vandusen, 1874, 47 Ind. 423; Meister v. Francisco, 1940, 233 Wis. 319, 289 N.W. 643, 127 A.L.R. 242; 3 Rest.Property, § 342, *Comment (c).* *Cf.:* Funk v. Eggleston, 1879, 92 Ill. 515; Rettig v. Zander, 1936, 364 Ill. 112, 4 N.E.2d 30, noted in 35 Mich.Law Rev. 1020 (1937).

59. Hopkins v. Fauble, 1964, 47 Ill.App.2d 263, 197 N.E.2d 725.

60. Farlow v. Farlow, 1896, 83 Md. 118, 34 A. 837; Underwood v. Cave, 1903, 176 Mo. 1, 75 S.W. 451.

61. Barnard v. Moore, 1922, 71 Colo. 401, 207 P. 332; Lister v. Lister, 1926, 47 R.I. 366, 133 A. 437. *Contra:* Prudential Inv. & Development Co. v. Hilton, 1922, 153 Ga. 415, 112 S.E. 464.

62. Hartford-Connecticut Trust Co. v. Thayer, 1926, 105 Conn. 57, 134 A. 155; In re Stork's Estate, 1943, 233 Iowa 413, 9 N.W.2d 273.

63. Grabbe v. St. Vincent's Home of Davenport, 1942, 232 Iowa 640, 5 N.W.2d 922; Patterson v. Wilson, 1885, 64 Md. 193, 1 A. 68; In re Central Home Trust Co., 1960, 61 N.J.Super. 109, 160 A.2d 186; 3 Rest.Property, § 343(1).

64. Harvard Trust Co. v. Frost, 1927, 258 Mass. 319, 154 N.E. 863; Adams v. D'Hauteville, 1947, 72 R.I. 325, 51 A.2d 92. See also, Emery v. Haven, 1893, 67 N.H. 503, 35 A. 940.

65. Fiduciary Trust Co. v. First Nat. Bank of Colorado Springs, 1962, 344 Mass. 1, 181 N.E.2d 6.

66. See, for example, California Trust Co. v. Ott, 1943, 59 Cal.App.2d 715, 140 P.2d 79; In re Summerfield's Estate, 1939, 172 Misc. 509, 15 N.Y.S.2d 418. For an enumeration of the various statutes, see 3 Rest.Property, § 343, *Comment d,* Statutory Note.

only with respect to a general power of appointment.

Interests Which May Be Created

Unless restricted by provisions in the instrument creating a power, the donee may exercise the power to its fullest extent or he may appoint an estate less than that authorized under the power.[67] For example, if a donee is authorized to appoint in fee simple, or absolutely, he may appoint a lesser estate, such as for life.

Creation of a New Power

A general power of appointment can properly be exercised by the creation of new powers, general or special. It is not necessary for the donee to appoint to himself first and then create new powers.[68]

Unless the authority is specifically restricted, the donee of a special power can properly exercise the power by creating a general power in the appointee.[69] So also, he may confer a life estate upon a qualified appointee and also give him a special power to appoint to persons who qualify as appointees under the original power.[70]

Lapse Statutes

In the absence of statute the exercise of a testamentary power fails if the appointee predeceases the donee.[71] A similar rule applies with respect to testamentary gifts. In a majority of states it is provided by statute that if a devisee or legatee predeceases the testator there is not necessarily a lapsed legacy. Designated relatives of the devisee or legatee, such as children, are entitled to take in his stead.

While these lapse statutes refer to "devises and legacies" and to "testators," they are generally applied to testamentary provisions involving the exercise of a general power of appointment. Because of the wide scope of the power it is not amiss to refer to the donee of a general power as a "testator," and to the exercise of the power as a devise or bequest. But this is not true with respect to a special power of appointment and, for that reason, a lapse statute is not applicable in the case of a special power. Further, in many situations application of the statute would permit benefits to persons not designated as appointees.[72]

SEGREGATION OF OWNED AND POWERED PROPERTY

180. If there is a blending clause in a will a general power of appointment is exercised "by the whole will." However, property owned by the testator may be segregated from powered property for certain purposes, such as for the purpose of applying the rule against perpetuities.

If the exercise of a general power is accomplished by the residuary clause, the powered property is not thereby made available for the payment of bequests that are not contained in the residuary clause.

67. Welch v. Morse, 1948, 323 Mass. 233, 81 N.E.2d 361, 4 A.L.R.2d 913; Massey v. Guaranty Trust Co., 1942, 142 Neb. 237, 5 N.W.2d 279, noted in 41 Mich. Law Rev. 985 (1943).

68. Lampkin v. Safe Deposit & Trust Co., 1949, 192 Md. 472, 64 A.2d 704; Garfield v. State Street Trust Co., 1947, 320 Mass. 646, 70 N.E.2d 705, 169 A.L.R. 719; 3 Rest.Property, § 357 (*Comment d* states that expressed intention of the donor to the contrary has no effect). *Contra:* DeCharette v. DeCharette, 1936, 264 Ky. 525, 94 S.W.2d 1018, 104 A.L.R. 1455 (relating to a testamentary power).

69. Stone v. Forbes, 1905, 189 Mass. 163, 75 N.E. 141; 3 Rest.Property, § 359.

70. In re Finucane's Will, 1950, 199 Misc. 1069, 100 N.Y.S.2d 1005; Lewis's Estates, 1921, 269 Pa. 379, 112 A. 454, 13 A.L.R. 1053; 3 Rest.Property, § 359 (2).

71. Harker v. Reilly, 1871, 4 Del.Ch. 72; Duke of Marlborough v. Lord Godolphin, [1750] 2 Ves.Sr. 61, 28 Eng.Rep. 41.

72. See Daniel v. Brown, 1931, 156 Va. 563, 159 S.E. 209, 75 A.L.R. 1377.

If there is a blending clause in a will a general power of appointment is exercised "by the whole will." That is the case, for example, if the will provides "I hereby devise and bequeath all property owned by me and all appointive property as follows . . .".

In spite of such a blending clause the property owned by a testator and the property over which he has a general power of appointment may be segregated for certain purposes, such as for the purpose of applying the rule against perpetuities. Assume that A's will gave B a general testamentary power with respect to $50,000. Assume also, that at the time of B's death his estate consisted of $50,000, plus the power of appointment authorized by A. B's will bequeathed $50,000 to his son S and gave his daughter, D, a life estate with respect to $50,000 and a power of appointment of $50,000 to her surviving children. The daughter, D, was not born until after the death of A. Since D was not a life in being at the time of A's death (the donor of the power), a gift to her surviving children, if applied to appointive property, would violate the rule against perpetuities in the state involved. In order to sustain this gift the property owned by B may be allocated to the gift made to D's children and the appointive property allocated to S.[73]

An allocation problem may also arise in connection with the satisfaction of testamentary dispositions. If a general power of appointment is exercised by the whole will, as in the case of a blending clause, the appointive property is available to satisfy bequests made in the will. However, there is authority for the view that this is not true if the power is exercised only by the residuary clause in a will. For example, in Slayton v. Fitch Home, Inc. (Mass.),[74] according to the local law a general power of appointment could be exercised by a residuary clause in a will, and the power was so exercised. Property owned by the testatrix was insufficient to satisfy the bequests made in the will. The conclusion is reached that appointive property is not available to make up the deficiencies.[75]

CREDITORS OF A DONEE OF A POWER

181. Except in the case of a "reserved power," the creditors of the donee of a special power cannot satisfy their claims out of the subject matter of the power. However, such claims may be recognized if the donee had a general power and exercised the power in favor of a volunteer.

Creditors of the donee of a special power of appointment cannot successfully assert a claim to the subject matter of a power.[76] It is not material whether or not the power is or is not exercised. Since the donee of a special power is not the owner of the property and his control over the property is restricted, the rights of ownership properly cannot be attributed to him. Additional rules are as follows:

First: If the owner of property creates an *inter vivos* trust (a living trust) reserving to himself the income for life with remainder over as he should appoint by will, his creditors may assert a claim to the property to the extent that other assets are not available to satisfy their claims. It is not material whether the power is exercised or not. Such a re-

73. Minor v. Paine, 1918, 230 Mass. 514, 120 N.E. 167, 1 A.L.R. 365; 3 Rest. Property, § 363, Illustration 1. *Cf.*: Amerige v. Attorney General, 1949, 324, 648, 88 N.E.2d 126 (the allocation rule is not applicable as to property acquired under a former will).

74. 293 Mass. 574, 200 N.E. 357, 104 A.L.R. 669 (1936).

75. See Simes & Smith, Future Interests (2d Ed.), § 975, p. 442.

76. 3 Rest.Property, § 326.

served power of appointment cannot be used as a means by which to defraud creditors.[77]

Second: If a general power of appointment is exercised in favor of a volunteer the creditors of the donee may satisfy their claims out of the powered property to the extent that other property is not available for this purpose.[78] A creditor of the donee is a "volunteer" within the meaning of this rule.[79] However, a *bona fide* purchaser for value from an appointee will be protected.[80] Claims against the donee's estate include the expense of administration and tax claims.[81] In State ex rel. Beardsley v. London & Lancashire Indemnity Co., (Conn.),[82] the donee of a general power incurred liability for the dissipation of the subject matter of the power. The court held that his surety was not a creditor within the meaning of the rule which permits the satisfaction of claims as against the appointee.

The general rule is based upon the ground that the donee of a general power has important "rights of ownership" and by exercising the power has elected to treat the property as his own. But if the power is not exercised the donee's creditors are not entitled to satisfaction out of the powered property.[83] The minority rule is that since the donee of a power is not the owner of the property his creditors have no right to the property even if the power is exercised.[84]

In a number of states it is provided by statute that, under varying circumstances, the creditors of the donee of a general power of appointment are in a position to satisfy their claims out of the powered property even if the power is not exercised.[85] Under provisions of the Bankruptcy Act, a power of appointment which a bankrupt could have exercised *in his own favor* passes to his trustee in bankruptcy.[86] The language of the Act indicates that this includes only a general power exercisable by deed (a power presently exercisable).

Third: An appointment to one who is entitled to take the property in default of appointment is not an exercise of the power of

77. Mackason's Appeal, 1862, 42 Pa. 330; Nolan v. Nolan, 1907, 218 Pa. 135, 67 A. 52; 3 Rest. Property, § 328.

78. Jackson v. Franklin, 1934, 179 Ga. 840, 177 S.E. 731, 97 A.L.R. 1064; Clapp v. Ingraham, 1879, 126 Mass. 200; U. S. Trust Co. of Newark v. Montclair Trust Co., 1943, 133 N.J.Eq. 579, 33 A.2d 901, noted in 42 Mich.Law Rev. 926 (1944); Thompson v. Towne, [1694], 2 Vern. 319, 23 Eng.Rep. 806; 3 Rest.Property, §§ 329, 330.

79. Vinton v. Pratt, 1917, 228 Mass. 468, 117 N.E. 919, L.R.A.1918D, 343; State Street Trust Co. v. Kissel, 1939, 302 Mass. 328, 19 N.E.2d 25, 121 A.L.R. 796.

80. Patterson v. Lawrence, 1889, 83 Ga. 703, 10 S.E. 355.

81. Olney v. Balch, 1891, 154 Mass. 318, 28 N.E. 258; 3 Rest.Property, § 329, *Comment f. Contra:* Seward v. Kaufman, 1935, 119 N.J.Eq. 44, 180 A. 857, noted in 84 Univ. of Pa.Law Rev. 431 (1936).

82. 124 Conn. 416, 200 A. 567 (1938), noted in 52 Harv.Law Rev. 533 (1939).

83. Gilman v. Bell, 1881, 88 Ill. 144; 3 Rest.Property, § 327. See Quinn v. Tuttle, 1962, 104 N.H. 1, 177 A.2d 391 (a power given to a life tenant to use principal for her "reasonable comfort and support).

84. St. Matthews Bank v. De Charette, 1935, 259 Ky. 802, 83 S.W.2d 471, 99 A.L.R. 1146; Com. v. Duffield, 1849, 12 Pa. 277; Rhode Island Hospital Trust Co. v. Anthony, 1928, 49 R.I. 339, 142 A. 531, 59 A.L.R. 1501; Humphrey v. Campbell, 1900, 59 S.C. 39, 37 S.E. 26

85. For an enumeration of these statutes, see 3 Rest. Property, § 327, *Comment d,* Statutory Note. See also, The Creditor's Rights against the Donee of a Power of Appointment, 27 Va.Law Rev. 1052, 1059 (1941).

86. Federal Bankruptcy Act § 70a, 11 U.S.C.A. § 110(a). See Montague v. Silsbee, 1914, 218 Mass. 107, 105 N.E. 611.

appointment because of the fact that it accomplishes nothing.[87]

FAILURE TO EXERCISE POWER AND DEFECTIVE APPOINTMENTS

182. Except as noted, if there is a failure to exercise a power, or if there is a defective appointment, the property is distributed to persons described as "takers in default." If provision is not made for takers in default the property belongs to the donor or to his estate.

    a. General power of appointment. Property subject to a general power of appointment may become a part of the estate of the donee because of a "blending clause" in his will. It will also be a part of his estate if an appointment is made in trust and the trust fails (capure doctrine).

    b. Special power of appointment. If a special power of appointment is mandatory (in trust), and is not exercised, the property is distributed to the appointees either on the theory of a trust or on the theory of a gift by implication.

In general, if there is a failure to exercise a power of appointment, or if there is a defective appointment, the property is distributed to persons described as "takers in default." If provision is not made for takers in default the property belongs to the donor of the power or to his estate.[88] Variations and exceptions to this rule are discussed in the following paragraphs.

General Power of Appointment

The donee of a general power of appointment may evidence the fact that his purpose was to commingle his own property with the property over which he had a power of appointment. In that event the subject matter of the power belongs to the donee of the power or to his estate. This purpose may be evidenced by a "blending clause" in his will.[89] For example, a will may contain a provision that property over which the testator has a general power of appointment is to be considered as a part of the residuary estate.[90]

Even in the absence of a "blending clause" the donee of a general power may "capture" the property and make it a part of his estate. This may be accomplished by an appointment in trust. Even if the trust fails in whole or in part the ownership of the property passes to the trustee and this effectively removes it from the scope of the power.[91] Such an "implied appointment" to the estate of the donee may arise even if the instrument creating the power provides for "takers in default."[92] The controlling factor is the intention of the donee of the power to appoint to himself or to his estate.

Special Power of Appointment

If a special power of appointment is mandatory (in trust), and it is not exercised, the property is distributed to the appointees either on the theory of a trust or on the theory

---

87. 3 Rest.Property, § 327, *Comment b*, § 369, *Comment a*. For criticism of this view see Moorhead, Book Review on Restatement of Property, Vol. III, 20 Tex.Law Rev. 252, 255 (1941).

88. In re Davies' Trusts, Ch. [1871] L.R. 13 Eq. 163.

89. Old Colony Trust Co. v. Allen, 1940, 307 Mass. 40, 29 N.E.2d 310, noted in 41 Col.Law Rev. 538 (1941), 21 Boston Univ.Law Rev. 364 (1941). See 3 Rest.Property, § 365, *Comment d*. See In re Breault's Estate, 1963, 291 Ill.2d 165, 193 N.E.2d 824

90. Willoughby Osborne v. Holyoake, 1882, 22 Ch.Div. 238.

91. Talbot v. Riggs, 1934, 287 Mass. 144, 191 N.E. 360, 93 A.L.R. 964; In re Van Hagan, 1880, L.R. 16 Ch.Div. 18; 3 Rest.Property, § 365(2).

92. Fiduciary Trust Co. v. Mishou, 1947, 321 Mass. 615, 75 N.E.2d 3, noted in 61 Harv.Law Rev. 715 (1948), 47 Mich.Law Rev. 93 (1948). *Contra*: Northern Trust Co. v. Porter, 1938, 368 Ill. 256, 13 N.E. 2d 487.

of a gift by implication.[93] If the special power is not mandatory, and if the donee fails to exercise the power, the property passes to the takers in default. If persons to take in default of appointment are not mentioned, the property belongs to the donor of the power or to his estate

Partial invalidity will not necessarily invalidate the entire appointment. In Greenough v. Osgood (Mass.),[94] the donee appointed in such a manner as to create future interests that were void under the rule against perpetuities. However, the validity of the life estate created by the same instrument was sustained. In some cases, however, the invalid part of an appointment is so interwoven with the valid part that the entire appointment will fail.[95]

---

93. See supra, § 173.

94. 235 Mass. 235, 126 N.E. 461 (1920).

95. Equitable Trust Co. v. Foulke, 1945, 28 Del.Ch. 238, 40 A.2d 713; Parker v. MacBryde, 4 Cir. 1942, 132 F.2d 932, certiorari denied 318 U.S. 779, 63 S. Ct. 859, 87 L.Ed. 1147 (1942).

CHAPTER 36

RULE AGAINST PERPETUITIES

THEORY UNDERLYING THE RULE AGAINST PERPETUITY

183. The weight of authority is that the rule against perpetuities is aimed against the remoteness of vesting of estates or interests in property. The minority rule is that a perpetuity involves the suspension of the power of alienation beyond the time permitted by law.

It has been seen that the Statute of Uses, passed in 1536, and the Statute of Wills, passed in 1540, made possible the creation of a new type of future estate called an executory interest.[1] The validity of an executory interest did not depend upon the existence of a supporting life estate or estate tail as did a contingent remainder. Accordingly, it was held that the doctrine of the destructibility of contingent remainders had no application to executory interests.[2] This led to the inevitable conclusion that some means would have to be found to regulate executory interests. The very existence of such interests is reflected in the alienability of property. Two theories regarding the matter were suggested in the early development of the law and each theory found its supporters.

According to one theory property is alienable if there are identified persons in being who have the power and the right to convey in fee simple or to transfer absolute ownership in the case of personal property. It is not material that this may require two or more persons to join in the conveyance. Until the time such a conveyance or transfer can be made there is a suspension of the power of alienation. If this extends beyond the permitted time it is a perpetuity. This view found expression in the early English case of Scatterwood v. Edge [3] where it is stated that a perpetuity is "an estate unalienable, though all mankind join in the conveyance." This theory is followed in the leading English case of Avern v. Lloyd,[4] decided in 1868, and is followed in a number of American states.[5]

According to another theory the "joint action" rule does not satisfy the requirements of alienability. There may be serious difficulties in bringing about such joint action. As a practical matter, so it is reason-

---

1. See supra, § 141.

2. Manning's Case, [1609] 8 Co. 94b, 77 Eng.Rep. 618; Pells v. Brown, [1620] Cro.Jac. 590, 79 Eng.Rep. 504.

3. 1 Salk. 229, 91 Eng.Rep. 203 (1699).

4. L.R. 5 Eq. 383 (1868).

5. See, for example, Dvorak v. School District, 1946, 237 Iowa 442, 22 N.W.2d 238; Mineral Land Inv. Co. v. Bishop Iron Co., 1916, 134 Minn. 412, 159 N.W. 966; Will of Butter, 1941, 239 Wis. 249, 1 N.W.2d 87; West's Ann.Cal.Civ.Code, § 715.8 (added in 1963).

ed, an interest impairs alienability until such time as it can be classified as vested (free from contingencies with respect to interest). An executory interest does not vest until it becomes possessory. An interest that may not vest or fail within the permitted time is classified as a perpetuity. This became the English rule after the decision in In re Hargreaves,[6] and represents the prevailing rule in the United States.

Many difficulties and uncertainties have been encountered in applying the "vesting" rule. Not the least of this is due to the ambiguous meaning of the word "vested." It has one meaning when used to define remainders and another when used in reference to executory interests. At times it is used to define remainders that are "transmissible at death" of the owner. These and other meanings have contributed to the confusion. Reform is in the making as evidenced by legislation enacted in a number of states.[7] Simplification can be attained by adoption of the "suspension of the power of alienation" rule and that step has been taken in recent legislation adopted in California. The change has been accomplished by merely changing the definition of the word "vested." The statute now provides that an "interest in real or personal property, legal or equitable, is vested if and when there is a person in being who could convey or there are persons in being, irrespective of the nature of their respective interests, who together could convey a fee simple title thereto."[8]

That a limitation may be void under one rule and valid under another may be illustrated by assuming a conveyance A to B and his

heirs for so long as the land is used for school purposes. When ceased to be used for that purpose the land is to revert to and become the property of the grantors or those claiming title under such grantors to the property out of which "the tract was carved." The gift over is void under the vesting rule because it may not vest or fail within the time permitted for the vesting of estates.[9] The gift over is valid under the rule against suspending the power of alienation.[10] This follows from the fact that at any time the owner of the possessory estate and the owner of the property out of which "the tract was carved" could join in a conveyance and the grantee would acquire a fee simple absolute.

STATEMENT OF THE RULE

184. **An interest is void in its inception unless it must vest, if at all, within life or lives in being, twenty-one years and gestation periods that may be involved. The possibilities pertaining to vesting are determined prospectively as of the date of the conveying instrument.**

From the outset it was considered that public inconvenience would not result if future interests were bound to vest or fail within the period of a life or lives in being, computed from the date upon which the interests were created. In Low v. Burron (Eng.),[11] the validity of a conveyance was sustained that postponed the vesting for three lives in being. The court states: "So, if instead of three, there had been twenty lives, all spending at the same time, all the candles lighted up at once, it would have been good;

---

6. 43 Ch.Div. 401 (1890).

7. See infra, § 184.

8. West's Cal.Ann.Civ.Code, § 715.8, as amended in 1963.

9. Barry v. Newton, 1954, 130 Colo. 106, 273 P.2d 735; Proprietors of the Church of Brattle Square v. Grant, 1855, 3 Gray (Mass.) 142; Donehue v. Nilges, 1954, 364 Mo. 705, 266 S.W.2d 553, 45 A.L.R. 2d 1150.

10. Dvorak v. School District, 1946, 237 Iowa 442, 22 N.W.2d 238.

11. 3 P.Wms. 262, 24 Eng.Rep. 1055 (1734).

for, in effect, it is only for one life, (viz.) that which shall happen to be the survivor.''

In Lloyd v. Carew (Eng.),[12] the proposition is declared that a conveyance is valid although it is not to take effect until some period of time in gross after the termination of lives in being. The period in gross involved was one year. That a period in gross of twenty-one years may be added was established in Cadell v. Palmer (Eng.).[13] This case also established the rule that while an actual period of gestation may be allowed, in addition to lives in being and twenty-one years, a period in gross cannot be allowed in this respect.

The measuring lives need not be persons who receive an interest under the conveying instrument.[14] In fact, the measuring lives need not be specifically mentioned in the conveying instrument. For example, if a testator directs that the income from a trust be paid to his grandchildren, the gift will be sustained even though children born after the death of the testator are included. The gifts are bound to vest within lives in being at the time of the testator's death. The measuring lives are the children of the testator.[15] In In re Villar (Eng.),[16] the suspension was for a period "ending at the expiration of 20 years from the day of the death of the last survivor of all the lineal descendants of Her Late Majesty Queen Victoria who shall be living at the time of my death. The validity of the conveyance is sustained. This is probably contrary to the rule declared in the Restatement of Property that the measuring lives

must not be "so numerous nor so situated that evidence of their deaths is likely to be unreasonably difficult to obtain." [17]

Professor Gray states the rule in its final form: "No interest subject to a condition precedent is good, unless the condition must be fulfilled, if at all, within twenty-one years after some life in being at the creation of the interest." [18] The possibility that vesting might be postponed beyond the permitted time is determined prospectively, as of the effective date of the conveying instrument. Statutory variations as to the time of vesting are to be found in some states.[19] It is generally recognized that vesting may be postponed for a flat period of twenty-one years because that is a shorter period than lives in being and twenty-one years. A California statute provides that vesting may be postponed for the period of lives in being and twenty-one years or vesting may be postponed for a flat period of 60 years.[20]

APPLICATION OF THE RULE

185. In general, the time permitted for the vesting of estates under the rule against perpetuities starts to run when the estates are created. Circumstances relating to the vesting of estates are also considered as of that date.

a. Possibility of issue. According to the common law rule there is a conclusive presumption that any person, regardless of age or physical condition, is capable of having issue.

b. Death of "wife" or "widow". Postponing the vesting of a gift until after the death of the "wife" or the "widow" of a living person violates the rule against perpetuities.

---

12. Prec.Ch. 72, 106, Show.P.C. 137, 24 Eng.Rep. 35 (1697).

13. 1 Cl. & F. 372, 6 Eng.Rep. 956 (1833).

14. Thellusson v. Woodford, [1805] 11 Ves. 112, 32 Eng.Rep. 1030.

15. B.M.C. Durfee Trust Co. v. Taylor, 1950, 325 Mass. 201, 89 N.E.2d 777.

16. 1 Ch. 243 (1929).

17. 4 Rest.Property, § 374.

18. Gray, Rule against Perpetuities, (3rd Ed.), § 201.

19. See, for example, N.Y.Laws of 1958, Chs. 152, 153, amending McKinney's Personal Property Law, § 11, and McKinney's Real Property Law, § 42.

20. West's Ann.Cal.Civ.Code, § 715.6 (added in 1963).

c.   **Happening of an event.** A contingent future interest is void if vesting is postponed until the happening of an event and that event might not take place within the time permitted for the vesting of estates.

d.   **"Wait and see" rule.** According to this rule future contingent interests do not violate the rule against perpetuities if they actually do vest within the permitted time.

In the case of testamentary dispositions the period of time allowed under the rule against perpetuities is computed from the time of the testator's death. In the case of an *inter vivos* trust computation is made as of the date of the conveyance. However, if the trustor reserves a power of revocation the period is computed from the time when such power becomes irrevocable.

Circumstances relating to the vesting of estates are also considered as of the time when an interest is created or when the conveyance becomes irrevocable. In Southern v. Wollaston (Eng.),[21] a testamentary trust directed that income was to be paid to B for life, remainder to B's children living at the time of B's death who should attain the age of twenty-five. Viewing conditions as they existed at the time of testator's death the gift to B's children did not violate the rule. It was shown that B predeceased the testator and all of B's children were, of necessity, lives in being when the interests were created.

Possibility of Issue

For purposes of applying the rule against perpetuities, any person, regardless of age or physical condition, is conclusively presumed capable of having issue.[22] In Jee v. Audley (Eng.),[23] testator bequeathed money to his wife for life, then to B and the issue of B's body "lawfully begotten, and to be begotten" and in default of such issue then equally to the daughters, then living, of John and Elizabeth Jee. At the time of the death of testator John and Elizabeth Jee, each seventy years of age, had four daughters living. The gift to the Jee daughters was held to be void because, should a daughter be born to the Jees after the death of the testator, that daughter might be the eventual taker under the gift and vesting in that daughter might conceivably be postponed beyond the permitted period. It is immaterial that John and Elizabeth Jee, at the death of the testator, were beyond the normal age for having children.

Since the gift involved personal property a construction was not possible that B acquired an estate tail followed by a valid remainder. Of course, if the court had construed the provision "in default of such issue" as meaning issue living at the time of the death of B, the gift over to the daughters of John and Elizabeth Jee would be valid. In that event the life of B would be the measuring life. At the time of this decision there was a preference for an "indefinite failure of issue" construction. At the present time, either by statute or otherwise, there is a preference for a "definite failure of issue" construction. Because of the fact that the testator was fully aware of the fact that John and Elizabeth Jee were not likely to have additional children it may be urged that he intended to limit the gift to the daughters

---

21.   16 Beav. 276, 51 Eng.Rep. 785 (1852).

22.   Lovering v. Lovering, 1880, 129 Mass. 97; Loud v. St. Louis Union Trust Co., 1923, 298 Mo. 148, 249 S.W. 629. *Contra:* Exham v. Beamish, 1939, Ir.R. 336, noted in 53 Harv.Law Rev. 490 (1940). See also,

United States v. Provident Trust Co., 1934, 291 U.S. 272, 54 S.Ct. 389, 78 L.Ed. 793 (such evidence admissible for the purpose of evaluating future interests)

23.   1 Cox 324, 29 Eng.Rep. 1186 (1787).

living at the time of his death. There is authority supporting such a conclusion.[24]

The common law rule as to "possibility of issue" resulted from the fact that uncertainty exists as to the "age limits" that should be applied. As for "physical condition," other than age, there is a possibility that expert testimony regarding the matter could be erroneous. Further, the consideration of matters relating to physical condition might lead to unnecessary operations that would not be in furtherance of public policy. Regardless of these various factors, there are decisions indicating that the common law rule is in the process of being abandoned.[25]

Death of "Wife" or "Widow"

Postponing the vesting of an interest until after the death of the "wife" or "widow" of a living person violates the rule against perpetuities.[26] The eventual "wife" or "widow" may be a person not in being at the effective date of the gift. However, there is authority for the view that such words are ambiguous. As such, extrinsic evidence is admissible to show that they were used as meaning the "present wife" of the named person.[27] In that event, the reference is to a life in being. But evidence as to such an intention must relate to facts existing at the time the will was executed or the deed delivered.[28]

Happening of an Event

The rule against perpetuities is not satisfied by proof of the fact that a contingent future interest *probably* will vest within the permitted time. The interest is void in its inception unless it must vest, if at all, within that time. An interest is void if vesting is postponed until the probate of the testator's will[29] or the distribution of his estate.[30] These are events that may not take place within the flat period of twenty-one years and the period is not measured by lives in being. The same result has been reached in other situations where the event was one which in all probability would occur within the permitted time.[31]

But a direction that the event involved must happen within a "reasonable time" satisfies the rule against perpetuities. As a matter of construction it is held that the "reasonable time" does not extend beyond twenty-one years.[32] An increasing number of decisions support the view that if there is

---

24. Snyder's Estate v. Denit, 1950, 195 Md. 81, 72 A.2d 757, 18 A.L.R.2d 663; Wright's Estate, 1925, 284 Pa. 334, 131 A. 188; Bryson v. Conn.Gen.Life Ins. Co., Tex.Civ.App., 1946, 196 S.W.2d 532, error refused. *Contra:* Ward v. Van Der Loeff, 1924, A.C. 653.

25. See, for example, Hicks v. Hicks Unborn Children, 1963, 259 N.C. 387, 130 S.E.2d 666 (litigation involving ownership of government bonds and cash); In re Bassett's Estate, 1963, 104 N.H. 504, 190 A. 2d 415, 98 A.L.R.2d 1281 (rule against perpetuities).

26. Easton v. Hall, 1926, 323 Ill. 397, 154 N.E. 216 (gift over after death of "widow" of a person living at the time of testator's death); Keefer v. McCloy, 1931, 344 Ill. 454, 176 N.E. 743, noted in 26 Ill.Law Rev. 826 (1932), (gift over after death of "wife"); American National Bank of Camden v. Morgenweck, 1933, 114 N.J.Eq. 286, 168 A. 598 (bequest over to "lawful wife"); Brookover v. Grimm, 1937, 118 W.Va. 227, 190 S.E. 697 (gift over to "widow").

27. In re Friend's Estate, 1938, 168 Misc. 607, 6 N.Y.S.2d 205.

28. In re Horton's Will, 1940, 175 Misc. 542, 24 N.Y. S.2d 278.

29. Miller v. Weston, 1920, 67 Colo. 534, 189 P. 610; Ryan v. Beshk, 1930, 339 Ill. 45, 170 N.E. 699.

30. Estate of Campbell, 1938, 28 Cal.App.2d 102, 82 P.2d 22, noted in 27 Cal.Law Rev. 86 (1938), 37 Mich. Law Rev. 814 (1939). *Cf.:* In re Sutton's Will, 1934, 150 Misc. 137, 268 N.Y.S. 458. *Contra:* Belfield v. Booth, 1893, 63 Conn. 299, 27 A. 585.

31. In re Wood, 1894, 3 Ch. 381.

32. West Texas Bank & Trust Co. v. Matlock, Tex. Com.App. 1919, 212 S.W. 937.

a probability that an event will take place within twenty-one years a "reasonable time" will be implied, and a "reasonable time" is something less than twenty-one years. This is especially true if the event involves some act to be performed, such as the construction of a building, and there is a direction that it is to be done "forthwith" and "continue expeditiously." [33] The "reasonable time" rule has also been applied as a means by which to sustain the validity of an option to purchase land. In Mattern v. Herzog (Tex.),[34] the court states: "When the wording of the option does not compel a construction that the parties intended that the time element should be unlimited, the court will not construe an option contract or a will provision granting an option to run for an indefinite time and thus destroy the validity of the option provision."

"Wait and See" Rule

The Pennsylvania Estates Act of 1947 [35] adopted a new theory with respect to the application of the rule against perpetuities. It abrogates the common law theory that if by any possibility interests might not vest or fail within the time allowed for vesting of estates such interests are void in their inception. The rule is adopted that if the created interests do, in fact, vest within the permitted time they do not violate the rule.[36] Similar statutes have been enacted in Connecticut,[37] Maine,[38] Massachusetts [39] and Ver-

mont.[40] A similar result has been reached in New Hampshire without the aid of statute.[41]

ALTERNATIVE CONTINGENCIES

186. If a conveying instrument expressly provides for two contingencies, one of which is void under the rule against perpetuities, the alternative gift, if valid, will be sustained. However, for this rule to apply the alternative contingencies must be expressly stated.

A gift may involve two or more contingencies that are expressed in the alternative. Some of the contingencies may violate the rule against perpetuities. However, a gift made on a contingency that does not violate the rule will be sustained.

In Springfield Safe Deposit & Trust Co. v. Ireland (Mass.),[42] testator died in 1891. His will directed that during January of 1922 his estate was to be distributed to B's then living children and to the issue of deceased children, or if B was then living distribution was to be made during the first January after B's death. B died in February of 1928 and was survived by his son, C. The validity of the gift to C was sustained. The condition that distribution was to be made in January of 1922 violated the rule against perpetuities because the period of postponement (1891 to 1922) was greater than twenty-one years. But the alternative contingency did not violate the rule and distribution was

---

33. Wong v. DiGrazia, 1963, 60 Cal.2d 525, 35 Cal. Rptr. 241, 386 P.2d 817.

34. —— Tex. ——, 367 S.W.2d 312, 319 (1963).

35. 20 P.S. § 301.4.

36. See Leach, Perpetuities: The Nutshell Revisited, 78 Harv.Law Rev. 973 (1965).

37. Conn.L.1955, P.A. 233.

38. Maine R.S. ch. 160, §§ 27–33.

39. Mass.—M.G.L.A. c. 184A.

40. Vermont Public Acts of 1957, No. 177.

41. Merchants Nat. Bank v. Curtis, 1953, 98 N.H. 225, 97 A.2d 207. See also, Story v. First Nat. Bank & Trust Co., 1934, 115 Fla. 436, 156 So. 101. See also, Leach, Perpetuities in Perspective: Ending the Rule's Reign of Terror, 56 Harv.Law Rev. 721, 730 (1952); Simes, Is the Rule against Perpetuities Doomed? The "Wait and See" Doctrine, 52 Mich. Law Rev. 179 (1953).

42. 268 Mass. 62, 167 N.E. 261, 64 A.L.R. 1071 (1929), noted in 10 Boston Univ.Law Rev. 256 (1930).

directed to be made on the alternative contingency.[43]

For this rule to apply the contingencies must be expressly stated to be in the alternative. Though a single stated contingency is such as necessarily to include another unnamed contingency, the validity of the gift will depend upon the validity of the named contingency. An intention to provide alternative contingencies will not be implied.

In Proctor v. Bishop of Bath and Wells (Eng.),[44] an advowson was devised to the first or other son of Thomas Proctor, who should be reared a clergyman and be in holy orders, but in case Proctor should have no *such* son, then to Moore in fee. Proctor died without having had a son. The court held that the gift to Moore was too remote. It was not measured by the life of Moore and the express contingency provided for an event which might not happen within life or lives in being and twenty-one years after the death of the testator. Since there was no express alternative contingency that in the event Proctor should die without having had a son the gift over was to go to Moore—a valid alternative contingency—the gift over failed.[45]

The situation is most frequently presented in cases where a testamentary gift is made to B for life, remainder to B's children who reach the age of twenty-five, with a gift over in default of *such* issue. The prevailing rule is that even if B dies without issue surviving

the gift over will fail.[46] To save the gift the testator must state the condition in the form of two contingencies.

If, in Proctor v. Bishop of Bath and Wells, the gift to Moore had been preceded by a life estate in Thomas Proctor, then, in the light of events as they occurred, the gift to Moore could be construed to be a remainder. As such, it would be valid. This exception to the general rule that alternative contingencies must be expressly stated is declared in Evers v. Challis (Eng.).[47] For example, if an estate is given to B for life, remainder to his unborn son, and then over to C if B left children who died under the age of twenty-three, as long as B has no children the contingent remainder in C is valid. In Evers v. Challis, Mr. Justice Wightman states the rule as follows: "No case or authority has been cited to show that where a devise over includes two contingencies which are in their nature divisible, and one of which can operate as a remainder, they may not be divided though included in one expression."

INTERESTS WITHIN THE SCOPE OF THE RULE

187. The rule against perpetuities applies with respect to both real and personal property and beneficial interests under a trust.

    a. **Destructible Interests. If a conveyor reserves a power of revocation the period under the rule against perpetuities is computed from the time when such power is released.**

    b. **Contracts. The rule against perpetuities has no application with respect to the time fixed for the performance of a contract.**

---

43. *Accord*: First Portland Nat. Bank v. Rodrique, 1961, 157 Me. 277, 172 A.2d 107; Longhead D. Hopkins v. Phelps, [1770] 2 W.Bl. 704, 96 Eng.Rep. 414; VI Am.Law of Property, § 24.54.

44. 2 H.Bl. 358, 126 Eng.Rep. 594 (1794). For a criticism of this case, see Freund, Three Suggestions Concerning Future Interests, 33 Harv.Law Rev. 526 (1920).

45. *Accord*: Thorne v. Continental Nat. Bank & Trust Co., 1940, 305 Ill.App. 222, 27 N.E.2d 302.

46. Easton v. Hall, 1926, 323 Ill. 397, 154 N.E. 216; Hancock v. Watson [1902] A.C. 14; Gray, The Rule against Perpetuities, (3rd Ed.), § 332. *Contra*: Edgerly v. Barker, 1891, 66 N.H. 434, 31 A. 900, 28 L.R.A. 328.

47. 7 H.L.Cas. 531, 11 Eng.Rep. 212 (1859).

c. **Unincorporated association.** A valid charitable trust may be created for an unincorporated association. A valid trust may also be created for a non-charitable association but, in that event, the trust may violate the rule against perpetuities if it is created to continue for a period longer than that allowed for the vesting of estates.

d. **Power of termination (right of entry).** A right of entry is not subject to the rule against perpetuities.

e. **Reversions and possibilities of reverter.** These interests are vested so the rule against perpetuities is not applicable.

f. **Option to purchase.** An option to purchase property must conform to the rule against perpetuities. However, as an exception to the rule, an option is valid if it is embodied in a lease and must be exercised, if at all, during the period of the lease.

g. **Option to renew or extend lease.** An option to renew or extend a lease is generally recognized as an exception to the rule against perpetuities.

The rule against perpetuities applies to the vesting of estates in land and also to the vesting of interests in personal property.[48] It also applies to the vesting of the beneficial interests under a trust.

If an executory interest is involved it must vest in possession within the time prescribed. Such an interest does not have the characteristic of vesting in interest before it vests in possession. However, if a remainder is created it satisfies the rule if it vests in interest within the permitted time even though it does not vest in possession. A gift to B for life, remainder to his children for life, remainder to C and his heirs, is valid as to all remainders. Though C's interest may not become possessory within the period of lives in being and twenty-one years, it is vested in

interest within the permitted time.[49] In order to prevent an undue postponement in possession, statutes have been passed in a few states providing that successive estates for life cannot be limited except to persons in being at the creation thereof and all life estates subsequent to those of persons in being are void.

Application of the rule against perpetuities with respect to specific interests are discussed in the following paragraphs.

Destructible Interests

One who creates a contingent future interest by an *inter vivos* conveyance may reserve a power of revocation. In that event the period under the rule against perpetuities is computed from the date upon which the power is released.[50] However, such a delayed computation is not authorized if the power of revocation is other than absolute.[51]

Contracts

The rule against perpetuities is concerned only with the vesting of estates and interest in property. Accordingly, it has no application

---

48. But see Kingston v. Home Life Ins. Co., 1917, 11 Del.Ch. 258, 266–267, 101 A. 898, affirmed 11 Del.Ch. 428, 104 A. 25 (1918).

49. Story v. First Nat. Bank & Trust Co., in Orlando, 1934, 115 Fla. 436, 156 So. 101 (where it appears that some of the interests were not vested either in possession or interest); Salisbury v. Salisbury, 1914, 92 Kan. 644, 141 P. 173; Seaver v. Fitzgerald, 1886, 141 Mass. 401, 6 N.E. 73; Evans v. Walker, [1876] 3 Ch.Div. 211. *Contra*: Feeney's Estate, 1928, 293 Pa. 273, 142 A. 284, criticized in Leach, Perpetuities in a Nutshell, 51 Harv.Law Rev. 638, 647, note (1938).

50. Manufacturers Life Ins. Co. v. von Hamm-Young Co., 1937, 34 Hawaii 288, noted in 51 Harv.Law Rev. 172 (1937) (revocable life insurance trust); Equitable Trust Co. v. Pratt, 1923, 117 Misc. 708, 193 N.Y.S. 152, affirmed 206 App.Div. 689, 199 N.Y.S. 921 (1923). See also, Sears v. Coolidge, 1952, 329 Mass. 340, 108 N.E.2d 563, noted in 33 Boston Univ. Law Rev. 119 (1953).

51. Ryan v. Ward, 1949, 192 Md. 342, 64 A.2d 258, 7 A.L.R.2d 1078.

with respect to the time fixed for the performance of a contract.[52]

Unincorporated Association

A valid charitable trust may be created for an unincorporated association. A valid trust may also be created for a non-charitable association but, in that event, there must be compliance with the requirements of the rule against perpetuities. Except as noted, the non-charitable trust violates the rule against perpetuities if it is created to continue for a period longer than that permitted for the vesting of estates. However, a violation of the rule is not involved if "an unqualified power to expend the corpus thereof for one or more of the purposes of the association is given to the trustee, or to the members of the association, or to some other person or persons." [53]

Power of Termination (Right of Entry)

The power of termination (right of entry) is not subject to the rule against perpetuities.[54] The reason why it should be considered as an exception to the rule is not clear.[55]

Reversions and Possibilities of Reverter

Reversions and possibilities of reverter are vested interests. Accordingly, the rule against perpetuities is not applicable. In Brown v. Independent Baptist church (Mass.),[56] it is held that a testator can devise a determinable fee and, by the same will, devise what the court designates as a possibility of reverter, without thereby violating the rule against perpetuities.

Option to Purchase

According to the English rule, an option to purchase land cannot be specifically enforced unless it must be exercised, if at all, within the time permitted for the vesting of estates. However, the rule against perpetuities is not a bar to the recovery of damages for breach of the option contract.[57]

The prevailing American rule is that an option to purchase land is void under the rule against perpetuities unless it conforms to the time permitted for the vesting of estates.[58] A conveyance of land may be rescinded if it is accompanied by an option to repurchase that is void under the rule against perpetuities.[59] In construing an option agreement it may be concluded that it is personal to the original contracting parties, and thus in compliance with the rule against perpetui-

---

52. Walsh v. Secretary of State for India, [1863], 10 H. of L. Cas. 367. See Holmes v. John Hancock Mutual Life Ins. Co., 1942, 288 N.Y. 106, 41 N.E.2d 909.

53. 4 Rest. Property, § 380(2) (b). See Wilbur v. Portland Trust Co., 1936, 121 Conn. 535, 186 A. 499; In re Drummond, 1914, 2 Ch. 90.

54. Hinton v. Gilbert, 1930, 221 Ala. 309, 128 So. 604, 70 A.L.R. 1192; Strong v. Shatto, 1919, 45 Cal. App. 29, 187 P. 159.

55. See Simes & Smith, Future Interests, § 1238.

56. 325 Mass. 645, 91 N.E.2d 922 (1950).

57. Worthing Corp. v. Heather, [1906] 2 Ch. 532, 75 L.J.Ch.,N.S., 761, 22 T.L.R. 750. Cf.: Blakeman v. Miller, 1902, 136 Cal. 138, 68 P. 587; In re Water Front on Upper N.Y. Bay, 1927, 246 N.Y. 1, 157 N.E. 911, reargument denied 246 N.Y. 549, 159 N.E. 646, certiorari denied 276 U.S. 626, 48 S. Ct. 320, 72 L.Ed. 738, noted in 41 Harv.Law Rev. 406. See also, Ospinach, Options as Perpetuities, 8 Cinn.Law Rev. 335 (1934).

58. Maddox v. Keeler, 1944, 296 Ky. 440, 177 S.W.2d 568, 162 A.L.R. 578; Gange v. Hayes, 1051, 193 Or. 51, 237 P.2d 196; Barton v. Thaw, 1914, 246 Pa. 348, 92 A. 312. See also, Eastman Marble Co. v. Vermont Marble Co., 1920, 236 Mass. 138, 128 N.E. 177, noted in 34 Harv.Law Rev. 440 (1921) (also void as a contract).

59. Pure Oil Co. v. Baars, 1944, 224 N.C. 612, 31 S. E.2d 854; Restatement of Law, 1948 Supplement, p. 528, § 394, Comment f.

ties, unless the covenant is made in behalf of a contracting party and his heirs.[60]

It is generally recognized that an exception is made with respect to the rule against perpetuities if an option to purchase is contained in a lease and is to be exercised, if at all, during the period of the lease.[61] Such an option encourages the improvement of leased land by the optionee and does not impair the alienability of the property.

Option to Renew or Extend Lease

The validity of an option to renew or extend a lease is generally recognized.[62] There are suggestions that the rule against perpetuities is not applicable because, for practical purposes, this merely involves a continuation of the original lease. But the privilege of securing such an extension constitutes an equitable estate and, theoretically, comes within the scope of the rule against perpetuities. However, it is recognized as an exception to the rule because of the utility of such options and the fact that the alienability of the property is not usually impaired by the option agreement.

CHARITABLE GIFTS

188. If a gift vests in a charity within the time permitted for the vesting of estates a valid provision may be made that upon the happening of an event the property is to pass to another charity. This "shift in interest" is not controlled by the rule against perpetuities.

From the very nature of a charitable gift there is uncertainty as to those who will eventually enjoy the benefits. The rule against perpetuities does not require the vesting of such interests within any specified time. However, with an exception to be noted, the legal ownership must vest within the permitted time either in a charitable corporation or in a trustee for a charitable purpose.[63]

An exception to this rule is recognized in a situation where the benefits are to shift from one charity to another upon the happening of a named event. The rule against perpetuities does not place a time limit with respect to such a "shift in interest." Of course, the rule is applicable in a case where a gift is made for a non-charitable purpose with a provision that upon the happening of a remote contingency the property is to be devoted to a charitable purpose.[64] So also, a gift for a non-charitable purpose is void if it follows a charitable gift and vesting may be postponed beyond the permitted time.[65]

In First Camden National Bank & Trust Co. v. Collins (N.J.),[66] a deed of trust directed that funds were to be accumulated until twenty-one years after the death of the survivor of

60. See Campbell v. Campbell, 1950, 313 Ky. 249, 230 S.W.2d 918; Herzog v. Mattern, Tex.Civ.App. 1962, 359 S.W.2d 86.

61. Keogh v. Peck, 1928, 316 Ill. 318, 147 N.E. 266, 38 A.L.R. 1151; Hollander v. Central Metal & Supply Co., 1908, 109 Md. 131, 71 A. 442. See Abbot, Leases and the Rule against Perpetuities, 27 Yale Law Journal 878, 885 (1918). *Contra*: First Huntington Nat. Bank v. Gideon-Broh Realty Co., 1953, 139 W.Va. 130, 79 S.E.2d 675.

62. Becker v. Submarine Oil Co., 1921, 55 Cal.App. 698, 204 P. 245; Todd v. Manufacturers' Light & Heat Co., 1922, 90 W.Va. 40, 110 S.E. 446. *Cf.*: Epstein v. Zahloute, 1950, 99 Cal.App.2d 738, 222 P.2d 318. See Abbot, Leases and the Rule against Perpetuities, 27 Yale Law Journal, 878, 883 (1918).

63. Thorne v. Continental National Bank & Trust Co., 1940, 305 Ill.App. 222, 27 N.E.2d 302; Matter of Roe, 1939, 281 N.Y. 541, 24 N.E.2d 322, 131 A.L.R. 707.

64. Institution for Savings in Roxbury v. Roxbury Home for Aged Women, 1923, 244 Mass. 583, 139 N.E. 301.

65. Proprietors of the Church of Brattle Square v. Grant, 1855, 69 Mass. (3 Gray) 142, 63 Am.Dec. 725. *Cf.*: Fidelity Union Trust Co. v. Egenolf Day Nursery Ass'n, 1960, 64 N.J.Super. 445, 166 A. 2d 402.

66. 114 N.J.Eq. 59, 168 A. 275 (1933).

named children. After the expiration of that time the property was to be delivered to a corporation to be organized under New Jersey law to operate a school that qualified as a charitable corporation. The court reaches the conclusion that the gift was void under the rule against perpetuities. Organization of the corporation and the vesting of the gift was postponed for a period beyond that permitted for the vesting of the estate.

This decision may be questioned upon the ground that the fund was committed to a charitable use prior to the organization of a corporation. The trust should not be permitted to fail for lack of a trustee because the court has the power to appoint a trustee to administer the trust.[67]

CLASS GIFTS

189. A gift to a class is treated as a gift to an entity insofar as the rule against perpetuities is concerned. The invalidity of a gift as to one potential member of the class invalidates the gift as to the entire class.

   a. Class membership. Either the membership in a class or the rule relating to the closing of a class may so limit class membership as to satisfy the requirements of the rule against perpetuities.

   b. Gift of a stated amount to each member of a class. In applying the rule against perpetuities, the gift of a stated amount to each member of a class is considered to be a "separate gift" transaction.

   c. Gift to sub-classes: rule of Cattlin v. Brown. If a gift is made to two or more classes, the invalidity of the gift as to one class will not invalidate the gift as to other classes.

Under the rule against perpetuities a class gift will fail in its entirety unless the estate of each potential member of the class must

vest or fail within the time permitted for the vesting of estates.

In the leading English case of Leake v. Robinson,[68] a testamentary trust provided that the income was to be paid to testator's grandson, William, for life and upon his death the subject matter of the trust was to be distributed to William's brothers upon attaining the age of twenty-five, and to his sisters upon attaining that age or upon marriage. The class gift violated the rule against perpetuities and was void in its entirety.[69] Class membership was not limited to William's brothers and sisters living at the time of the testator's death. A brother or sister born after the death of testator would qualify for class membership. Vesting in these new members might be postponed until these new members reached the age of twenty-five years.

William had five brothers and sisters at the time of the testator's death. Two additional brothers were born prior to the death of William. Thus, the share of each brother and sister in the gift ($\frac{1}{7}$) was ascertained during the lifetime of William. Because of this fact, it may be suggested that the gifts to the brothers and sisters living at the time of the testator's death should be sustained even though the gifts to those born thereafter would fail because of the rule against perpetuities.[70] In support of this view it may be contended that the gift vested in the children living at the time of the testator's death, subject to being divested in part by the birth of additional children. Under the rule de-

---

67. See In re Knouse's Will, 1963, 254 Iowa 1339, 121 N.W.2d 151.

68. 2 Mer. 363, 35 Eng.Rep. 979 (1817).

69. *Accord*: Taylor v. Crosson, 1916, 11 Del.Ch. 145, 98 A. 375; Beverlin v. First Nat. Bank of Wichita, 1940, 151 Kan 307, 98 P.2d 200, 155 A.L.R. 688.

70. See Leach, The Rule against Perpetuities and Gifts to Classes, 51 Harv.Law Rev. 1329, 1343 (1938).

clared in Church of Brattle Square v. Grant (Mass.),[71] a prior gift will not be divested by a gift over if the gift over is void because of the rule against perpetuities. Further, since the share of each brother and sister could be ascertained within the permitted time there is, in effect, a gift of a designated amount to each brother and sister. The invalidity of some of the gifts should not invalidate the gifts to others.[72]

While these various arguments tend to support the gifts made to William's brothers and sisters living at the time of the testator's death, it is not clear that the result thus attained would be in accord with the intention of the testator. There is nothing to indicate that he would have preferred a partial validity. In many cases of this type an equitable result can be attained by applying the rules of intestate succession to the entire subject matter of the gift.

Class Membership

A conveying instrument may lend itself to a construction that class membership is limited to persons properly qualified under the rule against perpetuities. A gift to "nieces and nephews" may be restricted to nieces and nephews living at the time of the death of the testator.[73] In Pippin v. Sams (S.C.),[74] testator created a life estate in his daughter and her children with a contingent gift over. The daughter's living children were mentioned in the will. The court held that the gift over was valid because the life estate was limited to the daughter's children who

were living at the time of the testator's death.[75]

A violation of the rule against perpetuities is not involved if the class closes within the permitted time. For example, in Picken v. Matthews (Eng.),[76] a testamentary gift was made to the children of testatrix's two daughters "who being sons shall live to attain the age of twenty-five, or being daughters shall attain that age or previously marry, whichever shall first happen." One of the children had attained the age of twenty-five at the time of the death of testatrix. Under established rules respecting class gifts, the class closed at the time of the death of testatrix and only children living at that time would be included. Thus, the gift did not violate the rule against perpetuities. However, the gift would have violated the rule if there were substitutional gifts to issue of the children who failed to reach the age of twenty-five unless all of the children were four years of age, or older, at the time of the testatrix's death. It is indicated in some decisions that the court may, as a salvaging process, apply a "class closing rule" as a means of avoiding invalidity of a class gift under the rule against perpetuities.[77]

Gift of a Stated Amount to Each Member of a Class

A gift of a stated amount to each member of a class is not a class gift within the scope of the rule against perpetuities. Rather, it is considered to be a separate gift to each member of the class. Accordingly, the

71.   69 Mass. (3 Gray) 142 (1855).

72.   Storrs v. Benbow, [1853] 3 De G.M. & G. 390, 43 Eng.Rep. 153.

73.   Wright's Estate, 1925, 284 Pa. 334, 131 A. 188.

74.   174 S.C. 444, 177 S.E. 659 (1934).

75.   *Accord*: Re Powell, 1898, 1 Ch.Div. 227.

76.   10 Ch.Div. 264 (1878).

77.   See Watson v. Goldthwaite, 1962, 345 Mass. 29, 184 N.E.2d 340.

validity of each gift is determined on an individual basis.[78]

Gift to Sub-classes: Rule of Cattlin v. Brown

For the purposes of applying the rule against perpetuities a gift may be severable as to classes. If it is possible to ascertain the portion of a gift that is to be distributed to one class it may be sustained to that extent even if it is otherwise void.

In the leading English case of Cattlin v. Brown,[79] testator devised land to his son, Thomas Cattlin, for life, then to the son's children for life, and at the death of each grandchild his respective share was to pass to his issue or heirs forever. Two children were born to Thomas before the death of the testator and two were born thereafter. Of course, the gift over to the issue of children born after the death of the testator was void under the rule against perpetuities. However, since the gift was *per stirpes* to the son's children, there were as many class gifts as there were grandchildren. It was not considered that the invalidity of some of these sub-class gifts should invalidate them all.[80] The share that each sub-class would be entitled to take could be determined at the time of the death of the son, Thomas Cattlin. If the gift had been to great-grandchildren on a *per capita* basis the entire gift would fail. In that event there would be but one class and membership was

not limited to those born within the limits of the rule.

POWERS OF APPOINTMENT

190. For purposes of applying the rule against perpetuities, a general power of appointment exercisable by deed or will is considered to be absolute ownership.

A general power of appointment exercisable by will only, and a special power, are void if exercisable beyond the time permitted for the vesting of estates.

In the case of a general power of appointment exercisable by will only, and in the case of a special power, the appointed interest must vest or fail within the permitted time computed from the date upon which the power was created. However, the validity of the appointment is governed by circumstances as they exist at the time of the appointment.

For the purpose of applying the rule against perpetuities, a general power of appointment exercisable by deed or will is considered to be absolute ownership. Accordingly, such a power is valid if the donee of the power qualifies as a person in being within the time permitted for the vesting of estates, computed from the time of the creation of the power. For example, a testator may properly devise or bequeath property to his son for life and create a general power of appointment, exercisable by deed or will, in an unborn child of the son.[81] It is not material that the power may not be exercised within life or lives in being and twenty-one years after the death of the testator.

But a special power of appointment, or a general power exercisable by will only, is void if it may be exercised beyond the time fixed for the vesting of estates under the rule against perpetuities.[82] In American Trust Co.

---

78. In re Helme's Estate, 1923, 95 N.J.Eq. 197, 123 A. 43; Storrs v. Benbow, [1853] 3 De G.M. & G. 390, 43 Eng.Rep. 153; Wilkinson v. Duncan, [1861] 30 Beav. 111, 54 Eng.Rep. 831.

79. 11 Hare 372, 68 Eng.Rep. 1319 (1853).

80. *Accord*: Turner v. Safe Deposit & Trust Co., 1925, 148 Md. 371, 129 A. 294; In re Harrah's Estate, 1950, 364 Pa. 451, 72 A.2d 587, noted in 4 Baylor Law Rev. 95 (1951); Smith's Estate v. Comm'r of Internal Revenue, 3 Cir., 1944, 140 F.2d 759.

81. Bray v. Bree, [1834] 2 Cl. & F. 453, 6 Eng.Rep. 1225.

82. Burlington County Trust Co. v. Di Castelcicala, 1949, 2 N.J. 214, 66 A.2d 164; In re Hargreaves, 1890 43 Ch.Div. 401. See 4 Rest.Property, § 390.

v. Williamson (N.C.),[83] testator gave his son, S, a general testamentary power. In exercising the power S gave his two children life estate and special powers of appointment. Since these children were born after the death of the testator the power conferred upon them was void.

A discretionary power given to a trustee authorizing him to determine the amount of income or principal to be paid beneficiaries is considered to be a special power of appointment. Accordingly, such a power is void if it may be exercised beyond the permitted time.[84]

Even if a power of appointment is valid insofar as the rule against perpetuities is concerned, the rule may nullify an appointment made in exercise of the power. Rules regarding this matter are as follows:

First: In determining the validity of an appointment under a general power *exercisable by deed or will,* the permitted time for vesting is computed from the time when the power is exercised. For the purpose of applying the rule against perpetuities the donee of such a power is considered to be the owner of the property.[85] If a general power is exercisable by will only the time is computed from the date upon which the power was created.[86] The English rule is that in applying the rule against perpetuities the time is computed from the date upon which a general power is exercised even if it is exercisable by will only.[87] There is some American authority that supports this view.[88]

In Fiduciary Trust Co. v. Mishou (Mass.),[89] a general testamentary power was exercised in such a manner as to blend the appointive property with property owned by the donee. The appointment also violated the rule against perpetuities insofar as the powered property was concerned. The court held that to permit the appointive property to pass into the trust established by the will would constitute an evasion of the rule that if a general power is exercisable by will only the time is computed from the date upon which the power was created.

Second: In the case of a special power the permitted time is computed from the date upon which the power was created.[90] This is also the rule with respect to a general power that is exercisable only by will. This conclusion is based upon the concept that the exercise of the power is an event that shifts ownership of the property from the donor of the power, or his estate, to the appointee.

Third: In determining the validity of an appointment facts are considered in the light

---

83. 228 N.C. 458, 46 S.E.2d 104 (1948).

84. Bundy v. United States Trust Co., 1926, 257 Mass. 72, 153 N.E. 337, noted in 40 Harv.Law Rev. 507 (1927).

85. Appeal of Mifflin, 1888, 121 Pa. 205, 15 A. 525.

86. Northern Trust Co. v. Porter, 1938, 368 Ill. 256, 13 N.E.2d 487, noted in 51 Harv.Law Rev. 1451 (1938), 36 Mich.Law Rev. 1411 (1938); Thorne v. Continental Nat. Bank & Trust Co., 1940, 305 Ill. App. 222, 27 N.E.2d 302; Minot v. Paine, 1918, 230 Mass. 514, 120 N.E. 167, 1 A.L.R. 365; St. Louis Union Trust Co. v. Bassett, 1935, 337 Mo. 604, 85

S.W.2d 569, 101 A.L.R. 1266, noted in 34 Mich.Law Rev. 1049, (1936); American Trust Co. v. Williamson, 1948, 228 N.C. 458, 46 S.E.2d 104.

87. Rous v. Jackson, 1885, 29 Ch.Div. 521.

88. See, for example, Miller v. Douglass, 1927, 192 Wis. 486, 213 N.W. 320.

89. 321 Mass. 615, 75 N.E.2d 3 (1947).

90. Brown v. Columbia Finance & Trust Co., 1906, 123 Ky. 775, 97 S.W. 421; Thomas v. Gregg, 1892, 76 Md. 169, 24 A. 418; Wilkinson v. Duncan, [1861] 30 Beav. 111, 54 Eng.Rep. 831. For a collection of cases applying this rule, see Foulke, Powers and Rule against Perpetuities, 16 Col.Law Rev. 627, 634n 61.

of circumstances as they exist when the power is exercised. For example, assume that property is devised or bequeathed to B for life, remainder to the issue of B as B might appoint. C, a child of B, was born after the testator's death. An appointment made to C for life remainder to C's children violates the rule against perpetuities insofar as appointment is made to C's children.[91] However, if B had appointed to C's children, and C predeceased B, the appointment would be valid.[92] The appointed interests would vest at the time of B's death and B was a life in being at the time of the testator's death. There is a minority rule to the contrary.[93] These authorities follow the view that the appointment, when made, is construed on the hypothesis that it had been embodied in the instrument that created the power.

Fourth: If a power of appointment is created by an *inter vivos* instrument the donor may retain the power of revocation. In that event, and for the purpose of applying the rule against perpetuities, computation of time starts from the date upon which the donor relinquishes the power of revocation.[94]

---

91. Leech, Perpetuities in a Nutshell, 51 Harv.Law Rev. 638, 653 (1938).

92. In re Warren's Estate, 1936, 320 Pa. 112, 182 A. 396, 104 A.L.R. 1345, noted in 49 Harv.Law Rev. 1011 (1936), 21 Cornell Law Quarterly 646 (1936).

93. Brown v. Columbia Finance & Trust Co., 1906, 123 Ky. 775, 97 S.W. 421; In re Baiter's Estate, 1934, 152 Misc. 177, 273 N.Y.S. 962.

94. Fitzpatrick v. Mercantile-Safe Deposit & Trust Co., 1959, 220 Md. 534, 155 A.2d 702.

PART 6

RESTRAINTS PERTAINING TO ALIENATION

CHAPTER 37

DIRECT RESTRAINTS ON ALIENATION

Sec.

IN GENERAL

191. Except to the extent permitted by statute, a direct restraint upon the alienation of an estate in fee, or an equivalent interest in things other than land, is void. Promissory and forfeiture types of restraints are valid in the case of life estates and less than freehold estates.

There are three types of direct restraints upon alienation.[1] A disabling restraint is one that impairs the power to alienate. A promissory type of restraint is one wherein an owner promises not to alienate. A violation of the promise results in a valid conveyance but a possible liability for breach of contract. A forfeiture type of restraint is involved if provision is made for termination of an estate upon a breach of the condition. Except in the case of beneficial interests under a trust (a spendthrift trust),[2] the general rule is that a disabling restraint is void under all circumstances. The validity or invalidity of a promissory or forfeiture restraint depends upon the type of estate involved.

The preferred view is that any type of a direct restraint upon alienation is null and void insofar as an estate in fee is concerned.[3] It is frequently stated that a restraint of this kind is repugnant to the rights of ownership in fee. In any event, the conclusion is in accord with a strong public policy in favor of free alienation. Attempts to avoid the rule against restraints upon alienation have been made by the formation of an association of property owners in a specific area. An association rule prohibits the sale of land by a member except to members of the association. Because of restrictions relating to membership in the association the arrangement involves a restraint upon alienation and is void.[4] However, a valid restraint

---

3. Bonnell v. McLaughlin, 1916, 173 Cal. 213, 159 P. 590; Northwest Real Estate Co. v. Serio, 1928, 156 Md. 229, 144 A. 245; Mandlebaum v. McDonell, 1874, 29 Mich. 78; Anderson v. Cary, 1881, 36 Ohio St. 506. See also, Tracey v. Franklin, 1949, 30 Del.Ch. 407, 61 A.2d 780, affirmed 31 Del.Ch. 477, 67 A.2d 56, 11 A.L.R.2d 990 (restraint pertaining to corporate stock). But see, Ink v. Plott, Ohio.App. 1960, 175 N.E.2d 94.

4. Mountain Springs Ass'n v. Wilson, 1963, 81 N.J. Super. 564, 196 A.2d 270; Lauderbaugh v. Williams, 1962, 409 Pa. 351, 186 A.2d 39. *Cf.*: Gale v. York Center Community Cooperative, Inc., 1961, 21 Ill.2d 86, 171 N.E.2d 30 (a co-operative housing ass'n had a preemptive right to purchase and the validity of the right was sustained).

---

1. 4 Rest.Property, § 404.

2. 1 Rest.Trusts, § 152.

upon alienation may be imposed if land is conveyed for a charitable purpose.[5]

A direct restraint upon alienation is distinguished from an indirect restraint, such as a restraint that may result from the imposition of various types of building restrictions. These indirect restraints are tolerated to the extent that they serve a useful purpose in land use and community development.[6] The minority rule is that a direct restraint upon alienation may be sustained even in the case of an estate in fee if the restraint is "reasonable" both as to time[7] and persons.[8]

In general, a direct restraint of the forfeiture type is sanctioned insofar as a life estate is involved.[9] Such a provision may be used as a means by which to protect future interests in the property. The situation is not unlike that in the case of a leasehold estate. Provisions against assigning and subleasing are valid.

PARTITION

192. **Reasonable restraints upon the rights of partition are valid.**

Restraints upon voluntary or compulsory partition are valid if they are reasonable.[10] Whether or not such restraints are reasonable is determined by reference to the length of time involved and the purpose of the restraint. An agreement between concurrent owners of land relating to partition is within the scope of the Statute of Frauds.[11]

A restriction relating to partition is not a direct restraint upon alienation because it leaves each concurrent owner free to convey his undivided interest. However, an indirect restraint is involved because there is not an "open market" with respect to a concurrent interest if the right to partition does not exist. This indirect restraint is tolerated in situations where it serves a useful purpose.

In Smith v. Smith (Mich.),[12] a conveying instrument created a joint tenancy and pro-

5. See Catholic Bishop of Chicago v. Murr, 1954, 2 Ill.2d 625, 120 N.E.2d 4 (but the *cy pres* doctrine is applicable); Ohio Society for Crippled Children & Adults v. McElroy, 1963, 175 Ohio St. 49, 191 N.E. 543.

6. Los Angeles Investment Co. v. Gary, 1919, 181 Cal. 680, 186 P. 596, 9 A.L.R. 115; Steward v. Cronan, 1940, 105 Colo. 393, 98 P.2d 999; Parmalee v. Morris, 1922, 218 Mich. 625, 188 N.W. 330, 38 A.L.R. 1180. *Cf.*: Shelley v. Kraemer, 1948, 334 U.S. 1, 68 S.Ct. 836, 92 L.Ed. 1161, 3 A.L.R.2d 441 (restrictions are not enforceable if they are based upon race, color or previous condition of servitude).

7. Hinshaw v. Wright, 1928, 124 Kan. 792, 262 P. 601, noted in 13 Cornell Law Quarterly 461; Kentland Coal & Coke Co. v. Keen, 1916, 168 Ky. 836, 183 S.W. 247, L.R.A.1916D, 924 (during lifetime of grantor); Furst v. Lacher, 1921, 149 Minn. 53, 182 N.W. 720 (during lifetime of grantor). For discussion of the validity of a provision in a will that the legatee's interest in the estate shall be inalienable pending administration of the estate, see Whiting, Validity of Clause Restricting Alienation of a Legacy During Administration, 40 Mich. Law Rev. 97 (1941).

8. Blevins v. Pittman, 1940, 189 Ga. 789, 7 S.E.2d 662; Morse v. Blood, 1897, 68 Minn. 442, 71 N.W. 682 (*dictum*); Overton v. Lea, 1901, 108 Tenn. 505, 68 S.W.2d 250. See 4 Rest.Property, § 406.

9. Conger v. Lowe, 1890, 123 Ind. 368, 24 N.E. 889, 9 L.R.A. 165 (indirect restraint); McCormick Harvesting Machine Co. v. Gates, 1888, 75 Iowa 343, 39 N.W. 657 (no provision for forfeiture); Bank of Powhattan v. Rooney, 1937, 146 Kan. 559, 72 P.2d 993 (disabling restraint). *Cf.*: Ehrisman v. Sener, 1894, 162 Pa. 577, 29 A. 719 (life estate not exempt from claims of creditors). See Restraints on the Involuntary Alienation of Legal Interests, 54 Harv. Law Rev. 466 (1941).

10. Miranda v. Miranda, 1947, 81 Cal.App.2d 61, 183 P.2d 61 (*dictum*); Guenther v. Roche, 1947, 238 Iowa 1348, 29 N.W.2d 222; Anderson v. Edwards, 1954, 239 N.C. 510, 80 S.E.2d 260; 4 Rest.Property, § 412.

11. Casolo v. Nardella, 1948, 193 Misc. 378, 84 N.Y.S. 2d 178. But see, Rowland v. Clark, 1949, 91 Cal. App.2d 880, 206 P.2d 59.

12. 290 Mich. 143, 287 N.W. 411, 124 A.L.R. 215 (1939), noted in 38 Mich.Law Rev. 875 (1940).

vided that neither joint tenant could dispose of his interest without the consent of the other. It is held that such a direct restraint upon alienation is null and void. There is authority for the view that such a provision may be sustained upon the ground that it merely constitutes a restraint upon partition.[13]

PRE-EMPTIVE RIGHT

193. **The validity of a pre-emptive right is generally sustained if it must be asserted, if at all, within the time permitted under the rule against perpetuities and at a fair market price.**

A pre-emptive right is involved if A conveys land to B and his heirs and the deed contains a provision that A has a right to repurchase the property in the event that B and his heirs should offer it for sale. It is generally held that this type of contract or promise is within the scope of the rule against perpetuities.[14] Of course, it is not void under that rule if the duration is limited to lives in being, such as in a case where it is personal as to A or to B.[15] It is also valid if it is to be exercised, if at all, within twenty-one years after lives in being, such as after the death of A or B.[16] The time may also be measured by a flat period of twenty-one years. If the right is expressed in the form of a condition the power of termination is exempt from the operation of the rule.

But the validity of a pre-emptive right must also be judged in the light of the common law rule against restraints upon alienation. The validity of a pre-emptive right is generally sustained if the contract requires payment of the prevailing market price or if the one asserting the right is required to meet the "best offer" made for the property by another.[17] However, a restraint upon alienation is involved if the property may be reacquired at the original purchase price or at any price that would be less than the fair market value at the time the pre-emptive right is asserted.[18] Under such circumstances there would be a lack of motive to sell.

TESTAMENTARY DISPOSITION AND INTESTATE SUCCESSION

194. **Important incidents of absolute ownership are rights relating to testamentary disposition and intestate succession. Restrictions on these rights are null and void.**

Important incidents of absolute ownership are rights relating to testamentary disposition and intestate succession. Provisions in a conveying instrument that limit or nullify these "rights of ownership" are repugnant and void.[19] In Basnight v. Dill (N.C.),[20] land was devised to husband and wife as tenants by the entireties. The will provided:

13. Rosenberg v. Rosenberg, 1952, 413 Ill. 343, 108 N.E.2d 766 (agreement between husband and wife in connection with divorce proceedings).

14. Neustadt v. Pearce, 1958, 145 Conn. 403, 143 A. 2d 437; Rocky Mountain Fuel Co. v. Heflin, 1961, 148 Colo. 415, 366 P.2d 577.

15. Old Mission Peninsula School District v. French, 1961, 362 Mich. 546, 107 N.W.2d 758.

16. New Haven Trap Rock Co. v. Tata, 1962, 149 Conn. 181, 177 A.2d 798.

17. Blair v. Kingsley, Fla.App.1961, 128 So.2d 889; Beets v. Tyler, Mo.1956, 290 S.W.2d 76.

18. Maynard v. Polhemus, 1887, 74 Cal. 141, 15 P. 451; Maddox v. Keeler, 1944, 296 Ky. 440, 177 S. W.2d 568, 162 A.L.R. 578, noted in 33 Ky.Law Jr., 118 (1945); In re Rosher, 1884, 26 Ch.Div. 801; 4 Rest.Property, § 413. *Contra*: Windiate v. Lorman, 1926, 236 Mich. 531, 211 N.W. 62; Kamas State Bank v. Bourgeois, 1963, 14 Utah 2d 188, 380 P.2d 931, *Cf.*: Schwartz v. Shapiro, 1964, —— Cal.App.2d ——, 40 Cal.Rptr. 189 (partnership agreement).

19. Luckey v. McCray, 1904, 125 Iowa 691, 101 N.W. 516; Jackson v. Littell, 1908, 213 Mo. 589, 112 S. W. 53; Gulliver v. Vaux, [1856] 8 De Gex.M. & G. 167, 44 Eng.Rep. 353.

20. 256 N.C. 474, 124 S.E.2d 159 (1962).

"But in the event the said (husband and wife) should die in possession of the property, then the same shall descend to the heirs of Mrs. Susan A. Churchill, my mother." The wife survived her husband and occupied the land until the time of her death. The land was then claimed by the devisees under the wife's will. In sustaining this claim it is held that the limitation in the instrument under which the wife claimed title was null and void.[21]

A valid limitation may follow a life estate even if the life tenant is also given a limited power to dispose of the property.[22] Such an interest falls short of absolute ownership. In fact, the general rule is that a life estate coupled with an unlimited power of disposition does not enlarge the life estate to ab- solute ownership. There may be a valid gift over after such a life estate.[23]

As a means by which to sustain the va- lidity of a gift over, there is an inclination on the part of the courts to find that the primary gift was only for life even if such was not evidenced on the face of the convey- ing instrument.[24] In a number of states it is held that a testamentary gift in fee simple, or absolute ownership in the case of personal property, may be followed by a valid gift over.[25]

---

21. *Accord:* Snodgrass v. Brandenburg, 1905, 164 Ind 59, 72 N.E. 1030; Van Horne v. Campbell, 1885, 100 N.Y. 287, 3 N.E. 316, reargument denied 101 N.Y. 608, 3 N.E. 901 (but see McKinney's N.Y.Real Property Law, § 57); Krumm v. Cuneo, 1943, 71 Ohio App. 521, 47 N.E.2d 1003; Mowery v. Coffman, 1946, 185 Va. 491, 39 S.E.2d 285.

22. Mayne v. Mayne, 1938, 28 Cal.App.2d 340, 82 P.2d 504; In re Britt's Will, 1947, 272 App.Div. 426, 71 N.Y.S.2d 405 (in express terms the power was absolute but the court implies the requirement of good faith in exercising the power).

23. Williams v. Jones, 1963, 219 Ga. 45, 131 S.E.2d 553; Hutchinson v. Farmer, 1948, 190 Md. 411, 58 A.2d 638; Julian v. Northwestern Trust Co., 1934, 192 Minn. 136, 255 N.W. 622; Morgan v. Meacham, 1938, 279 Ky. 526, 130 S.W.2d 992; Smiles v. Daube, 1938, 130 Pa.Super. 565, 198 A. 457; Edds v. Mitch- ell, 1945, 143 Tex. 307, 184 S.W.2d 823, 158 A.L.R. 470. *Contra:* Gibson v. Gibson, 1921, 213 Mich. 31, 181 N.W. 41; Van Deventer v. McMullen, 1928, 157 Tenn. 571. But see, Lockett v. Thomas, 1942, 179 Tenn. 240, 165 S.W.2d 375.

24. Morris v. Smith, 1954, 332 Mass. 34, 123 N.E.2d 212 (inquiry may always be made to determine whether or not the intention was to create only a life estate in the first taker); Krause v. Krause, 1924, 113 Neb. 22, 201 N.W. 670; In re Byrne's Es- tate, 1935, 320 Pa. 513, 181 A. 500, noted in 34 Mich.Law Rev. 1277 (1936); Washington Trust Co. v. Arnold, 1943, 69 R.I. 121, 31 A.2d 420.

25. See, for example, Mansfield v. Shelton, 1897, 67 Conn. 390, 35 A. 271; Roberts v. Mosely, 1930, 100 Fla. 267, 129 So. 835, 837.

CHAPTER 38

DURATION OF TRUSTS AND THE RULE AGAINST ACCUMULATIONS

DURATION OF TRUSTS

195. **The creation of a trust results in a suspension of the power of alienation.**

a. **Charitable trust. There are no durational limits with respect to a charitable trust.**

b. **Private trusts. The prevailing rule is that in the absence of statute there are no durational limits with respect to the creation of a private trust.**

From a practical point of view, there is a suspension of the power of alienation with respect to property held in trust. Insofar as the legal title is concerned, a trustee does not have complete freedom of action in connection with the alienation of trust property. Frequently, a court order is necessary to authorize alienation. Even a direct restraint upon the power of a trustee is not repugnant to the interest of a trustee within the meaning of the common law rule against restraints upon alienation.[1] There may also be a restraint upon the alienation of beneficial interests under the trust. This is the situation to the extent that recognition is extended to spendthrift trusts. Rules relating to the suspension of the power of alienation by the creation of a trust are discussed in the following paragraphs.

Charitable Trusts

It is recognized that there are no durational limits with respect to charitable trusts. Such trusts are looked upon with favor and are under the continued supervision of the court. This is a safeguard against any encroachments involving the public interest.

Private Trusts

According to the English rule, as declared in the leading case of Saunders v. Vautier,[2] a private trust may be terminated at any time at the instance of a beneficiary if all of the beneficiaries are competent adults and their interests are indefeasibly vested.[3] Under this view, there is no necessity for a rule that would place a time limitation on the duration of private trusts.

But the rule declared in Saunders v. Vautier has not been universally recognized in the United States. It was considered and repudiated in Claflin v. Claflin (Mass.).[4] In this case it is held that the intention of a trustor is the controlling factor. If he directs that a trust is to continue for a stated time that expression of intention is to be respected. This authority established the validity of indestructible trusts and the decision has been accepted in other American states.

---

1. But see, Blake-Curtis v. Blake, 1939, 149 Kan. 512, 89 P.2d 15 (a testamentary trust provided that land was not to be sold by the trustees until it would bring $20 per acre or an aggregate of $40,000. The restriction is held to be void).

2. 4 Beav. 115, 49 Eng.Rep. 282 (1841).

3. *Cf.*: In re Ridley, 1879, 11 Ch.Div. 645 (exception made if trust is created for the benefit of a married woman).

4. 149 Mass. 19, 20 N.E. 454 (1889).

Legislative action has been taken in a number of states. A usual provision is that the duration of a private trust is limited to the time permitted for the vesting of estates under the rule against perpetuities.

RULE AGAINST ACCUMULATIONS

196. In the absence of statute a trust may validly provide that the income is to be accumulated for a time not exceeding that permitted for the vesting of estates.

The rule against accumulations is not applicable in the case of charitable gifts.

In the absence of a statute a trust may validly provide that the income is to be accumulated for a time not exceeding that permitted for the vesting of estates. It was so held in the English case of Thellusson v. Woodford,[5] decided in 1805. Pending the decision in that case Parliament passed a statute (the Thellusson Act) [6] providing *alternative periods* during which a direction for accumulation could be made, *viz,* the life of the transferor, or twenty-one years from the death of a transferor, or during the minority of anyone living or *en ventre sa mere* at the death of the transferor or during the minori-

ty of the beneficiary who would otherwise be entitled to the income.

The Thellusson Act was passed too late to be considered a part of the adopted common law in the American states.[7] However, the matter is regulated by statute in many states. According to some statutes an accumulation that exceeds the permitted period is void in its entirety. Other statutes provide that invalidity attaches only as to the accumulation in excess of the permitted time. Some statutes prohibit accumulations as to land but not as to personal property.[8]

The rule against accumulations is not applicable in the case of charitable gifts.[9] This follows from the fact that such gifts are subject to judicial supervision and the court has the power to strike down an accumulations provision that is not for the best interest of the charitable purpose involved.[10]

---

5. 11 Ves.Jr. 112, 32 Eng.Rep. 1030 (House of Lords 1805).

6. 39 & 40 Goe. III, c. 98 (1800).

7. Gertman v. Burdick, App.D.C. 1941, 123 F.2d 924, noted in 36 Ill.Law Rev. 567 (1942).

8. See, for example, In re Hustad's Estate, 1941, 236 Wis. 615, 296 N.W. 74.

9. Ripley v. Brown, 1914, 218 Mass. 33, 105 N.E. 637; Collins v. Lyon, 1943, 181 Va. 230, 24 S.E.2d 572.

10. Frazier v. Merchants Nat. Bank, 1936, 296 Mass. 298, 5 N.E.2d 550; In re James' Estate, 1964, —— Pa. ——, 199 A.2d 275; Allaum v. First & Merchants Nat. Bank, 1949, 190 Va. 104, 56 S.E.2d 83.

TABLE OF CASES

References are to pages

A

B

G

H

M

N

X

Y

Z

INDEX